AN INTRODUCTION TO
MODERN PHILOSOPHY

AN INTRODUCTION TO

MODERN PHILOSOPHY

IN SEVEN PHILOSOPHICAL PROBLEMS

BY

ALBUREY CASTELL

PROFESSOR OF PHILOSOPHY
UNIVERSITY OF OREGON

SECOND EDITION

THE MACMILLAN COMPANY, NEW YORK

COLLIER-MACMILLAN LIMITED, LONDON

First Printing

Library of Congress catalog card number: 63-11788

The Macmillan Company, New York
Collier-Macmillan Canada, Ltd., Toronto, Ontario
DIVISIONS OF THE CROWELL-COLLIER PUBLISHING COMPANY

Printed in the United States of America

ACKNOWLEDGMENT is made to the authors and publishers cited below for permission to quote from the following copyrighted works:

"Demonstration of the Impossibility of Metaphysics," by A. J. Ayer, in *Mind*, XLIII (1934), reprinted by permission of the author and *Mind*.

The Decline of the West by Oswald Spengler, translated by Charles Francis Atkinson, copyright 1926, 1928, reprinted by permission of Alfred A. Knopf, Inc., and George Allen & Unwin, Ltd.

"The Concept of Artistic Expression" by John Hospers in *Proceedings of the Aristotelian Society* 1954-55, reprinted by permission of the author.

Principia Ethica by G. E. Moore, copyright 1903, reprinted by permission of Cambridge University Press.

(Acknowledgments continued)

The Principles of Art and *Metaphysics* by R. G. Collingwood, copyright 1938 and 1940 respectively, and reprinted by permission of The Clarendon Press, Oxford.

The State in Theory and Practice by Harold J. Laski, copyright 1935, reprinted by permission of The Viking Press, Inc., and George Allen & Unwin, Ltd.

The Philosophy of 'As If' by Hans Vaihinger, translated by C. K. Ogden, reprinted by permission of Harcourt, Brace & World, Inc., and Routledge & Kegan Paul, Ltd.

"The Role of Theory in Aesthetics" by Morris Weitz in *The Journal of Aesthetics and Art Criticism*, XV, No. 1 (September 1956), reprinted by permission of the author and *The Journal of Aesthetics and Art Criticism*.

Quest for Certainty by John Dewey, copyright 1929, reprinted by permission of G. P. Putnam's Sons.

Language, Truth and Logic by A. J. Ayer, 2nd ed., copyright 1943, reprinted by permission of Dover Publications, Inc., and Victor Gollancz, Ltd.

Lectures on Ethics by Immanuel Kant, translated by Louis Infeld, reprinted by permission of Methuen & Co., Ltd.

Essays on Truth and Reality by F. H. Bradley, reprinted by permission of The Clarendon Press, Oxford.

Life of Reason, Vol. II of *Reason in Religion* by George Santayana, reprinted by permission of Charles Scribner's Sons and Constable and Company, Limited.

The material from Hugh Elliott, pp. 114–118, appeared in *Modern Science and Materialism*, published by Longmans, Green & Co., Ltd., 1919.

To my friend and colleague,

There is nothing more wholesome for us than to find problems that quite transcend our powers.

–*Charles Peirce to William James, 1905*

A NOTE ON THE SECOND EDITION

The first edition of this textbook was published just twenty years ago, in 1943, and went through 26 printings. In preparing this second edition I have been made conscious of those intervening twenty years. So many things done then would be left undone now; so many things *not* done then, would be done now. It is one thing to see that, thereby learning some humility; it is another to try to make amends in a revision, thereby learning some more humility.

In preparing this second edition the following additions and changes have been made: (1) The reading questions have been revised; (2) The reading references have been brought down to recent years; (3) Notes on sources have been added; (4) Materials from T. H. Huxley, A. J. Ayer, R. G. Collingwood, G. E. Moore, and F. Engels have been added to the six original topics; (5) A seventh topic, "An Aesthetic Problem" has been added, using materials from Véron, Tolstoy, Collingwood, Hospers, and Weitz. It is to be hoped that students will derive as much from reading this new section as I did from putting it together.

In the preliminary chapter of the first edition I remarked on the difference between an introduction to modern philosophy and a modern introduction to philosophy. I still think there is a difference and that it is important; but I would not word the difference now as I did then. It seems to me that philosophizing is first the activity in which a person engages when he detects, or seeks to detect, the principles and presuppositions which are operative in his thinking and acting; and second, the activity in which he engages when he raises questions and proposes theses about these principles and presuppositions. I have found the philosophical writings of the late R. G. Collingwood perennially helpful in arriving at this conception of the character of philosophy considered as a distinctive mode of human activity.

ALBUREY CASTELL
UNIVERSITY OF OREGON
1963

TABLE OF CONTENTS

AN INTRODUCTION TO
MODERN PHILOSOPHY

INTRODUCTION

An Account of This Book

I

This book contains readings and comments on seven philosophical problems. The problems, in the order presented, are these: a problem in theology, a problem in metaphysics, a problem in epistemology, a problem in ethics, a problem in political theory, a problem in philosophy of history, and a problem in aesthetics.

1. *Theology* is the inquiry into the existence and nature of God. The term is derived from two Greek words meaning "God" and "discourse on." There are many problems in theology. Among these, attention is directed to the following: From our knowledge of the nature of things, is it possible to infer the existence of God? If not, why not? If so, can we go further and infer any of His attributes? If so, which? The matter could be put this way: Can you use what you know about nature to justify what you believe about God? The attempt to answer these questions is called *natural* theology. With reference to this question, we examine the views of Thomas Aquinas, Blaise Pascal, David Hume, John Stuart Mill, T. H. Huxley, and William James.

2. *Metaphysics* is the inquiry into the nature of ultimate reality and the categories in terms of which it may be most fittingly described. The derivation of the work is curiously accidental. Among the writings of the Greek philosopher Aristotle is a treatise in which he has analyzed the meanings of some terms in Greek physics. This treatise was lost after his death, and recovered by a later scholar. It bore no title. The discoverer bestowed upon it the title, *ta-meta-ta-phusika*, which is the Greek for "placed after the physics," the word *meta* meaning "after." The treatise became Aristotle's *metaphysics*. The problems with which he dealt, together with problems added by later philosophers, came to form the

field of metaphysics. From among these problems, attention is directed to the following: If we admit the distinction between a "reality" and its "appearances," if we hold that things in *reality* are so-and-so, whereas they *appear* to be otherwise, then what is this reality? And what is the relation between this reality and its appearances? For instance, it is possible these days to read that everything is "really" energy. This, however, is not what things appear to be. And what of energy? Is it, in turn, "really" something else? If so, what? With reference to this problem we examine the views of René Descartes, Thomas Hobbes, George Berkeley, Arthur Schopenhauer and A. J. Ayer.

3. *Epistemology* is the inquiry into the nature of knowledge. The term is derived from two Greek words meaning "knowledge" and "discourse on." You can ask many questions about knowledge. How does knowledge originate? Has knowledge any definable limits? Wherein does it differ from error? Wherein from opinion? Wherein from speculation? Suppose a man turns from a page of natural theology or metaphysics with the remark, "That is mere speculation." Clearly, he has a theory concerning the nature of knowledge, in the light of which he discriminates between knowledge and speculation, and dismisses theology and metaphysics as speculation. What might his theory be? Many philosophers have had views on the nature of knowledge. In some instances these views led them to repudiate theology and metaphysics as "mere speculation"; in some instances to recognize them as *knowledge*. Attention is directed to the problem of knowledge in the writings of John Locke, David Hume, Immanuel Kant, Auguste Comte, Hans Vaihinger, and R. G. Collingwood. Each of these thinkers holds a theory about knowledge. Each of them uses it to discriminate between knowledge and speculation.

The first three topics—theology, metaphysics, and epistemology—form a loosely connected set: God and nature, appearance and reality, knowledge and speculation. The next three topics form another loosely connected set: morals, politics, and history.

4. *Ethics* is the inquiry into the principles and presuppositions which are operative in our moral judgments. We say an act was wrong, or that its results were bad. What is the principle upon which this right-wrong distinction rests? Can it be defended? With reference to this problem we examine the writings of these modern moralists: William Paley, Immanuel Kant, John Stuart Mill, Friedrich Nietzsche, G. E. Moore, and A. J. Ayer.

5. It is a short step from morals to *politics*. The great fact which is encountered here is the state, which may be thought of as a community of persons organized to make law possible. The state differs from other institutions. It claims to possess a monopoly of legal violence. It alone issues absolute commands. It alone claims authority over life and death. It alone claims sovereign power. What is implied in this claim? Upon what grounds does it rest? Upon what grounds could it be challenged? Attention is here directed to James I of England, to Thomas Hobbes, to Jean Jacques Rousseau, to Edmund Burke, to Karl Marx, and to Harold Laski. Their writings lead from the theory of the divine right of kings, to the theory of government as resting upon the consent of the governed, and finally to the theory of the state as the organization of class domination.

6. Our sixth problem is usually described as "the philosophy of history." It arises thus: If one considers the enormous mass of details which constitute history, is there any pattern, any controlling regularity, any large movement within which the details find place and significance? One philosophy of history differs from another in respect to *what* the pattern is. Inasmuch as the pattern gives meaning to the details, we can say that one differs from another in respect to the meaning of history. Attention is directed to views on history to be found in the writings of George Santayana, Immanuel Kant, Georg Wilhelm Friedrich Hegel, Friedrich Engels, Oswald Spengler.

7. Our seventh problem is an aesthetic problem: What is art? You can think of art as an activity. Then you could have the question, what is the nature of this activity? What does it consist in doing? How does it differ from other activities? Or you can think of art as something produced by a certain kind of activity. In this sense art means work of art. Then you can have the question, what is a work of art? What makes something to be a work of art? Here we examine the views of Eugene Véron, Leo Tolstoy, R. G. Collingwood, Professor John Hospers, and Professor Morris Weitz.

As far as feasible, I have quoted the actual words of each of the philosophers. But it should be clearly understood that this has not always been done. I have not hesitated to drop, or change the order of, words, phrases, clauses, sentences, where to do so seemed to make the meaning clearer. In extreme cases, I have resorted to paraphrases. It is therefore never safe to assume that any passage is, word for word, exactly as it would be found in the original. For this reason the passages are not enclosed in quotation marks, but merely printed in a smaller type. For this reason, also, attention is drawn, at the end of each section, to the fact that the materials are quoted or abridged or paraphrased.

II

It is possible that the first result of working through these analyses and speculations will be confusion. The problems stand out. The presence of rival answers tends to unsettle one's mind. One is confronted by a sense of crosslights, of winding paths, not to say mazes, of claim and counterclaim, assertion and denial, proof and disproof, principle and prejudice, and the suspicion that finality may be apparent only. Is *that*, then, the last word? Are persuasive alternatives the essentials of modern philosophy? Is suspended judgment its parting counsel? Four reflections present themselves:

1. The first is this: Why not? If a survey of modern philosophical thought leaves one bewildered, and if the survey has been representative, what is gained by closing one's eyes to the fact? Modern philosophical thought appears to be chaotic, incoherent, confusing. Anyone who denies this is revealing his ignorance. This appearance may be deceptive, but it is at least the beginning of wisdom to allow for the possibility that it may be a reality.

2. The second point is this: Past and present discord are no grounds for asserting that such *must* be the case in the future. How old is the modern mind? Three or four centuries; younger, in point of time lived, than any of its predecessors. One possible protection against further chaos and more "alternatives" is an invincible skepticism bred from a knowledge of past and present efforts and failures.

3. The third point is this: To turn over in one's mind the thoughts brought together in this book is an intellectual experience of the first order. It is permissible for the present writer to say this because his own part in the book has been largely that of using scissors and paste pot. To read and meditate upon Hobbes, Pascal, Rousseau, Hume, Mill, James, Berkeley, Schopenhauer, Kant, Comte, Vaihinger, Nietzsche, Burke, Marx, Spengler, Huxley, Collingwood, Ayer, and Laski is to encounter large minds at moments when they are concerned with great issues.

4. The fourth point is this: Despite the disagreement and inconclusiveness which philosophy gives rise to, no person who is reflectively inclined can forswear it. There are principles and presuppositions operative in our thinking and acting. Philosophy is the attempt to detect

these, and express them clearly. To succeed in this is to rid oneself of naivete, to achieve sophistication. There is a perennial challenge here, which no amount of disagreement and inconclusiveness is likely to remove.

Two points by way of conclusion: (1) an introduction to modern philosophy is not a modern introduction to philosophy. This book is intended to say, in effect: These analyses and speculations are typical of what philosophers have been doing during the last three or four centuries. (2) A modern introduction to philosophy can be written and should be written. Its central problem would be an inquiry into the principles and presuppositions of criticism. It would note that criticism is a fundamental activity of the human soul, but that the nature of this activity is far from clear. It would note that criticism occurs in different forms, e.g., logical, ethical, political, aesthetic, etc.; but that the rationale of these varieties of critical experience is far from clear. It would note that criticism has presuppositions, e.g., freedom, objectivity, communicability, etc., but that inquiry into these matters is difficult and obscure. These matters, however, call for another and quite different book.

A Theological Problem

THE PROBLEM STATED

Men are religious. They have beliefs about God. Many times those beliefs make a difference in their actions. What is the rational foundation for these beliefs? It is customary to distinguish between *revealed* and *natural* or *rational* theology. Knowledge about God which rests upon revelations made directly to some man or group, and recorded in various sacred writings, constitutes *revealed* theology. Knowledge about God which is arrived at by reasoning from the facts of nature constitutes *natural* or *rational* theology. It is named *natural* theology because it purports to be knowledge of God derived from our knowledge of nature. It is named *rational* theology because it purports to be knowledge of God obtained by reasoning from what we know about nature. It is a worked-out answer to the question: "Can you use what you know about nature to justify what you believe about God?"

Our primary concern, in this topic, is with the central problem of natural or rational theology: Can a man, in an understanding of nature, find reasons for justifying a belief in the existence of God? With respect to revealed theology, it is possible to say relatively little. This limitation does not arise out of any inherent impossibility in the idea of God revealing His existence and nature to man. It arises out of the fact that a revelation, or the record of a revelation, is not open to the same kind of discussable verification which we can make, for example, of the claim that the earth is round or that Napoleon was defeated at the battle of Waterloo. This impossibility arises out of the fact that the revelation,

7

or its record in sacred writings, has to be taken at its face value. We cannot go "back" of it, to see whether its claims are true.

One turns, then, to the possibility of a natural or rational theology, which shall not claim to be revealed directly by God. Natural theology, so understood, is at least as old as the writings of Plato in the fourth century B.C. In examining this matter, therefore, we are breaking into a long and venerable tradition reaching down to our own day in the writings of contemporary philosophical theologians.

The citations [1] which follow these introductory remarks present six sets of reflections upon this central problem of natural theology. The first set, in which the competence of human reason to prove God's existence is unquestioned, has been drawn from the writings of St. Thomas Aquinas. The second set, in which the competence of human reason to prove God's existence is sharply questioned, and the argument advanced that man's helplessness without God is the surest proof of His existence, is from the writings of Blaise Pascal. The third set, in which the incompetence of human reason to prove God's existence is carefully argued for, is from the writings of David Hume. The fourth set, in which the hypothesis of a finite or limited God is advanced as the most that human reason can defend, is from the writings of John Stuart Mill. The fifth set, in which it is argued that it is immoral to believe where you cannot use what you *know* to justify your belief, is from T. H. Huxley. The sixth set, in which the whole notion of an "appeal to reason" is rejected in favor of an appeal to the *will* to believe, is from the writings of William James. These six sets span the modern period and provide examples characteristic of the analyses and speculations which this problem has evoked. Aquinas, one of the greatest of late medieval theologians, is included, from the thirteenth century, in order to provide the necessary background for those who follow. Pascal is seventeenth century; Hume is eighteenth century; Mill is nineteenth century; Huxley is nineteenth century; James is late nineteenth and early twentieth century. A careful perusal of what these men have said about this one problem should do two things: indicate the many sides which this problem presents when different minds make it the object of reflective analysis, and indicate the continuity of the problem over a period of several centuries.

---

[1] Let it be acknowledged, once and for all, that this is an awkward and possibly unusual use for the word "citation." The word "quotation" or "passage" would be better, except for the fact, mentioned already in the Introduction, that some of the original passages have been abridged, re-arranged, reworded. The results therefore are often not quotations in the full sense of that word. The word "citation" is an attempt to get around this difficulty.

1. THE PRINCIPLES OF NATURAL THEOLOGY —FROM ST. THOMAS AQUINAS

Biographical Note. Thomas Aquinas was born in Italy in 1225 and died in 1274 at the age of forty-nine. The story of his life can be summarized as follows: (1) His father was a nobleman. At the age of five, Thomas was sent for his education to the Benedictine monastery of Monte Cassino, where his uncle ruled as abbot. He studied grammar, poetry, rhetoric, logic, and some elementary philosophy. From the monastery he attended the University of Naples. While there, or shortly after, he formed the design of becoming a monk in the order of St. Dominic. His mother objected, even going so far as to imprison him for two years. However, he escaped and entered the order in 1243. (2) During the next dozen years or so he pursued advanced studies in theology and philosophy at various European universities. In 1256 or 1257 he received the degree of "master of sacred sciences" and began a career of teaching and writing and controversy. (3) His writings are many. Among these the most important was his huge *Summa Theologica* in which he provided his generation with an extraordinarily systematic digest of Christian theology and much ancient philosophy. This great work, which was unfinished at the time of his death, fills many volumes in its English translation. It begins with the question of God's existence, deals then with His attributes, traces the processes of things from God and the return of man to God through Christ by means of the sacraments which Christ instituted. This *Summa* soon became, and continues to be, the official presentation of Catholic theology and philosophy. (4) At the command of Pope Gregory X, Thomas undertook to be present at an ecclesiastical council to be held in Lyons. On the way he fell sick. He put up at a near-by monastery, but died after a few months' illness. In 1323, almost half a century after his death, Thomas was canonized by Pope John XXII. A recent translator remarks, "Whatever may be the proper statement of the grounds of his sainthood, his vast intellectual achievements are certainly events out of the natural order and appropriate to a miracle."

Why Theology? It may be well to ask ourselves why we begin the study of philosophy with a set of chapters on theology; and why, among theologians, we begin with Saint Thomas Aquinas. The answers to these questions are along these lines:

There are few methods better suited to introduce a student to

philosophy than to spend a little time with theology. The reason is that
in most ages men have sought to answer philosophical questions in terms
of theological beliefs. "What shall I believe?" has frequently been
answered by "The word of God." "What shall I do?" has frequently
been answered by "Obey the Will of God." "Where did the world come
from?" has frequently been answered by "It was created by God."
"What happens to me when I die?" has frequently been answered by
"You return to God." In these and many other ways, the notion of God
has entered into the questions men ask and the answers they accept; and
wherever it has entered, it has always been to answer some ultimate and
highly critical question. We can generalize by saying that the idea of
God has functioned as an ultimate principle of explanation and an
ultimate principle of criticism. Now, to the extent that philosophy is
the systematic inquiry into our principles and presuppositions, there has
always been a close connection between it and theology. If the answers
to ultimate questions of explanation and evaluation are to be found in
theology, it is a man's philosophical business to know this. If there is
reasonable doubt about these matters, it is likewise his philosophical business to inform himself that such is the case.

It is for this reason that theology provides a good beginning in
philosophy. The questions which *define* philosophy have frequently
been answered by theology. From a slight familiarity with the latter,
therefore, we may at least expect to discover what questions are philosophical in character.

Why Saint Thomas? The answer here is that he is in many ways the
prince among theologians. His two great works, *Summa Theologica*
and *Summa Contra Gentiles* are elaborate and painstaking and influential.
If we read Saint Thomas, we will confront ourselves with things which
are among the best which theology has to offer. The full text of his
Summa runs to about a score of volumes. We are concerned with the
first part of the first volume. There Saint Thomas poses, and endeavors
to answer the questions, Does God exist? How do we know that He
exists? Can this knowledge be demonstrated?

A Matter of Inference. Thomas's first claim is that the existence of
God is not something which we can know directly; it is not given as,
e.g., the color of this page is given; it is not known by intuition; it is
not known by direct insight. It is inferred or deduced. In other words,
belief in the existence of God rests upon an argument, upon discourse
having the form If-then, where the If-part is something directly given
and the then-part is something inferred from what is directly given. Such

being the case, we are naturally curious about the fact or facts, directly knowable, from which Thomas will infer the existence of God. He proposes five facts. Each gives rise to its proper argument. These are known as the argument from change; the argument from cause; the argument from contingency; the argument from degrees of excellence; and the argument from design. In considering these five theological arguments, we shall not quote Saint Thomas's own words, since his manner of stating them would be rather elusive and foreign. In place of direct quotation, we shall paraphrase and describe what he says.

(1) *The Argument From Change.* Change is an undoubted fact in nature. Wherever we look, things are changing. A-changing-into-B is a phrase which has a very wide application. How are we to explain or account for the fact of change? Any particular instance of change we can refer to some previous change; but this will not help us to account for the presence of change, as such. There are three possibilities: (a) We may accept change as an ultimate fact, neither requiring or permitting any explanation. (b) We may refer every case of change to some prior case, extending our reference backward to infinity. (c) We may postulate what Saint Thomas calls an Unmoved Mover, or Prime Mover, itself unchanging but the source from which all particular instances of change proceed.

The first two alternatives Thomas rejects. His reasoning is not so clear as one could wish it. He rejects the notion of change as an ultimate fact neither requiring nor permitting any explanation, because such a position would seem to be needless skepticism. Why *should* the fact of change in nature be allowed to fall outside the range of explanation? If there are going to be ultimate mysteries, why should change be among them? Is there any necessity in the claim that change is an ultimate, inexplicable fact? For these and similar reasons Thomas rejects the "skeptical" solution in favor of a more "rationalist" solution; that is, in favor of the claim that there is a reason for the fact of change.

He rejects the notion of explaining changes by referring them to prior changes, and so on back to infinity. His reasoning here seems to be that such an explanation is wrong in principle, and would hence break down and leave one in the first position of accepting change as an ultimate fact. The point here seems to be two-fold. First, that referring change to prior change is always to be left with change; whereas to be left with change is precisely the thing we are seeking to avoid. Second, the notion of an infinite regression is itself a highly unsatisfactory one. It involves the mind in many different puzzles and paradoxes which leave matters no better off than the skeptical solution. For these and similar reasons, Saint Thomas rejects the notion of infinite regression as required by the attempt to explain change by referring it to prior change.

If there is no fourth alternative, then he has a strong case for the remaining third explanation. If there are just three possibilities, and you show cause for rejecting two of them, you do not require any further justification for accepting the third. This, at any rate, seems to be Thomas's reasoning in respect to his argument from the fact of change to the existence of an Unmoved Mover, or Prime Mover, or God.

(2) *The Argument from Causation.* These arguments in natural theology, as their name suggests, are inferences *from* some fact about nature *to* the existence of God. From the fact of change, Thomas argued to the existence of God. His second argument, known as the argument from causation, is similar in form, but begins with a different fact. This time the fact selected is causation. Like change, causation is a large, obvious, ubiquitous fact. When we examine nature, our minds seem to detect the fact of causation almost everywhere. We have many different words and phrases for expressing this fact. This causes that. This is causally connected with that. The principle of causality is illustrated between this and that.

Granted this fact about nature, Thomas's procedure is the same as in the case of change. How are we to explain or account for the fact of causation? Any particular instance of causation we can refer to some previous instance. Suppose B is the cause of A. We can refer B itself back to C, as its cause; and C itself back to D, as its cause, and so on. But this will not help us to account for the fact of causation as such. The question is not, Does this cause that? It is, Why does this cause that? Why does anything cause anything? Why is there causation in nature? As in the case of change, there are three possibilities: (a) We may accept causation as an ultimate fact, neither requiring nor permitting any explanation. (b) We may refer every instance of causing to some prior instance, extending our reference back to infinity. (c) We may postulate what Saint Thomas calls a First Cause, itself uncaused.

There is no need to retrace his argument in further detail. He rejects the notion that causation is an ultimate fact neither requiring nor permitting any explanation. He rejects the notion of an infinite regression. He is left with the notion of a First Cause.

(3) *The Argument from Contingency.* We have seen that Thomas's procedure is to select some obvious fact about nature, and to argue from the existence of this fact to the existence of God. From the fact

of change, he argued the existence of God as unchanging First Mover. From the fact of causation, he argued the existence of God as uncaused First Cause. It will be noticed that these arguments begin with one sort of notion and conclude with the "opposite" notion. Thus from change, he argued an unchanging Being; from causation, he argued an uncaused Being. This inference from one sort of fact in nature, to God as an "opposite" sort of fact, characterizes Thomas's third argument.

The argument from contingency begins with the fact that in nature many things appear to be contingent, accidental, possible, dependent. A man is walking across a field. He encounters a stray bullet, fired by someone who was ignorant of his presence in that field. Death results. Speaking of this death, we say it was accidental. Among the things we mean when we say this is that it did not *have* to happen. Matters might have been, could have been, otherwise. The man might have been elsewhere when the bullet came by. The shot might have been fired in some other direction. The compresence of the victim and the bullet, at just that time and place, was not necessary. The man's presence, at just that time and place, did not necessitate the bullet's presence, at just that time and place. There were other possibilities. The way things actually happened did not exhaust all the possibilities. We have many different words and phrases which enable us to describe this sort of thing. We can say that his actual death was possible, but not necessary; that it was contingent or dependent upon the fact that he was there when the bullet came by; that it happened, but did not have to happen; that it was accidental, not necessary.

Like change and causation, contingency is an obvious fact about nature. Many things in nature exhibit this fact of contingency, or what Thomas sometimes calls "dependent being." It may be that *every* object and event in nature exhibits this fact of contingency. The question is, how are we to account for the fact of contingency in nature? The question is not, Was this contingent upon that? It is, Why are there contingent facts in nature? Why is anything contingent? We could put our question about contingency in the same form as our question about change and causation: Why is there change in nature? Why is there causation in nature? Why is there contingency in nature?

Once the *sort* of fact is clear, the rest of the argument is easily grasped. We have again three possibilities: (a) We may accept contingency as an ultimate fact about nature, neither requiring nor permitting any explanation. (b) We may refer every instance of contingency to some prior instance, extending our reference back to infinity. (c) We may postulate what Thomas calls a Necessary Being, itself not contingent upon anything.

There is again no need to retrace his argument in detail. He rejects the notion that contingency is an ultimate fact neither requiring nor permitting any explanation. He rejects also the notion of an infinite regression. He is left with the notion of a Necessary Being.

(4) *The Argument From Degrees of Excellence.* Thomas's fourth argument differs slightly from the first three. If we examine the nature of things, we notice the fact of degrees of excellence. This is more excellent than that. These are more excellent than those. What *sort* of excellence is not in question. Saint Thomas seems to suggest that there are kinds or sorts or classes of things, and that particular cases exhibit varying degrees of excellence, each according to its kind. Thus, one horse may be more excellent than another; one tree more excellent than another; one man more excellent than another. Thomas does not seem to suggest that this notion of degrees of excellence cuts across kinds or classes. Thus, his idea is not that a horse is more excellent than a tree, but rather that one horse is more excellent than another. However this may be, nature exhibits degrees of excellence. Degrees of excellence, like change and causation and contingency, is a fact about nature.

Granted this fact, he urges that the notion of degrees of excellence implies the notion of perfection. Unless we have the notion of perfection, we could not say that something was more or less excellent. Imperfect being, of no matter what sort, implies perfect being of that sort. Evaluation of the actual, in terms of degrees of excellence, implies a grasp of the ideal. Now the totality of actuals, exhibiting their degrees of excellence, make up nature. Nature is the whereabouts of degrees of excellence. But what can we say of perfection? Its whereabouts is obviously not nature; nothing in nature is perfect after its kind.

It is easier to state Thomas's problem here than it is to understand exactly what the answer means. What he seems to say is that nature is the realm of imperfect being, and God is the realm of perfect being. In nature, nothing is perfect. In God, all things are perfect. God is the whereabouts of perfect being, just as nature is the whereabouts of imperfect being. And our power to detect imperfect being (degrees of excellence) in nature implies our knowledge of perfect being in God. If knowing imperfect being entails the existence of imperfect being—if it did not exist you could not know it—then knowing perfect being entails the existence of perfect being.

This argument can be given the same formulation as we gave to the others. We can say, The fact in nature this time is degrees of excellence, or imperfect being. We have three possibilities: (a) We may accept this as an ultimate fact, neither requiring nor permitting any explanation. (b) We may refer every instance of a degree of excellence to some other instance of greater excellence, extending our reference to infinity. (c) We may postulate what Thomas calls Perfect Being, in whom all sorts of perfections live and move and have their being, and through knowledge of whom we are able to recognize the fact of imperfect being, or degrees of excellence, in nature.

(5) *The Argument from Harmony*. Thus far, Saint Thomas has argued from nature as changing being to God as unchanging being; from nature as caused being to God as uncaused being; from nature as contingent being to God as necessary being; from nature as imperfect being to God as perfect being. In each instance we begin with nature as the whereabouts of a certain sort of fact, and argue from that to God as the explanatory ground of this fact.

In the fifth and last argument, Thomas selects the fact of what he calls "accord" or "harmony" in nature. We sometimes call it "adaptation." What he refers to is this: Men require to see, and they have eyes; or, men have eyes and the nature of things is, in great part, visible to such eyes. There is "harmony" or "accord" or "adaptation" here. Polar bears require a covering to withstand arctic rigors, and they have a thick coat of fur; or, polar bears have a thick coat of fur, and arctic weather is, in great part, unable to penetrate such fur. There is adaptation here. A list of this sort of "accord" in nature could be extended indefinitely.

We have our fact, then. As in the other instances we have three possibilities: (a) We may accept adaptation as an ultimate fact, neither requiring nor permitting explanation. This is not to say that adaptation is to be "explained" by referring it to "chance," since such reference would either imply the legitimacy of the demand for explanation, or it would be only a covert way of denying the need or possibility of explanation. (b) We may refer each case of adaptation to some prior or some more general instance, extending our reference to infinity. (c) We may postulate what Saint Thomas calls "design"; that is, we may explain the fact of adaptation as the manifestation of intention or intelligence or foresight or providence.

The Nature of God. If we collect the conclusions to these five arguments, we have a general description of the nature of God. He is unchanging. He is uncaused. He is necessary. He is perfect. He is providential. We can add, by implication, that He is omnipresent and omnipotent: if

He is present in all things as their cause, it must be the case that in some
sense He *is* everywhere and *does* everything. So far, Thomas's argument
has proceeded tolerably smoothly. At this point, however, it begins to
generate problems. We may note two of these, namely, the problem of
evil and the problem of freedom.

   The Problem of Evil. We have seen that natural theology proceeds
by arguing from nature to God. Among the facts used by Saint Thomas
were change, causation, contingency, degrees of excellence, and adaptation or "accord." One of these facts gives rise to a problem. It is this: If
nature exhibits degrees of excellence, then it must be the case that nature
is not perfect. Indeed, nature is, for Thomas, the realm of the imperfect.
Here is a fact which needs to be accounted for. How account for the fact
that nature is not perfect? On the hypothesis that nature is God's handiwork, it ought to be perfect. But it is necessary for Thomas to insist that
nature is not perfect, otherwise the argument from degrees of excellence
loses its point; moreover, he was too sensible to deny the fact of imperfection in nature. Hence the problem: how square the imperfection of
the actual with the ideal perfection of the First Cause? If God is the
omnipotent and perfect author of the actual, why is the actual imperfect?

   Saint Thomas offers two lines of defense. Neither is satisfactory. The
first is that we must ascribe the imperfections in nature to the materials
with which the Great Artificer worked, as we might ascribe imperfections
in a statue to the tools or materials with which the human artist worked.
But this is to overlook the fact that the human artist did not create his
materials. The second is that we must ascribe the imperfections in nature
to the fact that they make possible some good things not otherwise possible, as we might say that trials are a necessary condition to the exercise
and development of patience, and patience is a good thing. On the hypothesis that some good things require imperfections in order that they
may come into being, Thomas argues that if all imperfections were excluded by divine providence, then the number of good things would be
diminished. It does not seem necessary to criticize this argument. Thomas
is in a dilemma, and there is no reason to prod him with the horns.

   The Problem of Free Will. Among the imperfections which are obvious to Saint Thomas is the fact of evil-doing, or sin, in the life of man.
This sort of imperfection Thomas could dispose of by ascribing it to a
man's free-will. However, if free-will is to be added to the facts of nature,
we are obliged to ask how it is to be reconciled with the omnipotence of
God. If God does *everything*, then in what sense does man do *anything*?
If God's will governs all things, in what sense is man's will responsible for

the evil acts which it performs? The argument would seem to require that Thomas sacrifice God's omnipotence to save man's freedom, if he proposes to use man's freedom to save God's righteousness. Thomas has three lines of defense, none of which are satisfactory. He says, in the first place, that the Scriptures tell us that God made man and left him in the hands of his own counsel, i.e., gave him free will to choose between good and evil. He says, in the second place, that man must have a free-will, since otherwise rewards and punishments would be inappropriate; i.e., if man's will is not free, then he is not responsible for his acts, and he should not be punished if those acts are evil, or rewarded if they are good. He says in the third place, that God made man rational, and that being rational includes having freedom of mind and will. These arguments are all irrelevant. The last two are good arguments in support of the thesis that man has a free will; but that was not Thomas's problem. His problem was how man's free-will is to be reconciled with God's omnipotence. The teaching of the Catholic Church is more forthright. It says that moral evil is a fact, explainable by reference to man's free-will, but that man's free-will, while a fact, is also a mystery.

Of Man's Last End. These snags and bucklings are, it would seem, essential ingredients in the argument of Saint Thomas's natural theology. However, once they have been noted one may pass on to further matters. Of these, in the voluminous *Summas*, there are many. One, selected here by way of conclusion, is the question of what Thomas calls man's last end. By that he means man's highest good, the term "end" being used in the sense of goal or object. Man's highest good, as set forth by Saint Thomas, is easily stated: it is the enjoyment of God. What this means is less easily stated. It is probably as follows: Man's last end is happiness. Wherein is true happiness to be found? It is to be found in those activities whereby man raises himself from a state of confusion and chaos about the world, to a grasp of the fact that the world's changeableness is rooted in God's unchangeableness; its causality rooted in God as first cause; its contingency rooted in God's necessity; its imperfection rooted in God's perfection; and its intelligibility rooted in God's intelligence. As the Spanish proverb has it, these are major words.

Thomas's writings exemplify one type of natural theology and one approach to the central problem. So long as the appeal to reason goes hand in hand with piety, his ideas are likely to be re-echoed in other men's minds, as in his mind they were echoes from classical Greek philosophy. The essentials are simple. God exists as the First Mover, the First Cause, the Author of the order and harmony in nature. His attributes include perfection, omnipotence, omniscience, omnipresence, benevolence, justice, rationality, prevision, and so forth. How these are to be squared with man's free will and the world's great evils are nice theoretical problems. In God's ordering of things, man stands a little lower than the angels and exercises dominion over the animals and plants and inanimate orders. With his Creator he shares an intelligence and a power to know good from evil. In the knowledge and enjoyment of God man finds his only true and lasting happiness.

Saint Thomas's five arguments or proofs for the existence of God will be found in Part I, Question 2, Article III, of his *Summa Theologica*. The title of Article III is "Whether God Exists?" So that the reader may not be at the mercy of my paraphrase, a translation of Saint Thomas's text is given here. The translation is from The English Dominican Translation of Saint Thomas, made by Father Laurence Shapcote, O.P., in 1911. Saint Thomas, at this point in his *Summa* has just asked whether God exists, and whether it can be demonstrated that God exists; and has answered: The existence of God can be proved in five ways. He then proceeds as follows:

THE FIRST WAY

The existence of God can be shown in five ways. The first and clearest is taken from the idea of motion. (1) Now it is certain, and our senses corroborate it, that some things in this world are in motion. (2) But everything which is in motion is moved by something else. (3) For nothing is in motion except in so far as it is in potentiality in relation to that towards which it is in motion. (4) Now a thing causes movement in so far as it is in actuality. For to cause movement is nothing else than to bring something from potentiality to actuality; but a thing cannot be brought from potentiality to actuality except by something which exists in actuality, as, for example, that which is hot in actuality, like fire, makes wood, which is only hot in potentiality, to be hot in actuality, and thereby causes movement in it and alters it. (5) But it is not possible that the same thing should be at the same time in actuality and in potentiality in relation to the same thing, but only in relation to different things; for what is hot in actuality cannot at the same time be hot in potentiality, though it is at the same time cold in potentiality. (6) It is impossible, therefore, that in relation to the same thing and in the same way anything should both cause movement and be caused, or that it should cause itself to move. (7) Everything therefore that is in motion must be moved by something else. If therefore the thing which causes it to move be in motion, this too must be moved by something else, and so on. (8) But we cannot proceed to infinity in this way, because in that case there would be no first mover, and in consequence, neither would there be any other mover; for secondary movers do not cause movement except they be moved by a first mover, as, for example, a stick cannot cause movement unless it is moved by the hand. Therefore it is necessary to stop at some first mover which is moved by nothing else. And this is what we all understand God to be.

THE SECOND WAY

The Second Way is taken from the idea of the Efficient Cause. (1) For we find that there is among material things a regular order of efficient causes. (2) But we do not find, nor indeed is it possible, that anything is the efficient cause of itself, for in that case it would be prior to itself, which is impossible. (3) Now it is not possible to proceed to infinity in efficient causes. (4) For if we arrange in order all efficient causes, the first is the cause of the intermediate, and the intermediate the cause of the last, whether the intermediate be many or only one. (5) But if we remove a cause the effect is removed; therefore, if there is no *first* among efficient causes, neither will there be a last or an intermediate. (6) But if we proceed to infinity in efficient causes there will be no first efficient cause, and thus there will be no ultimate effect, nor any intermediate efficient causes, which is clearly false. Therefore it is necessary to suppose the existence of some first efficient cause, and this men call God.

THE THIRD WAY

The Third Way rests on the idea of the "contingent" and the "necessary" and is as follows: (1) Now we find that there are certain things in the Universe which are capable of existing and of not existing, for we find that some things are brought into existence and then destroyed, and consequently are capable of being or not being. (2) But it is impossible for all things which exist to be of this kind, because anything which is capable of not existing, at some time or other does not exist. (3) If therefore *all* things are capable of not existing, there was a time when nothing existed in the Universe. (4) But if this is true there would also be nothing in existence now; because anything that does not exist cannot begin to exist except by the agency of something which has existence. If therefore there was once nothing which existed, it would have been impossible for anything to begin to exist, and so nothing would exist now. (5) This is clearly false. Therefore all things are not contingent, and there must be something which is necessary in the Universe. (6) But everything which is necessary either has or has not the cause of its necessity from an outside source. Now it is not possible to proceed to infinity in necessary things which have a cause of their necessity, as has been proved in the case of efficient causes. Therefore it is necessary to suppose the existence of something which is necessary in itself, not having the cause of its necessity from any outside source, but which is the cause of necessity in others. And this "something" we call God.

THE FOURTH WAY

The Fourth Way is taken from the degrees which are found in things. (1) For among different things we find that one is more or less good or true or noble; and likewise in the case of other things of this kind. (2) But the words "more" or "less" are used of different things in proportion as they approximate in their different ways to something which has the particular quality in the highest degree—e.g., we call a thing hotter when it approximates more nearly to that which is hot in the highest degree. There is therefore something which is true in the highest degree, good in the highest degree and noble in the highest degree; (3) and consequently there must be also something which has being in the highest degree. For things which are true in the highest degree also have being in the highest degree (see Aristotle, *Metaphysics*, 2). (4) But anything which has a certain quality of any kind in the highest degree is also the cause of all the things of that kind, as, for example, fire which is hot in the highest degree is the cause of all hot things (as is said in the same book). (5) Therefore there exists something which is the cause of being, and goodness, and of every perfection in all existing things; and this we call God. . . .

THE FIFTH WAY

The Fifth Way is taken from the way in which nature is governed. (1) For we observe that certain things which lack knowledge, such as natural bodies, work for an End. This is obvious, because they always, or at any rate very frequently, operate in the same way so as to attain the best possible result. (2) Hence it is clear that they do not arrive at their goal by chance, but by purpose. (3) But those things which have no knowledge do not move towards a goal unless they are guided by someone or something which does possess knowledge and intelligence—e.g., an arrow by an archer. Therefore, there does exist something which possesses intelligence by which all natural things are directed to their goal; and this we call God.

Note on Sources. The paraphrases of Saint Thomas's proofs are based on Part I, Question 2, Article III, of his *Summa Theologica*. The paraphrases of his remarks on Freewill are based on Part I, Question 83, Article I, of his *Summa Theologica*. The paraphrases of his remarks on man's last end are based on Book III, Chapters 37 and 59, of his *Summa Contra Gentiles*. The paraphrases of his remarks on evil are based on Part I, Question 19, Article IX, and Part I, Question 49, Article II.

Reading References. Thomas's writings have been studied and written about almost continuously since their publication. In the year 1879 Leo XIII issued a papal encyclical in which he enjoined upon Catholics the wisdom of reading the writings of scholastics in general and Thomas in particular. It is a difficult task to point to two or three books and say, "Above all, do not fail to look into these." Much of the literature on Thomistic thought is in Latin or Italian or German or French. Of this, rather little has been translated. There are, however, two treatises, written by English scholars, which will repay any time spent on them: *The Conception of God in the Philosophy of Thomas Aquinas,* by R. L. Patterson, and *Thomas Aquinas* by M. C. D'Arcy. The same may be said for the translation of M. Gilson's *Le Thomisme.* Anyone who finds these books difficult should turn to the translation of M. Maritain's *Le docteur Angelique* or to G. K. Chesterton's charming little volume *Thomas Aquinas.*

The following are some books published since 1940:

Adler, M. J. *Saint Thomas and the Gentiles.*
Ardley, G. *Aquinas and Kant.*
Bryar, W. *Saint Thomas and the Existence of God.*
Copleston, F. C. *Aquinas.*
Gardeil, H. D. *Introduction to the Philosophy of Saint Thomas Aquinas.*
Gilson, E. *The Christian Philosophy of Saint Thomas Aquinas.*
Gerstein, G. C. *On the Conception of God in the Philosophy of Maimonides and Saint Thomas Aquinas.*
Herrlin, O. *The Ontological Proof in Thomistic and Kantian Interpretation.*
Lyttkens, H. *The Analogy Between God and the World.*
Maritain, J. *Saint Thomas and the Problem of Evil.*
———. *Saint Thomas Aquinas, Angel of the Schools.*
Noon, W. T. *Joyce and Aquinas.*
Pegis, A. C. *Saint Thomas and the Greeks.*
Ryan, J. K. *The Reputation of Saint Thomas Aquinas Among English Protestant Thinkers of the 17th Century.*
Walz, A. M. *Saint Thomas Aquinas: A Biographical Study.*

READING QUESTIONS

1. Distinguish between revealed and natural theology.
2. Why is *rational* synonymous with *natural* in this connection?

3. Formulate the central problem of natural theology.
4. Why ignore the question of revealed theology?
5. How would you distinguish between theism and atheism?
6. How between atheism and skepticism?
7. If you wanted to establish a case for atheism, what would you use for evidence?
8. What is the argument from change?
9. From causation?
10. From contingency?
11. From degrees of excellence?
12. From harmony?
13. Why does Thomas reject the idea of an infinite regression?
14. Aside from Thomas's five, can you think of any other arguments for the existence of God?
15. What qualities does Thomas ascribe to the Deity?
16. What is the problem of evil in natural theology?
17. Along what lines does Thomas seek to deal with it?
18. What criticism is his position open to?
19. What is the problem of free will in natural theology?
20. Do you see any connection between these two problems?
21. Why would Thomas hesitate to deny man's free will?
22. How does he seek to deal with this problem?
23. What two attributes of Deity raise these two problems?
24. What does Thomas mean by man's last end?
25. Wherein does he believe man will find it?
26. Formulate one or more problems you would put to Thomas.
27. What questions does the following question give rise to: "Can you use what you know about nature to justify what you believe about God?"

2. THE RELIGIOUS WAGER
—FROM BLAISE PASCAL

From Thomas to Pascal. Thomas Aquinas wrote in an age of Christian faith. His trust in reason to find out God was a trust shared by most of his contemporaries and readers. This, however, was in the thirteenth century. The Renaissance and the Reformation succeeded the Middle Ages. The new science of Copernicus, Kepler, Galileo, succeeded the old science of Aristotle, Ptolemy, and the medieval scholars. The new philosophy of Montaigne, Descartes, Hobbes, Bacon succeeded the old philosophy of Augustine, Anselm, Abélard, and Aquinas. It was only to be expected that the placid argumentation by which Thomas built up his

Summa should be replaced by something more vibrant and uneasy. This change is seen clearly in the religious writings of Blaise Pascal.

Biographical Note. Pascal was born in 1623 and died in 1662 at the age of thirty-nine. It is convenient to consider his life in three periods. (1) He was educated at home. His parents, especially his father, were devout Catholics, pious but stern. Blaise early displayed a remarkable precocity in physics and mathematics; at the age of fifteen he was producing monographs on conic sections which were thought important enough to be read to "the most learned and scientific men in Paris." He was counted one of the outstanding physicists and mathematicians of his time. His discoveries were made during the years when most scientists are still mastering the known facts of their field. (2) The elder Pascal died in 1650 leaving a patrimony to Blaise and his sister Jacqueline. Jacqueline entered a convent; Blaise went off to Paris. During the next four years he lived among scholars, scientists, wits, and the nobility. On November 23, 1654, he had what is termed a mystical experience. That he had this experience, there is no reason to doubt; that it meant what he interpreted it to mean is perhaps open to debate. (3) That hour, described for posterity in a note which was found sewn into the coat he was wearing at the time of his death, wrought a complete change in Pascal's life. Austerity, self-denial, boundless almsgiving, and absolute obedience to his spiritual director replaced his previous routine of scientist and man-about-town. He threw himself into the defense of the Cistercian abbey of Port Royal des Champs, which was being persecuted by the hierarchy for a number of real or supposed heresies. The case for the Port Royalists was stated by Pascal in his celebrated *Letters to a Provincial*. The closing years of his life were given to planning and sketching in what was to have been, had he lived to complete it, an apologia for the Christian faith in an age of unbelief and indifference. The book was never finished. It consists of hundreds of loosely grouped fragments, aphorisms, jottings. It has always been known, in French, by the title *Pensées;* in English, by the title *Thoughts.* The citations which follow are drawn from this unfinished defense of Pascal's religious beliefs.

The Argument of the Citations. The citations given below do not trace the argument of Pascal's entire book. Much of that volume deals with special topics, for example, the relation of other religions to Christianity, the significance of miracles, prophecy, revelation, and so on. With these we are not concerned. Our interest is limited to the question: Can a man, by the use of his reason, argue the existence of God from the existence of nature? Can you use what you know about nature to justify what you believe about God? To this question Thomas had answered in the affirmative. Pascal, an equally devout Christian and Catholic, answers in the negative The movement of his thought is as follows: Some persons are skeptical or indifferent in matters of religious belief. Such persons are to be pitied and scorned. But no appeal to reason, no natural theology in the manner of Thomas, will avail to dissolve their doubts, denials, indifference. This for two reasons: They are too hardened, and in any case, human reason is frankly unequal to the task of elaborating a rational theology. Pascal soliloquizes at some length on the littleness of man and the impotence of reason. If not through his rational powers, then through what can the doubting and indifferent soul be brought to a knowledge of God? Pascal's answer is this: through his emotions. In a famous line he remarks: "The heart hath its reasons, which the reason knows not of." The utmost that reason can do is to pose and defend what Pascal describes as a "wager," that is, a bet that God exists. Man must see for himself that his happiness lies in belief in and love of God. When he has seen this fact, his skepticism and indifference will be replaced by faith and happiness and true goodness.

He begins with those who have doubts about the existence of God and are not particularly worried over it:

Before entering on the proofs of the Christian religion, I find it necessary to set forth the unfairness of men who are indifferent to the search for truth in a matter which is so important to them and which touches them so nearly. Among all their errors, this most proves them to be fools and blind.

We know well enough how men of this temper behave. They believe they have made a great effort after their instruction when they have spent a few hours reading some book of Scripture and putting a few questions to some ecclesiastic. Whereupon they boast that they have "in vain consulted books and men." Such carelessness is intolerable.

Among unbelievers I make a vast distinction. I can have nothing but compassion for all who sincerely lament their doubt, who look upon it as the worst of evils, who spare no pains to escape it, who make these matters their chief and most serious occupation. But those who pass their lives without thinking of this ultimate end of existence, who neglect to examine whether these are matters which people receive through credulous simplicity or have a solid and impregnable basis, such persons I regard in a wholly different manner. Their negligence irritates me much more than it excites my pity. It astonishes and overwhelms me; it is for me something monstrous.

There are but three classes of persons: those who have found God and serve Him; those who have not found God, but do diligently seek Him; and those who have not found God, and live without seeking Him. The first are happy and wise. The second are unhappy, but wise. The third are unhappy and fools.

It is a sorry evil to be in doubt. It is an indispensable duty to seek when we are in doubt. Therefore he who doubts and neglects to seek to dispel these doubts, is at once in a sorry plight and guilty of great perversity. If he is calm and contented in his doubt, if he frankly avows it, if he boasts of it, if he makes it the subject of vanity and delight, I can find no terms with which to describe him.

How do men come by these sentiments? What delight is there in such things? What is there to be proud of in beholding ourselves in the midst of impenetrable darkness? How can any rational man reason in this way: "I know not who has put me in the world, nor what the world is, nor what I am myself. I am in terrible ignorance of all these things. I view the awful spaces of the universe that surround me, I find myself fixed to a corner of this vast extent, I see nothing but infinities on every side enclosing me like an atom. All that I know is that I must soon die. Such is my state—full of misery, weakness, obscurity. And from this I conclude that I ought to pass all the days of my life without thinking of what is to happen to me hereafter. It may be that I could find some answers to my doubts; but I am unwilling to take the trouble."

Who would desire to have for a friend a man who discourses in such a fashion? Who would select such a person to be the confidant of his affairs? Who would have recourse to such a one in his afflictions? In fine, for what use in life could such a man be destined? It is the glory of religion to have such irrational men for its enemies. Such strange insensibility for the greatest things is something monstrous. It is an incomprehensible delusion.

There must be a strange revulsion in the nature of man, to make him glory in such a state. Most of those who are thus involved are people who have heard that fine worldly manners consist in what they call "throwing off the yoke." This they try to imitate. But, what good does it do us to hear a man say that he has "thrown off the yoke," that he does not believe there is a God, that he is answerable in his conduct to none but himself? Is this a thing to be said gaily? On the contrary, is it not a thing to be said with sadness, as of all things the saddest? It requires all the love of the religion which they despise, not to despise such persons and abandon them in their folly.

So much for perverse doubts and callous indifference. Pascal knows that there is a long tradition of rational theologizing which, in its heyday, triumphed easily over such skepticism and infidelity. But that day has passed. Since then, Montaigne had written. Doubt had taken too firm a hold to be dislodged by appeals to man's reason in support of religious belief. To what point, he seems to ask, to what point such intellectual circumgyrations as the argument from design, or the argument from first cause, when a man has really ceased to believe in God?

I wonder at the boldness of those who undertake to speak of God to the irreligious. Their first chapter is to prove the existence of God by reference to the works of nature. I should not be astonished if they addressed their argument to those who already believe; for those who have a lively faith in their heart see at once that all that exists is none other than the handiwork of God. But for those who are destitute of faith—to tell them that they need only look at nature around them in order to see God unveiled, to give them the course of the sun and the moon as the sole proof of this important matter, to imagine with such an argument we have proved anything, is only to give grounds for believing that the proofs of our religion are very feeble. Indeed, I see by reason and experience that nothing is more fitted to excite contempt.

This is what I see, and what troubles me. I look on all sides, and see nothing but obscurity; nature offers me nothing but matter for doubt. If I saw nothing in nature which marked a Divinity, I should decide not to believe in him. If I saw everywhere the marks of a Creator, I should rest peacefully in faith. But I see too much to deny, and too little to affirm; so my state is pitiful. A hundred times I have wished that God would mark His presence in nature unequivocally, if He upholds nature; or that nature would wholly suppress the signs which she gives of God, if those signs are fallacious; that she would either say all or say nothing, so I might see what part I should take. While in my present state, ignorant of what I am and of what I ought to do, I know neither my condition nor my duty.

The metaphysical proofs of God are so far apart from man's reason, and so complicated, that they are but little striking. If they are of use to any, it is only during the moment that the demonstration is before them. An hour afterwards they fear they have been mistaken. Therefore I do not here undertake to prove by natural reason the existence of God. I do not feel myself strong enough to find in nature proofs to convince hardened atheists. All who seek God in nature find no light to satisfy them. They fall either into atheism or into deism, two things which the Christian religion almost equally abhors.

What then? Revealed theology, as Pascal well knows, is a dead horse when one is chasing doubters and deniers. Rational theology, in the sense of a reasoned appeal from nature to God, he has himself rejected as barren and unconvincing if a man does not already feel God in his heart. His answer worked out bit by bit in the fragments of his unfinished *Thoughts*, comes to this: The strongest proof for the existence of God is the great need felt by the human soul for the sustaining presence of such a Being in an otherwise empty universe.

He begins this step in his argument by drawing attention to the immensity of the spatio-temporal universe in which man finds himself:

Let a man contemplate nature in her full majesty. Let him extend his view beyond the objects which surround him. Let him regard the sun. Let him consider the earth whereon he lives as a point in comparison with the vast orbit described by the sun. Let him learn that this vast orbit is but a point compared with that embraced by the stars which roll in the firmament. Let his imagination pass beyond. All this visible cosmos is but a point in the ample bosom of nature. In vain we extend our conceptions beyond imaginable spaces: We bring forth but atoms in comparison with the reality of things. For the universe is an infinite sphere whose center is everywhere and whose circumference is nowhere.

From the vastness of things, he passes to the other extreme. Compared to the whole of nature, man may be a mere speck. But compared to the infinitely small particles which compose the material world, he is a colossus.

There is another aspect, equally astonishing. Let a man seek things the most minute. Let him consider a mite, in the exceeding smallness of its body: parts incomparably smaller, limbs with joints, veins in those limbs, blood in those veins, humors in this blood, globules in these humors, gases in the globules. Let him divide these globules. Let him exhaust his powers of conception. He will think perhaps that he has arrived at the minutest atom of nature. I will show him therein a new abyss. I will picture to him the inconceivable immensity of nature in the compass of this abbreviation of an atom. Let him view therein an infinity of worlds, each with its own firmament, its planets, its earth, in the same proportion as the visible world. Let him lose himself in these wonders, as astonishing in their littleness as the others in their magnitude. His body, which just before was imperceptible in the universe, is now a colossus in comparison with the infinitely small at which it is possible to arrive.

With this contrast in mind, Pascal pauses to ask: What is man, amid all this? If he had completed his argument, he would doubtless have used the words of the Psalmist, "What is man that Thou art mindful of him?" But at this point, that would be a begging of the question: It is precisely that "Thou" that is in question.

What is man, in the midst of these two infinities? A nothing compared with the infinitely large, all compared with the infinitely small. A mean between all and nothing, infinitely far from comprehending the extremes. Let us, then, know our range. Such is our true state. This is what renders us incapable, alike of absolute knowledge and absolute ignorance.

Nature confounds the skeptics, and reason confounds the dogmatists. What will become of you, O man, who would search out your true condition by your natural reason? You can avoid neither skepticism nor dogmatism; but, alas, you can live with neither!

Our intelligence holds the same position as our body, in the vast extent of nature. This middle state between two extremes is common to all our weaknesses: Our senses can perceive no extreme; too much noise deafens us, too much light blinds us, too far or too near interferes with our vision, too much brevity or too much prolixity obscures our understanding, too much truth overwhelms us, too much pleasure cloys on us, too many benefits annoy us, we feel neither extreme heat nor extreme cold, too much and too little teaching hinder our minds—in a word, all extremes are for us as though they were not. They escape us or we escape them.

Man is a creature full of natural error. Nothing shows him the truth, everything deceives him. His reason and his senses deceive each other. The senses trick the reason by false appearances; reason in turn avenges herself and deceives the senses. His emotions trouble his senses and make false impressions on him. Reason, senses, emotions, lie and deceive, outdoing each other.

What a chimera is man! Strange and monstrous! A chaos, a contradiction, a prodigy. Judge of all things, yet a weak earthworm. Depository of truth, yet a cesspool of uncertainty and error; the glory and the scrapings of the universe.

Who will unravel such a tangle? It is beyond the power of dogmatism, of skepticism, of philosophy. Man is incomprehensible by man. We grant that to the skeptics. Truth is not within our reach, nor to our taste; her home is not on earth.

We sail on a vast expanse of being, ever uncertain, ever drifting, ever hurried from one goal to another. If we seek to attach ourselves to any one point, it totters and fails us; if we follow, it eludes our grasp, vanishing forever. Nothing stays for us. This is our natural condition. Yet, it is the condition most contrary to our inclination; for we burn with desire to find a steadfast place and a fixed basis whereon we may build. But our whole foundation breaks up, and the abysses open before us.

When I consider the short duration of my life, swallowed up in an eternity before and after, the small space I fill engulfed in the infinite immensity of spaces whereof I know nothing, and which know nothing of me, I am terrified. The eternal silence of these infinite spaces alarms me. I wonder why I am here, rather than there, now rather than then. Who has set me here? By whose order and design have this place and time been destined for me?

When I see the blindness and misery of man; when I survey the whole dumb universe; when I see man left to himself without a light unto his path, lost in this corner of the cosmos, ignorant of who placed him here, of what he has come here to do, of what will overtake him when he dies, I fall into terror. And my terror is like that of a man who should awake upon a terrible desert island with no means of escape. And I wonder why men do not fall into despair. I see others around me, of like nature. I ask if they are better informed than I am; and they say they are not.

We may not, then, look for certainty or stability. Our reason is always deceived by changing shows. It matters not that man should have a trifle more knowledge of the universe; if he has it, he but begins a little higher; but he is always infinitely distant from the end. In regard to the infinities, all finites are equal, and I see no reason why we should fix our imagination on one more than on another.

Who would not think, when we declare that man consists of mind and matter, that we really understood this combination? Yet—it is the one thing we least understand. Nothing is more obscure than just this mixture of spirit and clay. Man is, to himself, the most marvelous object in nature, for he cannot conceive what matter is, nor what mind is, nor how a material body should be united to an immaterial mind. This is the crown of all his difficulties; yet it is his very being.

These are some of the causes which render man so totally unable to know nature. For nature has a twofold infinity, while he is finite. Nature is permanent, while he is fleeting and mortal. All things change and fail; he sees them only as they pass. All things have their beginning and their end; he sees neither the one nor the other. Things are simple and homogenous. He is complex and composed of two different elements.

Not from space must I seek my dignity. I should have no more if I possessed whole worlds. By space the universe encompasses and swallows me as an atom. Man is but a reed, weakest in nature, but a reed which thinks. A thinking reed. It needs not that the whole universe should arm to crush him. A vapor, a drop of water is enough to kill him. But were the universe to kill him, man would still be more noble than that which has slain him, because he knows that he dies, and that the universe has the better of him. The universe knows nothing of this.

Know then, proud Man, how great a paradox thou art to thyself. Bow down thyself, impotent reason; be silent, thou foolish human nature. Learn that man is altogether incomprehensible by man.

Let man now estimate his value. Let him love himself, because he has a nature capable of good. But let him not love the vileness which exists in that nature. He has in himself the capacity of knowledge and happiness, yet he finds no last truth or satisfaction. I would lead him to desire it; to be freed from passions, to know how his passions obscure his knowledge and his achievement of happiness. I would have him hate in himself the desires which bias his judgment, that they might neither blind him in choosing nor obstruct him when he has chosen.

The net result of all this is that man, of himself, is ignorant and helpless and alone. The blind forces of nature offer him no haven. The universe at large cares as little for his living as for his dying. In his quest for happiness and goodness, he is confronted by an alien, indifferent, even hostile world. Pascal might have let it go at that. Many have; for example, Schopenhauer and Thomas Hardy and Bertrand Russell. Not so Pascal. In such a plight, his soul could find no peace and rest. So he picks up the argument again, reminding man that the conquest of true happiness is at stake:

All men seek happiness. To this there is no exception. Our will makes no step, except toward this object. This is the motive of every action of every man. And yet, after so many years no one has arrived, without faith, at the point to which all eyes are turned. All complain, rulers and ruled, nobles and commons, old and young, strong and weak, learned and ignorant, sound and sick, of all countries, all times, all ages, and all conditions.

A trial so long, so constant, so uniform, should have convinced us of our inability to arrive at our complete happiness by our own strength. But example teaches us little. We expect that our efforts will not be foiled on this occasion, as before. Thus while the present never satisfies us, experience never teaches us; and from misfortune to misfortune we are led on to death, the eternal crown of our sorrows.

This desire, and this weakness, cry aloud to us that there is an empty space in man which he seeks vainly to fill from all that surrounds him, seeks vainly to find in things absent the happiness which he finds not in things present.

Peace of mind, happiness of soul, are nowhere within reach so long as these are sought for among the things of this world. Who can deny that? But who is prepared to let it go at that? Not Pascal, at any rate. It is at this point that his argument becomes a record of his personal findings:

Man finds his lasting happiness only in God. Without Him, there is nothing in nature which will take His place; neither the stars, nor heaven, nor earth, nor the elements; not plants, cabbages, animals, insects, calves, serpents, fever, pestilence, war, famine, vices, adultery, incest. Since man has lost track of his true happiness, all things appear equally good to him, even his own destruction, though so contrary to God, to right reason, and to the whole course of nature.

There is no good without knowledge of God. Only as we approach Him are we happy; and our ultimate good is to know Him certainly. We are unhappy, in proportion as we are removed from Him; and the greatest evil would be the certainty of being cut off from Him.

WAGER

These reflections bring Pascal to the terms of his famous religious wager. It may be well to restate his position before proceeding: Some men doubt God's existence, and are indifferent to their doubts. For them Pascal has nothing to say. But others doubt, and are concerned. Like the man in the New Testament they cry, paradoxically: "Lord, I believe, help Thou my unbelief!" To those who feel this cry, Pascal addresses himself. They must recognize the futility of attempting a "rational" solution to their doubts: Renaissance skepticism, personified in Montaigne, has blown up that bridge. It remains to face squarely the utter loneliness and littleness of man. Left to himself, his hopes and joys and values and aspirations are doomed to extinction. In God alone, if there be a God, can he hope to find a friend and protector. But, good skeptic that he is, Pascal knows that there is a gap between the fact of our need for God and God's inferred existence to fill that need. Hence his genuine intellectual honesty. He is himself satisfied to argue from our need for God to the existence of God. But he does not ask his reader to follow him in that jump. He proposes a wager:

If there be a God, He is infinitely incomprehensible, since, having neither parts nor limits, He has no relation to us. We are, then, incapable of knowing either that He is or what He is.

Let us examine this point: "Either God is, or is not," we can say. But to which side shall we incline? Reason cannot help us. There is an infinite gulf fixed between creature and creator. What will you wager? It is like a game in which heads or tails may turn up. There is no reason for backing either the one possibility or the other. You cannot reasonably argue in favor of either.

If you know nothing either way, it might be urged, the true course is not to wager at all. But you must wager; that does not depend on your will. You are embarked in this business. Which will you choose?

Let us see. Since you must choose, your reason is no more affronted in choosing one way than the other. That point is clear. But what of your happiness? Let us weigh the gain and the loss in wagering that God does exist. If you wager that He does, and He does, you gain all; if you wager that He does, and He does not, you lose nothing. If you win, you take all; if you lose, you lose nothing. Wager then, unhesitatingly, that He does exist. This is demonstrable, and if men are capable of any truths, this is one.

If we ought to do nothing except on a certainty, we ought to do nothing for religion, because it is not a matter of certainty. But it is false to say, "We ought to do nothing except on a certainty." In a voyage at sea, in a battle, we act on uncertainties. If it be the case that we ought to do nothing except on a certainty, then we ought to do nothing at all, for nothing is certain.

You may object: "My hands are tied, my mouth is gagged. I am forced to wager, I am not free. But, despite this, I am so made that I cannot believe. What then would you have me do?"

I would have you understand your incapacity to believe. Labor to convince yourself, not by more "proofs" of God's existence, but by disciplining your passions and wayward emotions. You would arrive at faith, but know not the way. You would heal yourself of unbelief, yet know not the remedies. I answer: Learn of those who have been bound as you are. These are they who know the way you would follow, who have been cured of a disease you would be cured of. Follow the way by which they began, by making believe what they believed. Thus you will come to believe.

Now, what will happen to you if you take this side in the religious wager? You will be trustworthy, honorable, humble, grateful, generous, friendly, sincere, and true. You will no longer have those poisoned pleasures, glory and luxury; but you will have other pleasures. I tell you that you will gain this life; at each step you will see so much certainty of gain, so much nothingness in what you stake, that you will know at last that you have wagered on a certainty, an infinity, for which you have risked nothing.

If my words please you, and seem to you cogent, know that they are the words of one who has thrown himself on his knees before and after to pray to that infinite Being to whom he submits all; know too that you also would submit to Him your all for your own good and His glory, and that this strength may be in accord with this weakness.

Thus Pascal. Between the two of them, Thomas and this seventeenth-century religiously minded skeptic, they leave little more to be said on the question of natural theology. Hume, who follows in the eighteenth century only articulates more delicately the case against "reason" in these matters. Mill, in the nineteenth century, advances a startling hypothesis designed to save men like Thomas from the emotionalism of Pascal and the skepticism of Hume. James, in the twentieth century, comes full circle back to Pascal in a pragmatic approach to this perennial question.

Note on Sources. The Pascal material in this section is quoted, abridged, or paraphrased from his book, *Thoughts.* That book consists of 923 numbered items. The following items have been used in this chapter:

Numbers 194, 195, 205, 206, 229, 233, 347, 348, 434, 437—and a few here and there among the remaining items.

Reading References. Aldous Huxley, the English novelist, has written what amounts to a small book on Pascal. It is to be found in his volume of essays, *Do What You Will*. In this study, Huxley attempts to "take Pascal to pieces" to see just precisely what it is that "makes the wheels go round." The result is catastrophic—for Huxley, if you agree with Pascal; for Pascal, if you agree with Huxley. Such highly seasoned and partisan treatment should be balanced by something more conventional and appreciative. Several first-rate monographs exist. Among these are *Pascal* by Jacques Chevalier and *Pascal—the Life of Genius* by Morris Bishop. Bishop's volume is more suited to those who come to the study of Pascal from Anglo-American traditions.

The following are some books published since 1940:

Cailliet, E. *Pascal: Genius in the Light of Scripture.*
———. *The Clue to Pascal.*
Fletcher, F. T. H. *Pascal and the Mystical Tradition.*
Hubert, M. L. *Pascal's Unfinished Apology.*
Maggioni, M. J. *The Pensées of Pascal.*
Mauriac, F. (ed). *Living Thoughts of Pascal.*
Mesnard, J. *Pascal, His Life and Works.*
Patrick, D. G. *Pascal and Kierkegaard.*
Stewart, H. F. *Blaise Pascal.*
———. *Secret of Pascal.*
Waterman, M. *Voltaire, Pascal and Human Destiny.*
Woodgate, M. V. *Pascal and His Sister Jacqueline.*

READING QUESTIONS

Pascal differs significantly from Thomas; in nothing, perhaps, more than in that elusive thing called *spirit* or *mood.* As one reads Thomas, one feels the presence of what is essentially a teacher, one who has the facts in hand and proposes to impart them in an orderly and dispassionate manner. One result is that it is comparatively easy to cross-question one's self on the points that are made and the general conclusions reached. It is sometimes otherwise with Pascal. He is articulating a mood, as well as arguing a case. To catch the mood it is important to get *en rapport* with the author. However, it is still important to see the steps through which his thought proceeds.

1. As a first step toward his wager, he classifies people into three groups. To which group will he address his wager? Why not to the other groups?
2. His second step is to undermine natural or rational theology. How this prepares for the wager.
3. He argues against theology, first from the side of nature and then from the side of man. Which argument you consider most incisive in each of these two lines of attack.
4. His third step is to insist that man seeks happiness but to deny that he will find it in either nature or himself. How this prepares for the wager.
5. Why you do or do not agree with Pascal that man cannot find true happiness in either nature or himself.
6. At this point he proposes his wager. State it.
7. Sense in which doubt, not belief, is a premise of the wager.
8. If you cannot believe, then make believe. Why? What good will come of it?
9. Suggest what Aquinas might have thought of Pascal's wager.
10. Pascal's point in each of the following:
    (a) Among all their errors, this most proves them to be fools and blind.
    (b) Too much to deny, too little to affirm.
    (c) An hour afterwards they fear they have been mistaken.
    (d) Nature confounds the skeptics and reason confounds the dogmatists.
    (e) Nothing is more obscure than just this mixture.
    (f) Not from space must I seek my dignity.
    (g) If men are capable of any truths, this is one.
    (h) Learn of those who have been bound as you are.
    (i) It requires all the love of religion not to despise such persons.
    (j) All who seek God in nature find no light to satisfy them.
    (k) The two infinities.
    (l) It is like a game in which heads or tails may turn up.
    (m) It might be urged (that) the true course is not to wager at all.
11. If belief comes hard and doubt persist, Pascal recommends behaving like a believer, "by taking holy water, having masses said, etc." He added: "*Naturellement même cela vous fera croire et vous abetira.*" Why? His early editors deleted that sentence. Why?
12. Pascal speaks of "true" happiness. Does this imply that there is, or might well be, "false" happiness? If so, what would it be like?
13. What do you know of the seventeenth century that makes Pascal a plausible figure?
14. Wherein you find Pascal (a) most convincing (b) least convincing.

3. A SKEPTICAL CRITIQUE OF NATURAL THEOLOGY —FROM DAVID HUME

From Pascal to Hume. The problem of natural theology continued to command attention. We have examined, in St. Thomas, what is perhaps the most typical orthodox presentation of these matters. We have seen their repudiation by Pascal; a repudiation, however, which left no bitter taste in the devout reader's mouth, since Pascal strove earnestly to restore with one hand what he had swept aside with the other. By the middle of the eighteenth century times and tempers had changed. The "Age of Reason" had set in. The French Revolution was drawing nearer. The sciences, from their small beginnings with Galileo and Bacon and Harvey in the seventeenth century, had come to exercise considerable dominion over the imaginations of the intellectual classes. It was in this somewhat more chilly climate of opinion that David Hume turned his critical attention to the central problem of natural theology.

Biographical Note. Hume was born in Scotland in 1711 and died in 1776 at the age of sixty-five. Although he was destined, along with Immanuel Kant, to mark the opening of an as yet unclosed chapter in the history of philosophy, his early life was passed in obscurity, and his fame, among his contemporaries, was based principally upon his writings in the field of political history. (1) He was intended by his father for the law, and to that end was educated in Edinburgh. However he abandoned the study of law and tried his hand in a Bristol counting-house. This, too, proved uncongenial. He went to France, where he proceeded to write one of the epoch-making books in modern philosophy, his *Treatise of Human Nature.* The theme of this philosophical masterpiece is simply stated in the form of a question: How much of human knowledge, human emotional preferences and aversions, human morality, is what it is for no better reason than the fact that human nature is what it is? The suggestion, that once you have taken the "human" out of these things there is nothing left over, was too much for his generation to entertain. It contained too many skeptical implications. The *Treatise* fell, as though stillborn, from the press. (2) Hume now set about to find some employment which would put him in a position of independence. He applied, without success, for the chair of moral philosophy in the University of Edinburgh. For two years he tutored an almost insane Scottish marquis. He accompanied a diplomatic expedition to France. He applied, again without success, for the chair of logic in the University of Glasgow. At last he secured the position of Keeper of the Advocates' Library in Edinburgh. The access to books and original authorities which this gave him suggested the idea of writing a work on history. This he proceeded to do and, between 1754 and 1762, produced his famous *History of England* which ranked, in that century, with Gibbon's *Decline and Fall of the Roman Empire.* (3) In the lean years before he became Keeper and turned historian, Hume continued reworking and expanding the ideas of his original philosophical treatise. These were published in a series of short monographs and collections of essays. In this form they gained a gradual acceptance. But it was still the historian who overshadowed the philosopher in the minds of his generation. He retired from active life in 1769, on a combined income and pension of £1,000 a year. He spent the remainder of his days, the recognized head of the intellectual and literary society in Edinburgh, admired by those who read his *History* and his miscellaneous essays, distrusted or misunderstood by those who tried their hand at his philosophy.

The Argument of the Citations. The selections which follow provide a skeptical examination of the principles of natural theology. They are, for the most part, from Hume's essay *On Miracles* and from *Dialogues Concerning Natural Religion.* They presuppose, as a starting point, that the reader is familiar with the stock arguments for the existence of God.

The position finally occupied by Hume is somewhat complex. We may imagine him saying, "Either we have knowledge of God's existence and nature, or we do not. If we do not possess such knowledge, there is no call for a skeptical examination. If, however, we do possess, or claim to possess, such knowledge, then it must rest on some sort of evidence. What is this evidence? It is formulated, usually, in three arguments.' There is the argument from miracles, the argument from design, and the argument from first cause. A skeptical examination of the claims of national theology will resolve itself into a skeptical examination of these three arguments. We shall advance two lines of criticism with respect to each: first, that the argument itself is questionable; second, that even if it were accepted without question, it does not prove what it claims to prove."

It is well to remember the limitations of the task which Hume sets himself. He is not attempting to prove that God does not exist; that is, he is not stating the case for atheism. Nor is he seeking to discredit all belief in God. His claim is the more modest one, namely, that such belief, whether true or false is not susceptible of the traditional argumentative justification; that no "appeal to reason," can be made in support of the claims of natural theology.

Belief in God has, in times past, been supported by what is called the *argument from miracles.* It is to this effect: Miracles, violations of natural laws, occur from time to time. An explanation of such events must therefore refer to something outside or beyond nature. That is, miracles point to a miracle-worker, namely, God. Hence Hume's interest in the question of miracles. His approach is indirect. He does not deny that miracles ever happen. He directs attention to the nature of the evidence upon which we believe that miracles happen and claims that the evidence in question is not strong enough to support the belief:

> I flatter myself I have discovered an argument which will be an everlasting check to all kinds of superstitious delusion, all accounts of miracles and prodigies sacred and profane.
>
> A miracle is a violation of the laws of nature. Now, as a firm and unalterable experience has established our belief in those laws, the proof against miracles, from the very nature of the case, is as entire as any argument from experience can possibly be imagined. There must be a uniform experience against any miracle; otherwise it would not be so described. Now, as a uniform experience amounts to a proof, there is here a full proof against the occurrence of any miracle. Nor can such a proof against any miracle be weakened or destroyed, except by an opposite proof which would be superior to it.
>
> The plain consequence is this: No testimony is sufficient to establish a miracle unless the testimony be of such a kind that its falsehood would be as miraculous as, or more miraculous than, the fact which it endeavors to establish. Even in that case there is a mutual destruction of arguments; and the superior only gives us an assurance suitable to that degree of evidential force which remains after deducting the inferior.
>
> A man tells me he saw one dead restored to life. I ask myself: Is it more probable that he should deceive or be deceived, or that the fact which he relates should really have happened? I weigh one miracle against the other, and reject the greater. If the falsehood of his testimony would be more miraculous than the event which he relates, then (but not until then) can he command my belief.

There are two parts to Hume's criticism of the evidence for believing that miracles happen. The first, and most incisive, has been given already: Miracles purport to be violations of the laws of nature. Our evidence for believing in the uniformity of nature is very great; so great, in fact, that no evidence for doubting it could possibly be strong enough, since it would have to be stronger than the evidence for believing in nature's uniformity and this latter includes practically all our experience. He moves on to a second criticism:

We have supposed in the foregoing that the evidence for a miracle may be so strong that its falsehood would itself be a miracle. But it is easy to show that we have been a great deal too liberal in our concessions, and that no miracle has ever been established on so full an evidence.

First: There is not to be found in all history any miracle attested by a sufficient number of men of such unquestioned good sense, education, and learning, as to secure us against all delusion in themselves; of such undoubted integrity as to place them beyond all suspicion of any design to deceive others; of such credit and reputation as to have a great deal to lose in case of being detected in any falsehood; and, at the same time, attesting facts in such a manner and in so celebrated a place as to render that detection unavoidable.

Second: The many instances of mistaken or fraudulent miracles which have been detected show that mankind have a strong propensity to believe in the extraordinary and marvelous. This fact ought reasonably to beget a suspicion against all narratives concerning such matters.

Third: Reports of miracles abound chiefly among ignorant and barbarous peoples; or if such reports have been admitted by civilized and educated peoples they will be found to have received them from ignorant and barbarous peoples who transmitted them with that sanction and authority which, among such peoples, attends received opinions. This fact constitutes a strong presumption against all accounts of miracles.

Fourth: There is no *a priori* case in favor of the miracles peculiar to any one religion. The miracles of all religions stand on the same footing. If any such should be mutually incompatible, they simply cancel each other out. Nor is there any *a priori* case in favor of religious over secular miracles.

Fifth: The records of miracles in ancient times are not to be placed on an equal level with the records of nonmiraculous events in ancient times. Because some human testimony has the utmost force and authority in some cases, as when it relates to the battle of Philippi or Pharsalia, the assassination of Caesar or the execution of Socrates, it is not therefore reasonable that all kinds of testimony must, in all cases, have equal force and authority.

It appears, then, that no testimony for any kind of miracle has ever amounted to a probability, much less a proof. Experience only gives authority to human testimony, and it is experience which assures us of the laws of nature. When, therefore, these two kinds of experiences are contrary, we can only subtract the one from the other and embrace the opinion with that assurance which arises from the remainder. But, according to the measures of probability above established, this subtraction amounts to entire annihilation. Therefore no human testimony can have such force as to prove a miracle and make it a just foundation for any system of religion.

Mere reason is not sufficient to convince us of the miracles of the Christian religion. Whoever is moved by faith to assent to it, is conscious of a continued miracle in his own person, which subverts all the principles of his understanding and gives him a determination to believe what is most contrary to custom and experience.

The net result thus far is this: Belief in God rests in part on belief in miracles. Belief in miracles rests on questionable grounds. Belief in God, therefore, insofar as it rests on belief in miracles, rests on questionable grounds. Hume's case against the argument from miracles ends at that point. He might have rounded out his argument with greater force. This was done by T. H. Huxley, Hume's biographer, in the next century. Huxley's argument proceeded along this line: Suppose the evidence for believing in miracles is left unquestioned. Suppose we admit without argument, that miracles do take place. What follows? Belief in the Deity described by orthodox Christian theology? It would seem not. For miracles are an equivocal kind of evidence. They point frequently to a Deity who befriends some people at the expense of others. Consider, for example, the Old Testament miracle of the taking of Jericho. What kind of evidence would this be, in the eyes of a citizen of Jericho? Or consider the miracle of the Gadarene swine recorded in the New Testament. What kind of evidence would this be, in the eyes of the unfortunate individual who owned those swine, or (to stretch a point) in the eyes of the still more unfortunate swine? These, and similar miracles, are equivocal testimony to Deity's universal benevolence. Moreover, if miracles are evidence of His benevolence, why do they fail to occur in so many cases where benevolence would seem to be in order, for example, when a vessel is sinking in a storm at sea? The point does not need elaboration: miracles, even if not disputed, do not provide us with decisive evidence one way or the other about God. And, when evidence is ambiguous, it is wiser to omit it altogether.

Hume proceeds, in his examination of natural theology, to a statement and refutation of the *argument from design.* This is one of his most famous pieces of destructive criticism.

The chief argument for divine existence is derived from the order of nature. Where there appear marks of intelligence and design, you think it extravagant to assign for its cause either chance or the blind unguided force of matter. This is an argument from effects to causes. From the order of the work, you infer there must have been project and forethought in the workman.

Look around the world. Contemplate the whole and every part of it. You will find it to be nothing but one great machine, subdivided into an infinite number of lesser machines, which again admit of subdivisions to a degree beyond what human senses can trace and explain.

All these various machines, and even their most minute parts, are adjusted to each other with an accuracy which ravishes into admiration all men who have ever contemplated them. The curious adapting of means to ends, throughout all nature, resembles exactly, though it much exceeds, the productions of human contrivance, human design, human thought, wisdom, intelligence.

Anatomize the eye. Survey its structure and contrivance. Does not the idea of contriver immediately flow in upon you with the force like that of a sensation? Behold the male and female of each species, their instincts, their passions, the whole course of their life before and after generation. Millions of such instances present themselves through every part of the universe. Can language convey a more intelligible, more irresistible meaning than the curious adjustment of means to ends in nature?

Since the effects (natural productions and human productions) resemble each other, you are led to infer, by analogy, that the causes also resemble; that the author of nature is somewhat similar to the mind of man, though possessed of larger powers, proportioned to the grandeur of the work He has created.

You compare the universe to productions of human intelligence, to houses, ships, furniture, machines, and so forth. Since both terms of the comparison exhibit adaptation and design, you argue that the cause of the one must resemble the cause of the other.

The argument from design, he says, is an argument from analogy: We examine a watch, a house, or a ship, and we conclude that such things were produced by beings possessing intelligence and controlled by purposes. We can, if we wish, verify this inference by acquainting ourselves with watchmakers, architects, and shipwrights. We examine the universe, or parts of it, and conclude that it too must have been produced by a being possessing intelligence and controlled by purposes. Our reason for drawing this inference is that we find the universe, or parts of it, intelligible and answering to our needs and purposes. That is, we draw the analogy watch-watchmaker and universe-Deity. From the intelligibility and utility of a watch, we infer intelligence and purposiveness in the watchmaker. By analogy, from the intelligibility and utility of nature we infer intelligence and purposiveness in the author of nature. Hume's criticisms are directed toward undermining the strength of the proposed analogy between human-product-human-producer, on the one hand, and nature-author-of-nature on the other. "Is the analogy entire and perfect?" he asks and proceeds to show in what respects he thinks it is weak:

When two things (human intelligence and the products of human intelligence) have been observed to be conjoined, you can infer, by custom, from the one to the other. This I call an *argument from experience*. But how this argument can have place in the present case, may be difficult to explain. If you see a house, you can conclude it had an architect or builder because such effects, you have experienced, proceed from such causes.

But does the universe resemble a house so closely that we can with the same certainty infer a similar cause? Is the analogy entire and perfect? Can you pretend here to more than a guess, a conjecture, a presumption, concerning a similar cause? To ascertain such reasoning, it were necessary that you have had experience in the origin of the world. Have worlds ever been formed under your eye? Have you experienced the generation of the universe as you have experienced the building of a house?

If you survey a ship, you form an exalted idea of the ingenuity of the builder. You find him a stupid mechanic who imitated others, who copied an art which through a long succession of ages, after multiplied mistakes, corrections, deliberations, and controversies has been gradually improving. On your argument, then, many worlds might have been botched and bungled ere this one was arrived at; much labor lost; many fruitless trials made; a slow improvement during infinite ages in the art of world-making.

When you read a book, you enter into the mind and intention of the author, and have an immediate feeling and conception of those ideas which revolved in his imagination while employed in that composition. Is it thus when you read the book of nature?

By this argument from analogy, how prove the unity of Deity? Many men join in building a house or ship or city or commonwealth. Why may not several deities have combined in framing a world? This is only so much greater similarity to human affairs, to the operation of human intelligence. By dividing thus the work among several, you would get rid of that extensive power and knowledge which must be supposed in one deity.

Were one deity, who possessed every attribute necessary to the production of the universe, and not many deities, proved by this argument from analogy, it would be needless to suppose any other deity. But while it is still an open question whether all these attributes are united in one deity or dispersed among several independent deities, by what phenomena in nature can you pretend to decide the controversy? On this kind of argument from nature, polytheism and monotheism are on a like footing. Neither has any advantage over the other.

By this method of reasoning from analogy you renounce all claim to perfection in any of the attributes of the Deity. Imperfections in human productions you ascribe to imperfections in human producers. There are many inexplicable difficulties in the work of nature. Are you to ascribe these to the imperfections of the author of nature?

By representing Deity as so intelligible and comprehensible, so similar to a human mind, you make ourselves the model. Is this reasonable? The sentiments of the human mind include gratitude and resentment, love and hate, friendship and enmity, blame and approval, pity and scorn, admiration and envy. Do you propose to transfer such sentiments to a Supreme Being? Or suppose Him actuated by them? Do you propose to ascribe to Him only knowledge and power but no virtues?

The above citations bring out several difficulties in the proposed analogy which, Hume thinks, lies at the heart of the argument from design. The criticism continues, the point of attack being shifted slightly. From the nature of the product, you infer certain characteristics in the producer; from a man's handiwork you infer that the man is of such-and-such character. Hume has no objection to this. His next point is merely that we should extend the same reasoning to the world and the maker of the world. What sort of place is this world, anyway? Is it such that we are obliged to argue that its author must have possessed the benevolent and providential attributes ascribed to him by traditional theology?

Can any man, by a simple denial, hope to bear down the united testimony of mankind? The whole earth is cursed and polluted. A perpetual war is kindled among all living creatures. Necessity, hunger, want, stimulate the strong and courageous; fear, anxiety, terror, agitate the weak and the infirm. The first entrance into life gives anguish to the newborn infant and to parent. Weakness, impotence, distress, attend each stage of many lives which are finished at last in agony and horror.

Is it not thus in nature? Observe the curious artifices of nature to embitter the life of living beings. The stronger prey upon the weaker, and keep them in perpetual terror and misery. The weaker, too, often prey upon the stronger. Consider those species of insects which are bred on the body of animals, or flying about, infix their stings into them. These insects have others, still more minute, which torment them. On every hand animals are surrounded with enemies which cause their misery and seek their destruction.

Why should man pretend to be exempted from the lot which befalls all other animals? Man is the greatest enemy of man. Oppression, injustice, contempt, slander, violence, sedition, war—by these men torment each other. The external ills of humanity, from the elements, from other animals, from men themselves, form a frightful catalogue of woes; but they are nothing compared with those that arise from conditions within. How many lie under the lingering torment of disease? How many suffer remorse, shame, anguish, rage, disappointment, fear, despair? How many suffer those deep disorders of mind, insanity, idiocy, madness? Who has passed through life without cruel inroads from these tormentors?

Were a stranger to drop into this world, I would show him, as a specimen of its ills, a hospital full of diseases, a prison crowded with malefactors, a battlefield strewn with carcasses, a fleet floundering in the ocean, a nation languishing under tyranny, famine, or pestilence. Labor and poverty are the certain lot of the far greater number, while the few who enjoy riches and ease never reach contentment or true felicity. All the good things of life taken together make a man very wretched indeed.

You ascribe an author to nature, and a purpose to the author of nature. What, I beseech you, is the object fulfilled by these matters to which attention has been drawn? Our sense of music, harmony, beauty, has some purpose. But what of gout, gravels, megrims, toothaches, rheumatisms? How does divine benevolence and purpose display itself here? Why argue for the power and knowledge of the Deity while His moral qualities are in doubt?

You say: But this world is only a point in comparison of the universe; this life is but a moment in comparison of eternity. Present evils are rectified in other regions and future times. And the eyes of men, being then opened to large views of things see the whole connection of general laws, and trace with adoration the benevolence and wisdom of the Deity through all the mazes and intricacies of his providence.

I answer: The only method of supporting divine benevolence is for you to say to me, "Your representations are exaggerated; your melancholy views are mostly fictitious; your inferences are contrary to fact and experience; health is more common than sickness; pleasure, than pain; happiness, than misery; for one vexation we meet, we attain a hundred enjoyments."

I add: Can such apologetics be admitted? Even allowing your claim that human happiness exceeds human misery, yet it proves nothing. For an excess of happiness over misery is not what we expect from infinite power coupled with infinite wisdom and infinite goodness.

The questions asked by Epicurus, of old, are yet unanswered. Is Deity willing to prevent evil, but not able? Then He is not omnipotent. Is He able, but not willing? Then He is malevolent. Is He both able and willing? Then whence cometh evil? Is He neither able nor willing? Then why call Him Deity?

Evil and unhappiness are the rocks upon which all arguments for Deity must finally come to wreck. Why is there any misery and wickedness at all in the world? Not by chance, surely. From some purpose or cause then? Is it from the intention of the Deity? But He is perfectly benevolent. Is it contrary to his intention? But He is almighty. Nothing can shake the solidity of this reasoning, so short, so clear, so decisive; unless we agree that these matters lie beyond human capacity, that our human reason is not applicable to them. This is the counsel of skepticism that I have all along insisted on.

In the above citations Hume has been making capital out of the problem of evil. He has, by this time, made his two principal criticisms of the argument from design: The analogy upon which it rests cannot be admitted; and even if it were admitted, it would come to grief over the problem of evil. However, he cannot let it go at that. The next seven citations give a different line of criticism. The point which they make is sufficiently evident to require little comment. From God as Designer, he turns to God as Soul, of the world.

You have argued, thus far, on the principle that like effects have like causes. But there is another you might try, based no less on experience: Where several known parts are observed to be similar, the unknown parts will also be found similar. Thus, if you see the limbs of a human body, you conclude that it is attended with a human head, though hid from you. If you see a small part of the sun, through a chink in the wall, you conclude that, were the wall removed, you should see the rest. Within the limits of experience, this method of reasoning is obvious and reliable.

Now I say, if you survey the universe, so far as it falls under your knowledge, it bears a great resemblance to an animal, or organized body, and seems actuated by a like principle of life and motion. A continual circulation of matter produces no disorder. A continual waste in every part is incessantly repaired. Each part, in performing its proper offices, operates both to its own preservation and that of the whole. From all this, why not infer that the world is an organism, an animal, and that Deity is the soul of the world, actuating it and being actuated by it?

If it be legitimate to argue thus by analogy from part to whole, I affirm that other parts of the world bear a greater resemblance to the structure of the world than do matters of human invention; and, therefore, should afford a better conjecture concerning the origin and nature of the whole. These parts are animals and vegetables. The world resembles more an organism than a clock or a knitting loom. Its cause, therefore, more probably resembles the cause of the former, namely, generation.

As a tree sheds its seed into neighboring fields, so the great system of the world produces certain seeds which, being scattered into the surrounding chaos, grow into new worlds. A comet, for instance, may be taken as such a seed. After it has been fully ripened, by passing from sun to sun and star to star, it is at last tossed into the unformed elements which surround this universe, and sprouts into a new system.

Or, for variety (for I see no other advantage), suppose this world to be an animal instead of a vegetable. A comet then would be an egg. And, in like manner as an ostrich lays its egg in the sand, which without any further care hatches the egg, so . . .

You protest: What wild, arbitrary suppositions are these? What data have I for such extraordinary conclusions? Is the slight resemblance of the world to a vegetable or animal sufficient basis for an argument as to further resemblances? You are right. This is what I have been insisting on, all along. We have no data, or insufficient data, for any such speculations. Our experience, from which alone we can argue safely, is so limited in extent and duration as to afford us no probable conjecture concerning the whole of things.

If you agree that our limited experience is an unequal standard by which to judge of the unlimited extent of nature, a too narrow stretch upon which to erect hypotheses concerning so vast a matter, you entirely abandon your case, and must admit of the absolute incomprehensibility of the author of nature.

The whole matter is summarized in the two following citations:

In a word, a man who follows this kind of argument from analogy, where one of the terms of the analogy lies beyond his experience, may perhaps be able to conjecture that the universe arose from something like design. But beyond that he cannot go, except by the utmost license of thought.

On this argument, for all you know to the contrary, this world may be a very faulty and imperfect copy compared to a superior standard; only the first rude essay of some infant deity who afterwards abandoned it, ashamed of his lame performance; only the work of some dependent, inferior deity, the object of derision to his superiors; only the product of old age and dotage in some superannuated deity, and ever since his death running on at adventures from the first impulse it received from him.

Thus far, the argument from miracles and the argument from design. The argument from the analogy of human producers led one to deny or left one unable to account for the facts of evil and misery, and led one to admit or left one unable to deny the absurd speculations which he suggested regarding the organic nature and origin of the world. If this *a posteriori* argument presented so many difficulties, would one fare better with the *a priori* argument from first Cause? By this argument could one prove the infinity, the unity, and the perfection, of the author of nature? Hume states this argument as follows:

The argument from first cause is this. Whatever exists must have a cause of its existence. Nothing can produce itself. In mounting up, therefore, from effects to causes, we must go on tracing an infinite regression without any ultimate cause, or must finally have recourse to an ultimate cause. Now, it is insisted, the conception of an infinite regression, of utterly no beginning cause to which all others can be traced, is absurd. We must, therefore, have recourse to a necessarily existent being, the first cause of all things, who carries the reason of His existence in Himself, and whom we cannot suppose not to exist without embracing an absurdity. Such a being is the Deity.

His criticism is brief and to the point:

Wherein do we find the absurdity of an infinite regression? It leads us beyond our powers of conceiving? So also does the conception of an infinite deity.

Let us admit its absurdity. Let us admit the necessity of a first cause. Shall we then ask for a cause of this cause? If not, then may we not argue a material first cause of this material universe? If not, may we ascribe to the spiritual first cause the origin of evil and misery and waste which we noted in our analysis of the argument from analogy? If not, to what cause then are they to be traced? If so, wherein do we fare better with the argument from the necessity of a first cause than from the probability of an intelligent designer?

His conclusion to the whole business is a frank plea for skepticism in natural theology:

All religious systems are subject to insuperable difficulties. Each disputant triumphs in his turn, exposing the absurdities, barbarities, and pernicious tenets of his antagonist. But all of them prepare a complete triumph for the skeptic who tells them no system ought ever to be embraced with regard to such questions. A total suspense of judgment is here our only reasonable recourse.

The upshot of Hume's critique of natural theology is skepticism. Its historical importance is to be seen along several lines. In the first place, it was a nemesis visited upon the Age of Reason; for what Hume showed was the helplessness of reason to cope with the problems of natural theology. In some minds this work has never been undone. For them, Hume administered a deathblow to the speculations at which he directed his attention. Rational theology, in the grand manner has never been completely restored to its former intellectual respectability. In the second place, Hume's handling of these questions led to an interesting attempt, by John Stuart Mill in the following century, to introduce into theology the conception of a finite God; in the twentieth century, to the pragmatic approach to these matters in the writings of the American, William James.

Note on Sources. The Hume material in this section is quoted, abridged, or paraphrased from the short essay "On Miracles" in his book *An Enquiry Concerning Human Understanding;* and from his small book *Dialogues Concerning Natural Religion.* The *Dialogues* is divided into twelve Parts. The present section is based on Parts 2, 3, 4, 5, 6, 7, 8, 9, and 10.

Reading References. Hume's skeptical examination of natural theology forms only one part of his general philosophy. He cultivated comparable doubts in other fields. The reading from Hume given in the third chapter of this book, the chapter dealing with epistemology, provides the premises from which he approached all problems. These will be looked at at that point, and some bibliographical references noted. There are, however, one or two pieces of philosophical commentary which deal with Hume as critic of natural theology. The first of these is A. E. Taylor's lecture, *David Hume and the Miraculous.* This lecture is published in the form of a little book, and again in a volume of essays, *Philosophical Studies.* The second is Chapter 6, of Volume 2, of Sir Leslie Stephen's *English Thought in the Eighteenth Century.*

For some books published since 1940, see list under Hume in the chapter on "Epistemological Problem."

READING QUESTIONS

1. Why Hume is interested in a criticism of belief in miracles.
2. Where we get our evidence for believing in the uniformity of nature. Why, then, the proof against miracles is "as strong as any argument from experience could be."
3. Five reasons for saying that the evidence for belief in miracles cannot be so strong that its falsity would be a miracle.
4. Why the Christian who believes in miracles is conscious of a miracle in himself. Does Hume use the term "miracle" in the same sense each time here?
5. What addition to Hume's criticism is contained in Huxley's criticism?
6. In what way the Jericho episode and the Gadarene episode are equivocal as evidence.
7. Distinguish between criticizing the evidence *for* miracles, and criticizing miracles *as* evidence. Which of these two, if valid, would be the more devastating?
8. Why Hume does well to criticize the evidence for belief in miracles rather than to try to prove that miracles do not happen.

9. Which: (a) You believe that God exists because you believe that miracles happen; or (b) you believe that miracles happen because you believe that God exists.
10. Hume defines a miracle as a violation of the laws of nature. How about this? Need it be so defined?
11. State the analogical argument to which Hume reduces the so-called "design argument."
12. His primary criticism of the analogy is contained in the paragraphs "When two" and "But does." State this criticism.
13. He then makes four supplementary criticisms: (a) On this argument many worlds might have been botched and bungled. (b) On this argument how prove the unity of the Deity? (c) On this argument how prove the perfection of the Deity? (d) On this argument you make ourselves the model. Bring out his point in each case.
14. He then has a long aside on the ills of nature, society, and man. Why this gloomy review?
15. What come-back ("you say") a reader might make. Hume's come-back to such a come-back. ("I answer." "I add.")
16. Set of questions he ascribes to the Greek philosopher Epicurus. Hume's point here.
17. Restate the following in the form of a dilemma: Why is there any misery and wickedness in the world? Is it from the intention of the Deity? But He is perfectly benevolent. Is it contrary to His intention? But He is almighty.
18. Having considered and rejected the argument which would make God the designer of the world, he then considers the argument which would make Him the soul of the world. On what grounds he rejects it also.
19. His two criticisms of the argument which says that the world must have a first cause and that the first cause is God.
20. Wherein you find Hume (a) most (b) least convincing.

4. AN ARGUMENT FOR LIMITED THEISM
—FROM JOHN STUART MILL

From Hume to Mill. The student who has followed these readings thus far should find himself, by now, becoming familiar with natural theology. With Thomas, he examined the great tradition. With Pascal, he noted the appeal from reason to feeling and need. With Hume he reviewed skeptically the arguments from miracles, from design, and from first cause. This brings matters to the close of the eighteenth century. In the century which followed, several interesting variations were proposed.

Not least among these was John Stuart Mill's celebrated attempt to save natural theology from skepticism by advancing the challenging hypothesis that an appeal to reason might be made in support of belief in a finite or limited Deity.

Biographical Note. John Stuart Mill was born in England in 1806 and died in 1873 at the age of sixty-seven. Lord Morley, in a review of Mill's life and work, referred to him as "the saint of Victorian rationalism." He might well have added "and of Victorian liberalism." For a great portion of Mill's contribution to modern liberalism is summed up in two propositions: that human reason applied to the data of human experience is the only source of human knowledge; and that a maximum of individual liberty of thought and action is the surest means of extending knowledge and increasing happiness. In the elaboration and defense of these claims he wrote book after book which came, in time, to form the staples of British liberalism in the nineteenth century. That all knowledge comes from experience is the thesis of his *System of Logic.* That the distribution of wealth is the fundamental problem in economics is the thesis of his *Principles of Political Economy.* That freedom of thought and action is the safest guarantee of individual and social well-being is the thesis of his essay *On Liberty.* That an act is right if, and only if, it produces more happiness than any other act possible, is the thesis of his *Utilitarianism.* That government by elected representatives is preferable to either constitutional monarchy or an enlightened aristocracy is the thesis of his *Considerations on Representative Government.* That women have as much right to votes and careers as men, is the thesis of *The Subjection of Women.* That the evils of a capitalistic economy give some point to the doctrines of socialists is the thesis of his *Socialism.* And that only so much as can be grounded in experience should be retained in a living theology, is the thesis of *Three Essays on Religion.* For further biographical material, see page 286.

The Argument of the Citations. Mill seeks to establish (1) that Deity is a Being of "great but limited power"; (2) that He is a Being of "great and perhaps unlimited knowledge and intelligence"; (3) that benevolence but not justice is one of His attributes; (4) and that a theology centering in this conception has several things to recommend it over the more traditional views. The citations are from his essay on theism. The argument opens as follows:

The most important quality of an opinion on any momentous subject is its truth or falsity. It is indispensable that the subject of religion should be reviewed from time to time, and that its questions should be tested by the same methods, and on the same principles as any of the speculative conclusions drawn by physical science.

From this introductory remark, Mill passes at once to a consideration of the argument from design. He prefers it because it "is grounded wholly on our experience of the appearances of the universe"; that is, we can see order and harmony and adaptation of some sort by merely observing the nature of things, whereas we have no experience whatever of such things as first causes and unmoved movers.

Whatever ground there is to believe in an author of nature is derived from the appearances of the universe. The argument from design is grounded wholly on our experience of the appearances of the universe. It is, therefore, a far more important argument for theism than any other.

Mill's formulation of the argument from design, given in the next six citations, is more elaborate than we have met hitherto. His words bear close attention:

The order of nature exhibits certain qualities that are found to be characteristic of such things as are made by an intelligent mind for a purpose. We are entitled from this great similarity in the effects to infer similarity in the cause, and to believe that things which it is beyond the power of man to make, but which resemble the works of man in all but power, must also have been made by intelligence armed with a power greater than human.

The argument from design is not drawn from mere resemblances in nature to the works of human intelligence, but from the special character of those resemblances. The circumstances in which it is alleged that the world resembles the works of man are not circumstances taken at random, but are particular instances of a circumstance which experience shows to have a real connection with an intelligent origin; the fact, namely, of conspiring to an end or purpose.

To show this, it will be convenient to handle, not the argument from design as a whole, but some one of the most impressive cases of it, such as the structure of the eye or the ear. It is maintained that the structure of the eye proves a designing mind. The argument may be analyzed as follows:

1. The parts of which the eye is composed, and the arrangement of these parts, resemble one another in this very remarkable respect, that they all conduce to enabling the animal to see. These parts and their arrangement being as they are, the animal sees. This is the only marked resemblance we can trace among the different parts of the eye; beyond the general likeness in composition which exists among all other parts of the animal.

2. Now, the combination of the parts of the eye had a beginning in time and must therefore have been brought together by a cause or causes. The number of instances (of such parts being brought together to enable organisms to see) is immensely greater than is required to exclude the possibility of a random or chance concurrence of independent causes. We are therefore warranted in concluding that what has brought all these parts together was some cause common to them all. And, since the parts agree in the single respect of combining to produce sight, there must be some connection between the cause which brought the parts together, and the fact of sight.

3. Now sight, being a fact which follows the putting together of the parts of the eye, can only be connected with the production of the eye as a final cause, not an efficient cause; since all efficient causes precede their effects. But a final cause is a purpose, and at once marks the origin of the eye as proceeding from an intelligent will.

At this point we should expect Mill to proceed with his evaluation of the design argument. But he proposes, instead, to develop an alternative explanation covering the type of facts which would be explained by the hypothesis of God's existence if that hypothesis were accepted. This alternative to "creative forethought," or "intelligent will," is the hypothesis of "natural selection" suggested by Mill's contemporary, Charles Darwin. The important point to notice is the way in which natural selection, if granted as an hypothesis, would account for the type of fact which seems to demand explanation in terms of intelligent will.

Of what value is this argument? Is intelligent will, or creative forethought, the only hypothesis that will account for the facts? I regret to say that it is not. Creative forethought is not the only link by which the origin of the mechanism of the eye may be connected with the fact of sight. There is another connecting link on which attention has been greatly fixed by recent speculation. This is the principle of natural selection, of "the survival of the fittest."

This principle of the survival of the fittest does not pretend to account for the origin of sensation, or of animal or vegetable life. It assumes the existence of some one or more very low forms of organic life, in which there are no complex adaptations. It next assumes, as experience warrants us in doing, that many small variations from those simple types would be thrown out, which would be transmissible by inheritance, some of which would be advantageous to the creature in its struggle for existence and others disadvantageous. The forms which are advantageous would always tend to survive; and those which are disadvantageous, to perish. Thus there would be a constant, though slow, general improvement of the type as it branched out into many different varieties, until it might attain to the most advanced examples which now exist.

It must be acknowledged that there is something very startling, and *prima facie* improbable in this hypothetical history of nature.

With reference to the eye, for example, it would require us to suppose that the primeval animal could not see, and had at most such slight preparation for seeing as might be constituted by some chemical action of light upon its cellular structure; that an accidental variation (mutation) would produce a variety that could see in some imperfect manner; that this peculiarity would be transmitted by inheritance while other variations continued to take place in other directions; that a number of races would thus be produced who, by the power of even imperfect sight, would have a great advantage over all other races which could not see and would in time extirpate them from all places except perhaps from a few very peculiar situations underground. Fresh variations would give rise to races with better and better seeing powers until we might at last reach as extraordinary a combination of structures and functions as are seen in the eye of man and of the more important animals.

Of this theory, when pushed to this extreme point, all that can now be said is that it is not so absurd as it looks; and that the analogies which have been discovered in experience, favorable to its possibility, far exceed what anyone could have supposed beforehand. Whether it will ever be possible to say more than this is at present uncertain.

Leaving this remarkable speculation to whatever fate the progress of discovery may have in store for it, I think it must be allowed that, in the present state of our knowledge, the adaptions in nature afford a large balance of probability in favor of creation by intelligence. It is equally certain that this is no more than a probability.

Having noted these two hypotheses, creative forethought and natural selection, and rejected the latter as less probable, Mill turns to the question of the nature of the being whose creative forethought is under consideration:

The question of the existence of a Deity standing thus, it is next to be considered what sort of Deity the indications point to. What attributes are we warranted, by the evidence which nature accords of a creative mind, in assigning to that mind?

The first attribute is great but limited power:

It needs no showing that the power, if not the intelligence, must be so far superior to that of man as to surpass all human estimate. But from this to omnipotence and omniscience there is a wide interval. And the distinction is of immense importance.

For I shall argue that the net result of natural theology, on the question of the divine attributes is this: a Being of great but limited power; how, or by what, limited we cannot even conjecture; of great, perhaps unlimited intelligence; who desires and pays some regard to the happiness of His creatures but who seems to have other motives of action for which He cares more, and who can hardly be supposed to have created the universe for that purpose alone.

Then follow the passages in which this claim is supported by a series of ingenious arguments:

Every indication of design in the cosmos is so much evidence against the omnipotence of the designer. For what is meant by *design?* Contrivance, the adaptation of means to end. But the necessity for contrivance, the need of employing "means" to achieve an "end," is a consequence of the limitation of power.

Who would have recourse to means, to attain his end, if his mere wish or word was enough? The very idea of *means* implies that the means have an efficacy which the direct action of the being who employs them has not. Otherwise, they are not means but an encumbrance.

A man does not use machinery to move his arms; unless he is paralyzed, i.e., has not the power to do so directly by his volition.

But, if the use of contrivance is a sign of limited power, how much more so is the careful and skillful choice of contrivance? Could we speak of "wisdom in the selection of means," if he who selects them could, by his mere will, have achieved the same results without them, or by any other means? Wisdom and contrivance are shown in overcoming difficulties, and there is no room for difficulties, and so no room for wisdom or contrivance, in an omnipotent being.

Any evidences of design in nature, therefore, distinctly imply that the author of nature worked under limitations; that he was obliged to adapt himself to conditions independent of his will, and to attain his ends by such arrangements as those conditions admitted of.

On this hypothesis, the Deity had to work out His ends by combining materials of given nature and properties. This did require skill and contrivance; and the means by which it is effected are often such as justly excite our wonder and admiration. But, exactly because it requires wisdom, skill, contrivance, it implies limitation of power.

It may be said: An omnipotent Creator, though under no necessity of employing contrivances such as man must use, thought fit to do so in order to leave traces by which man might recognize his Creator's hand.

The answer is: This equally supposes a limit to the Deity's omnipotence, for it is a contrivance to achieve an end. Moreover, if it was His will that man should know that they and the world are His work, He, being omnipotent, had only to will that they should be aware of it.

From the question of God's power, Mill turns to the question of His knowledge and wisdom. The claim here is that there are probably no grounds for ascribing infinite knowledge or intelligence to Deity:

Omnipotence, therefore, cannot be predicated of the Creator on the evidences of design in nature. But what of omniscience? If we suppose limitation of power, must we also suppose limitation of knowledge and wisdom?

To argue that Deity possesses only limited power does not preclude us from ascribing unlimited knowledge and wisdom to Him. But there is nothing to prove it. The knowledge and wisdom necessary to planning and arranging the cosmos are, no doubt, as much in excess of human knowledge as the power implied is in excess of human power. But nothing obliges us to suppose that either the knowledge or the skill is infinite.

We are not even obliged to suppose that the contrivances and arrangements were always the best possible. If we judge them as we judge the work of human artificers, we find abundant defects. The human body, for example, is one of the most striking instances of artful and ingenious contrivance which nature offers. But we may well ask whether so complicated a machine could not have been made to last longer, and not get out of order so easily and frequently.

We may ask why the human race should have been so constituted as to grovel in wretchedness and degradation for countless ages before a small portion of it was enabled to lift itself into the very imperfect state of intelligence, goodness, and happiness which we enjoy.

If, however, Deity, like a human ruler, had to adapt Himself to a set of conditions which He did not make, it is as unphilosophical as it is presumptuous in us to call Him to account for any imperfections in His work; to complain that he left anything in it contrary to what (if indications of design prove anything) He must have intended.

Great but limited power. Great, perhaps unlimited, knowledge and intelligence. What moral attributes? To settle this question Mill suggests a consideration of the probable purposes of the author of nature. The idea here is that one's moral qualities will be embodied in, and therefore inferable from, whatever one devotes time and forethought to making or doing. The only conclusion Mill is able to reach is "some benevolence but no justice." The argument is as follows:

Assuming then, that while we confine ourselves to the evidences of design in nature, there is no ground for ascribing infinite power, and probably no grounds for ascribing infinite knowledge or intelligence to Deity, the question arises as to the same evidence afforded with regard to His moral attributes. What indications does nature give of the purposes of its author?

This question bears a very different aspect to us from what it bears to those are encumbered with the doctrine of the omnipotence of Deity. We do not have to attempt the impossible problem of reconciling infinite benevolence and justice with infinite power and knowledge in such a world as this. The attempt to do so involves a contradiction, and exhibits to excess the revolting spectacle of a jesuitical defense of enormities.

To what purpose, then, do the expedients and contrivances in the construction of animals and vegetables appear to tend? These are the "adaptations" which most excite our admiration. If they afford evidence of design, of purpose, in nature, we can best hope to be enlightened by examining such parts of nature.

There is no blinking the fact that these animal and vegetable adaptations tend principally to no more exalted object than to make the structure remain in life and in working order for a certain time: the individual for a few years, the species for a longer but still limited period.

The greater part of the design or adaptation in nature, however wonderful its mechanism, is, therefore, no evidence of any moral attributes in the author of nature; because the end to which it is directed is not a moral end: it is not the good of any creature but the qualified permanence, for a limited period of the work itself.

The only inference that can be drawn from most of nature, respecting the character of the author of nature, is that He does not wish His work to perish as soon as created. He wills it to have a certain duration.

In addition to the great number of adaptations which have no apparent object but to keep the organism going, there are a certain number of provisions for giving pleasure and a certain number for giving pain. These, perhaps, should be included among the contrivances for keeping the creature or its species in existence; for both the pleasures and the pains are generally so disposed as to attract to the things which maintain existence and deter from the things which would destroy it.

When these matters are considered, a vast deduction must be made from the facts usually cited as evidence of the benevolence of the Creator; so vast, indeed, that some may doubt whether any remains.

Yet, viewing the matter impartially, it does appear that there is a preponderance of evidence that the Creator desired the pleasure of His creatures. This is indicated by the fact, which cannot itself be denied, that pleasure of one description or another, is afforded by almost all of the powers, mental and physical, possessed by the creature.

The author of these pleasure-giving and pain-preventing adaptations is no doubt accountable for having made the creature susceptible of pain. But this may have been a necessary condition of its susceptibility to pleasure: a supposition which avails nothing on the theory of an omnipotent creator, but is extremely probable in the case of a limited creator.

There is, therefore, much evidence that the creature's pleasure is agreeable to the Creator; while there is very little if any evidence that its pain is so. There is, then, justification for inferring that benevolence is one of the attributes of the Creator.

But to jump from this to the inference that his sole or chief purposes are those of benevolence, and that the single end and aim of creation was the happiness of his creatures, is not only not justified by any evidence but is a conclusion in opposition to such evidence as we have.

If the motive of the Deity for creating sentient beings was the happiness of those beings, His purpose, in our corner of the universe at least, must be pronounced to have been thus far an ignominious failure. If God had no purpose but our happiness, and that of other living creatures, it is incredible that He would have called them into existence with the prospect of being so completely baffled.

If man had not the power, by the exercise of his own energies, to improve himself and his circumstances, to do for himself and other creatures vastly more than God had in the first instance done, then He [God] would deserve something very different from thanks at his [man's] hands.

Of course, it may be said that this very capacity of improving himself was given to man by God, and that the changes which man will be able ultimately to effect will be worth purchasing by the sufferings and wasted lives.

This may be so; but to suppose that God could not have procured these blessings for man at a less frightful cost is to make a very strange supposition concerning the Deity. It is to suppose that God could not, in the first instance, create anything better than a primitive savage, and was yet able to endow this primitive savage with the power of raising himself into a Newton or a Fénelon. We do not know the nature of the barriers which limit the divine omnipotence; but it is a very odd notion of them that they enable the Deity to confer on a primitive savage the power of producing what God Himself had no other means of creating.

Such are the indications respecting the divine benevolence. If we look for any other moral attribute, for example, justice, we find a total blank. There is no evidence whatever in nature of divine justice, whatever standard of justice we may hold. There is no shadow of justice in the general arrangements of nature. Whatever justice exists in human society is the work of man himself, struggling upwards against immense natural difficulties into civilization, and making to himself a second, and far better and more unselfish nature than he was created with.

Looking back, Mill summarizes his finding:

These, then, are the net results of natural theology on the question of the divine attributes. A Being of great but limited power, how or by what limited we cannot even conjecture; of great and perhaps unlimited intelligence; who desires, and pays some regard to the happiness of His creatures, but who seems to have other motives of action which He cares more for, and who can hardly be supposed to have created the universe for that purpose alone. Such is the Deity whom natural religion points to; and any idea of God more captivating than this comes only from human wishes, or from the teaching of either real or imaginary revelation.

There are several considerations in favor of this hypothesis of a finite Deity. It eliminates the problem of evil and the problem of free will. These problems, it will be recalled, were raised by the claim that Deity combines in Himself the two attributes of omnipotence and complete benevolence. It keeps close to what experience actually tells us about the world we live in. And, by way of conclusion, it gives meaning to the notion of helping or working with God:

This religious idea admits of one elevated feeling, which is not open to those who believe in the omnipotence of the good principle in the universe, the feeling of helping God—of requiting the good He has given by a voluntary cooperation which He, not being omnipotent, really needs, and by which a somewhat nearer approach may be made to the fulfillment of His purposes. This is the most invigorating thought which can inspire a human creature.

A contemporary of Mill had argued "that even if the investigation of the concept of God as the absolute, infinite, all-powerful, all-good Being, leads to self-contradiction, yet we must believe in such a Being, since neither human logic nor human ethics are applicable to such a being." To this Mill replied:

Convince me that the world is ruled by a being whose attributes are infinite, but what they are we cannot learn (except that the highest human morality which we are capable of conceiving does not sanction them) and I will bear my fate as I may. But when I am told that I must believe this, and at the same time call this being names that affirm the highest human morality, I say in plain terms that I will not. Whatever power such a being may have over me, there is one thing which he shall not do; he shall not compel me to worship him. I will call no being good who is not what I mean when I apply that epithet to my fellow creatures; and if such a being can sentence me to hell for not so calling him, to hell I will go.

Note on Sources. The Mill material in this section is quoted, abridged, or paraphrased from the long essay "Theism," in his book *Three Essays on Religion*. The essay, "Theism," is 132 pages in length. It is divided into five Parts. Part I is itself divided into an Introduction and six brief chapters. The present section is based on Part I, especially the Introduction and Chapter 6; and Part II, entitled "Attributes." The concluding ("to hell I will go") paragraph is from Mill's book, *An Examination of Sir William Hamilton's Philosophy*.

Reading References. There are not many valuable commentaries on Mill's handling of this particular theological problem. The notion of a finite or limited deity did not originate with Mill; indeed, it is to be found as far back as Plato's *Republic* in the fourth century B.C.[2] But Mill did set himself more deliberately to argue the case for the conception than any of his predecessors had done. Since his day, it has passed into the writings of William James and has been used by H. G. Wells as the theme of his little book, *God the Invisible King*.

When J. S. Mill was still exercising a great influence in England, his work was subjected to considerable critical overhauling by one of his fellow countrymen, F. H. Bradley. In the course of many years' study and writing Bradley declared himself upon most of the major themes in Mill's general philosophy. In a volume, *Essays on Truth and Reality*, he has a chapter "On God and the Absolute" which contains some suggestive remarks on the conception of a limited God. It is instructive to watch another philosopher at work on the idea. Moreover, in the concluding sentences, Bradley raises a point which forms, so to speak, a beginning for William James's pragmatic approach to this question. Says Bradley:

> There is a fundamental inconsistency in religion. For, in any but an imperfect religion, God must be perfect. God must be at once the complete satisfaction of all finite aspiration, and yet on the other hand must stand in relation to my will. Religion (at least in my view) is practical, and on the other hand in the highest religion its object is supreme goodness and power. We have a perfect real will, and we have my will, and the practical relation of these wills is what we mean by religion. And yet, if perfection is actually realized, what becomes of my will which is set over against the complete good will? While, on the other hand, if there is no such will, what becomes of God? The inconsistency seems irremovable. . . .

---

[2] Plato, *Republic, Book II:* "Then God, if he be good, is not the author of all things, as the many assert, but he is the cause of a few things only, and not of most things that occur to men. For few are the goods of human life, and many are the evils, and the good is to be attributed to God alone; of the evils, the causes are to be sought elsewhere, and not in him."

An obvious method of escape is to reject the perfection of God. God will remain good, but in a limited sense. He will be reduced to a person who does the best that is in Him with limited knowledge and power. Sufficiently superior to ourselves to be worshipped, God will nevertheless be imperfect, and, with this admitted imperfection, it will be said, our religion is saved. . . .

Now certainly on such terms religion still can persist, for there is practical devotion to an object which is taken to be at a level far above our own. Such a religion even in one sense, with the lowering of the Deity, may be said to have been heightened. To help a God in His struggle, more or less doubtful and blind, with resisting evil, is no inferior task. And if the issue were taken as uncertain, or if even further the end were known to be God's indubitable defeat and our inevitable disaster, our religion would have risen thereby and would have attained to the extreme of heroism.

But on the other hand, if religion is considered as a whole and not simply from one side, it is not true that with the lowering of God religion tends to grow higher. A principal part of religion is the assured satisfaction of our good will, the joy and peace in that assurance, and the added strength which in the majority of men can come perhaps from no other source. To sacrifice altogether or in part this aspect means on the whole to set religion down to a lower level. And it is an illusion to suppose that imperfection, once admitted into the Deity, can be stopped precisely at that convenient limit which happens to suit our ideas. The assertor of an imperfect God is, whether he knows it or not, face to face with a desperate task or a forlorn alternative. He must try to show (how, I cannot tell) that the entire rest of the universe, outside his limited God, is known to be still weaker and more limited. Or he must appeal to us to follow our Leader blindly and, for all we know, to a common and overwhelming defeat. In either case, the prosepct offered entails, I should say, to the religious mind, an unquestionable loss to religion.

And yet it will be urged that we have ourselves agreed that all other ways of escape are closed. For, if God is perfect, we saw that religion must contain inconsistency, and it was by seeking consistency that we were driven to a limited God. But our assumption here, I reply, is precisely that which we should have questioned from the first. Is there any need for our attempt to avoid self-contradiction? Has religion really got to be consistent theoretically? Is ultimate theoretical consistency a thing which is attainable anywhere? And, at all events, is it a thing attainable in life and in practice? That is the fundamental question upon which the whole issue depends. And I need not pause here to ask whether it is quite certain that, when God is limited, the universe becomes theoretically consistent. . . .

Viewed thus, the question as to what may be called religious ideas is seriously changed. To insist upon ultimate theoretical consistency, which in no case can we reach, becomes once for all ridiculous. The main question is as to the real nature and end of religion, and as to the respective importance of those aspects which belong to it. The ideas which best express our highest religious needs and their satisfaction, must certainly be true. Ultimate truth they do not possess, and exactly what in the end it would take to make them perfect we cannot know.

READING QUESTIONS

1. Why Mill prefers the design-argument in theology.
2. He says: "It is maintained that the structure of the eye proves a designing mind." Spell out the argument here.
3. Which: (a) The design-argument proves that a process in nature is purposive; or (b) the design-argument argues from the fact that a process in nature is purposive.
4. Why Mill pauses at this point to consider the hypothesis of natural selection in nature. Why he does not adopt it.
5. The lines along which he revises the traditional conception of God.
6. Why evidence *for* design in nature is evidence *against* the omnipotence of the author of nature.
7. Mill's rejoinder to this: "The Creator left traces in nature by which man might recognize His hand."
8. Why he thinks it is not necessary to infer that the Deity is either all-knowing or all-wise.
9. Why he is unwilling to ascribe unlimited benevolence to the Deity.
10. On what grounds he would be willing to ascribe limited benevolence.
11. The two claims about the Deity which pose an impossible problem, involve a contradiction, lead to jesuitical defence of enormities.
12. The claim about the Deity which would force you to infer that He had failed ignominiously and was completely baffled.
13. Why Mill comes down hard on the question of the Deity's justice.
14. What bearing Mill's limited theism might have on the problem of evil and the problem of free will in theology.
15. The elevated feeling, the invigorating thought, which he derives from his limited theism.
16. What would lead him to say "to hell I will go."
17. Where you find Mill (a) most (b) least convincing.
18. What Bradley has to say (a) for (b) against the notion of a finite Deity.
19. Show that his handling of limited theism turns on the question whether there is any need to avoid self-contradiction in religion. Is there, would you say?
20. Does Bradley help the situation any?

5. THE AGNOSTIC APPROACH
—FROM T. H. HUXLEY

From Mill To Huxley. Two famous books, both published in 1859, entered into popular discussion of our question. The first was Charles Darwin's *Origin of Species;* the second, John Stuart Mill's *On Liberty.* Our question has been: Can you use what you know about nature to justify what you believe about God? Both books bore on that question.

Darwin's book caused many persons to revise their conception of nature, thus causing them to question their conception of God. The book pictured plants and animals engaged in a ruthless and life-long struggle for existence. In one way or another they must eat or be eaten, kill or be killed. Tennyson's phrase "Nature red in tooth and claw" described the situation. Under the pressure of this struggle for existence some species were eliminated and some survived. This was "natural selection": nature "selected" the fit and eliminated the unfit. If nature is created and sustained by God, then this natural selection is Divine Selection: God, through the struggle for existence, selects the fit and eliminates the unfit; in so doing, He brings about an evolution from the lowest beginnings of life up to the present stage of the higher animals and man. Suppose this is what we know about nature. Can we use this knowledge to justify what we believe about God? Can we, as one writer asked, proceed "through nature to God"?

Mill's book, especially in its famous second chapter, argued for the right of the individual to think for himself. It provided the classic plea for "the right to pro and con," on all questions, no matter how important or sacred or long established. Darwin's "down-grading" of nature, particularly if you thought about God as the author of nature, produced a crisis in public discussion of these matters. Mill's chapter was a timely warning against obscurantism and intolerance.

That was in 1859. In 1877 William Kingdon Clifford published a paper, *The Ethics of Belief,* in which he argued that ethics as well as logic has something to say on the justification of belief: if you are not logically entitled to hold a particular belief, then you are not morally entitled to hold that belief. Clifford included religious beliefs in this winnowing demand. The result was something of a paradox for many of his readers: they were familiar with the claim that in these matters doubt or disbelief was a sin, and here was Clifford insisting that in the absence of logical justification belief was immoral and sinful.

Thomas Henry Huxley's *Agnosticism,* which repeated and extended

Clifford's thesis, became a symbol for the state of mind in which many found themselves. Huxley commanded a wider hearing, spoke with greater authority, and ranged over a wider field. The papers in which he stated and applied his agnosticism provided Victorian England with one of its liveliest controversies. Since Clifford's paper expressed so much of what Huxley meant by agnosticism, we shall begin by looking at what he has to say:

Clifford

A shipowner was about to send to sea an emigrant ship. He knew that she was old, not overwell built, and often had needed repairs. It had been suggested to him that possibly she was not seaworthy. He thought that perhaps he ought to have her overhauled and refitted, even though this should put him to great expense.

Before the ship sailed, however, he said to himself that she had gone safely through so many voyages and weathered so many storms, that it was idle to suppose that she would not come safely home from this trip also. He would put his trust in Providence, which could hardly fail to protect all these unhappy families that were leaving their fatherland to seek for better times elsewhere. He would dismiss ungenerous suspicions about the honesty of builders and contractors. In such ways he acquired a sincere and comfortable conviction that his vessel was safe and seaworthy; he watched her departure with a light heart, and benevolent wishes for the success of the exiles in their new home; and he got his insurance money when she went down in mid-ocean and told no tales.

What shall we say of him? Surely that he was guilty of the death of those men. He sincerely believed in the soundness of his ship; but the sincerity of his conviction can in nowise help him, because he had no *right* to believe on such evidence as was before him. He had acquired his belief not by honestly earning it in patient investigation, but by stifling his doubts.

Let us alter the case a little, and suppose that the ship was not unsound after all; that she made her voyage safely, and many others after it. Will that diminish the guilt of her owner? Not one jot. The man would not have been innocent; he would only have been not found out. The question of right or wrong has to do not with whether his belief turned out to be true or false, but whether he had a *right* to believe on such evidence as was before him.

Although he had sincerely and "conscientiously" believed, yet he had no *right* to believe on such evidence as was before him. His sincere convictions, instead of being honestly earned, were stolen. The question is not whether his belief was true or false, but whether he entertained it on wrong grounds.

If he chose to examine himself *in foro conscientiae*, he would know that he had acquired and nourished a belief, when he had no *right* to believe on such evidence as was before him; and therein he would know that he had done a wrong thing.

No real belief, however trifling and fragmentary it may seem, is ever truly insignificant; it prepares us to receive more of its like, confirms those which resembled it before, and weakens others; and so gradually lays a stealthy train in our inmost thoughts, which may some day explode into overt action, and leave its stamp upon our character forever.

It is wrong to believe on insufficient evidence, or to nourish belief by suppressing doubts and avoiding investigation. Since no belief, however seemingly trivial, and however obscure the believer, is ever actually insignificant or without its effect, we have no choice but to extend our judgment to all cases of belief whatever. Belief, that sacred faculty, which prompts the decisions of our will, and knits into harmonious working all the energies of our being, is ours not for ourselves but for humanity. It is *rightly* used on truths which have been established by long tradition and waiting toil, and which have stood in the fierce light of free and fearless questioning. It is desecrated when given to unproved and unquestioned statements, for the solace and private pleasure of the believer; to add a tinsel splendor to the plain straight road of our life and display a bright mirage beyond it; or even to drown the common sorrows of our kind by a self-deception which allows them not only to cast down, but also to degrade us. Whoso would deserve well of his fellows in this matter will guard the purity of his belief with a very fanaticism of jealous care, lest at any time it should rest on an unworthy object, and catch a stain which can never be wiped away.

It is not only the leader of men, statesman, philosopher, or poet, that has this duty to mankind. Every rustic who delivers in the village alehouse his slow infrequent sentences, may help to kill or keep alive the fatal superstitions which clog his race. No simplicity of mind, no obscurity of station, can escape the universal *duty* of questioning all that we believe.

It is the sense of power attached to a sense of knowledge that makes men desirous of believing, and afraid of doubting. This sense of power is the highest and best of pleasures when the belief on which it is founded has been fairly earned. But if the belief has been accepted on insufficient evidence, the pleasure is a *stolen* one. Not only does it deceive ourselves by giving us a sense of power which we do not really possess, but it is *sinful*, because it is *stolen* in defiance of our *duty*. That *duty* is to guard ourselves from such beliefs as from a pestilence, which may shortly master our own body and then spread to the rest of the town. What would be thought of one who, for the sake of a sweet fruit, should deliberately run the risk of bringing a plague upon his family and his neighbors?

Every time we let ourselves believe for unworthy reasons, we weaken our powers of self-control, of doubting, of judicially and fairly weighing evidence. We all suffer severely enough from the maintenance of false beliefs and the fatally wrong actions which they lead to. The evil born when one such belief is entertained is great and wide. But a greater and wider evil arises when the credulous character is maintained, when a habit of believing for unworthy reasons is fostered and made permanent.

It is *wrong* always, everywhere, and for any one, to believe anything upon insufficient evidence. Habitual want of care about what I believe leads to habitual want of care in others about the truth of what is told to me. The credulous man is father to the liar and the cheat.

If a man, holding a belief which he was taught in childhood or persuaded of afterwards, keeps down doubts which arise about it in his mind, purposely avoids the reading of books and the company of men that call in question or discuss it, and regards as impious those questions which cannot easily be asked without disturbing it; the life of that man is one long *sin* against mankind.

If this judgment seems harsh when applied to those simple souls who have never known better, who have been brought up with a horror of doubt, and taught that their eternal welfare depends on *what* they believe; then it leads to the very serious question, *Who hath made Israel to sin?*

Inquiry into the evidence of a doctrine is not to be made once for all, and then taken as finally settled. It is never *lawful* to stifle a doubt; for either it can be honestly answered by means of the inquiry already made, or else it proves that the inquiry was not complete.

"But," says one, "I am a busy man; I have no time for the long course of study which would be necessary to make me in any degree a competent judge of certain questions, or even able to understand the nature of the arguments." Then he should have no time to believe.

The beliefs about right and wrong which guide our actions in dealing with men in society, and the beliefs about physical nature which guide our actions in dealing with animate and inanimate bodies, these never suffer from investigation; they can take care of themselves, without being propped up by "acts of faith," the clamor of paid advocates, or the suppression of contrary evidence.

Since it is not enough to say, "It is wrong to believe on unworthy evidence," without saying also what evidence is worthy, we shall now go on to inquire under what circumstances it is lawful to believe on the testimony of others; and more generally when and why we may believe that which goes beyond our own experience, or even beyond the experience of mankind.

The Argument in Huxley. In reading Huxley on these matters it is well to keep Mill and Darwin and Clifford in mind. In what follows there are five extended quotations from Huxley. In the *first* he tells how he arrived at the position which he calls agnosticism, and why he coined that word as a name for it. In the *second* he gives a carefully worked out statement of the essential ideas which he wants held together by the term agnosticism. To put it briefly, agnosticism is the claim that if you cannot use what you know to justify what you believe, then it is immoral to go on believing. Suppose a man asks himself "Am I *morally* entitled to entertain a certain belief of mine?" Agnosticism asks him: "Are you *logically* entitled to entertain the belief to which you refer?" If the answer is "No," then agnosticism says to him: "Then you are not *morally* entitled to entertain the belief. You have no *moral* right to a belief which you cannot justify logically." In the *third* set of quotations Huxley presents three examples of the winnowing results of insisting that what you *believe* shall rest on, be justified by, what you *know.* (a) Are the Gospel records an historically reliable source for the narrative which they set forth? (b) Given what we know about evolution in nature, what are we entitled to believe about the Author of nature? (c) Given what we know about nature, are we entitled to argue that an act is right if and only if it is according to nature? Can we say that "nature's ways," the "cosmic process," provide us with any model of the good for man?

I

Looking back nearly fifty years, I see myself as a boy, whose education has been interrupted, and who, intellectually, was left, for some years, altogether to his own devices. At that time, I was a voracious and omnivorous reader; a dreamer and speculator, endowed with that courage in attacking any and every subject, which is the blessed compensation of youth and inexperience. Among the books and essays, on all sorts of topics from metaphysics to heraldry, which I read at this time, two left indelible impressions on my mind. One was Guizot's "History of Civilization," the other was Sir William Hamilton's essay "On the Philosophy of the Unconditioned." The latter was strange reading for a boy, and I could not possibly have understood a great deal of it; nevertheless, I devoured it with avidity, and it stamped upon my mind the strong conviction that, on even the most solemn and important of questions, men are apt to take cunning phrases for answers; and that the limitation of our faculties, in a great number of cases, renders real answers to such questions, not merely actually impossible, but theoretically inconceivable.

When I reached intellectual maturity and began to ask myself whether I was an atheist, a theist, or a pantheist; a materialist or an idealist; a Christian or a freethinker; I found that the more I learned and reflected, the less ready was the answer; until, at last, I came to the conclusion that I had neither art nor part with any of these denominations, except the last. The one thing in which most of these good people were agreed was the one thing in which I differed from them. They were quite sure they had attained a certain "gnosis,"—had, more or less successfully, solved the problem of existence; while I was quite sure I had not, and had a pretty strong conviction that the problem was insoluble. And, with Hume and Kant on my side,

I could not think myself presumptuous in holding fast by that opinion.

This was my situation when I had the good fortune to find a place among the members of that remarkable confraternity of antagonists, long since deceased, but of green and pious memory, the Metaphysical Society. Every variety of philosophical and theological opinion was represented there, and expressed itself with entire openness; most of my colleagues were -*ists* of one sort or another; and, however kind and friendly they might be, I, the man without a rag of a label to cover himself with, could not fail to have some of the uneasy feelings which must have beset the historical fox when, after leaving the trap in which his tail remained, he presented himself to his normally elongated companions. So I took thought, and invented what I conceived to be the appropriate title of "agnostic." It came into my head as suggestively antithetic to the "gnostic" of Church history, who professed to know so much about the very things of which I was ignorant; and I took the earliest opportunity of parading it at our Society, to show that I, too, had a tail, like the other foxes. To my great satisfaction, the term took; and when the (*Spectator*) had stood godfather to it, any suspicion in the minds of respectable people, that a knowledge of its parentage might have awakened was, of course, completely lulled.

That is the history of the origin of the terms "agnostic" and "agnosticism."

2

Agnosticism is properly described as a creed in so far as it expresses absolute faith in the validity of a principle which is as much ethical as intellectual. This principle may be stated in various ways, but they all amount to this: that it is wrong for a man to say that he is certain of the objective truth of any proposition unless he can produce evidence which logically justifies that certainty. This is what agnosticism asserts; and, in my opinion, it is all that is essential to agnosticism.

That which agnostics deny and repudiate as immoral is that there are propositions which men ought to believe, without logically satisfactory evidence; and that reprobation ought to attach to the profession of disbelief in such inadequately supported propositions. The justification of the agnostic principle lies in the success which follows upon its application, in natural or in civil history; and in the fact that, so far as these topics are concerned, no sane man thinks of denying its validity.

Agnosticism is a creed, in so far as its general principle is concerned. The application of that principle results in the denial of, or the suspension of judgment concerning, a number of propositions respecting which contemporary "gnostics" profess entire certainty.

The extent of the region of the uncertain, the number of the problems the investigation of which ends in a verdict of not proven will vary according to the knowledge and the intellectual habits of the individual agnostic. What

I am sure about is that there are many topics about which I know nothing, and which, so far as I can see, are out of reach of my faculties. Relatively to myself, I am quite sure that the region of uncertainty is far more extensive than I could wish. Materialism and idealism; theism and atheism; the doctrine of the soul and its mortality or immortality—appear in the history of philosophy like the shades of Scandinavian heroes, eternally slaying one another and eternally coming to life again. It is getting on for twenty-five centuries, at least, since mankind began seriously to give their minds to these topics. Generation after generation, philosophy has been doomed to roll the stone up hill; and, just as all the world swore it was at the top, down it has rolled to the bottom again. All this is written in innumerable books; and he who will toil through them will discover that the stone is just where it was when the work began. Hume saw this; Kant saw it; since their time, more and more eyes have been cleansed of the films which prevented them from seeing it; until now the weight and number has begun to tell in practical life.

Between agnosticism and clericalism, there can be neither peace nor truce. The cleric asserts that it is morally wrong not to believe certain propositions, whatever the results of a strict scientific investigation of the evidence of these propositions. He tells us that "religious error is, in itself, of an immoral nature." He declares that he has prejudged certain conclusions, and looks upon those who show cause for arrest of judgment as emissaries of Satan. It necessarily follows that, for him, the attainment of faith, not the ascertainment of truth, is the highest aim of mental life. And, on analysis, it will be found to be the "power of saying you believe things which are incredible." Now I, and many other agnostics, believe that faith in this sense is an abomination; and we feel that the disagreement between ourselves and those who hold this doctrine is even more moral than intellectual. It is desirable there should be an end of any mistakes on this topic.

Those who appreciate our position will see that when any one declares that we ought to believe this, that, and the other, and are wicked if we don't, it is impossible for us to give any answer but this: We have not the slightest objection to believe anything you like, if you will give us good grounds for belief; but, if you can not, we must respectfully refuse, even if that refusal should wreck morality and insure our own damnation several times over.

3(a)

I find, in the second Gospel (chap. v.), a statement, to all appearance intended to have the same evidential value as any other contained in that history. It is the story of the devils who were cast out of a man, and ordered, or permitted to enter into a herd of swine, to the loss and damage of the innocent Gadarene pig owners. There can be no doubt that the narrator intends to convey his conviction that this casting out and entering in were effected by the agency of Jesus of Nazareth; that, by speech and action, Jesus

enforced this conviction; nor does any inkling of the legal and moral difficulties of the case manifest itself.

On the other hand, everything that I know of physiological and patho-
logical science leads me to entertain a very strong conviction that the phenomena ascribed to [demoniacal] possession are as purely natural as those
which constitute smallpox; everything that I know of anthropology leads me
think that the belief in demons and demoniacal possession is a mere survival
of a once universal superstition, and that its persistence, at the present time,
is pretty much in the inverse ratio of the general instruction, intelligence, and
sound judgment of the population among whom it prevails. Everything that
I know of law and justice convinces me that the wanton destruction of other
people's property is a misdemeanor of evil example. Again, the study of
history, and especially of that of the fifteenth, sixteenth, and seventeenth
centuries, leaves no shadow of doubt on my mind that the belief in the reality
of possession and of witchcraft, justly based, alike by Catholics and Protes-
tants, upon this and innumerable other passages in both the Old and New
Testaments, gave rise, through the special influence of Christian ecclesiastics,
to the most horrible persecutions and judicial murders of thousands upon
thousands of innocent men, women, and children.

If the testimony of the Gospel, is sufficient to do away with all rational
doubt as to a matter of fact of the utmost practical and speculative importance—belief or disbelief in which may affect, and has affected, men's lives
and their conduct towards other men, in the most serious way—then I am
bound to believe that Jesus implicitly affirmed himself to possess a "knowledge
of the unseen world," which afforded full confirmation of the belief in demons and possession current among his contemporaries. If the story is true,
the medieval theory of the invisible world may be, and probably is, quite
correct; and the witch-finders, from Sprenger to Hopkins and Mather, are
much-maligned men.

On the other hand, humanity, noting the frightful consequences of this
belief; common sense, observing the futility of the evidence on which it is
based, in all cases that have been properly investigated; science, more and
more seeing its way to inclose all the phenomena of so-called "possession"
within the domain of pathology—all these powerful influences concur in
warning us, at our peril, against accepting the belief without the most careful
scrutiny of the authority on which it rests.

I can discern no escape from this dilemma: either Jesus said what he
is reported to have said, or he did not. In the former case, his authority on
matters connected with the "unseen world" should be roughly shaken; in the
latter, the blow falls upon the authority of the Gospels. If their report on a
matter of such stupendous and far-reaching practical import as this is un-
trustworthy, how can we be sure of its trustworthiness in other cases?

The choice then lies between discrediting those who compiled the Gospel biographies and disbelieving the Master, whom they, simple souls, thought to honor by preserving such traditions of the exercise of his authority over Satan's invisible world. This is the dilemma. No deep scholarship, nothing but a knowledge of the revised version (on which it is to be supposed all that mere scholarship can do has been done), with the application thereto of the commonest canons of common sense, is needful to enable us to make a choice between its alternatives.

I am not aware that I have been influenced by any more bias in regard to the Gadarene story than I have been in dealing with other cases of like kind the investigation of which has interested me. I was brought up in the strictest school of evangelical orthodoxy; and when I was old enough to think for myself, I started upon my journey of inquiry with little doubt about the general truth of what I had been taught; and with that feeling of the unpleasantness of being called an "infidel" which, we are told, is so right and proper. Near my journey's end, I find myself in a condition of something more than mere doubt about these matters.

3(b)

The vast and varied procession of events, which we call Nature, affords a sublime spectacle and an inexhaustible wealth of attractive problems to the speculative observer. If we confine our attention to that aspect which engages the attention of the intellect, nature appears a beautiful and harmonious whole, the incarnation of a faultless logical process, from certain premises in the past to an inevitable conclusion in the future. But if it be regarded from a less elevated, though more human, point of view; if our moral sympathies are allowed to influence our judgment, and we permit ourselves to criticize our great mother as we criticize one another; then our verdict, at least so far as sentient nature is concerned, can hardly be so favorable.

In sober truth, to those who have made a study of the phenomena of life as they are exhibited by the higher forms of the animal world, the optimistic dogma, that this is the best of all possible worlds, will seem little better than a libel upon possibility. It is really only another instance to be added to the many extant, of the audacity of *a priori* speculators who, having created God in their own image, find no difficulty in assuming that the Almighty must have been actuated by the same motives as themselves. They are quite sure that, had any other course been practicable, He would no more have made infinite suffering a necessary ingredient of His handiwork than a respectable philosopher would have done the like.

But even the modified optimism of the time-honored thesis of physico-theology, that the sentient world is, on the whole, regulated by principles of benevolence, does but ill stand the test of impartial confrontation with the facts of the case. No doubt it is quite true that sentient nature affords hosts of examples of subtle contrivances directed towards the production of pleasure or the avoidance of pain; and it may be proper to say that these are evidences of benevolence. But if so, why is it not equally proper to say of the equally numerous arrangements, the no less necessary result of which is the production of pain, that they are evidences of malevolence?

If a vast amount of that which, in a piece of human workmanship, we should call skill, is visible in those parts of the organization of a deer to which it owes its ability to escape from beasts of prey, there is at least equal skill displayed in that bodily mechanism of the wolf which enables him to track, and sooner or later to bring down, the deer. Viewed under the dry light of science, deer and wolf are alike admirable; and, if both were non-sentient automata, there would be nothing to qualify our admiration of the action of the one on the other. But the fact that the deer suffers, while the wolf inflicts suffering, engages our moral sympathies. We should call men like the deer innocent and good, men such as the wolf malignant and bad; we should call those who defended the deer and aided him to escape brave and compassionate, and those who helped the wolf in his bloody work base and cruel. Surely, if we transfer these judgments to nature outside the world of man at all, we must do so impartially. In that case, the goodness of the right hand which helps the deer, and the wickedness of the left hand which eggs on the wolf, will neutralize one another: and the course of nature will appear to be neither moral nor immoral, but non-moral.   AMORAL

This conclusion is thrust upon us by analogous facts in every part of the sentient world; yet, inasmuch as it not only jars upon prevalent prejudices, but arouses the natural dislike to that which is painful, much ingenuity has been exercised in devising an escape from it.

From the theological side, we are told that this is a state of probation, and that the seeming injustices and immoralities of nature will be compensated by and by. But how this compensation is to be effected, in the case of the great majority of sentient things, is not clear. I apprehend that no one is seriously prepared to maintain that the ghosts of all the myriads of generations of herbivorous animals which lived during the millions of years of the earth's duration, before the appearance of man, and which have all that time been tormented and devoured by carnivores, are to be compensated by a perennial existence in clover; while the ghosts of carnivores are to go to some kennel where there is neither a pan of water nor a bone with any meat on it. Besides, from the point of view of morality, the last stage of things would be worse than the first. For the carnivores, however brutal and sanguinary, have only done that which, if there is any evidence of contrivance in the world, they were expressly constructed to do. Moreover, carnivores and herbivores alike have been subject to all the miseries incidental to old age, disease, and over-multiplication, and both might well put in a claim for "compensation" on this score.

On the evolutionist side, on the other hand, we are told to take comfort from the reflection that the terrible struggle for existence tends to final good, and that the suffering of the ancestor is paid for by the increased perfection of the progeny. There would be something in this argument if, in Chinese fashion, the present generation could pay its debts to its ancestors; otherwise it is not clear what compensation the *Eohippus* gets for his sorrows in the fact that, some millions of years afterwards, one of his descendants wins the Derby. And, again, it is an error to imagine that evolution signifies a constant tendency to increased perfection. That process undoubtedly involves a constant remodeling of the organism in adaptation to new conditions; but it depends on the nature of these conditions whether the direction of the modifications effected shall be upward or downward. Retrogressive is as practicable as progressive metamorphosis. If what the physical philosophers tell us, that our globe has been in a state of fusion, and, like the sun, is gradually cooling down, is true; then the time must come when evolution will mean adaptation to an universal winter, and all forms of life will die out, except such low and simple organisms as the Diatom of the arctic and anarctic ice and the Protococcus of the red snow. If our globe is proceeding from a condition in which it was too hot to support any but the lowest living thing to a condition in which it will be too cold to permit of the existence of any others, the course of life upon its surface must describe a trajectory like that of a ball fired from a mortar; and the sinking half of that course is as much a part of the general process of evolution as the rising.

From the point of view of the moralist the animal world is on about the same level as a gladiator's show. The creatures are fairly well treated, and set to fight—whereby the strongest, the swiftest, and the cunningest live to fight another day. The spectator has no need to turn his thumbs down, as no quarter is given. He must admit that the skill and training displayed are wonderful. But he must shut his eyes if he would not see that more or less enduring suffering is the meed of both vanquished and victor. And since the great game is going on in every corner of the world, thousands of times a minute it seems to follow that, if the world is governed by benevolence, it must be a different sort of benevolence from that of John Howard.

If the optimism of Leibnitz is a foolish though pleasant dream, the pessimism of Schopenhauer is a nightmare, the more foolish because of its hideousness. Error which is not pleasant is surely the worst form of wrong.

This may not be the best of all possible worlds, but to say that it is the worst is mere petulant nonsense. A worn-out voluptuary may find nothing good under the sun, or a vain and inexperienced youth, who cannot get the moon he cries for, may vent his irritation in pessimistic moanings; but there can be no doubt in the mind of any reasonable person that mankind could, would, and in fact do, get on fairly well with vastly less happiness and far more misery than find their way into the lives of nine people out of ten. If each and all of us had been visited by an attack of neuralgia, or of extreme mental depression, for one hour in every twenty-four—a supposition which many tolerably vigorous people know, to their cost, is not extravagant—the burden of life would have been immensely increased without much practical hindrance to its general course. Men with any manhood in them find life quite worth living under worse conditions than these.

There is another sufficiently obvious fact, which renders the hypothesis that the course of sentient nature is dictated by malevolence quite untenable. A vast multitude of pleasures, and these among the purest and the best, are superfluities, bits of good which are to all appearances unnecessary as inducements to live, and are, so to speak, thrown into the bargain of life. To those who experience them, few delights can be more entrancing than such as are afforded by natural beauty, or by the arts, and especially by music; but they are products of, rather than factors in, evolution, and it is probable that they are known, in any considerable degree, to but a very small proportion of mankind.

The conclusion of the whole matter seems to be that pessimism is as little consonant with the facts of sentient existence as optimism. If we desire to represent the course of nature in terms of human thought, and assume that it was intended to be that which it is, we must say that its governing principle is intellectual and not moral; that it is a materialized logical process, accompanied by pleasures and pains, the incidence of which, in the majority of cases, has not the slightest reference to moral desert. That the rain falls alike upon the just and the unjust, and that those upon whom the Tower of Siloam fell were no worse than their neighbors, seem to be Oriental modes of expressing the same conclusion.

We are more than sufficiently familiar with modern pessimism, at least as a speculation; for I cannot call to mind that any of its present votaries have sealed their faith by assuming the rags and the bowl of the mendicant Bhikku, or the wallet of the Cynic. We also know modern speculative optimism, with its perfectability of the species, reign of peace, and lion and lamb transformation scenes; but one does not hear so much of it as one did forty years ago; indeed, I imagine it is to be met with more commonly at the tables of the healthy and wealthy, than in the congregations of the wise. The majority of us, I apprehend, profess neither pessimism nor optimism. We hold that the world is neither so good, nor so bad, as it conceivably might be; and, as most of us have reason, now and again, to discover that it can be. Those who have failed to experience the joys that make life worth living are, probably, in as small a minority as those who have never known the griefs that rob existence of its savor and turn its richest fruits into mere dust and ashes.

3(c)

There is a fallacy which appears to me to pervade the so-called "ethics of evolution." It is the notion that because, on the whole, animals and plants

have advanced in perfection of organization by means of the struggle for
existence and the consequent "survival of the fittest"; therefore men in society,
men as ethical beings, must look to the same process to help them towards
perfection. I suspect that this fallacy has arisen out of the unfortunate ambiguity of the phrase "survival of the fittest." "Fittest" has a connotation of
"best"; and about "best" there hangs a moral flavor. In cosmic nature, however, what is "fittest" depends upon the conditions. Long since, I ventured
to point out that if our hemisphere were to cool again, the survival of the
fittest might bring about, in the vegetable kingdom, a population of more and
more stunted and humbler and humbler organisms, until the "fittest" that
survived might be nothing but lichens, diatoms, and such microscopic organisms as those which give red snow its color; while, if it became hotter,
the pleasant valleys of the Thames and Isis might be uninhabitable by any
animated beings save those that flourish in a tropical jungle. They, as the
fittest, the best adapted to the changed conditions, would survive.

Men in society are undoubtedly subject to the cosmic process. But the influence of the cosmic process on the evolution of society is the greater the
more rudimentary its civilization. Social progress means a checking of the
cosmic process at every step and the substitution for it of another, which may
be called the ethical process; the end of which is not the survival of those
who may happen to be the fittest, in respect of the whole of the conditions
which obtain, but of those who are ethically the best.

The practice of that which is ethically best—what we call goodness or
virtue—involves a course of conduct which, in all respects, is opposed to that
which leads to success in the cosmic struggle for existence. In place of ruthless
self-assertion it demands self-restraint; in place of thrusting aside, or treading
down, all competitors, it requires that the individual shall not merely respect,
but shall help his fellows; its influence is directed, not so much to the survival
of the fittest as to the fitting of as many as possible to survive. It repudiates
the gladiatorial theory of existence. It demands that each man who enters into
the enjoyment of the advantages of a polity shall be mindful of his debt to
those who have laboriously constructed it; and shall take heed that no act
of his weakens the fabric in which he has been permitted to live. Laws and
moral precepts are directed to the end of curbing the cosmic process and
reminding the individual of his duty to the community, to the protection and
influence of which he owes, if not existence itself, at least the life of something
better than a brutal savage.

Let us understand, once for all, that the ethical progress of society depends not on imitating the cosmic process, still less in running away from it,
but in combating it. It may seem an audacious proposal thus to put the microcosm against the macrocosm and to set man to subdue nature to his higher
ends; but I venture to think that the great intellectual difference between the
ancient times and our day, lies in the solid foundation we have acquired for

the hope that such an enterprise may meet with a certain measure of success.

The history of civilization details the steps by which men have succeeded in building up an artificial world within the cosmos. Fragile reed as he may be, man, as Pascal says, is a thinking reed: there lies within him a fund of energy operating intelligently and so far akin to that which pervades the universe, that it is competent to influence and modify the cosmic process. In virtue of his intelligence, the dwarf bends the Titan to his will. In every family, in every polity that has been established, the cosmic process in man has been restrained and otherwise modified by law and custom.

Note on Sources. The Clifford material in this section is quoted or abridged from his essay "The Ethics of Belief." The Huxley material is quoted from his essays "Agnosticism," "Agnosticism and Christianity," "The Struggle for Existence in Human Society," and "Prolegomena to Evolution and Ethics."

Reading References. Huxley is eminently readable. Almost any collection or selection of his essays will be found worth reading. The essays and parts of essays brought together in the Huxley volume in the Crofts Classics series make a good starter.

People have written interesting books and essays on Huxley. The following are examples: Clarence Ayres, Huxley; Houston Peterson, Huxley—Prophet of Science; William Irvine, Apes, Angels and Victorians; T. H. Huxley and Julian Huxley, Touchstone for Ethics 1893–1943; John Fiske, Through Nature to God, Chap. 2; Leonard Huxley, Life and Letters of T. H. Huxley.

READING QUESTIONS

1. Relevance of Darwin's book and Mill's book to a study of Huxley's agnosticism and its applications.
2. Point of Clifford's parable of the shipowner.
3. Point of the title of Clifford's essay.
4. How both logic and ethics enter into what Clifford wants to say about belief.
5. How Huxley came to invent the term agnostic.
6. His point here: "I too had a tail like the other foxes."
7. What agnosticism asserts. What it denies and repudiates.
8. What the application of agnosticism does or would do to contemporary "gnostics."
9. Why there can be neither peace nor truce between agnosticism and clericalism.

10. What was the episode of the Gadarene swine?
11. What physiology and pathology, anthropology, law and justice, history, suggest to him about such an episode or story.
12. "I can discern no escape from this dilemma. . . . This is the dilemma." Namely.
13. What is meant by "evolution by natural selection."
14. He says nature can be looked at from two points of view. Namely.
15. Why men felt called upon to explain away the gladiatorial aspect of nature.
16. Name and formulate the two arguments by which they tried to do that.
17. Give Huxley's most incisive criticism of each.
18. Why he won't settle for either Leibniz (optimism) or Schopenhauer (pessimism).
19. His thesis about the behavior of "ethical man" and the "cosmic process." Bearing of this on the theological problem examined in this Topic I.
20. Wherein you find Huxley (a) most (b) least convincing.

6. THE PRAGMATIC APPROACH TO NATURAL THEOLOGY —FROM WILLIAM JAMES

From Huxley to James. It will be recalled that Pascal, writing in the seventeenth century, repudiated the possibility of rational theology but clung to orthodox convictions. He rejected the appeal to reason in theology, but he retained the theology. John Stuart Mill, writing two centuries later, reversed the procedure. He clung to the idea of a rational theology, but repudiated the orthodox convictions. He rejected the orthodox theology, but he retained the appeal to reason. The most man can rationally justify, he argued, is the belief in a finite God. Now, William James, writing toward the close of the nineteenth century and in the opening years of the twentieth century, combined Pascal's rejection of reason and Mill's hypothesis of a limited Deity. James stands at the end of a line of rational theologians stretching back to Thomas Aquinas and beyond. He was familiar with Thomas, Pascal, Hume, Mill, and Huxley. Dispassionate consideration convinced him that the appeal to reason in theology was bankrupt. No one had ever properly answered Hume on his own grounds. But James found himself believing wholeheartedly in the existence of God. That, he could not shake off. Accordingly, he sought to combine the two compromises offered by Pascal and Mill respectively: an appeal to what he called "the will to believe" in support of the belief in a finite God.

On the face of it, James's "will to believe," later his pragmatism, is closely related, historically, to Huxley's agnosticism. That is apparent on reading James's essay. Huxley had said that if you couldn't logically justify what you believe, then it was immoral to believe. Such belief would be "stolen." It is this note of moral censure in Huxley's agnosticism that caught James's attention. His argument is that among Huxley's own beliefs are some which he (Huxley) could not justify "logically," "intellectually"; but which he (Huxley) nevertheless will not abandon. Such beliefs embody "the will to believe." Beliefs which are *appropriate* objects of the will to believe are not open to the moral criticism proposed by Huxley's agnosticism.

Biographical Note. William James was born in 1842 and died in 1910 at the age of sixty-eight. He was educated at Harvard and in Europe. He was appointed to the teaching staff in Harvard in the department of physiology. From physiology he moved later to psychology, writing his brilliant and epoch-making *Principles of Psychology* and *Varieties of Religious Experience.* From psychology he moved on to philosophy. His best-known and most controversial books were written during his years as professor of philosophy. He gathered about him, at Harvard, what was perhaps the most brilliant group of teachers and writers in philosophy ever assembled at any one time in any university in this country. These philosophical colleagues included Josiah Royce, George Herbert Palmer, George Santayana, and (in psychology) Hugo Münsterberg.

Although James was trained as physiologist and psychologist, he was essentially a moralist and theologian. His robust assurance that the good life, in the long run, provides the deepest and most lasting satisfaction; his passionately felt need for a "Friend" sustaining the universe and reaching out to man in his struggle for righteousness and truth, are convictions which pervade many of his writings. His three books, *The Will To Believe and Other Essays, The Varieties of Religious Experience,* and *Pragmatism,* contain popular and persuasive presentation of these views.

The Argument of the Citations. The citations quoted or abridged hereunder are, for the most part, from James's essay, "The Will to Believe." He states somewhere that it might better have been called "The Right to Believe." His aim is to point out that, in certain cases, where the evidence is insufficient to justify belief on "rational" grounds, there may nevertheless be other grounds. In a word, sufficient evidence is not the only thing which justifies belief, is not the only thing which gives us a "right to believe." Agnosticism may not be the last word here. In such

cases upon what does our right to believe rest? Where the evidence is insufficient, is it necessary to say, with agnosticism, that belief is everywhere and always immoral?

That is the central problem of the essay. James begins by a few remarks on hypotheses in general. The purpose of these remarks is to explain what he means by a "genuine option" between rival hypotheses.
Where we are faced with a genuine option between rival hypotheses, neither of which is backed by sufficient evidence, upon what principle may
we legitimately exercise our will to believe? James then formulates the
principle which, he thinks, justifies belief under such circumstances. The
question now is: Are there any beliefs which present themselves for acceptance on this principle? James notes that moral judgments are of this
nature. If this is so, then the moral judgments proposed by agnosticism, or
moral principles embodies in such judgments, would be important exceptions to the rule laid down by agnosticism. However, and more important,
the "religious hypothesis" is of this nature. He then states the terms of this
hypothesis. In what follows, he deals with two possible lines of criticism
which, he knows, will be directed against his position. The first of these
is the objection of the skeptic, namely, that where evidence is insufficient
to justify belief, we have no right to believe. The second objection is to
the effect that once you set up any principle designed to justify belief on
insufficient grounds, you have (in principle) obliterated the distinction
between intelligent belief and any but the wildest superstition. Finally,
in a few citations, we note his acceptance of Mill's limited theism.

James begins:

Let us give the name of *hypothesis* to anything that may be proposed
to our belief. And, just as electricians speak of live and dead wires, let us
speak of an hypothesis as either live or dead. A live hypothesis is one which
appeals as a real possibility to him to whom it is proposed.

Next, let us call the decision between hypotheses an *option*. Options may
be of several kinds. They may be living or dead, forced or avoidable, momentous or trivial.

A living option is one in which both hypotheses are live. If I say to you:
"Be a theosophist or be a Mohammedan," it is probably a dead option, because for you neither hypothesis is likely to be live. But if I say: "Be an
agnostic or be a Christian," it is otherwise. Trained as you are, each hypothesis
makes some appeal, however small, to your belief.

A forced option is one which arises when there is no standing outside
of the alternative hypotheses. If I say to you: "Choose between going out
with your umbrella or without it," I do not offer you a forced option. You

can easily avoid it by not going out at all. But if I say: "Either accept this truth or go without it," I put on you a forced option, for there is no third alternative and no standing outside of these two alternatives.

A momentous option is one that is presented when the opportunity is unique, when the stake is significant, or when the decision is irreversible if it later prove unwise. If I were Dr. Nansen and proposed to you to join my North Pole expedition, your option would be momentous; for this would probably be your only opportunity, and your choice now would either exclude you from the North Pole sort of immortality altogether, or put at least the chance of it into your hands. *Per contra*, the option is trivial when the opportunity is not unique, when the stake is insignificant, or when the decision is reversible if it later prove unwise.

An option is genuine when it is of the living, forced, momentous kind.

So much for hypotheses and options. Suppose, now, that a man is confronted by a pair of rival beliefs, neither of which can be said to rest on sufficient evidence to justify belief. What is he to do? Upon what principle can he justify himself in accepting the one or the other? It is the following:

The thesis I defend is this: Our passional [emotional] nature not only lawfully may, but must, decide an option between propositions, whenever it is a genuine option that cannot by its nature be decided on intellectual grounds.

The essence of the matter is contained in this principle. We are curious to know where, among our beliefs, we shall find some which call for acceptance on this principle. One example would be our moral beliefs: that it is better to do this than that, better to be this sort of man than that, and so on.

The question arises: Are there any such forced options in our speculative opinions? Are there some options between opinions in which this passional influence must be regarded both as an inevitable and as a lawful determinant of our choice?

Moral questions immediately present themselves. A moral question is a question not of what exists, but of what is good, or would be good if it did exist.

Science can tell us what exists; but to compare the worths, both of what exists and what does not exist, we must consult not science, but what Pascal calls our "heart," i.e., our passional nature. Science, herself, consults her heart when she lays it down that the infinite ascertainment of fact and correction of false belief are the supreme goods for man. Challenge the statement, and science can only repeat it oracularly, or else prove it by showing that such ascertainment and correction bring man all sorts of other goods which man's heart in turn declares desirable.

Moral beliefs. Is that all? What about religious beliefs? Are they appropriate objects of our sheer "will to believe"?

Let us pass to the question of religious faith. What do we mean by the religious hypothesis? Broadly it is this: Science says things are: morality says some things are better than other things: religion says that the best things are the more eternal things, the things in the universe that throw the last stone, so to speak, and say the final word: and that we are better off, even now, if we believe her first affirmation to be true.

Now let us consider what the logical elements of this situation are in case the religious hypothesis in both its branches be really true. We must admit that possibility at the outset.

We see, first, that religion offers itself as a momentous option. We are supposed to gain, even now, by our belief, and to lose by our nonbelief, a certain vital good.

We see, second, that religion is a forced option so far as that vital good is concerned. We cannot escape the issue by remaining skeptical, because although we do avoid error in that way if religion be untrue, we lose the good, if it be true. Skepticism, then, is not an avoidance of the option.

In these matters, the skeptic's position is this: Better risk the loss of truth than the chance of error. But in this he is actively playing his stake as much as the believer is. He is backing the field against the religious hypothesis, just as the believer is backing the religious hypothesis against the field.

Now, to most of us, religion comes in a still further way. What I mean is this. The more perfect and more eternal aspect of the universe is represented in our religions as having a personal form. The universe is no longer a mere It, but a Thou, if we are religious; and any relation that may be possible from person to person might be possible here. We feel, too, as if the appeal of religion were made to our own active good will, as if evidence for its truth might be forever withheld from us unless we met the hypothesis halfway.

This feeling, forced on us we know not whence, that by obstinately believing that there are gods we are doing the universe the deepest service we can, seems part of the living essence of the religious hypothesis.

God is the natural appellation, for us Christians at least, for the supreme reality, so I will call this higher part of the universe by the name of God. We and God have business with each other; and in opening ourselves to His influence our deepest destiny is fulfilled. The universe, at those parts of it which our personal being constitutes, takes a turn genuinely for the worse or for the better in proportion as each one of us fulfills or evades God's demands.

God's existence is the guarantee of an ideal order that shall be permanently preserved. This world may indeed some day burn up or freeze up; but if it is part of His order, the old ideals are sure to be brought elsewhere to fruition, so that where God is, tragedy is only provisional and partial, and shipwreck and dissolution are not the absolutely final things.

Only when this farther step of faith concerning God is taken, and remote objective consequences are predicted, does religion, as it seems to me, get wholly free from subjective experience, and bring a real hypothesis into play.

What is this but to say that religion, in her fullest exercise of function, is a postulator of new facts? The world interpreted religiously is not the materialistic world over again, with an altered expression. It must have, over and above the altered expression, a natural constitution different at some point from that which a materialistic world would have. It must be such that different events can be expected in it, different conduct must be required.

All this on the supposition that our passional nature may be prophetic and right: and that the religious hypothesis is a live hypothesis which may be true.

We are now in possession of the essentials of James's position. We know what he means by a genuine option between rival hypotheses. We know the principle by which he would justify belief in such circumstances. We know that he considers the religious hypothesis a case in point. We know, finally, what he means by this religious hypothesis. His defense of the whole position is still to be made. He deals first with the skeptic. The point here is this: It may be all very well to talk about the demands of our "passional nature," but, as a matter of fact, why is it not just as legitimate to refuse to believe either hypothesis when neither is backed by sufficient evidence? Why may a skeptic not take the stand, in all conscience, that under the circumstances stipulated by James, the proper attitude is one of suspended judgment? Let us hear, through James, the skeptic's statement of the case:

It does seem preposterous on the very face of it, to talk of our opinions being modifiable at will. Can our will either help or hinder our intellect in its perceptions of truth? . . . Indeed, the talk of believing by our volition seems from one point of view, simply silly. From another point of view it is worse than silly, it is vile. When one turns to the magnificent edifice of the physical sciences, and sees how it was reared, what thousands of disinterested moral lives of men lie buried in its mere foundations; what patience and postponement, what choking down of preference, what submission to icy laws of outer fact are wrought into its very stones and mortar; how absolutely impersonal it stands in its vast augustness—then how besotted and contemptible seems every little sentimentalist who comes blowing his voluntary smoke wreaths! Can we wonder if those bred in the rugged and manly school of science should feel like spewing such subjectivism out of their mouths? The whole system of loyalties which grow up in the schools of science go dead against its toleration; so that it is only natural that those who have caught the scientific fever should pass over to the opposite extreme and write sometimes as if the incorruptibly truthful intellect ought positively to prefer bitterness and unacceptableness to the heart in its cup.

Clough sings:

> It fortifies my soul to know
> That, though I perish, Truth is so

while Huxley exclaims: "My only consolation lies in the reflection that, however bad our posterity may become, so far as they hold by the plain rule of not pretending to believe what they have no reason to believe, because it may be to their advantage so to pretend, they will not have reached the lowest depth of immorality."

And that delicious *enfant terrible*, Clifford, writes: "Belief is desecrated when given to unproved and unquestioned statements for the solace and private pleasure of the believer. Whoso would deserve well of his fellows in this matter will guard the purity of his belief with a very fanaticism of jealous care, lest at any time it should rest on an unworthy object, and catch a stain which can never be wiped away. If a belief has been accepted on insufficient evidence, even though the belief be true, the pleasure is a stolen one. It is sinful because it is stolen in defiance of our duty to mankind. That duty is to guard ourselves from such beliefs as from a pestilence which may shortly master our body and then spread to the rest of the town. It is wrong, always, everywhere, and for everyone, to believe anything upon insufficient evidence."

Now, all of this strikes one as healthy, even when expressed by Clifford with somewhat too much of robustious pathos in the voice. Willing and wishing do seem, in the matter of our beliefs, to be only fifth wheels to the coach.

How shall this indictment be answered? It will be noticed that James has been scrupulously fair to the skeptic in admitting the genuine possibility here of an ethical issue. The skeptic's claim is not, at its best, that we are merely foolish to believe on insufficient evidence. It is the more serious claim that we *ought* not to believe on insufficient evidence; that belief, in such cases, is positively immoral. That is the point which agnosticism adds to skepticism. That is the charge with which James is faced. The first move in his defense is to note that in this unique case of the religious hypothesis doubt is the equivalent of denial; and, the point is, denial is not suspended judgment. (It may be necessary to reread James's wording of the religious hypothesis, especially its *second* part, to follow his argument here.)

To preach skepticism in these matters is tantamount to telling us, when in the presence of the religious hypothesis, that to yield to our fear of its being false is wiser and better than to yield to our hope that it may be true.

As James points out, this puts a slightly different face on the matter. Why is it "wiser and better" to refrain from belief on all occasions where the evidence is insufficient? It should be noted that, by developing the moral case for skepticism, James is jockeying the skeptic into a "moral" question. He has already explained that moral questions must be decided on "emotional" grounds.

This is not a case of "intellect" against "passion." It is only intellect, with one passion—the dread or horror of believing what may be false— laying down its law—never to believe what may be false when there is no evidence that it may be true.

And by what, forsooth, is the supreme wisdom of this passion warranted? Dupery for dupery, what proof is there that dupery through hope is so much worse than dupery through fear? I, for one, can see no proof; and I simply refuse to imitate the skeptic's option in a case where my own stake is important enough to give me the right to choose my own form of risk.

And what it comes down to is this:

We may regard the case for truth as paramount, and the avoidance of error as secondary; or we may treat the avoidance of error as more imperative, and let truth take its chance. Clifford exhorts us to the latter course. Believe nothing, he tells us, keep your mind in suspense forever, rather than, by closing on insufficient evidence, incur the awful risk of believing lies. You, on the other hand, may think that the risk of being in error is a very small matter when compared with the blessings of real knowledge, and be ready to be duped many times rather than postpone indefinitely the chance of guessing true.

This being so, he knows where he stands:

For my own part, I have also a horror of being duped. But I can believe that worse things than being duped may happen to a man in this world. So Clifford's exhortation has to my ears a thoroughly fantastic sound. Our errors are surely not such awfully solemn things. In a world where we are so sure to incur them, a certain lightness of heart seems healthier than this excessive nervousness on their behalf.

If the religious hypothesis be true, and the evidence for it still insufficient, I do not wish, by putting a skeptical extinguisher upon my nature, to forfeit my sole chance of getting upon the winning side; that chance depending, of course, on my willingness to run the risk of acting as if my passional need of taking the world religiously might be prophetic and right.

When I look at the religious hypothesis, as it really puts itself to men, and when I think of all the possibilities which it involves, then the skeptical command to put a stopper on our heart and wait—acting meanwhile more or less as if religion were not true—wait till doomsday, or till such time as our intellect and senses may have raked in enough evidence—this command, I say, seems to me the queerest idol ever manufactured in the philosophic cave.

If the religious hypothesis were true, then pure intellectualism, with its veto on our willingness to make advances, would be an absurdity; and some participation of our sympathetic nature would be logically required. I, therefore, for one, cannot see my way to accepting the agnostic rules for truth-seeking (never to believe any hypothesis when there is no evidence or insufficient evidence) or to willfully agree to keep my willing nature out of the game.

I cannot do so for this plain reason: A rule of thinking which would prevent me from acknowledging certain kinds of truth if those kinds of truths were really there, would be an irrational rule. That, for me, is the long and short of the logic of the situation.

The great empiricists are only empiricists on reflection; left to their instincts, they dogmatize like infallible popes. When the Cliffords tell us how sinful it is to be Christians on such "insufficient evidence," insufficiency is really the last thing they have in mind. For them the evidence is absolutely sufficient, only it makes the other way. They believe so completely in an anti-Christian order of the universe that there is no living option: Christianity, for them, is a dead hypothesis from the start.

As a kind of Parthian shot, James throws a question at the skeptics themselves:

Our belief in truth itself, for instance, that there is a truth and that our minds and it are made for each other—what is it but a passionate affirmation of desire in which our social system backs us up? We want to have a truth; we want to believe that our experiments and studies and discussions must put us in a continually better and better position toward it; and on this line we agree to fight out our thinking lives.

But if a skeptic asks us how we know all this, can our logic find a reply?

It cannot. It is just one volition against another; we are willing to go in for life upon a trust or assumption which he, for his part, does not care to make. As a rule we disbelieve all facts and theories for which we have no use. Clifford's cosmic emotions find no use for Christian feelings. Huxley belabors the bishops because there is no use for sacerdotalism in his scheme of life. But Newman goes over to Romanism, and finds all sorts of reasons good for staying there, because a priestly system is for him an organic need and delight.

So Clifford notwithstanding, our nonintellectual nature evidently does influence our convictions. The state of things is far from simple, and pure insight and pure logic, whatever they may do ideally, are not the only things that really do produce our creeds.

If we had an infallible intellect, with its objective certitudes, we might feel ourselves disloyal to such a perfect organ of knowledge in not trusting to it exclusively, in not waiting for its releasing word. But if we believe that no bell in us tolls to let us know for certain when truth is in our grasp, then it seems a piece of idle fantasticality to preach so solemnly of our duty of waiting for the bell.

James has still to deal with another sort of critic, no less hostile in his way than the skeptic. The charge this time is not that where evidence is lacking it is wiser and better to suspend judgment. It is, rather, to this effect: If you start justifying belief on this basis, where and how are you going to draw the line? The justification is not, by its nature, the peculiar property of the man who desires to believe in God. It would seem to be equally available, as a principle of justification, for other beliefs as well, some of which might be incompatible with those beliefs which James used it to defend. A man who advances a principle which would justify incompatible beliefs has some explaining to do. James knew this. Although convinced that his argument was sound, he knew that others would not be. Thus:

I confess I do not see how this logic can be escaped. But sad experience makes me fear that some of you may still shrink from saying with me that we have the right to believe at our own risk any hypothesis that is live enough to tempt our will.

If this is so, however, I suspect it is because you have got away from the logical point of view altogether, and are thinking of some particular religious hypothesis which for you is dead. The freedom to "believe what we will" you apply to the case of some patent superstition; and the faith you think of is the faith defined by the schoolboy when he said: "Faith is when you believe something that you know ain't true."

I can only repeat that this is a misapprehension of my position. The freedom to "believe what we will," for which I have been arguing, can only cover living options which the intellect by itself cannot resolve; and living options never seem absurd or superstitious to him who has them to consider.

Where there is no such forced option, the dispassionately judicial intellect with no pet hypothesis, saving us, as it does, from dupery, at any rate, ought to be our ideal.

It would appear that James has only restated his difficulty. It is still open to anyone to point out: "Yes, what you have said, you have said. The point is, however, that what you have not said, you have not said. What about the man whose passional nature inclines him to embrace, as true, a proposition which is incompatible with one which your passional nature has inclined you to embrace? As between two passional natures having divergent inclinations, how do you decide?" A glance through the published letters of William James shows that he was bothered by this point. Writing to his brother Henry, the novelist, he protests:

When *I say* that, *other things being equal,* the view of things that seems more satisfactory morally will legitimately be treated by men as truer than the view that seems less so, *they quote me as saying* that anything morally satisfactory can be treated as true, no matter how unsatisfactory it may be from the point of view of its consistency with what we already know or believe to be true about physical or natural facts, which is rot!!

James has drawn a two-edged sword. To vary the metaphor, his principle may be used to reinforce either theism or atheism, or for the matter of that, some third alternative equally removed from either, say skepticism or polytheism. In the last analysis he merely reinforces the most deeply congenial belief; he does not state which belief is or ought to be the most congenial. However, he is not done protesting. Writing to an English philosopher, he has much the same thing to say:

Would to God I had never thought of that unhappy title for my essay. What I meant by the title was the state of mind of the man who finds an impulse in him toward a believing attitude, and who resolves not to quench it simply because doubts of its truth are possible. Its opposite would be the maxim: Believe in nothing which you can possibly doubt.

My essay hedged the license to indulge in private overbeliefs with so many restrictions and sign boards of danger that the outlet was narrow enough. It made of tolerance the essence of the situation. It defined the permissible cases. It treated the faith attitude as a necessity for individuals, because the total "evidence" which only the race can draw include their experiments among its data. It tended to show only that faith cannot be absolutely *vetoed*, as certain champions of "science" had claimed it ought to be.

I cry to heaven to tell me of what insane root my "leading contemporaries" have eaten, that they are so smitten with blindness as to the meaning of printed texts.

In my essay the evil shape was a vision of "Science" in the form of abstraction, priggishness and sawdust, lording it over all. Take the sterilest scientific prig and cad you know, compare him with the richest religious intellect you know, and you would not, any more than I would, give the former the exclusive right of way.

There are two parts to a man's exposition of his ideas concerning God. In the first place, he should make clear why he believes that God exists. In the second, he should make clear what he conceives God's nature to be. So far as God's existence goes, we know where James stands in this essay. "Why do I believe in God? Is it because I have experienced his presence? No; rather because I need that it be true." Before quitting James, it is worth noting that he used his principle to justify his belief in God's finiteness. Like Mill, and many other recent and contemporary theologians, James repudiated the celebrated "omni's" of traditional theology.

I simply refuse to accept the idea of there being no purpose in the objective world. On the other hand, I cannot represent the existence of purpose except as based in a mind. The "not-me," therefore, so far as it contains purpose, must spring from a mind; but not necessarily a *One and Only* mind.

In saying God exists, all I imply is that my purposes are cared for by a mind so powerful as on the whole to control the drift of the universe. That is . . . merely a practical emotional faith.

The only difficulties of theism are the moral difficulties and meanness; and they have always seemed to me to flow from the gratuitous dogma of God being the all-inclusive reality. Once think possible a pluralism of which He may be one member, and piety forthwith ceases to be incompatible with manliness, and religious faith with intellectual rectitude.

In short, the only theism I defend is that of simple unphilosophic mankind. God, in the religious life of ordinary men is the name, not of the whole of things, heaven forbid, but only of the ideal tendency in things. . . . He works in an external environment, has limits, and has enemies. . . . If there be a God, how the devil can we know what difficulties he may have had to contend with? Possible difficulties! They save everything. But what are they if not limitations to the all-inclusiveness of any single being!

Having an environment, being in time, and working out a history just like ourselves, He escapes from the foreignness from all that is human, of the static, timeless, perfect absolute.

My God, being part of a pluralistic system, is responsible only for such things as He knows enough and has enough power to have accomplished. The "omniscient" and "omnipotent" God of theology I regard as a disease of the philosophy shop.

The line of least resistance, as it seems to me, both in theology and in philosophy, is to accept, along with the Superhuman Consciousness, the notion that It is not all embracing; the notion, in other words, that there is a God, but that He is finite, either in power or in knowledge, or in both at once.

Note on Sources. The James material in this section is quoted or abridged from his essay "The Will to Believe." The concluding passages (pages 86–87 of this book) are from the chapters entitled "Conclusion" and "Postscript" in his book, *Varieties of Religious Experience.*

Reading References. The best thing to do with William James is to read him. In many respects, he is his own best commentary. The volume, *The Will to Believe and Other Essays,* from which this chapter has been largely drawn, is a delightful collection. (See also *Essays in Pragmatism,* edited by the present writer.) But one may desire to know what other people think about an author whom one has read. A book here is Julius Bixler's *Religion in the Philosophy of William James.* The only complete account of James's life and times is to be found in R. B. Perry's two monumental volumes, *The Life and Thought of William James.* The chapter in which Perry gives an account of "The Will to Believe" will repay immediate perusal.

The following are some books published since 1940:

Compton, Charles Herrick. *William James: Philosopher and Man.*
In Commemoration of William James.
Knight, Margaret. *William James.*
Mathiessen, Francis Otto. *The James Family.*
Moore, Edward C. *American Pragmatism: Peirce, James, and Dewey.*
Morris, Lloyd. *William James: The Message of The Modern Mind.*
Roback, A. A. *William James: His Marginalia, Personality and Contribution.*
William James: The Man and The Thinker.

READING QUESTIONS

1. What James means by (a) an hypothesis, (b) a live hypothesis, (c) an option, (d) a genuine option.

2. He distinguishes between genuine options which can be decided on intellectual grounds and genuine options which cannot be so decided. Give an example of the first sort. What he would have us do about genuine options of the first sort. Quote any three passages in support of your answer.

3. His thesis about genuine options of the second sort, i.e., those which cannot be decided on intellectual grounds.

4. Give three examples—your own, not James'—of genuine options which cannot be decided on intellectual grounds.

5. When you decide a genuine option which cannot be decided on intellectual grounds, you exercise the "will to believe." By "will" here, do you understand simply "desire" or "wish"? Is the "will to believe" simply another name for "wishful thinking"?

6. James says that moral questions present genuine options which cannot be decided on intellectual grounds. (a) Give an example of his point here. (b) Why, looking forward to Clifford and Huxley, he does well to include moral questions at this point.

7. He says that the religious hypothesis has two parts to it, both necessary: (a) A personal God exists, over and above nature. (b) We are better off, even now, if we believe that. If that is the religious hypothesis, do you find it, in James' sense, "live"? If that is the religious hypothesis, how would you state the religious option? Would it be, in James' sense, a genuine option? Of the second sort?

8. A genuine option that cannot be decided on intellectual grounds might be called an "open" question which you see no intellectually defensible way of "closing." The skeptic advises suspended judgment: on grounds of prudence such options should be avoided, such questions be left "open." James' rejoinder to him.

9. The agnostic (Clifford, Huxley) goes further. He says that it is *immoral* to exercise the will to believe in the case of genuine options that cannot be decided on intellectual grounds. James' rejoinder to him.

10. The atheist goes further than either the skeptic or the agnostic. Suggest what James would say to him.

11. If you decide a genuine option which cannot be decided on intellectual grounds, you exercise the "will to believe." What is the "two-edged sword" objection?

12. State James's "piece-meal" supernaturalism. His reasons for adhering to it.
13. Wherein James invites comparison with Pascal and Mill, but contrast with Thomas Aquinas and Hume.
14. Wherein you find James (a) most (b) least convincing.

The following are two lists of books containing popular (i.e., not technical) discussions of questions in theology. There is no reason that only professional theologians should write and read books about God. If you have found St. Thomas, Pascal, Hume, Mill, Huxley, and James worth reading, then you should extend your holdings. If your thinking runs with Pascal and Mill and James, you will perhaps prefer to browse in the first list; if, however, with Hume and Huxley, then the second list.

LIST I

Chesterton, G. K. *Orthodoxy; The Everlasting Man.*
Eddington, Sir Arthur. *Science and the Unseen World.*
Fiske, John. *Through Nature to God.*
Hocking, W. E. *Science and the Idea of God.*
Joad, C. E. M. *God and Evil.*
Lewis, C. S. *The Problem of Pain; Miracles.*
More, Paul Elmer. *The Skeptical Approach to Religion.*
Paton, H. J. *The Modern Predicament.*
Shaw, Bernard. *Infidel Half Century.*
Stace, W. T. *Time and Eternity; Religion and the Modern Mind.*

LIST II

Bury, J. B. *History of Freedom of Thought.*
Dewey, John. *A Common Faith.*
Freud, Sigmund. *The Future of an Illusion.*
Mencken, H. L. *Treatise on the Gods.*
Russell, Bertrand. *Religion and Science.*
Santayana, George. *Reason in Religion.*
Stephen, Sir Leslie. *An Agnostic's Apology; Freethinking and Plain Speaking.*

TOPIC TWO

A Metaphysical Problem

THE PROBLEM STATED

One of the best-known remarks in the history of philosophy is ascribed to the Greek thinker, Thales. He is said to have held that "all things are made of water." On the face of it, this seems both unimportant and false. Whence its historical importance? Why has Thales been bracketed, along with Copernicus and Darwin, as having initiated a line of thought which marked an epoch in human speculation?

The reason is this. It required, in the first instance, a bold mind to conceive any proposition having the general form "All things are made of . . ."; because if there is one proposition which would appear to be justified by the facts of our everyday experience, it is that all things are not made of any one thing. Multiplicity and variety are the obvious facts about the everyday world. The effort of thought required to break down the testimony of the everyday world must have been considerable, as it certainly was subsequently fruitful.

Thales probably had his reasons. Such apparently diverse things as ice, snow, mist, vapor, steam are all "made of" water, if we use the term loosely. Why not other things too? Whatever his reasons may have been, his remark, once made, continued to re-echo in the minds of generations which came after him. "All things are made of . . ."

In fact, the problem is with us to this day. What are all things made of? What do we intend by the phrase *made of?* If we brush aside Thales' answer, what do we propose in place of it? Speculations on this question constitute part of the general topic of metaphysics. That is, metaphysics is, in part, an inquiry into the question what all things are "made of."

Suppose we consider a miscellaneous collection of things, a clay pipe, a bird's egg, a rainbow, a copy of *Hamlet*, an uprising in Central China, an act of mercy, a cry in the night, a new planet. What are all these things made of? Varying the words, to what common substance are these all reducible? Of what "underlying reality" are they all manifestations? Is this underlying reality itself further reducible?

The notion that the observed multiplicity and variety of the everyday world are reducible to something common and uniform and *not* given as part of the everyday world is not an unreasonable notion. Few persons would care to deny it in principle, much as they might argue over what that something is to which all things are reducible. Granted the propriety of the notion of an ultimate reality, a "real" world in contrast to the "everyday" world, it is necessary to go one step further. In some sense or other, the everyday world is an appearance or a manifestation of the real world. They are the appearances; it is the real.

It is then possible to restate our central problem: What is the nature of that ultimate reality, that real world, of which the everyday world is the appearance?

Answers to this question vary. If it is held that there is *an* ultimate reality, we have what is called *monism* in metaphysics, the belief that ultimate reality is one in kind. If it is held that there are at least two ultimate realities, we have what is called *dualism* in metaphysics, the belief that ultimate reality is two in kind. If it is held that there are three or more ultimate realities, we have what is called *pluralism* in metaphysics, the belief that ultimate reality is three or more in kind.

Within these classifications others will occur. You and I might agree that monism is a true belief. Our agreement might extend no further. When we came to the question of the nature of this ultimate reality, we might differ. I might claim that it was matter; you might claim that it was mind; a third person might claim that it was neither, but something more ultimate of which both matter and mind are manifestations.

In this topic we are to be concerned with such inquiries. A metaphysical hypothesis is a claim about the nature of ultimate reality. In considering any such hypothesis, it will be helpful to ask: Is it a form of monism, or dualism, or pluralism? What reasons are given, or may be given, in support of it? What reasons against it? What consequences follow from it? Do these agree with common sense? Or do they make nonsense of it? Reflection upon the nature of ultimate reality is not the whole of metaphysics, but it is a large part of it. For a beginner in metaphysics, two things are of primary importance: to demand reasons for accepting any hypothesis, and to note consequences which follow from accepting the hypothesis.

The readings and comments which follow are grouped, in an historical way, around the problem stated above. They provide material for thinking about this problem, comparable to the readings and comments grouped around the theological problem in the sections which preceded. There are six sets of them: two from the seventeenth century (Descartes and Hobbes), one from the eighteenth century (Berkeley), one from the nineteenth century (Schopenhauer), and two from the twentieth century (Ayer and Elliott). These men have been chosen because, among them, they provide a varied gallery in which to roam. No two are alike. Each is convinced of his views and eager to spread them among "all rational minds." Each realizes that he must be prepared to argue his case. There is, among them, no appeal to emotions; at least, not intentionally. They are all, in this respect, "hardheaded rationalists." Here, for the eye which can detect it, is one of man's supreme intellectual sports insofar as he is a "rational" animal. Here are corrosive skepticism, caustic (if obscure) wit, resounding thwacks, closely built arguments, relentless determination to "begin at the beginning" and "think it through," and proud gestures directing attention to "positions established" and "positions overthrown." A taste for metaphysics and a flare for the practice of metaphysics are not widely diffused, but the genuine article, like a love for poetry or painting, is irrepressible once it has become aware of itself.

The readings which follow are in chronological order, but the chronological order itself exhibits development. Conceive each of these six authors confronted with the inquiry: What is the nature of ultimate reality? The answer of Descartes is the most conventional. Reality consists of three substances, namely, God, human souls, and matter. The position taken up by Hobbes represents a selection of one of the elements argued for by Descartes. All things, his argument runs, are matter: materialism, as full blown as one could wish it. The position taken up by Berkeley represents a deliberate rejection of Hobbes' materialism. All things, runs the argument here, are mind or spirit. Hobbes' materialism and Berkeley's idealism, between them, account for an enormous amount of modern metaphysics. The term *voluntarism*, associated with Schopenhauer in metaphysics, covers the conviction that neither matter nor spirit but "will" is the ultimate substance, the ultimately real stuff, of which all things are merely manifestations. Ayer's *positivism* proposes an abandonment of metaphysics, a refusal to admit that the metaphysical problem is a genuine problem, susceptible of a meaningful answer.

DESCARTES — God, human souls, matter
Hobbes — matter
Berkeley — mind, or spirit.
Shopenhauer — will (voluntarist)
Ayer — refuses problem (positivist)

1. DUALISM AND ITS IMPLICATIONS
—FROM RENE DESCARTES

In point of time, and with respect to content, it is well to begin with the speculations of René Descartes. This, for two reasons: He lived in a "climate of opinion" which is still widely prevalent, despite the lapse of three centuries, and hence brings to his task the presuppositions which most persons still possess; and he has served as the point of departure for almost all metaphysicians since his day.

Biographical Note. Descartes was born in France in 1596 and died in Sweden in 1650 at the age of fifty-four. His biography reveals three periods: years of education, years of wandering and learning, and years of maturity and production.

(1) His formal education, from eight to sixteen, was received at the Jesuit college of La Flèche. Here he acquired the essentials of a "gentleman's education," which he subsequently devoted much time to erasing. Before he had turned seventeen he put aside his books and after a few lessons in fencing and horsemanship went to "the great world of Paris." Here he remained for about five years, living at first the usual life of gaiety and gambling, but retiring after a while to the quiet and seclusion of an obscure lodging house. His thoughtful temper reasserted itself. Habits of reflection acquired at La Flèche, and roused once more by a Catholic friend, one Father Mersenne, took possession of him again.

(2) In 1618 Descartes left Paris, determined to see the world. He became a soldier, serving in three different European armies, in the Netherlands, in Bavaria, and in Hungary. It was a life which gave him much time for thought during the months of idleness in winter quarters. He stuck to soldiering for three or four years, then resolved "no longer to carry a musket." Army days over, he continued his travels for five or six years more, visiting Switzerland and Italy, until, in 1628, he decided that he had read enough in the "great book of the world."

(3) In 1629, his mind crowded with ideas demanding to be written down, he settled in Holland. He was seeking quiet and seclusion once more. His European retirement, as he called it, lasted twenty years. These were the years of fruitful production. Book followed book. His reputation spread. He had the intellectuals of his generation for his readers, and its rulers for his patrons and friends. In rapid succession he wrote his *Quest for Truth*, his *Rules for the Direction of the Mind*, his *Discourse on Method*, his *Meditations on First Philosophy*, his *Principles*

of Philosophy, his *Treatise on the Passions;* and many other volumes which soon became stock in trade for the philosophically minded of his day. In 1649 he was invited by Queen Christina of Sweden to visit her at Stockholm and expound the principles of the "new philosophy." After much hesitation, and against the advice of his friends, he agreed to go. It cost him his life, for he caught a cold in his lungs which brought about his death in the following year.

The Argument of the Citations. The following citations are taken for the most part from Descartes' little book *Meditations on First Philosophy.* The thought of these six short soliloquies might be paraphrased as follows: I was given the usual gentlemen's education in my youth. Presently I became skeptical of most of what had been taught me. Accordingly, I determined to abandon all my learning and begin again with a clean slate upon which no one but myself should write, and upon which nothing should be written that was not clear and distinct. I needed, as a starting point, something which could stand against skepticism, something not doubtable. To that end I set about the cultivation of doubt. My doubts were brought to an end by the fact of my own existence. The fact that I was doubting entailed necessarily my own existence as a doubter. From this *indubitandum* my reconstruction must proceed. Could I use the fact of my own existence to prove the existence of anything else? Two great steps were in order: to demonstrate the existence of God and the existence of the material world. The steps by which I moved from doubts about things taught me at school, to the demonstrated existence of myself, God, and the external world, constitute the theme of these *Meditations.*

The first group of citations supply some autobiographical facts with which Descartes wishes to begin.

I had been nourished on letters since my childhood, and since I was given to believe that by their means a clear and certain knowledge could be obtained of all that is useful in life, I had an extreme desire to acquire instruction.

But as soon as I had achieved the entire course of study at the close of which one is usually received into the ranks of the learned, I entirely changed my opinion. I found myself embarrassed with so many doubts and errors that it seemed to me that the effort to instruct myself had no effect other than the increasing discovery of my own ignorance. And yet I was studying at one of the most celebrated schools in Europe, where I thought there must be men of learning if such were to be found anywhere in the world.

I learned there all that others had learned. Moreover, not being satisfied with the sciences that we were taught, I even read through all books which fell into my hands, treating of what is considered most curious and rare. Along with this, I knew the judgments which others had formed of me, and I did not feel that I was esteemed inferior to my fellow students. And finally, our century seemed to me as flourishing, and as fertile in great minds, as any which had preceded it.

These reflections combined to make me take the liberty of judging all others by myself, and of coming to the conclusion that there was no learning in the world such as I had formerly believed it to be.

That is why, as soon as age permitted me to emerge from the control of my tutors, I entirely quitted the study of letters. I resolved to seek no other knowledge than that which could be found in myself, or at least in the great book of the world. I employed the rest of my youth in travel, in seeing courts and armies, in intercourse with men of diverse temperaments and conditions, in collecting varied experiences, in testing myself in the various predicaments in which I was placed by fortune. In all circumstances I sought to bring my mind to bear on the things that came before it so that I might derive some profit from my experience.

For nine years I did nothing but roam hither and thither, trying to be a spectator rather than an actor in all the comedies which the world displays. Especially did I ask myself, in each matter that came before me, whether anything could make it subject to suspicion or doubt.

I considered the manners and customs of other men, and found nothing to give me settled convictions. I remarked in them almost as much diversity as I had formerly seen in the opinions of philosophers. So much was this so, that I learned to believe nothing too certainly of which I had been convinced only by example and custom.

I thus concluded that it is much more custom and example that persuade us than any certain knowledge. And this despite the fact that the voice of the majority affords no proof of any value in matters a little difficult to discover. Such truths are like to have been discovered by one man, more than by a nation. But I could not, however, put my finger on a single person whose opinions seemed preferable to those of others.

I found I was constrained, so to speak, to undertake the direction of my own inquiries.

As regards all the opinions which, up to that time, I had embraced, I thought I could not do better than try once for all to sweep them completely away. Later on they might be replaced, either by others which were better, or by the same when I had made them conform to the uniformity of a rational scheme. I firmly believed that by this means I should succeed much better than if I had built on foundations and principles of which I had allowed myself to be persuaded in youth without having inquired into their truth. My design has never extended beyond trying to reform my own opinions and to build on a foundation which is entirely my own.

I was not seeking to imitate the skeptics, who only doubt for the sake of doubting and pretend always to be uncertain. On the contrary, my design was only to provide myself with good ground for assurance, to reject the quicksand and the mud in order to find the rock or clay.

These remarks give us the terms of his self-imposed task. It was twofold. On the one hand, to work himself free from the opinion which he had accepted as part of a normal education; on the other, to avoid mere skepticism. The execution of this design called for a definite procedure. This Descartes outlines:

Like one who walks alone and in the twilight, I resolved to go slowly, to use so much circumspection that even if my advance was very small at least I guarded myself from falling. I did not wish to reject any opinion finally until I had planned out the task I had undertaken, and until I had sought out the true method of arriving at a knowledge of the things of which my mind was capable.

In my younger days I had studied logic and geometry and algebra—three sciences which, it seemed, ought to contribute something to the design I had in view.

But, in examining them, I observed in respect to logic, that syllogisms and the rest served better to explain those things which one already knows than to learn something new. As to geometry and algebra, they embrace only the most abstract matters, such as appear to have no actual use. This made me feel that some other method must be found exempt from their fault. So, in place of the many precepts of which logic is composed, and the many rules and formulae of which mathematics is composed, I settled on four rules for the direction of the understanding.

My first rule was to accept nothing as true which I did not clearly recognize to be so; to accept nothing more than what was presented to my mind so clearly and distinctly that I could have no occasion to doubt it. The second rule was to divide each problem or difficulty into as many parts as possible. The third rule was to commence my reflections with objects which were the simplest and easiest to understand, and rise thence, little by little, to knowledge of the most complex. The fourth rule was to make enumerations so complete, and reviews so general, that I should be certain to have omitted nothing.

Those long chains of reasoning which geometricians make had caused me to imagine that all parts of human knowledge might be mutually related in the same fashion; and that, provided we abstain from receiving anything as true which is not so, and always deduce one conclusion from some other, there can be nothing so remote that we cannot reach it, nor so recondite that we cannot discover it.

But what pleased me most, in this method which I was determined to follow, was that I was certain by its means to exercise my reason in all things; if not perfectly, at least as well as was in my power. I felt that, in making use of it, my mind would gradually accustom itself to think about its objects more accurate and distinctly.

The first of the above rules is perhaps the important one: to accept nothing as true which he did not clearly recognize to be so. It is one thing to lay this rule down. It is another to abide by it. The difficulty is in knowing where to start searching for one indubitable fact. But, the search is under way.

. . . it is necessary for me to reject as false everything as to which I can imagine the least ground of doubt, in order to see if anything remains that is entirely certain. So I set myself seriously and freely to the general upheaval of all my former opinions.

To that end it is not requisite that I examine each opinion in particular. That would be an endless undertaking. Owing, however, to the fact that the destruction of the foundations bring with it the downfall of the rest of the edifice, I shall only attack those principles upon which all my former opinions rested.

All that up to the present time I have accepted as most true and certain I have learned either from the senses or through the senses. But it is sometimes proved to me that these senses are deceptive. And it is wiser not to trust entirely to anything by which we have once been deceived.

But it may be objected that, although the senses sometimes deceive us concerning things which are hardly perceptible or are very far away, there are yet many things as to which we cannot reasonably have any doubt although we recognize them by their means. For example, there is the fact that I am here, seated by the fire, attired in a dressing gown, having this paper in my hand. And how could I deny that these hands and this body are mine?

At the same time I must remember that I am in the habit of sleeping, and in my dreams representing to myself the same things. How often has it happened that I dreamt I was in this particular place, dressed and seated near the fire, while in reality I was lying undressed in bed. On many occasions I have in sleep been deceived by similar illusions. In thinking carefully about this fact, I see that there are manifestly no certain indications by which we may clearly distinguish wakefulness from sleep.

Suppose we assume, then, that we are asleep; that all these particulars, e.g., opening our eyes, shaking our head, extending our hand, are but false delusions; that possibly neither our hands nor our body are such as they appear to us to be.

There is a point, however, which we must not overlook. We must admit that the things which are represented to us in sleep are like painted representations which can only have been formed as the counterparts of something real and true, i.e., not illusory. It would follow from this admission that those general things at least, i.e., eyes, head, hands, body, are not imaginary things but things really existent.

We are bound, at the same time, to confess that there are some objects yet more simple and universal than eyes, a head, a body, etc., namely, colors, shapes, size, number, etc., which are real and true. For, whether I am awake or asleep, red is not blue, two and three make five, squares have only four sides, and so on. It does not seem possible that truths so clear can be suspected of any falsity.

Nevertheless, I have long had fixed in my mind the belief that an all-powerful God existed by whom I have been created such as I am. But how do I know that He has not brought it to pass that there is no earth, no heaven, no extended body, no magnitude, no place; and that, nonetheless, I possess perceptions of all these things which seem to me to exist just exactly as I now see them?

It might be urged against this suggestion that God has not desired that I should be thus deceived. For is He not said to be supremely good? However, if it is contrary to His goodness to have made me such that I am constantly deceived, it would also seem to be contrary to His goodness to permit me to be sometimes deceived; and yet it cannot be denied that He does permit this.

There may indeed be those who, rather than believe that all other things are uncertain, would prefer to deny the existence of a God so powerful. Let us not oppose them. Let us suppose, then, not that God (who is supremely good and the fountain of truth) but some evil genius not less powerful than deceitful, has employed his whole energies in deceiving me.

I shall suppose, then, that some evil genius not less powerful than deceitful is employing His whole energies to deceive me. I shall consider that the heavens, the earth, colors, shapes, sounds, and all other external things, are nothing but illusions and dreams by which this evil genius has laid traps for my credulity. I shall consider myself as having no hands, no eyes, no flesh, no blood, nor any senses; yet falsely believing myself to possess all these things. I shall remain obstinately attached to this idea. If, by this means, it is not in my power to arrive at the knowledge of any truth, I may at least do what is in my power, namely, suspend judgment, and thus avoid belief in anything false and avoid being imposed upon by this arch deceiver, however powerful and deceptive he may be.

Determined to "doubt everything," until doubt becomes impossible of being pushed further, Descartes has had recourse to heroic measures. The senses have been discredited, and with them the credibility of the external world revealed by the senses. This, one might have thought, would have sufficed. But assurance must be made doubly sure. Hence the hypothesis of a malignant genius who deceives him. At this point the eagerly sought *indubitandum* begins to appear.

I suppose, then, that all the things that I see are false. I persuade myself that nothing has ever existed of all that my fallacious memory represents to me. I consider that I possess no senses. I imagine that body, figure, extension, motion, and place are but the fictions of my mind. What, then, can be esteemed as true? Perhaps nothing at all, unless that there is nothing in the world that is certain.

But immediately I notice that while I wish to think all things false, it is nonetheless absolutely essential that I, who wish to think this, should truly exist. There is a powerful and cunning deceiver who employs his ingenuity in misleading me? Let it be granted. It follows the more that I exist, if he deceives me. If I did not exist, he could not deceive me. This truth, "I think, therefore I am; *cogito, ergo sum,*" is so certain, so assured, that all the most extravagant scepticism is incapable of shaking it. This truth, "I am, I exist," I can receive without scruple as the first principle of the philosophy for which I am seeking.

I think, therefore I am. But what am I? I do not yet know; and hence I must be careful lest I imprudently take some other object in place of myself and thus go astray in respect of this knowledge which I hold to be the most certain of all that I formerly believed.

What then did I formerly believe myself to be? I considered myself as having a face, hands, arms, and all that system of members which I designate by the name of body. In addition to this, I considered that I was nourished, that I walked, that I felt, and that I thought.

But what am I, now that I assume that there is an evil and malicious genius who employs all his powers to deceive me? Can I affirm, with as much certainty as I can affirm my existence, that I possess any of the least of all those things which I have just now ascribed to myself? I pause to consider. I resolve all these things in my mind. I find none of the bodily attributes which I can ascribe to myself.

What of thinking? I find that thought alone is an attribute which cannot be separated from me. I am, I exist; that is certain. But this certainty reposes on the "I think" which preceded. I am trying here not to admit anything which is not necessarily true. To speak thus strictly, I am nothing more than a thing which thinks, that is, to say, a mind, an understanding. I am a real thing. I really exist. But what am I? I have answered: a thing which thinks.

I am a thing which thinks. And what more? What is a thing which thinks? It is a thing which doubts, understands, conceives, affirms, denies, wills, refuses, imagines, feels. Certainly it is no small matter if all these things pertain to my nature.

But why should they not so pertain? Am I not that being who now doubts nearly everything, who nevertheless understands certain things, who affirms that only one thing is true, who denies all other things, who desires to know more, who is averse from being deceived, who imagines many things, who perceives many things? Is there, in all this, anything which is less certain than that I exist? Indeed, it is so evident that it is I who doubt, who understand, who desire, and so on, that there is no reason here to add anything to explain it. From this time I begin to know what I am with a little more clearness and distinctness than before.

Doubt has been explored and exploited. Self has been isolated as the single indubitable fact. The nature of self, a thinking thing, has been noted. Can this be used as a steppingstone? Does the fact of himself and his thoughts imply any other fact?

I shall now close my eyes; I shall stop my ears. I shall call away all my senses. I shall efface from my thoughts all images of material things—or, since that is hardly possible—I shall esteem them as vain and false. Thus holding converse only with my self, and considering my own nature, I shall try to reach a better knowledge of what I am.

I am a thing which thinks; that is to say, that doubts, affirms, denies, knows, is ignorant, wills, desires, imagines, perceives. For, as I remarked before, although the things which I perceive and imagine are perhaps nothing apart from me, yet the perceptions and imaginings certainly reside in me. And in the little that I have just said, I think I have summed up all that I really know, or was hitherto aware that I knew. To extend my knowledge further, I shall look around more carefully and see whether I cannot still discover in myself some other things which I have not hitherto perceived.

I am certain that I am a thing which thinks. But if I am indeed certain of this I must know what is requisite to render me certain of anything. I must possess a standard of certainty. In this first knowledge which I have gained, what is there that assures me of its truth? Nothing except the clear and distinct perception of what I state. This, indeed, would not suffice to assure me that what I state is true if it could ever happen that I should clearly and distinctly perceive to be true something which was in fact false. Accordingly, I can establish as a general rule that all things which I perceive very clearly and very distinctly are true.

All things which I perceive very clearly and very distinctly, are true. If I have heretofore judged that such matters could be doubted, it was because it came into my mind that perhaps a God might have endowed me with such a nature that I might have been deceived even concerning things which seemed to me most manifest. I see no reason to believe that there is a God who is a deceiver; however, as yet I have not satisfied myself that there is a God at all.

I must inquire whether there is a God. And, if I find that there is a God, I must also inquire whether He may be a deceiver. For, without a knowledge of these two truths, I do not see that I can ever be certain of anything.

Now, it is obvious that there must be at least as much reality in any cause as in its effect. For whence could the effect derive its reality, if not from its cause? From this it follows that something cannot proceed from nothing; and that the more or the greater cannot proceed from the less.

The longer and more carefully I investigate these matters, the more clearly and distinctly do I perceive their truth. But what may I conclude from it all, finally? It is this: If I have any idea which I myself cannot be the cause of, it follows of necessity that I am not alone in the world, that there is some other being which exists as the cause of this idea. Have I any such idea?

There is the idea of God. Is this idea something that could have originated in, been caused by, me? By the name *God* I understand a being that is infinite, eternal, immutable, independent, all-knowing, all-powerful, by which I myself and everything else (if anything else does exist) have been created.

Now, all these qualities are such that the more diligently I attend to them, the less do they appear capable of originating in me alone. Hence, from what was premised above, we must conclude that God necessarily exists as the origin of this idea I have of Him. For, to consider but one point, the idea of a being or a substance is within me owing to the fact that I am myself a being or substance; nevertheless, I would not have the idea of an infinite being, since I am myself finite, unless it had proceeded from some being who was infinite.

I see nothing in all that I have just said which, by the light of nature, is not manifest to anyone who desires to think attentively on the subject. It only remains to examine into the manner in which I have acquired this idea from God.

I have not received it through the senses; nor is it a fiction of my mind, for it is not in my power to take from or add to it. The only alternative is that it is innate in me, just as the idea of myself is innate in me.

It is not strange that God, in creating me, placed this idea within me to be like the mark of the workman imprinted on his work. For, from the fact that God created me it is most probable that He has placed His image and similitude upon me. The whole strength of the argument which I have here used to prove the existence of God consists in this: It is not possible that my nature should be what it is, and that I should have in myself the idea of a God, if God did not exist. God, whose idea is in me, possesses all those supreme perfections of which our mind may have some idea but without understanding them all; is liable to no errors or defects, and has none of those marks which denote imperfection. From this it is manifest that He cannot be a deceiver, since fraud and deception proceed from some defect.

Before I pass on to the consideration of other truths which may be derived from this one, it seems to me right to pause for a while to contemplate God Himself, to ponder at leisure His marvelous attributes, to consider and to admire and to adore the beauty of His light. Faith teaches us that supreme felicity of the life to come consists in this contemplation of the Divine Majesty. Even so we continue to learn by experience that a similar meditation, though less perfect, causes us to enjoy the greatest satisfaction of which we are capable in this life.

Disillusionment. Systematic doubt. Existence of self as a thinking thing. Existence of God, no longer the deceiving genius of the early part of the argument. There remains only the external world, revealed by the senses. Can this be reinstated? Can its existence be shown to be part of the network, inextricably bound up with his own and Deity's nature and existence?

And so I see that the certainty and truth of all knowledge depends alone upon the knowledge of the true God. Before I knew Him, I could not have a perfect knowledge of any other thing. Now that I know Him I have the means of acquiring a perfect knowledge of an infinitude of things.

Nothing further now remains but to inquire whether material things exist. And first of all I shall recall those matters which I hitherto held to be true, as having perceived them through the senses; in the next place I shall examine the reasons which have since obliged me to place them in doubt; and in the last place I shall consider which of them I must now believe.

First of all, I perceived that I had a head, hands, feet, and all other members of which this body is composed. Further, I was sensible that this body was placed amid many others. In them, in addition to extension, figure, and motion, I remarked hardness, heat, light, color, scents, sounds, and so forth.

Considering the ideas of all these qualities which presented themselves to my mind, it was not without reason that I believed myself to perceive objects quite different from my thought, to wit, bodies from which those ideas proceeded. For I found by experience that these ideas of all these qualities presented themselves to me without my consent being needed. Thus, I could not perceive any object unless it were present to the organs of sense; nor could I help but perceive it, when it was present.

Furthermore, because these ideas which I received through my senses were clearer, more lively, more distinct, than any ideas I could myself frame in meditation or find in memory, it appeared as though they could not have proceeded from my mind. So, therefore, I concluded that they must have been produced in me by some other things. And, since I had no knowledge of these objects except the knowledge which the ideas themselves gave me, nothing was more likely to occur to my mind than that the objects themselves were similar to the ideas which were caused.

But afterwards many experiences destroyed, little by little, all the faith which I had rested in my senses. For example, I observed that towers, which from afar appeared to me to be round, seemed square when more closely observed; that colossal statues seemed quite tiny when viewed from a distance; that persons whose legs or arms had been cut off seemed to feel pain in the part which had been amputated; that my dreams, which could not be caused by outside objects, closely resembled my waking moments; and so on.

Now, however, that I begin to know myself better ("I am a thing which thinks") and to discover more clearly the author of my being, I do not think I should rashly admit all the things which the senses seem to teach me, nor do I think that I should doubt them all universally.

This much is certain, i.e., clear and distinct: There is in me the capacity to receive and recognize the ideas of sensible things. The active cause of these ideas which I passively receive cannot be in me, since those ideas are often produced in me without my contributing in any way to the same, often even against my will. It follows that the power which produces these ideas resides in some substance different from me. This substance is either a material object or God or some other creature.

But, I have argued already, God is no deceiver. He has given me a very great inclination to believe that my ideas of sensible objects are sent or conveyed to me by external material objects. I do not see how He could be defended from the accusation of deceit if these ideas were produced in me by any cause other than material objects. Hence we must allow that material objects exist.

Descartes' meditations have brought him full circle. It is well to remember that he wrote in the seventeenth century, and to appreciate the gesture of impatience and sincerity with which he seeks to abandon old traditions and to start over again. The full weight of tradition was pressing upon him from the past. The new sciences and new world were beckoning toward the future. A clean break with the past seemed required. The *Meditations* were an attempt to see what ideas of the past must be allowed for by the future.

Note on Sources. The Descartes material in this section is quoted, abridged, or paraphrased from his *Discourse on Method* and his *Meditations*. The autobiographical account and the statement of the rules is from the *Discourse*, Parts I, II, III. The rest is from *Meditations* I, II, III, and VI.

Reading References. There is little point in trying to read an entire book on Descartes at this stage. Much of what he himself wrote is

dated; however, there are some valuable secondary items. Short of attempting a thorough study of Descartes and his influence on later
speculation, one does best to concentrate on the ideas presented in the
little books from which the citations in this chapter were taken, his
Meditations and his _Discourse on Method._ These are still readable and
valuable. An old volume by a German historian of philosophy, Kuno
Fischer, translated into English under the title _Descartes and His School,_
is lively and interesting. In T. H. Huxley's volume of essays, _Method and
Results,_ there is a good study of Descartes as a thinker.

The following are some books published since 1940:

Balz, A. G. A. _Cartesian Studies._
———. _Descartes and the Modern Mind._
Beck, L. J. _The Method of Descartes._
Joachim, H. H. _Descartes' Rules for the Direction of the Mind._
Keeling, S. V. _Descartes._
Koyré, A. _Descartes after 300 Years._
Maritain, J. _The Dream of Descartes._
Rosenfield, L. D. _From Beast-machine to Man-machine._
Scott, J. F. _Scientific Work of René Descartes._
Smith, N. K. _New Studies in the Philosophy of Descartes._
Vartanian, A. _Diderot and Descartes._
Versfeld, M. _An Essay on the Metaphysics of Descartes._

READING QUESTIONS

It cannot be repeated too often: Descartes repays study. Master him,
and you are in a fair way to proceed to other thinkers. Study his way of
thinking. It is typical of many others. Be sure that no turn in his total
argument goes unnoticed.

1. What realization on Descartes' part touched off the reflections which
led him to the _Cogito?_
2. In these reflections he "was not seeking to imitate the skeptics."
Wherein he differs from them.
3. To guide him in these reflections he laid down four rules. Namely.
Why the first rule is the most important.
4. Show that his first rule required him to track down an _indubitandum,_
something not doubtable.
5. Why, in this search for an _indubitandum,_ he did not examine each of
his particular beliefs separately.

6. His motive and his reason for deciding to doubt his senses.

7. Why he sets up his hypothesis of an evil genius who systematically deceives him.

8. How he arrives finally at the *Cogito* as an *indubitandum*.

9. Why the *indubitandum* has to be a *res cogitans* and not a *res extensa*.

10. Why, having arrived at the *Cogito*, he then tackles the question of God's existence. Argument by which he seeks to prove His existence.

11. Why at this point Descartes could not have made use of the design argument for the existence of God.

12. Having established his own existence and God's existence he turns to establish the existence of material things. His argument here.

13. Wherein you find Descartes (a) most (b) least convincing.

2. MATERIALISM AND ITS IMPLICATIONS —FROM THOMAS HOBBES   Monism

From Descartes to Hobbes. The problem we have been considering is stated in the question: What is the nature of ultimate reality? We have seen Descartes' answer. This, one suspects, is the metaphysics most congenial to the unsophisticated person. But not all men are unsophisticated in these things. There have therefore been several alternative metaphysical positions. One of the most familiar of these is a straight materialism: the belief, namely, that reality consists of particles of matter moving in space and time according to necessary laws. This metaphysical hypothesis is as old as the history of European philosophy. In modern times it came early to the fore, in the seventeenth century, and allowing for a certain quaintness of language, it has never received a more wholehearted exposition than is to be found in the pages of Thomas Hobbes, contemporary and friend and critic of Descartes.

Biographical Note. Thomas Hobbes was born in England in 1588 and died in 1679 at the age of ninety-one. During a long and busy life he was a close student of revolutionary politics and the new physical sciences. His life's work was a sustained attempt to formulate a philosophy which, he felt, would be more adequate to the new times than either the medieval traditions persisting from St. Thomas and others or the somewhat compromising position adopted by Descartes and his followers. The story of his own life is crowded with interest, but it is a reflected interest arising largely out of the stirring times through which he lived.

He was educated at Oxford. Thereafter he became tutor and secretary to the Earl of Devonshire. In this capacity he made the acquaintance of Francis Bacon, Ben Jonson, and other literary figures. He published a translation of Thucydides. When his patron died, Hobbes took over the education of his son with whom he took the Grand Tour, making the acquaintance of Galileo, Gassendi, and other scientific luminaries on the Continent. He returned to England to study politics. It was the time of England's civil war against Charles I. Hobbes was Royalist, siding against Cromwell. Circulation of his book, *The Body Politic*, obliged him to leave England and reside in Paris. This time he met Descartes and engaged him in metaphysical controversy. The exiled Prince of Wales, afterwards Charles II, was also in Paris. Hobbes became his tutor. He published again on the subject of politics, this time rousing the wrath of some of the Royalists. He returned to England and enjoyed such peace as obtained under Cromwell's regime, making friends with William Harvey, who discovered the circulation of the blood, with the poet Cowley, and others. Upon the restoration of Charles II to the English throne, Hobbes moved once more to a place in the sun and on the pension list. He was one of the most influential men of his day among persons who were open to ideas. There is not space to outline his position in seventeenth-century thought, but this much may be summarized: He believed that matter is the ultimate reality; that our sense organs are transformers, not revealers; that man does not have a free will; that all human action is motivated by complete selfishness; that an absolute sovereign is needed, whether in the form of a monarch or a parliament, to insure peace under law; and that religion is a "pill which it is better to swallow without chewing."

The Argument of the Citations. The following citations give a simple formulation of metaphysical materialism. From a statement of the essential point, that all is matter moving according to laws, the passages follow Hobbes through the principal turns of his belief. They present a development and, in some cases, a defense of the implications of the fundamental belief. It should be remembered that Hobbes is writing here as a philosopher, not as a scientist. In the strict sense of the word, he was not a scientist, either by temperament or training. He is, where it is relevant, restating or referring to the labors of Copernicus, Kepler, Galileo, Harvey, and the rest. But the point of his writings, in effect, is this: If what such men are finding out, is once accepted without reservation, then over all we are committed to these more comprehensive beliefs.

Think not, courteous reader, that the philosophy which I am going to set in order is that which makes philosophers' stones. It is the natural reason of man, busily flying up and down among the creatures, and bringing back a true report of their order, causes, and effects. Philosophy is therefore the child of the world and your own mind. Like the world, its father, as it was in the beginning, it is a thing confused. If you will be a philosopher in good earnest, let your reason move upon the deep of your own cogitations and experience; those things that lie in confusion must be set in order, distinguished, and stamped everyone with its own name.

Philosophy excludes theology, I mean the doctrine of God. It excludes the doctrine of angels and also such things as are neither bodies nor properties of bodies. It excludes history, natural as well as political, because such knowledge is but experience or authority and not reason. It excludes astrology and all such divinations. It excludes all such knowledge as is acquired by divine inspiration, or revelation, as not derived to us by reason but by some supernatural sense. Lastly it excludes the doctrine of God's worship as being not to be known by the light of natural reason but by the authority of the church.

I am not ignorant how hard a thing it is to weed out of men's minds inveterate opinions that have taken root there, and been confirmed by the authority of eloquent writers; especially since true philosophy rejects the paint and false colors, the ornaments and graces, of language. The first grounds of knowledge are not only not beautiful; they are poor and arid, and, in appearance, deformed. Nevertheless, there being some men who are delighted with truth and strength of reason, I thought I might do well to take these pains for the sake of even those few. I proceed therefore and take my beginning from the definition of philosophy.

With these preliminary observations, Hobbes closes in on his theme:

The subject of philosophy is every body [i.e., piece of matter] of which we can conceive any beginning, which we can compare with other bodies, or which is capable of composition and resolution; that is to say, every body of whose beginning or properties we can have any knowledge.

The definition of body may be this: a body is that which, having no dependence upon our thought, is coincident or coextended with some part of space.

The world—I mean the whole mass of things that are—is corporeal, that is to say, body; and that which is not body is no part of the universe. . . . The universe being the aggregate of all bodies, there is no real part thereof that is not also body.

The basic thesis once stated, Hobbes moves on to a series of implications, propositions which follow from the fundamental position.

(1) The first of these is that motion is the one thing that "really" takes place; all else is mere appearance, thrown off, so to speak, by matter in motion.

There can be no cause of motion except in a body contiguous and moved.

Mutation, that is, change, can be nothing but motion of the parts of that body which is changed. We say that that which appears to our senses is otherwise than it appeared formerly. Both appearances are effects produced in the sentient creature; and, if they be different, it is necessary that some part of the agent which was formerly at rest is now moved, and so the mutation consists in the motion; or some part which was formerly moved, is now otherwise moved, and so the mutation consists in this new motion; or which, being formerly moved, is now at rest, and so again mutation is motion.

(2) A second corollary is rigid determinism, that is, the belief that everything happens of necessity, or inevitably.

Whatever effect is produced at any time, the same is produced by a necessary cause. For whatsoever is produced had an entire cause, had all those things which, being supposed, it cannot be understood but that the effect follows; that is, it had a necessary cause. In the same manner, whatsoever effects are hereafter to be produced, shall have a necessary cause, so that all the effects that have been or shall be produced have their necessity in things antecedent.

From this determinism it would follow that, given enough knowledge of the past and present one could predict all future events in the greatest detail. Hobbes is aware of this claim. It has been made, off and on, ever since his time. Better than a century later the French astronomer, LaPlace, wrote:

We ought to regard the present state of the universe as the effect of its antecedent state and as the cause of the state that is to follow. An intelligence, who for a given instant should be acquainted with all the forces by which nature is animated, and with the several positions of the beings composing it, if his intellect were vast enough to submit these data to analysis, would include in one and the same formula the movement of the largest bodies in the universe and those of the lightest atom. Nothing would be uncertain for him, the future as well as the past would be present to his eyes.

Before resuming the elaboration of his views, Hobbes pays his lip service to natural theology:

He that from any effect he seeth come to pass, should reason to the next and immediate cause thereof, and from thence to the cause of that cause, and plunge himself profoundly into the pursuit of causes, shall come at last to this, that there must be, as even the heathen philosophers confessed, one first mover, one first cause of things which is that which men mean by the name of God.

3) Having disposed of that, Hobbes turns to noting further implications of his materialism. All living organisms, it would follow, are just so many complicated machines:

Seeing that life is but a motion of limbs and organs, why may we not say that all automata (engines that move themselves by springs and wheels as doth a watch) have an artificial life? For what is the heart but a spring, and the nerves but so many strings, and the joints but so many wheels, giving motion to the whole body?

(4) Materialism in metaphysics, he urges, implies sensationism in epistemology; implies, that is, that all knowledge originates in sensations.

The original of men's thoughts is sense, for there is no conception in a man's mind which hath not, totally or by parts, been begotten upon the organs of sense. The rest are derived from that original.

As I said before, whatsoever we conceive, hath been perceived first by sense, either all at once or by parts. A man can have no thought representing anything, not subject to sense.

Imagination is nothing but decaying sense. From whence it followeth that the longer the time is after the sense, the weaker is the imagination.

Imagination being only of those things which have been formerly perceived by sense, it followeth that imagination and memory are but one thing which for divers considerations hath diverse names.

Materialism. Determinism. Mechanism. Sensationism. And now the doctrine of representative perception, that is, the belief that sensations represent but do not reveal the real nature of the external world. Hobbes labors this point at great length.

The cause of sense is the external object which presseth the organ proper to each sense either immediately or mediately. This pressure, by the mediation of the nerves and other strings and membranes, continueth inward and causeth there a reaction or counter-pressure; which endeavor because outward, seemeth to be some matter without. This seeming is that which men call sense; and consisteth, as to the eye, in a light or colored figure; to the ear, in a sound; and so on. All which qualities, called sensible qualities, are, in the object that causeth them only so many several motions of the matter by which it presseth our organs diversely. Neither in us that are pressed, are they anything else but divers motions; for motion produceth nothing but motion. For if these sensible qualities (colors, sounds) were in the object which causeth them, they could not be severed from them as by mirrors and echoes they are.

The cause of perception consisteth in this: When the uttermost part of the organ is pressed, it no sooner yields but the next part within it is pressed also. In this manner the pressure or motion is propagated through all the parts of the organ to the innermost. Also, the pressure of the uttermost part proceedeth from the pressure of some more remote body, and so continually till we come to the object. Sense therefore is some internal motion in the sentient organism, generated by some internal motion of the parts of the object, and propagated through all the media to the innermost part of the organ.

I shall endeavor to make plain these points: that the object wherein color is inherent is not the object seen; that there is nothing without us, really, which we call image or color; that color is but the apparition unto us of the motion, agitation, or change which the object worketh in the brain or some internal substance of the head; that as in vision, so also in the other senses, the subject of their inherence is not the object but the sentient creature.

As a color is not inherent in the object, but an effect thereof upon us, caused by motion in the object, so neither is sound in the thing we hear, but in ourselves. The clapper hath no sound in it, but action, and maketh motion in the internal parts of the bell; so the bell hath motion, and not sound, that imparteth motion to the air; and the air hath motion, but no sound, which it imparteth by the ear and nerve unto the brain; and the brain hath motion, but not sound.

From hence it followeth that whatsoever qualities our senses make us think there be in the world, they be not there, but are seeming and apparitions only; the things that really are in the world without us are those motions by which these seemings are caused. And this is the great deception of sense.

Hobbes is stopped by a problem. If the sensation, say the red color of a cherry, is really so much motion of particles in the observer's head, how can we explain the fact that it appears out there in space, located where the cherry is? As Hobbes asks, "Why doth the sensation appear as something situated without the organ?" His answer is:

Why doth the sensation appear as something situated without the organ? It is thus: There is in the whole organ, by reason of its own internal natural action some reaction against the motion which is propagated from the object to the innermost part of the organ. In the organ there is an endeavor opposite to the endeavor which proceedeth from the object. That endeavor inwards is the last action in the act of sense. Then from the reaction, an idea hath its being, which by reason that the endeavor is now outward, doth always appear as something situated without the organ.

But though all sense be made by reaction, as I have said, it is not necessary that everything that reacteth should have sense. I know there have been philosophers, and those learned men, who have maintained that all bodies are endued with sense. Nor do I see how they can be refuted if the nature of sense be placed in reaction only.

The argument turns from the subjectivity of sensations to the question of desires. These too must be admitted to be merely so much matter in motion.

As that which is really within us, in sensation, is only motion caused by the action of external objects, so that which is really within us in appetite or desire is nothing but motion. But the appearance of that motion we call either pleasure or pain.

When appetites and aversions arise alternately concerning the same thing, so that sometimes we have an appetite to it and sometimes an aversion from it, then the whole sum of desires and aversions is what we call *deliberation.*

In deliberation, the last appetite or aversion, immediately adhering to the act or the omission thereof, is what we call *will.*

If this be the whole story of man's preferences and desires, Hobbes is in a position to make short shrift of any lofty moral idealism. This he proceeds to do:

Moral philosophy is nothing else but the science of what is good and evil in the conversation and society of mankind. Good and evil are names that signify our appetites and aversions; which in different tempers, customs, and doctrines of men, are different, and divers men differ not only in their judgment, on the sense of what is pleasant and unpleasant to the taste, smell, hearing, touch, and sight, but also what is conformable or disagreeable to reason in the actions of common life. Nay the same man, in divers times differeth from himself and at one time praiseth, that is, calleth good what at another time he dispraiseth, that is, calleth evil.

Every man calleth that which pleaseth him, *good;* and that which displeaseth him, *evil.* Since every man differeth from another in constitution, they differ also from one another concerning the common distinction of good and evil. Nor is there any such thing as absolute goodness considered without relation.

Whatsoever is the object of any man's appetite or desire, that it is which he for his part calleth good; and the object of his hate and aversion, evil. For these words *good* and *evil* are ever used with relation to the person that useth them, there being nothing simply and absolutely so, nor any rule of good and evil to be taken from the nature of objects themselves; but from the man, where there is no commonwealth.

To the commitments adduced thus far, Hobbes adds one more: a categorical denial of man's free will:

I conceive that nothing taketh beginning from itself, but from the action of some other immediate agent without itself. Therefore, when a man hath an appetite or will to something, to which before he had no appetite or will, the cause of his will is not the will itself but something else not in his own disposing.

Neither is the freedom of willing or not willing greater in man than in other living creatures. For where there is appetite, the entire cause thereof hath preceded, and, consequently, the appetite could not choose but follow; that is, hath of necessity followed. Therefore such a liberty as is free from necessity is not to be found in the will.

If by *freedom* we understand the power, not of willing but of doing what we will, then certainly that freedom is to be allowed to both men and animals.

The ordinary definition of a *free agent* is that he is one that when all things are present which are needful to produce an effect, can nevertheless not produce it. This implies a contradiction that is nonsense, being as much as to say the cause of anything may be sufficient and yet the effect shall not follow. There is no such thing as an "agent," which when all things requisite to action are present, can nevertheless forbear to produce it. Or, which is all one, there is no such thing as freedom from necessity.

The essentials of Hobbes's materialism are now before us. The position bristles with difficulties. With unerring instinct Hobbes places his finger upon the one point which, more than any other perhaps, will be disputed. I mean the denial of man's free will. The following citations show Hobbes attempting to defend his determinism against anticipated objections:

To deny necessity is to destroy the power and foreknowledge of God Almighty. For whatsoever God hath purposed to bring to pass by man, or foreseeth shall come to pass, a man might frustrate and make not come to pass if he have freedom from necessity. Then would God foreknow such things as never shall be, and decree such things as shall never come to pass.

Liberty and necessity are consistent: as in the water, that hath not only liberty but a necessity to descend by the channel. So likewise in the actions men voluntarily do; which because they proceed from their will are termed *voluntary*. And yet, because every act of man's will and every desire and inclination proceedeth from some cause, and that from some other cause, in a continual chain, it proceedeth from necessity. To him that could see the connection of those causes, the necessity of all men's voluntary actions would appear manifest.

The necessity of an action doth not make the laws that prohibit it unjust. Whatsoever necessary cause precede an action, yet if the action be forbidden, he that doth it willingly may justly be punished. For instance, suppose the law on pain of death prohibit stealing. Suppose there be a man who by the strength of temptation is necessitated to steal, and is thereupon put to death. Doth not this punishment deter others from theft? Is it not a cause that others steal not? Doth it not frame and make their wills to justice? To make the law is therefore to make a cause of justice, and so to necessitate justice. The intention of the law is not to grieve the delinquent for that which is past and not to be undone; but to make him and others just who might otherwise not be so. It respecteth not the evil act past, but the good to come. But you will say, how is it just to kill one man to amend another, if what were done were necessary? To this I answer: men are justly killed, not because their actions are not necessitated, but because their actions are noxious. We destroy, without being unjust, all that is noxious, both beasts and men.

Repentance is nothing but a glad returning into the right way, after the grief of being out of the way. Even though the cause that made a man go astray were necessary, there is no reason why he should not grieve. So likewise, even though the cause that made a man return into the right way were necessary, there remaineth still the cause of joy. So that I say the necessity of actions taketh away neither of those parts of repentance, neither grief for the error nor joy for the returning.

As for praise and dispraise, they depend not at all on the necessity of the action praised or dispraised. For what is it to praise, but to say a thing is good? Good for me, good for someone else, or good for the commonwealth. What is it to say an act is good, but to say it is as I wish it, or as another wish it, or according to the law of the commonwealth? Can no action please me, or another, or the commonwealth, that should happen of necessity? Doth not praise and dispraise, reward and punishment, make and conform the will to good and evil by example?

Materialism is always with us. It is as old as the records of Western philosophy, having received an elaborate presentation in the fifth century

B.C. among the Greeks. Our task is to grasp the meaning of materialism and its implications. To recapitulate: It is the belief that reality is moving particles of matter. Its adherents have usually felt committed to certain further claims, as, for example, all events are rigidly predictable; all organisms are only mechanisms; all knowledge, originating in sensations, is knowledge of appearances only, since sensations are entirely subjective; human conduct is strictly determined by antecedent and concomitant events; human motives are essentially egocentric; and the achievement of happiness, in the sense of the satisfaction of desire, is the only finally good thing. These assorted doctrines are not, of course, as logically interdependent as the materialist would have us believe. But they are temperamentally interdependent. They give expression to a mood or a temperament or a frame of mind which is sufficiently widespread to demand a courteous hearing.

Hobbes wrote in the seventeenth century. Materialism had its defenders in the eighteenth century, the nineteenth century, and the twentieth century. Hugh Elliott's *Modern Science and Materialism* (1919) is a vigorous restatement of this perennial metaphysical position. The following, quoted from Chapter 5, pp. 137–46, of his book provides assurance that the spirit of Hobbes' materialism is still with us. Says Mr. Elliott:

The main purpose of the present work is to defend the doctrine of materialism. . . . The outlines of this system are not new; the main features of it, indeed, have been admittedly associated with scientific progress for centuries past. An age of science is necessarily an age of materialism; ours is a scientific age, and it may be said with truth that we are all materialists now. The main principles which I shall endeavour to emphasize are three.

1. The uniformity of law. In early times events appeared to be entirely hazardous and unaccountable, and they still seem so, if we confine atttention purely to the passing moment. But as science advances, there is disclosed a uniformity in the procedure of Nature. When the conditions at any one moment are precisely identical with those which prevailed at some previous moment, the results flowing from them will also be identical. It is found, for instance, that a body of given mass attracts some other body of given mass at a given distance with a force of a certain strength. It is found that when the masses, distances, and other conditions are precisely repeated, the attraction between the bodies is always exactly the same. It is found, further, that when the distance between the bodies is increased the force of their attraction is diminishd in a fixed proportion, and this again is found to hold true at all distances at which they may be placed. The force of their attraction again

varies in a different but still constant proportion to their masses. And hence results the law of gravitation, by which the force of attraction can be precisely estimated from a knowledge of the masses and distances between any two bodies whatever. A uniformity is established which remains absolute within the experience of Man, and to an equivalent extent the haphazard appearance of events is found to be only an appearance. Innumerable other laws of a similar character are gradually discovered, establishing a sort of nexus between every kind of event. If oxygen and hydrogen in the proportion by weight of eight to one are mixed together, and an electric spark is passed through them, water is formed; and on every occasion where precisely the same conditions are realized precisely the same result ensues. This truth is the basis of the experimental method. If from similar conditions it were possible that dissimilar results should follow on various occasions, then experiments would be useless for advancing knowledge.

This uniformity of sequence confers the power of prophesy; and the more we learn about the nexus of natural phenomena, the greater becomes our power of prophesying future events. Such prophesies are made and fulfilled at the present day in all departments of knowledge where the data or conditions are sufficiently few and simple to be dealt with by calculation, as, for instance, in many astronomical problems. They are made even when the data are numerous and complicated, though with much less accuracy. We can foretell at what minute on what day an eclipse of the Sun will begin to take place. We can equally foretell that a rise in the bank rate will, under normal conditions, cause an influx of gold; but precisely how much gold we cannot tell. With a larger knowledge of the conditions, we could arrive at a closer approximation to the amount of the influx. With an absolute knowledge of all the conditions at work, we could prophesy the exact number of ounces of gold that any specified rise of bank rate would divert into this country. Such a knowledge, of course, is for ever impossible, since the factors concerned are innumerable and severally minute; to apply mathematical analysis to them, even if they could all be collected, would infinitely transcend our powers. Nevertheless, we shall be led to adopt the proposition of Laplace, to the effect that if we knew the precise disposition at any moment of all the matter and energy existing in the Universe, and the direction of motion of every moving particle, and if we were armed with a mathematics of infinite power, we should be able to prophesy the exact disposition of all the matter and energy in the Universe at any future time. Any being who possessed such powers, and who, a myriad ages ago, had acquired absolute knowledge at some moment of the nebula from which the solar system arose, would have been able to prophesy that at this present moment there would exist a being identical with myself who would be writing the words that are now flowing from my pen; he would have been able to prophesy that a little later other beings, identical with my readers, would be perusing those words, and he would be aware of what emotions would be excited within them by the perusal. In other words, the uniformity of Nature and the paramountcy of law are universal and without exception.

2. The denial of teleology. Scientific materialism warmly denies that there exists any such thing as purpose in the Universe, or that events have any ulterior motive or goal to which they are striving. It asserts that all events are due to the interaction of matter and motion acting by blind necessity in accordance with those invariable sequences to which we have given the name of laws. This is an important bond of connection between the materialism of the ancient Greeks and that of modern science. Among all peoples not highly cultivated there reigns a passionate conviction, not only that the Universe as a whole is working out some pre-determined purpose, but that every individual part of it subserves some special need in the fulfilment of this purpose. Needless to say, the purpose has always been regarded as associated with human welfare. The Universe, down to its smallest parts, is regarded by primitive superstition as existing for the special benefit of man. To such extreme lengths has this view been carried that even Bernardin de Saint-Pierre, who only died last century, argued that the reason why melons are ribbed is that they may be eaten more easily by families.

The reason for this early teleology is obvious. We all of us survey the Universe from the standpoint of our own centrality. Subjectively we all do stand actually at the centre of the Universe. Our entire experience of the Universe is an experience of it as it affects ourselves; for if it does not affect ourselves, we know of it only indirectly, and in primitive stages we do not know of it at all. As our education endows us with a wider outlook and a wider knowledge, we come to see that the objective Universe is very different from our own private subjective Universe. At first we discover that we as individuals are not the centre of the Universe, as appears to uncorrected experience, but that we are merely one individual among many others of equal status constituting a nation or society. We then perhaps regard our own society as the centre of the Universe, as many primitive peoples do, such, for instance, as the ancient Romans and the modern Chinese. Or we may regard our own sex as the purposed product of the Universe, as in many Mohammedan peoples, who hold that women have not souls like men, and that they exist purely for the benefit or use of men, in the same way that cattle exist in order to be eaten, or that melons are ribbed to indicate the proper amount of one portion.

With still further cultivation, the entire human species becomes regarded as the centre and object of all events in the Universe. This is the stage now reached by the masses in modern civilizations. Just as the existence of one particular individual has not the world-wide or cosmic importance that that individual is apt to suppose; just as the existence of a particular tribe or society is not of the profound historic import that that tribe or society very commonly imagines; so too the human species as a whole is far from being, as it too often believes, the sole object for which the Universe was created, with all things in it, great and small. The human species is, indeed, a mere incident in the universal redistribution of matter and motion; its existence has not the smallest cosmic significance. Our species is biologically very modern. Neither in numbers nor in antiquity can it compare with infinitely numerous species of other animals inhabiting the Earth. The Earth itself is one of the smaller planets, revolving round a minor star. The entire solar system, of which the Earth is so insignificant a portion, is itself a system of contemptible minuteness, set among other luminaries and other systems which surpass it many times in magnitude, in brightness and in every other ascertainable quality that we are accustomed to admire. . . . Most men have as yet not shaken off the habit, which all men necessarily start from, that they themselves, or their family, nation or kind, are in fact, as in appearance, the very centre of the cosmos.

3. The denial of any form of existence other than those envisaged by physics and chemistry, that is to say, other than existences that have some kind of palpable material characteristics and quality. It is here that modern materialism begins to part company with ancient materialism, and it is here that I expect the main criticisms of opponents to be directed. The modern doctrine stands in direct opposition to a belief in any of those existences that are vaguely classed as "spiritual." To this category belong not only ghosts, gods, souls, *et hoc genus omne* [and everything of the kind], for these have long been rejected from the beliefs of most advanced thinkers. The time has now come to include also in the condemned list that further imaginary entity which we call "mind," "consciousness," etc., together with its various sub-species of intellect, will, feeling, etc., in so far as they are supposed to be independent or different from material existences or processes. . . .

The proposition which I here desire to advance is that every event occurring in the Universe, including those events known as mental processes, and all kinds of human action or conduct, are expressible purely in terms of matter and motion. If we assume in the primeval nebula of the solar system no other elementary factors beyond those of matter and energy or motion, we can theoretically, as above remarked, deduce the existing Universe, including mind, consciousness, etc., without the introduction of any new factor whatsoever. The existing Universe and all other things and events therein may be theoretically expressed in terms of matter and energy, undergoing continuous redistribution in accordance with the ordinary laws of physics and chemistry. If all manifestations within our experience can be thus expressed, as has for long been believed by men of science, what need is there for the introduction of any new entity of spiritual character, called mind? It has no part to play; it is impotent in causation. According to Huxley's theory it accompanies certain physical processes as a shadow, without any power, or any reason, or any use. The world, as Huxley and the great major-ity of physiologists affirm, would be just the same without it. Now there is an ancient logical precept which retains a large validity: *entia non sunt multi-plicanda praeter necessitatem* [no more entities should be posited than are necessary]. It is sometimes referred to as William of Occam's razor, which cuts off and rejects from our theories all factors or entities which are super-fluous in guiding us to an explanation. "Mind" as a separate entity is just such a superfluity. I will not deny—indeed I cordially affirm—that it is a direct datum of experience; but there is no direct datum of experience to the effect that it is anything different from certain cerebral processes. . . . The ancient materialists believed to a certain extent in an unseen world; they believed even in the existence of souls. They asserted their materialism only by the theory that these entities were material in character. Democritus con-ceived the soul as consisting of smooth, round, material particles. The scientific materialist of today does not believe in any separate existence of this kind whatever. He regards what is called soul or mind as *identical* with certain physical processes passing in a material brain, processes of which the ancient Greeks knew nothing, and, indeed, which are still entirely unknown to all who have not acquired some smattering of physiology. . . .

The materialism which I shall advocate, therefore, is centred round three salient points: the uniformity of law, the exclusion of purpose, and the assertion of monism; that is to say, that there exists no kind of spiritual substance or entity of a different nature from that of which matter is com-posed.

Note on Sources. The Hobbes material in this section is quoted, abridged, or paraphrased from the relevant chapters in his *The Elements of Philosophy*, his *Human Nature*, his *Of Liberty and Necessity*, and his *Leviathan*. The Molesworth Edition of Hobbes' English Works was used for these texts.

Reading References. A good small book on Hobbes is by Sir Leslie Stephen. It is in the series, *English Men of Letters*. The literature on materialism itself is very large. One can only suggest a few things. A good beginning may be made in T. H. Huxley's volume mentioned already under Descartes, *Method and Results*. The third and fifth essays deal with phases of materialism. Hugh Elliott's *Modern Science and Materialism* is a competent and aggressive presentation of the case. Elliott has the virtue of *caring* whether his reader believes in materialism or does not. Santayana has remarked of himself that he is today perhaps the sole surviving materialist. The volume, *Reason in Science*, in his five-volume treatise, *The Life of Reason*, provides a statement of his materialism. It is also to be found in his later book, *The Realm of Matter*.

The following are some books published since 1940:

Bowle, J. *Hobbes and His Critics: A Study of Seventeenth Century Constitutionalism.*
Childs, A. H. *Making and Knowing in Hobbes, Vico and Dewey.*
Gooch, Sir G. P. *Hobbes.*
James, D. G. *The Life of Reason: Hobbes, Locke, Bolingbroke.*
McDonald, H. and Hargreaves, M. *Thomas Hobbes: A Bibliography.*
Peters, R. *Hobbes.*
Thorpe, C. A. *The Aesthetic Theory of Thomas Hobbes.*
Warrendon, H. *Political Philosophy of Hobbes.*

READING QUESTIONS

1. He begins by excluding from philosophy (a) theology, (b) angelology, (c) history, (d) astrology, (e) things known by inspiration or revelation, (f) doctrines of worship. On what principle? *[Based on exp, or authority Not Reason]*
2. Philosophy, then, appeals only to what and talks only about what?
3. He proposes a reductive analysis—"A is nothing but B"—of many things. Change is nothing but what? Organisms are nothing but what? Knowledge is nothing but what? Imagination is nothing but what? Sensation is nothing but what? Will is nothing but what? Good and evil are nothing but what?
4. Why he is led to propose these and similar reductions.
5. Why determinism is a corollary of materialism.
6. "And this is the great deception of sense." What is? What theory leads Hobbes to the conclusion that sense perception is sense deception?
7. Are sense-organs best thought of as transformers or revealers?
8. How Hobbes would correlate the distinction between primary and secondary qualities with the distinction between objective and subjective.
9. If you say that sense qualities are secondary and subjective, and that knowledge originates in sense experience, what problem have you set yourself in regard to "matter"?
10. He asks why a sensation—say, color or sound—appears as something situated outside the sense-organ. (a) Why this is a problem for him. (b) His explanation.
11. Hobbes' reasons for denying man's free will.
12. How he seeks to get theology on his side in this denial of man's free will.
13. The definition of "liberty" which enables him to say "liberty and

necessity are consistent"; and to use the analogy of water in the
channel.

14. Why, in connection with his denial of man's free will, Hobbes deals
with (a) punishment, (b) repentance, (c) praise and dispraise. How
he handles each of these points.

15. If you punish a person for wrong-doing, do you, according to
Hobbes, presuppose that the person could have done otherwise?

16. Wherein you find Hobbes (a) most (b) least convincing.

17. How you would account for the persistence and popularity of materialism?

3. IDEALISM AND ITS IMPLICATIONS
—FROM GEORGE BERKELEY

From Hobbes to Berkeley. It was inevitable that Hobbes's tough-
minded materialism should provoke protest and criticism. Throughout
the seventeenth and eighteenth centuries, it is not too much to say,
materialism was the "specter" which haunted Western metaphysics.
Some resorted to the simple expedient of ignoring such views. Some
reviled the personal characters of those who held them. Some attacked
the premises and disputed the validity of the conclusions which com-
prised the materialist's position. Among these, in the eighteenth century,
was George Berkeley, the founder of modern idealism, and one of the
shrewdest metaphysicians of modern times.

Biographical Note. George Berkeley was born in Ireland in 1685,
and died in 1753 at the age of sixty-eight. He was educated at the Trinity
College, Dublin, where while yet an undergraduate, he conceived the
necessity of "refuting atheists and materialists." At the age of twenty-five
he published *A Treatise Concerning the Principles of Human Knowledge*,
and three years later his *Three Dialogues Between Hylas and Philonous*.
These two small volumes, by the youngest and brightest philosophical
mind of his generation, contain the statement and defense of his case
against materialism and his case for idealism. For a while he was laughed
at, as readers of Boswell's *Johnson* will remember. But the scattered ranks
of those who had been troubled by the fashionable materialism launched
by Hobbes and others in the preceding century soon closed to his support.
Shortly after publication, Berkeley visited England and was received
into the circle of Addison, Pope, and Steele. He traveled on the continent
in various capacities, and on his return was appointed lecturer in divinity
and Greek in Trinity College, Dublin. He received a D.D. He was made

an ecclesiastical dean. He was promised aid to found a college in Bermuda
for training clergymen for the colonies and missionaries for the Indians.
He was made, finally, Bishop of Cloyne. He died at Oxford, beloved and
respected, if not clearly understood, by all who knew him.

The Argument of the Citations. Berkeley desires to establish the
proposition that reality is spiritual, that a man's mind provides him with
a better example of the constituent "stuff" of things than is provided by
a lump of matter. This is his idealism. The first step, is a critique of
materialism. This Berkeley proceeds to construct. He starts from premises
which the materialists themselves admit (any others would be irrelevant)
and seeks to show that their conclusions (1) are either incompatible with
these premises, or (2) do not follow from these premises. He then approaches materialism from another angle, seeking, this time to explain
how materialists have come to hold their "misguided" conclusions.
Methodologically this procedure is usable. A communist might apply it
to capitalism as the first step in a general statement of the case for communism. A free trader might apply it to protectionism as the first step
in a general statement of the case for free trade. A liberal might apply
it to conservatism as the first step in a general statement of the case for
liberalism. The same remarks are applicable to capitalists, protectionists,
and conservatives.

The case against materialism stated, Berkeley's argument moves on
to the case for idealism. He formulates a few premises which anyone,
he thinks, will admit. From these he seeks to deduce his idealism. He
turns then to consider possible objections which might be urged against
it before they are made.

The case against materialism stated, the case for idealism stated,
the possible objections anticipated, he closes in on what, after all, he
considers to be the most important part of the whole business, namely,
an elucidation of the implications of his metaphysical idealism, an enumeration of the propositions which are also true if his idealism is true.

The total argument begins as follows:

It is plain that the notion of what is called *matter* or *corporeal substance*
involves a contradiction,[1] so much so that I should not think it necessary to
spend time exposing its absurdity. But belief in the existence of matter seems
to have taken so deep a root in the minds of philosophers, and draws after

---

[1] The "contradiction" would seem to be in saying that all knowledge is from sense-
data, and at the same time admitting that matter is not a sense-datum. How then do
we know of it?

it so many ill consequences, that I choose rather to be thought prolix and tedious than to omit anything that might conduce to the discovery and extirpation of that prejudice.

The following distinction between primary and secondary qualities and the claim that primary qualities are alone real, whereas secondary qualities are merely subjective, were familiar notions in Berkeley's day.

Some there are who make a distinction between primary and secondary qualities. By *primary qualities* they mean extension, figure, motion, rest, solidity, and number. By *secondary qualities* they mean sensible qualities, as colors, sounds, tastes, and so forth.

Our ideas of secondary qualities they acknowledge not to be the resemblances of anything existing without the mind or unperceived. But they will have our ideas of the primary qualities to be patterns or images of things which exist without the mind in an unthinking substance which they call *matter*. By *matter*, therefore, we are to understand an inert, senseless substance in which extension, figure, and motion do actually exist.

Colors, sounds, heat, cold, and such like secondary qualities, they tell us, are sensations existing in the mind alone, depending on and occasioned by the different size, texture and motion of the minute particles of matter. This they take for an undoubted truth, which they can demonstrate beyond all exception.

By *materialism*, then, Berkeley proposes to mean the belief in an inert, senseless substance possessing primary qualities in its own right but not possessing secondary qualities in the same intimate fashion. His first criticism of this belief is as follows:

But can anyone conceive the extension and motion of a body without any of its secondary qualities? It is not in my power to frame an idea of a body extended and moving but I must withal give it some color or other secondary quality which is acknowledged to exist only in the mind. In short, primary qualities abstracted from secondary qualities are inconceivable. Where therefore the secondary qualities are, to wit, in the mind and nowhere else, there must the primary qualities be also.

His second criticism is this:

Great and small, swift and slow, degrees of extension and motion, are allowed to exist only in the mind, being entirely relative, and changing as the frame or position of the sense organs varies. The extension therefore which exists independently of the mind is neither great nor small; the action, neither swift nor slow. That is, they are nothing at all.

His third criticism is this:

Number is entirely a creature of the mind. Even though the other primary qualities be allowed to exist without, it will be evident that the same thing bears a different denomination of number as the mind views it with different respects. Thus the same extension is one, or three, or thirty-six, according as the mind considers it with reference to a yard, a foot, or an inch. Number is so visibly relative and dependent on men's understanding that it is strange anyone should give it an absolute existence without the mind.

His fourth criticism is this:

One argument whereby modern philosophers would prove that secondary qualities do not exist in matter but in our minds may be turned likewise against primary qualities. Thus, it is said that heat and cold are affections only of the mind and not at all qualities of real things; for the same body which appears cold to one hand seems warm to another. Thus, too, it is proved that sweetness is not really in the sapid thing; because, the thing remaining unaltered, the sweetness is changed to bitterness, as in the case of a fever or otherwise vitiated palate.

Now, why may we not as well argue that figure and extension are not real qualities existing in matter? To the same eye at different stations, or to eyes of a different texture at the same station, they appear various. By parity of reasoning, therefore, they cannot be ideas of anything settled and determinate without the mind.

In short, those arguments which are thought to prove that secondary qualities (colors, tastes, etc.) exist only in the mind, may with equal force be brought to prove the same thing of primary qualities (extension, figure, motion, etc.).

His fifth criticism is this:

Suppose it were possible that material substances possessing only primary qualities do exist independent of the mind. Yet how is it possible for us to know this? Either we know it by our senses or by our reason. As for our senses, by them we have knowledge only of our sensations: but they do not inform us that things exist independent of the mind, or unperceived by the mind, like to those which are perceived. This the materialists themselves acknowledge; nay, insist.

It remains, therefore, that, if we have any knowledge at all of material substances, it must be by our reason inferring their existence from what is immediately perceived by sense. But I do not see what reason can induce us to believe in the existence of bodies independent of the mind, from what we perceive, since the very patrons of matter themselves do not pretend there is any necessary connection betwixt them and our ideas.

His sixth criticism is this:

It may be thought easier to explain the production of our sensations by supposing external bodies, rather than otherwise; and so it might be at least probable that there are such things as bodies that excite ideas in our minds. But neither can this be said. For, though we give the materialists their "external bodies," they by their own confession are no nearer knowing how our ideas are produced, since they own themselves unable to comprehend in what manner body can act upon spirit (or mind) or how it could imprint any idea in the mind.

Hence it is evident that the production of ideas or sensations in our minds can be no reason why we should suppose matter or corporeal substances; since their production is acknowledged to remain equally inexplicable with or without this particular supposition. If therefore it were possible for bodies to exist without the mind, yet to hold that they do so must needs be a very precarious opinion. In short, if there were external bodies, it is impossible we should come to know it; and if there were not, we might have the very same reasons to think there were that we have now. Which consideration were enough to make any reasonable person suspect the strength of whatever arguments he may think himself to have, for the existence of external bodies independent of the mind.

His conclusion is this:

It is on this, therefore, that I insist, to wit, that the absolute existence of unthinking things are words without a meaning, or which include a contradiction. This is what I repeat and inculcate, and earnestly recommend to the attentive thoughts of the reader.

He turns now to an exploration of the probable reasons which led men "to suppose the existence of material substance":

It is worth while to reflect on the motives which induced men to suppose the existence of material substance; so that having observed the gradual ceasing and expiration of those motives, we may withdraw the assent that was grounded on them.

First, it was thought that the sensible qualities did really exist without the mind. And for this reason it seemed needful to suppose that some unthinking substratum or substance wherein they did exist, since they could not be conceived to exist by themselves.

Then, in process of time, men being convinced that secondary qualities had no existence without the mind, they stripped this substratum or material substance of those qualities, leaving only the primary ones, which they still conceive to exist without the mind and consequently to stand in need of a material support.

But now, it having been shown that none even of these can possibly exist otherwise than in a spirit or mind which perceives them, it follows that we have no longer any reason to suppose the being of "matter," nay, that it is utterly impossible that there should be any such thing so long as that word is taken to mean an unthinking substratum or substance for qualities wherein they exist without mind. It is an extraordinary instance of the force of prejudice that the mind of man retains so great a fondness, against all the evidence of reason, for a stupid, thoughtless Somewhat as a support of the qualities we perceive.

Thus Berkeley on materialism. One is moved to ponder its effect upon Thomas Hobbes. A smile perhaps, a sharpening of his controversial quill as he prepared to do battle with this newcomer. For Berkeley, having "dethroned" matter, sets about to "enthrone" spirit. His first step is to secure one or two propositions which "any rational man" would admit.

It is evident to anyone who takes a survey of the objects of human knowledge, that they are either ideas imprinted on the senses; or such as are perceived by attending to the passions and operations of the mind; or lastly, ideas formed by help of memory and imagination—compounding, dividing, or merely representing those originally perceived in the aforesaid ways.

As several such ideas are observed to accompany each other, they come to be marked by one name, and so reputed as one thing. Thus a certain color, taste, smell, figure, and consistence having been observed to go together, are accounted one distinct thing, signified by the name *apple*. Other collections of ideas constitute a stone, a tree, a book, and the like.

Besides the ideas or objects of knowledge, there is something which knows or perceives them, and exercises divers operations as willing, imagining, remembering, about them. This perceiving active being I call *mind, spirit, soul*, or *myself*.

The existence of an idea consists in its being perceived. Its *esse* is *percipi*. The table I write on I say "exists"; that is, I see and feel it; and if I were out of my study, I should say it "existed"; meaning that if I was in my study,

"To be is to be perceived"

I might perceive it, or that some other spirit actually does perceive it. There was an odor, that is, it was smelt; there was a sound, that is, it was heard; there was a color or figure, that is, it was perceived by sight or touch. That is all I can understand by these and like expressions. Their *esse* is *percipi*. Nor is it possible they should have any existence out of the minds which perceive them.

All our ideas and sensations are visibly inactive. There is nothing of power or agency included in them. One idea or sensation cannot produce or alter another. The very being of an idea implies passiveness and inertness in it; insomuch that it is impossible for an idea to do anything, or be the cause of anything.

We perceive a continual succession of ideas. Some are excited anew, others are changed or totally disappear. There is therefore some cause of these ideas, whereon they depend, and which produces and changes them.

Having premised the above facts, Berkeley proceeds to argue from them:

It is clear, from what hath been said, that this cause cannot itself be any idea or sensation since all such are passive and inert. It must therefore be a substance. But it has been shown that there is no corporeal or material substance. It remains therefore that the cause of our ideas and sensations is an incorporeal active substance, or spirit.

I find I can excite some of my ideas in my mind at pleasure, and vary and shift the scene as oft as I think fit. This making and unmaking of ideas doth very properly denominate the mind active. Thus much is certain and grounded on experience. But when we talk, as do materialists, of unthinking substances producing ideas, we only amuse ourselves with words.

But whatever power I have over some of my ideas, I find that others have not a like dependence on my will. When, for example, I open my eyes in broad daylight, it is not in my power to choose whether I shall see or no, nor to determine what I shall see. It is likewise as to hearing and the other senses. The ideas imprinted on them are not creatures of my will. There is, therefore, some other will or mind or spirit that produces them.

These ideas which I cannot control, these ideas of sense, are more strong, more lively, more distinct than those which I can control. They have, likewise, a steadiness, order, and coherence which belong not to those that are the effects of my will. They speak themselves the products of a Mind more powerful and wise than human minds.

Some truths there are so near and obvious to the human mind that a man need only open his eyes to see them. Such I take this important one to be, namely, that all the choir of heaven and furniture of the earth, in a word, all those bodies which compose the mighty frame of the world, have not any subsistence without a mind; that their being is to be perceived or known; that, consequently, so long as they are not actually perceived by me, or do not exist in my mind or the mind of any other created spirit, they must either have no existence at all or else subsist in the mind of some Eternal Spirit. For it is unintelligible to attribute to any single part of them an existence independent of (perception by a) Spirit.

Until his premises are effectively questioned, or his reasoning from these premises shown to be fallacious, Berkeley may now survey his work with satisfaction. Are there any loopholes? The citations which follow show Berkeley at work on this question.

Before we proceed any farther, it is necessary that we spend some time in answering objections which may probably be made against the principles we have hitherto laid down. In this, if I seem too prolix, I desire I may be excused, since all men do not equally apprehend things of this nature; and I am willing to be understood by every man.

It might be objected:

By the foregoing principles all that is real and substantial in nature is banished out of the world. All things that exist, it will be said, exist only in the mind, that is, are purely notional. What therefore becomes of the sun, moon, and stars? What must we think of houses, rivers, mountains, trees, stones, nay even of our own bodies? Are all these but so many chimeras and illusions?

To this objection he has an answer:

We are not deprived of any one thing in nature. Whatever we see, hear, feel, or any wise conceive or understand remains as secure as ever, and is as real as ever. I do not argue against the existence of any one thing that we can apprehend either by sense or reflection. That the things I see with my eyes and touch with my hands do really exist, I make not the least question. The only thing whose existence I deny is that which philosophers call *matter*. There are minds which will or exite ideas in themselves at pleasure. Other ideas, which they do not so excite, speak themselves the effects of a mind more powerful and wise than human spirits. These latter are said to be more real than the former. In this sense the sun I see is the real sun. In this sense, everything in the world is as much a real being by our principles as by any other. If the word *substance* be taken for a combination of sensible qualities, we cannot be accused of denying its existence.

It sounds harsh to say we eat and drink ideas, and are clothed with ideas.

But, in common discourse, the word *idea* is not used to signify the several combinations of sensible qualities which are called *things*. But this concerns not the truth of the proposition, which says no more than that we are fed and clothed with those things which we perceive immediately by our senses. The sensory qualities which, combined, constitute the several sorts of victuals and apparel, have been shown to exist only in the mind that perceives them. This is all that is meant by calling them *ideas*. If you agree that we eat and drink and are clad with the immediate object of sense, which cannot exist unperceived, I shall readily grant that it is more conformable to custom that they should be called *things* rather than *ideas*.

"I will still believe my senses and will never suffer any argument, how plausible soever, to prevail over the certainty of them." Be it so. Assert the evidence of your senses. We are willing to do the same. That what I see, hear, feel, etc., doth exist, I no more doubt of than I do of my own being. But, I do not see how the testimony of sense can be alleged as a proof for the existence of anything which is not perceived by the senses. We are not for having any man turn skeptic and doubt his senses.

Again, it might be objected:

From these principles it follows that things are every moment annihilated and created anew. The objects of sense exist only when they are perceived. The trees are in the garden, the chairs in the parlor, only while there is someone there to perceive them. Upon shutting my eyes it is all reduced to nothing, and upon opening them it is again created.

His answer:

It is thought absurd that, upon closing my eyelids, all the visible objects around me should be reduced to nothing. Yet, is not this what my very critics and opponents commonly acknowledge when they agree on all hands that light and color, which are the immediate objects of sight, are mere sensations, mere "subjective states" which exist no longer than they are perceived?

Indeed we hold the objects of sense to be nothing else but ideas which cannot exist unperceived. Yet we may not hence conclude that they have no existence except only when they are perceived by us; there may be some other spirit that perceives them though we do not. It would not follow, hence, that bodies are annihilated and created every moment, or exist not at all during the intervals between our perception of them.

It might be objected:

If primary qualities exist only in the mind, it follows that mind is extended, since extension is a primary quality of things.

The answer:

It no more follows that the mind is extended because extension is in it alone, than that it is red or blue because those qualities exist in it alone and nowhere else. Yet my opponents admit that secondary qualities exist in the mind alone; i.e., are "subjective."

It might be objected:

There have been a great many things explained by matter and motion. Take these away and you destroy the whole atomic theory, and undermine those principles of mechanics which have been applied with so much success to account for things. In short, whatever advances have been made in the study of nature, do all proceed on the supposition that "matter" doth exist.

To which Berkeley replies:

To "explain" things is all one as to show why, upon such and such occasions, we are affected with such and such ideas. But, how "matter" operates on mind, or produces any idea in it, is what no philosopher will pretend to explain. Of what use is it, therefore? Besides, things are accounted for by figure, motion and other qualities; not by "matter." Such qualities are no more than ideas, and therefore cannot be the cause of anything, since ideas cannot be the cause of anything.

It might be objected:

Does it not seem absurd to take away "natural causes" and ascribe everything to the operation of spirit? To say, not that fire heats or water cools, but that a spirit heats or a spirit cools, etc. Would not a man be deservedly laughed at who should talk after this manner?

To which Berkeley rejoins:

In such things we ought to think with the learned and speak with the vulgar. Those who are convinced of the truth of Copernican astronomy do nevertheless say "the sun rises," and "the sun sets." Yet it doth not. But if such persons affected a contrary style in common talk, it would appear ridiculous. It is the same with our tenets.

It might be objected:

Is not the universal assent of mankind an invincible argument on behalf of matter? Must we suppose the whole world to be mistaken? If so, what cause can be assigned of so widespread and predominant an error?

To which Berkeley responds:

It will perhaps not be found that so many do really believe in the existence of "matter." Strictly, to believe that which involves a contradiction, or
has no meaning, is impossible. I admit men act as if the cause of their sensations were some senseless, unthinking being. But, that they clearly apprehend
any meaning thereby, that they have formed a settled speculative opinion, is
what I am not able to conceive.

Adding, too:

Even though we should grant a notion to be universally and steadfastly
held to, yet that is but a weak argument for its truth. A vast number of
prejudices and false opinions are everywhere embraced by the unreflecting
part of mankind. There was a time when the antipodes and the motion of the
earth were looked upon as monstrous absurdities even by men of learning.
    It is demanded that we assign a cause of this prejudice that matter exists
and is the cause of our sensations. I answer: Men, knowing they perceived
several ideas whereof they themselves were not the author, nor depending
on their wills, first maintained that those ideas had an existence independent
of and external to the mind. But, seeing that the immediate objects of perception do not exist except they are being perceived, they then argued that
there are objects, distinct from the colors, etc. immediately perceived by the
mind, of which those latter are images or resemblances or effects imprinted
on us by those objects. So the notion of an imperceived and unthinking
"matter" owes its origin to the consciousness that we are not the authors of
our sensations, which must therefore have some cause distinct from our minds
upon which they are imprinted.

It might be objected:

You say: Though the ideas themselves do not exist without the mind,
yet there may be things like them whereof they are copies or resemblances,
which exist without the mind in an unthinking substance.

To which Berkeley counters:

It is indeed an opinion strangely prevailing among men that houses,
mountains, rivers, in a word, all sensible objects, have an existence distinct
from their being perceived by the understanding. But this principle involves
a manifest contradiction. For what are the aforementioned objects but the
things we perceive by sense? And what do we perceive besides our own ideas
or sensations? Could any of these exist unperceived? There was an odor, that

is, it was smelt; there was a sound, that is, it was heard; there was a color or figure, that is, it was perceived by sight or touch. That is all I can understand by these and like expressions. Their *esse* is *percipi*. Nor is it possible they should have any existence out of the minds which perceive them.

An idea can be like nothing but an idea; a color can be like nothing but a color. It is impossible for us to conceive a likeness except only between our ideas.

I ask whether the supposed originals or external things, of which our ideas are pictures or representations, be themselves perceivable or no? If they are, then they are ideas, and we have gained our point. If they are not, I appeal to anyone whether it be sense to say a color is like something which is invisible; to say hard or soft is like something intangible; and so of the rest.

It might be objected:

Let us admit that the notion of "matter" as the cause or support of the perceived qualities of things, is not needed. Yet there may perhaps be some inert, unperceiving substance, as incomprehensible to us as colors to a man born blind; supporting, it may be, qualities of which we know nothing because we have no senses adapted to them, but which, if we had other senses we should know of.

To which Berkeley replies:

If by *matter* you mean the unknown (and unknowable) cause or support of unknown (and unknowable) qualities, I see no point in affirming or denying its existence. I see no advantage in disputing about something we know not what and we know not why.

And adds:

If we had those other senses, they could only furnish us with new ideas or sensations. In which case we should have the same reason against their existing in an unperceiving substance that has been already offered with relation to such qualities as we do perceive: they would exist only in a mind perceiving them. This is true not only of ideas we are acquainted with at present but likewise of all possible ideas whatsoever.

The case is by now almost completed. He has stated and refuted materialism. He has stated and established idealism. He has anticipated and parried every objection which he can imagine. He proceeds to draw some conclusions.

Having posed and met possible objections, we proceed to take a view of our principles with regard to their consequences. After what hath been premised, I think we may lay down the following conclusions.

First: It is plain that men amuse themselves in vain when they inquire for any natural cause distinct from a mind or spirit.

Second: Since the whole creation is the workmanship of a wise and good Agent, it should seem to be in order to employ our thoughts about the final causes, or purposes of things. This not only discovers to us the attributes of the Creator and Sustainer, but may also direct us to the proper uses and applications of things.

Third: The natural immortality of the soul is a necessary consequence of these principles. To assert natural immortality is not to assert that it is incapable of annihilation by the Creator who first gave it being but only that it is not liable to be broken or dissolved by the laws of nature or motion. Bodies are ideas in the mind or soul. The latter is indivisible, incorporeal, unextended, and consequently indissoluble. Changes, decays, dissolutions, which we see in bodies cannot affect a spirit which hath none of their properties. Such a being, a mind or soul or active spirit, is therefore indissoluble by the forces of nature.

Fourth: From what hath been said, it is plain that we cannot know the existence of other minds or spirits otherwise than by their operations or the ideas excited by them in us. I perceive combinations of ideas, and changes thereof, that inform me that there are agents like myself which accompany them and concur in their production. But the knowledge I have of these other spirits or minds is hence indirect; not as is the knowledge of my ideas, but depending on the intervention of ideas by me referred to minds as spirits distinct from myself.

Fifth: Though there be some things (i.e., combinations of sensations) which convince us that human agents are concerned in producing them, yet it is evident that nature, that is, the far greater part of the ideas or sensations perceived by us, is not produced by or dependent on the wills of men. There is therefore some other Spirit that causeth them. But if we consider the regularity, order, and concatenation of natural things, the surprising magnificence, beauty, and perfection of the larger, and the exquisite contrivance of the smaller parts of creation, we shall clearly perceive that the attributes One, Eternal, Infinitely Wise, Good, and Perfect, belong all of them to the aforesaid Spirit, who "works in all" and "by whom all things consist."

Hence it is evident that God is known as certainly and immediately as any other mind or spirit, distinct from ourselves. We may even assert that the existence of God is more evident than the existence of men; because the effects of nature are more numerous and considerable than those ascribed to men. There is not any one mark which denotes a man, or effect produced by him, that does not more strongly evince the being of that Spirit which is the author of nature. A human spirit is not perceived by sense: when we perceive the color, size, etc. of a man, we perceive only sensations or ideas excited in our own minds. These being exhibited to our view in sundry distinct collections, serve to mark out unto us the existence of finite spirits like ourselves. And after the same manner we see God. All the difference is that whereas some one finite and narrow assemblage of ideas denotes a particular human mind, on the other hand wherever we direct our view we perceive manifest tokens of the Divinity, "in whom we live and move and have our being."

It will be objected here that monsters, untimely births, fruits blasted in the blossom, rains falling in desert places, waste, miseries incident to human life, and so on, are evidence that the whole frame of nature is not actuated and superintended by a Spirit of infinite wisdom and goodness. If, that is to say, God is the author of all things, is He not the author of evil and undesirable things? Is this coherent with His infinite wisdom and goodness?

I answer: The very blemishes and defects of nature are not without their use. They make an agreeable variety and augment the beauty of the rest of creation, as shadows in a picture serve to set off the brighter parts.

I add: We do well, before we tax the author of nature with wastefulness, to examine whether such accusation be not the effect of prejudice contracted by our familiarity with impotent and saving mortals. In man, thriftiness with what he cannot easily secure may be wisdom. But, an Omnipotent Spirit can produce everything by a mere fiat. Hence nature's splendid profusion should not be interpreted as wastefulness in the author of nature. Rather is it an evidence of the riches of His power.

I add: As for the pain which is in the world, pursuant to the general laws of nature and the actions of finite imperfect Spirits, this is indispensably necessary to our well-being. We consider some one particular pain and account it an evil. But our view is too narrow. If we enlarge our view, so as to comprehend the various ends, connections, and dependencies of things, we shall be forced to acknowledge that those particular things which, considered in themselves, appear to be evil, have the nature of good when considered in connection with the whole system of beings.

From what hath been said, it will be manifest that it is merely for want of attention and comprehensiveness of mind that there are any atheists or Manichaeans. Little and unreflecting souls may indeed burlesque the works of Providence, the beauty and order whereof they have not the capacity or will not be at the pains to comprehend. But those who are masters of any justness and extent of thought can never sufficiently admire the traces of wisdom and goodness that shine through the economy of nature.

Since it is downright impossible that a soul pierced and illumined with a thorough sense of the omnipresence, holiness, and justice of that Spirit, should persist in a remorseless violation of His laws, we ought therefore earnestly to meditate on those important matters, that so we may attain conviction without scruple.

For, after all, what deserves the first place in our studies, is the consideration of God and duty; which to promote, was the main drift and design of my labors.

What is to be said of this flight of the metaphysical imagination? A generation later it caught the attention of David Hume. He observed, somewhat tartly, "The speculations of the ingenious Dr. Berkeley—they admit of no refutation, but they produce no conviction," and proceeded to deal with idealism as Berkeley had dealt with materialism, rejecting spiritual substance as Berkeley had rejected material substance. But of that, more later. Meanwhile, one does well to know the argument. It has long served as a kind of rallying point for the like-minded in each generation. He provided an apparently coherent case against the "specter" of materialism. He gave articulation to that perennial temperament which dreads and despises and mistrusts the "appeal to matter." For his premises, others have been substituted. To his conclusions, especially his repudiation of materialism, little of importance or variety has been added.

Note on Sources. The Berkeley material in this section has been quoted, abridged, or paraphrased from his small book, *A Treatise Concerning the Principles of Human Knowledge*, Part I. This book, usually referred to as the *Principles*, consists of 156 numbered paragraphs. The order of my quotations, and so on, does not follow the order in Berkeley's book.

Reading References. A great number of books and chapters have been written about and against the philosophical position taken up by Berkeley. Mention might be made of four items. The first is a book by T. H. Huxley, *Hume, with Helps to the Study of Berkeley*. The "helps" part of this book is interesting and illuminating, inasmuch as Huxley is ordinarily credited with views which fall short of Berkeley's religiously motivated idealism. The second is a book by John Wild, *George Berkeley, a Study of His Life and Philosophy*. This is a careful and elaborate exposition of Berkeley. The third is the chapter on Berkeley in Mary Whiton Calkins' book, *The Persistent Problems of Philosophy*. The fourth is G. E. Moore's well-known essay, "The Refutation of Idealism," contained in his book, *Philosophical Studies*.

The following are some books published since 1940:

Aristotelian Society. *Berkeley and Modern Problems.*
Bender, F. *George Berkeley's Philosophy Re-examined.*
Brayton, A. *George Berkeley in Newport.*
Broad, C. D. *Berkeley's Argument about Material Substance.*

Laky, J. J. *A Study of George Berkeley's Philosophy in the Light of the Philosophy of Thomas Aquinas.*
Luce, A. A. *Berkeley's Immaterialism.*
———. *The Life of George Berkeley.*
Sillem, E. A. *George Berkeley and the Proofs for the Existence of God.*
University of California Publications in Philosophy. *George Berkeley.*
Warnock, G. J. *Berkeley.*
Wisdom, J. O. *The Unconscious Origin of Berkeley's Philosophy.*

READING QUESTIONS

1. Enumerate the four large steps in Berkeley's argument. Show how that four-step pattern could be used by (a) a socialist, (b) a hedonist, (c) an evolutionist, (d) a fundamentalist, (e) a determinist, (f) an atheist.
2. He begins by reminding his reader of the distinction between primary qualities which are objective, and secondary qualities which are subjective. Would a materialist admit this distinction?
3. What sound principle of criticism is illustrated by Berkeley's use of claims admitted by the materialist?
4. State the materialist thesis which Berkeley proposes to criticize.
5. His first claim is that the primary qualities, extension and motion, are intellectual abstractions. What use does he make of that?
6. His second claim is about *degrees* of those primary qualities. State it. Use to which he puts said claim.
7. His third claim is about number. State it. Use to which he puts said claim.
8. His fourth claim is that an argument used to prove that secondary qualities are subjective may be turned against primary qualities. Show.
9. His fifth claim is that even if the materialists's "matter" does exist, we could not know it. Show.
10. It might be at least probable that the materialists matter exists. Why so? Berkeley's rejoinder.
11. Why it is worth while to reflect on the motives which induced men to suppose the existence of material substance. What those motives were.
12. Which of Berkeley's criticisms of materialism you find (a) most (b) least convincing.
13. We have ideas. Their "*esse est percipi.*" What that means. Would a materialist admit it? How Berkeley uses the claim as a step in his argument for idealism.

14. "We have ideas. Their *esse est percipi*. They must have some cause." You take it from there.
15. Why Berkeley's idealism should not be called solipsism.
16. He formulates a number of objections which he thinks will be offered. State each briefly. Which objections strike you as the most telling?
17. Show how he handles each objection.
18. Which objection, or objections, he handles (a) most effectively (b) least effectively.
19. Having criticized materialism, argued for idealism, met objections to idealism, he concludes by drawing five consequences. State each.
20. Why he becomes involved in the problem of evil. How he seeks to dispose of it.
21. Wherein you find Berkeley (a) most (b) least convincing.

4. VOLUNTARISM AND ITS IMPLICATIONS —FROM ARTHUR SCHOPENHAUER

From Berkeley to Schopenhauer. It is sometimes argued that metaphysics is a question of temperament. There is a half truth in the claim. What it comes to is something like this: Descartes was a somewhat conventional individual, inclined to safe, middle-of-the-road opinions. This is reflected in his orthodox metaphysics of God, human souls, and matter. Hobbes was a hardheaded, realistically minded individual, inclined to discount flights of imagination and to stick to the "facts." What more natural, then, than his unvarnished materialism? Berkeley was a devout and genial Anglican cleric, inclined to share the pious aspirations enshrined in the institution for which he was a spokesman. Why not an idealism, under these circumstances? Why not the firm conviction that this world is, in the last analysis, but the manifestation of a Supreme Mind? Hume was a canny, skeptically minded Scot, impressed, above everything else, with man's seemingly boundless credulity. What more natural than his carefully reasoned refutation of Descartes, Hobbes, and Berkeley? And so one might continue, seeking to "psychologize" away any claim of metaphysics to rational consideration. There is a flaw in this notion. No explanation in terms of nature and training, of why any man believes anything, has any relevance to the question of whether the beliefs are true or false. It is well to raise this point here for two reasons: (1) One's introduction to a variety of alternative metaphysical hypotheses is usually marked by a sense of confusion and a ready ear to the dissolving suggestion that, "After all, it's only a question of temperament." The best reply is that the truth of an opinion has nothing to do with the temperament of the man who holds the opinion. (2) In the case of Arthur Schopenhauer, there is a great tendency to "explain away" his doctrine by reference to his biography. It is known that in life he was bitter, disillusioned, cynical, pessimistic. It is also known that his metaphysical views amount to the claim that the nature of ultimate reality is such as to justify his cynicism and pessimism. The result has sometimes been that persons who reject his metaphysics, with something approaching abhorrence, do so on the ground that "his temperament explains his views." Perhaps it does, but that is not the important point. What one should ask is, "Does the nature of things justify his views?"

Biographical Note. Arthur Schopenhauer was born in Germany in 1788 and died in 1860 at the age of seventy-two. His life was filled with selfishness, suspiciousness, and bitterness. He spent some time in a commercial house before going to the universities at Göttingen, Jena, and Berlin. He left his business career in disgust. He berated most of his fellows and teachers at the universities. Upon the death of his father, his mother had moved to Weimar. Schopenhauer followed her, quarreled with her, and took separate lodgings; met Goethe, quarreled with him, and left town to settle a while in Dresden. Here he wrote his great work, *The World as Will and Idea.* As soon as it was published, he left for Italy. There he fumed jealously over the reputation and the gallantries of Lord Byron. He returned to Germany to find his book almost unnoticed. He raged at the obtuseness of his contemporaries and set himself up as a privatdocent at the university in Berlin. Here he was outclassed by the famous Hegel, whom he denounced as a "windbag," and left Berlin for Frankfort. In Frankfort, despite squabbles with persons who shared his rooming house, he spent the remaining years of his life writing brilliant essays on various themes in his own philosophy, compiling a scrapbook of all articles and notices dealing with his work, preparing for a second and third edition of his treatise, and watching his doctrines and fame spread slowly over the Western world.

The Argument of the Citations. Schopenhauer's metaphysics is called *voluntarism.* It may be contrasted with materialism. It is the belief that will, not matter, is the ultimate reality of which all things are manifestations. Reality is *will,* manifested as nature and present in man. The following citations fall into two groups. The first, given immediately below, without any comment, comprises what might be called the *data.* The second sets forth what might be called the *theory.* The first group requires no elucidation. Collectively, they might be inscribed "cynicism and pessimism." They are random reflections on the rottenness of things. As I read him, Schopenhauer would have these disconnected observations on nature and life fall, like so many drops of acid, into the reader's mind, preparing him to understand and appreciate the metaphysical theory which is to follow. "See," he seems to say, "see—these are the facts. Think them over. Then, but not until then, I'll give you a theory that will fit them."

Unless suffering is the direct and immediate object of life, our existence must entirely fail of its aim. It is absurd to look upon the enormous amount of pain that abounds everywhere in the world, originating in needs and necessities inseparable from life itself, as serving no purpose, as being the result of mere chance.

Let us consider the human race. Here life presents itself as a task to be performed. Here we see, in great and in small, universal need, ceaseless wars, compulsory activity, extreme exertion of mind and body. Millions united into nations, striving for a common good, each individual on account of his own. But thousands are sacrificed. Now silly delusions, now intriguing politics, excite them to wars. Then sweat and blood must flow to carry out someone's ideas or expiate someone's folly. In peace time it is industry and trade. Inventions work miracles, seas are navigated, delicacies are brought from the ends of the earth, waves engulf thousands. The tumult passes description. And all to what end? To sustain life through a brief span, and then to reproduce and begin again.

From whence did Dante take the materials for his hell but from our actual world? And a very proper hell he was able to make of it. When, on the other hand, he came to describe heaven and its delights, he was confronted with a difficulty, for our world affords no materials for this.

In early youth we are like children in a theater before the curtain is raised, sitting in high spirits and eagerly waiting for the play to begin. It is a blessing we do not know what is actually going to happen . . . the longer you live, the more clearly you feel that life is a disappointment, nay, a cheat.

We are like lambs in a field, disporting under the eye of the butcher who chooses first one and then another. In our good days we are unconscious of the evil which fate may have in store for us—sickness, poverty, mutilation, blindness, insanity, and so on.

It is folly to try to turn this scene of misery into a garden of pleasure. It is folly to aim at joy and pleasure instead of the greatest possible freedom from pain. There is some wisdom in taking a gloomy view of things, in looking upon the world as a kind of hell and in confining one's efforts to securing a little room not too exposed to the fire.

Human life? It is like a drop of water seen through a microscope, teeming with infusoria; or a speck of cheese full of mites invisible to the naked eye.

We laugh as they bustle about, and struggle. It is only in the microscope that our life looks so big. It is an almost invisible point, drawn out and magnified by the powerful lenses of time and space.

Unrest is the mark of human existence. We are like a man running down hill who cannot keep on his legs unless he runs on. We are like a pole balanced on the tip of one's finger, or like a planet which would crash into its sun the moment it should cease to hurry on its way.

As far as real physical pleasure is concerned, man is no better off than the brute. The higher possibilities of his brain and nervous system make him sensitive to more and intenser kinds of pleasure, but also to more and intenser kinds of pain. Boredom is a form of suffering unknown to brutes, except perhaps when they are domesticated. Whereas, in man it has become a scourge. Of a truth, need and boredom are the two poles of human life.

In every man there dwells, first and foremost, a colossal egotist who snaps the bands of right and justice with consummate ease. Newspapers show it every day. History shows it on every page. Does not the need of a balance of power in Europe demonstrate it? If it were egotism only, it would be bad enough. But to the egotist in man is joined a fund of hatred, anger, envy, rancor, malice, accumulated like the venom in a serpent's tooth.

I have been reading a book on the condition of the slaves in the southern states. This book constitutes one of the heaviest indictments against the so-called human race. No one can put it down without a feeling of horror. Whatever you may have heard will seem small when you read of how those human devils, those bigoted, church-going, Sabbatarian rascals treated their black brothers whom they had gotten into their clutches.

What is our civilized world but a big masquerade, where you meet knights, priests, soldiers, scholars, lawyers, clergymen, philosophers and so on? But they are not what they pretend to be. They are only masks, and behind the masks, as a rule, you will find moneymakers. It is merchants and moneylenders alone who, in this respect, constitute an honest class.

Formerly faith was the chief support of a throne. Now it is credit. The pope himself is scarcely more concerned over the faithful than over his creditors. In times past it was the guilty debt of the world which was lamented. Now it is the financial debt which arouses dismay. Formerly it was the Last Day which was prophesied. Now it is the great repudiation, the bankruptcy of nations.

Leibnitz, you know, argued that this is the best of all possible worlds. Those who agree with him are optimists. If I could conduct a confirmed optimist through hospitals, infirmaries, operating rooms, asylums; through prisons, torture chambers, and slave kennels; over battlefields, places of execution and sudden death; if I were to open to him all the dark abodes where misery hides from cold curiosity—he might come finally to understand the nature of this "best of all possible worlds."

Nature has appointed that the propagation of the species shall be the business of men who are young, strong, and handsome; so that the species may not degenerate. There is no law older or more powerful than this. Woe to the man who sets up claims and interests that conflict with it; they will be unmercifully crushed at the first serious encounter.

If we contemplate life, we behold a turmoil where most are occupied with want and misery, straining to dodge or ward off its multifarious sorrows. In the midst of this tumult, we see the stealthy glance of two lovers. Why so fearful, so secret? Because—unrealized by them, perhaps—these lovers are traitors who seek to perpetuate whole sordid rounds of want and drudgery which would otherwise come to an end.

If children were brought into the world by an act of pure reason, would human life continue to exist? Are not most of us trapped into life? Would not a man rather have so much sympathy with the coming generation that he would spare it the burden of existence?

Kant speaks much of the dignity of man. I have never seen it. It seems to me that the notion of dignity can be applied to man only in an ironical sense. His will is sinful. His intellect is limited. His body is weak and perishable. How shall a man have dignity whose conception is a crime, whose birth is a penalty, whose life is toil, whose death is a necessity?

Human life must be some kind of mistake. Else why is man a compound of needs and necessities so hard so satisfy? And why, if perchance they should be satisfied, is he thereby abandoned to boredom? This is direct proof that existence has no real value. For what is boredom but the feeling of the emptiness of life? The fact that this most perfect manifestation of life, the human organism, with the infinite cunning and complex working of its machinery, must oscillate between need and boredom and finally fall to dust and extinction, this fact, I say, is eloquent to him who has the mind to understand it.

Disillusion is the mark of old age. By that time the fictions are gone which gave life its charm and spurred on the mind to activity. By that time the splendors of the world have proved themselves null and vain. Its pomp, grandeur, ideals, and enthusiasms are faded. Not till a man has attained his three score years and ten does he quite understand the first verse of Ecclesiastes.

The world and man is something that had better not have been. This may sound strange. But it is in keeping with the facts. And it reminds us of that which is, after all, the most necessary thing in life—the tolerance, patience, regard, love of neighbor, which everyone needs and which everyone owes to his fellow.

You need only look at the way woman is formed to see that she is not meant to undergo great labor either of mind or body. She pays the debt of life not by what she does but by what she suffers: by the pains of childbearing, by caring for the child, by submission to her husband to whom she should be a patient and cheering companion.

That woman is meant by nature to obey may be seen by the fact that every woman who is placed in the unnatural position of complete independence immediately attaches herself to some man by whom she allows herself to be guided and ruled. If she is young, it will be a lover; if she is old, it will be a priest or a lawyer.

The institution of monogamy, and the marriage laws which it entails, bestow upon women an unnatural position of privilege by considering her as the full equivalent of a man, which is by no means the case. Seeing this, men who are shrewd and prudent often scruple to make so great a sacrifice and to acquiesce in so one-sided an arrangement.

The nobler and more perfect a thing is, the later and slower it is to mature. A man reaches the maturity of his reasoning powers hardly before the age of twenty-eight; a woman at eighteen—and then it is only reason of a sort, very niggard in its dimensions.

This weakness of woman's reasoning power explains why she shows more sympathy for the unfortunate than men do; present circumstances have a stronger hold over her, and those concrete things, that lie directly before her eyes, exercise a power which is seldom counteracted to any extent by abstract principles of thought, by fixed rules of conduct, or in general by consideration for the past and the future.

Women are dependent, not upon strength but upon craft. Hence their instinctive capacity for cunning and their inveterate tendency to say what is not true. For as lions are provided with claws and teeth, elephants with boars and tusks, cuttlefish with clouds of inky fluid, so nature has equipped woman with the arts of dissimulation. Therefore a perfectly truthful and straightforward woman is perhaps an impossibility. It may indeed be questioned whether women should be allowed to take an oath in court.

It is only the man whose intellect is clouded by his sexual impulses that could give the name of "fair sex" to that undersized, narrow-shouldered, broad-hipped, short-legged race. For the whole beauty of women is bound up with that impulse.

Nature proceeds with her usual economy. Just as the female ant, after fecundation, loses her wings which are then superfluous, nay, a danger to the business of breeding; so, after giving birth to one or two children, a woman generally loses her beauty; probably for similar reasons.

What can you expect of women, when you consider that the most distinguished intellects among them have never produced a single achievement in the fine arts that is really great, genuine, and original? Not even in painting, where mastery of technique is as much within their power as within man's, and where they have diligently cultivated it. The case is not altered by a few partial exceptions. Taken together, women are and remain thorough Philistines and incurable.

There is no proportion between the troubles of life and the gains of life. In the lives of the brute creation, the vanity of life's struggle is easily grasped. The variety and ingenuity of adaptation contrasts sharply with any lasting

aim. Only momentary comfort, only fleeting pleasures conditioned and succeeded by want, much suffering, long strife, war of all against all as Hobbes
has it, each one a hunter and a hunted, everywhere pressure, need, anxiety,
shrieking, howling, and sudden death. And this, *in secula seculorum* or till
once again the crust of the planet breaks.

The bulldog ant of Australia affords us a most instructive example. If it
is cut in two, a battle begins between the head and the tail. The head seizes
the tail with its teeth; the tail defends itself by stinging the head. The battle
may last for half an hour, until they die or are dragged off by other ants.

Yunghahn relates that he saw in Java a plain, as far as the eye could reach,
entirely covered with skeletons. He took it for a battlefield. They were, however, merely the skeletons of large turtles which come out of the sea to lay
their eggs and are then attacked by wild dogs who drag them over onto their
backs, strip off the small shell from the stomach, and devour them alive. For
this, these turtles are born. Thus life preys upon itself, and in different forms
is its own nourishment.

Under the firm crust of the planet dwell powerful forces of nature. Some
accident affords them free play. The crust is destroyed, with every living
thing on it. The earthquake of Lisbon, the destruction of Pompeii, are only
playful hints of what is possible.

The only thing that reconciles me to the Old Testament is the story
of the Fall. In my eyes, that is the only metaphysical truth in the book, even
though it appears as an allegory. There seems to me no better explanation
of our existence than that it is the result of some false step, some sin for which
we are paying the penalty.

Vanini, whom his contemporaries burned, finding that easier than refuting him, put the same matter in a very forcible way: "Man is so full of
misery that, if it were not contrary to the Christian religion, I should say
that evil spirits, if there are any, have passed into human form and are now
atoning for their crimes."

Tragedy is the summit of poetical art. The pain and wail of humanity,
the triumph of evil, the mastery of chance, the fall of just and innocent, are
here presented for us. And in it lies a significant hint of the nature of the
world and man: the strife of the will against itself comes here into prominence.
It is shown in the sufferings of men due to chance and error, reaching sometimes even the appearance of design. This we are led to see in the noblest
works of the tragic muse.

Religious teachers tell us that suicide is cowardice, that only a madman
could be guilty of it, and other insipidities of the same kind. Or else they
make the nonsensical remark that suicide is wrong, when obviously there is
nothing to which every man has a more unassailable title than to his own
life and person.

The ancients did not regard the matter in that light. Pliny says "Life is
not so desirable as to be protracted at any cost. Whoever you are you are

sure to die, even though your life has been full of abomination and crime. The chief remedy for a troubled mind is the feeling that there is no greater blessing than an opportune death; and that every one can avail himself of."

Two Chinamen traveling in Europe paid their first visit to the theater. One of them spent all his time studying the machinery. He succeeded in finding out how it was worked. The other tried to get at the meaning of the piece being presented, in spite of his ignorance of the language. There you have the scientist and the philosopher.

The citations thus far have been expressions of Schopenhauer's pessimism and cynicism. They form a prolegomenon to his metaphysical voluntarism. His general argument is to this effect: Metaphysical voluntarism is the only hypothesis which will account for the many facts upon which I base my cynicism and pessimism. The next four citations set forth his fundamental thesis.

I teach that the inner nature of everything is will.

That which makes itself known to us in the most immediate knowledge as our will is also that which objectifies or manifests itself at different grades in all the phenomena of the world.

If we observe the unceasing impulse with which the waters hurry to the ocean, the persistence with which the magnet turns to the pole, the readiness with which iron flies to the magnet; if we see the crystal take form, the attraction and repulsion of bodies; if we feel how a burden which hampers us by its gravitation toward the earth presses and strains in pursuit of its one tendency—if we note all these things, it requires no great effort of the imagination to recognize in nature what is will in us.

As the magic lantern shows many different pictures made visible by one and the same light, so in all the multifarious phenomena which fill the world, or throng after each other as events, only one will manifests itself, of which everything is the visibility, the objectivity, the manifestation. It is that which is identical in all this variety and change.

To throw his position into bolder relief, Schopenhauer contrasts it with pantheism, the belief that reality is God Himself manifested in everything.

Pantheism is the belief that God is the world—a belief which has always puzzled me. Taking an unprejudiced view of the world as it is, who would regard it as a god? A very ill-advised god, surely, who knows no better than to turn himself into such a world as ours, such a mean, shabby world; there to take the form of countless millions who are fretted and tormented, who live only by preying upon one another. What a pastime for a god!

With the pantheist, I have that One-in-All in common; but my One is not God. I do not go beyond experience, taken in its widest sense; and still less do I fly in the face of the facts which lie before me. The "God" of pantheism is, and must ever remain, an unknown "X." The will, on the other hand, is the one thing known most immediately in experience and therefore exclusively fitted for the explanation of the rest. What is unknown should always be explained by what is better known, not conversely.

The "God" of pantheism manifests himself to unfold his glory. What glory! Apart from the vanity here attributed to him by pantheism, there is immediately created the obligation to sophisticate away the colossal evil of the world. With me, there is none of this. With me alone, the evil of the world is honestly confessed in its whole magnitude. I alone have no need to have recourse to palliatives and sophistries.

From pantheism, he turns to the more orthodox alternative of theism, the belief, namely, that nature is God's handiwork:

There are two things which make it impossible to believe that this world is the successful work of a wise, good and all-powerful Being. The first is the misery which abounds everywhere. The second is the obvious imperfection of its highest product, man, who is a burlesque of what he should be.

In its explanation of the origin of the world—creation by God—Judaism is inferior to any other form of religious doctrine professed by a civilized people. That Jehovah should have created this world of misery and woe, because he enjoyed doing it, and should then have clapped his hands in praise of his own work, declaring everything to be good—that will not do at all!

I shall be told that my philosophy is comfortless—because I speak the truth. People prefer to be assured that everything the Lord has made is good. Go to the priests, then. Or go to your university professors; they are bound to preach optimism; and it is an easy task to upset their theories.

These matters of contrast noted, he resumes the exposition of his own metaphysical thesis:

That which, in us, pursues its ends by the light of knowledge, strives in nature blindly and dumbly in a one-sided and unchangeable manner. Yet in both cases it may be brought under the conception of will; just as the first dim light of dawn must share the name of sunlight with the rays of full midday.

The lowest grades of the objectification of the will are to be found in those most universal forces of nature which partly appear in all matter, as gravity, impenetrability, and so on, which it is the work of physics and chemistry to discover. They are the simplest modes of its objectification.

The conception of "will" has hitherto been subordinated to the conception of "force." I reverse the matter. I desire that every force in nature be understood in terms of will. This is not mere quibbling. For at the basis of the conception of force, as of all conceptions except will, there lies the sense-perceptual knowledge of the objective world, and the conception is constructed out of this. It is hence an abstraction from what is given in sense-perception. We have no direct experience of "forces" in nature, only of connections and sequences. The conception of will, however, is of all conceptions the one which does not have its origin in sense perception, in ideas of things. It comes from within, and proceeds from our immediate consciousness. If therefore, we refer the conception of will to the conception of force we have referred the better known to the less known.

From inanimate nature, Schopenhauer passes to the world of living things. It, too, is only a higher manifestation of the same underlying will:

Every species of animal is a longing of the will-to-live. For instance, the will is seized with a longing to live on trees, to hang from ther branches, to devour their leaves. This longing becomes objectified in the sloth. It can hardly walk, being only adapted for climbing. It is helpless on the ground, agile on trees, looks like moss so as to escape its pursuers.

The will is active in nature where no knowledge guides it. This we see in the instincts and mechanical skills of animals. The ends toward which they strive are to them unknown. The bird of a year old has no idea of eggs for which it builds a nest. The young spider has no idea of the prey for which it spins its first web. Ants, marmots, bees, lay in provision for the winter they have never experienced. Insects deposit their eggs where the coming brood finds future nourishment. The larva of the stag beetle makes the hole in the wood, in which it is to await its metamorphosis, twice as big if it is going to be a male beetle as it would if it were gong to be a female beetle— so that there will be room for the horns which no female beetle possesses. Has it knowledge thus in advance? The point is merely this: Knowledge is not necessary to guide will. It acts instinctively at some levels.

The instincts of plants and animals give us the best illustration of what is meant by teleology in nature. An instinct is an action like that which is guided by a purpose, and is yet entirely without this purpose. So all constructions of nature resemble that which is guided by an aim, and yet is entirely without it. What we think to be means and end is, in every case, the manifestation of the unity of the one will.

Everywhere in nature pervading this adaptation we see strife. In this we can recognize that variance with itself which is essential to the will. Every grade of objectification fights for the matter of the others. The permanent matter must continually change its form. This strife may be followed through the whole of nature. It is most visible in the animal kingdom. For animals have the whole of the vegetable kingdom for their food, and within the animal kingdom one order is the prey and food of another. Thus the will everywhere preys upon itself and in different forms is its own nourishment.

From the lower forms of animal life, Schopenhauer turns to consider the higher levels at which instinct and impulse are somewhat modified by the emergence of intellect and knowledge.

From grade to grade, yet still without consciousness, as an obscure striving force, the will rises through matter and the vegetable kingdoms to the point at which the individuals in whom it is manifested can no longer receive food through mere movement following upon stimuli. The chances of the individual that is moved merely by stimuli would be too unfavorable. Its food must be sought out and selected. For this purpose movement following upon motive, and therefore consciousness, becomes necessary.

Consciousness, called in at this stage for the conservation of the individual, appears. It is represented by the brain, just as every other effort of the will is represented by an organ. With this new addition, the "world as idea" comes into existence at a stroke, with all its forms and categories, its subject and object, its time and space and causality and multiplicity. The world now shows its second side.

Till now mere will, it becomes now also idea, object to a knowing conscious subject. Up to this point the will followed its tendency in the dark with unerring certainty. But at this grade it kindles for itself a light as a means to an end, as an instrument needed to deal with the throng and complication of its prior manifestations; a need which would have accrued precisely to its highest manifestation.

The hitherto infallible certainty and regularity with which will worked in unorganized and vegetable matter, rested upon the fact that it alone was active in its original nature as blind impulse, as unconscious will, without interruption from a second and entirely different world, the world of perception. But with consciousness, its infallible certainty comes to an end. Animals are thereby exposed to deception and error. They have, however, only ideas arising out of perception. They have no conceptual powers, no reflective powers, and are therefore bound to the present.

This "knowledge without reason" becomes insufficient. When the will has attained to the highest grade of its objectification, the kind of knowledge which arises out of mere perception confined to what is immediately present to the senses, does not suffice. That complicated and many-sided imaginative being, man, with his many needs, exposed to innumerable dangers, must, if he is to exist, be lighted by a double knowledge. A higher power than mere perception must be given him.

With this new power of reasoning, of framing and using abstract conceptions, there has appeared reflection, surveying the past, anticipating the future, deliberation, care, premeditated action, and finally the full and distinct awareness of one's own deliberate volition as such.

With mere knowledge of perception there arose the possibility of illusion and error, by which the previous infallibility of the blind striving of the will was done away with. With the entrance of reasoning powers that certainty and infallibility are almost entirely lost. Instinct diminishes. Deliberation, supposed to supplant everything from physical causation to instinctive reaction, begets irresolution and uncertainty. Errors become widely possible, and in many cases obstruct the will in action.

Thus knowledge, rational as well as sensuous, proceeds originally from the will itself, belongs to the inner being of the higher grades of its objectification as an instrument of selection and adaptation, a means of supporting the individual and the species like any other organ. Destined to forward the aims of the will, it remains almost entirely subject to its service. It is so in all brutes and in almost all men.

In all grades of its manifestations, from the lowest inorganic forms to the highest organic forms, the will is controlled by no final goal or aim. It always strives, for striving is its sole nature which no attaining can put to an end. Therefore it is not capable of any final satisfaction, but only of obstruction. This endless striving, of the will-to-be, the will-to-live, the will-to-conquer, the will-to-reproduce, we see everywhere, and see hindered in many ways. Wherever blocked, we see suffering. So if there be no final aim and no final satisfaction, there are no measure and end of suffering.

We ask: For what purpose does all this torment and agony exist? There is only one consideration that may serve to explain. It is this: The will-to-live, which underlies the whole world of phenomena, must satisfy its cravings by feeding on itself. This it does by forming a graduated scale of phenomena in which one level exists at the expense of another. Note two animals, one of which is engaged in eating the other.

By now man's place in nature has been indicated. Two citations conclude this somewhat evolutionary account.

In the life of man all this appears with greatest distinctness, illumined by the clearest knowledge. As the manifestation of the will rises higher, the suffering becomes more apparent. In the plant there is no sensibility and therefore no pain. In the lowest forms of animal life, a small degree of suffering may be experienced. As the level rises, sensitivity becomes wider and deeper. It appears in a high degree with the complete nervous system of backboned animals, and increases as intelligence develops. Thus, as knowledge increases, as consciousness attains to greater distinctness, pain also increases, and reaches its highest degree in man. And the more intelligent and finely formed a man is, the more pain he is open to.

Every human being is only another short dream of that endless spirit of nature, the persistent will-to-live; only another fleeting form carelessly sketched on an infinite page, and obliterated to make room for new. And every one of these fleeting forms must be paid for with many deep and long-drawn sufferings, and finally with a relentless death. Do you wonder why the sight of a corpse is never funny?

From the vantage point of his metaphysical hypothesis Schopenhauer feels himself in a position to account for the futility, the restlessness, the unhappiness and boredom which mark human life. If mankind is nothing but an objectification of a blindly striving universal will, what else could be expected?

Man's appetites are insatiable. Every satisfaction he gets lays the seeds of some new desire. There is hence no end to the wishes of any individual will. Why is this? The reason is simple. Will is the lord of all worlds. Everything is but a manifestation of will. Therefore no one single thing can ever give it satisfaction. Only the totality of things—which is endless.

The basis of all willing and striving is need, deficiency, pain. Thus the nature of man is subject to pain originally and in its essence. If, on the other hand, it lacks objects of desire, a terrible void and boredom comes over it. Thus man's life swings like a pendulum, backwards and forwards, between uneasiness and boredom. (Hence, in his speculations, after man had transferred all pains to hell, there remained nothing over for heaven but boredom.)

Real boredom is by no means an evil to be lightly esteemed. In the end it depicts on the countenance a real despair. It makes beings who love each other so little as men do, seek each other eagerly. Like its opposite evil, famine in every form, it provokes us to elaborate precautions. People require *panem et circenses*—bread and circuses. As want is the constant scourge of the lower classes, boredom is the lash laid across the back of the fashionable world. In the great middle classes, boredom is represented by Sunday and want by the six weekdays.

Thus, between desiring and attaining, all human life flows on. The wish is, in its nature, uneasiness. The attainment soon begets satiety. The end was only apparent, and possession drives away the charm.

It should be added to this that satisfaction, or what is commonly called *happiness*, is never positive. It is not something original, growing out of itself, so to speak; but must always be the satisfaction of some wish or longing. The wish, the want, the need, the desire, these are the positive things; and these precede, condition, and follow every satisfaction.

The life of every individual, surveyed as a whole, is a tragedy. Here and there in detail, it may have the character of a comedy. The restless irritations of a moment, the needs and vexations of a day, the mishaps and fears of a week, are scenes in a comedy. But the overarching, never-satisfied wishes, the frustrated efforts, the crushed and abandoned hopes, the deep errors of a whole life, with increasing pain or boredom, and death at the close, are always a tragedy. As if the fates would add derision to the miseries of our existence, our life must contain all the ingredients of a tragedy while in detail it will have the foolish look of a comedy.

That happiness is not something positive, that it is merely the satisfaction of some want, to be followed by another or by ennui, finds support in art, that true mirror of the world and life. Every epic and dramatic poem can only represent struggle, effort, fight for happiness; never enduring and complete happiness. It conducts its heroes through a thousand difficulties and dangers to the goal. But, as soon as this is reached, the curtain falls, for now there remains nothing for it to do but show that what lured the hero on as happiness, materialized as disappointment.

Everyone who has awakened from the first dream of youth will realize, if his judgment is not paralyzed, that this world is the kingdom of chance and error, of folly and wickedness. Hence, everything better only struggles through with difficulty. What is noble and wise seldom attains to expression. The absurd and perverse in thought, the dull and tasteless in art, the wicked and deceitful in action, assert a real supremacy broken only by brief interruptions. In vain the sufferer calls on his gods for help. This irremediable evil is only the mirror of the will, of which himself is the objectification.

To me, optimism, when it is not merely the thoughtless verbalizing of those who have nothing but words under their low foreheads, is not merely absurd; it is wicked. It is a bitter mockery of the unspeakable misery of mankind. To me, as to the writers of the Gospels, the *world* and *evil* are almost synonymous terms.

Thus far Schopenhauer the metaphysician. Now Schopenhauer the moralist. The latter directs the argument from this point to its despairing conclusion. In our own day Thomas Hardy has expressed in poetry what Schopenhauer, up to this point, has been arguing in prose.

Given this view of things, what is Schopenhauer's message for mankind? It is one of pity and self-mortification. His argument turns to these matters, beginning with an explanation of the origin of humanity's pervasive egoism and selfishness, working around gradually to counsels of despair.

What I have been saying comes to this: In the whole of nature, at all the grades of the objectification of the will, there is a necessary and constant conflict, expressing the inner contradiction of the will with itself. This phenomenon exhibits itself with greater distinctness at the highest level of the will's objectification, namely in man. What I propose now is to trace to its source that egoism which is the starting point of all conflict.

The will everywhere manifests itself in separate individuals. But this sepa-

produces,
egoism

rateness does not concern the will as it is in itself. The will itself is present, whole and undivided, in every one of these—as the color red is present, whole and undivided, in any red object—and beholds around it the innumerably repeated images of its own nature. Therefore everyone desires everything for himself, and would destroy whatever would oppose it. Every individual feels himself the center of the world, has a primary and inextinguishable regard for his own existence and well-being.

This disposition, which I call *egoism*, is essential to everything in nature. It is by reason of this primary fact that the inner conflict of the will with itself attains such terrible proportions. Yet this egoism has its being and continuance in that opposition of the microcosm and the macrocosm, in the fact that the objectification of the will has individualization as its form, in the fact that it manifests itself in the same way in innumerable individuals. In the highest grade of consciousness all this appears in its sharpest form.

We see the consequences of this basic fact everywhere in human life, in small things and great. We see its terrible side in the lives of great tyrants and miscreants, and in world-desolating wars. We see its absurd side in conceit, vanity, and minor selfishness. We see it writ large in history, which is the record of struggles ranging from vast armies to pairs of human alley cats. We see it when any mob of men is set free from law and order and restraint. Then that "war of all against all" which Hobbes has described so admirably, shows itself. This is the highest expression of egoism.

This "primary and ineradicable egoism" is the fact upon which Schopenhauer proceeds to build a moral philosophy, an ethics of pity and despair.

Out of this primary and ineradicable egoism arise both misery and wickedness. Do we desire to know what men so constituted, are worth in moral terms? We have only to consider their fate as a race. This is want, wretchedness, affliction, misery, and death. There is a species of eternal justice in it all. In this sense the world is the judgment of the world. Could we lay the misery of the world in one scale of the balance, and the guilt of the world in the other, the needle would point to the center.

I referred to an eternal justice in the scheme of things. To him who has grasped in all of its ramifications the thought which I have been developing, this will be evident. The world, in all its parts, is the manifestation of one will. The will is free. The will is almighty. The world is its mirror. As the will is, so is the world. It alone bears the responsibility for what comes into being.

However, the world does not stand thus revealed to the knowledge of him whose mind is still bound to the service of his will, as it does to him who has risen to an entirely objective contemplation. The vision of the uncultured individual is clouded. He does not see the reality behind the phenomenon in time and space. He sees not the inner unity and identity of things, but only its separated, individualized, disunited, opposed, manifestations. For him pleasure is one thing and pain another. He sees one manifestation of the will live in abundance and ease, while at his door another dies of want and cold. He asks, "Where is Justice?"

But the vision of eternal justice is beyond him. He sees no inner connection. He sees the wicked flourish and the oppressed suffer. He cannot rise above these individual differences. Hence he does not understand the nature of this world's justice. That man only will grasp and comprehend eternal justice who raises himself above particular things, who sees through the individualizations of the real. He alone sees that the difference between him who inflicts suffering and him who bears it, is phenomenal only and concerns not the will as thing-in-itself. The inflicter of suffering and the sufferer are one. If the eyes of both were opened, the inflicter of suffering would see that he lives in all that suffers pain. The sufferer would see that all the wickedness in the world proceeds from that will which constitutes his own nature.

The comprehension of this eternal justice, of the tie that unites the evil of my crime with the evil of your misery, demands the power to rise above the limits of individuality. Therefore it will always remain unattainable by most men.

What I have been arguing is this: Hatred and wickedness are conditioned by egoism, and egoism rests on the entanglement of knowledge in the principle of individuation, in the fact that the will realizes itself in separate individuals.

If this penetration of the principle of individuation, this direct knowledge of the identity of the will in its diverse manifestations, is present in a high degree of distinctness, it will show an influence upon the will of the individual who has achieved this insight. If the veil is lifted from his eyes so that he no longer makes the egotistical distinction between his self and other selves, then he will regard the infinite suffering of all sufferers as his own.

To such a man no suffering is any longer strange. All the miseries of others work upon his mind like his own. It is no longer the changing joy and sorrow of his own person that he has in view. All lies equally near him. He knows the ultimately real, and finds that it consists in a constant passing away, a vain striving, an inward conflict, a continual suffering. Wherever he looks he sees suffering humanity and a world in passage. But all this now lies as near him as his own person lies to the man who is still in bondage to egoism.

The moralist, backed by the metaphysician, is now in a position to ask pointedly: Why should man, with this knowledge of ultimate reality, accept life on such terms? Why should man be a yea-sayer? Why not a nay-sayer?

Why should he, now, with this knowledge of ultimate reality, assert this very life through constant acts of will? Knowledge of the nature of the thing-in-itself becomes a quieter of the individual will. The individual will now turns away from life, now shudders at the pleasures in which it once recognized the assertion of life, now attains to voluntary renunciation, resignation, indifference, will-less-ness.   *give up trying*

If we compare life to a course which we must run, a path of red-hot coals with here and there a cool spot, then he who is still entangled in the egoistic delusion is consoled by the cool places and sets out to run the course. But he who sees through individualization to the one will which is identical in all is no longer susceptible to such consolation. He sees himself in all places at once, and withdraws. His will turns round, no longer asserts itself, but denies.

This denial of the will by an individual manifestation of it follows the recognition of the real nature of the thing-in-itself. It is the transition from virtue to asceticism. This is to say, when a man has once seen, it no longer suffices for him to love others as himself. There arises within him a horror of that will of which he is himself a manifestation.

Nothing but a manifestation of the will, the individual ceases now to will anything. His body he denies. His health he is indifferent to. His desires he ignores. He desires no gratification of any appetite in any form.

More concretely, what is meant by this exhortation to suppress and deny the will-to-live? Schopenhauer is clear enough about it all. Upon unhappy man he urges a program of chastity, asceticism, self-chastisement, and ultimate starvation:

Voluntary and complete chastity is the first step in asceticism, the first move in the denial of the will-to-live. It denies the assertion of the will which extends beyond the individual's own life. It gives assurance that the life of this body, the will whose manifestation it is, ceases.

Asceticism shows itself further in voluntary and intentional poverty; not only *per accidens* as when possessions are given away to mitigate the sufferings of others, but directly to serve as a constant mortification of the will, so that the satisfaction of desires, the sweet things of life, shall not rouse the will of which a penetrating self-knowledge has conceived a horror.

Asceticism extends further as humility and patience. He who denies the will as it appears in his own person will not resist if another does wrong to him. Suffering, insult, ignominy, he will receive gladly, as the opportunity of learning that he no longer stands behind his will. Patience and meekness will replace impatience and pride and anger.

Asceticism culminates in self-chastisement, fasting, and starvation. By constant privation and suffering he who has seen the nature and source of the evil of life in the will-to-live is able more and more to break down and destroy that manifestation in himself; to crush in himself that which he recognizes and abhors as the source of his own and humanity's misery and wickedness.

When death comes to such a one, it is most welcome. Here it is not, as in the case of others, merely the manifestation of the will that ends in death. The inner nature of the will has long been restrained, denied, crushed. The last slight bond is now broken. For him who ends thus, the world also ends.

With a backward glance over the whole argument of his metaphysics and moral philosophy, Schopenhauer concludes:

What I have described here with feeble tongue and only in general terms, is no philosophical fable. It is the moral of the life of saints and ascetics in all ages and all religions. The inner nature of holiness, self-renunciation, mortification, is here expressed, abstractly and free from mythology, as the denial of the will-to-live, appearing after the complete knowledge of its own nature has become a quieter of all volition.

Before us there is certainly only nothingness. We look with deep and painful longing upon the perfect calm of the spirit which has strangled and subdued the will-to-live. Beside it, the misery and evil of life is thrown into clear contrast. Yet, only when we have recognized the incurable suffering and endless wickedness which follows upon the assertion of the will, and have ordered our days to its denial, do we attain any lasting consolation. To those in whom the will has turned against itself, this world of planets, suns, and milky ways is nothing.

Note on Sources. The Schopenhauer material in this section is quoted, abridged, or paraphrased from his *World as Will and Idea*, especially Book IV; his Supplements to *The World as Will and Idea;* his *On the Will in Nature;* and his two volumes of miscellaneous essays, *Parerga and Paralipomena*—e.g., "On Women," "On Suicide," "On Pantheism," and so forth.

Reading References. In a book by R. A. Tsanoff, *The Nature of Evil,* will be found a good, brief account of Schopenhauer's life and thought. Tsanoff writes on a gallery of pessimists, but his tenth and eleventh chapters are on Schopenhauer alone. A book by V. J. McGill, *Schopenhauer: Pessimist and Pagan,* is a popular biographical study. There is an edition of Schopenhauer, by Will Durant, which contains good selections. There is a single-volume collection of essays, *Essays of Schopenhauer,* in which seven small volumes are bound in one. These are more easily read than the selections from *The World as Will and*

Idea. Much criticism of Schopenhauer is either narrowly technical, in which case the whole point of the man is somehow overlooked, or is so pious and horror-stricken that one feels that after all there must be something to what Schopenhauer says. An exception to this might be found in the "Pessimism" chapter of Paulen's *System of Ethics*. A valuable little book, *Thomas Hardy's Universe*, by Ernest Brennecke, will show the way in which Schopenhauer's metaphysics forms a basis upon which Hardy's poems, tales, and novels can be understood.

The following are some books published since 1940:

Adams, J. S. *The Aesthetics of Pessimism*.
Copleston, F. *Arthur Schopenhauer, Philosopher of Pessimism*.
Taylor, R. (ed.). *The Will to Live: Selected Writings of
                Arthur Schopenhauer*.

READING QUESTIONS

1. Berkeley died in 1753. Schopenhauer published in 1819. Just for the record, how much "public strife" marked the years between?
2. What point brings each of the following into the first long group of quotations from Schopenhauer: (a) Dante, (b) children in a theatre, (c) the two poles of human life, (d) the southern states, (e) Leibniz, (f) lovers, (g) Kant, (h) Ecclesiastes, (i) woman, (j) monogamy, (k) the bull-dog ant, (l) the wild dogs of Java, (m) Lisbon and Pompeii, (n) the Old Testament, (o) tragedy, (p) suicide, (q) two Chinamen.
3. Use the distinction between "manifested as" and "present in" to state Schopenhauer's metaphysical thesis.
4. Contrast his position with (a) materialism, (b) theism, (c) pantheism.
5. Why intellect succeeds instinct in the hierarchy of being. What happens to the world at that point? What is his "instrumentalist" theory of the intellect?
6. Between what alternatives human life swings. Why happiness is never positive. What he has to say about optimism.
7. What he means by "egoism" in relation to the will. In what sense egoism is an illusion. Illusory or not, however, what consequences follow from this egoism?
8. An all-pervading will. Manifested as separate individual persons. Hence misery and wickedness. Whence, then, the "eternal justice" of it?

9. How the recognition of the illusory character of egoism gives rise to morality. And then to asceticism. With what final outcome?
10. Why Schopenhauer's doctrine of the will is a fitting metaphysical prelude to the Age of Darwin, Marx, and Freud.
11. Wherein you find Schopenhauer (a) most (b) least convincing.

5. DOUBTS ABOUT METAPHYSICS —FROM A. J. AYER

From Schopenhauer to Ayer. The writers examined thus far in this topic claim to tell you about "reality" in contrast to "appearances." I have expressed this by saying that they work with the distinction between two "worlds," the real world and the everyday world. Once this distinction has been proposed, one is curious about the real world and about its relation to the everyday world. In a general way our authors aim to satisfy such curiosity. Hobbes tells you that the real world is matter; Berkeley, that it is spirit; Schopenhauer, that it is will. They would all agree that the real world "transcends" the everyday world; is, therefore, a "transcendent" or "transcendental" or "trans-empirical" world. Now, discourse about a real world, which transcends the everyday world, has a highly speculative ring to it. It will be a standing invitation to cautious persons to suspend judgment as to whether it is true or false. That is, traditional metaphysics has encountered skepticism, doubts about its truth, or doubts that you can settle whether it is true or false. In this respect metaphysics has been comparable to theology. Each has met with considerable skepticism. This is not to be wondered at. If you say, e.g., that the real world is spirit which is "manifested as" nature, and "present in" individual selves, you must not be surprised if people say "I doubt that" or "How do you know that?"

In our day, however, metaphysics has encountered more than skepticism. It has met with repudiation; and the repudiation has been based, not on the grounds that metaphysics is doubtable or doubtful, but on the grounds that it is meaningless. This is more radical than skepticism. It is one thing to say: "I doubt the truth of your claim. I am skeptical about it"; it is another to say "The question whether your claim is true or false, probable or improbable, does not arise, because your claim is meaningless." If a person utters what sounds like a meaningful statement, you might say "I doubt that"; but if you suspect that you were mistaken in thinking that it was a meaningful statement, that, in fact, it was so much meaningless jargon, you would not say "I doubt that." You would say, "Talk sense if you want me to believe or doubt or deny what you say."

This is to go beyond skepticism. The thesis "Metaphysical statements are meaningless" is more radical than the thesis "Metaphysical statements are doubtable, or doubtful, or false." This is not itself metaphysics. It is a thesis about metaphysics. Let us refer to it as anti-metaphysics. The anti-metaphysician does not have doubts *in* metaphysics. He has doubts *about* metaphysics.

Biographical Note. Alfred Jules Ayer was born in 1910. He was educated at Eton and Oxford. For fourteen years (1932–46) he held teaching, research, and administrative positions in Oxford colleges. For thirteen years (1946–1959) he was Grote Professor in philosophy in the University of London. In 1959 he was appointed Wykeham Professor of philosophy in Oxford University. His best known book, proposing an extended critique of metaphysics and related modes of thinking, was published in 1936. Professor Ayer has done as much as anyone to secure a wide and sympathetic hearing for anti-metaphysics in the English-speaking world. He writes with clarity and vigour and great personal conviction. This makes him interesting and persuasive. "He that is not with me is against me" sounds through his lively pages. His writings have done more than stimulate; they have challenged. Many persons relish metaphysics. Professor Ayer has given them a bad conscience, or stirred them to indignation. This was all to the good. It made the years between the two world wars memorable. One of the great debates in philosophy was metaphysics versus anti-metaphysics. Ayer's book, *Language, Truth and Logic,* and Collingwood's book, *An Essay on Metaphysics,* are excellent handlings, pro and con, of this issue.

Ayer's Anti-Metaphysics. Professor Ayer has published several books and a great number of papers. His doubts about metaphysics, his campaign against it, will be found in many of these. But two items in particular let you in on the argument—namely, "Demonstration of the Impossibility of Metaphysics," published in 1934 in the English philosophical journal *Mind;* and "The Elimination of Metaphysics," published in 1936 as Chapter I of his book, *Language, Truth and Logic.* These, you might say, are anti-metaphysics in the grand manner. As the titles indicate, Professor Ayer does not pull his philosophical punches.

His purpose is the same in both papers, namely to evict metaphysics from the mansion of philosophy. The 1934 paper aims to demonstrate that metaphysics is impossible. The 1936 paper aims to eliminate metaphysics. In either case, whether eliminated or shown to be impossible, metaphysics is in for a rough time.

He proposes to achieve this purpose by showing that metaphysics is meaningless. This will show that it is impossible. Now, how do you show that discourse is meaningless? Professor Ayer suggests that you need a criterion of meaning, of meaningfulness. This will enable you to settle the question. If discourse satisfies the criterion, then it is meaningful; if not, then not. What then is the criterion of meaning? How do you get at it? Professor Ayer outlines a procedure.

First, you take cases which everyone agrees are meaningful, and cases which everyone agrees are meaningless. These are "given," that is, you do not choose them by having the criterion of meaning and finding that they do or do not satisfy it. You get them first. Then you ask what it is the meaningful statements have in common, by virtue of which they are meaningful; and what it is the meaningless statements lack, by virtue of which they are meaningless. This gives you the criterion of meaning. An analogy might help. Suppose you want the criterion of rightness, satisfying which you judge an act right. You take cases which everyone agrees are right, and cases which everyone agrees are wrong. These are "given"; that is, you do not choose them by having a criterion of rightness and finding that they do or do not satisfy it. You get them first. Then you ask what it is the right acts have in common, by virtue of which they are right; and what it is the wrong acts lack, by virtue of which they are wrong. This gives you the criterion of rightness. You would proceed similarly if you wanted to get at the criterion for judging whether something is or is not a work of art. It seems to me that this is sound procedure. It insists that you know what it is you are talking about before you begin to philosophize about it.

Thus far, then, you have statements whose meaningfulness is not doubtful, statements whose meaninglessness is not doubtful, and the criterion of meaning which the first cases satisfy and the second cases do not. At this point you consider what Professor Ayer calls "doubtful" cases. These would be statements about which you would not be sure, at first glance, whether they were meaningful or meaningless. You apply your criterion to these cases. If they fail to satisfy it, they are meaningless, nonsensical; and out they go. (See *Mind*, p. 345, Vol. 43, 1934.)

So much for procedure. When Professor Ayer followed this procedure, what criterion of meaning did he arrive at? Having ascertained it, he gave it a name: the Verifiability Criterion of Meaning. But we need more than the name. What is the criterion so designated? Here the going is more difficult. Professor Ayer spends many pages in an attempt to find words which will enable him to state the criterion satisfactorily. We will not follow him through the details of this search.

Metaphysics + discussion is meaningless

②

statements
(1) empirical
(2) analytic
or
tautological

Perhaps this will suffice: he discovers that all unquestionably mean-ingful statements may be divided into two groups. The first consists of those statements which you would verify or refute by an ~~appeal~~ to ex-perience, an appeal to "observation statements." This verification or refu-tation would be either direct or indirect. For example, "My neighbor's house is colored green" would be verified directly, by confronting the statement with the experienced fact of the green color of the house. How-ever, "There was a tree there before he cut it down and built his house where the tree stood," or "There are mountains on the far side of the moon," could not be verified directly. The tree is no longer there; and you can't see the other side of the moon. Direct confrontation of statement with experienced fact is not possible. In such cases you show that the statements about the tree and the mountains can be *inferred* from some *other* statements which can be verified directly. In this way the statements about the tree and the mountains are said to be verified indirectly.

To put all this negatively, you would not satisfy yourself of their truth or falsity, probability or improbability, by merely reflecting on their meaning. Their truth or falsity does not stare up at you from their meaning alone. If I say "There are mountains on the far side of the moon," you do not verify or refute my statement by merely reflecting on its meaning. From a knowledge of its meaning alone you do not get a knowl-edge of its truth or falsity. Evidence for such statements is not obtained by reflecting on their meaning. This is sometimes expressed in popular speech by saying that they are not their own evidence, are not "self-evident." Professor Ayer calls such statements "empirical." Empirical statements are those which can be verified or refuted either directly or indirectly by an appeal to experience.

The second group stands in sharp contrast. It consists of those state-ments which you would verify or refute by an appeal to their meaning alone. You would see that they were true or false by reflecting on their meaning. Nothing further would be relevant. To put it negatively, you would not settle their truth or falsity by an appeal, direct or indirect, to any "observation statements." If I say "All fathers are parents," or "All circles have equal radii," you do not "check" on these statements by in-vestigating examples of fathers or circles. You reflect on the meaning of what is said and that settles it. From a knowledge of their meaning alone you can arrive at a knowledge of their truth or falsity. Here "evidence" is obtained by reflecting on their meaning. This is sometimes expressed in popular speech by saying that they are, or contain, their own evidence, are "self-evident." Professor Ayer calls such statements "tautologies," or "analytic."

His claim is that all unquestionably meaningful statements are either empirical or tautological, empirical or analytic. The basis for this division is the way in which you would go about to verify or refute them. If they are meaningful, they are verifiable or refutable in either of the two ways explained above; and conversely, if they are verifiable or refutable in either of those two ways, they are meaningful. Since Professor Ayer concedes no third way in which any meaningful statement can be verified or refuted, he speaks of their verifiability, or the mode of their verifiability, as the criterion of their meaningfulness. Further, it will be found that no unquestionably meaningless statement can be verified or refuted in either of these two ways; and, conversely, that any statement that cannot be verified or refuted in either of these two ways, is unquestionably meaningless. This is the Verifiability Criterion of Meaning, and its derivation from admittedly meaningful and meaningless statements. As suggested above, it might as a theory in semantics, be compared, *mutatis mutandis*, to a theory in ethics, for example the Utility Criterion of Rightness, and its derivation from admittedly right and wrong acts.

At this point the argument, now possessed of a criterion of meaning, turns from admittedly meaningful and meaningless statements to doubtful cases. Their fate is to be settled by seeing whether they satisfy the Verifiability Criterion of Meaning in either of its modes; that is, by seeing whether they are empirical or tautological. Professor Ayer closes in on metaphysics. Give him any statement from metaphysics and he puts it to the question: Is it empirical or tautological? Is its claim to be true directly or indirectly, supported or supportable by any fact of experience? Is it claimed to be true because self-evident, true by virtue of its meaning alone? If so, either way, it is meaningful; if not, it is meaningless.

Once the chips are down, Professor Ayer extends no quarter. The stakes are high and he plays for keeps. His purpose is to exhibit the bankruptcy of traditional metaphysics, to remove metaphysics from philosophy. One metaphysical claim after another is audited and declared bankrupt. This is his "demonstration that metaphysics is impossible," his "elimination of metaphysics" from philosophy. If any so-called metaphysical claim satisfies the criterion, that is, makes sense, is found to be meaningful, it is not declared bankrupt but it is ordered out of philosophy on the grounds that it belongs in some empirical science or in mathematics or in formal logic. By the time Professor Ayer is finished he has, by one or the other of these arguments, emptied philosophy of metaphysics. It is thrown out either on the grounds that it is meaningless or on the grounds that it is not philosophy.

Professor Ayer did not stop at metaphysics. He used the same criterion and the same argument to demonstrate the impossibility, the semantic bankruptcy, of theology, ethics, aesthetics, and much traditional philosophical psychology. As with metaphysics, their claims were tested, found meaningless, and thrown out of philosophy; or found meaningful, therefore empirical or analytic, and declared part of some inductive or deductive science. Their traditional problems and propositions were written off as pseudo-problems and pseudo-propositions, which hustled them into bankruptcy; or they were unmasked as bonafide scientific problems and propositions masquerading as philosophy. In either case they were eliminated from philosophy. All that was left was semantics and logic. Semantics stayed because the Verifiability Criterion of Meaning was needed to initiate these evictions. Logic stayed because its propositions were found to be analytic and hence meaningful.

It seems to me that anyone who has the interests of philosophy at heart will feel grateful to Professor Ayer and the "logical positivists." At least they stirred things up. They made a bonfire of much old lumber. They thinned out the traffic in vague, obscure, and pretentious thinking. They forced those interested in philosophy to put up or shut up. And these things were all to the good.

It would be misleading to suggest that Professor Ayer and the friends of "logical positivism" had things all their own way. In these matters it is possible to win the battles and yet lose the war. The attack raised some valuable questions.

(1) Consider, for example, the procedure, described by Professor Ayer in his 1934 paper, for arriving at criteria, in his case the criterion of meaning. You start with positive and negative cases agreed to without benefit of the criterion. Everything hinges on that. This places a premium on knowing what you are talking about before beginning to philosophize about it. If there is serious disagreement about the cases, there is no way to derive the criterion. And you cannot use the criterion to enforce agreement about the cases. If there is serious disagreement about the cases, all you can do is establish "party lines." You cannot arrive at a knowledge of the criterion that would enable you to rise above such party lines. What is the status of this knowledge which precedes the derivation of the criterion? Is it "above the battle?"

(2) Again, consider the statement of a criterion once it has been ar-

rived at. Let it be the criterion of meaning: "a proposition is meaningful, if and only if . . ." and finish it any way you have to. The completed statement is itself meaningful. No one would want it that a statement of the criterion of meaning was itself meaningless. Therefore the statement itself is either empirical or tautological. If it is empirical, then it does not belong in philosophy, but in some empirical science. If it is a tautology ("all fathers are parents," "all circles have equal radii," and so on) then it is "true by definition," to use one of Professor Ayer's expressions. But what is the status of definitions? If they are "arbitrary," you cannot use them to enforce agreement. If they are not arbitrary, what constrains them? [2]

(3) One of Professor Ayer's older contemporaries, Professor G. E. Moore, had argued in his *Principia Ethica* that the basic concept in ethics, "good," is indefinable. There is no logically prior concept which you can use to arrive at a definition of "good." Given "good" as indefinable you can use it to define other ethical concepts, for example, right. Now you have here the notion of a basic concept and the thesis that it is indefinable. Does this apply in semantics? If not, why not? If so, is it indefinable? If not, why not? If so, can you use the criterion of meaning, as Professor Ayer proposes, to arrive at a definition of meaning? If so, the "structural analogy" between ethics and semantics does not hold. If not, what is the distinction between and relation between a criterion and a definition?

(4) Professor Ayer's elimination of metaphysics requires that metaphysical statements be subject to verification; that the notion of verification should apply to them; and that if it doesn't, the trouble lies with metaphysical statements and not with verification. This is to say that every meaningful statement is either empirical or tautological. Is this true? Are there no meaningful statements which are neither empirical nor tautological? How about the statement itself? How about such statements as the following: (a) Every proposition is either true or false. (b) No true proposition is inconsistent with any other true proposition. (c) Every event has a cause. (d) Miracles never happen. (e) Same cause, same effect.

---

[2] The friends of the Verifiability Criterion of Meaning have sought to side-step this objection by saying that the verbal formulation of the criterion is itself not a statement, not a proposition, therefore neither true nor false. Instead, they say it is a "proposal" or an "imperative." You don't verify or refute proposals or commands; you act on them or refuse to act on them. Therefore they are not amenable, not answerable, to the Verifiability Criterion of Meaning. They are not meaningful by virtue of satisfying it. It applies only to statements, propositions. However, proposals, commands, petitions, imperatives and the like *are* meaningful. So, this postpones the agony by leaving unsettled the question of the criterion by which proposals, and so on, are to be declared meaningful or meaningless.

(f) Matter does not cease to exist. (g) No surface is both red all over and green all over. (h) Change occurs according to law. (i) In the last analysis you always do what you want to do. (j) Space and time are infinite. (k) I ought to implies I can. (l) If nothing is necessary, then nothing is probable. (m) A liar and a thief ought to change his ways (n) If H_1 accounts for more facts than any other H, then it is probably true.

(5) Verifying and refuting are activities. Are there any principles and presuppositions operative in these activities? If not, why not? If so, then their status is crucial. They make these activities possible. Remove them, and the activities do not get under way. Now, assuming that there are such principles and presuppositions, are they subject to the Verifiability Criterion of Meaning? Are they either empirical or tautological? If so, there is no problem. But suppose they are neither empirical nor tautological. Then the Verifiability Criterion does not cover them. Are they, then, meaningless? Must one say that principles and presuppositions which are operative in "getting to know," in verifying and refuting, are themselves meaningless? The alternative would be to say that they are meaningful, but that in their case some *other* criterion of meaning is involved. Now (a) What is this other criterion? (b) If there is *this* exception to the Verifiability Criterion, can we be sure that there are no other exceptions? How?

Consider this second alternative further. It opens up the possibility that there are principles and presuppositions operating in knowing, proving, refuting, which are not themselves candidates for verification. They make verification possible. Therefore the question "Can they themselves be verified?" does not arise. What principles and presuppositions are thus operative in the activities called getting to know, verifying, refuting, and the like? Let the job of metaphysics be to run them down. Call them "ultimate" or "absolute" to indicate the difference between their status and the status of the empirical statements whose discovery or verification or refutation they make possible. They are operative in verifications, but are not themselves verifiable. They enter into the verification of empirical statements but are themselves not open to verification. Then you could say that the task of metaphysics is to ascertain the "ultimate" or "absolute" principles and presuppositions of empirical knowledge. And metaphysics would be back in business again.

The following passage is quoted from Professor Ayer's article "Demonstration of the Impossibility of Metaphysics":

The views expressed in this paper are not original. The work of Wittgenstein inspired it. The arguments which it contains are for the most part such as have been used by writers in *Erkenntnis*, notably by Moritz Schlick in his *Positivismus und Realismus* and Rudolf Carnap in his *Überwindung der Metaphysik durch logische Analyse der Sprache*. But some may find my presentation of them the clearer. And I hope to convince others by whom the work of Wittgenstein and the Viennese school has so far been ignored or misunderstood.

DEFINITION OF METAPHYSICS

My purpose is to prove that any attempt to describe the nature or even to assert the existence of something lying beyond the reach of empirical observation must consist in the enunciation of pseudo-propositions, a pseudo-proposition being a series of words that may seem to have the structure of a sentence but is in fact meaningless. I call this a demonstration of the impossibility of metaphysics because I define a metaphysical enquiry as an enquiry into the nature of the reality underlying or transcending the phenomena which the special sciences are content to study. Accordingly if I succeed in showing that even to ask whether there is a reality underlying the world of phenomena is to formulate a bogus question, so that any assertion about the existence or nature of such a reality is a piece of nonsense, I shall have demonstrated the impossibility of metaphysics in the sense in which I am using the term. If anyone considers this an arbitrary definition, let him refer to any work which he would call metaphysical, and consider how it differs from an enquiry in one of the special sciences. He will find, not that the authors are merely using different means to derive from the same empirical premises the same sort of knowledge, but that they are seeking totally different types of knowledge. The metaphysician is concerned with a reality transcending the phenomena about which the scientist makes his generalisations. The metaphysician rejects the methods of the scientist, not because he believes them to be unfruitful in the field in which the scientist operates, but because he believes that by his own metaphysical methods he will be able to obtain knowledge in his own metaphysical field. It will be shown in this paper not that the metaphysician ought to use scientific methods to attain his end, but that the end itself is vain. Whatever form of reasoning he employs, he succeeds in saying nothing.

COMPARISON WITH KANT'S PROCEDURE

That the speculative reason falls into self-contradiction when it ventures out beyond the limits of experience is a proposition maintained by Kant. But by his formulation of the matter he is committed to a view different from that which will here be maintained. For he implies that there is a transcendent reality, but the constitution of our speculative reason is such that we cannot hope to gain knowledge of it: he should therefore find no absurdity in imagining that some other being, say a god, had knowledge of it, even though the

existence of such a being could not be proved. Whereas on our view to say
that there is or that there is not a transcendent reality is to utter a pseudo-
proposition, a word-series empty of logical content: and no supposition about
the knowledge of a higher reality possessed by a higher being is for us even
a significant hypothesis. The difference between the two views is best expressed by saying that while Kant attempted to show that there were certain
problems which the speculative reason was in virtue of its own nature incapable of solving, our aim is to show that these are not genuine problems.

No criticism of Kant's transcendental philosophy will be undertaken in
this paper. But the method by which we demonstrate the impossibility of
metaphysics, in the sense in which Kant too held it to be impossible, serves
also to show that no knowledge is both synthetic and *a priori*. And this is
enough to prove the impossibility of metaphysics, in the special sense which
Kant reserved for the term, though it in no way discredits the excellent pieces
of philosophical analysis which the *Critique of Pure Reason* contains.

FORMULATION OF A CRITERION OF SIGNIFICANCE

The method of achieving these results lies in the provision of a criterion
by which the genuineness of all *prima facie* propositions may be tested. Having laid down the conditions which must be fulfilled by whatever is to be
a significant proposition, we shall find that the propositions of metaphysics fail
to satisfy the conditions and are therefore meaningless.

What is it, then, that we are asking when we ask what is the meaning
of a proposition? I say "ask the meaning of a proposition" rather than "ask
the meaning of a concept," because questions about the meaning of concepts
reduce themselves to questions about the meanings of propositions. To discover the meaning of a concept we form its corresponding primary proposition, i.e., the simplest proposition in which it can significantly occur, and
attempt to analyse this. I repeat "what is it that we are asking when we ask
what is the meaning of a proposition?" There are various ways in which the
correct answer can be formulated. One is to say that we are asking what are
the propositions to which the proposition in question is reducible. For instance, if "being an amphisbæna" means "being a serpent with a head at
both ends," then the proposition "X is an amphisbæna" is reducible to (or
derivable from) the propositions "X is a serpent" and "X has a head at either
end of its body." These propositions are in turn reducible to others until we
reach the elementary propositions which are not descriptive at all but os-
tensive. When the analysis reaches its furthest point the meaning of the
proposition can no longer be defined in terms of other propositions but only
pointed to or shown. It is to this process that those philosophers refer who
say that philosophy is an activity and not a doctrine.

Alternatively the procedure of definition may be described by saying that to give the meaning of a proposition is to give the conditions under which it would be true and those under which it would be false. I understand a proposition if I know what observations I must make in order to establish its truth or falsity. This may be more succinctly expressed by saying that I understand a proposition when I know what facts would verify it. To indicate the situation which verifies a proposition is to indicate what the proposition means.

APPLICATION OF THE CRITERION

Let us assume that some one says of my cat that it is corylous. I fail to understand him and enquire what circumstances would make it true to say that the cat was corylous. He replies "its having blue eyes". I conclude that in the sense in which he uses the word corylous "X is corylous" means "X has blue eyes". If he says that, although the fact that my cat has blue eyes and no other fact makes it true to say that it is corylous, nevertheless he means by "corylous" something more than "blue-eyed," we may infer that the use of the word "corylous" has for him a certain emotional value which is absent when he merely says "blue-eyed". But so long as its having blue eyes is all that is necessary to establish the truth of the proposition that something is corylous, and its having eyes of another colour all that is necessary to establish its falsehood, then "having blue eyes" is all that "being corylous" means.

In the case when something is called corylous and no description or indication can be given of the situation which verifies the proposition, we must conclude that the assertion is meaningless. If the speaker protests that he does mean something, but nothing that mere observation can establish, we allow that he has certain feelings which are in some way connected with the emission of the sound "corylous": and it may be a matter of interest to us that he should express these feelings. But he does not thereby make any assertion about the world. He utters a succession of words, but they do not form a genuine proposition. His sentence may provide good evidence of his feelings. In itself it has no sense.

So in every case where we have a series of words which seems to be a good grammatical sentence, and we wish to discover whether it really makes sense—i.e., whether it expresses a genuine proposition—we must consider what are the circumstances in which the proposition apparently expressed would be called true or false: what difference in the world its truth or falsity would entail. And if those who have uttered it or profess to understand it are unable to describe what in the world would be different if it were true or false, or in any way to show how it could be verified, then we must conclude that nothing has been asserted. The series of words in question does not express a genuine proposition at all, but is as much a piece of nonsense as "the moon is the square root of three" or "Lenin or coffee how". The difference is merely that in some cases where a very slight transformation of the phrase, say the alteration of a single word, would turn it into a propositional sign, its senselessness is harder to detect.

MEANINGLESS OF EVERY METAPHYSICAL ASSERTION

In this way it can quickly be shown that any metaphysical assertion is nonsensical. It is not necessary to take a list of metaphysical terms such as the Absolute, the Unconditioned, the Ego, and so forth, and prove each of them to be meaningless: for it follows from the task metaphysics sets itself that all its assertions must be nonsense. For it is the aim of metaphysics to describe a reality lying beyond experience, and therefore any proposition which would be verified by empirical observation is *ipso facto* not metaphysical. But what no observation could verify is not a proposition. The fundamental postulate of metaphysics "There is a super- (or hinter-) phenomenal reality" is itself not a proposition. For there is no observation or series of observations we could conceivably make by which its truth or falsehood would be determined. It may seem to be a proposition, having the sensible form of a proposition. But nothing is asserted by it.

An example may make this clearer. The old conflict between Idealism and Realism is a fine instance of an illusory problem. Let us assume that a picture is unearthed, and that the finder suggests that it was painted by Goya. There are definite means of settling this question. The critics examine the picture and consider what points of resemblance it has to other works of Goya. They see if there is any contemporary or subsequent reference to the existence of such a work—and so on. Suppose now that two of the experts have also read philosophy and raise a further point of dispute. One says that the picture is a collection of ideas (his own or God's): the other that its colours are objectively real. What possible means have they of settling this question? Can either of them indicate any circumstances in which to the question "are those colours a collection of ideas?" or to the question "are those colours objective sensibilia?" the answer "yes" or "no" could be given? If they cannot then no such questions arise. And plainly they cannot. If it is raining now outside my window my observations are different from what they would be if it were fine. I assert that it rains and my proposition is verifiable. I can indicate the situation by which its truth or falsity is established. But if I ask "is the rain real or ideal?" this is a question which no observations enable me to answer. It is accordingly not a genuine question at all.

It is advisable here to remove a possible source of misunderstanding. I am not maintaining that if we wish to discover whether in a *prima facie* proposition anything is really being asserted, we must consider whether what seems to be asserted is practically verifiable. As Professor Schlick has pointed out, it makes perfectly good sense to say "there is a mountain 10,000 feet high on the other side of the moon," although this is a proposition which through practical disabilities we are not and may never be in a position to verify. But it is in principle verifiable. We know what sort of observations would verify or falsify it. If we got to the other side of the moon we should know how to settle the question. But the assertions of metaphysics are in principle unverifiable. We may take up any position in space and time that our imagination allows us to occupy, no observation that we can make therefrom makes it even probable in the least degree that any answer to a metaphysical question is correct. And therefore we conclude that there are no such questions.

METAPHYSICAL ASSERTIONS NOT HYPOTHESES

So the conclusion is not that metaphysical assertions are uncertain or arbitrary or even false, but they are nonsensical. They are not hypotheses, in the sense in which general propositions of law are hypotheses. It is true that assertions of such general propositions are not assertions of fact in the way that assertions of singular propositions are assertions of fact. To that extent they are in no better case than metaphysical assertions. But variable hypotheticals (general propositions of law) make sense in a way in which metaphysical assertions do not. For a hypothesis has grounds. A certain sequence of events occurs and a hypothesis is formulated to account for it—i.e., on the strength of the hypothesis, when we make one such observation, we assume that we shall be able to make the others. It is the essence of a hypothesis that it admits of being used. In fact, the meaning of such general propositions is defined by reference to the situations in which they serve as rules for prediction, just as their truth is defined by reference to the accuracy of the predictions to which believing them gives rise. A so-called hypothesis which is not relevant to any situation is not a hypothesis at all. As a general proposition it is senseless. Now there is no situation in which belief in a metaphysical proposition bridges past and potential observations, in the way in which my belief in the poisonousness of arsenic connects my observation of a man's swallowing it with my expectation that he will shortly die. Therefore metaphysical propositions are not hypotheses. For they account for nothing.

READING QUESTIONS

1. Use Descartes or Hobbes or Berkeley or Schopenhauer, to illustrate what it is about traditional metaphysics that invites skepticism.
2. What is a "criterion of meaning"? Why Professor Ayer is interested

in formulating one. How he goes about to do so. What criterion of meaning resulted.

3. Elucidate the phrase: "The Verifiability Theory of Meaning." In what sense is it, as a theory in semantics, comparable to a theory in ethics, e.g., Utilitarianism?

4. How would you distinguish between these two statements: (a) Every father is a parent. (b) Every father is happy.

5. How Professor Ayer uses the Verifiability Theory of Meaning, a doctrine in semantics, to eliminate all doctrines in metaphysics.

6. Point here: "If there is disagreement about the cases."

7. Point here: "The statement itself is either empirical or tautological."

8. Point here: "A basic concept and the thesis that it is indefinable."

9. Point of the (a–n) statements on pages 161–162.

10. Point here: The status of principles and presuppositions operative in such activities as getting to know, verifying, refuting, and so on.

11. How the demand that metaphysical statements be confirmable leads to Professor Collingwood's notion of pseudo-metaphysics (v. pages 253–254).

12. Point of Professor Ayer's contrast between himself and Kant.

13. Professor Ayer: "Metaphysical Assertions (are) not Hypotheses." (a) Why not? (b) What then are they?

14. Wherein you find Professor Ayer (a) most (b) least convincing.

TOPIC THREE

An Epistemological Problem

THE PROBLEM STATED

The word *epistemology* is derived from two Greek words meaning "knowledge" and "the rationale of." It means an inquiry into the nature of knowledge. If the intention were carried out, it would provide us with knowledge of the nature of knowledge. In the conception of epistemology, knowledge turns in upon itself and seeks to formulate a "theory" of itself. Here knowledge is itself made the object of investigation. How did philosophers find themselves involved in such an inquiry?

From an acquaintance with the theological and metaphysical speculations which comprise the first two divisions of this book, one can see in a general way how epistemology came about. There is a cautious turn of mind to which all such speculations seem to be of doubtful value. Such a mind is impressed finally with the futility of such matters, and with the confusion which emerges when men seek to clarify their beliefs about such things. Out of this attitude toward speculation, two widely different things have resulted. There have come, in the first place, the genial and undisciplined doubts of such persons as Montaigne and Anatole France. Here the procedure is largely one of banter and ridicule. But that has not been the doubter's only defense against the speculator. For, in the second place, there has come the demand that flights of speculation be put aside until a preliminary inquiry is made into the nature of knowledge itself, and the question faced: Can it be shown, from an analysis of the nature of knowledge itself, whether such speculations are legitimate, whether they lie within the actual or possible grasp of the mind?

The chapters that follow may, therefore, be considered as approaches to a single problem: Can we make an inquiry into the nature of knowledge? From the findings of such an inquiry can we say anything about the scope or reach of knowledge? Can we show that some speculations carry the quest for knowledge beyond a legitimate possibility?

The authors chosen for consideration are John Locke, from the seventeenth century; David Hume and Immanuel Kant, from the eighteenth century; Auguste Comte, from the nineteenth century; and Hans Vaihinger and R. G. Collingwood, from the twentieth century.

1. THE APPEAL TO EXPERIENCE —FROM JOHN LOCKE

Empiricist

Epistemology is by no means a modern inquiry. Indeed, one of the finest pieces of epistemological analysis ever written may be found in Plato's dialogue "The Theaetetus"; but not all of Plato was continuously read by the generations which came after him, with the result that much that appeared in the early modern centuries was taken to be new. It is in this sense that John Locke is described as the founder of modern epistemology. Questions of priority aside, however, there is no reasonable doubt that the enormous literature which has grown up around this problem owes its inspiration, directly or indirectly, to Locke's epoch-making *Essay Concerning Human Understanding*. This famous old book is long, wordy, and repetitious, but its historical importance is great, for it drew attention, from the year it was published, to the central place in all philosophy of the problem of knowledge. What it said, in so many words, was this: Before any man launches into speculation, he should pause to inquire concerning the human understanding itself. What things is it capable of knowing? How does knowledge arise? Are there not some questions the answers to which lie beyond the reach of human understanding? Would not a cool hour spent in a reflective consideration of the nature of knowledge reveal this?

Biographical Note. John Locke was born in England in 1632 and died in 1704 at the age of seventy-two. His life may be divided into three periods: years of education and educating, years of politics and governmental affairs, years of authorship. (1) He was educated at Westminster School and at Oxford University. After graduation he was made lecturer on Greek, and two years later, lecturer on rhetoric. While still a student, he had turned from the ancient and medieval authors and doctrines which then formed the basis of a university education. From Aristotle and the medieval schoolmen, for example, he felt drawn to Hobbes, Descartes, Bacon, and the new experimental sciences. These were the molders of progressive opinion in his day. (2) In 1664 he left his work at the university and accepted the post of secretary to an Embassy to Brandenburg. This was the beginning of a long political and governmental career. The great political event of the times was the "bloodless" revolution of 1688. Locke allied himself, through the house of Shaftesbury, with the party which was to engineer the deposition of King James II and the invitation to King William of Holland. (3) The revolution took place in 1688. Thereafter John Locke shared the prestige which attached to those who were instrumental in bringing it about. He was now a man of fifty-six, widely read, widely traveled, widely respected. He turned to publishing a series of treatises which gave expression to the ideas and aspirations of British liberalism in education, politics, religion, and philosophy. He had been writing these books for many years, but had not thus far ventured to publish. Now in rapid succession he issued *Letters Concerning Toleration, Essay Concerning Human Understanding, Two Treatises of Government, Some Thoughts Concerning Education,* and *The Reasonableness of Christianity.* These volumes were published between 1689 and 1695. In six years, near the close of his life, Locke produced books which influenced liberal thought for the next century.

The Argument of the Citations. The citations which follow pose the modern problem of knowledge. They do not solve it, but they point to the need for a solution, and they express the spirit in which this inquiry has been carried on. Locke, like Descartes before him, begins by explaining why an inquiry concerning human understanding is important. He then asks the primary question: How does the human mind come by its knowledge? He pauses to state and refute one answer to this question current in his century, the hypothesis of innate ideas. He returns then to propound his own thesis: All knowledge comes from experience. This is known in philosophy as *empiricism.* He elaborates this claim in some detail. From the question of the origin of knowledge, he turns to the question of its limits. If knowledge arises in experience, how far can it reach? He distinguishes, to begin with, between intuitive and demonstrative knowledge. This suggests a further distinction between demonstrative and probable knowledge. With these distinctions made, Locke's theory of knowledge is complete; however, there were some who talked of a kind of knowledge, namely, *revelation,* which appeared not to fall anywhere within his scheme. His argument closes with some reflections on revelation and its relation to knowledge obtained through experience.

The argument begins with a series of reflections on the value of an inquiry into the nature of mind and knowledge:

Since it is the understanding that sets man above the rest of sensible beings, and gives him all the advantage and dominion which he has over them, it is certainly a subject, even for its nobleness, worth our labor to inquire into.

This therefore is my purpose: to inquire into the original, certainty, and extent of human knowledge, together with the degrees of belief, opinion, and assent. It is worth while to search out the bounds between opinion and knowledge, and examine by what measures in things, whereof we have no certain knowledge, we ought to regulate our assent and moderate our persuasions.

If I can discover the powers of the understanding, how far they reach, to what things they are in any degree proportionate, and where they fail us, I suppose it may prevail with the busy mind of man to be more cautious in meddling with things exceeding its comprehension; to stop when it is at the utmost extent of its tether; and to sit down in a quiet ignorance of those things which, upon examination, are found to be beyond the reach of our capacities.

I shall imagine I have not wholly misemployed myself, if, in this historical, plain method, I can give any account of the ways whereby our understandings come to attain those notions of things we have, and can set down any measures of the certainty of our knowledge, or the grounds of those persuasions which are to be found among men, so various, different, and wholly contradictory.

We should not then perhaps be so forward, out of an affectation of an universal knowledge, to raise questions and perplex ourselves and others with disputes about things to which our understandings are not suited, and of which we cannot frame in our minds any clear or distinct perceptions, or whereof we have not any notion at all.

If we can find out how far the understanding can extend its view, how far it has faculties to attain certainty, and in what cases it can only judge and guess, we may learn to content ourselves with what is attainable by us in this state.

When we know our own strength, we shall the better know what to undertake with hopes of success. When we have well surveyed the powers of our own mind, and made some estimate of what we may expect from them, we shall not be inclined either to sit still and not set our thoughts on work at all, in despair of knowing anything; or, on the other side, question everything and disclaim all knowledge because some things are not to be understood.

It is of great use to the sailor to know the length of his line, though he cannot fathom all the depths of the ocean with it. It is well he knows that it is long enough to reach the bottom at such places as are necessary to direct his voyage and caution him against running upon shoals that may ruin him.

So much for purpose and plan. Before proceeding, Locke pauses to narrow and sharpen the inquiry:

Thus much I thought necessary to say concerning the occasion of this inquiry into human understanding. But, before I proceed to what I have thought on this subject, I must here in the entrance beg pardon of my reader for the frequent use of the word *idea*. It being that term which, I think, serves best to stand for whatsoever is the object of the understanding when a man thinks, I have used it to express whatever it is which the mind can be employed about in thinking; and I could not avoid frequently using it.

I presume it will be easily granted me that there are ideas in men's minds. Everyone is conscious of them in himself, and men's words and actions will satisfy him that they are in others.

Our first inquiry shall be how ideas come into the mind.

The problem has been brought to a focus: How does the mind come by its ideas? Before advancing his own hypothesis, Locke glances at an alternative explanation:

It is an established opinion amongst some men that there are in the understanding certain innate principles, primary notions, characters as it were stamped upon the mind of man, received in its very first being, brought with it into the world.

This "established opinion" to which Locke refers will be found in the writings of several of his predecessors. The most typical example is perhaps Lord Herbert of Cherbury, the author of a book, *On Truth*. In this book Lord Herbert maintains that there are certain "common notions." Some of these common notions are formed without any assistance from experience or reason; others are developed by experience and reason, but do not originate therein. These common notions were supposed to yield the first principles of morality and religion. His book emphasizes in particular five common notions which Locke has in mind at this point. They were the notions (1) that there is a supreme Deity; (2) that He ought to be worshiped; (3) that the chief part of divine worship is virtue combined with piety; (4) that men should repent of their sins and turn from them; (5) that reward and punishment follow from the goodness and justice of God, both in this life and hereafter. With these historical references in mind, we may return to Locke's paragraphs:

It would be sufficient to convince unprejudiced readers of the falseness of this supposition if I should only show how, barely by the use of their natural faculties, men may attain to all the knowledge they have without the help of any innate impressions, and may arrive at certainty without any such original notions or principles.

But, because a man is not permitted without censure to follow his own thoughts in the search for truth when they lead him ever so little out of the common road, I shall set down the reasons that made me doubt the truth of the supposition of innate ideas.

Locke's refutation of the hypothesis of innate ideas is too long to be reproduced here. It comes to this: (1) It is a useless hypothesis, since the steps to knowledge are all discoverable. If this be the case, why assume innateness for some ideas? (2) Many ideas for which innateness is claimed are not perceived by infants. How account for this? If any ideas are genuinely innate, one would expect very young children to be in conscious possession of them. (3) Many ideas for which innateness is claimed are not known till the person "comes to the use of reason." How account for this? Why do some ideas, said to be innate, require for their discovery or recognition the use of powers which develop comparatively late in the person's life? (4) Many ideas for which innateness is claimed are said to be "self-evident"; and their self-evidence is advanced as proof of their innateness. Locke objects. It is risky to claim self-evidence for any ideas. Self-evident to whom? Moreover, granting self-evidence, what of it? "Self-evident" is not the same as "innate"; and who shall say, without assuming the point at issue, that it is evidence of innateness? Further, are all self-evident ideas (for example, $2 + 2 = 4$) to be taken as innate? If not, by what do we distinguish, among self-evident ideas, which are innate? (5) The "universal assent of mankind" to some ideas is advanced as evidence of their innateness. Locke objects again. To what ideas do all men give assent? One genuine dissenter would be enough to spoil the argument from consensus. Moreover, that all men assent to an idea is one thing; that the idea is therefore innate is another thing. Upon what grounds are we justified in arguing from the one to the other? (6) Finally, Locke suspects that this whole notion of innate ideas has arisen from men's anxiety to place some ideas, particularly moral and religious ideas, beyond the scope of reasonable inquiry and doubt. Having disposed thus of the arguments in support of the hypothesis of innate ideas, he resumes his original inquiry:

Let us then suppose the mind to be, as we say, white paper, void of all characters, without any ideas. How comes it to be furnished? Whence comes it by that vast store which the busy and boundless fancy of man has painted on it with an almost endless variety? Whence has it all the materials of reason and knowledge? ~thru senses~

To this I answer in one word: experience. All our knowlege is founded in experience, and from experience it ultimately derives itself.

This experience is of two sorts. Our observation is employed either about external sensible objects or about the internal operations of our mind, perceived and reflected on by ourselves. This observation supplies our understandings with all the materials of thinking. These two are the fountains of knowledge from whence all the ideas we have, or can naturally have, do spring.

First, our senses, conversant about particular sensible objects, do convey into the mind several distinct perceptions of things, according to those various ways wherein those objects do affect them: and thus we come by those ideas we have of yellow, white, heat, cold, soft, hard, bitter, sweet, and all those which we call sensible qualities. This great source of most of our ideas I call *sensation*.

Secondly, the other fountain from which experience furnisheth the understanding with ideas, is the perception of the operations of our own mind within us. Such operations are perceiving, thinking, doubting, believing, knowing, willing, and all the different actings of our own minds. We, being conscious of these operations, do from them receive into our understandings ideas as distinct as we do from bodies affecting our senses. As I call the other source *sensation*, so I call this *reflection*, the ideas it affords being such only as the mind gets by reflecting on its own operations within itself.

These two, I say, namely, external material things as the objects of sensation, and the operations of our own minds within as the objects of reflection, are to me the only originals from whence all our ideas take their beginnings. The understanding seems to me not to have the least glimmering of any ideas which it doth not receive from one of these two.

Mind is passive in receiving sensations

Having satisfied himself that all knowledge consists of ideas, that all ideas are derived from experience, that all experience is either sensation or reflection, Locke settles down to map out the entire field. His argument, at this point, becomes too detailed to permit of adequate reproduction by citation. Highly condensed, it comes to the following:

Considered with reference to their origin, ideas come to the mind either by way of sensation or reflection, or a combination of the two. From sensation, the mind gets ideas of the primary qualities of objects, e.g., solidity, extension, figure. These are qualities of the objects perceived. From sensation the mind gets also ideas of the secondary qualities of objects, e.g., sounds, tastes, colors, smells. These are not qualities of the objects perceived in the same sense that primary qualities are: they are

I   All knowledge is ideas
II All ideas come from experience
III All experience is either sensation or Reflection

effects, arising out of the operation of the object on the senses. From reflection the mind gets ideas of its operations. These operations include perceiving, retaining, discerning or discriminating, comparing, compounding or enlarging, abstracting, willing.

Considered with reference to their objects, ideas are either simple or complex. By *simple ideas* Locke means such qualities as coldness, hardness, sweetness, redness, as perceived in some particular object on some particular occasion. These simple ideas, either of sensation or reflection, are "the materials of all our knowledge." These simple ideas are sheer data, given to the mind in experience: "The mind can neither make nor destroy them." In the reception of simple ideas, the mind is passive.

By *complex ideas*, Locke means combinations of simple ideas; made by the mind out of its simple ideas, by repeating, combining, abstracting, and so on. Complex ideas "may all be reduced under three heads: modes, substances, relations."

I Modes are complex ideas which "do not contain in them the supposition of subsisting by themselves, but are considered as depending on or affections of things." Such are "ideas of triangle, gratitude, murder, etc." The point is, modes exist as properties or accidents or qualities of things, not in their own right. There are triangular things, grateful persons, murderers, and so on, but none of these qualities exists independently.

II Substances are "collections of qualities existing together" considered as "inhering" in some one thing. Thus, the color, shape, taste, weight, and other qualities of an apple exist together and "inhere" in the apple as a substance. The notion of substance causes Locke great perplexity and distress. It corresponds to no simple idea. It is nowhere given in experience. He refers to it as "something we know not what." "The idea to which we give the name *substance* is nothing but the supposed unknown support of those qualities we find existing, which, we imagine, cannot subsist without something to support them. We call that support *substance*." The need for the category is obvious. Its justification is obscure. He adds: "Whether anyone has any other clear idea of substance, beyond certain simple ideas coexisting together, I appeal to everyone's own experience." To repeat: "Because we cannot conceive how various sensible qualities, of which we have ideas, could exist alone, or in one another, we suppose them existing in and supported by some common subject which we denote by the name *substance*, though it is certain we have no clear or distinct idea of that thing we suppose a support."

III Relations, the third kind of complex ideas, are many and various. Examples are identity and diversity, cause and effect, time and place,

owner and owned, father and son, larger and smaller, and so on. Relations
are described as "the work of the mind." Locke examines them at great
length, classifies them, arranges them, defines them. They occur between
two things at least. All things are capable of some kind of relation. Relations are often clearer than the things related. Relations terminate in simple ideas. Relations may change when the relata remain unchanged, and
so on.

Having surveyed ideas with reference to their origin, i.e., sensation
and reflection, their objects, i.e., modes, substances, relations, Locke turns
to a consideration of the nature and degrees of human knowledge. Here
we may resume our citations:

Since the mind, in all its thoughts and reasonings, hath no other immediate object but its own ideas, which it alone does or can contemplate, it
is evident that our knowledge is only conversant about them.

Knowledge, then, seems to me to be nothing but the perception of the
agreement or disagreement, connection or repugnance, of any of our ideas.
In this alone it consists. Where this perception (of agreement or disagreement of our ideas) is, there is knowledge; where it is not, we come short of
knowledge.

Locke's argument may be recapitulated. All knowledge may be analyzed into ideas. All ideas arise in experience. None are innate. Ideas are
either simple or complex, the latter being combinations of the former. In
knowing, the mind notes only ways in which its ideas agree or disagree.
Upon the basis of this general analysis, Locke proceeds to discriminate
between intuitive and demonstrative knowledge:

Omit to p. 181

I have said that all knowledge consists in the view the mind has of its
own ideas. It may not be amiss to consider a little the degrees of its evidence.
The different clearness of our knowledge seems to me to lie in the different
ways of perception the mind has of the agreement or disagreement of any of
its ideas. There are three different ways.

1. Sometimes the mind perceives the agreement or disagreement of two
ideas immediately, without the intervention of any other. Thus the mind
perceives that white is not black, that a circle is not a triangle, that three are
more than two, and so on. This we may call *intuitive* knowledge, for in this
the mind is at no pains of proving or examining, but perceives the truth, as
the eye doth light, merely by being directed toward it.

This intuitive kind of knowledge is the clearest and most certain that
human frailty is capable of. On this kind of knowledge depends all the cer-

tainty and evidence of all our knowledge. He that demands a greater certainty than this, demands he knows not what, and shows only that he has a mind to be a skeptic, without being able to be so. In the next degree of knowledge, which I call *demonstrative*, this intuitive knowledge is necessary in all the intermediate ideas.

2. The next degree of knowledge is where the mind perceives the agreement or disagreement of any ideas, but not immediately. Thus, the mind being willing to know the agreement or disagreement in bigness between the three angles of a triangle and two right angles, cannot by an immediate view and comparing them do it. The three angles of a triangle cannot be brought at once and be compared with two right angles. In this case the mind is fain to find out some other angles, to which the three angles of a triangle have an equality, and, finding those equal also to two right angles, comes to know their equality to two right angles. And so, of the equality of the three angles of a triangle, to two right angles, the mind does not have immediate, intuitive knowledge. This mediated kind of knowledge we may call *demonstrative* knowledge.

When the mind cannot bring two ideas together in immediate comparison, to perceive their agreement or disagreement, it is fain, by the intervention of other ideas, to discover the agreement or disagreement which it searches. This is what we call *reasoning*. Those intervening ideas which serve to show the agreement or disagreement of any two others, are called *proofs*. Where the agreement or disagreement is by this means clearly perceived, it is called *demonstration*. A quickness in the mind to find out these intermediate ideas (that shall discover to it the agreement or disagreement which it searches) is called *sagacity*.

In every step which reason makes in demonstrative knowledge, there is an intuitive knowledge of that agreement or disagreement it seeks with the next intermediate idea which it uses as a proof. Without this intuitive knowledge of each step in reasoning, there would be no knowledge produced. If the connection between each step be perceived immediately, it is intuitive knowledge; if not, there is need of some intervening idea. This knowledge by intervening proofs, though it be certain, is thus not so clear and bright, nor assent so ready, as in intuitive knowledge.

These two, intuition and demonstration, are the degrees of our knowledge. What ever comes short of these, with what assurance so ever embraced, is but faith or opinion.

• Had Locke stopped at this point, or been satisfied merely to develop it in more detail, all might have been well. But he stumbled upon a further distinction which led him deeper and deeper into difficulties which he was never able finally to clear up. The next five citations are included merely to suggest something of what is meant.

3. There is, indeed, another perception of the mind, which I shall call *sensitive* knowledge. It is the perception of the existence of particular things about us, e.g., the sun, a rose, a fire, a table. I think we may add this knowledge of particular external objects, that by perception and consciousness we have of the actual entrance of ideas from them, to the two former sorts of knowledge, and allow these three, namely, intuitive, demonstrative, sensitive.

There is a difficulty connected with sensitive knowledge of the existence of external objects. It is this. There can be nothing more certain than that the idea we receive from an external object is in our minds. Of this fact we have intuitive knowledge. But whether there be anything more than barely the idea in our minds; whether we can thence certainly infer the existence of anything without us, which corresponds to that idea; of this some men think there may be a question made. They think so because men may have such ideas in their minds when no external thing exists, when no object affects their senses.

I think we are provided with an evidence that puts us past doubting. For I ask anyone, whether he be not invincibly conscious to himself of a different perception when he looks on the sun by day and thinks on it by night; when he actually tastes wormwood or smells a rose and thinks on that savor or odor? We find the difference between an idea revived in our mind by our memory and one actually coming into our minds by our senses, as plainly as we do between any two distinct ideas.

If any one say, a dream may do the same thing, and all these ideas may be produced in us without any external object; he may please to dream that I make him this answer: (1) Where all is dream, reason and argument are of no use, truth and knowledge nothing; so it is no great matter whether I remove this scruple or no. (2) He will allow a very manifest difference between dreaming of being in the fire, and actually being in it.

If he be resolved to appear so skeptical as to maintain that what I call "being actually in the fire" is nothing but a dream, and that we cannot certainly know that any such thing as fire actually exists without us, I answer: We certainly find that pleasure or pain follows upon the application of certain objects to us, whose existence we perceive or dream we perceive. The certainty with which we know this is as great as the pleasure or the pain. Beyond this we have no concernment to know or to be. So, I think, we may add sensitive knowledge of external objects to the two former kinds of knowledge.

Locke returns to the main argument of his inquiry. He has traced knowledge to experience. He has distinguished between intuitive and demonstrative knowledge: The former is the basis of the latter. There is, however, another possibility. Knowledge may fall short of demonstrative rigor, in which case it is "probable knowledge." Thus:

The understanding being given to man, not barely for speculation but also for the conduct of life, man would be at a great loss if he had nothing to direct him but what has the certainty of true knowledge. For that being very short and scanty, as we have seen, he would be often utterly in the dark had he nothing to guide him in the absence of clear and certain knowledge.

The faculty which supplies the want of clear and certain knowledge, in cases where it cannot be had, is judgment. In judgment the mind takes its ideas to agree or disagree (or, which is the same, any proposition to be true or false) without perceiving a demonstrative evidence in the proofs. The mind sometimes exercises this judgment out of necessity, where demonstrative proofs are not to be had; and sometimes out of laziness, unskillfulness, or haste even where demonstrative proofs are to be had.

As demonstration is showing the agreement or disagreement of two ideas by the intervention of one or more proofs, so probability is nothing but the appearance of such an agreement or disagreement by the intervention of proofs. For example, we may have a demonstration of the equality of the angles of a triangle to two right angles, or we may take the word of some mathematician that it is so, in which case the foundation of our judgment or assent is the probability of the thing.

Probability is likeness to be true. The entertainment the mind gives this sort of proposition is called *belief, assent, opinion.* Herein lies the difference between probability and certainty: In all the parts of certainty there is intuition, each step has its visible connection; in belief, not so. That which makes me believe is something extraneous to the thing I believe, something not evidently joined on both sides to those ideas that are under consideration.

Probability, being to supply the defect of our knowledge and to guide us where that fails, is conversant about propositions whereof we have no certainty but only some inducements to receive them for true. The grounds of probability are two: conformity with our own experience, or the testimony of the experience of others.

The propositions which we receive upon inducements of probability are of two sorts: concerning some particular existence falling under observation and hence capable of human testimony; concerning things which, being beyond our senses, are not capable of any such testimony.

Concerning the first of these, the concurrent experience of all other men with ours produces assurance approaching to knowledge; failing this, the concurrence of unquestionable testimony with our experience produces confidence; failing for the most part this, fair testimony in support of a proposition having no great initial improbability. When, however, experience and testimonies clash, the degrees of probability vary indefinitely.

The above probabilities are only such as concern things capable of observation and testimony. There remains that other sort, where the things are not capable of such testimony. In these matters, analogy is the only help we have, and it is from this alone that we draw all our grounds of probability.

One large question remains. Locke lived in an age when men traced some of their most valued knowledge, not to experience, but to revelation. This is not to be confused with the doctrine of "innate ideas." Many who held to revelation as a source of knowledge would take no stock in innate ideas. Locke was himself a devout person. He realized the important role which revealed knowledge played in the religious life of his friends and contemporaries. It was, however, not compatible with a thoroughgoing empiricism. Hence his rather grudging remarks:

Besides those we have hitherto mentioned, there is one sort of proposition that challenges the highest degree of our assent upon bare testimony. I mean where the testimony is of God Himself. This is called by a peculiar name, *revelation;* and our assent to it, *faith.*

Properly understood, faith is a settled and sure principle of assent and leaves no manner of room for doubt. Only, we must be sure (1) that it is a revelation from God, and (2) that we understand it aright. Otherwise we shall expose ourselves to all the error of wrong principles and all the extravagance of enthusiasm if we have faith in what is not divine revelation. Our assent, therefore, can be rationally no higher than the evidence of its being a revelation, and that we do understand the meaning of the expression by which it is delivered. If the evidence of its being a revelation, or that we do understand its true meaning, be only on probable proofs, our assent can rise no higher than that probability.

From these things thus premised I think we may come to lay down the measures and boundaries between faith and reason; the want whereof may possibly have been the cause of great disputes and perhaps mistakes in the world. For, till it be resolved how far we are to be guided by reason and how far by faith, we shall in vain dispute and endeavor to convince one another.

I find that every sect, as far as reason will help them, make use of it gladly; and where it fails them, they cry out, "It is a matter of faith and above reason." And I do not see how they can argue with anyone, or ever convince a gainsayer who makes use of the same plea, without setting down strict boundaries between faith and reason.

Reason I take to be the discovery of the certainty or probability of such truths as the mind has got by sensation or reflection, or has arrived at by deduction from such ideas. Faith is the assent to any proposition not thus arrived at but accepted upon the credit of the proposer as coming from God in some extraordinary way of communication. This way of discovering truths to men we call *revelation.*

First, I say that no man inspired by God can by any revelation communicate to others any new simple ideas which they had not before from sensation and reflection. For whatsoever impressions he himself may have received from the immediate hand of God, if it be of new simple ideas, cannot be conveyed to another either by words or any other signs; because words and other signs recall to our minds those ideas only which to us they have been wont to be signs of. They cannot introduce any new and formerly unknown simple ideas.

For our simple ideas, then, which are the foundation and sole matter of all our notions and knowledge we must depend wholly upon our natural faculties; and can by no means receive them from traditional revelation. I say traditional revelation, in distinction to original revelation. By the former I mean those impressions delivered over to others in words; by the latter I mean that first impression which is made immediately by God on the mind of any man, to which we cannot set any bounds.

Second, I say that the same truths may be discovered and handed down by revelation which are discoverable to us by reason. So God might by revelation discover the truth of any proposition in geometry, as well as men might make the discovery themselves.

Third, I say nothing can, under title of revelation, shake or overrule plain knowledge, or rationally prevail with any man to admit for true anything directly contradictory to the clear evidence of his own understanding. A proposition supposed revealed which contradicts our knowledge or reason will always have this objection hanging to it, namely, that we cannot conceive that to come from God, the bountiful author of our being, which, if received for true, must overturn all the principles and foundations of knowledge He has given us, render our faculties useless, wholly destroy the most excellent part of His workmanship (our understandings), and put a man in a condition wherein he will have less light than the beast which perisheth.

If anything shall be thought revelation which is contrary to the plain principles of reason and the evident knowledge the mind has of its own ideas, there reason must be hearkened to. And this because a man can never have so certain a knowledge that a proposition contradictory to reason was divinely revealed, or that he understands rightly the words wherein it is delivered, as he has that the contrary is true. So he is bound to consider it, and judge of it, as a matter of reason, and not swallow it, without examination, as a matter of faith.

In all things, therefore, where we have clear evidence from our ideas and principles of knowledge, reason is the proper judge. Revelation may, in consenting with it, confirm it; yet it cannot in such cases invalidate it. Nor can we be obliged, where we have the clear and evident sentence of reason, to quit it for the contrary opinion under the pretense that it is a matter of faith.

Fourth, I say that things wherein we have imperfect notions or none at all, being beyond the discovery of our natural powers and above reason, are, when revealed, the proper matter of faith. Thus, that some of the angels rebelled against God, and thereby lost their first happy state; that the dead shall rise and live again—these and the like, being beyond the discovery of reason, are purely matters of faith. With them reason has nothing to do.

if can't get something by reason when revealed must get by Faith

Thus John Locke on the problem of knowledge. A few paragraphs gather up the threads of his argument:

If, then, knowledge lies in the perception of the agreement or disagreement of any of our ideas, it follows that we can have knowledge no farther than we have ideas; and no farther than we can have perception of their agreement or disagreement.

It follows from this that we cannot have an intuitive knowledge that shall extend itself to all our ideas because we cannot examine and perceive all the relations they have one to another by an immediate comparison. Some knowledge, at least, must always remain mediated.

It follows also that our demonstrative knowledge cannot reach to the whole extent of our ideas because between two different ideas we cannot always find such intervening ideas as we can connect one to another with an intuitive knowledge. Wherever that fails, we come short of demonstrative knowledge.

From all which it is evident that the extent of our knowledge comes not only short of the reality of things, but even of the extent of our own ideas.

Nevertheless, I do not question but that human knowledge, under the present circumstances of our beings and constitutions, may be carried much farther than it has hitherto been, if men would sincerely, and with freedom of mind, employ all that industry and labor in improving the means of discovering truth which they employ to support a falsehood, to maintain a system, interest, or party they are once engaged in.

These ideas should be studied and thought about carefully.

Their simplicity tends to lull one's critical faculties. All seems too straightforward and inevitable. Only here and there does the argument show signs of getting out of hand. But, as subsequent chapters in the history of the problem were to show, these difficulties pointed to problems from which epistemology is still seeking to extricate itself.

Note on Sources. The Locke material in this section is quoted, abridged, or paraphrased from his treatise, *An Essay Concerning Human Understanding.* This treatise is divided into four Books. In Book I he out-

Locke accepts idea that not all understanding comes by Reason that thru revelation by Faith get some notions or form of knowledge lines his over-all purpose and states his case against innate ideas. In Book II he proposes to reduce knowledge to ideas and derive ideas from experience. It is almost as long as the other three Books taken together. His argument in Book II, while the heart of the *Essay*, is too detailed to be either quoted or abridged. I have done what I can with a two-page summary (pp. 175–177). In Book III he deals with ideas in relation to words and language; and with problems and difficulties that arise out of this relation. In Book IV he deals with the extent or limits of knowledge and its relation to faith. This over-all order has been followed in selecting and arranging the materials in this section.

Reading References. John Locke's *Essay Concerning Human Understanding* had both a popular and a technical influence. In this respect it was comparable in philosophy to Adam Smith's *Wealth of Nations* in economic theory. It was widely read by the educated laity, not only in Great Britain, but also on the continent and in the American colonies. Its influence, for example on Voltaire in France and on Jonathan Edwards in the colonies, is a matter of common knowledge. It was made the subject of an extended chapter-by-chapter commentary by Locke's contemporary, the German philosopher Leibniz. It exercised the minds of Berkeley, Hume and Kant, to mention only a few outstanding names in the history of eighteenth-century philosophy. To the general reader it brought clarification and emancipation. For the philosopher, as will be seen, it raised difficult problems. The history of this two-fold influence has not yet been adequately studied. Suggestions of its manifold variety may be gained by reading, e.g., Gibson's *Locke's Theory of Knowledge* or Hefelbower's *Locke and English Deism*, or Leibniz's *New Essays*. An interesting and valuable article by F. J. E. Woodbridge, "Locke's Essay," is to be found in the third volume of the Columbia University *Studies in the History of Ideas*. The standard two-volume life is by Fox Bourne. Good general accounts of Locke's life and writings are to be found in Aaron's *John Locke*, in Fraser's *Locke*, and in Fowler's *Locke*.

The following are some books published since 1940:

Cjaikowski, C. J. *The Theory of Private Property in John Locke's Political Philosophy.*
Cranston, M. W. *John Locke, a Biography.*
Gough, J. W. *Locke's Political Philosophy.*
James, D. G. *The Life of Reason: Hobbes, Locke, Bolingbroke.*
Kendall, W. *John Locke and the Doctrine of Majority Rule.*
McLachlan, H. *The Religious Opinions of Milton, Locke and Newton.*

O'Connor, D. J. *John Locke.*
Yolton, J. W. *John Locke and the Way of Ideas.*

READING QUESTIONS

1. What value does Locke see in an inquiry into human knowledge?
2. What was the hypothesis of innate ideas?
3. By whom was it held?
4. What items were so described?
5. What motive would Locke have in criticizing such a doctrine?
6. What criticisms does he offer?
7. What alternative hypothesis does he advance?
8. What does he mean by *simple* in contrast to *complex* ideas?
9. What by *modes, substances,* and *relations*?
10. What problem does he note in connection with substances?
11. What is his distinction between intuitive and demonstrative knowledge?
12. What is the relation between them?
13. What does he have in mind by sensitive knowledge?
14. What problem does he note in this connection?
15. Is his reasoning here open to any criticism?
16. How does he distinguish between demonstrative and probable knowledge?
17. What does he say about probable knowledge?
18. Why is he called upon to deal with the doctrine of revelation?
19. How would you distinguish it from the doctrine of innate ideas?
20. What four points does he make with respect to revelation?
21. Why would you expect Locke's empiricism in epistemology to ramify into a general liberalism in other fields, e.g., politics, religion, education?
22. Formulate two or more questions you would put to Locke.
23. (a) He defines _____ as the perception of agreement or disagreement between or among our _____.
    (b) His claim is that the mind comes by all of its ideas by way of _____.
    (c) This leads him to criticize and reject the then current theory that some ideas are _____.
    (d) The hypothesis regarding the origin of some ideas, referred to in item (c), was popularized in Locke's day by Lord Herbert of Cherbury in his book _____.
    (e) The ideas so accounted for were supposed to yield the first principles of _____ and _____.

(f) Locke distinguishes between a mind's experience of (1) external things, and (2) itself and its own operations. The first sort of experience yields ideas of _____; the second sort, ideas of _____.

(g) From its experience of external things, the mind gets ideas of two sorts of qualities, _____ and _____.

(h) _____ qualities belong to or inhere in the thing experienced. _____ qualities are effects arising out of the operation of the object on the senses.

(i) Color or taste illustrates what is meant by a _____ quality; whereas, shape or size are example of _____ qualities.

(j) Locke distinguishes between _____ and complex ideas.

(k) We have complex ideas of _____, _____, and _____.

(l) Qualities which "do not contain in them the supposition of subsisting by themselves," e.g., gratitude in contrast to grateful persons, Locke calls _____.

(m) A collection of qualities existing together, considered as inhering in some one thing, he calls a _____.

(n) The idea of _____ causes Locke considerable perplexity. He refers to it as "something we know not what."

(o) If a _____ is anything more than a collection of qualities existing together, then we do not have _____ of it, hence have no _____ of it, hence no _____ of it.

(p) To repeat from item (a). Locke defines _____ as the perception of agreement or disagreement between or among our _____.

(q) When this agreement or disagreement is not mediated by an intervening term, you have _____ knowledge.

(r) In contrast to this, where the agreement or disagreement is mediated by intervening terms, you have _____ knowledge.

(s) Each step in a case of _____ knowledge is itself a case of _____ knowledge.

(t) He calls the mind's search for the needed intervening ideas _____. When these are found, he calls them _____. Quickness in the mind to find them, he calls _____.

(u) Knowledge may fall short of demonstrative rigor, in which case it is called _____ knowledge.

(v) He speaks at one point of knowledge of the relation between our ideas and their objects. This he calls _____ knowledge.

(w) He calls knowledge which rests upon the testimony of God Himself, _____; and our assent to it he calls _____.

(x) The notion of knowledge based upon revelation leads him to try to set boundaries between the two human capacities involved, namely _____ and _____.

(y) Three of the four principles introduced to do this item (x) make _____ superior to or independent of _____.

2. EMPIRICISM INTO SKEPTICISM —FROM DAVID HUME

From Locke to Hume. Epistemology is an inquiry into the nature of knowledge. It is an inquiry which is motivated by the desire to discover, from an analysis of knowledge, what range and scope we may ascribe to knowledge. All this was set forth in the previous section. For most readers, during the closing years of the seventeenth and most of the eighteenth century, the problem of knowledge meant John Locke's *Essay Concerning Human Understanding.* His general common-sense tone, his homely appeal to experience, his determination not to be led into unverifiable speculations, all combined to secure for him a wide circle of readers and followers. It was only natural, therefore, that the next stage in the development of epistemological theory should take the form of an attempt to "begin where Locke left off." His position briefly was this: All knowledge may be analyzed into ideas. All ideas come to us from experience. All experience is by way of the senses. This *empiricism,* as it is called, was Locke's contribution to epistemological theory. His successor in these matters, David Hume, wrote for a generation which was familiar with the problem as Locke had stated it, and the appeal to experience as Locke had formulated it. Hume set himself a simple task: to deduce more rigorously the implications of Locke's position.

Biographical Note. See under "A Theological Problem," pages 35–36.

The Argument of the Citations. Hume will be remembered, from an earlier chapter, as the critic of natural theology. His method there was to show what happens in natural theology if one sticks closely to the terms laid down by traditional speculation in these matters. He applies the same method in epistemology. It is proposed to make an appeal to experience, he writes; let the appeal be made, then, and not abandoned because it is found to lead to inconvenient consequences. The argument of his position is simple and direct. All knowledge may be analyzed into impressions and ideas. All ideas are derived from earlier impressions. We have certain metaphysical ideas, such as ₁"matter," ₂"mind," ₃"causal connection," ₄"free will," ₅"the uniformity of nature." These ideas play a *nothing*

Like Ayer their meaningless

large part in human thinking and speculating. In fact, they are the fundamental terms in the modern man's general reflections upon the world about him. What are they worth? From what "impressions" are they derived? What corresponds to them in that actual experience to which Locke proposed to appeal? In each case Hume's answer is "they have no basis in experience." They are unjustifiable knowledge claims, and any speculation which incorporates them is mere waste of ink and paper. He begins, in the manner of Locke, by explaining that an inquiry into the nature of knowledge is directed toward eliminating as mere speculation all abstruse ideas which clutter up human thinking:

Like Locke

> The only method of freeing learning from abstruse questions is to inquire seriously into the nature of human understanding and show, from an exact analysis of its powers and capacity, that it is by no means fitted for such subjects.

(1) \The premises of his theory of knowledge are to be the following:

> We may divide all perceptions into two classes: impressions and ideas. By impressions I mean all our perceptions when we hear, see, feel, love, hate, desire, etc. Ideas are those less lively perceptions of which we are conscious when we reflect on any of those sensations mentioned above.
>
> All ideas are copies of impressions. . . . Even those ideas which seem most wide of this origin are found, upon a nearer scrutiny to be derived from it. . . . We shall always find that every idea is copied from a similar impression . . . it is impossible for us to think of anything which we have not antecedently felt by our senses.

The test of all ideas is to be "show me the impression":

> When we entertain any suspicion in a philosophical term, we need but inquire from what impression is that supposed idea derived. If it be not possible to assign any, this will serve to confirm our suspicion that it is employed without meaning. . . . By this means we can throw light upon ideas and render them precise. Produce the impressions or originals from which the ideas are copied.

The first idea to be tested by the appeal to impressions is the now familiar idea of substance or matter:

I

> Some philosophers found much of their reasonings on the distinction of *substance* and *quality*. I would fain ask them whether the idea of substance be derived from impressions of sensations or impressions of reflection. Does

it arise from an impression? Point it out to us, that we may know its nature and qualities. But if you cannot point out any such impression, you may be certain you are mistaken when you imagine you have any such idea.

If the impression from which we derive our idea of substance be conveyed to us by our senses, I ask, by which of them? If by the eyes, it must be a color. If by the ears, it must be a sound. If by the palate, it must be a taste. And so of the other senses. But I believe none will assert that substance is either a color, a sound, or a taste.

Is the idea of substance, then, derived from an impression of reflection [i.e., introspection]? But impressions of reflection resolve themselves into our feelings, passions, and emotions, none of which can possibly resemble a substance. We have, therefore, no idea of substance, apart from that of a collection of qualities.

The idea of substance is nothing but a collection of ideas of qualities, united by the imagination and given a particular name by which we are able to recall that collection. The particular qualities which form a substance are commonly referred to an unknown something in which they are supposed to "inhere." This is a fiction. *Substance is not a Reality*

We may well ask what causes us to believe in the existence of body [i.e., matter]. 'Tis certain there is no question in philosophy more abstruse. By what argument can it be proved that perceptions must be caused by external objects entirely different from them? By an appeal to experience? But here experience is and must be entirely silent. The mind has never anything present to it but its perceptions and cannot possibly have any experience of their connection with objects. The supposition of such a connection is, therefore, without any foundation in reasoning.

Philosophers distinguish betwixt *perceptions* and *objects*. The perceptions are supposed to be caused by the object, and to be interrupted, perishing and different at different times and for different people. The objects are supposed to cause the perceptions, and to be uninterrupted, continuous, and identical. But, however this new view may be esteemed, I assert that there are no principles, either of the understanding or the fancy which lead us to embrace this opinion of the double existence of perceptions and objects.

This hypothesis of the double existence of perceptions and objects has no primary recommendation to reason. The only existences of which we are certain are perceptions. Being immediately present to us by consciousness, they command our strongest assent, and must be the foundation of all our reasonings. But, as nothing is ever present to the mind but perceptions, it follows that we can never observe any "object," or any connection, causal or otherwise, between perceptions and objects.

The idea of substance as something underlying a set of qualities is unable to produce its credentials. Away with it, then. As Hume remarks of all such ideas, "Commit it to the flames." From material substance he turns to the idea of mind or spiritual substance:

II   There are some philosophers (e.g., Berkeley) who imagine we are every
moment intimately conscious of what we call our *self;* that we feel its existence and its continuance in existence, and are certain of its identity and simplicity.

Unluckily all these positive assertions are contrary to that very experience which is pleaded for them. Have we any idea of a self? From what impression could it be derived? It must be some impression that gives rise to every idea. But self or person is not any one impression. If any impression gives rise to the idea of one's self, that impression must continue to be the same, since one's self is supposed to continue to be the same. But there is no such continuing, constant impression.

For my part, when I enter most intimately into what I call my *self,* I always stumble on some particular perception or other, of heat or cold, light or shade, love or hatred, pain or pleasure, color or sound, etc. I never catch my self, distinct from some such perception.

If anyone thinks he has a different notion of his self, I must confess I can no longer reason with him. He may perceive something simple and continued which he calls his *self;* though I am certain there is no such principle in me.

Setting aside metaphysicians of this kind, I may venture to affirm of the rest of mankind that they are nothing but a bundle or collection of different perceptions which succeed each other with an inconceivable rapidity and are in a perpetual flux and movement. Our eyes cannot turn in their sockets without varying their perceptions. Our thoughts are still more variable. And all our other senses and powers contribute to this change.

The mind (or self) is a kind of theater where perceptions make their appearance, pass, repass, glide away, and mingle in an infinite variety. But there is no simplicity, no one simple thing present or pervading this multiplicity; no identity pervading this process of change; whatever natural inclination we may have to imagine that there is. The comparison of the theater must not mislead us: it persists, while the actors come and go. Whereas, only the successive perceptions constitute the mind.

The idea of mind or self or Spirit fails to reveal any basis in immediate impressions. That seals its fate. But the question persists: Why do we entertain such a notion? It is one thing to show that an idea is a mere fiction. It is another thing to account for its widespread presence in human thinking.

Why do we ascribe an identity amid these successive perceptions, and suppose our selves possessed of an invariable and uninterrupted existence through the whole course of our life? The identity which we ascribe to minds and selves is only a fictitious one, but why do we ascribe it?

Suppose we could see clearly into the mind of another, and observe that succession of perceptions which constitutes his mind. Suppose, too, that he always preserves the memory of a considerable part of past perceptions. It is evident that nothing could more readily contribute to bestowing a relation between these successive perceptions. Would not the frequent placing of these remembered perceptions in the chain of thought convey our imagination more easily from one to another? And so make the whole seem like the continuance of one object?

As memory alone acquaints us with the continuance and extent of a succession of perceptions, it is to be considered, on that account chiefly, as the source of personal identity. Had we no memory, we should never have any notion of that succession of perceptions which constitutes our self or person. But having once acquired this notion from the operation of memory, we can extend the same beyond our memory and come to include times which we have entirely forgot. And so arises the fiction of person and personal identity.

Material substance is gone. Mental substance is gone. Hume turns to the notion of causal connection between events. He is here proposing to invade the citadel of eighteenth-century science, a structure which was believed to rest squarely on the notion of causal connection. Hume's handling of this idea should be observed closely. His first question is: What do people mean by the idea of causal connection? His answer is, By causal connection they mean necessary connection; they believe that there is a necessary connection between a cause and its effect. His next question is the inevitable one: What evidence, open to our senses, have we for believing that there is any necessity in causal connection? His answer is: None whatever.

III. There is no idea in metaphysics more obscure or uncertain than *necessary connection* between cause and effect. We shall try to fix the precise meaning of this term by producing the impression from which it is copied.

When we look at external objects, and consider the operation of causes, we are never able, in a single instance, to discover a necessary connection; any quality which binds the effect to the cause, and renders the one a necessary consequence of the other. We find only that the effect does, in fact, follow the cause. The impact of one billiard ball upon another is followed by the motion of the second. There is here contiguity in space and time, but nothing to suggest necessary connection.

The scenes of the universe are continually shifting, and one object follows another in an uninterrupted succession. But any "force" or necessary connection pervading the whole machine never discovers itself in any of the sensible qualities of body. We know that heat is a constant attendant of flame. But as to any necessary connection between them, we have no room so much as to conjecture or imagine.

In single instances of causal connection we never, by our utmost scrutiny, discover anything but one event following another. We detect no necessary connection between the cause and its effect. All events seem loose and separate. One event follows another. But we observe no tie between them, beyond contiguity in space and time. They are contiguous, thus; but never connected. As we can have no idea of anything of which we have had no correspondent impression, the conclusion seems to be that we have no idea of necessary connection, and that these words are absolutely without meaning.

We are apt to imagine that we could discover effects from their causes by the mere operation of our reason, without experience. We fancy that, were we brought on a sudden into this world, we could have inferred that one billiard ball would communicate motion to another upon impact; and that we need not have waited for the event, in order to pronounce with certainty concerning it.

Knowledge of this relation arises entirely from experience. We find that particular objects are constantly conjoined with each other. Knowledge of this relation is not, in any instance, attained by reasonings *a priori*. Causes and effects are discoverable by experience, not by reason. Every effect is a distinct event from its cause. It could not, therefore, be discovered in the cause (prior to experience of their conjunction). Without the assistance of observation and experience, we should in vain pretend to determine any single event or infer any cause or effect. A man must be very sagacious who could discover by reasoning that ice is the effect of cold, without being previously acquainted with the operation of these qualities.

Hence no philosopher who is rational and modest has ever pretended to assign the ultimate cause of any natural operation. Ultimate springs and principles (causes) are totally shut off from human curiosity and enquiry.

As in the case of our idea of mind or self, Hume pauses to inquire why we ascribe to the connection between cause and effect something which is not revealed in experience.

Why do we imagine a necessary connection? From observing many constant conjunctions? But what is there in a number of instances which is absent from a single instance? Only this: <u>After a repetition of similar instances</u> <u>the mind is carried by habit, upon</u> the appearance of the cause, <u>to expect</u> the effect. This connection, which we feel in the mind, this customary and habitual transition of the imagination from a cause to its effect, is the impression from which we form the idea of necessary connection. There is nothing further in the case.

When we say a cause is necessarily connected with its effect, we mean, therefore, that <u>they have acquired a connection in our thought:</u> a conclusion which is somewhat extraordinary, <u>but seems founded on sufficient evidence.</u>

<u>Every idea is copied from some impression.</u> In all single instances of causal connection <u>there is nothing that can suggest any idea of necessity.</u> But when <u>many instances have been experienced, we begin to entertain the idea.</u> We then feel a new impression, to wit, a customary transition in our thoughts or imagination between the cause and its effect. This impression is the original of that idea which we seek for. For, as this idea arises from a number of similar instances, it must arise from that circumstance in which the number of instances differ from each single instance. This customary transition is the only circumstance in which they differ.

His rejection of the idea of cause as <u>necessary connection</u> suggests at once that he may be in a position to say something about the longstanding controversy over <u>free will</u> and <u>determinism</u>. That dispute arises because men hold (a) that <u>human acts are caused</u>, and (b) that <u>causes are</u> <u>necessary connections</u>. Hume's claim here is not that he can solve the problem but that he can dissolve it. *If no necessary connection; then*

The question of man's <u>free will</u> has been long disputed among philosophers. Does man have freedom of will? Or are his acts determined? If motives determine acts, are motives themselves determined? This dispute has been much canvassed on all hands, and has led into such labyrinths of obscure sophistry that a sensible reader inclines to turn a deaf ear to the question, expecting neither instruction nor entertainment. I hope to make it appear that the whole controversy has hitherto turned merely upon words.

We ascribe necessity to matter. The degree and direction of every motion are prescribed with exactness. Do we similarly ascribe necessity to persons? Are the degree and direction of every action prescribed with exactness?

Two circumstances form the whole of the necessity we ascribe to matter: a constant conjunction between cause-events and effect-events, and a consequent inference in our minds from the one to the other. Beyond these two circumstances we have no notion of any necessity in the motion of matter.

Do not these two circumstances take place in the voluntary actions of men? Are not similar motives followed by similar actions? Are there not detectable uniformities in human action? Is it impossible to collect any general observations concerning mankind? Has experience of human affairs, however accurately digested by reflection, no purpose?

The most irregular and unexpected resolutions of men may be accounted for by those who know every particular circumstance of their character and situation. A genial person, contrary to expectation, may give a peevish answer, but he has a toothache or has not dined. Even when, as sometimes happens, an action cannot be accounted for, do we not put it down to our ignorance of relevant details?

Thus it appears that the conjunction between motive and action is as regular and uniform as between cause and effect in any part of nature. In both cases, constant conjunction and inference from one to the other.

Though constant conjunction and customary transition be all that is discoverable between a cause and an effect in nature, men believe they perceive something like a necessary connection. Then, when they consider the operations of their own wills and feel no such necessary connection between motive and action, they suppose there is a difference between the cause-effect relation and the motive-action relation. And are hence led to say that man's will, unlike matter, is free.

But our knowledge of causation, like our knowledge of motivation, is merely of a constant conjunction and a consequent inference in our minds from one to the other. It is the same in both cases. It is different only if it be pretended that the mind can perceive, in the operation of matter, some other connection between cause and effect than has place in the voluntary actions of intelligent beings. It is incumbent on those who pretend thus to make good their assertion. So long as we rashly suppose that we have an idea of some necessity in the operations of external nature, beyond constant conjunction and an habitual inference in our minds; and, at the same time, admit we can find nothing such in the voluntary actions of the mind, we shall continue in confusion.

Thus far Hume has examined the ideas of material substance, of mental substance, of causal connection, of free will. Of each in turn he has asked one question: Upon what impression, received by the senses, does it rest? From each in turn he has received only silence for an answer. One more idea remains, namely, the idea of a uniformity of nature, the unquestioned premise of all our inductions and generalizations from nature. Why do we believe, so unquestioningly, that the "future will resemble the past"? Why do we argue, for instance, that fire will always melt ice, when our only grounds for this belief is the fact that it has done so in the past?

All our conclusions from experience proceed on the supposition that the future will resemble the past. To prove that the future will resemble the past, by arguing from experience, is evidently going in a circle, and taking that for granted which is the very point in question.

As to past experience, it can be allowed to give direct and certain information of those precise objects only, and that precise period of time only, which fell under its cognizance. But why this experience should be extended to future times and other objects, is the question on which I would insist. So to extend it is a process of mind or thought of which I would willingly know the foundation.

Not by an argument from experience can we prove this resemblance of the past to the future, for all such arguments are founded on the supposition of that resemblance. Let the course of things be allowed hitherto ever so regular. That alone, without some new inference, does not prove that for the future it will continue so.

My practice, you say, refutes my doubts. But you mistake the purport of my question. In practice I am satisfied. As a philosopher, who has some share of curiosity, I will not say skepticism, I want to learn the foundation of this inference. No reading, no inquiry, has yet been able to remove my difficulty. Upon what grounds can we argue that the future will resemble the past? Upon what grounds expect similar effects from causes which are similar?

Geometry (or any mathematics), when taken into the assistance of science, is unable to remedy this defect. Every part of applied mathematics proceeds on the supposition that certain laws are established by nature in her operations. Mathematical reasonings are employed to assist experience in the discovery of these laws, or to determine their influence in particular instances. But the discovery of the law itself is owing merely to experience, and all the mathematical reasoning in the world could never lead one step toward the knowledge of it.

In all reasonings from experience, then, there is a step taken by the mind (that the future resembles the past) which is not supported by any argument. Nevertheless, we take this step. There must therefore be some other principle (than rational or demonstrative argument).

Though none but a fool or madman will ever pretend to dispute the authority of experience, it may surely be allowed a philosopher to have so much curiosity as to examine the principle of human nature which gives authority to experience.

This principle is custom, or habit. Wherever repetition produces a propensity to renew the same act, without being impelled by any reasoning, we say this propensity is the effect of custom or habit. That habit or custom is the ultimate principle of all our conclusions from experiences, seems to be the only hypothesis which explains why we draw from many instances an inference which we are not able to draw from one instance that is in no respect different from them.

All inferences from experience are, therefore, effects of habit or custom, not of reasoning. The conclusions which we draw, based on reasoning, from considering one circle, are the same which we would draw from surveying all circles. But no man, having seen only one body impelled by another, could infer that every other similar body would move after a like impulse.

Custom, then, not reason, is the great guide of human life. It is that principle alone which renders our experience useful to us, and makes us expect, for the future, a similar train of events with those which have appeared in the past. Without the influence of custom, we should be entirely ignorant of every matter of fact beyond what is immediately present to the memory or the senses.

What, then, is the conclusion of the whole matter? A simple one, though, it must be confessed, pretty remote from the common theories of philosophy. All belief concerning matters of fact or real existence, is derived merely from some object present to the memory or the senses, and a customary conjunction btween that and some other object. Having found, in many instances, that two kinds of objects have been conjoined (say, flame and heat), the mind is carried by custom to expect the same in the future. This is the whole operation of the mind in all our conclusions concerning matters of fact and existence.

Here, then, is a kind of pre-established harmony between the course of nature and formation of our beliefs. Custom or habit is the principle of human nature by which this correspondence, so necessary to the subsistence of our species and the regulation of our conduct, has been effected. Did not the presence of an object excite in us the ideas of other objects commonly conjoined with it, all human knowledge would be limited to the narrow sphere of our memory and senses. Those who delight in the discovery of purposes in nature have here ample subject to employ their wonder and admiration.

As this operation of the mind, whereby we infer like effects from like causes, is so essential to human life, it is not probable that it could be trusted to the fallacious deductions of our reason, which is slow in its operation and extremely liable to error and mistake. It is more conformable to the ordinary wisdom of nature to secure so necessary an act of the mind by some instinct or mechanical tendency which may be infallible in its operations and independent of all the labored deductions of understanding.

Hume is now at the end of his review:

By way of conclusion to these reflections on diverse questions: When we run over libraries, persuaded of the principles here expounded, what havoc must we make? If we take in hand any volume, of divinity or metaphysics, for instance, let us ask: Does it contain any reasoning concerning quantity or number? No. Does it contain any experimental (probable) reasoning concerning matter of fact? No. Commit it then to the flames: for it can contain nothing but sophistry and illusion.

I am at first affrighted and confounded with that forlorn solitude in which I am placed by my philosophy, and fancy myself some strange uncouth monster, utterly abandoned and disconsolate. Fain would I run into the crowd for shelter and warmth. I call upon others to join me. But no one will hearken to me. Everyone keeps at a distance, and dreads that storm which beats upon me from every side. I have exposed myself to the enmity of all metaphysicians, logicians, mathematicians, and theologians. Can I wonder at the insults I must suffer? I have declared my disapprobation of their systems. Can I be surprised if they should express a hatred of my ideas and my person? When I look about me, I foresee on every hand, dispute, contradiction, anger, calumny, detraction. When I turn my eye inward, I find only doubt and ignorance. Every step I take is with hesitation; every new reflection makes me dread an error and absurdity in my reasoning.

Note on Sources. The Hume material in this section is quoted, abridged, or paraphrased from his book, *An Enquiry Concerning Human Understanding*, particularly Sections 1, 2, 4, 5, 7, 8, and 12. However, since Hume had already, in an earlier book, *A Treatise of Human Nature*, worked over much of the materials in those Sections of the *Enquiry*, I have sometimes drawn on corresponding Sections of the *Treatise* to replace or supplement passages in the *Enquiry*.

Reading References. It would be advantageous to consult the pages on Hume in B. A. G. Fuller's *History of Philosophy*. They form a section in a chapter on Locke, Berkeley, Hume. The Hume portion should be read straight through. It brings together his critique of natural theology and his theory of knowledge. T. H. Huxley's little book on Hume, recommended elsewhere, is noted again here. Time given to C. W. Hendel's *Studies in the Philosophy of David Hume* will be well spent.

The following are some books published since 1940:

Glathe, A. B. *Hume's Theory of the Passions and of Morals.*
Heinemann, F. *David Hume: The Man and His Science of Man.*
Kydd, R. M. *Reason and Conduct in Hume's Treatise.*
MacNabb, D. G. *David Hume: His Theory of Knowledge and Morality.*
Mossner, E. C. *The Forgotten Hume.*

————. *The Life of David Hume.*
Passmore, J. A. *Hume's Intentions.*
Price, H. H. *Hume's Theory of the External World.*
Ross, W. *Human Nature and Utility in Hume's Social Philosophy.*
Smith, N. K. *The Philosophy of David Hume.*

READING QUESTIONS

1. Hume proposes to free learning from abstruse questions. (a) What are the marks of an "abstruse" question? (b) How he proposes to free learning from such questions.
2. He begins by distinguishing between "impressions" and "ideas." What is the distinction here?
3. He then says that all ideas are copies of impressions. Is this an empirical generalization? Does it presuppose in any way that the future will resemble the past?
4. What test does he propose for all ideas? Unless he knows that all ideas do originate in, are copies of, impressions, how good is this test?
5. If he does not know that all ideas originate in, are copies of, impressions, then should his test be worded somehow thus: "If an idea originates in, is a copy of, an impression, then and only then is it to be validated by tracing it to its impression"?
6. Enumerate the "abstruse" ideas to which he applies his proposed test.
7. His criticism of the traditional idea of material substance. His final redefinition of it.
8. His criticism of the traditional idea of the self as a spiritual substance. His final redefinition of it. How he accounts for the traditional, albeit mistaken, idea of the self as a substance.
9. If you criticize or punish a person for wrong-doing, do you presuppose that the person criticized (or punished) is the same person who did the wrong act?
10. His criticism of the traditional idea of a "necessary connection" between a cause and its effect. His final redefinition of it. How he accounts for the traditional, albeit mistaken, idea of causal connection as necessary connection.
11. The impression of "customary transition" is the origin of the idea of "necessary connection." Is there more to the idea of necessary connection than simply constant conjunction? If so, then how did this "more" get there? Do impressions give rise to ideas which contain "more" than the impressions? When they do this, is the result an "abstruse" idea? Has Hume provided for the power in impressions

to produce "abstruse" ideas? Toward the end of his account he traces all thinking about matters of fact to the operation of a certain "mechanical tendency." Do we, then, owe our "abstruse" ideas to the presence and operation of this "mechanical" tendency?

12. Which: (a) Constant conjunction is the meaning of causal connection; or (b) constant conjunction is evidence of causal connection.

13. Why, probably, Hume's rejection of the idea of necessary connection between causes and effects jolted some persons more than his rejection of the idea of substance.

14. How he dissolves the traditional problem of free will.

15. When we act we frequently get the impression that we could have done otherwise. Hence our idea that we could have done otherwise. Would Hume deny that we do get this impression? Or that we are therefore entitled to the corresponding idea?

16. When something in "external nature" acts, e.g., a stone rolling down a hill, do *we* get the impression that *it* could have done otherwise? If not, why *should* we have the idea that it could have? If we shouldn't, then are the two cases analogous?

17. His criticism of the traditional idea ("supposition") that the future will resemble the past.

18. He ascribes this traditional idea (that the future will resemble the past) to the operation of a "mechanical tendency." What is a "mechanical" tendency? Are there any tendencies which are not mechanical? Are we to suppose that Hume's efforts to think about thinking, to rid the mind of abstruse questions, is itself simply the working out of a mechanical tendency? If we owe our abstruse ideas to the operation of this mechanical tendency in human thinking, then how are we to know that Hume's own ideas are not themselves abstruse?

19. My practice, you say, refutes my doubts. How so? His rejoinder.

20. Wherein you find Hume (a) most (b) least convincing.

3. MIND AND THE WORLD ORDER
—FROM IMMANUEL KANT

From Hume to Kant. The problem of knowledge was, to all intents and purposes, posed for modern times by John Locke in his *Essay Concerning Human Understanding.* That problem, stated simply, was to suggest a theory of the nature and origin of knowledge, and from that theory to indicate the limits of human understanding. The problem persisted. It is with us yet. It has come, indeed, to occupy the center of philosophy. Hume and Kant, between them, have been, in large measure, responsible for this fact. For that reason it is important to grasp clearly what these two thinkers sought to accomplish.

Locke, it will be remembered, was led to pose the problem of knowledge as a measure of caution. His words reveal this motive:

> If by this inquiry into the nature of the understanding I can discover the powers thereof, how far they reach, to what things they are in any degree proportionate and where they fail us, I suppose it may be of use to prevail with the busy mind of man to be more cautious in meddling with things exceeding its comprehension, to stop when it is at the utmost extent of its tether, and to sit down in a quiet ignorance of those things which, upon examination, are found to be beyond the reach of our capacities.

Nothing could be more straightforward than that. From an insight into the nature of knowledge, to recognize that some things lie beyond its reach. The hypothesis which Locke advanced was this: All knowledge comes from experience and all experience is by way of the senses.

By the middle of the eighteenth century, in Hume's writings, things had undergone a subtle change. Indeed, it would perhaps be more accurate to say that they had come to something of an impasse. What Hume did, in effect, was to take Locke's appeal to experience and push it to its "logical conclusion." This conclusion was that much of the familiar furniture of man's world was dissolved into a series of question marks. The metaphysical notions of material substance and mental substance were declared to be so much verbiage. No appeal to experience showed any grounds for believing in their existence. The notion of free will went the same way. Only the come-and-go of impressions and ideas remained. The generally accepted notions of cause and uniformity of nature met a like fate; they were mere habits, mere effect of custom. The theological notions of God as first cause and designer were weighed and found wanting. Hume tried, indeed, to undermine the credibility even of mathematics, by arguing, for example, that such geometrical notions as straight line, circle, equal angles, and so on, were "mere notions" to which nothing discoverable in experience could be said to correspond. Hume's own consternation at this reduction of Locke's empiricism was genuine. His words will be recalled:

> I am at first affrighted and confounded with that forlorn solitude in which I am placed by my philosophy, and fancy myself some strange uncouth monster, utterly abandoned and disconsolate. Fain would I run into the crowd

for shelter and warmth. I call upon others to join me. But no one will hearken to me. Everyone keeps at a distance, and dreads that storm which beats upon me from every side. I have exposed myself to the enmity of all metaphysicians, logicians, mathematicians, and theologians. Can I wonder at the insults I must suffer? I have declared my disapprobation of their systems. Can I be surprised if they should express a hatred of my ideas and my person? When I look about me, I foresee on every hand, dispute, contradiction, anger, calumny, detraction. When I turn my eye inward, I find only doubt and ignorance. Every step I take is with hesitation; every new reflection makes me dread an error and absurdity in my reasoning.

These conclusions, which filled Hume with grave doubts about the whole epistemological enterprise, were meanwhile being reflected upon by the German philosopher, Immanuel Kant. They did not fill his mind with any fright and confusion. Their effect was, to quote his well-known words, "to rouse me from my dogmatic slumbers." Where Hume was "affrighted and confounded," Kant was stimulated and enlightened. For he detected an element of irony in the whole affair. Here was Hume, in the name of a theory of knowledge, denying that there is any knowledge. Knowing that it is the function of a theory to account for that of which it is a theory, not to deny it, Kant was moved to say, in effect, "So much the worse for Hume's theory." If the appeal to experience will not serve as a satisfactory hypothesis, by means of which to account for the fact of knowledge, then so much the worse for the appeal to experience; surely, not so much the worse for knowledge. Hume's conclusions served only to convince Kant that unrelieved empiricism must somehow be mistaken.

That is the first fact to be kept in mind with respect to Kant. There is another fact, equally important. It was this: Kant believed firmly in the existence of God, in the freedom of the will, and in the immortality of the soul. But, being also a man of wide reading in modern philosophy he knew that his age, the Age of Reason, was unsympathetic with such convictions. The age was willing, in theory, that a man should entertain these convictions as a matter of faith. But it would not in practice let it go at that. It was inclined to challenge, even to ridicule, such faith. It urged an appeal to reason, confident that in such an appeal faith would come off second best. Everything was to be tried at the "bar of reason." Kant's answer to all this was to carry the war into the enemies' country. He determined to put reason itself on trial. To this end he wrote his large and epoch-making treatise, *Critique of Pure Reason*. The thesis of this book, in one sentence, was this: An examination of reason itself will show that it is powerless to deny, to challenge, or to ridicule the beliefs which devout men hold on faith.

Kant's handling of the problem of knowledge was motivated, then, by these two considerations. First, a theory of knowledge was required to replace the empiricism of Hume. Second, a theory of knowledge was required to deflate the appeal to reason which was placing obstacles in the way of religious convictions. What Kant proposed was this: to replace the appeal to experience and the appeal to reason by a critical analysis of the function of reason in experience.

Biographical Note. Immanuel Kant was born in Germany in 1724 and died in 1804 at the age of seventy-nine. His parents were members of a German sect known as Pietists. This meant that he was associated from infancy with persons of a devout turn of mind. This devotion to the "fundamentalism" of his parents did not outlast his adolescence, but it was succeeded by an equally rigorous adherence to the fundamentals of morality. His early education was intended to direct his thoughts toward the church. University years directed them along more secular lines. He graduated in classics, mathematics, science, and philosophy. At the age of thirty-one he became a privatdocent in the University at Königsberg. Here, for fifteen years, he provided coaching in mathematics, physics, physical geography, logic, and metaphysics. During these years he was gradually awakened to the dilemmas of the modern mind. He took his mathematics and his natural sciences with great seriousness; he found, on the one hand, that the kind of world to which they pointed was "incompatible" with his belief in God, free will, immortality, and the supremacy of a high-minded morality; and he found, on the other, that the unquestioned appeal to experience among progressive minds cast doubts on the reliability of mathematics and the sciences. This was not the only respect in which the "modern mind" was at sixes and sevens with itself. In the fields of theology and metaphysics, confusion reigned. In the name of reason there were claims and counterclaims; theism, atheism, skepticism with respect to Deity; dualism, materialism, idealism, skepticism, with respect to the nature of ultimate reality. All these eddies and cross-currents met in the mind of this young man whose business was to provide instruction in science and philosophy. The thought which gradually took shape in his speculations was this: The modern mind appears to be divided against itself. Used in one field, it has provided us with the beauties and achievements of mathematics and science; used in another field, it has created endless confusion in which unverifiable speculation is met with unverifiable denial. He looked into his own mind and found two unshakable convictions: on the one hand, mathematics and the sciences must be "saved" from the skeptics; on the other, the normal beliefs of a conscientious and God-fearing soul must be "saved" from both the sciences and the skeptics. As these various dilemmas clarified themselves, he saw his task: What was required, apparently, was an examination of the human mind itself. His thoughts began to shape themselves along these lines. He was, at the age of forty-six, appointed to the chair of philosophy in his university. In his inaugural address he communicated to his fellow professors his intention to devote himself to a critical analysis of the mind's power to know. For the next eleven years he did just that, and in 1781, at the age of fifty-seven, published his long-awaited *Critique of Pure Reason*.

The Argument of the Citations. Kant's problem, in its general outlines, was clear enough. The question was where to begin. He found a starting point in the distinction between *a priori* and *a posteriori* knowledge. Both he held to be undoubted facts, but the current appeal to experience would account only for the latter; the former it either ignored or sought to deny. This point gave Kant the opening he required. It is time to let him speak for himself. As the citations begin, he is reflecting upon metaphysics. As his thoughts move around, he hits upon the distinction between *a priori* and *a posteriori* knowledge.

My object is to persuade all those who think metaphysics worth studying, to pause, and, neglecting everything that has been done, to propose the preliminary question: Is metaphysics possible?

How does it come about that metaphysics, unlike other sciences, cannot obtain universal and permanent recognition? It seems almost ridiculous that, while every other science is continually advancing, we should, in metaphysics, move constantly around on the same spot without gaining a single step. We do not find men, confident of their ability to shine in other sciences, venturing their reputation here. And so its followers have melted away.

Time was when metaphysics held a royal place among all the sciences. If the will were taken for the deed, the importance of her subject matter might well have secured her that place of honor. But at present it is the fashion to despise her; and like Hecuba, she languishes forsaken and alone. Time was when her rule was despotic. But intestinal war and anarchy broke out. The skeptics, a kind of nomad tribe, despising all settled cultivation of her lands, broke up all civil society. Fortunately their number was small; they could not prevent the old settlers from returning to till the ground afresh. But the old settlers returning had no fixed plan or agreement. At present there reign in metaphysics weariness and indifference, the mother of chaos and night. Near-

reforms, ill-applied study, have rendered her counsels dark, confused, and useless.

It is vain, however, to assume a kind of artificial indifference with respect
to inquiries to which human nature cannot be indifferent. Nay, even those who
pretend indifference, if they think at all, fall back inevitably into those very
metaphysical dogmas which they profess to despise.

Nevertheless, this widespread indifference to metaphysics is worth attention and consideration. It is, clearly, not the result of carelessness but of matured judgment. Our age will no longer rest satisfied with the mere appearance
of knowledge in these matters. Its patience has run out. This fact constitutes a
powerful challenge, a powerful appeal to reason to undertake anew the most
difficult of her duties, to institute a court of appeal which, while it will protect
her own rights, will dismiss all groundless claims. This court of appeal is no
other than a critique of pure reason.

By a *critique of pure reason* I do not mean a criticism of books and systems. I mean a critical analysis of the power of reason itself, touching that
whole class of knowledge which it may strive after unassisted by experience.
This must decide the question: Is metaphysics possible or impossible?

Since the origin of metaphysics nothing has ever happened which was
more decisive to its fate than the attack made upon it by David Hume. He
started from a single, but important concept, namely causal connection. He
challenged reason, which pretends to have given birth to this idea, to tell him
by what right she thinks anything to be so constituted that it is necessarily connected with something else; for that is the meaning of causal connection. He
demonstrated, beyond refutation, that it is impossible for us to see why, in
consequence of the existence or occurrence of one thing, another thing must
necessarily exist or occur also.

Hence he inferred that reason was deluded with reference to this conception of causal connection; that she erroneously considered it one of her children; that, in reality, it was nothing but a bastard child of imagination im-
pregnated by experience; that a subjective necessity of habit was mistaken for
an objective necessity arising from insight. I frankly confess, the suggestion of
David Hume was the very thing which, many years ago first interrupted my
dogmatic slumber, and gave my investigations in the field of speculative philosophy quite a new direction.

Hume's question was not whether the conception of causal connection was
right, useful, even indispensable for our knowledge of nature. This he had
never doubted. His question was whether that conception could be thought,
by reason, *a priori;* whether it thus possessed an inner truth, independent of
all experience. That was Hume's problem. It was, as we see, a question concerning the origin of the conception, not its indispensability.

I tried whether Hume's objection could not be put in a general form, and
soon found that the conception of causal connection was by no means the only
idea by which the understanding thinks the connection of things *a priori.*

It may be advisable to interrupt the movement of Kant's thought at this point. He has already used this fundamental term *a priori* twice. He is going to explain what it means, give an illustration of its use, and contrast it with *a posteriori*. The entire argument of his position revolves around this idea. It may therefore be well to try to fix its meaning for ourselves. If we say that some fact is known, or can be known, *a priori*, we mean that it is known or can be known in advance of experience of it. Thus, we might say, "I don't know whether there are any triangles on the far side of the moon; but if there are, I can say *a priori* that the sum of their interior angles will equal two right angles." Or, we might say, "I don't know whether a slave economy was the cause of the fall of the Roman Empire, but I can say *a priori* that there was a cause." Or, we might say, "I don't know whether there are two chairs in the next room, and two in the hall; but if there are, I can say *a priori* that they will add up to four chairs." Or, we might say, "I don't know what happened either before or after I ate my dinner, but I can say *a priori* that something happened both before and after." These illustrations could be extended indefinitely. As Kant will indicate, the problem which they present is this: How does it happen that we can know certain sorts of facts *a priori*?

It is a question worth investigating, whether there exists any knowledge independent of experience and all sense impressions. Such knowledge is called *a priori* and is distinguished from *a posteriori* knowledge which has its sources in experience. That there is genuine *a priori* knowledge, that we can advance independent of all experience, is shown by the brilliant example of mathematics.

This term *a priori* requires closer definition. People are wont to say, even with regard to knowledge derived from experience, that we have it or might have it *a priori*. They mean we might derive it from a general rule. Thus, of one who undermines the foundations of his house, they would say he might have known *a priori* that it would tumble down; know it, that is, from the general rule that unsupported bodies fall. But this general rule has itself been derived from experience. Whoever knows this general rule had first to learn it from experience. He could not have known this entirely *a priori*. (This Hume has shown.) In what follows, we shall use the term more strictly. We shall understand by *a priori* that which is absolutely independent of all experience, and not of this or that experience only. Opposed to this is *a posteriori* or empirical knowledge, such as is derived from experience.

Experience tells us what is, but not that it must necessarily be as it is. It therefore never gives us any necessary, *a priori*, knowledge. Experience never imparts to its judgments any strict universality, but only relative universality (by means of induction) so that we ought always to say, "so far as we have experienced, there is no exception to this or that rule." Necessity and universality are criteria of the *a priori*. If, therefore, a judgment is thought with strict universality and necessity so that no exception is admitted as possible, it cannot have been derived from experience.

We have here a mystery. We must discover the ground of *a priori* judgments. We must understand the conditions which render them possible. The real problem is contained in the question: How is *a priori* knowledge possible? That metaphysics has hitherto remained in so vacillating a condition of ignorance and contradiction is due entirely to the fact that this problem has been ignored.

David Hume, who among all philosophers approached nearest to this problem, arrived at the conclusion that *a priori* knowledge is impossible. According to his reasoning everything we call metaphysics would turn out to be mere delusion. But if he had grasped clearly the problem of the *a priori* he would never have thought of an assertion which destroys all metaphysics, because he would have seen that, according to such an argument, neither was mathematics possible (since it contains *a priori* judgments). And from such an assertion his good sense would probably have saved him.

It is to be noted that our problem is not: Are *a priori* judgments possible? For there are enough of them to hand, of undoubted certainty, that we need not argue for their possibility. (What is actual must be possible.) We must inquire into the grounds of the possibility of their existence. The proper problem, upon which all depends, when expressed precisely is this: How are *a priori* propositions possible?

It again seems advisable to break in upon Kant's meditations. The justification must be this: He is saying things which cut very deep. He began by admitting a sort of bankruptcy on all hands in matters philosophical. He added, however, that no philosopher worth his salt would therefore feel justified in crying quits. He realized that Hume had been an important factor, despite his negative conclusions. He wants, above all, a toe hold, some fact upon which he can take a stand. His eye catches sight of this apparently neglected distinction between *a priori* knowledge and *a posteriori* knowledge. He fastens on this, realizing that this may have important implications. He sees, also, that the fact of the *a priori* raises a problem. The *a priori* is a fact. The problem is how to account for it.

Although all our knowledge begins *with* experience, it does not follow that it arises entirely *from* experience. For it is quite possible that our empirical knowledge is a compound of that which we receive through impressions and that which our own faculty of knowing (incited by impressions) supplies from itself—a supplement to impressions which we do not distinguish from that raw material (i.e., impressions) until long practice has roused our attention and rendered us capable of separating one from the other.

Hitherto it has been supposed that all our knowledge must conform to the objects, but, under that supposition, all attempts to establish any knowledge about them *a priori* have come to nothing.

The experiment therefore ought to be made, whether we should not succeed better by assuming that objects must conform to our forms of knowledge. For this would agree better with the required possibility of an *a priori* knowledge of objects; that is, with the possibility of settling something about those objects before they are given us in experience.

We have here the same case as with the first thought of Copernicus. Not being able to explain the movements of the heavenly body so long as he assumed that the stars moved around the spectator, he tried assuming the spectator to be turning around and the stars to be at rest. A similar experiment may be tried in metaphysics, so far as our knowledge of objects is concerned. If our knowledge has to conform to the nature of objects, I do not see how we could know anything *a priori*. But if the object of knowledge has to conform to the constitution of our power of knowing, I can very well conceive the possibilities of such *a priori* knowledge.

If Copernicus had not dared, by an hypothesis which contradicted the senses, to seek the observed movements in the spectator instead of in the heavenly bodies, the laws of planetary motion would have remained for ever undiscovered. I propose my own view, which has so many analogies with the Copernican hypothesis, as, at first, an hypothesis only.

Kant's argument at this point becomes too complicated for reproduction in quotation. For that reason, the next passages are mere descriptions of his argument, not selections or paraphrases from his *Critique*. Thus far, what he has been saying comes to this: Metaphysical speculation is in disrepute. Hume's criticism seems to have put an end to it. His conclusions followed from his dogma that all knowledge comes from experience. Since, on this premise, he could not account for *a priori* knowledge, he denied it. But a theory of knowledge which issues in a denial of knowledge is a poor theory. *A priori* knowledge is a fact to be accounted for, not an illusion to be denied. Since the appeal to experience has failed, something else must be tried. A new theory of knowledge is required to account for the fact of *a priori* knowledge. Kant's hypothesis is this: That knowledge is a joint product of mind and external world, arising in experience. This hypothesis raises the following problem: If knowledge is a joint product of mind and external world, then what part of the joint product is contributed by the mind? Kant answers by distinguishing between the form and the content of knowledge. The form of knowledge is contributed by the mind. The content is contributed by the external world. In the production of knowledge the mind acts to impose form on content supplied by the external world. This leads to a new problem: If knowledge is a joint product of mind and world, and mind's contribution is the form, can these formal elements in knowledge be isolated and analyzed? What, in other words, is the form which mind contributes?

Kant answers by distinguishing between perceptual, conceptual, and speculative knowledge. To our perceptual knowledge, mind contributes the forms of space and time. These Kant calls *forms of sensibility*. To our conceptual knowledge mind contributes the forms of quantity, quality, relation, and modality. These, when further analyzed, he calls *categories of understanding*. To our speculative knowledge, mind contributes the forms of self, universe, and God. These he calls *ideas of reason*. I shall refer to them as *forms of speculation*. Space and time are forms of perception, not things perceived. Things are always perceived spread-out-and-strung-along, are always perceived in a background-foreground and a before-and-after setting. This invariable spatial and temporal character is the form of all perceptual knowledge. On Kant's hypothesis, it is due to the "diffracting" action of mind or consciousness. Except as forms of consciousness, these words have no meaning. They are forms of awareness, not things of which we are aware. In Kant's words, space and time are "empirically real, but transcendentally ideal," that is, real in experience but otherwise only ideal. Quotations are here possible once more:

Space does not represent any property of things in themselves, nor does it represent them in their relation to one another. . . . Space is nothing but the form of all appearances of outer sense. It is the subjective condition of sensibility under which alone outer perception is possible for us.

Since the capacity to be affected by objects must precede all perceptions of these objects, it can readily be understood how the form of all appearances (i.e., space) can be given prior to all perceptions, and so exist in the mind *a priori;* and how, as a pure intuition, in which all objects must be determined, it can contain, prior to all experience, principles which determine the relations of these objects. It is, therefore, solely from the human standpoint that we can speak of space, of extended things. If we depart from the subjective, the representation of space stands for nothing whatsoever.

This predicate (i.e., space) can be ascribed to things only insofar as they appear to us; that is, to objects of sensibility. Since, however, we cannot treat the special conditions of sensibility as conditions of the possibility of things, but only of their appearances, we can indeed say that space comprehends all things that appear to us as external, but not all things in themselves. For we cannot judge in regard to the perceptions of other kinds of thinking beings, whether they are bound by the same conditions as limit us.

The proposition that all things are side by side in space is valid under the limitation that these things are viewed as objects of our perception. Our exposition claims the reality, the objective validity, of space in respect of whatever can be presented us; but also, at the same time, the ideality of space in respect of things when they are considered in themselves, that is, without regard to the constitution of our sensibility.

We assert, then, the empirical reality of space, as regards all possible outer experience, and, at the same time, its transcendental ideality, i.e., that it is nothing at all, immediately we withdraw the said condition, namely limitation to possible experience, and look upon it as something that underlies things in themselves.

The transcendental conception of appearances in space is a critical reminder that nothing perceived in space is a thing in itself; that space is not a form inhering in things in themselves as their intrinsic property; that objects in themselves are nothing but mere representations of our sensibility, the form of which is space. The true correlate of sensibility, the thing in itself, is not known, and cannot be known, through these representations; and in experience no question is ever asked in regard to it.

Kant's remarks on the status of time, which parallel, roughly, his remarks on the status of space, may be quoted in part:

Time is not an empirical conception that has been derived from any experience. For neither coexistence nor succession (the two modes of time) would ever have come within our perception, if the representation of time were not presupposed as underlying them *a priori.*

Time is not something which exists of itself or inheres in things. Were it a determination (i.e., property) of things in themselves, it could not be known *a priori.* But such *a priori* knowledge is quite possible if time is nothing but the subjective condition under which alone perception can take place in us. For, that being so, this form of intuition can be represented prior to the objects and therefore *a priori.*

Time is a purely subjective condition of our human perception, and, in itself, apart from the subject, is nothing. . . . What we are maintaining is the empirical reality of time, its objective validity of all objects which allow of ever being given to our senses. Since our perception is always sensible (i.e., by the senses), no object can ever be given to us in experience which does not conform to the condition of time. On the other hand, we deny to time any claim to absolute reality; that is to say, we deny that it belongs to things absolutely, as their condition or property independently of any reference to the form of our perception. Properties that belong to things in themselves can never be given to us through the senses. This, then, is what constitutes the ideality of time.

What we mean by the *ideality of time* is this: If we abstract from the subjective conditions of sensuous perception, time is nothing, and cannot be ascribed to the objects in themselves apart from their relation to our perception, neither in the way of subsistence nor of inherence.

By *categories* Kant means such forms of understanding things as unity and plurality, substance and quality, cause and effect, and so on. He enumerates twelve. The number is not as important as his recognition that conceptual knowledge has form as well as content, and his hypothesis that the form is the mind's contribution. Thus, to consider one of these categories, causation is a form of understanding, not a reality in its own right. When a drop in temperature causes the water to freeze, there are not three things, namely, dropping temperature, freezing water, and a cause connecting the two. Rather, there are two things understood in terms of a category. Our understanding of anything involves many such categories. Kant's point is the simple, but revolutionary, suggestion that categories of understanding are not objects of knowledge but forms of knowledge; not things known but ways of knowing. Our understanding of things given in experience is conditioned by the categories in terms of which our minds work. These categories are forms of understanding what is given in experience; they are, themselves, not given in experience.

Speculation is the attempt to carry understanding beyond the limits of experience. Since the categories are only forms to which experience gives content, any such attempt is doomed to fail. To use a common expression, it can never be anything more than "mere speculation." Kant notes, and condemns, three forms of speculation, three ways in which the mind perennially seeks to transcend the limits of experience.

(1) The first of these is the attempt to speculate on the nature of the mind itself, to seek to understand the nature of that which contributes form to knowledge. Beyond detecting the forms, we cannot go. The mind itself is outside of experience. It is, itself, never given in experience. It can never be content for its own forms. The attempt to formulate a rational psychology, that is, to gain an understanding of the mind, soul, self, ego, is, on Kant's theory of knowledge, to attempt the impossible. We cannot pierce beyond the stream of consciousness, to a knowledge

of the factors which make it to be the kind of thing it is. That there is a mind, beyond the stream of consciousness, Kant is prepared to argue, as against Hume. His reason for refusing to stop short with Hume is simple. The latter, it will be recalled, "reduced" mind to a succession of awarenesses. To this Kant has a rejoinder. The fact to be accounted for, he points out, is not a succession of awarenesses, but an awareness of succession. If that which is aware passed with the awareness, there could be no awareness of succession. But there is precisely this, namely, awareness of succession. Time indeed is one of the forms of knowledge.

The second attempt to extend knowledge beyond experience, is to speculate on the nature of the whole of things, beyond what is given piecemeal in experience. The attempt to formulate a rational cosmology, that is, to extend the categories beyond experience is to attempt the impossible. The mind's categories are valid only within experience. As the universe comes within the grasp of experience, it becomes understood in terms of the categories. Beyond that, as in the case of rational psychology, is "mere speculation."

The third attempt to extend knowledge beyond experience is to speculate on the nature of God. For reasons which will appear later, Kant believed in the existence of God, but he is prepared to argue that such belief is not to be confused with knowledge. To attempt to formulate a rational theology, that is, to know God as we know things which fall within our experience, is to attempt the impossible. Kant reiterates and extends Hume's destructive criticism of the grounds for theism. Like rational psychology and rational cosmology, rational theology is "mere speculation." A quotation from Kant is possible here:

> Human reason begins with principles which, in the course of experience it must follow. With these again, according to the necessities of its nature, it rises higher and higher to more remote conditions. Thus it becomes involved in darkness and contradictions. It may conclude that errors must be lurking somewhere, but it is unable to discover them because the principles which it follows go beyond all limits of experience and so beyond all experimental verification. Metaphysics is the battlefield of these endless controversies.

Kant contrasts the forms of sensibility and the categories of understanding with these three ideas of speculation. The two former are constitutive of knowledge. That is, within the limits of experience, they enter into and contribute to genuine knowledge. The latter, however, are merely regulative. This distinction between constitutive and regulative forms of knowledge is important. The ideas of self, cosmos, and

God are regulative goals toward which knowledge moves but to which it never attains.

Kant's distinction between *phenomena* and *noumena*, between things as known and things-in-themselves, follows as a corollary from this general theory of knowledge. It arises thus: Knowledge is a joint product of mind and external world arising in experience. There are here two contributing factors: the mind and external world. The latter "appears" through the forms and categories of the former. The word *phenomena* is derived from a Greek word meaning "that which appears." Hence reality as known is appearance, is phenomenal, is to be contrasted with reality as it is, which is noumenal. As Kant sweepingly remarks, "We only know phenomena."

We are now in a position to return to the one basic fact which this elaborate theory was invoked to account for, namely, *a priori* knowledge. Our *a priori* knowledge is formal only, and arises out of the dual origin of knowledge. We know *a priori* that things perceived will be perceived as spread-out-and-strung-along. We know *a priori* that things will be understood as effects of causes. We know *a priori* that things will be understood as qualities inhering in substances. We know *a priori* that things will be understood in terms of part-whole relations. And so on through the categories. But this knowledge is purely formal. We do not know *a priori* what the content of future experiences will be. We know that it will exhibit the various forms referred to, because, by hypothesis, knowledge is a joint product of mind-imposed forms filled with experience-given content. Thus did Kant "answer" Hume. At this point we can resume quoting directly from his writings.

I must, therefore, even before objects are given me in experience, presuppose the "rules of the understanding," or the "principles of knowledge" as existing within me *a priori*. These rules are expressed in *a priori* concepts to which all objects of experience must necessarily conform and to which they must agree. By thus changing our point of view, the possibility of *a priori* knowledge can well be explained.

After a superficial view of this work, it may seem that its results are negative only, warning us against venturing beyond the limits of experience. Such is no doubt its primary use. But its results are seen to be positive, when we perceive that it leads inevitably to a narrowing, a limiting, of the employment of reason; to the impossibility of going by it beyond the frontier of possible experience.

But thus and thus alone can we cut away the very root of materialism, idealism, skepticism, fatalism, atheism, fanaticism, and superstition. If governments ever think proper to interfere with the affairs of the learned, it would be consistent with their wise regard for science and society, to favor the freedom of such a criticism as can establish the labors of reason on a firm footing.

To deny that this service, setting limits to the speculative use of reason, is a positive advantage, would be the same as to deny that the police confer any positive advantage on us in preventing that violence which citizens have to fear from citizens. The police protection enables each to pursue his vocation in peace and security. The critique of reason does as much for the powers of the mind.

To illustrate this, let us suppose that the necessary distinction, established in our critique, between things as phenomena and things-in-themselves, had not been made. In that case the principle of causality, and with it the mechanical interpretation of nature, would apply to all things and not to their appearances only. I should then not be able to say of one and the same thing, for instance, the human soul, that it is both free and subject to necessity, without involving myself in a contradiction.

If, however, we may legitimately take an object in two senses, namely, as phenomenon and as thing-in-itself; and if the principle of causality applies to things only as phenomena and not as noumena, then we can, without any contradiction, think one and the same thing when phenomenal as necessarily conforming to the principle of causality and so far not free, and yet, in itself not subject to that principle and therefore free.

Suppose morality necessarily presupposed freedom of the will while speculative reason had proved that such freedom cannot even be thought. In such case freedom, and with it morality, would have to make room for the mechanical interpretation of nature. But our critique has revealed our inevitable ignorance of things-in-themselves, has limited our knowledge to mere phenomena. So, as morality requires only that freedom should not entail a contradiction, there is no reason why freedom should be denied to the will, considered as thing-in-itself, merely because it must be denied to it as phenomenon. The doctrine of morality may well hold its place, and the doctrine of nature too; which would have been impossible without our theory of the nature and limitations of knowledge.

If I cannot deprive speculative reason of its pretensions to transcendent insight, I cannot even assume freedom of will, not even in the interests of morality. I had, therefore, to remove the possibility of knowledge of what lies beyond experience, in order to make room for faith. This question of free will is but one of many which derive positive advantage from the limitations imposed by my theory of knowledge, on the speculative reach of pure reason beyond experience.

Let any reader who finds these inquiries obscure consider that not every one is bound to study metaphysics; that many minds will succeed very well in the exact sciences more closely allied to practical experience while they cannot succeed in investigations dealing exclusively with abstract conceptions. In such cases men should apply their talents to other subjects.

The following citations from John Dewey's *Quest For Certainty* describe rather pointedly the motive and the main turns of Kant's theory of knowledge:

Kant's position bristles with points of internal difficulty; many of these are objects of controversy. Ignoring these, however, it can fairly be asserted that the main characteristic of his position is a division of territory between the objects of cognitive certitude and the objects of equally complete moral assurance.

He aims in the first place to make secure, on rational *a priori* grounds, the foundation of natural knowledge; in the second, to perform a like office for the foundations of moral and religious conceptions. Science is limited to phenomena in space and time in order that the world of higher and noumenal realities may be appropriated by ideals and spiritual values. Each has complete jurisdiction and undisputed sovereignty in its own realm.

His argument in justification of the certitude of the foundations of knowledge is couched at every point so as to indicate the necessity of a higher although intellectually unapproachable realm. There was nothing factitious, in Kant's own conception, in the way in which the two kingdoms excluded each other and yet made each other necessary. On the contrary, the neat way in which the elements of each dovetailed into those of the other was to him a convincing proof of the necessity of the system as a whole. If the dovetailing was the product of his own intellectual carpentry, he had no suspicion of the fact.

He thought he had disposed, once for all, of many of the most perplexing problems of earlier philosophy. Upon the scientific side he was concerned to provide a final philosophical justification, beyond the reach of skepticism, for the Newtonian science.

His conception of space and time as necessary forms of the possibility of perception was the justification of the application of mathematics to natural phenomena. Categories of thought, necessary to understand perceived objects —an understanding necessary to science—supplied the foundation of permanent substances and causal connection demanded by Newtonian science. The tendency of the mind to pass beyond the limits of experience to the thought of unconditioned and self-sufficient totalities, "Ideas" of the universe, soul and God, was explained; and while cognitive validity was denied these "Ideas," they were admitted as regulative ideals which directed inquiry and interpretation. Above all, the thought of these transempirical realities left room that the postulate of free choice could fill.

In its essential framework, the Kantian scheme thus agreed marvelously well with the needs of the historic crisis. It gave freedom to both science and morals, with a guarantee that they could never interfere with each other. The traditional belief was that security of moral authority depends upon some source in being apart from the experiences by which values are incarnated in concrete objects and institutions. Granted this traditional belief, the Kantian scheme has such merits that it is safe to predict that as long as this belief continues to have vitality, the main elements of the Kantian position will have devoted disciples.

Thus Kant on the problem of knowledge in his *Critique of Pure Reason*. His ideas here are closely connected with the ideas which he was to put into his second *Critique*. The latter was directed toward a clarification and defense of his convictions in the field of ethics. Since his philosophy comprises both of these *Critiques*, together with much more, we shall return to him later on in connection with the ethical problem.

Note on Sources. The Kant material in this section is quoted, abridged, or paraphrased from his *Critique of Pure Reason*, particularly from the preface to the first edition, the preface to the second edition, and the introduction. In the present volume that carries you to page 207, Kant's argument, at that point, becomes too complicated for anything but a brief outline summary (pp. 207–208). The material on space and time is derived from the Transcendental Aesthetic (Critique, immediately following the Introduction.) Pages 210–212 again give only a brief outline summary of Kant's doctrines about the categories and the forms of speculation. Then, by way of conclusion, pages 212–213 give further material from Kant's Prefaces and Introduction to his *Critique*. Finally, page 214 presents some reflections on Kant's historical significance by John Dewey in his *Quest for Certainty*.

Reading References. It has been said that more books have been written on Shakespeare, Goethe, and Kant than on any three other persons. Kant is a perennially attractive figure. Anyone who is familiar with the main turns of modern philosophy can feel the tug which his ideas exert even when had at second hand. The accounts of Kant to be found in Will Durant's *Story of Philosophy*, in Mary Whiton Calkins's *The Persistent Problems of Philosophy*, in Royce's *Lectures on Modern Idealism* are good introductory presentations. These are for beginners. For those who desire to go a little further, Lindsay's *Kant*, Paulsen's *Immanuel Kant*, the extended account in Volume Two of Hoffding's *History of Modern Philosophy*, and the chapters on Kant in Collingwood's *Metaphysics* are recommended. Beyond that, one arrives soon at specialized treatises.

The following are some books published since 1940:

Ardley, G. *Aquinas and Kant: The Foundations of the Modern Sciences.*
Cassirer, H. W. *Kant's First Critique.*
Collingwood, R. G. *Metaphysics* (the chapters on Kant).
Das, R. *Handbook to Kant's Critique of Pure Reason.*
Hendel, C. W. (ed.). *The Philosophy of Kant and Our Modern World.*
Herrlin, O. *The Ontological Proof in Thomistic and Kantian Interpreta-
     tion.*
Klinke, W. *Kant for Everyman.*
Kroner, R. (tr., J. E. Smith). *Kant's Weltanschauung.*
Martin, G. *Kant's Metaphysics and Theory of Science.*
Mattern, C. D. *Personal Freedom Within the Third Antinomy.*
Miller, O. W. *The Kantian Thing-in-itself.*
Smith, A. H. *Kantian Studies.*
Tulane University. *Symposium on Kant.*
Weldon, T. D. *Introduction to Kant's Critique of Pure Reason.*

READING QUESTIONS

1. Why Kant felt that Hume's philosophical investigations were important.
2. What Kant means by *a priori* knowledge. Give an example. The problem which such knowledge raised for him.
3. What was Kant's "Copernican" revolution in philosophy? Why he proposed it. What was revolutionary about it? What was "Copernican" about it?
4. Knowledge, he says, is a joint product. What factors combine to produce it? Problem raised by this "joint-product" conception of knowledge.
5. How close to Kant do you come in Leibniz' remark: "*Nihil est in intellectu quod non prius erat in sense; nisi intellectus ipse.*"
6. Kant's distinction between form and content. How related to his distinction between *a priori* and *a posteriori.*
7. What he means by (a) the forms of sensibility, (b) the categories of understanding, (c) the ideas of reason.
8. Use the notion of either cause or substance to explain what Kant means by calling them categories.
9. How he uses his theory of the "Ideas" to liquidate (a) rational psychology, (b) rational cosmology, (c) rational theology.
10. Point of his distinction between constitutive and regulative.

11. Point of his distinction between phenomena and noumena.
12. Point of his remark: "We only know phenomena."
13. Point of his policeman analogy.
14. Point of his aside on free will.
15. He says he wanted to make room for faith—(a) why (b) how.
16. Why many persons have boggled at Kant's notion of noumenal object, ding-an-sich.
17. Dewey remarks that Kant's position bristles with points of internal difficulty. Can you suggest some?
18. Wherein you find Kant (a) most (b) least convincing.

4. POSITIVISM —FROM AUGUSTE COMTE

From Kant to Comte. Each century tackles the problem of knowledge in its own way. The seventeenth century, represented most completely in Locke's essay, differs in method from the eighteenth. The eighteenth, represented by the twin stars of Hume and Kant, differs again from the nineteenth represented in the writings of Auguste Comte. By the 1830's, it seemed unnecessary to reopen the hectic controversies which inspired and followed from earlier epistemologies. At least, Comte appears to have felt as much. The picture is altered. Comte approaches the question of knowledge from the point of view of a man who is interested primarily in the range and organization of the various bodies of science. He pins a controversial tag on himself, no doubt; for *positivism*, as will be seen, means "no more metaphysics." But he is inclined to sweep controversy to one side and ask several new leading questions: What common method has the growth of science revealed? What relations, if any, exist among the different sciences? What significance, for general education, may be ascribed to the sciences as a whole? In what fields, if any, may we look for the emergence of new sciences? For these reasons, among others, Comte is perhaps more convincing to one who is either innocent of Hume and Kant or who has lost those peculiar sensibilities which respond to their anxieties and convictions.

Biographical Note. Auguste Comte was born in France in 1798, and died in 1857 at the age of fifty-nine. He showed an early aptitude for mathematics, which he began to teach in Paris. When he was twenty-eight, he embarked on a series of public lectures designed to offer a synoptic account of the principal sciences. These attracted considerable attention; but after the third lecture, his brain temporarily gave way, and he tried to commit suicide. Two years later he had sufficiently recovered to resume his lectures. In 1830 he began the publication of his great survey of the sciences. It was completed in six large volumes and served through several generations as a storehouse of fact and generalization for students in France and abroad. He continued to maintain himself by teaching mathematics and serving as an examiner in that subject. Unfortunately, however, he became embroiled in controversies which caused him to lose a great part of his means of living. The English philosopher, J. S. Mill, who had been impressed by the value of Comte's work, was instrumental in securing a considerable sum of money from Comte's admirers in England. This tided him over his immediate difficulties. When this was used up, Comte faced poverty; however, aid came eventually from admirers in France who banded together to provide the lonely polymath with a small income for the rest of his life.

Comte's interest in epistemology was not direct. To get this point as clearly and, at the same time, as sympathetically as possible, we need to recall a bit of French history. Comte wrote for the first generation after Napoleon. The old regime, the epoch of the grand monarchy, formed a remote background. It had been swept away by the French Revolution. Liberal hopes had run high, only to be disappointed by the autocratic domination of Napoleon; and now, following the Congress of Vienna, France had been made over once more into a monarchy under Louis XVIII and Charles X. These drastic changes appear to have inspired Comte with the dream of a new era in which they would no longer be possible. This new era was to be built upon science and the application of science to industry. But, as Comte saw it, several obstacles blocked the path of the new age. They were remnants from the past. They were, more particularly, beliefs or mental sets which still lingered from the Middle Ages, the period of the grand monarchy, the Age of Reason, the French Revolution, and Napoleon. They were beliefs about such matters as God, the soul, ultimate reality, immortality, natural laws, inalienable rights, men of destiny, and so forth. These beliefs, Comte felt, were not only groundless, they were harmful. They had been responsible for continuous tyranny, revolt, suppression, war, and they would continue to be. What the world needed was a riddance of such beliefs, and Comte would supply it under cover of this new term *positivism*, which was to abolish the old loyalties and controversies, to set up the ideal of scientific method and its application to nature in the interests of human welfare.

The Argument of the Citations. Comte begins by elaborating what he calls the *law of the three stages.* This enables him to dispose of metaphysics and theology. He turns then to a statement of his theory of the sciences. The citations tell their own story from that point on:

In order to understand the true value and character of positivism, we must take a brief general view of the progress of the human mind; for no conception can be understood otherwise than through its history.

From the study of the development of human understanding, in all directions and through all times, the discovery arises of a fundamental law. The law is this: that each of our leading conceptions, each branch of our knowledge, passes through three different theoretical conditions: the theological or fictitious, the metaphysical or abstract, the scientific or positive. This fundamental law should henceforth be, in my opinion, the starting point of all philosophical researches about man and society.

The human mind employs in its progress three methods of philosophizing, the characteristics of which are essentially different and even radically opposed: the theological, the metaphysical, and the scientific. Hence arise three philosophies, or three general systems of thought, each of which excludes the other. The first is the mind's necessary point of departure; the second is merely a state of transition; the third is the mind's fixed and definitive state.

An instance of what Comte means might be the following: In the early stages of man's study of the heavens, he accounted for their motion in terms of various deities. Later he envisaged them as controlled by the force of gravitation. Finally he repudiates explanation in terms of gods and forces and is satisfied to describe the motion in terms of formulae which enable him to locate and predict:

Different departments of our knowledge have passed through the three stages at different rates. The rate depends on the nature of the knowledge in question. Any kind of knowledge reaches the positive stage early in proportion to its generality, simplicity, and independence of other branches of knowledge. Thus astronomy, which is above all made up of facts which are general, simple, and independent of other facts, was the first science to attain the positive stage, then physics, then chemistry, and finally physiology.

In the theological stage, the human mind, seeking the essential nature of things, their first and final causes, supposes all things to be produced by the immediate action of supernatural beings. Here imagination predominates over observation.

A natural and irresistible instinct disposes the human race to adopt theological ideas as its earliest principles of explanation. The personal action exerted by man on other things is, at first, the only kind he is able to understand. He is thus led to conceive, in an analogous way, the action of external bodies on himself and on each other. This is animism. Continued observation leads him to convert this primitive hypothesis into another, less enduring one: that of a "dead" inert nature guided by invisible superhuman agents, distinct and independent of one another. This is polytheism. Continued observation and reflection disposes him gradually to reduce the number of these supernatural agencies until he is led from polytheism to monotheism. The theological system arrived at its highest perfection when it substituted the providential action of a single supreme Being for the varied operations of numerous divinities; when, that is, it passed from polytheism to monotheism.

The entire theological system is based on the supposition that the earth is made for man, and the whole universe made for the earth. Remove this supposition, and the system crumbles. Hence the true astronomical theory, proposed by Copernicus and proved by Kepler, Galileo, and Newton, would alone have sufficed to demolish the theological system. In the light of the fact that our planet, one of the smallest, is in no respect different from the others, revolving like them around the sun, the hypothesis that nature is made for mankind alone so shocks good sense and contradicts fact that it must appear absurd and collapse. With it falls the theological edifice.

In the metaphysical stage, which is only a modification of the first, the mind supposes abstract forces, personified abstractions, inherent in all things and capable of producing them, instead of supernatural beings. What is called the *explanation* of anything is, in this stage, a reference of it to its proper force, principle, or abstraction.

To explain sleep, for example, in terms of what used to be called the *dormitive principle* is to explain observed phenomena by reference to what Comte would call a *metaphysical abstraction*. Many such phrases are to be found strewn through the annals of science and philosophy. Thus Hegel's *reason* or *time-spirit*, Schopenhauer's *will*, Bergson's *élan vital*, Freud's *censor*, the erstwhile *vis viva*, *vis inertia*, and *entelechy* are, I suspect, all instances of what Comte would call *metaphysical abstractions*. His objection to them is that they are attempts to explain the known by the unknown, to postulate something which is not revealed in experience to account for what is revealed in experience.

Even today, after all our advance in positive knowledge, if we try to understand how the fact which we name a cause produces the fact which we name its effect, we should be compelled, as Hume points out, to resort to images similar to those which serve as the basis of primitive human theories. (Cause is a metaphysical notion; regularity of succession is the positive notion.) The metaphysical system arrived at its last stage when men substituted the one great entity—nature—as the cause of everything.

In the scientific or positive stage the mind has given over the vain search after absolute knowledge; abandoned the quest for knowledge of the origin and destination of the universe, of causes and forces; and applies itself solely to the study of laws, to the study of relations of succession and resemblance. Reasoning and observation, duly combined, are the means of this knowledge. What is now called the *explanation* of anything is the establishment of a connection between it and some general laws, the number of which continually diminishes with the progress of science.

Observation of fact is the only solid basis for human knowledge. Taking this principle in its most rigorous sense, we may say that a proposition which does not admit of being reduced to a simple enunciation of fact, particular or general, can have no real or intelligible sense.

The first characteristic of positivism is that it regards all things as subject to invariable laws. Our business—seeing how vain is any search into what are called causes, either first or final—is to pursue an accurate discovery of those laws, with a view to reducing them to the smallest possible number. The best illustration of this is in the case of the law of gravitation. We say things are explained by it, because it connects an immense variety of facts under one head.

The positive system would attain its ultimate perfection if men could represent all particular facts as instances of one general law, e.g., the law of gravitation.

There is no science, which, having attained to the positive stage, does not bear marks of having passed through the two previous stages. At some earlier period it was composed of metaphysical abstractions; and, further back in its evolution, it took its form from theological conceptions. Our most advanced sciences still bear traces of the earlier stages through which they have passed.

In mentioning just now the four principal categories of phenomena—the astronomical, the physical, the chemical, the physiological—there was an omission. Nothing was said of social phenomena. These demand a distinct classification, by reason of their importance and difficulty. They are the most complicated and the most dependent on others. Their science, therefore, will be the latest to attain positivity.

This branch of science has not hitherto entered the domain of positive knowledge. Theological and metaphysical conceptions and methods, exploded and abandoned in other departments, are still used in the treatment of social subjects, though the best minds are weary of disputes about "divine rights," "sovereignty of the people," and so on. This is the great, the only, gap to be filled to constitute solid and entire the positive philosophy. This is what men have now most need of.

This once done, the philosophical system of the moderns will be complete. There will then be no phenomena which do not enter into one of the five great categories—astronomical, physical, chemical, physiological, and sociological.

So much then, for the law of the three stages. For Comte, its principal virtue seems to reside in the fact that it eliminates, at one fell swoop, a whole army of clamorous hypotheses and controversies which constitute a large portion of modern philosophy. Comte now turns his attention to the question of the classification of the positive sciences. (It should be noted that, as Comte uses it, the term *physiology* has the broader meaning which we extend today to the term *biology*.)

We propose to classify the fundamental sciences. They are six, as we shall see. We cannot make them less; and most scientists would make them more. To classify the sciences is not so easy as may appear. It always involves something, if not arbitrary, at least artificial; and in so far, it will always involve imperfection. It is perhaps impossible to exhibit the sciences, quite rigorously, in their natural relations and mutual dependence so as to avoid, in some degree, the danger of overlapping.

What we seek to determine is the dependence of scientific studies. Does physics depend upon physiology? Does sociology depend upon chemistry? Dependence among the sciences can result only from dependence among the corresponding phenomena. For a principle in terms of which to classify the sciences, then, we must look to the different orders of phenomena through which science discovers the laws which are her object.

All phenomena may be included within a very few natural categories, so arranged that the study of each may be grounded on the principle laws of the preceding and serve as the basis of the next ensuing. We have now obtained our rule. We proceed next to our classification.

We are first struck by the clear division of all natural phenomena into two classes: inorganic and organic. Each of these two great halves has subdivisions. Inorganic phenomena may be divided into two classes: celestial and terrestrial. Terrestrial inorganic phenomena may be divided into two classes according as we regard bodies in their mechanical or chemical character. Organic phenomena may be divided into two classes: those which relate to the individual and those which relate to groups.

Thus we have five basic sciences in successive dependence: astronomy, physics, chemistry, physiology, and sociology. The first considers the most general, simple, and remote phenomena known to us, and those which affect all others without being affected by them. The last considers the most particular, complex, and nearest phenomena. Between these two the degrees of speciality and complexity are in regular proportion to the place of the respective sciences in the scale exhibited. This we must regard as the true filiation of the sciences.

It is proposed to consolidate the entire body of positive knowledge into one body of homogeneous doctrine. But it must not be supposed that we are proposing to study this vast variety as proceeding from one single law. There is something so chimerical in attempts at explanation in terms of one single law, that it may be as well to repudiate any such notion. Our intellectual resources are too narrow, and the universe too complex, to justify any hope that it will ever be within our power to carry scientific perfection to this last degree of simplicity.

This notion of all phenomena referable to a single law is by no means necessary to the systematic formation of science. The only necessary unity is that of method. And this is already, in great part, attained: The scientific method of thought is the same for all fields of knowledge, however widely they may vary and however irreducible they may be in content.

Comte's meaning is probably this: In the scientific exploration of any field, the method is the same. Initial data are collected, usually in the light of some tentatively held hypothesis; this hypothesis is then assumed to be true, and its consequences or implications deduced; facts subsequently acquired, by observation or experiment, verify the deductions made from the hypothesis. The hypothesis may be with regard to some particular fact or some general law.

The most interesting point in our hierarchical classification is its effect on education, both general and scientific. This is its direct and unquestionable result. No science can be effectually pursued without a competent knowledge of the anterior sciences upon which it depends.

Your competent physicist must have at least a general knowledge of astronomy. Chemists cannot properly understand chemistry without physics and astronomy. Physiologists require some knowledge of chemistry, physics, and astronomy. Above all, students of social science require a general knowledge of the anterior sciences. As such conditions are rarely fulfilled, there is among us, no genuinely rational scientific education. To this may be attributed, in part, the imperfection of even the most important sciences at this day.

In our enumeration of the basic sciences there is one prodigious omission. We have said nothing of mathematics. The omission was intentional, and the reason was the vast importance and unique status of mathematics. It is, however, less a constituent part of the body of positive knowledge than a basis for the whole of that knowledge. It is the most powerful instrument that the human mind can employ in the investigation of the laws of natural phenomena. It must, therefore, hold the first place in the hierarchy of the sciences and be the point of departure for all education in any of the sciences.

From the question of the classification of the sciences, Comte addresses himself to certain advantages which, he thinks, will arise from the unified view which results. It is interesting to note that these include the elimination of logic and the reduction of psychology to behaviorism.

math
astronomy
Physics
Chem
Physiology
Sociology

We have now considered philosophically the articulation of the positive sciences. The order that results is this: mathematics, astronomy, physics, chemistry, physiology, and sociology. We must glance at the principal advantages to be derived from a study of them. Of these advantages, four may be pointed out.

I In the first place, the study of the positive sciences affords the only rational means of exhibiting the logical laws of the human mind. Looking at all scientific theories as so many great logical facts, it is only by the observation of these facts that we can arrive at the knowledge of logical laws.

behavior—Psychology pretends to discover the laws of the human mind by contemplating the mind itself. Such an (introspective) attempt, made in defiance of the physiological study of our intellectual organs, cannot succeed. The mind may observe all phenomena but its own. There can be nothing like scientific observation of mental phenomena except from without, and by another. The observing and observed organ are here the same. In order to observe its activity, your mind must pause from activity; yet it is this very activity that you want to observe. If you cannot pause, you cannot observe; if you do pause, there is nothing to observe. The results of such a method are in proportion to its absurdity.

After two thousand years of psychology, no one proposition is established to the satisfaction of psychologists. To this day they are divided into a multitude of schools, still disputing about the very elements of their doctrine. The psychologists have done some good in keeping up the activity of our understandings when there was no better work for our minds to do.

What we have said with regard to psychology as a positive science applies yet more strikingly to logic, that is, to the "study" of scientific method. Scientific method can be judged of only in action. It cannot be studied apart from the work on which it is employed. Such a study would be dead, could produce nothing of value in the mind which loses time on it. We may talk forever about scientific method, and state it in terms very wise and learned, without knowing half so much about it as the man who has once put it into practice upon a single piece of research. Thus have logicians, by dint of reading the aphorisms of Bacon and the discourses of Descartes mistaken their own dreams for science. We cannot explain the great logical procedures apart from their applications.

II In the second place, a study of positive science as here conceived will regenerate education. The best minds are agreed that our European education, still essentially theological, metaphysical, and literary, must be superseded by a scientific education conformable to our time and needs.

Everything yet done to this end is inadequate. What is required is an organic conception of the sciences such as positivism presents. The exclusive specializing tendencies of our sciences spoil our teaching. If any student desires to form a conception of science as a whole, he is compelled to go through each *Positive Sciences* department as it is now taught, as if he were to be only an astronomer or only a

I. Pos. science best means to logical discovery
II Regenerate ed.
III Study of related science will help progress each separate
IV Offers solid basis for social reorganization   *Sci*

chemist. The result, be his intellect what it may, is unsatisfactory when what he requires is a general conception of the entire range of positive knowledge.

It is such a general conception of the entire range of the sciences which must henceforth be the permanent basis of all human combinations. It will constitute the mind of future generations. But to this end it is necessary that the sciences, considered as branches from one trunk, should yield us as a whole, their chief methods and results.

III In the third place, the proposed study of the organically related generalizations of the positive sciences will aid the progress of each separate science. The divisions we establish between the sciences are, though not arbitrary, essentially superficial. The subject of our researches is one; we divide it for convenience, in order to deal more easily with separate problems. But it sometimes happens that we need what we cannot obtain under the present isolation of the sciences, namely a combination of several special points of view. For want of this, important problems wait for their solution.

To go into the past for an example: Descartes' grand conception with regard to analytical geometry, a discovery which has changed the whole face of mathematics, issued from the union of two sciences which had before been separately studied and pursued.

Again, it was undecided whether azote is a simple or a compound body. Almost all chemists held that azote is a simple body. But the illustrious Berzelius, influenced by the physiological observation that animals which receive no azote in their food have as much of it in their tissue as carnivorous animals, was able to throw new light on the question. Thus must physiology unite with chemistry to inform us whether azote is simple or compound, and to institute a new series of researches upon the relation between the composition of living bodies and their mode of alimentation.

IV In the fourth place, philosophy based on the positive sciences offers the only solid basis for that social reorganization which must succeed the critical condition in which even the most civilized nations are now living.

It cannot be necessary to argue that ideas govern the world or throw it into chaos, that all social mechanism rests upon opinions held by the members of society. The great political and moral crisis that societies are now undergoing proceeds from intellectual anarchy. Stability in fundamental principles is the first condition of genuine social order: We witness an utter disagreement on all such matters. Till a certain number of general ideas can be acknowledged as a rallying point for social doctrine, nations will remain in a revolutionary state whatever palliatives may be advised, and their institutions only provisional and makeshift.

But when the necessary agreement on first principles can be obtained, appropriate institutions will issue from them without shock or resistance. It is in this direction that those must look who desire a natural, regular, normal state of society.

Now, the existing disorder is abundantly accounted for by the existence, all at once, of three incompatible philosophies—the theological, the metaphysical, and the positive. Any one of these might alone secure some sort of social order. But while the three coexist, it is impossible for us to understand one another upon any essential point whatever. If this is true, we have only to ascertain which of the philosophies must, in the nature of things, eventually prevail.

Comte's point here might be illustrated by controversies centering in such questions as birth control, sterilization of the subnormal and criminal, and so on. Consider the case of sterilization. A sincere Catholic might oppose the measure as contrary to the will of God; a sincere democrat might oppose it as contrary to the rights of man; a social scientist disregarding both grounds of opposition, might simply argue that offspring born to such parents are likely to prove a needless burden and menace to a society which must, in the end, either support them or imprison them.

This problem, once recognized, cannot remain long unsolved; for all considerations point to a philosophy based on the positive sciences as the one destined to prevail. It alone has been advancing during the course of centuries, while others have been declining. The fact is incontestable. Some may deplore it, but none deny it or destroy it, nor neglect it save on pain of being betrayed by illusory speculations.

This general revolution of the human mind is nearly accomplished. We have only to complete the hierarchy of the positive sciences by bringing the facts and problems of society within its comprehension. The preference which almost all minds, from the highest to the commonest, accord to positive knowledge over vague and mystical conceptions, is a pledge of what this philosophy will receive when it is once completed by the addition of a positive social science. When this has been accomplished, its supremacy will be automatic and will establish order throughout society.

Note on Sources. The Comte material in this section is quoted, abridged, or paraphrased from his treatise, *The Positive Philosophy*, Introduction and Chapters I and II.

Reading References. Comte's influence has been considerable. Many unphilosophically-minded scientists are Comteans, in the sense that they would endorse his positivism. Further reading in Comte should be done in those writings in which he sets forth his conception of the new social sciences, the new social order, and the new religion of humanity. John Morley's essay on Comte in one of the volumes of his *Miscellanies* is worth while. John Stuart Mill's *Auguste Comte and Positivism*, published shortly after Comte's death, is still an illuminating account and, with respect to what Mill describes as Comte's "later aberrations," a vigorous polemic. The account of Comte in Volume Two of Hoffding's *History of Modern Philosophy* is excellent. The standard work on Comte is by Lucien Lévy-Bruhl.

The following are books published since 1940:

De Lubac, H. *The Drama of Atheistic Humanism*, Part II.
Gilson, E. *The Unity of Philosophical Experience* (chapters on Comte).

READING QUESTIONS

1. What Comte means by (a) a theological explanation, (b) a metaphysical explanation, (c) a positive or scientific explanation. Which of these explanations was, or could be, teleological. Why neither of the others could be.
2. His law of the three stages. The three sub-stages of the first main stage. Contrast the last stage of each of the three main stages.
3. Bearing of Copernican astronomy on the first main stage.
4. Basis on which he classifies the six positive sciences. The resulting hierarchy.
5. Bearing on education of the hierarchical classification of the sciences.
6. Why he eliminates (a) logic (b) psychology from the hierarchy of the positive sciences.
7. The four principal advantages to be derived from the study of the hierarchy of the positive sciences.
8. Show how Hume, Kant, and Comte reach anti-metaphysical conclusions from different premises.
9. Comte's positivism provided no place for logic or psychology. Would it have a place for ethics?
10. Wherein you find Comte (a) most (b) least convincing.

5. THE ROLE OF FICTIONS IN KNOWLEDGE —FROM HANS VAIHINGER

From Comte to Vaihinger. We began with Locke, and have thus far read our way from him through Locke, Hume, Kant, and Comte. With Comte's positivism matters seemed likely to reach a dead end. What Comte did, in effect, was to settle the problem of knowledge by definition. That is, he described the method of natural science (observation, hypothesis, deduction, verification) and the method of mathematics (postulation, definition, deduction), and then said that anything not obtained by these methods is not knowledge. Comte was then able to write off all beliefs which he could not certify in terms of these methods, as vestiges of the theological or metaphysical stages through which the mind of man has passed, but from which, here and there, some traces yet remain.

One must go back to Kant in order to make a new beginning with Vaihinger. It will be recalled that Kant conceived of his *Critique of Pure Reason* as having set limits to knowledge in order to make room for faith. There were consequences. The first was that knowledge could deal only with the world of appearances. The second was that all beliefs concerning the real world were mere speculations. It will be recalled that he describes such notions as God, the soul, and the cosmos as regulative ideas. They were regulative, in contrast to constitutive. This was a way of stating that these ideas were useful fictions, or so, at least, our next author takes it. In this concept of a useful fiction, one passes directly from Immanuel Kant to Hans Vaihinger.

Vaihinger seized upon this notion of Kant's, and elaborated it into the general theory that all knowledge rests on useful fictions. This hypothesis was stated and documented in his treatise, *The Philosophy of As-If*. By an *as-if*, the author means a useful fiction.

Biographical Note. In place of the usual biographical facts, I am substituting an abridgment of Vaihinger's account of his own life. This account is also an account of his opinions. Anyone who has read through this volume of selections thus far is in possession of most of the names and ideas to which Vaihinger refers. This makes his autobiography both interesting and valuable to read.

I was born in a Swabian parsonage near Tübingen in 1852, and so I grew up in a very religious atmosphere. It was not exactly bigoted, but it had a limited horizon. When I was twelve years old I was given into the charge of an excellent master and teacher. I was his favorite pupil. He was especially interested in the great Mahabharata epic; and occasionally he would tell us how this Indian epic contained the same sort of legends as the New Testament. The stories of the Old and New Testament had already awakened doubts in my mind, so I was gradually led to the ethical value of the myth. During this period of transition I came across Herder's book on the history of mankind. I owe a great deal to it. It gives a wide and lofty view of the whole history of mankind from the earliest origins through all kinds and varieties of civilization. The idea of evolution became one of the fundamental elements of my mental outlook. Herder draws special attention to the evolution of spiritual life out of its first animal origins; and he regards man always as linked up with that nature from which he has gradually evolved. Thus when I first heard Darwin's name, and when my school friends told me about the new theory of man's animal ancestry, it was no surprise to me. From that time onward, one of the fundamentals in my philosophy has been this fact of man's animal ancestry.

About this time I came under the influence of Plato, which acted as a counterbalancing factor. I read the usual dialogues and the *Apology*. Our professor was old, and, though very thorough, he was dull. His routine teaching made nothing like the impression on me that was made by three lectures from a young man who came to replace him during an illness. This young man read us the myth on the nature of the soul, in the *Phaedrus*, and the description of the cave from the *Republic*. These opened a new world to me, and as he spoke of Plato's myths, the seed was sown of that conception which later I myself named the "World of as-if."

I must mention Schiller's poems and treatises, for they too had an important influence on me. His philosophic poems, in which he contrasts the ideal world of pure form with the empirical world, were easily linked up with Plato. Many of his verses made an indelible impression on me; for instance, the words "in error only is there life, and knowledge must be death" have, in certain respects, become the foundation of my theory of fictions.

Thus equipped, I entered the University as a student in the resident theological college. My first term was devoted to ancient philosophy; the second to later philosophy up to Kant; the third to the period from Kant to Hegel; and the fourth from Schleiermacher onwards. No obstacles were placed in the path of my philosophical development. I was encouraged when I started a prize essay on recent theories of consciousness. For this work, I received first prize. This enabled me to travel in Switzerland and North Italy. This prize essay was also the decisive factor in making me abandon my theological studies. I had started them with much hesitation anyway. My transition to philosophy was made easier for me in every way.

The impression made upon me by Kant was very different from the rest. In every respect he freed my mind. What impressed me most was his discovery of the contradictions with which human thought is faced when it ventures into the realm of metaphysics. His theory of antinomies had a profound influence upon me. I derived permanent value from his theory of the limitation of knowledge to experience, and also from his doctrine that action, the practical, must take first place.

The official plan of studies passed from Fichte, Schelling, and Hegel, to Schleiermacher. But I followed my own course and turned to Schopenhauer, who, until then, had been ignored, even despised, by the faculty. I studied Schopenhauer thoroughly. He gave me much that was new and lasting: pessimism, irrationalism, and voluntarism.

1. Schopenhauer's pessimism became, with me, a fundamental and lasting

state of mind. I am one of those whom only pessimism enables to endure life. Pessimism gives me the moral strength to work and fight for myself, as well as to help others. I believe that pessimism has given me a more objective view of reality. Even in Kant, as I noticed, there is a strong undercurrent of pessimism.

2. The impression which Schopenhauer made upon me was greater than that made by Kant. In the systems of philosophy which I had hitherto met, the irrational aspect of the world and of life had not received adequate attention. The ideal of philosophy was to explain everything rationally, to prove it rational, significant, fitting. This ideal had failed to satisfy me. I had come across countless manifestations of the irrational. I therefore considered it to be a lack of sincerity in systems of philosophy if they tried to hide the irrational side. Now, in Schopenhauer I came across one who recognized irrationality openly and honorably, and attempted to explain it in his philosophy. His love of truth was a revelation to me. I did not follow his metaphysical theories because, since I had studied Kant, the impossibility of all metaphysics had seemed to me to be obvious. But that part of Schopenhauer's teaching which can be established empirically became my lasting possession, particularly as it could be linked up with the theory of evolution and the struggle for existence.

3. What appealed to me most in Kant was his emphasis on the practical. In Schopenhauer I found this same tendency, but clearer, stronger, more comprehensive. With him "the will" was placed in the forefront. To me, much that had hitherto been inexplicable seemed suddenly to be explained, or at least capable of explanation. What struck me most was his proof that originally thought is only used by the will as a means to its own end, and that only in the course of evolution does thought free itself and become an end in itself. The theory of evolution corroborated Schopenhauer's contention.

This theory of Schopenhauer's, that thought is dependent on the purposes of the Life-Will, and has developed into an end in itself only as it were against all laws, became linked up in my mind with Kant's theory that human thought is bound by certain limits and that metaphysical knowledge is impossible. This limitation of human knowledge to experience, which Kant emphasizes over and over again, no longer struck me as a deplorable deficiency in the human mind. It seemed to me now to be a necessary and natural result of the fact that thought and knowledge are originally only a means to attain the life purpose. Indeed, the independence of thought signifies a breaking away from its original purpose; and by the fact of this breaking loose thought is confronted with impossible problems which are not merely insoluble to human thought but to all forms of thought as such. This conviction has become one of the foundations of my conception of the universe.

Another influence, along these lines, was Adolf Horwicz. He claimed that all psychology is based on a scheme of reflexes: stimulation, sense impressions, ideas leading up to thought, expressive movement, and volitional action. The simplest reflexes are motor phenomena following upon stimulation. These stimuli must result in elementary feelings, which release corresponding movements, representing the most elementary beginning of volitional actions. In the interval between these impressions and the motor expression, ideas come to the surface, first in an elementary form, but growing more and more complicated so that in their highest form they may be described as thought processes. Thus idea and thought appear as intermediary between impression and expression. This theory fitted in very well with the idea I had derived from Schopenhauer that thought is, originally, only a means for the purposes of the will. And both ideas coincided with the conviction I had gained from Kant as to the supremacy of the practical.

These comments bring Vaihinger to the year 1873. During the next three years he prosecuted his studies on a variety of fronts.

Toward the latter part of the year 1876 I wrote down my thoughts in a large manuscript to which I gave the title *Logical Studies. Part I: The Theory of Scientific Fictions.* This work is exactly the same as what was published in 1911 as *Part I: Basic Principles of The Philosophy of As-If.* In it I developed the whole system of scientific fictions and tried to give an exhaustive theory of this manifold as-if process.

I regarded this dissertation as only a rough outline, in need of much supplementing and correction. I made use of the next two years to work at it as much as my lectures would allow me to.

Other things intervened. His father's death obliged him to look for more remunerative work. He arranged with a publisher to write a commentary on Kant's *Critique of Pure Reason.* The first volume of this commentary was recognized at once as a great work of its kind. The author was appointed "special professor" at the University of Halle. Bad health delayed the publication of the second volume of the *Commentary* until 1892. In 1894 the author was made "regular professor" at Halle. In 1896 he founded a journal, *Kant Studien,* as a means of helping his work along. He was getting away from his 1876 essay on the theory of fictions. But events brought him back to it.

In 1906, in the midst of all these complications, a misfortune enabled me after twenty-seven years to return to my original plan which I had given up in 1879. The misfortune was the weakening of my eyesight so that it became impossible for me to continue my lectures. I had to give up my official duties. The eyesight still remaining to me was just sufficient to allow me to work on my manuscript. It was the spring of 1911 before the work appeared.

I called this work *The Philosophy of As-If*. That seemed to express what I wanted to say: that the *as-if*, the consciously false, plays an enormous part in science, in philosophies, and in life. I wanted to enumerate the methods in which we operate intentionally with consciously false ideas; to reveal the secret life of these extraordinary methods; to give a complete theory of as-if.

I will end by summarizing all the conclusions which are expressed in *The Philosophy of As-If*, or which form its basis, or arise out of it:

1. Philosophical analysis leads to sensational contents. Psychological analysis leads to sensations, feelings, and strivings or actions. Scientific analysis leads to matter and the smallest constituents and motions of matter. It is impossible for the mind to bring these two spheres of reality into a rational relation, although in intuition and experience they form a harmonious unity.

2. The strivings which probably exist in the most elementary physical processes develop in organic beings into impulses. In man, who has sprung from the animal, these impulses have evolved into will and action, which is expressed in movements and caused by stimuli or by the sensations arising from stimuli.

3. Ideas, judgments and conclusions, i.e., thought, act as a means in the service of the will to live and dominate. Thought is originally only a means in the struggle for existence and to this extent only a biological function.

4. It is a universal phenomenon of nature that means which serve a purpose often undergo a more complete development than is necessary for the attainment of that purpose. In this case the means can emancipate itself and become an end in itself. This I call the law of the preponderance of the means over the end.

5. The preponderance of the means over the end has taken place in thought, which, in the course of time, has gradually lost sight of its original practical purpose and is finally practiced for its own sake as theoretical thought.

6. As a result, this thought, which appears to be independent and theoretical in its origins, sets itself problems which are impossible, not only to human thought, but to every form of thought. An instance of what I mean is the problem of the origin and nature of the universe. Another is the question of the relation between sensation and motion, popularly known as mind and matter.

7. These senseless questions, can be "answered" by showing how they arose psychologically within us.

8. If rationalism is the assumption of an original theoretical reason, an inherent human faculty with certain problems to be determined by it, then my position must be termed *antirationalism* or even *irrationalism*.

9. From this standpoint all thought processes and thought constructs appear to be not essentially rationalistic but biological phenomena.

10. In this light many thought processes and thought constructs appear

to be consciously false assumptions, which either contradict reality or are even contradictory in themselves, but which are intentionally thus formed to overcome difficulties of thought by this artificial deviation and reach the goal of thought by roundabout ways and bypaths. These artificial thought constructs are called *scientific fictions* and are distinguished as conscious creations by their as-if character.

11. The as-if world, which is formed in this manner, is just as important as the so-called real or actual world. Indeed, it is far more important for ethics and aesthetics. This aesthetic and ethical world of as-if becomes finally for us a world of values which, particularly in the form of religion, must be sharply distinguished in our mind from the world of becoming.

12. What we usually term *reality* consists of our sensational contents which press upon us with greater or less irresistibility and as "given" can generally not be avoided.

13. In these given sensational contents, which include what we call our body, there is an abundance of regularity in coexistence and succession, investigation of which forms the content of science. By means of the sensational contents which we call our body, we can exercise greater or less influence on the world of the other sensational contents.

14. In this world we find relations of fitness and much that is not fitting. We have to take this as we find it for there is little we can alter. It is a satisfying fiction for many to regard the world as if a more perfect Higher Spirit had created or at least regulated it. But this implies the supplementary fiction that the order created by the Higher Divine Spirit had been destroyed by some hostile force.

15. It is senseless to question the meaning of the universe.

The Argument of the Citations. There is no need to restate the argument of the passages quoted below. It has already been given above in Vaihinger's own words. Numbers indicate that the author is beginning a new line of thought at that point.

I

Scientific thought is a function of the psyche. It is an active appropriation of the outer world, a useful organic elaboration of the material of sensation.

The psyche is not merely a receptacle into which foreign matter is poured. It may be compared to a machine with a chemical retort which uses foreign matter most fittingly for its own maintenance. Just as the physical organism breaks up the matter which it receives, mixes it with its own juices, so the psyche envelops the thing perceived with categories. As soon as an external stimulus reaches the psyche, it responds as though provided with delicate feelers, inner processes start, the outcome of which is the appropriation of the thing perceived for some purpose.

The procedures of the psyche are carried on, for the most part, unconsciously; are chiefly, in the beginning, instinctive and unconscious, even if later they press forward into consciousness.

It is the purpose of the eye to transform various waves into sensations, to make reduced images of the objective world through refraction and reflection of rays. It is suitably arranged to achieve this purpose and is able to carry out independent movements of accommodation and modification as circumstances require. In the same way, the logical or scientific function of the psyche is an activity which hast a purpose and can adapt itself to circumstances and objects for the fulfillment of this purpose.

The function of the psyche is to change and elaborate perceptional material into ideas, associations of ideas and conceptual constructions consistent and coherent among themselves. Since, however, we do not know objective reality directly but only infer it, we are obliged to say that thought has fulfilled its purpose when it has elaborated the given sensations into valid conceptions and generalizations and has produced such a world that objective happenings can be calculated and our behavior successfully carried out.

2

Thought must be recognized as a mechanism, a machine, a tool, an instrument, in the service of life. The test of the correctness of a logical construct lies in practice. The purpose of thought must be sought, not in the reflection of a so-called objective world, but in rendering possible the calculation of events and of operations upon them.

The purpose of the psyche in logical procedures is to keep us in a position to deal with things so that, given certain conditions and relations, we may receive an ascertainable sense impression; so that, by a certain impulse, we may produce an ascertainable effect. Sensations are the starting point of all logical activity and the terminus to which they must run.

We lay most stress on practical corroboration, on the experimental test of the utility of the logical constructions produced by the psyche. It is not the correspondence with an assumed objective reality (never directly accessible to us); it is not the theoretical representation of an outer world in the mirror of the mind, which, in our view, guarantees that thought has fulfilled its purpose. It is the practical test: Is it possible, with the help of the psyche's products, to calculate events and to realize our impulses?

3

To attain the purpose of its activity—to deal with events and render them dependent on our will—the psyche employs the most diverse means. It undertakes ingenious operations, invents brilliant expedients, introduces complicated processes. The raw material—sensations—is remodeled, recoined, compressed. We emphasize the utility of the psyche's procedures because we shall be dealing with logical constructions in which this purposiveness is strikingly manifested.

It must be remembered that the purpose of the world of ideas is not to portray reality—an utterly impossible task—but to provide us with an instrument for finding our way about more easily in this world. Subjective processes of thought represent the highest result of organic development, and the world of ideas is the fine flower of the whole process; but, for that very reason it is not a copy of reality in the ordinary sense. Its purpose is the preservation and enrichment of life. It serves as an intermediary between living beings. It is an edifice, well calculated to fulfill such purposes. But to regard it as a copy of reality is to indulge in a hasty and unjustifiable comparison.

It would indeed be strange if these concepts were actually pictures of objective reality. We need only make clear to ourselves what this term *picture* or *copy* is supposed to mean, and to ask how a logical construct could be a copy of an event in the real world. These concepts are not copies of events. They are themselves events. The world as we conceive it is only a secondary or tertiary construction. This conceptual world is not a picture of the real world, but an instrument for grasping, dealing with, understanding, that world; an auxiliary construct formed by the psyche in order to take its bearings. This construct can be substituted for the actual world, and in practice we do that. But it is not a picture; it is only a sign used to deal with reality, a logical expedient devised by the psyche to enable us to act in the real world.

4

There are methods employed in scientific procedure which have not been duly considered in logical theory. They are employed less in the natural sciences than in the mathematical and social sciences, i.e., in the most exact and the least exact sciences. They may be described as irregular. In logic, a veil of secrecy has been woven about them.

5

We may distinguish between rules and artifices of thought. Rules are operations in virtue of which any function is able to attain its objective directly. Artifices, on the other hand, are operations of a somewhat mysterious character which run counter to ordinary procedure in more or less paradoxical ways. They give an onlooker the impression of magic if he be not himself initiated. They are able to overcome, indirectly, the difficulties which beset the ordinary activities. Thought has such artifices. They are strikingly purposive expressions of the organic function of thought.

Among these artifices is one which is our special concern, namely, the fiction. Fictions are mental constructs, woven by the psyche itself. It introduces these hybrid and ambiguous thought structures in order to attain its purpose indirectly where the material which it encounters resists a direct procedure.

We shall try to give a typical example of every variety of fiction, and to use it to study the scheme of the construct and the methodology employed.

6

I   A standard example is the well-known assumption of Adam Smith, according to which all human actions are dictated by egoistic motives. Human actions are excessively complicated. They present insuperable obstacles when we try to understand them and reduce them to laws. This was Smith's problem. He realized that the main cause lay in egoism. He therefore formulated the assumption that all human actions, and particularly those of an economic nature, could be looked upon as if egoism were their sole motive. Thus all other factors were neglected. By means of this as-if he succeeded in bringing economics into an ordered system. He assumed the egoism, and then deduced from it the relations in trade and commerce which followed from that assumption.

II   Another typical example may be found in Thünen's fiction of an imaginary city. He introduced it into economics, at the beginning of the nineteenth century, in order to explain the relations between agriculture, transportation, etc. It was this: Grant an imaginary city. Around it, in concentric zones, are arranged the different spheres of activity from which the requirements of the city are drawn. By means of this ingenious artifice agricultural and economic laws are then systematically deduced. The fictions of an isolated man, an isolated state, etc., belong to the same group.

III   Another instructive example of the fictional method is offered by Bentham's treatment of the problems of political science. Bentham based his general theory of the state on the assumption that men act always from self-interest. In order, then, to work up the case for constitutionalism and parliamentariasm, he reasoned as follows: If men's actions are determined by selfish interests, then the only rulers who govern in the interests of the governed are those whose selfish interests coincide with those of the governed. The interests of the rulers are brought into harmony with the interests of the ruled only by responsibility, i.e., through the dependence of the rulers upon the will of the ruled. The wish on the part of rulers to retain power and the fear of losing it are the only motives which can inspire a policy in agreement with the interests of the ruled. From this Bentham deduced representative government, responsibility of ministers, frequent elections, and so forth.

IV   Another example of the fictional method is to be found in Condillac's statue. In his *Treatise on Sensations* he sought to show that all beliefs and conceptions could be reduced to an origin in experience. To this end he imagines a statue, similar to a human being whose mind is as yet devoid of ideas. To admit and exclude impressions at will, this imaginary man is enclosed in a marble case which prevents him from using his sense organs. In this way Condillac is able to isolate those ideas which would result from each of the senses. He limits his statue to the sense of smell, and then, in succession, to hearing, taste, sight, and touch. He then combines the various senses by opening or closing the means of access to the statue. By this means he can show the contribution of each particular sense, trace the development of consciousness, attention, memory, judgment, imagination, abstraction, reflection, and so forth.

The term *fiction* is nowhere better known than in jurisprudence. The juristic fiction consists in submitting a single case under a construct not intended for it. The basis for this is as follows: Since laws cannot include all cases, certain special examples are treated as if they belonged under them. For instance, in a recent German commercial code we find a provision that goods not returned to the sender within a specified time are to be regarded as if the recipient had definitely authorized and accepted them. Again, it is assumed, in England, that a husband is the father of a child if it can be proved that he was in the country at the time of the child's conception. This, however, is rather a *praesumptio juris* than a genuine *fictio juris*. In England in the eighteenth century every crime could be treated as if it were directed personally at the king and every plaintiff had the right to bring action under this fiction. The Code Napoléon contains a number of legal fictions, e.g., that a woman's household goods are *immobilia,* that an *enfant conçu* can under certain circumstances be regarded as an *enfant né*, etc. Elsewhere we encounter such legal fictions as that the defendant who does not put in an appearance is regarded as if he admitted the charge; an adopted son is regarded as if he were a real son; an heir who is deemed unfit to inherit is regarded as if he had died before the testator; and so forth.

In these juristic fictions the behavior of the psyche is identical with what we have seen it to be in other fields. Practically, the importance is great; theoretically, there is a deviation from reality. Without such deviations thought cannot attain its purposes.

7

On of the most important fictions ever formed by man is the idea of free will. Human actions are regarded as "free," and therefore responsible, in contrast with the "necessary" course of natural events. In spite of all the contradictions which this concept contains, we use it constantly in ordinary life in making judgments, and it is the foundation of criminal law. Our judgment of our fellow men is so bound up with this construct that we can no longer do without it. Only on this basis is a high degree of culture and morality and law possible. But this does not prevent us from realizing that it is itself a logical monstrosity, a contradiction, a fiction. There is nothing in the real world corresponding to the idea of free will, but in practice it is an exceedingly necessary fiction.

Ideals are working fictions, in contradiction with reality. Morality rests upon fictions. We must act as if duty were imposed by God, as if we would be judged by Him for our conduct, as if we would be punished for immorality, etc. But as soon as we transform these as-ifs into so many "becauses," morality loses its purely ethical character and becomes merely a matter of calculating our interests. Thus, before our very eyes does a small artifice of the psyche develop into a mighty source of all the idealistic belief and behavior of mankind.

The importance of our theory for practical philosophy is obvious. Fictions enter profoundly into our practical life. Indeed, they are necessary. They are a consequence of human imperfection. But all the nobler aspects of our life are based upon fictions. A pure ethics can only be established by the recognition of its fictional basis. How closely truth and illusion thus approach one another is apparent. What we call *truth* is really only the most expedient form of error. It is an error to suppose that an absolute truth, an absolute criterion of knowledge and behavior, can be discovered. The higher aspects of life are based upon noble delusions.

8

The fundamental conceptions of mathematics are all fictions. Thus, e.g., empty space, empty time, points without extension, lines without breadth, surfaces without depth, spaces without content, are all imaginary and fictional conceptions. Upon these as foundations the psyche has constructed the entire edifice of this amazing science. Mathematicians have occasionally realized that they were dealing with fictions, but seldom have they made this the subject of study. Recognition of the fictional nature of its basic concepts is, however, essential for mathematical progress. The efforts made to conceal this fact have worn threadbare.

Another ingenious mathematical fiction is that of considering lines and surfaces as composed of elements of infinitely small extension. This fiction enables us, e.g., to subsume a curve under a straight line, to subsume an ellipse under a circle, and so forth.

The same applies to such mathematical notions as zero, negative numbers, fractions, irrational numbers, imaginary numbers, infinite series, and so forth. Their very names indicate that they are constructs. The history of mathematics is full of examples of the superstitious awe with which these number-constructs have been regarded.

9

In mechanics we are confronted with many fictions. For example, such concepts as the rigid bar, the Alpha body (the immovable central point of absolute space), the center of gravity, absolute space and time, absolute motion, *actio in distans,* and so on, are, all of them, imaginary constructs, useful in the elaboration of theoretical mechanics, but corresponding to nothing in reality.

One of the most important fictions is that notorious product of the imagination, the concept of "force." If two events are constantly conjoined, we call that peculiarity of the first event which consists in its being followed by the other event, its *force;* and we measure this force in terms of the magnitude of its effect. In reality, of course, only the sequence exists. The forces that objects are supposed to possess are nothing but a necessary consequence of succession. They are raised to the rank of real entities, placed as a permanent background, given a separate existence, all in contrast with the transitory events. What we call *force,* so far as it is thought of as the cause of motion or change is nothing but a disguised outlet for our tendency to personify.

Force is a fiction. It is nothing but a reduplication of the facts, namely, of the causal relations of succession. We interpolate this construct, and imagine we have added something. The assumption of forces that "determine" the sequence of phenomena in no way aids us in giving a theoretical explanation. As the critical, positive attitude develops, these abortive branches on the tree of knowledge wither and fall off.

All the specific forces are included here. Gravitational force, life force, sleeping force, and so on. Newton himself looked upon gravitation as a fiction. The phenomena which it correlated are, of course, real enough, but to attribute some gravitational force to them is simply a summary expression for the regularity of the correlations.

10

Such terms as *soul, psychic force, vital force, vis inertia, vis dormitiva,* etc., are names of fictions. The concept soul, for example, is a glaring fiction. We still use it. We still speak of a soul as if there were a separate, integral, simple entity, though we know there is no such reality.

What we call a *natural law* is a fiction. It is nothing but an expression for the totality of relations existing in a group of phenomena. It is a summational fiction. If by *law* we intend anything more than the regular sequence of events of which it is a summary, if we intend any "force" or "power" which determines the sequence, we are misleading ourselves by a typical fiction.

11

All abstractions are fictions. By an *abstraction* is meant a quality or property which belongs to some particular thing but may be considered in abstraction from that thing; e.g., goodness, color, smoothness, equality, etc. Abstractions get built into the language and conceal their fictional nature. We begin to apply adjectives to them, and add verbs. We say, "War destroys men." We speak of "deeds of fame," of "qualities of virtues, wisdom, justice," etc. We come thus to impart substance to what are merely abstractions. We speak of them as if they were realities existing independently of the objects with which they are always, in fact, connected. In themselves they are no more real than the square root of minus one.

All generalizations are fictions. Generalization is another favorite device of thought, closely connected with abstraction. Such words as *stone, plant, book, tree, ship* are names of general concepts, or generalizations, formed from particular instances. But the particular instance is alone real. No perception exists covering, e.g., the notion "tree." There is this tree and that tree, but not tree in general. These general concepts are psychical constructs, extracted by thought from the particulars of experience; pure fictions, for nothing real can be proved to exist corresponding to them in the external world. It would not be necessary to waste words on this subject, were it not for the fact in philosophy it has been held that there is something objective corresponding to these constructs.

12

Our view gains importance and value through its application to the favorite ideas of philosophers, e.g., the ideas of God, free will, immortality, thing-in-itself, the Absolute, and so on. These gain their true significance when they are considered as fictions. The value of our inquiry lies in the rigorous application of the notion of fictions to certain popular thoughts and famous ideas.

The German theologian, Schleiermacher, made use of fictions in his interpretation of Christianity. The actual relationship, e.g., between God and the world, and between God and men, he holds to be incomprehensible. Take the relationship between God and men. For Schleiermacher, the philosopher, this is completely unknowable. But by Schleiermacher, the theologian, it is conceived of as if it were the relation of father to son. God is not the father of men, but He is to be regarded and treated as if He were. By means of this as-if Schleiermacher held thousands of people to Christianity. Such an interpretation proved to be of tremendous importance for the practice of religion. Schleiermacher was well aware of the artificial aspect of his method, although he did not describe it quite as bluntly as we do here.

Schleiermacher further argues that prayer is a meaningful act so long as it is interpreted as if God would hearken to it. It is clear, however, that the conception of praying to an omnipotent and omniscient God contains a contradiction, i.e., is a fiction. This quite apart from the contradiction involved by the idea of prayer in relation to natural laws.

The materialistic conception of the world is a necessary and useful fiction. It proceeds as if the external world did assuredly exist outside ourselves, and as if, even without us as subjects, things would be as they appear; although, in reality, all that we experience is merely our sensations which thus have validity only in relation to us as subjects. Not only does the world of color and sound exist merely through and in our sensations, but the world of touch also. The old truth that secondary qualities are merely relative has been extended to primary qualities also.

The idea of substance is a fiction. We speak of things having qualities; e.g., we speak of this tree as having the quality of hardness, smoothness, a given size, shape, etc. Now what is the *thing* which has these qualities? It is absolutely equivalent to the indefinite series of those qualities. If the qualities were all removed, there would be no thing. A thing is merely the sum of the qualities. A thing in any other sense is a mere fiction, and when we say that a thing "has" certain qualities, we are making use of a fiction if thereby we intend something outside of and beyond the qualities.

13

We must discuss one other idea, the last and greatest fiction, namely the thing-in-itself, Kant's *Ding-an-sich*. From all that has preceded, it is clear what our attitude must be: that the thing-in-itself is a fiction. In the first edition of his *Critique of Pure Reason* Kant indeed, in one place, calls it a "mere idea," i.e., a fiction. It is a device by means of which the whole world of reality can be dealt with. It is an x to which a y, our ego, corresponds. By means of these two the real world of sensations is ordered and understood. To explain the world of ideas Kant assumes that the real world consists of things-in-themselves, mutually interacting. On the basis of this interacting he explained the genesis of sensations. We must remember, however, that Kant had the right to say only that we must regard real existence as if things-in-themselves existed, as if they influenced us and gave rise to our idea of the world. In that case the thing-in-itself was a necessary fiction since only thus can we imagine actual reality or think and speak of it at all.

The division of the world into things-in-themselves and egos, into objects and subjects, is the primary fiction upon which all others depend. From the standpoint of a critical positivism sensations alone are real, and out of these the whole subjective world is constructed with its division into physical and psychical complexes. A critical positivism asserts that any further claim is fictional. For it, only the observed sequence and coexistence of phenomena exist, and upon these alone it takes its stand. Any explanation going beyond this can do so only by the instrumentalities of fictions. A critical positivism is the only fictionless doctrine.

14

The treatment of all ideational constructs as mere products of the psyche was originally accomplished by Hume and Kant and continued by Schopenhauer. We go further in pointing out that they are, from a logical point of view, identical with scientific fictions, i.e., with constructs that are practically useful and necessary though theoretically false, deviations from reality. This point is implicit in Hume and Kant but is not stressed by them. The view here presented we call *critical positivism*.

15

It is well to distinguish between semifictions and genuine fictions. The former is illustrated in Adam Smith's assumption that all human action is selfishly motivated; the latter in the notion that the circumference of a circle is composed of an infinite number of infinitely short straight lines, or in Kant's notion of a thing-in-itself nowhere revealed to experience but conditioning experience.

We can note four main characteristics of fictions:

1. The first is their deviation from reality. In the case of semifictions this deviation is partial. Thus, recurring to Adam Smith, some human action is selfishly motivated, and some is not. In the case of genuine fictions this deviation is complete; and, furthermore, they contain a self-contradiction. This discloses itself in the antinomies to which they give rise.

2. A second main characteristic is that they disappear in the course of history or through the operation of logic. The former holds for semifictions, the latter for genuine fictions. Those which partially contradict reality have value only if they are used provisionally until experience has become richer or methods of thought more refined and definitive. Those which completely contradict reality, and contain a self-contradiction, are allowed for, when recognized for what they are, because our aim is to obtain noncontradictory results.

3. The third main feature of a fiction is the awareness that it is a fiction. This holds only of normal fictions; or rather, of fictions normally held. In the history of the sciences this is frequently not the case. The first authors of a fiction are not themselves clear whether they have a fiction or an hypothesis on their hands. The realization of its fictional nature develops later.

4. The fourth characteristic of a fiction is that it is a means to an end, that it is expedient, or useful, not to say necessary. Where there is not such utility the fiction is unscientific, i.e., merely aesthetic. That fictions in scientific thought have this character of utility is the kernel of our position, and distinguishes it fundamentally from previous positions, e.g., Hume's or (to a less extent) Kant's. The essential element in a scientific fiction is not the fact of its being a deviation from reality; it is that it is a useful or necessary deviation.

These four characteristics distinguish fictions from hypotheses. With them as criteria, every fiction can be recognized. If a survey of science were made today, many fictions which we have not mentioned would be discovered.

16

Fictions are useful for scientific thought. It is wrong to reject them as useless once their objective impossibility has been recognized. This shows the prejudice which dominates philosophy today; namely, that because a construct is logically contradictory, it is therefore of no value. Precisely the contrary is true. These contradictory concepts are the most valuable.

As we have seen, many of the fundamental ideas with which science operates are fictions. The problem is not how to do away with these contradictions—that would be futile—but to show that their utility and advantage to thought. It is an error to imagine that only what is logically noncontradictory is logically fruitful. Such an attitude, if consistently adhered to, would bring us to the conclusion that all science is valueless, since so many of the fundamental concepts are contradictory. Our position must be sharply distinguished from this. Many fundamental scientific concepts are fictional and contradictory and do not "reflect" the world of reality. But this in no way renders them valueless. They are psychical constructs which not only give rise to the illusion that the world is being comprehended but also enable us to orient ourselves in the realm of the actual.

17

Because our conceptual world is a product of the real world it cannot be a reflection of the real world. On the other hand, it can serve as an instrument by which we can move about. It is a symbol by which we orient ourselves. It is in the interests of science to make this symbol more adequate and useful, but a symbol it will remain.

There is no reply to the argument that the conceptual world cannot be identical with the real world because it is a product of the real world. There is no identity of thought and reality. The "world" which the psyche constructs is merely an instrument, and for that reason, the world of ideas is not the ultimate goal of thought. The ultimate purpose of thought is not thought itself, but behavior and ultimately ethical behavior. The real world, symbolized in the form of a world of ideas, is the means thereto.

The final purpose of thought is action and the facilitation of action. The world of ideas, is simply a means, and its constituent elements are also merely a means. It is a system of expedients of thought which help and support one another. It is an extremely sensitive machine constructed by the psyche. It is related to a prescientific world of ideas as a modern hammer to a prehistoric stone hammer. Both are instruments and, though very different as regards delicacy and elegance, are yet identical in kind. They are instruments, products of the psyche, of the logical instinct.

The conceptual world, the world of ideas, lies between the two poles of sensation and motion, perception and action. The psyche continually adds new members between these two poles.

The conceptual world, the world of ideas, lies between the sensory and the motor nerves, an intermediate world, serving merely to make the interconnection between them richer and easier, more delicate and more serviceable. Science is concerned with the elaboration of this intermediate world, and with the adjustment of this instrument to the objective relations of sequence and coexistence which make themselves perceptible. But when science goes further, making this instrument an end in itself, when it is no longer concerned merely with the perfecting of the instrument, it is to be regarded as a luxury and a passion.

It is a pardonable weakness in science to believe that its ideas are concerned with reality itself. It deals with reality only to the extent of detecting sequences and coexistences. But the concepts, the ideas, which encompass and embrace reality are of a fictional nature, the additions of man, forming merely the frame in which man encloses the reality in order that he may thus manipulate it better.

This attitude can free us from the pressure of the contradictions concealed in the basic principles of science. It is not these which really matter, for they are but a means. The psyche creates more and more delicate means of encompassing and dealing with reality. It is an error to confuse the means, the instrument, with what the instrument was created to deal with.

18

The psyche is not merely a receptacle into which foreign matter is poured. It may be compared to a machine with a chemical retort which uses foreign matter for its own maintenance. Just as the physical organism breaks up the matter which it receives, mixes it with its own juices, so the psyche envelops the thing perceived with categories. As soon as an external stimulus reaches the psyche, it responds as though provided with delicate feelers; inner processes start, the outcome of which is the appropriation of the things perceived for some purpose.

Vaihinger has some defensive comments to make on his own position:

1. The term *skepticism* has occasionally been applied to the philosophy of as-if. This is not a correct description. Skepticism raises doubting or questioning to the dignity of a principle. The as-if philosophy has no trace of this attitude. It claims that consciously false conceptions and judgments are applied in all sciences, and it shows that these scientific fictions are to be distinguished from hypotheses. Hypotheses are assumptions which are probable, assumptions the truth of which can be proved by further experience. They are therefore verifiable. Fictions are never verifiable, because they are assumptions which are known to be false but which are employed because of their utility. When a series of assumptions in mathematics, mechanics, physics, chemistry, ethics, or the philosophy of religion are shown in this way to be useful fictions, and so to justify themselves, this does not imply skepticism. The application of the term *skepticism* to the as-if philosophy has been made, partly, no doubt, because of the doubt with which this philosophy treats God and immortality. But, as in the case of the sciences, the above consideration applies here also. The as-if philosophy does not deny that these conceptions are fictions of ethical value.

2. Many people think they can discover not exactly skepticism but agnosticism in the as-if philosophy. Agnosticism is the belief that human knowledge is confined within more or less narrow limits. It speaks of the Unintelligible, the Unknowable. Now, the as-if philosophy holds that knowledge has certain limits, but not in the sense that these limits bound only human knowledge but do not bound a superhuman knowledge. My opinion is that the limitations are not implicit in the specific nature of man (as compared with possible minds of a higher order) but are part of the nature of thought itself. If there are higher forms of mind, these limitations will affect them, and even the highest mind of all. For thought originally only serves the will to life as a means to an end. But when, according to the law of the preponderance of the means over the end, thought has broken loose from its original aim and has become an end in itself it sets itself problems to which it is not equal because it was not developed for this purpose, for example, such problems as the origin of the world, the formation of matter, the beginning of motion, the meaning of the world, the purpose of life, etc. If thought is regarded as a biological function, it is obvious that these are impossible problems for thought to solve, and quite beyond the natural boundaries which limit thought as such. I have no inclination to fall back on the old grievance about the limitations of human knowledge. At most, we may complain that the law of the preponderance of the means over the end has led us to ask questions that are unanswerable.

3. Another objection raised against the as-if philosophy is that the concept of reality implied in it is not unified. On the one hand all reality is reduced to sensations; on the other hand, to the motion of matter and the smallest constituents of matter. The question is how to unify these two notions. The criticism is that the as-if philosophy does not unify them.

I ask a question in return. Has *any* philosophical system ever succeeded in bringing these two spheres into a rational relation? The answer is no. They will never be unified by any rational formula. We stand here at a point where an impossible problem confronts our reason. This question is as impossible of solution by rational methods as the question of the purpose of existence. Although we, who ask this question, unite in our nature these two halves of reality, our mind is not in a position to answer it satisfactorily. He who would criticize *any* system of philosophy for not answering this question, is in the same intellectual position as a man who would reproach a mathematician for not solving the problem of squaring the circle, or an engineer for not solving the problem of a perpetual-motion machine.

Naturally, the human mind is tormented by this insoluble contradiction between the world of motion and the world of consciousness, and this torment can eventually become very oppressive. One would be well advised to remember that Kant had already pointed out that there are problems which mock us perpetually, but which we cannot get rid of. But there is one solution of this and similar torturing questions, for in intuition and in experience all this contradiction and distress fade into nothingness. Experience and intuition are higher than human reason. When I see a deer feeding in the forest, when I see a child at play, when I see a man at work or sport, but above all when I am myself working or playing, where are the problems with which my mind has been torturing itself? We do not understand the world when we are pondering over its problems, but when we are doing the world's work.

Note on Sources. The Vaihinger material in this section is quoted, abridged, or paraphrased from his *The Philosophy of 'As-If.'* The German title is *Philosophie des Als Ob.* Vaihinger's book contains an autobiographical chapter, a general introduction, and three Parts. Part I, Basic Principles; Part II, Amplified Study of Special Problems; Part III, Historical Confirmations. The volume has a long (12 pages) and detailed Analytical Table of Contents. The order of the present section was obtained by following the Analytical Table of Contents. The materials were selected from the text to fill out the resulting scheme.

Reading References. Books and articles expounding the ideas of Hans Vaihinger are few in number, unless one is prepared to read them in German. The translation of the treatise itself, and a chapter in a book by Havelock Ellis, are all that this author has encountered: Hans

Vaihinger, *The Philosophy of 'As-If.'* Havelock Ellis, "The Art of Think-ing," in *The Dance of Life*. The student is recommended to browse in R. G. Collingwood's *Metaphysics*. Vaihinger's "fictions" and Colling-wood's "absolute presuppositions" invite both comparison and contrast.

READING QUESTIONS

1. Point of his comparison of the psyche to (a) a machine with a chemi-cal retort, (b) the eye.
2. He seems to use "purpose" and "function" as equivalent notions. (a) Are they? (b) If not, which would he be better to stick to?
3. What guarantees that thought has fulfilled its function? Two other "guarantees" thereby ruled out.
4. Three stages: (a) sensations (b) logical constructs, thought-con-structs (c) prediction, control. Which stage is not a picture, not a copy? What, then, is it?
5. At which of the three stages just mentioned, fictions occur. Why the word "fiction," in both its ordinary meaning and its etymological meaning, is a good word here. Point of his phrase "as-if."
6. Examples of fictions in (a) economic theory, (b) political theory, (c) psychological theory, (d) legal theory.
7. How he uses (a) free will, (b) moral ideals, (c) absolute truth, to bring out his notion of a fiction, an as-if.
8. Mathematics and mechanics as happy hunting-grounds for the theory of fictions.
9. Speaking of the soul he says, "We know there is no such reality." Should he have said, "We do not know that there is any such reality"?
10. Sense in which abstractions and generalizations are fictions.
11. Many philosophical ideas prove to be sitting ducks for Herr Vaihin-ger. How many "favorite ideas" does he pick off?
12. Why he reckons Hume, Kant, and Schopenhauer among his prede-cessors.
13. Some synonyms for the term "fiction."
14. His distinction between a semi-fiction and a genuine fiction.
15. Four main characteristics of fictions. How these enable you to distin-guish between a fiction and an hypothesis.
16. "Our conceptual world cannot be a reflection of the real world be-cause it is a product of the real world." How about this?
17. He says that our conceptual world (a) is a product of the real world, and (b) is constructed by the psyche. Is he here trying to eat his cake and have it too?

18. The intermediate, in between, means-to-an-end, character of the conceptual world.
19. He says that his "philosophy of as-if" should not be confused with either skepticism or agnosticism. Why?
20. His point about trying to square the circle or invent a perpetual motion machine.
21. Wherein you find Vaihinger (a) most (b) least convincing.

6. KNOWLEDGE HAS PRESUPPOSITIONS
—FROM R. G. COLLINGWOOD

From Vaihinger to Collingwood. The claim which Vaihinger had made about knowledge was that it "contained" or "rested on" fictions. These he called "As-ifs," and had sought them in almost every important branch of knowledge. For example, in economics, one may ask "What determines the selling price of a commodity in a freely competitive market?" However, there is no such thing as an *entirely* freely competitive market: there is always some element, however slight, however concealed or unsuspected, of monopoly. One proceeds, nevertheless, "as if" there were such a thing as a freely competitive market. If an answer to the originating question is obtained, it will not hold of any actual market. It will hold only of the "imaginary" market taken to be entirely "freely competitive." R. G. Collingwood's interesting and important book, *An Essay on Metaphysics,* provides a fresh approach to this aspect of knowledge.

Biographical Note. R. G. Collingwood was born in England in 1889, and died in 1943 at the age of fifty-four. Professor T. M. Knox, concludes his memorial paper for the British Academy with the statement: ". . . his was the most original and constructive mind in English philosophy since Bradley." Collingwood was educated at Eton and Oxford. He became a fellow and tutor of Pembroke College at Oxford in 1912. He served with the Admiralty Intelligence during World War I, and returned to his college when the war was over. In 1934 he was appointed Waynflete Professor of Metaphysical Philosophy to succeed J. A. Smith, and was elected a Fellow of the British Academy. In 1938 he received an Honorary L.L.D. from St. Andrews University in Scotland. He retired in 1941. His most important philosophical books were *Speculum Mentis* (1924), *Outlines of a Philosophy of Art* (1925), *An Essay on Philosophical Method* (1933), *The Principles of Art* (1937), *An Autobiography* (1939), *An Essay on Metaphysics* (1940), *The New Leviathan* (1942), *The Idea of Nature* (1945), and *The Idea of History* (1946). These books provide ample support for Professor Knox's remark about Collingwood's place in English philosophy since Bradley.

The Argument for the Citation. The following passages are taken from Professor Collingwood's book, *An Essay on Metaphysics.* The thesis of the book is that scientific thinking, thinking productive of science, rests upon presuppositions which are not themselves pieces of knowledge. The title is intended to suggest that the term *metaphysics* be reserved for the name of the activity whereby a knowing mind diagnoses—analyzes out—its presuppositions. Since these presuppositions cannot be verified or refuted, they are never known to be either true or false. They are never proved. When presupposed, however, they make proof possible. Collingwood calls them "absolute presuppositions," and his book deals with the role which such presuppositions play in the activity called "getting to know." To try to prove an absolute presupposition is to treat it as an hypothesis. This is to mistake its character in relation to knowledge. Ferretting out absolute presuppositions Collingwood calls "metaphysics"; trying to prove them, once they have been tracked down, he calls "pseudo-metaphysics," and warns against it as the besetting mistake of empiricism or positivism when it seeks to promote presuppositions into knowledge, or, seeks to abandon them when it finds that such promoting is not possible. His book on these matters is an interesting alternative to Professor Ayer's *Language, Truth and Logic.* It is related to that lively book in something the same way that Kant's *Critique* and *Prolegomena* were related to Hume's *Treatise* and *Inquiry.* Professor Collingwood's absolute presuppositions invite comparison with Kant's synthetic *a priori* propositions.

SCIENTIFIC THINKING

In proportion as a man is thinking scientifically, when he makes a statement, he knows that his statement is the answer to a question and knows what that question is. To ask questions, knowing that you are asking them, is the first stage in high-grade thinking.

HAS PRESUPPOSITIONS

Whenever anybody states a thought there are more thoughts in his mind than are expressed in his statement. Among these, some stand in a peculiar relation to the thought he has stated: they are its presuppositions.

250 AN INTRODUCTION TO MODERN PHILOSOPHY

One can make presuppositions without knowing it, and without knowing what presuppositions one is making.

In low-grade or unscientific thinking we hardly know that we are making any presuppositions at all.

Every question involves a presupposition from which it "arises." This presupposition in turn has other presuppositions, which are thus indirectly presupposed by the question. Unless this presupposition were made, the question to which it is logically prior could not be logically asked.

SOME OF THESE ARE "ABSOLUTE"

A presupposition is either relative or absolute. By a relative presupposition I mean one which stands to one question as its presupposition and to another question as its answer.

To question a presupposition, to demand that it be "verified," is to demand that a question be asked to which the affirmative answer would be that presupposition itself. To verify the presupposition that my measuring-tape is accurate is to ask a question admitting of the answer "the tape is accurate." Hence to speak of verifying a presupposition involves supposing that it is a relative presupposition.

An absolute presupposition is one which stands, relatively to all questions to which it is related, as a presupposition, never as an answer. Thus if you asked a pathologist about a certain disease "What is the cause of the event E which sometimes happens in this disease?" he would reply "The cause of E is C. That was established by So-and-so." You might go on to ask: "I suppose before So-and-so found out what the cause of E was, he was quite sure it has a cause?" The answer would be "Quite sure, of course." If you now say "Why?" he will probably answer, "Because everything that happens has a cause." If you ask "But how do you know that everything that happens has a cause?" he will probably blow up right in your face, because you have put your finger on one of his absolute presuppositions, and people are apt to be ticklish in their absolute presuppositions. But if he keeps his temper and gives you a civil and candid answer, it will be to the following effect: "That is a thing we take for granted in my job. We don't question it. We don't try to verify it. It isn't a thing anybody has discovered, like microbes or the circulation of the blood." He is telling you that it is an absolute presupposition of the science he pursues.

An absolute presupposition is not a "dodge," and people who "start" a new one do not start it because they "like" to start it. People are not ordinarily aware of their absolute presuppositions, and are not, therefore, aware of changes in them; such a change, therefore, cannot be a matter of choice. Nor is there anything superficial or frivolous about it. It is the most radical change a man can undergo, and entails the abandonment of all his most firmly established habits and standards for thought and action.

Why do such changes happen? Briefly, because the absolute presuppositions of any given society, at any given phase of its history, form a structure which is subject to "strains" of greater or less intensity, which are "taken up" in various ways, but never annihilated. If the strains are too great, the structure collapses and is replaced by another, which will be a modification of the old with the destructive strain removed; a modification not consciously devised but created by a process of unconscious thought.

PECULIAR STATUS OF ABSOLUTE PRESUPPOSITIONS

Absolute presuppositions are not verifiable. This does not mean that we should like to verify them but are not able to; it means that the idea of verification is an idea which does not apply to them; because, to speak of verifying a presupposition involves supposing that it is a relative presupposition.

The distinction between truth and falsehood does not apply to absolute presuppositions. Putting the same point differently: absolute presuppositions are never propounded; they are presupposed. To be propounded is not their business; their business is to be presupposed. The scientist's business, as we shall see, is not to propound them but to propound the proposition that this or that one of them is presupposed.

We do not acquire absolute presuppositions by arguing; on the contrary, unless we have them already, arguing is impossible to us. Nor can we change them by arguing; unless they remained constant all our arguments would fall to pieces. We cannot confirm ourselves in them by "proving" them; proof depends on them, not they on proof.

Absolute presuppositions are not "derived from experience," but are catalytic agents which the mind must bring out of its own resources to the manipulation of what is called "experience" and the conversion of it into science.

An absolute presupposition cannot be undermined by the verdict of "experience," because it is the yard-stick by which "experience" is judged.

METAPHYSICS IS THE STUDY OF SUCH PRESUPPOSITIONS

There are absolute presuppositions. The analysis which detects them I call metaphysical analysis.

Metaphysics is the science which deals with the presuppositions underlying science.

The business of metaphysics is to reveal the absolute presuppositions that are involved in any given piece of thinking. The general class of study to which metaphysics belongs is thus the study of thought. Metaphysics is one branch of the science of thought.

There are two things you can do with absolute presuppositions. One of them is what the scientist does, and the other what the metaphysician does. You can presuppose them, which is what the scientist does; or you can find out what they are, which is what the metaphysician does. I mean finding out what absolute presuppositions are in fact made.

Metaphysics arises out of the pursuit of knowledge. That pursuit, science, involves disentangling the presuppositions of our thought. This again involves discovering that some of them are relative presuppositions which have to be justified, and that others are absolute presuppositions which neither stand in need of justification nor can in fact be justified. A person who has made this discovery is already a metaphysician.

Science and metaphysics are inextricably united, stand or fall together. The birth of science, the establishment of orderly thinking, is also the birth of metaphysics. As long as either lives the other lives; if either dies the other must die with it.

Metaphysical analysis, the discovery that certain presuppositions are absolute, is an integral part of scientific work. In the interests of science it is necessary that the work of metaphysics should be done.

Physics has become a science by obtaining a firm grasp on its own presuppositions, asking questions that arose from them, and devising experiments by which these should be answered.

It is important for every one who either thinks scientifically, or profits by the fruits of another people's scientific thinking, that the work of metaphysics should be done, and well done.

People do not need to analyse their thoughts very deeply in order to find out that there are a good many things they take for granted. Further analysis, however, is needed to settle the question whether the things are taken relatively for granted or absolutely for granted. It might seem that the question should be an easy one to answer, because presupposing is a thing people do in their minds, and the distinction between presupposing relatively and presupposing absolutely is a distinction between two ways of doing it, so that a man need only be ordinarily intelligent and truthful, one might think, to give an accurate answer to the question which of them he is doing.

But it is not quite so simple as that. To begin with, people may have a motive for deceiving themselves and each other. In modern Europe absolute presuppositions are unfashionable. The smart thing is to deny their existence. Even people who regard this as a silly fashion may be so far influenced by it as to weaken at the critical moment when every available ounce of determination is needed in order to decide whether a given presupposition is absolute or relative; and may allow a kind of mass-suggestion to decide them in favour of its being relative.

It is only by analysis that any one can come to know either that he is making absolute presuppositions or what absolute presuppositions he is making. Such analysis may in certain cases proceed in the following manner. If the inquirer can find a person to experiment upon who is well trained in a certain type of scientific work, intelligent and earnest in his devotion to it, and unaccustomed to metaphysics, let him probe into various presuppositions that his "subject" has been taught to make in the course of his scientific education, and invite him to justify each or to abandon it. If the "inquirer" is skilful and the "subject" the right kind of man, these invitations will be contemplated with equanimity, and even with interest, so long as relative presuppositions are concerned. But when an absolute presupposition is touched, the invitation will be rejected, even with a certain degree of violence.

The rejection is a symptom that the "subject," cooperating with the work of analysis, has come to see that the presupposition he is being asked to justify or abandon is an absolute presupposition; and the violence with which it is expressed is a symptom that he feels the importance of this absolute presupposition for the kind of work to which he is devoted. This is what I called being "ticklish in one's absolute presuppositions." This ticklishness is a sign of intellectual health combined with a low degree of analytical skill. A man who is ticklish in that way is a man who knows, "instinctively" as they say, that absolute presuppositions do not need justification.

This is a precarious method, because the qualifications it demands in the "subject" are too delicate. As soon as the "subject" understands what is going on he will lose the ticklishness on which his value depends. The only altogether satisfactory method is for the analyst to experiment on himself; because this is the only case in which familiarity with the experiments will make the subject more valuable, instead of less. But it demands great resolution, and the temptation to cheat is stronger than one would expect. The purpose of the experiments is to find out what absolute presuppositions are made. Presuppositions are brought to light, and about each the question is raised and settled whether it is relative or absolute.

It is a mistake to fancy that by investigating the truth of their absolute presuppositions a metaphysician could show that one school of science was fundamentally right and another fundamentally wrong.

Some persons think there are two things you can do with absolute presuppositions: presuppose them, which is what the ordinary scientist does with them; or find out whether they are true or false, which is what the metaphysician does with them. I deny this. The second thing cannot be done. To inquire into the truth of a presupposition is to assume that it is a relative presupposition. Such a phrase as "inquiry into the truth of an absolute presupposition" is nonsense.

I distinguish between metaphysics and pseudo-metaphysics. Pseudo-metaphysics will ask such questions as this, where AP stands for any absolute presupposition: Is AP true? Upon what evidence is AP accepted? How can we demonstrate AP? What right have we to presuppose it if we can't? Answers to questions like these are neither metaphysical truths nor metaphysical errors. They are nonsense: the kind of nonsense which comes of thinking that what is absolutely presupposed must be either true or false. That kind of nonsense I call pseudo-metaphysics. Let the distinction between metaphysics and pseudo-metaphysics be firmly grasped. Let it be understood that the business of metaphysics is to find out what absolute presuppositions have actually been made by various persons at various times in doing various pieces of scientific thinking.

METAPHYSICS IS AN HISTORICAL INVESTIGATION

All metaphysical questions are historical questions, and all metaphysical propositions are historical propositions.

Metaphysics is the attempt to find out what absolute presuppositions have been made by this or that person or group of persons, on this or that occasion or group of occasions, in the course of this or that piece of scientific thinking. Arising out of this, it will consider (for example) whether absolute presuppositions are made singly or in groups, and if the latter, how the groups are organized; whether different absolute presuppositions are made by different individuals or races or nations or classes; or on occasions when different things are being thought about; or whether the same have been made *semper, ubique, ad omnibus*. And so on.

The metaphysician is not confined to one single constellation of absolute presuppositions. He has before him an indefinite number of them. He can study the presuppositions of European science at any phase in its history for which he has evidence. He can study the presuppositions of Arabic science, of Indian science, of Chinese science; again in all their phases, so far as he can find evidence for them. He can study the presuppositions of the science practised by "primitive" and "prehistoric" peoples. All these are his proper work; not an historical background for his work, but his work itself.

When he has some knowledge about several different constellations of absolute presuppositions, he can compare them. This has its uses. It will convince the metaphysician that there are no "eternal" or "crucial" or "central" problems in metaphysics. It will rid him of the parish-pump idea that the metaphysical problems of his own generation, or, more likely, the one next before his own, are the problems that all metaphysicians have been worrying about. It will give him a hint of the way in which different sets of absolute presuppositions correspond not only with differences in the structure of what is generally called scientific thought but with differences in the entire fabric of civilization.

Anti positivist

REFLECTIONS ON POSITIVISM

Positivism is the doctrine that the only valid method of attaining knowledge is the method used in the natural sciences, and hence that no knowledge is genuine unless it either is natural science or resembles natural science in method.

Positivists say that scientific thought has no presuppositions.

They never discovered that there were such things as absolute presuppositions. Presuppositions they misunderstood as general propositions about matters of fact, advanced upon credit and awaiting verification. This would do at a pinch as an account of relative presuppositions, in whose case verification is a word that has meaning. As an account of absolute presuppositions, which are neither in need of verification nor susceptible of it, the description of them as generalizations is nonsensical.

The positivist says either of two things about an absolute presupposition. (1) He describes it as a generalization about matters of fact; and consequently maintains that by observing facts one could hope to verify it. Indeed, it must have been arrived at by observing facts; for here it is; and there was no other way in which that could have been arrivel at. Heads I win. (2) He says that it was not arrived at by observing facts, for it was not a record of observations; and that, since there was no other way in which it could have been arrived at, it had not been arrived at; consequently, although it looks like a significant statement, it could not be one; it is just a piece of nonsense. Tails you lose.

They take absolute presuppositions and play "heads I win" with them, in order to exhibit them as generalizations from observed facts. Their reason for playing "heads I win" with them, arises from the fact that, having consituted themselves philosophical patrons of natural science, they thought themselves bound to justify any presuppositions which natural science thought fit to make. "Metaphysics," said Bradley, "is the finding of bad reasons for what we believe upon instinct." If I understand this epigram correctly, it is an accurate description of what the positivist does when he attempts to justify some absolute presupposition inductively. What Bradley seems to be saying is this: "Why we believe things of that kind I do not know. Let us give this ignorance a name by saying that we believe them upon instinct; meaning that it is not because we see reason to believe them. Metaphysics is the attempt to find reasons for these beliefs. Experience shows that the reasons thus found are always bad ones.

It is not the business of metaphysics to find reasons for "what we believe upon instinct," to raise the presuppositions of ordinary scientific thinking to the level of ascertained and demonstrated truths.

The positivistic mistake about metaphysics is the mistake of thinking that metaphysics is the attempt to justify by appeal to observed facts the absolute presuppositions of our thought. This attempt is bound to fail because absolute presuppositions cannot stand as the answers to questions, and therefore the question whether they are justifiable, which in effect is identical with the question whether they are true, is a question that cannot logically arise. To ask it is the hall-mark of pseudo-metaphysics.

If metaphysics were an attempt to provide empirical justification for the presuppositions of science, it might prove detrimental to science itself, not by its success but by its failure; for when the discovery was made that no justification of this kind is to be had, the belief that it is nevertheless necessary might lead to the false conclusion that the whole fabric of scientific thought is rotten at the core.

It is a characteristic of modern European civilization that metaphysics is habitually frowned upon and the existence of absolute presuppositions denied. If this denial ever achieves the eradication of metaphysics, the eradication of science and civilization will be accomplished at the same time.

The result of thinking systematically according to any given set of presuppositions is the creation of science. The result of thinking systematically about what presuppositions are actually in use is the creation of metaphysics. The result of simply presupposing our presuppositions, clinging to them by a sheer act of faith, whether or not we know what they are, whether or not we work out their consequences, is the creation of a religion.

Note on Sources. The above materials are quoted, with an occasional abridgment or paraphrase, from Collingwood's book *An Essay on Metaphysics.* The passages are almost all from Part I and Part II of that book.

Reading References. Collingwood, like Plato and William James and a small number of other writers on philosophy, is a joy to read. The student is recommended, therefore, to secure a copy of *An Essay on Metaphysics* and read for himself as much as he will. Collingwood conceives of philosophy, in general, as the activity whereby a mind gets to know the principles and presuppositions which are operative in its thinking and acting. Thus *An Essay on Metaphysics* does this for the activity called "getting to know." His *Principles of Art* does this for the activity whereby an artist produces, or "creates," a work of art. His *The New Leviathan* does this for man considered as a political animal. His *The Idea of History* does it for the activity by which the historian produces some history—i.e., seeks to make the past intelligible. His *Autobiography* contains an account of the activities and experiences which led him to entertain and elaborate this conception of the activity called philosophizing.

READING QUESTIONS

1. His distinction between absolute and relative presupposition.
2. Do absolute presuppositions change? If so, why?
3. He says they are neither true nor false. Why not?
4. His distinction between metaphysics and pseudo-metaphysics.
5. His distinction between what the scientist does and what the metaphysician does.
6. "Science and metaphysics stand or fall together." How so?
7. Why people are "ticklish" in their presuppositions.
8. Sense in which "metaphysics" is an historical science, according to Collingwood.
9. Sense in which positivists play "heads I win" and "tails you lose" with absolute presuppositions. Why they do this.
10. His distinction here: (a) science, (b) metaphysics, (c) religion.
11. Wherein you find Collingwood (a) most (b) least convincing.

TOPIC FOUR

An Ethical Problem

THE PROBLEM STATED

Ethics may be defined an an inquiry into the principles and the presuppositions which are operative in your moral judgments. Not to know your principles and presuppositions is to be naïve. To get to know them is to achieve sophistication.

Upon what principle do we discriminate between right and wrong? Compile a list of acts or ways of acting which you would judge to be wrong. What fact, about all of these acts, is your reason for calling them cases of wrong doing? The fact that they are contrary to the will of God? The fact that they are contrary to custom or convention? The fact that they are contrary to nature, "unnatural"? The fact that they militate against human happiness? Whatever the fact is, call it X. You can then say, "An act is wrong if and only if it is X or an X." When you spell out that X, you have formulated the principle which is operative in your moral judgments. You use such a principle when you authorize moral judgments on conduct, on character, on institutions, on laws, on customs. We say, of a given act, that it is right or wrong; of a type of character, that it is the right type or the wrong type; of an institution, for example, private property, that it is right or wrong; of a law, say, capital punishment, that it is right or wrong; of a custom, that it is right or wrong. Our present problem is not which particular act, or character, or institution, or law, or custom is right or wrong. Our problem is the more general one: On what principle do we judge these things right or wrong?

The sets of citations which follow present six different approaches to this question. The first set, drawn from the writings of an eighteenth-century moralist, William Paley, argues that *right* means "according to the will of God." This way of grounding morality in theology is something with which we are all familiar. Paley's statement is therefore valuable as a starting point.

The second set, drawn from the writings of Immanuel Kant, argues that *right* means "according to reason," or "what reason prescribes." Kant wrote in the Age of Reason which produced such characteristic figures as Voltaire, Rousseau, Thomas Paine, and others. His attempt to ground morality on an appeal to reason, with no reference to theological doctrine, represents one perennial possibility. In any age which understands by *reason* what Kant intended by that term, his appeal would be instant and profound.

The third set, drawn from the writings of John Stuart Mill, argues that *right* means "producing human happiness." Mill was a spokesman for an age of social reform. His position in moral philosophy was inspired by his experience of great and far-reaching changes in the social order, widespread wealth and poverty, the rise of nineteenth-century democratic governments, the emergence of new economic classes, and the rapid decay of old customs and institutions. It is in this context that we must understand his somewhat abrupt and impatient dismissal of the moral philosophies typified by Paley and Kant, and his forthright appeal to happiness as the foundation principle of human morality.

In the fourth set, Friedrich Nietzsche argues that *right* means "productive of or giving expression to the superman." The notion that man has evolved from lower animals suggested that something higher may evolve from man. This, when it comes, will be the superman, and anything is right which either hastens his arrival or expresses his nature when arrived.

The fifth set of citations, drawn from the writings of G. E. Moore, presents a curious outcome to the argument from Paley to Mill. It seems clear that Professor Moore recognizes the problem common to these other writers: what is the fundamental concept operative in moral judgments? But his argument is that because it *is* fundamental it is logically simple and therefore indefinable.

In the sixth set, A. J. Ayer presents a repudiation of the entire problem as common to Paley, Kant, Mill, and Moore. In this regard Professor Ayer has affinities with Nietzsche. His thesis is that moral judgments are meaningless expressions of emotion, and hence call for a psychological theory to account for them, not an ethical theory to elucidate them.

1. MORALITY GROUNDED IN THEOLOGY —FROM WILLIAM PALEY

One important question we can direct at any human act, is this: "Was it right or wrong? Did the agent do as he ought to have done, or as he ought not to have done?" Implicit in any answer to this question is a moral principle; that is, a criterion in terms of which we distinguish between right and wrong. As long as men entertain a lively belief in the existence of God, and ascribe to Him an interest in human affairs, many are likely to base their moral judgments upon what they consider to be His will. They are going to say that *right* means "according to the will of God," and *wrong* means "contrary to the will of God." William Paley, a popular moralist in the eighteenth century, was a man of precisely this turn of mind. One can do worse than examine the essentials of the appeal to theology as these are to be found in his writings. Any virtues which reside in this view will be obvious in the simplicity and sincerity of his language. Any shortcomings can be the more readily pointed out, since his stand is clear and bold. The following passage by Sir Leslie Stephen in his *History of English Thought in the Eighteenth Century* is worth reading before proceeding to Paley.

The different religions of the world tell us, each in its own fashion, what is the plan and meaning of this universe. Thence believers may infer what is the best method of employing our brief existence within it. We ought to be good, say all moralists, and the question remains: What is meant by *ought* and by *goodness*? Theology, so long as it was a vital belief in the world, affords a complete and satisfactory answer to these questions. Morality was, of necessity, its handmaid. Believe in an active ruler of the universe, who reveals his will to men, who distributes rewards and punishments to the good and the evil, and we have a plain answer to most of the problems of morality. God's will, so far as known to us, determines what is good. We are obliged to be good, whether from love or from fear.

Biographical Note. William Paley was born in England in 1743 and died in 1805 at the age of sixty-two. His father was headmaster of the school of Giggleswick in Yorkshire. His early education was obtained under the paternal eye. At the age of fifteen, young Paley went to the University of Cambridge. That his father had great expectations may be gathered from a remark he made to a friend: "My son is now gone to college. He'll turn out a great man. Very great, indeed. I am certain of it.

He has by far the clearest head I ever met in my life." Paley spent four
years at Cambridge, obtaining his B.A. in 1762. The following anecdote
suggests that he was a normal young man during these years:

> I spent the first two years of my undergraduate life happily, but unprofit-
> ably. I was constantly in society, where we were not immoral, but idle and
> rather expensive. At the commencement of my third year, however, after hav-
> ing left the usual party at a rather late hour in the evening, I was awakened
> at five in the morning by one of my companions, who stood at my bedside.
> He said: "Paley, I have been thinking what a fool you are. I could achieve
> nothing worth while, even were I to try, and anyway I can afford the idle
> life I lead. You could achieve anything, if you were to try, and you cannot
> afford to waste your time. I have had no sleep during the whole night on
> account of these reflections, and am now come solemnly to inform you that if
> you persist in your indolence, I must renounce your society." I was so struck
> with the visit and the visitor that I laid in bed a great part of the day, and
> formed my plan. I ordered my bedmaker to prepare my fire every evening, in
> order that it might be lighted by myself the next morning. I rose at five
> o'clock, read during the whole of the day, except such hours as chapel and
> lectures required, allotting to each portion of time its peculiar branch of study;
> and, just before the closing of the gates (9:00 P.M.) I went to a neighboring
> coffeehouse, where I constantly regaled upon a mutton chop and a dose of milk
> punch.

After graduating, Paley rose slowly but steadily in the ecclesiastical
world. In 1785 he published his *Principles of Moral and Political Philosophy.* It passed through fifteen editions during his own lifetime. One of
his contemporaries remarked of this book: "It may be said to be the only
work on moral philosophy fitted to be understood by every class of
readers."

The Argument of the Citations. Paley's formulation of the fundamental principle of morality is simple and clear: Right is that which agrees
with the will of God; wrong is that which does not. Having stated this
controlling idea, he sets himself to elaborate it. He provides first a definition of *virtue*, consistent with his basic propositions; he moves on, then,
to examine the meaning of moral obligation and the distinction between
prudence and duty. These matters settled, he turns to the question: if
right means "according to the will of God," how are we to tell what is
and is not the will of God? His answer here is twofold: scriptural revelation and the "light of nature." The sense in which God's will may be
gathered from Scripture is then explained. But what of the light of nature;
what, that is, about the morality of acts where we do not have God's ex-

press declaration? Here Paley meets a real problem, and knowing, as he did, that many occasions arise with respect to which Scripture is silent, he could not treat this matter lightly. To solve his problem he adopts the assumption that human happiness is God's primary concern. Realizing, as he says, that "this assumption is the foundation of the whole system," he sets himself to "explain the reasons upon which it rests." The explanation in question occupies the remainder of the citations. The following quotation from a seventeenth-century moralist expresses clearly the idea which Paley proposes to develop:

That God has given a rule whereby men should govern themselves, I think there is no one so brutish as to deny. He has a right to do it. We are His creatures. He has goodness and wisdom to direct our actions to what is best, and He has power to enforce it by rewards and punishments of infinite weight and duration in another life; for nobody can take us out of His hands. This is the only touchstone of moral rectitude, and by comparing them to this law, it is that men judge of the most considerable moral good or evil of their actions; that is, whether as duty or as sins, they are like to procure them happiness or misery from the hands of the Almighty.

Now Paley. First, as to ethics in general:

Ethics is that science which teaches men their duty and the reasons of it. The use of such a study depends upon this, that, without it, the rules of life by which men are ordinarily governed, oftentimes mislead them, through a defect in either the rule or in the application.

Then, as to the meaning of *right:*

Right signifies being consistent with the will of God.
Right is a quality of persons or of actions. Of persons, as when we say, "He has a right to his property"; of actions, as when we say, "His action was right on that occasion." Whether of persons or of actions, *right* means "consistent with, or according to, the will of God." In the one case, substituting the definition for the term, you may say, "It is consistent with or according to the will of God that he have his property"; in the other case, "His action, on that occasion, was consistent with or according to the will of God."

From this it follows that:

Virtue is doing good to mankind, in obedience to the will of God, and for the sake of everlasting happiness.

The division of virtues to which we are nowadays most accustomed is into duties: duties toward God; duties toward other men; duties toward ourselves. There are more of these distinctions, but it is not worth while to set them down.

And we are now in a position to explain what is meant by *duty* or *moral obligation*.

What are we to understand by *moral obligation?* Truthfulness, we say, is a moral obligation. What do we intend by this expression? Why am I obliged to keep my word?

When I first turned my thoughts to moral speculations, an air of mystery seemed to hang over the whole subject. This arose, I believe, from hence—that I supposed that to be obliged to do a thing was very different from being induced or urged to do it; that the obligation to practice virtue, for example, was quite another thing, and of another kind, than the obligation which a soldier is under to obey his officer, or a servant his master. Now in what does the difference consist?

I shall argue to the following effect: A man is said to be *obliged* when he is urged by a violent motive resulting from the command of another. First, the motive must be violent, strong, powerful. A person has done me some little service. Suppose, then, he asks me for my vote. From a motive of gratitude, or expectation, I may give it to him. But I should hardly say I was obliged to give it to him; because the motive, or incentive, or inducement, does not rise high enough. Second, it must result from the command of another. Offer a man a gratuity for doing anything. He is not obliged by your offer to do it. But if a magistrate were to command it, he would then consider himself obligated to do it.

Wherever, then, the motive is violent enough and is coupled with the idea of a command, an authority, a law, a will, there, I take it, we always reckon ourselves to be obliged. Let it be remembered that to be obliged is to be urged by a violent motive resulting from the command of another.

And then let it be asked: Why am I "obliged" to keep my word? The answer will be: Because I am urged by the expectation of being rewarded after this life if I do, and punished if I do not, follow, in this respect, the command of God. This solution goes to the bottom of the subject, as no further question can reasonably be asked.

There is always understood to be a difference between an act of prudence and an act of duty. Thus, if I distrusted a man who owed me money, I should reckon it an act of prudence to get another bound with him; but I should hardly call it an act of duty. On the other hand, it would be a loose kind of language to say that, as my friend had placed a box of jewels in my hands when he went abroad, it would be prudent of me to preserve it for him until he returned.

Now, wherein does the difference consist? The difference, and the only difference, is this, that, in the one case, we consider what we shall gain or lose in the present world; in the other case, we consider also what we shall gain or lose in the world to come. Prudence has regard to the former; duty, to the latter. Those who would establish a system of morality, independent of a future state, must look out for some different idea of moral obligation.

To us, therefore, there are two great questions: Will there be, after this life, any distribution of rewards and punishments at all? If so, what actions will be rewarded and what actions will be punished? The first question comprises the credibility of the Christian religion. Proof of an affirmative answer to it, although we confess that it is the foundation upon which the whole fabric rests, must in this treatise be taken for granted. The second question comprises morality itself, and to this we shall now address ourselves.

By now the fundamental role of the will of God in Paley's moral philosophy should be clear. From it proceed all the principal terms in such a moralists's vocabulary. The question hence, begins to press: How do we determine what is and is not the will of God? _Scripture_

As the will of God is our rule, to inquire, in any instance, what is our duty or what we are obliged to do, is, in effect, to inquire what is the will of God in that instance. This consequently becomes the whole business of morality.

Now, there are two methods of coming at the will of God on any point: by his express declarations, when they are to be had, and which must be sought for in Scripture; by what we can discover of his designs and disposition from his works, or, as we usually call it, the light of nature. The object of both is the same—to discover the will of God; and, provided we do but discover it, it matters nothing by what means.

An ambassador may guide himself in many cases with safety by judging only from what he knows of his sovereign's disposition, by arguing from what he has observed of his conduct or what he knows of his designs. But if he have his commission and instructions in his pocket, it would be strange never to look into them. He will, naturally, conduct himself by both rules. When his instructions are clear and positive, there is an end of all further deliberation, unless, indeed, he suspects their authenticity. Where his instructions are silent or dubious, he will endeavor to supply or explain them by what he has been able to collect from other quarters of his master's general inclination or intentions.

Whoever expects to find in the Scriptures particular directions for every moral doubt that arises looks for more than he will meet with. Such a detail of particular precepts would have so enlarged the sacred volume that it would have been too bulky either to be read or circulated; or rather, as St. John says, "even the world itself could not contain the books that should be written."

Morality is taught in the Scriptures in this wise: General rules are laid down, of piety, justice, benevolence, and purity. Several of these rules are occasionally illustrated, either in fictitious examples, as in the parable of the good Samaritan; or in instances which actually presented themselves, as in Christ's reproof of his disciples or his praise of the poor widow; or, in the resolution of questions proposed to Christ, as in his answer to the young man who asked him, "What lack I yet?"

This is the way in which all practical sciences are taught, as arithmetic, grammar, navigation, and the like. Rules are laid down, and examples are subjoined, by way of explaining the principle of the rule, and as so many specimens of the method of applying it.

So far, so good. By reference to the will of God we determine what is right and wrong. By reference to Scripture we determine, in part, what is the will of God. But what of that part which is not provided for by Scripture?

The method of coming at the will of God concerning any action, where we do not have this express declaration, is to inquire into the tendency of the action to promote or diminish the general happiness. This rule proceeds on the assumption that God Almighty wills and wishes the happiness of His creatures, and, consequently, that those actions which promote that will and wish must be agreeable to Him; and the contrary.

As this assumption is the foundation of the whole system, it becomes necessary to explain the reasons upon which it rests.

When God created the human species, either He wished their happiness or He wished their misery or He was indifferent to both.

If He wished their misery, He might have made sure of His purpose, e.g., by forming our senses to be as many sores and pains to us as they are now instruments of gratification and enjoyment. He might, e.g., have made everything we tasted, bitter; everything we saw, loathsome; everything we touched, a sting; every smell, a stench; every sound, a discord.

If He had been indifferent to our happiness or misery, we must impute to our good fortune both the capacity of our senses to receive pleasure and the supply of external objects fitted to excite it. But either of these—and still more both of them—is too much to be attributed to accident, i.e., mere "good fortune." Nothing remains, therefore, other than the first supposition; namely, that when God created the human species, He intended their happiness.

The same argument may be proposed in different terms, thus: The world abounds in contrivances, and all the contrivances with which we are acquainted are directed to beneficial purposes. Evil, no doubt, exists. But it is never, that we can perceive, the object of contrivance. Teeth are contrived to eat, not to ache. Their aching now and then is incidental to the contrivance, perhaps inseparable from it, perhaps even a defect in it; but it is not the object of it.

This is a distinction which well deserves to be attended to. In describing implements of husbandry, you would hardly say of a sickle that it is made to cut the reaper's fingers, though from the construction of the instrument, and the manner of using it, this mischief often happens.

On the other hand, if you had occasion to describe instruments of torture, the case would be different. This, you would say, is to stretch the sinews; this, to dislocate the joints; this, to break the bones; this, to scorch the soles of the feet; and so forth. Here pain and misery are the very objects of the contrivance.

Now, nothing of this sort is to be found in nature. We never discover a contrivance whose object is to bring about pain and misery. No anatomist ever discovered anything in the organism calculated to produce pain and disease. No anatomist, in explaining the parts of the human body, ever said, "This is to irritate, this is to inflame, this is to conduct stones to the kidneys, this is to secrete the humor which forms gout." The most he will say is that he does not understand some part or other, or that it is useless. He never suspects that it is put there to incommode, to annoy, to torment.

Since, then, God hath called forth His consummate wisdom to contrive and provide for our happiness, and the world appears to have been constituted with this design at first, then, so long as this consitution is upheld by Him, we must suppose the same design to continue.

We conclude, therefore, that God wills and wishes the happiness of His creatures. This conclusion being once established, we are at liberty to go on with the rule built upon it, namely, that the method of coming at the will of God concerning any action, where we do not have his express declaration, is to inquire into the tendency of that action to promote or diminish the general happiness.

By virture of the two principles, that God wills the happiness of His creatures, and that God's will is the measure of right and wrong, we arrive at certain conclusions. These conclusions become rules. And soon we learn to pronounce actions right or wrong according as they agree or disagree with our rules, without looking any further.

Paley is of interest for the difficulties which his position suggests. Stated briefly, what he says comes to this: "*Right* means according to God's will. An act is right if and only if it is according to the will of God. This is the principle of morality. The phrase 'if and only if' indicates that you are trying to define rightness in principle. God's will is to be found in the Scriptures, or discovered by the light of nature. The light of nature tells us that God intends above all to produce and promote human happiness. Where, therefore, the Scriptures are silent, we determine the rightness of an act by the fact that it produces more happiness than any other act possible at the time." This is both clear and confused. It raises more questions than it settles. For example, does Paley mean that an act is right because it agrees with God's will, or that it agrees with God's will because it is right? These two are not the same. Also, what is the relation between a man's will and God's will? Does Paley believe that God's will causes and governs all things? If so, could a human act ever be contrary to God's will? If it could not, then it would follow that no act is ever wrong. Does Paley want *that?*

Then, of course, there is the problem connected with detecting God's will in the Scriptures. Why the Scriptures? Why not in Plato's dialogues? Or in the Mohammedan *Koran?* In which parts of the Scriptures? In those parts which enjoin an eye for an eye? Or in those parts which enjoin the golden rule? If in both, what about clashes? If in one, how choose which? Passing to the second half of his argument, has he proved, at all conclusively, that God's will is directed to creating and promoting human happiness? This hypothesis may account for some of the facts. But it does not account for all of them. See Hume and Schopenhauer on the misery of man's estate. Going a step further, and admitting his argument, are we justified in arguing that an act is right, if and only if, it produces more happiness than any other act possible under the circumstances? Is this not to formulate a moral principle that swings clear of the first part of Paley's argument, and could stand on its own feet, without any aid from Scripture? If so, what about cases where the "appeal to Scripture" and "the appeal to happiness" appear to clash? Finally is it or is it not the case that we are more sure of what is right and wrong than we are of God's very existence? If so, would it not be wiser to begin with what we are more sure of, than to begin with what we are less sure of? These, and other problems which suggest themselves, were engaging the attention of Immanuel Kant during the years in which Paley was writing his *Principles of Moral and Political Philosophy*. Paley published in 1785. Kant had published his *Critique of Pure Reason* in 1781, and was meanwhile engaged on a second *Critique,* directed, this time, not at the problem of knowledge but at the problem of morality. From this prosperous and rather worldly Anglican divine one turns with something like eagerness to the austere and searching professorial moralist at Königsberg.

Note on Sources. The Paley materials in this section are quoted, abridged, or paraphrased from his volume, *The Principles of Moral and Political Philosophy*. That work is divided into six Books. The materials in this section are from Books I and II. Each Book is divided into brief chapters. The titles of the chapters in Books I and II will indicate the points at which material has been used for this section.

READING QUESTIONS

1. Use the "If and only if" formula to state Paley's principle.
2. Two ways of getting to know the will of God.
3. Is Paley's principle the same as the Golden Rule?
4. Suppose you affirm Paley's principle. Mention at least three things you thereby presuppose. Can you mention more than three?
5. Relation between Paley's principle and (a) the Scriptures (b) the light of nature. Does he cite either (a) or (b) as authority for his principle?
6. Why he wants to prove that God wills the happiness of men. Why it would not do for him to use the Scriptures to prove that. What logical fallacy would have been involved?
7. How in the course of his argument Paley uses the contrast between a sickle and an instrument of torture.
8. What fact common to all cases of wrong-doing would, according to Paley, be the reason for calling them cases of wrong-doing?
9. What fact common to all cases of wrong-doing would, according to the light of nature, be the reason for calling them cases of wrong-doing?
10. Why Paley should hesitate to judge any act wrong unless he is willing to presuppose free will in man.
11. Which of Paley's presuppositions would be placed in jeopardy by a strict theological determinism?
12. Use Paley's position to illustrate (a) the distinction (b) the relation between a principle and a presupposition.
13. If you were inclined to reject Paley's principle, which presupposition(s) would incline you to do so?
14. Which of these statements Paley would endorse: (a) God wills a line of action because it is right; (b) a line of action is right because God wills it.
15. What you would do with this question if you were Paley: "Why does agreeing with the will of God make an act right?"
16. Wherein you find Paley (a) most (b) least worth your while.

2. MORALITY GROUNDED IN DUTY —FROM IMMANUEL KANT

From Paley to Kant. While Paley was engaged in arguing that morality has its roots in theology, Immanuel Kant was engaged in showing that such is not the case. Paley, it will be remembered, published in 1785. Kant, who had been developing his views in lecture form since 1775, published in 1785 and again, at greater length, in 1788. The efforts made by these two moralists to formulate the principle of morality provide an excellent starting point for the study of modern analysis and speculation in these matters.

Kant lived in the Age of Reason, the age of Hume and Rousseau and Voltaire and the revolutions in America and France. He is a firm believer in the rationality of man. He seeks to develop the notion of a rational morality: what, in the way of action, does reason require of man? He works with the conception of man as a rational animal. By *rational* as applied to man he meant two things: having (1) the power to discover what is the case, and to guide conduct by such knowledge, i.e., to develop pure and applied sciences; (2) the power to discover what ought to be the case, and to guide conduct by such knowledge, i.e., to make moral judgments and act them out. Just as he could speak of rational science, so he would speak of rational conduct or rational morality. Just as, by *rational science* he would mean knowledge valid and binding for all rational minds, so by *rational morality* he would mean morality valid and binding for all rational minds. To the first kind of rationality he devoted his *Critique of Pure Reason;* to the second, his *Critique of Practical Reason.*

Biographical Note. At the end of the biographical note on Kant in the previous topic, page 203, we left him finishing his *Critique of Pure Reason* and publishing it in 1781. This treatise was the first of three, all directed to the analysis and exploration of a single theme, namely, mind and its place in nature. The first critique dealt with mind and the world order; the second is to deal with mind and the moral order; the third with mind and the aesthetic order. In other words, the relation of mind to the true, the good, and the beautiful; or to science, morality, and art. The elaboration of the ideas contained in these three studies brought Kant to a ripe old age, crowned with honors and influence. He became, and remains, one of the great formative thinkers in the history of modern philosophy.

The Argument of the Citations. Kant's handling of the problem of moral principle follows from his conception of what morality is. Without a firm grip of this, one is likely to miss the point of his analysis. For that reason, it is necessary to emphasize his starting point. He begins by assuming that morality, whatever it may be in detail, is something which is universally binding on all rational minds, comparable, in this respect, to science. Thus, if it is true that two and two make four, then it is binding on all rational creatures to accept this proposition. If this is a truth, it is true for everyone, not merely true for those who care to believe it. If it is true, it is true necessarily and always. It is true, in and of itself, without any reference to why it is true, without any reference to who does or does not believe it, without any reference to consequences that follow from its being true or from its being believed. It is, to use a favorite phrase of Kant's, true categorically, without any strings or qualifications. To repeat, it is not true because God commands it, nor because it is according to nature, nor because it pays in the long run to believe it, nor because all or most people agree to it, nor for any other reason. It is simply true because it is true. Moreover, it is true of all cases of two's and two's. There are no possible exceptions. It is not something which holds for one period of time and not for another, for one pair of two's and not for another, for one stage of civilization and not for another. In this universality, necessity, objectivity, which we detect readily enough in the proposition that two and two make four, Kant finds the differential mark of rational knowledge. He has his own word for it. It is, he says, true *a priori*. It will be recalled that he began his *Critique of Pure Reason* by accepting and exploring the implications of *a priori* knowledge.

This notion of *a priori* he carries over into the field of morality. If there is such a thing as rational science, it is *a priori*. If there is such a thing as rational morality, it is *a priori*. Moreover, just as in the case of *a priori* knowledge he did not undertake to prove that there is such a thing, but assumed its existence as a fact, so in the case of morality he does not undertake to show that there is such a thing, but assumes its existence as a fact. His argument is after this manner: If you admit that there is any rational knowledge, then you must admit that it is *a priori* in character, and if you admit that there is any rational morality, you must admit that it is *a priori* in character. If you admit that there is any rational knowledge, you must recognize that it is binding on all rational beings; so, by analogy, if you admit that there is any rational morality, you must recognize that it is binding on all rational beings. He is content to accept both rational knowledge and rational morality as facts to be recognized, not as hypotheses to be proved.

Once the notion of a rational morality is admitted, Kant is in a position to formulate his problem. It is this: What must be its principle? It will be noticed that he is not seeking to justify morality, any more than one would seek to justify arithmetic; not seeking to explain why right is right and wrong is wrong, any more than one would seek to explain why true is true, or false is false. He is merely saying: The facts of morality are categorical facts, not dependent for their moral quality upon anything beyond themselves. Such being the case, we ask again, what principle must run through all the cases of morality, and be absent from all the cases of immorality?

His answer is simple: An act is moral if and only if the principle which it embodies is capable of universalization without self-contradiction. This notion once stated, Kant proceeds to illustrate his meaning by some examples. His next step is to approach this same notion of categorical rightness from two other angles, namely, duty and good will. When these matters have been settled, he turns to consider a question that had been hanging fire since his studies in the problem of knowledge. I mean the problem of man's free will. Here the findings of the first *Critique* are called in to help solve the difficulty. As a moralist, his fundamental problem is, "What ought I to do?" But if, as would appear from the "scientific" view of the world, everything happens "of necessity," what sense is there to claiming that some things "ought" or "ought not" to be done? Here Kant is at once clarifying and baffling. Clarifying because he has the insight and tenacity to hold on to the "ought" as being every bit as much a reality as the "is," baffling because he concludes by admitting his inability to solve the paradox involved in their joint acceptance. His treatment of this question would require too much space to be summarized here. From freedom he passes on to God and immortality. As in the case of Kant's handling of the problem of knowledge, it will be necessary to state a few of his claims in the form of a condensed summary. His own language is too involved to permit direct citation. Wherever possible, however, his own words will be introduced.

Morality, the rightness and wrongness of actions, is categorical (not dependent upon anything) and *a priori* (valid for all persons and all times and all cases). In this it resembles rational knowledge. To quote: "The morality of an action is quite a peculiar thing. When we are considering the goodness of an action, we are concerned with what constitutes the goodness in and of itself."

If morality is of this categorical and *a priori* nature, then we can rule out several misleading attempts to formulate its principle. For example, the morality of an act is said, by some, to reside in the "feeling" which one has about the act. But this could not be for two reasons: (1) If morality is a matter of someone's feelings, then it is not categorical; that is, an act would depend, for its morality, upon the fact (external to the act itself) that it was or was not felt about in some way or other by some person or other. (2) If morality is a matter of feeling, then it is not anything universally binding and valid for all men, because feelings vary notoriously from time to time and from person to person; that is, one and the same act could be both right and wrong provided merely that two persons had opposite feelings about it. But this is to rob morality of its categorical nature, to give as the defining characteristic of morality a quality in virtue of which it would fail to be categorical and *a priori.*

Much the same line of reasoning is adduced by Kant against those who seek to locate the rightness of an act in its agreement with God's will. He says:

There are those who argue that we must first have God and then morality —a very convenient principle. But ethics and theology are neither of them a principle of the other. We are not discussing, here, the fact that theology is a motive for ethics—which it is—but we are asking whether the principle of ethical discrimination is theological—and it cannot be that.

Were it so, then before a nation could have any conception of duties it would first have to know God. Nations which had no right conception of God would have no duties, and this is not the case. Nations had a right idea of their duties, e.g., were aware that lies were detestable, without having the proper notion of God. Duties must therefore be derived from some other source.

If we do as God commanded, because He has commanded, and because He is so mighty that He can force us to, or punish us if we do not, we act under orders from fear and fright, not appreciating the propriety of our actions and knowing why we should do as God has commanded. Might cannot constitute a *vis obligandi.* Threats do not impose a (moral) obligation; they extort. Such conduct does not make the heart better.

Moral laws can be right without any commander, promulgator, obligator. How do we know the divine will? None of us feels it in his heart. We cannot know the moral law from any revelation, for if we did so, then those who had no revelation would be wholly ignorant of it.

We imagine God as possessing the most holy and most perfect will. But what then is the most perfect will? The moral law shows us what it is. We say the divine will accords with the moral law and is, therefore, holiest and most perfect. Thus we recognize the perfection of the divine will from the moral law. God wills all that is morally good and proper, and His will is, therefore, holy and perfect. But what is it that is morally good? Ethics supplies the answer to this question.

These strictures may be summarized. To locate the rightness of an act in its agreement with God's will is to deny its categorical nature, i.e., to make it depend, for its rightness, upon something other than or outside of itself. It is, too, to render morality an impossibility for all who do not know what God's will is, or who have a wrong notion of that will, or (it may be) deny His existence. There is, Kant would say, such a thing as morality apart from God's existence or our knowledge of the same. Finally, the view fails to take into account that when we say, "God is good," we are making goodness prior to and independent of God. He is good because His will or His action corresponds to the good; not vice versa.

There remains for consideration what Kant calls the *pragmatic* view of morality. The pragmatic view of morality is that an act is right because of the nature of its consequences; not right in itself, but because of the results that do or do not follow from it. Kant does not need to concern himself with the question of the nature of the results. He has two objections to doing so: (1) To locate the rightness of an act in the nature of its consequences is to deny the categorical nature of morality. It is to make its morality depend upon something other than the act. (2) To find the morality of an act in its consequences is to deprive morality of its *a priori* nature, because we can never know the consequences of an act until after the act is done, and even then never know them completely. This would reduce morality to a matter of probability; make it, as Kant says, *a posteriori*, instead of *a priori*. At this point, we can get closer to Kant's own words.

Having examined what the principle of morality is not, we must now examine what it is.

What is the one principle of morality, the criterion by which to judge everything and in which lies the distinction between moral goodness and all other goodness? What is the principle upon which we establish morality, and through which we are able to discriminate between what is moral and what immoral?

In this connection we must first notice that there are two points to be considered: the principle upon which we discriminate, and the mainspring or motive of performance. We must distinguish between the measuring rod and the mainspring. The measuring rod is the principle of discriminating; the mainspring is the motive of the performance of our obligation. If we ask, "What is morally good and what is not?" it is the principle of discrimination that is in question; but if we ask, "What is it that leads me to be moral?" it is the motive that is in question. We must guard against confusing the principle of morality with the motive to morality. The first is the norm. The second is the incentive.

The essence of morality is that our actions are motivated by a general rule. If we make it the foundation of our conduct that our actions shall be consistent with a universal rule, valid at all times and for everyone, then our actions exemplify the principle of morality.

In all moral judgments the idea which we frame is this: What is the character of the action taken by itself? If the principle of the action can, without self-contradiction, be universalized, it is moral; if it cannot be so universalized without contradicting itself, it is immoral. That action is immoral whose principle cancels and destroys itself when it is made a universal rule.

From this general statement of the nature of rightness Kant turns to some concrete illustrations. He considers the case of lying and suicide. These, being instances of wrongness, illustrate his notion of rightness only indirectly.

May I, when in distress, make a promise with the intention not to keep it? Considerations of prudence aside, would such an act be moral? The shortest way to answer this question is to ask, "Would I be content that the principle (getting out of difficulties by making false promises) should hold good as a universal law, for myself and all others?"

If I ask, "Can the principle of making deceitful promises to get out of difficulties be universalized?" I realize that it cannot. For with such a law there would be no promises at all. With such a principle made universal, it would be in vain to allege my intentions in regard to future actions. As soon as it were made a universal law, the principle would necessarily destroy itself, necessarily defeat its own end.

A man finds himself forced to borrow money. He knows that he will not be able to repay it, but he sees also that nothing will be lent to him unless he promises to repay it. Would it be right to promise? The principle of his action would be: When in need, to borrow and promise to repay, knowing that I cannot do so. Could this principle become a universal law? I see at once that it could not. As a universal law, it would contradict itself. For if this principle were a universal law, such promises would become impossible. For no one would consider such promises as binding, and all would ridicule them as vain pretenses.

A man reduced to despair by a series of misfortunes feels wearied of life. Would it be right to take his own life? Could the principle of his action become a universal law of nature? The principle would be: To shorten life when its longer duration is likely to bring more evil than satisfaction. Could this principle become a universal law of nature? Clearly not. A system of nature in which it was a law to destroy life by means of the very feeling whose special office it is to impel to the improvement of life, would contradict itself, and therefore could not exist as a system of nature. Hence that principle could not possibly exist as a universal law of nature. Hence it would be wholly inconsistent with the supreme principle of all duty.

If we attend to ourselves, on occasion of any transgression of duty, we shall find that we do not will that the principle of our action should become a universal law. On the contrary, we will that the opposite should remain a universal law, only we assume the liberty of making an exception in our own favor—just for this time only, it may be. This cannot be justified to our own impartial judgment, and it proves that we do recognize the validity of the moral principle I have formulated, even while we allow ourselves a few exceptions which we think important and forced upon us.

Thus far Kant has been developing the notion of a rational morality as something categorical and *a priori*. He has used this conception of morality to eliminate certain other theories which are incompatible with it, e.g., the theory that morality is a matter of feeling or emotion. He has disentangled what he takes to be the underlying principle of morality so conceived and advanced a few illustrations of his thesis. He returns again and again throughout his ethical writings to these basic claims. One example of such a reworking is contained in his distinction between hypothetical and categorical imperatives. The statement of this is given below. But a word first on Kant's use of these terms. The term *imperative*, used as a noun, means "a command." Kant inclines to use it in this sense. We shall, I think, come closer to his real meaning if we construe it by the word *ought*. We do, as a matter of everyday usage, employ the term *ought* in precisely the sense Kant would appear to have in mind. We say, for example, "If you wish to be there on time, you *ought* to leave early." Here the force of the *ought* is hypothetical; that is, it depends on whether you do or do not wish to get there on time. But there are occasions, Kant would claim, when we do not so use the term; when, for instance, we are pointing out what we take to be a duty. Thus, "you *ought* to be honest," "you *ought* to respect the rights of others." Here, we might feel, the *ought* is not dependent upon any *if*. It is not an hypothetical *ought*. It is, Kant would say, a categorical *ought*. The same idea could also be expressed in the distinction between an hypothetical obligation and a categorical obligation. Kant says:

All imperatives command either hypothetically or categorically. The former represent the practical necessity of a possible action as means to something else that is willed or might be willed. The latter would be that which represented an action as obligatory of itself without reference to some other end.

If an action is good only as a means to something else, then the imperative which commands it is hypothetical only; but if it is conceived to be good in itself, that is, without reference to any further end, the imperative which commands it is categorical.

The hypothetical imperative only says that the action is good for some purpose, actual or possible. The categorical imperative declares an action to be binding in itself, without reference to any purpose or end beyond itself.

All sciences have a practical part, consisting of problems connected with ends or purposes possible for us, and of imperatives directing how these may be attained. Here there is no question whether the end is good or rational, but only what one must do in order to attain it. The precepts for the physician to make his patient healthy and for a prisoner to insure his victim's death, are of equal value in this respect, namely that each serves to effect its purpose.

There is one imperative which commands certain conduct immediately, without having as its condition any other purpose to be attained by it. This imperative is categorical. It concerns not the matter of the action, nor its intended result, but its form and principle. This imperative may be called the imperative of morality.

There is but one categorical imperative, namely, "Act only on that principle which thou canst will should become a universal law."

This imperative of duty may be expressed, by analogy with natural laws, as follows: "Act as if the principle of thy action were to become by thy will a universal law of nature."

If there is a supreme practical principle or categorical imperative it must be one which constitutes an objective principle, and can therefore serve as a universal practical law. From this, as a supreme practical law, all laws of the will must be capable of being deduced. Accordingly the categorical imperative may be stated in a third way: "So act as to treat humanity, whether in thine own person or in the person of another, as an end withal, never as a means only."

If all the imperatives of duty can be deduced from this one imperative, from it as their principle, then, although it should remain undecided whether what is called *duty* is not merely a vain notion, yet at least we shall be able to show what we understand by it; be able, that is, to show what the notion means.

To act out of respect for this principle constitutes duty. To this every other motive must give place, because it is the condition of a will being good in itself, good absolutely, good without qualification; and the worth of such a will is above everything.

The direct opposite of acting on the principle of morality is acting on the principle of private happiness. This would ruin morality altogether, were not the voice of reason so clear, so irrepressible, so distinctly audible even to the commonest men. That action should be based on the principle of private happiness can only be maintained by such as are bold enough to shut their ears against that heavenly voice in order to support a theory that costs no trouble.

Two things fill the mind with ever new and increasing admiration and awe, the oftener and more steadily we reflect on them: the starry heavens above and the moral law within. I have not to search for them and conjecture them as though they were veiled in darkness or in a region transcending my horizon. I see them before me and connect them directly with the consciousness of my existence.

Duty! Thou sublime and mighty name! Thou seekest not to move the will by threatening nor by charming. Thou merely holdest forth a law which finds entrance into the mind, a law before which all inclinations and desires are dumb. What origin is worthy of thee? Where is to be found the root of thy noble descent? [1]

I do not, therefore, need any far-reaching penetration to discern what I have to do in order that my will may be morally good. Inexperienced in the course of the world, incapable of being prepared for all its contingencies, I need only ask, "Can I will that the principle of my action should become a universal law?" If not, then it must be rejected.

A second reworking of his fundamental insight is contained in his remarks on the intrinsic goodness of a good will. This thought requires a few words of explanation. Kant has spoken thus far of the morality of acts and wherein it resides. He has, also, restated the same notion in terms of *ought* and *ought not*. But, he is quite aware, there is no such thing as an act apart from someone who does the act. We may analyze and define the morality of an act, but we must end by addressing our remarks, not to acts, but to persons who act. There can be right acts only insofar as persons act rightly; hence the need to restate the matter in terms of will or intention. Every moralist, no matter what his principle of morality, is brought around at last to this point; hence Kant's genuine concern over a good will, i.e., a will inspired and controlled by the principle he has defined.

Nothing can be called *good*, without qualifications, except a good will. We now proceed to examine what exactly constitutes that will, simply good in itself, on which moral goodness depends.

Intelligence, wit, judgment, courage, resolution, perseverance, and so on, are no doubt good and desirable in many respects. But these gifts of nature may also be bad and mischievous if the will which is to make use of them is not good.

It is the same with gifts of fortune. Power, riches, honor, even health and happiness, inspire pride and often presumption if there is not a good will to check their influence.

A good will is good, not because of what it performs or accomplishes, not because of its usefulness or fruitfulness, but is simply good in itself. Even if it should happen that, owing to a special disfavor of fortune or the niggardly provision of a stepmotherly nature, a good will should wholly lack power to

[1] See Matthew Arnold's poem, *Morality*.

achieve its purpose, should by its greatest efforts achieve nothing, yet, like a jewel it would shine by its own light as a thing which has its whole value in itself.

We have, then, to develop the notion of a will good in itself and without reference to anything further. This notion already exists in the sound natural understanding, and requires rather to be clarified than taught or proved. In order to define more closely the notion of a good will, we will consider the wider notion of duty which includes the notion of a good will.

To have moral worth an act must be done from a sense of duty alone. We must distinguish between acts which accord with what duty requires, and acts done because duty requires. The latter alone have moral worth. We must distinguish between doing what duty requires, and doing because duty requires. Only the latter possesses moral worth.

If I do a thing because it is commanded, or because it brings advantage, my action is not moral. But if I do a thing because it is absolutely right in itself, my disposition is a moral one. We ought to do a thing, not because God wills it, but because it is righteous and good in itself.

Thus, it is a matter of duty that a dealer should not overcharge an inexperienced customer. Refraining from so doing for any other motive than that duty requires it, has no moral worth. It is one's duty to maintain life and happiness. Doing so for any other reason than that duty requires it, has no moral worth. It is one's duty to be generous, kind, honest, and so on. Being so for any reason except that duty requires it, has no moral worth. An action done from a sense of duty must wholly exclude the influence of inclination. An action, to be wholly moral, must exclude wholly the influence of inclination.

Take for instance a man who pays his debts. He may be swayed by the fear of being punished if he defaults, or he may pay because it is right that he should. In the first case his conduct is legally right, but it is only in the latter case that it is morally right.

It is a very beautiful thing to do good to men out of love for them or to be just from love of order. But this is not the true moral principle, suitable to our position among rational beings as men. To pretend it were, would be to set ourselves, with fanciful pride, above the thought of duty, like volunteers independent of command; to want to do, of our own pleasure, what we think we need no command to do.

An action done from a sense of duty derives its moral worth, not from the purpose which is to be attained by it, but from the principle upon which it is done. . . . The moral worth of an action does not lie in the results expected from it, but from the principle which it embodies.

What sort of principle, or moral law, can that be, the conception of which must determine the will, without regard to expected consequences, in order that the will may be called *good* absolutely and without qualifications?

It is this: "So act that the principle of your action might become a universal law." Canst thou will that the principle of thy action should become a universal law? If not, then it must be rejected.

Kant has now declared himself on one fundamental problem in moral philosophy. Another problem remains. It grows out of his remarks on the nature and importance of a good will. A *good* will may be defined, after Kant, as a will to do what ought to be done. Here the crucial term is *ought.* And it is crucial because it implies that the will in question is a free will. There would be no point to the remark that a man ought to do so-and-so if, as a matter of fact, he cannot; i.e. has no free will. Furthermore, we hold a man responsible for his action, but only if his action expresses his free will in the matter. The moralist in all of us is brought up short by any denial of man's free will. Such a denial would deprive much of our everday ethical language of meaning. If you doubt this, try some time to be a moralist about your own or other people's conduct, and refrain from using such words as *ought, ought not, obligation, responsible, accountable, answerable, deserved, undeserved,* and so on.

Without freedom of the will, no moral law and no moral responsibility are possible.

A man commits a theft. By the physical law of causality this deed is a necessary result of the causes preceding it in time; it was impossible that it could not have happened. How then can the moral judgment make any difference, and suppose it could have been omitted? The moral judgment says it ought to have been omitted. How can this be? How can a man be called free, at the same moment and with respect to the same act in which he is subject to an inevitable physical necessity?

Actions which are not free, and do not involve one's personality, do not give rise to obligations. Thus no man can be placed under an obligation to give up swallowing for the very reason that it would not be within his powers. Obligation, therefore, presupposes the use of freedom.

That is the difficulty. No free will, no morality. Deny freedom of will, and you annihilate morality. This is not to say that by denying freedom of will you "discourage" people, so that they will "give up trying to do what is right"; but rather that you make the term *morality* a meaningless term. Kant spent years thinking out a theory of knowledge which would legitimate the notion of free will. In this sense his *Critique of Pure Reason* was thought out with an eye to the *Critique of Practical Reason* which followed it. In the next sentence, we are back in the ideas of the first *Critique:*

If we take things in time as things-in-themselves, as is commonly done, then it is impossible to reconcile the necessity of the causal relation with freedom. They are contradictory. From the former, it follows that every event, every action, is a necessary result of what existed in time preceding. So, since time past is no longer in my power, it would follow that every action I perform is the necessary result of causes which are not in my power. That is, it would follow that at the moment in which I act, I am never free.

Obligation expresses a sort of necessity which occurs nowhere else in nature except in man. It is impossible that anything in nature *ought to be* other than in fact it is. In truth, obligation, if one has before one's eyes only the succession in nature, has simply and solely no meaning. We can as little ask what ought to happen in nature as what attributes a circle ought to have.

If existence in time, that is, existence as phenomena, were the only kind we could ascribe to things-in-themselves, freedom would have to be rejected as a vain and impossible suggestion.

Consequently, if we would save freedom, no other way remains but to consider that the existence of a thing in time and therefore according to the law of physical necessity, is appearance only. Freedom we must attribute to the thing as a reality, as a thing-in-itself. This is inevitable, if we would retain both these contradictory conceptions of necessity and freedom. However, when we try to explain their combination in one and the same action, great difficulties present themselves.

Now, in order to remove the apparent contradiction between freedom and mechanism in one and the same action, we must recall what was said in the *Critique of Pure Reason*, or what follows from what was said there. It was said there that the necessity of nature—which cannot coexist with the freedom of the will—pertains only to things as phenomena. The category of causation, it was argued, extends to phenomena or appearances only. The possibility of freedom was thus left open, although its reality was not thereby proved.

Kant's words are important. He says, "The possibility of freedom was thus left open." That is all the help he claims from his theory of knowledge. It is sufficient, however. As his discourse shows, he proposes to use the undeniable *ought*. That we ought to do some things and ought not to do others is a point upon which all moralists would agree. They might differ as to what we ought or ought not to do. The essential point is that they would all use the notions of "oughtness" and "ought-notness." Returning to the argument, the only point is to change this "may be free," which Kant's theory of knowledge permits, into an "is free" which his moral insight demands.

The only point is to change this "may be free" into "is free." That is, to show, in an actual case, that certain actions do imply freedom. Now, it is a duty to realize the moral law in our acts. Therefore it must be possible. ("I ought" implies "I can.") Therefore every rational being must assume whatever is implied by this possibility. Freedom of the will, independence of causal necessity, is implied by this possibility. The assumption is as necessary as the moral law, in connection with which alone it is valid.

Freedom and duty reciprocally imply each other. It is the moral law, of which we become directly conscious, that leads directly to the conception of freedom. It is morality that first discovers to us the notion of freedom. The moral law—"I ought"—which itself does not require any proof, proves the actuality of freedom in those who recognize it as binding on themselves. A man judges he can do, or refrain from doing, a certain act because he is conscious that he ought to. No one would ever have been so rash as to introduce freedom into science had not the moral law forced it upon us.

Morality requires us only to be able to think freedom without self-contradiction, not to understand it. It is enough that our notion of the act as free puts no obstacle in the way of the notion of it as mechanically necessary. Our notion is that the act stands in quite a different relation to freedom from that in which it stands to the mechanism of nature. From the point of view of my *Critique of Pure Reason* this is possible; the doctrine of nature and necessity and the doctrine of morality and freedom may each be true in its own sphere.

How freedom of the will is possible, how we are to conceive it theoretically and positively, how man is a member of two worlds, how man's moral actions must always appear necessitated while they are nonetheless free—all this is not discoverable. Only that there is such a freedom, is postulated by the moral law. How freedom is possible no human intelligence will ever fully fathom. That freedom is possible, on the other hand, no sophistry will ever wrest from the conviction of even the commonest man.

It will be said that the solution here proposed to the problem of freedom involves great difficulty. But is any other solution easier and more intelligible?

Thus far Kant gives a clarifying and convincing presentation of what is implied in moral judgment. A transition from moral philosophy to theology comes about in connection with his account of two other "postulates" of morality. One of these postulates we have already seen, namely, free will. But there are two more to come, namely, immortality and God. It is perhaps as well to let Kant tell his own story. First, immortality:

The immortality of the soul is also a postulate of the moral law. By a *postulate* I mean a theoretical proposition, not demonstrable as such, but which is an inseparable result of an unconditional, *a priori*, practical (i.e., moral) law.

The connection is this. The moral law commands the perfect accordance of the will with it. This must be possible, since it is commanded. But perfect accordance of the will with the moral law is a perfection of which no rational being of the sensible world is capable at any moment of his existence. Since, nevertheless, it is commanded, it can only be realized in an infinite progression toward that perfect accordance. Now, this endless progress is only possible on the supposition of an endless duration of the existence and personality of the same rational being. This is called the *immortality of the soul.* The highest good for man, the perfect accord of his will with the moral law, is only possible on the supposition of the immortality of the soul. Consequently, this immortality, being inseparably connected with the moral law, is a postulate of pure practical reason.

For a rational but finite being, the only thing possible is an endless progress from the lower to higher degrees of perfection. . . . And thus he may hope, not indeed here nor at any imaginable point of his future existence, but only in the endlessness of his duration, to be perfectly adequate in his will.

This principle of the moral destination of our nature, namely, that it is only in an endless progress that we can attain perfect accordance with the moral law, is of the greatest use, not merely for supplementing the impotence of speculative reason, but also with respect to religion.

It is interesting to note that Kant has here reversed the usual order of things. Paley, it will be recalled, deduced morality from theology. Kant is deducing theology from morality. Some amends, one must suppose, were required in order to square accounts: from his theory of knowledge he had deduced an agnosticism with respect to speculative theology; in his analysis of the conception of a rational morality he had demonstrated its independence of theology. The argument continues:

The existence of God is also a postulate of the moral law. We proceed to exhibit this connection in a convincing manner.

Happiness is the condition of a rational being in the world with whom everything goes according to his wish and will. It rests, thus, on the harmony of physical nature with his ends and purposes. But the rational being in the world is not the cause of the world and of physical nature. There is, therefore, not the least ground in the moral law for any necessary connection between morality (i.e., virtue) and proportionate happiness.

To repeat: In a being that belongs to the world as part of it, is therefore dependent on it, and for that reason cannot by his will be a cause of nature nor by his own power make it completely harmonize, as far as his happiness is concerned, with his practical (i.e., moral) principles, in such a being there is not the least ground for any connection between morality and proportionate happiness.

Therefore, *the summum bonum,* the union of virtue and happiness, is possible in the world only on the supposition of a Supreme Being having a causality corresponding to moral character.

Accordingly, the existence of a cause of nature, distinct from nature itself, and containing the principle of this connection, this exact harmony of happiness with morality, is postulated.

Now, a being that is capable of acting on the conception of laws is an intelligence, and the causality of such a being according to this conception of laws, is his will. Therefore, the supreme cause of nature, which must be pre-supposed as a condition of the *summum bonum* (the union of virtue and happiness) is a being who is the cause of nature by intelligence and will, that is, its author; that is, God.

Now, in as much as it is a duty for us to promote the *summum bonum*, it is not merely allowable but a duty to presuppose the possibility of this *summum bonum*. And so, as this is possible only on condition of the existence of God, it is morally necessary, it is a matter of duty, to assume the existence of God.

These postulates of immortality, freedom, and the existence of God, all proceed from the principle of morality which is itself not a postulate but a law, an imperative. . . . These postulates are not theoretical dogmas, but suppositions practically necessary, i.e., required in the interests of practice. While they do not extend our speculative knowledge, they do give objective reality to the ideas of speculative reason in general, do give it a right to conceptions the possibility of which it could not otherwise venture to affirm. . . . Thus respect for the moral law leads, through these postulates, to conceptions which speculation might indeed present as problems but could never solve.

By way of conclusion it might be well to repeat the main turns of Kant's argument. He begins by assuming that a rational morality is the only morality. He shows that this means categorical and *a priori*. This enables him to eliminate three misleading conceptions—that it is a matter of feelings, that it is a matter of consequences, that it is a matter of agreeing with God's will, since on these counts it would be neither categorical nor *a priori*. He returns again to the conception of rational morality as categorical and *a priori*, and formulates its principle. This central thesis he then works over in terms of the notion of *ought* or *duty*, and in terms of the *good will*. These considerations raise the problem of free will. He sharpens the point of this problem. He then reaches back into his theory of knowledge for justification of the claim that free will "may be so." He returns, finally, to the conception of morality as necessitating free will as a postulate. There his moral philosophy proper stops, and his theology begins. Kant's moral philosophy, I think, contains some of the soundest and most clarifying analyses to be found anywhere in the history of human thought.

It is customary, among historians of these matters, to distinguish between the morality of principles and the morality of consequences. This distinction cannot be pressed very far, but it serves to set Kant off from those who attempt to determine the morality of actions in terms of the consequences which follow from those actions. Of moralists who have developed the latter approach, one stands out pre-eminent among the rest, and forms an instructive contrast to Immanuel Kant. I mean John Stuart Mill, who is the subject of the next chapter.

Note on Sources. The Kant materials in this section are quoted, abridged, or paraphrased from three books: *Lectures on Ethics*, translated by Louis Infield and published (1930) by Methuen and Co., Ltd.; *Fundamental Principles of The Metaphysics of Morals;* and *Critical Examination of Practical Reason.* The Kant material, pages 273–274 this section, is from Kant's essay, "The Supreme Principle of Morality" in the volume of Kant's essays translated by Louis Infield, pages 36–46. The material expounding and illustrating the categorical imperative is from the first two sections of Kant's *Fundamental Principles.* The material setting forth the postulates of morality is from the third section of the same work, and from Part I, Book II, Chapter II, of Kant's *Critique of Practical Reason.*

Reading References. The references given under the Kant section, in the third topic, are valuable here also. A few titles are here added which have special reference to Kant as a moralist, e.g., J. W. Scott's *Kant on the Moral Life;* A. K. Rogers' *Morals in Review,* chapter on Kant; discussion of Kant in Paulsen's *System of Ethics;* discussion of Kant in Rashdall's *Theory of Good and Evil.*

The following are some books published since 1940:

Beck, L. W. *A Commentary on Kant's Critique of Practical Reason.*
Cassirer, E. *Rousseau, Kant and Goethe.*
Duncan, A. R. C. *Practical Reason and Morality: A Study of Immanuel Kant's Foundations for the Metaphysics of Morals.*
Jones, W. T. *Morality and Freedom in the Philosophy of Immanuel Kant.*
Mattern, C. D. *Personal Freedom Within the Third Antinomy.*
Miller, R. D. *Schiller and the Idea of Freedom.*
Paton, H. J. *The Categorical Imperative: A Study in Kant's Moral Philosophy.*
——. *The Moral Law; or Kant's Groundwork of the Metaphysic of Morals.*

Ross, Sir W. D. *Kant's Ethical Theory.*
Schilpp, P. A. *Kant's Pre-Critical Ethics*, 2nd ed. (1960.)
Teale, A. E. *Kantian Ethics.*

READING QUESTIONS

1. Kant begins by considering three theories about what makes an act right. Use the "If and only if" formula to state each.
2. Show that according to each of those theories an act is right because of its relation to something external to the act.
3. Kant's claim is that an act is right if and only if it is done out of respect for the moral law. Does this "internalize" the criterion?
4. Suppose defenders of the three positions mentioned above were to say that an act is right if and only if it is done (a) out of respect for how I feel about the act, (b) out of respect for the will of God, (c) out of respect for the consequences of the act. Would they thereby "internalize" their criteria, and so meet Kant's objections?
5. "Out of respect for the moral law." Which is (a) mainspring (b) measuring rod.
6. Does acting "out of respect for" mean (a) doing what the moral law says, or (b) doing it because the moral law says to.
7. How Kant formulates the moral law.
8. Given his formulation of the moral law, he says: "I do not need any far-reaching penetration to discern what I have to do in order that my will may be morally good." Why not?
9. Is Kant's moral law the same as the Golden Rule?
10. He says that acting on the principle of private happiness is the direct opposite of acting on the principle of morality. His point here.
11. He says that the moral law confronts us as a "categorical" imperative. What that means. If a categorical imperative, then not what other kind of imperative?
12. He says that obeying the moral law is not a "hypothetical" imperative. What that means. If not a hypothetical imperative, then what other kind?
13. Use Kant's notion of acting out of respect for the moral law to show what he would mean by (a) right act, (b) good will, (c) categorical imperative, (d) duty.
14. Use courage (a gift of nature) and wealth (a gift of fortune) to explain Kant's claim that only a good will is good unconditionally, good without qualification.
15. How Kant's moral law differs from a scientific law. Which is descriptive? Which is prescriptive?

16. Why Kant is concerned with the free will problem. What makes it a problem?

17. How he uses his distinction between phenomenon and thing-in-itself to show *that* freedom is possible. What about "*how* freedom is possible"?

18. What it means to say that free will is a "postulate" of morality. Kant mentions two other postulates. Namely.

19. Wherein you find Kant (a) most (b) least convincing.

3. MORALITY GROUNDED IN HAPPINESS —FROM JOHN STUART MILL

From Kant to Mill. Our subject is still the principle of morality. We began with Paley's attempt to ground morality in theology, to distinguish between right and wrong by reference to God's will: that is right which agrees, and wrong which disagrees with God's will. Difficulties latent in Paley's position were noted and need not be repeated here. In Kant's attempt to argue that morality is categorical, that it is not grounded in anything, but "stands on its own feet," we met a complete antithesis to the position represented by Paley. Kant's effort to disengage morality from theology, as well as from happiness, stands alone. The trend of moral philosophizing has been for the most part away from Kant. In J. S. Mill one meets a moralist who is prepared to argue that an act is right if, and only if, it produces more happiness than any other act possible under the circumstances.

Biographical Note. John Stuart Mill grew up in the group which included Jeremy Bentham, James Mill (father of J. S.), T. R. Malthus, David Ricardo, George Grote, and others. These men were interested primarily in political, economic, and social reform. They were the driving force behind the first Reform Bill, the early Factory Acts, and so on. They were known, in their own day, as the Utilitarians and as the Philosophical Radicals: Utilitarians because they enquired of any law, custom, or institution, "What is its utility? Of what use is it?" If no answer were forthcoming, beyond some vague statement about its prestige or its long standing, they proposed to scrap it. Philosophical radicals because they aimed to go to the roots of things, the word *root* being English for the Latin word *radix*. The root to which these men proposed to go was human happiness. That, for them, was the "root question" to be addressed to any law, custom, or institution. For the most part they did not spend time seeking to justify this principle. This task J. S. Mill undertook to do. They applied the principle that right means "producing human happiness." He undertook to clarify and defend the principle in his book *Utilitarianism*. Most of his other writings are related to his *Utilitarianism*. Thus, in his essay *On Liberty*, written a few years before his *Utilitarianism*, but based on the principles subsequently given in the later book, he argued that the greatest happiness of the greatest number is more likely to be achieved by allowing as much freedom of thought and action as possible. In his treatise, *Considerations on Representative Government*, he argued that government by elected representatives would offer a better guarantee of human happiness than government by monarchs or aristocrats. In his monograph *On the Subjection of Women* he argued that the purpose of representative government was, in part, frustrated by refusing votes to women. The range and sincerity of his writings have given him great influence in the past hundred years. For other biographical notes, see page 49.

The Argument of the Citations. Mill's exposition and defense of the appeal to happiness as the basis of morality moves through five turns. He first states the problem: What is the basis or principle of morality? He then explores two "false leads," and shows grounds for rejecting them. He then states his own position at some length. He then asks the question: Is this belief open to any kind of proof or disproof? and answers as best he can. He turns then to a review of objections and misunderstandings which, he knows, will be brought against his claim. These he seeks to answer. With this accomplished, he is in a position to say, "I have posed an age-long problem. I have criticized two widely held theories. I have advanced my own answer. I have shown what sort of proof it is amenable to. I have stated and removed as many objections as I can think of. The defense rests."

The *Utilitarianism* begins as follows:

There are few circumstances more significant of the backward state of speculation than the little progress which has been made in the controversy respecting the criterion of right and wrong.

From the dawn of philosophy the question concerning the foundation of morality has been accounted the main problem in speculative thought, has occupied the most gifted intellects, and divided them into sects and schools carrying on a vigorous warfare against one another.

After more than two thousand years the same discussions continue. Philosophers are still ranged under the same contending banners. Neither thinkers nor mankind at large seem nearer to agreement than when the youthful Socrates listened to the old Protagoras.

The problem is now before us: What is the foundation of morality?
He proposes to examine two familiar answers. The first of these is the
observation that this is a matter of personal opinion. Thus one reads the
remarks, "There's nothing right or wrong, but thinking makes it so."
"Right you are, if you think you are." That is, an act is right if you, or
the community, or all mankind, think it is; right and wrong are mere matters of opinion, are merely subjective. There are many different ways of
stating this notion. Of all moralists, who hold this view Mill says:

> They all, in one phrase or another, place the test of right and wrong in a
> feeling of approval or disapproval . . . they find certain feelings of approval
> and disapproval in themselves . . . a great part of all the ethical reasoning in
> books and in the world is of this sort.

His criticism of this appeal to moral feeling to settle the matter is
short and pointed:

> All experience shows that "moral feelings" are eminently artificial, and
> the product of culture; that the most senseless and pernicious "feelings" can be
> raised to the utmost intensity by inculcation, as hemlock and thistles could be
> reared to luxuriant growth by sowing them instead of wheat.
> Things which have been really believed by all mankind have been proved
> to be false, as that the sun rises and sets. Can immunity from similar error be
> claimed for the "moral feelings"?
> I do not found the morality of actions upon anybody's opinion or feeling
> of them. I found it upon facts.

What facts, we ask. Let us first glance at another doctrine: the appeal
to nature. A thing is right, it will be said, if it is according to nature, if it
is natural; wrong, if it is contrary to nature, if it is unnatural.

> We will inquire into the truth of the doctrines which make nature a test
> of right and wrong, good and evil, or which in any mode or degree attach
> merit or approval to following, imitating, or obeying nature. A reference to
> that supposed standard is the predominant ingredient in the vein of thought
> and feeling which was opened by Rousseau, and which has infiltrated itself
> most widely into the modern mind.
> That any mode of thinking, feeling, or acting is "according to nature" is
> usually accepted as a strong argument for its goodness. If it can be said, with
> any plausibility, that "nature enjoins" anything, the propriety of obeying the
> injunction is considered to be made out. And, conversely, the imputation of
> being "contrary to nature" is thought to bar the thing so designated from being

tolerated or excused. It is thought that nature affords some criterion of what we ought to do.

Mill's handling of the appeal to nature is a good example of condensed refutation. He first points out that the term *nature*, or ~~according to nature~~, is ambiguous. He states the two senses in which it might be used. He then shows that, given the first sense, the appeal to nature is meaningless; and, given the second sense, it is irrational and immoral.

The word *nature* has two principal meanings: it either denotes the entire system of things, with the aggregate of all their properties, or it denotes things as they would be, apart from human intervention.

Such being the two principal senses of the word *nature*, in which of these is it taken when the word and its derivatives are used to convey ideas of commendation, approval, and even moral obligation?

In the first of these senses, the doctrine that man ought ~~to follow nature~~ is unmeaning, since man has no power to do anything else than follow nature; all his actions are done through, and in obedience to, ~~some one or many of~~ nature's physical or mental laws.

In the other sense of the term, the doctrine that man ought to follow nature, or in other words, ought to make the spontaneous course of things the model of his voluntary actions, is equally irrational and immoral.

Irrational, because all human action whatever, consists in altering, and all useful action in improving the spontaneous course of nature. Immoral, because the course of natural phenomena being replete with everything which when committed by human beings is most worthy of abhorrence, any one who endeavored in his actions to imitate the natural course of things would be universally seen and acknowledged to be the wickedest of men.

The doctrine that the existing order of things is the natural order, and that, being natural, all innovation upon it is criminal, is vicious. Conformity to nature has no connection whatever with right and wrong. The idea can never be fitly introduced into ethical discussions at all. That a thing is unnatural is no argument for it being blamable.

At this point we may give Mill's own position. We have now two alternatives with which to compare it. He says:

All action is for the sake of some end, and rules of action must take their whole character and color from the end to which they are subservient.

The creed which accepts the greatest happiness principle as the foundation of morals holds that actions are right in proportion as they tend to promote happiness, wrong as they tend to produce the reverse of happiness. By happiness is intended pleasure, and the absence of pain; by unhappiness, pain, and the privation of pleasure. This theory I propose to expound and defend.

The standard is not the agent's own greatest happiness, but the greatest amount of happiness altogether. As between his own happiness and that of others, utilitarianism requires him to be as strictly impartial as a disinterested and benevolent spectator.

The test of morality is not the greatest happiness of the agent himself. Utilitarianism does not dream of defining morality to be the self-interest of the agent. The greatest happiness principle is the greatest happiness of mankind and of all sentient creatures. (all living creatures)

He who does anything for any other purpose than to increase the amount of happiness in the world is no more deserving of admiration than the ascetic mounted on his pillar. He may be an inspiring proof of what men can do, but assuredly not an example of what they should do.

Pleasure and freedom from pain are the only things desirable as ends, and all desirable things are desirable either for the pleasure inherent in them or as means to the promotion of pleasure and the prevention of pain.

Mill has stated that morality is a matter of consequences. An act is right or wrong, according to its consequences, not because it agrees with someone's opinion, or with universal opinion, or with nature, or (by implication) with God's will. He pauses a moment to elaborate this point:

By "calculating the consequences" is meant, generally, calculating the consequences of classes of actions. There are, as we shall note, exceptions to this, but over all we must look at actions as though multiplied, and in large masses. Take murder for example. There are many persons, to kill whom would be to remove men who are a cause of no good to any human being, who are a cause of cruel physical and moral suffering to several, and whose whole influence tends to increase the mass of unhappiness and vice. Were such a man to be murdered, the balance of traceable consequences would be greatly in favor of the act. But, the counter consideration, still on the principle of utility, is that unless persons were punished for killing, and taught not to kill, nobody's life would be safe.

We say, "generally," not "universally." For the admission of exceptions to rules is a necessity equally felt in all systems of morality. To take an obvious instance: The rule against homicide, the rule against deceiving, the rule against taking advantage of superior strength, are suspended against enemies in the field and partially against malefactors in private life. In each case, the rule is suspended as far as is required by the peculiar nature of the case. That the moralities arising from special circumstances of the action may be so important as to over-rule those arising from the class of acts to which it belongs, is a liability common to all ethical systems.

The existence of exceptions to moral rules is no stumbling block peculiar to the principle of utility. The essential is that the exception should itself be a general rule; so that, being definite, and not left to the partial judgment of the individual, it might not shake the stability of the wider rule in the cases to which the reason of the exception does not extend. This is an ample foundation for "the construction of a scheme of morality."

With respect to the means of inducing people to conform in their actions to the scheme so formed, the utilitarian system depends, like all other schemes of morality, on the external motives supplied by law and opinion and the internal motives produced by education or reason.

The greatest happiness principle is now before us. Is the principle open to any kind of proof? Mill's answer amounts to a denial. The rationale of this denial is as follows:

Of what sort of proof is this principle of the greatest happiness susceptible?

It is evident that it cannot be proof in the ordinary and popular meaning of the term. Questions of ultimate ends are not amenable to direct proof. Whatever can be proved to be good must be shown to be a means to something admitted to be good without proof.

The medical art is proved to be good by its conducing to health. But how is it possible to prove that health is good? The art of music is good, for the reason among others, that it produces pleasure. But what proof is it possible to give that pleasure is good?

No comprehensive formula, including all things good in themselves and not as means to things good in themselves, is a subject of what is commonly meant by *proof*. It may be accepted or rejected, but not proved in the usual sense of that term.

There is a larger meaning of the word *proof* in which this question of ultimate principles is as amendable to proof as any other of the disputed questions of philosophy. The subject is within the cognizance of the rational faculty. Its acceptance or rejection does not depend on blind impulse or arbitrary choice.

The problem has been stated. False solutions have been exposed. His own solution has been given. The meaning of *proof* in these matters has been made clear. He turns to objections that may be raised. A study of these objections and replies will clarify and fix the doctrine in one's mind.

It may not be superfluous to notice a few of the common misapprehensions of utilitarian ethics, even those which are so obvious and gross that it might appear impossible for any person of candor and intelligence to fall into them.

The first objection is that such a moral philosophy is a godless doctrine:

Utilitarianism is a godless doctrine: The appeal to happiness, instead of the appeal to the will of God, is a godless, i.e., irreligious, principle of morality.

Mill's answer is to carry the war into the enemy's camp:

The question [whether the appeal to happiness is a godless doctrine] depends upon what idea we have formed of the moral character of the Deity. If it be a true belief that God desires above all things the happiness of His creatures, and that this was His purpose in their creation, then utilitarianism is not only not a godless doctrine, but more profoundly religious than any other.

Although the existence of God as a wise and just lawgiver is not a necessary part of the feelings of morality, it may still be maintained that those feelings make His existence eminently desirable. No doubt they do, and that is the great reason why we find that good men and women cling to the belief and are pained by its being questioned.

If the objection [that utilitarianism is a godless doctrine] means that utilitarianism does not recognize the revealed will of God as the supreme law of morals, I answer: An utilitarian who believes in the perfect goodness and wisdom of God, necessarily believes that whatever God has thought fit to reveal on the subject of morals must fulfill the requirements of utilitarianism in a supreme degree.

A second objection:

To suppose that life has no higher end than pleasure, no better and nobler object of desire and pursuit, is utterly mean and groveling; a doctrine worthy only of swine.

Mill's answer:

This supposes that human beings are capable of no pleasure except those of which swine are capable. If this supposition were true, the charge could not be denied; but it would then be no charge, for if the sources of pleasure were precisely the same for human beings and for swine, then the rule of life which is good enough for the one would be good enough for the other.

The comparison is felt to be degrading precisely because a beast's pleasures do not satisfy a human being's conception of happiness. Human beings have faculties more elevated than the animal appetites, and do not regard anything as happiness which does not include their gratification.

A third objection:

That utilitarianism [the appeal to the pleasure-pain consequences of action] renders men cold and unsympathizing; that it chills their moral feelings toward individuals; that is makes them regard only the consequences of actions, not taking into account the personal qualities from which those actions emanate.

Mill's answer:

If this means that utilitarians do not allow their judgment concerning the rightness or wrongness of an act to be influenced by their opinion of the quality of the person who does it, then it is a complaint not against utilitarianism but against having any standard of morality at all. For certainly no known ethical standard decides an action to be good or bad because it is done by a good or bad man; still less because it is done by an amiable, brave, or benevolent man, or the contrary. These considerations are relevant, not to the estimation of actions, but of persons; and there is nothing in utilitarianism inconsistent with the fact that there are other things which interest us in persons besides the rightness or wrongness of their actions.

The stoic moralists, indeed, were fond of saying that he who has virtue has everything. But no claim of this description is made for the virtuous man by the utilitarian moralist. There are other desirable possessions and qualities besides virtue. A right action does not necessarily indicate a virtuous character. Actions that are blamable often proceed from qualities entitled to praise. When this is so in any particular case, it modifies one's moral estimation of the agent, but not of the act.

A fourth objection is that the morality of an action depends upon the motive, not upon the consequences. Mill answers:

As to motive, the utilitarian position is this: Motive has nothing to do with the morality of the action, though much with the worth of the agent. He who saves a fellow creature from drowning does what is morally right, whether his motive be duty or the hope of being paid for his trouble.

A fifth objection:

A stock argument against utilitarianism consists in saying that an utilitarian will be apt to make his own particular case an exception to moral rules, and when under temptation, will see an utility in the breach of a rule, greater than he will see in its observance.

Mill's answer:

But is utilitarianism the only creed which is able to furnish us with excuses for evil doing and means of cheating our own conscience? They are afforded in abundance by all doctrines which recognize as a fact in morals the existence of conflicting considerations; which all doctrines do that have been believed by sane persons.

It is not the fault of any creed, but of the complicated nature of human affairs, that rules of conduct cannot be so framed as to require no exceptions, and that hardly any kind of action can safely be laid down as either always obligatory or always condemnable.

There is no ethical creed which does not temper its laws by giving a certain latitude, under the moral responsibility of the agent, for accommodation to peculiarities of circumstances. At the opening thus made, self-deception and dishonest casuistry get in.

There exists no moral system under which cases of conflicting obligation do not arise. These are the real difficulties, the knotty points, both in a theory of ethics and in the conscientious guidance of personal conduct. But is any one less qualified to deal with cases of conflicting obligations by reason of the fact that he possesses an ultimate standard to which such cases can be referred?

A sixth objection:

Utilitarianism is only an appeal to expedience, and an appeal to expedience is not as high morally as an appeal to principle.

Mill's answer:

This objection rests on a loose use of the term *expedience*. Generally, the *expedient* means that which is expedient for the particular interests of the agent himself; as when a minister of state sacrifices the interests of his country to keep himself in place. The expedient in this sense is a branch of the hurtful; and to claim that utilitarianism is an appeal to the expedient, in this sense, is simply to misunderstand or misrepresent its meaning.

Utilitarianism does recognize in human beings the power of sacrificing their own greatest good for the good of others. I must repeat again, what critics seldom have the justice to acknowledge, that the happiness which forms the standard of what is right in conduct, is not the agent's own happiness but the happiness of all concerned.

Utilitarianism does, however, refuse to admit that sacrifice of one's own good is itself a good. A sacrifice which does not increase the sum of happiness is wasted. The only sacrifice which utilitarianism applauds is that which is made in the interests of the happiness either of mankind or of individuals within the limits imposed by the interests of mankind.

A seventh objection:

Happiness cannot be the rational purpose of life, because it is unattainable.

Mill's answer:

This objection, were it well founded, would go to the root of the matter; for if no happiness is to be had at all by human beings, the attainment of it cannot be the end of morality. However, the assertion that it is impossible that human life be happy is an exaggeration.

If by *happiness* he meant a continuity of highly pleasurable excitement, it is evident that this is impossible. A state of exalted pleasure lasts only for a few moments, or in some cases for somewhat longer periods. If this kind of intense rapture be meant by *happiness*, then happiness is unattainable.

But this is not what philosophers have meant by *happiness* when they taught that happiness was the end of life. The happiness which they meant was not a life of rapture, but moments of such in an existence made up of few and transistory pains, many and various pleasures, with a decided predominance of the active over the passive, and having as the foundation not to expect more from life than it is capable of bestowing. A life thus composed, to those who have been fortunate enough to obtain it, has always appeared worthy of the name of happiness. And such an existence is even now the lot of many.

An eighth objection:

We cannot calculate all the consequences of any action and thus cannot estimate the degree in which it promotes human happiness.

Mill's answer:

Is there any department of human affairs in which we can do all that is desirable? Because we cannot foresee everything, is there no such thing as foresight? Can no estimate be formed of consequences, which would be any guide for our conduct, unless we can calculate all consequences? Because we cannot predict every effect which may follow from a person's death, are we to say that we cannot know that murder would be destructive to human happiness? Whether morality is or is not a question of consequences, it cannot be denied that prudence is a question of consequences, and if there is such a thing as prudence, it is because the consequences of actions can be calculated.

A ninth objection:

There is not time, previous to action, for calculating and weighing the effects of any line of conduct on the general happiness.

Mill's answer:

This is exactly as if any one were to say that it is impossible to guide our conduct by Christianity, because there is not time, on every occasion on which everything has to be done, to read through the Old and New Testaments.

The answer to the objection is that there has been ample time, namely, the whole past duration of the human species. During all that time mankind have been learning by experience the tendencies of action; on which experience all the prudence, as well as all the morality, of life is dependent.

Nobody argues that the art of navigation is not founded on astronomy, because sailors cannot wait to calculate the nautical almanac. Being rational creatures, they go to sea with it ready calculated, and all rational creatures go out upon the sea of life with their minds made up on the common questions of right and wrong.

There is no difficulty in proving any ethical standard whatever to work ill, if we suppose universal idiocy to be conjoined with it, but on any hypothesis short of that, mankind must by this time have acquired positive beliefs as to the effects of some actions on their happiness. To inform a traveler respecting the place of his ultimate destination is not to forbid the use of landmarks and direction posts on the way.

A tenth objection:

If happiness is made the ultimate standard by which other things are judged to be good or bad, then we are not in a position to distinguish among kinds of happiness with respect to their goodness or badness.

Mill's answer:

It is quite compatible with the principle of utility to recognize the fact that some kinds of pleasure are more desirable and more valuable than others. It would be absurd that while, in estimating all other things, quality is considered as well as quantity, the estimation of pleasures should be supposed to depend on quantity alone.

Of two pleasures, if there be one to which all or almost all who have experience of both give a decided preference, irrespective of any feeling of moral obligation to prefer it, that is the more desirable pleasure.

Now it is an unquestionable fact that those who are equally acquainted with, and equally capable of appreciating and enjoying, both, do give a most marked preference to the manner of existence which employs their higher faculties. It is better to be a human being dissatisfied than a pig satisfied; better to be Socrates dissatisfied than a fool satisfied. And if the fool, or the pig, is of a different opinion, it is because they know only their side of the question. The other party to the comparison knows both sides.

Few human creatures would consent to be changed into any of the lower animals for a promise of the fullest allowance of an animal's pleasures. No intelligent human being would consent to be a fool, no instructed person would consent to be an ignoramus, no person of feeling and conscience would consent to be selfish and base, even though they should be persuaded that the fool, the dunce or the rascal is better satisfied with his lot than they are with theirs.

From this verdict of the only competent judges, I apprehend there can be no appeal. On the question which of two pleasures is the best worth having, which of two modes of existence is the most grateful to the feelings, the judgment of those who are qualified by knowledge of both must be admitted as final. . . . There is no other tribunal to be referred to.

Note on Sources. The Mill material in this section is quoted, abridged, or paraphrased from his essay, "Nature," and from Chapters I, II, and IV of his *Utilitarianism.*

Reading References. It is not easy to find a sympathetic account of Mill as a moralist. In a little book by George Santayana, *Some Turns of Thought in Modern Philosophy*, there is a passage, beginning on page 55, "With this dissolution always in prospect . . . ," which is an exception to this rule. The trouble arose, even in Mill's own day, over his somewhat unsatisfactory handling of the tenth objection: The appeal *to* happiness does not permit criticism *of* happiness. Nor does it. F. H. Bradley's *Ethical Studies*, Chapter 3, "Pleasure for Pleasure's Sake," contains a criticism of Mill's argument. Mill's *Autobiography* is splendid reading. It gives a picture of the man who made a bold stand for happiness in moral philosophy. Courtney's *Life of Mill* and the third volume of Stephen's *English Utilitarians* are good books on Mill. The subsequent elaboration and defense and modification of Mill's position is to be traced in Henry Sidgwick's *Method of Ethics* and G. E. Moore's *Principia Ethica.*

The following are some books published since 1940:

Anschutz, R. P. *The Philosophy of J. S. Mill.*
Baumgardt, D. *Bentham and the Ethics of Today.*
Borchard, R. *John Stuart Mill: The Man.*
Britton, K. *John Stuart Mill.*
Hayek, F. A. *John Stuart Mill and Harriet Taylor.*
Jackson, R. *An Examination of the Deductive Logic of John Stuart Mill.*
MacMinn, N., et al. *Bibliography of the Published Writings of John Stuart Mill.*
Mill, J. S. (D. Fosdick, ed.). *On Social Freedom.*
Mueller, I. W. *John Stuart Mill and French Thought.*

Packe, M. *The Life of John Stuart Mill.*
Pankhurst, R. K. P. *Saint Simonians, Mill and Carlyle.*
Plamenatz, J. P. *The English Utilitarians.*
Rees, J. C. *Mill and His Early Critics.*
Russell, Bertrand. *John Stuart Mill* (a lecture).

READING QUESTIONS

1. Mill begins by considering two theories about what makes an act right. Use the "If and only if" formula to state each.
2. His criticism of the first theory is that "moral feelings" can be mistaken, are not infallible. But, to speak strictly, can a feeling, simply as a feeling, ever be either true or false? How, for example, is the feeling of hunger, simply as a feeling, ever either true or false?
3. Suppose the first theory is revised: "An act is right if and only if I judge or state that it is right." (A judgment or statement, unlike a feeling, can be either true or false.) Mill's criticism, revised to meet this reformulation, would be that judgments or statements can be mistaken, are not infallible. Would that dispose of the theory? If not, what criticism of the theory would you propose?
4. His criticism of the second theory is (a) its key phrase ("according to nature") is ambiguous. How so? (b) If you develop this ambiguity you get a dilemma. Namely?
5. Use the "If and only if" formula to state Mill's own theory. Why this theory is called "Utilitarianism."
6. What points about his own theory is he making in his reference to (a) a disinterested and benevolent spectator, (b) an ascetic mounted on his pillar.
7. Mill seems willing to admit exceptions to particular moral rules. For example. One general moral rule, however, to which he would admit no exceptions.
8. The principle of utility admits of (a) no exceptions, (b) no proof. Show why, in each case.
9. The principle of utility, he says, admits of no proof. However, its acceptance or rejection, he goes on to say, does not depend on blind impulse or arbitrary choice. On what does it depend, then?
10. If you were Mill, what would you do with this question: "Why does producing the greatest amount of happiness make an act right?"
11. Mill is seeking to formulate the first or ultimate principle of morality. It is a mark of such a principle, when found, that it admits of no exceptions and no proof. Would this hold of first or ultimate principles in other fields besides morality?

12. Mill meets the first objection to Utilitarianism ("It is a godless doctrine") by arguing that it is no objection if God is Himself a Utilitarian. But suppose God is Himself not a Utilitarian. Then what?

13. Suppose a person has a swinish conception of happiness. What would Mill be entitled to say to him? On what grounds would he be entitled to say it?

14. "A right action does not necessarily indicate a virtuous character." Why not?

15. "The motive has nothing to do with the morality of the action." (a) Why not? (b) Would Kant agree to this?

16. What Mill would say to the statements (a) The road to hell is paved with good intentions. (b) The end justifies the means.

17. What, precisely is an act, considered apart from the agent's purpose or intention? How would you tell what act it was? Would it differ from an event in nature, e.g., a stone rolling down a hill? If not, should we speak of a stone's behavior as moral or immoral, depending on the consequences?

18. How he meets the objections (a) Happiness is unattainable. (b) We cannot calculate all the consequences of any action.

19. He says it is quite compatible with the principle of utility to recognize that some kinds of pleasure are more desirable, more valuable, than others. Is it? If not, why not? If so, on what grounds?

20. Wherein you find Mill (a) most (b) least convincing.

4. MORALITY GROUNDED IN POWER —FROM FRIEDRICH NIETZSCHE

From Mill to Nietzsche. We have examined three attempts to formulate the principle of morality. Paley found the rightness of an act to depend upon its agreement with the will of God. Kant denied that the rightness of an act depended upon anything, asserting that an act, if right, is so categorically, without reference to anything outside of itself. Mill found the rightness of an act to depend upon its consequences, these consequences being the amount of happiness which it brought about. We have now to examine the claim of a fourth moralist whose findings differ radically from any of the other three. The difference is so great that it is rather difficult to institute a comparison. The point may be approached in terms of an example. Consider honesty, the habit of telling the truth and being "square" in one's dealings. Let us suppose each of our moralists to be asked, "Why is it right to be honest and wrong to be dishonest?" "Because it agrees with God's will," Paley would say. "There is no reason why honesty is right," Kant would say, "It is right simply because it is right." "Because it makes for the greatest amount of happiness in the long run and for the most people," Mill would say. Now our fourth moralist would be inclined to answer the question by asking another: "Who said that honesty is right, and dishonesty wrong?" That is, he would ask whether the very wording of the question doesn't beg the question. You first accept certain things as right and wrong, he would argue, then you ask what principle is involved in thus distinguishing them. That is to beg the question. In other words, you can only ask this question by first assuming, without inquiry, that some things are right and others wrong; but if you query *that* fact, then where are you?

Biographical Note. Friedrich Nietzsche was born in Germany in 1844 and died in 1900 at the age of fifty-six. His biography may be epitomized in terms of three periods: years of preparation, years of production, and years of insanity. (1) He was born into a puritanical, religious family and was intended by his parents to enter the church. To this end he was educated privately and at a denominational school. In the University at Bonn he broke completely with his family in doctrinal matters. He moved on to the University at Leipzig. There he met Wagner, the German composer, and became a fervent Wagnerite. He discovered Schopenhauer's writings in a second-hand bookshop and became a convinced Schopenhaurian. He met Erwin Rhode, the historian of Greek culture, and became engrossed in the problems and perspectives of the cultural history of mankind. He did military service for a year in a war with Austria, returning to the University at Leipzig to complete his studies. The following year he was appointed to the chair of classical philology in the university at Bâle, received his Ph.D., and began work on his important book, *The Birth of Tragedy.* The next year he was called once more into military service in the Franco-Prussian War which had just begun, 1870. He was head of an ambulance corps, but did only three weeks' service. Diphtheria ended his military career. He returned to the university at Bâle and resumed lectures. For eight years he remained at this work. During this period he was arriving at conclusions which formed the basis of his future writings. He published *The Birth of Tragedy.* It met with a chilly reception. His prestige began to decline. His next book, *Thoughts Out of Season,* contained four essays in which he criticized Strauss, Schopenhauer, German historians, and others. Two years later for reasons of poor health he retired on a small pension from the university.

(2) It should never be forgotten that Nietzsche was, first and last, a cultural historian; that is, he was interested in, and drew his inspiration

from, the study of the cultures achieved by various peoples, ancient and modern. He wrote a series of books which develop really one theme. His investigations into mankind's cultural history, understanding by the term *culture* such things as art, religion, science, morality, government, and so on, left him profoundly impressed, in the first place, by the enormous diversity which has obtained in these things at different times and places. But that was not all. He was equally impressed with the fact that cultural values are local and transitory affairs. He expressed this in the notion of the relativity of cultural values. By this he meant that cultural values are relative to time and place, relative to the needs peculiar to the peoples among whom they flourish. In other words, there is nothing eternal or absolute or immutable about them, and this, he felt, holds for values of all descriptions: religious, artistic, social, moral, scientific, and so on. On the rebound from his earlier orthodox training, he dismissed them with a flourish of his pen in his book, *Humna, All Too Human.* That was his "great discovery." Values, one and all, are "human-all-too-human." The rest of his work may be described as a series of studies in the natural history of human values. *Human, All Too Human,* was followed by *Dawn of Day,* and it in turn by *Joyful Wisdom.* Clearly, a new note was being struck. What idea was Nietzsche working out in these books?

It was something like this: The cultural history of mankind shows that aristocratic qualities flourish in the early stages of a culture and disappear gradually as that culture becomes old. In Homer's time, the Greeks were "heroes"; by the time of Pericles and the Spartan war, they had become mere "sophists" and "philosophers" and "scientists." In early Roman history there were great kings who founded a race which conquered the ancient world, but centuries later, in the days of imperial decline, this nation of "strong, silent men" had become helpless victims of their own weakening civilization and the new races of barbarians as yet "untouched" by such things. These newcomers swept over Europe, and another page in cultural history was begun, but with the same result. By the nineteenth century these "Germanic" peoples who had made over the civilization of ancient Rome had become democratic, even socialistic; they cultivated "science," "art," "morality" or (in some instances) decadent forms of "immorality," wealth, ease, the "emancipation of women," optimism, pessimism, philosophy, and so on.

There is no quarreling with Nietzsche's likes and dislikes in these matters. The sight of Achilles sulking in his tent was simply something he admired more than the sight of Karl Marx sulking in the library of the British Museum. A Greek athlete or a Roman warrior was simply not in the same degenerate class with J. S. Mill pleading for representative government and the political enfranchisement of women, or Schopenhauer brooding over the misery and folly of human affairs. Hence, the titles of his books. To "see through" modern degeneration was "the dawn of day"; to realize that "real virtues" belong in the context of fresh and vigorous young cultures was the first step in "joyful wisdom." Nietzsche was carried away on the wings of this sort of thing. Lonely, poor, sickly, unpopular, a bachelor *malgré lui*, he nevertheless lived on in the private world of "transvalued values," heaping scorn on "art" and "science" and "morality" and "religion" and "emancipation" and "democracy" and "socialism" and "humanitarianism." He poured his soul into the mold of one beautiful book, *Thus Spake Zarathustra.* This was the fine flower of his genius. Through the mouth of Zarathustra, the prophet of his doctrine, he preached and exhorted and satirized in pages of marvelous beauty and suggestiveness. But the nineteenth century passed Zarathustra by on the other side. Only a handful took the trouble to read him, and even these few were puzzled and disturbed. For their enlightenment, Nietzsche wrote two more books, *Beyond Good and Evil* and *The Genealogy of Morals*. They were intended as commentaries on the *Zarathustra*. The substance of their argument is given in the citations which follow. The balance of Nietzsche's writings carry further the ideas presented already. The Zarathustra group was followed by *The Twilight of the Idols, Antichrist, The Will to Power* (unfinished), and his own autobiography bearing the significant title *Ecce Homo*.

(3) In 1889, now forty-five, Nietzsche began to lose the use of his mind. For the next eleven years he was caught in the toils of a steadily increasing insanity. The picture brings to mind Schopenhauer's gloomy hypothesis and leaves one impatient with the century which had allowed the man's genius to flicker out alone and unheeded.

The Argument of the Citations. The following passages, chosen principally from Nietzsche's *Beyond Good and Evil* and *The Genealogy of Morals*, exhibit six turns of thought. He begins by repudiating the whole notion of trying to formulate any principle of morality, in the sense that moralists have traditionally sought to do this. He insists that there is no such thing as morality having one fundamental principle running through it; that, on the contrary, there have been and are many moralities; and that any attempt to think philosophically about morality must begin by recognizing its diversity and the fact of its having had a history like any other phase of human culture. He propounds then a tentative natural history or genealogy of morals. From this he undertakes to draw some far-reaching conclusions. These he calls collectively his *immoralism*, or *transvaluation of values*. One fundamental distinction, arising out of his account of the natural history of morals and forming the foundation of his immoralism, is that between master morality and slave morality. The characteristics of each he then describes at some length. The doctrine is now substantially complete. However, to illustrate it more concretely, he applies it in a critical way to two phenomena of modern morality, namely, the emancipation of woman, and the close connection between modern morality and Christianity. He closes with a few reflections on his own significance.

The opening citations are fundamental. In these Nietzsche draws the searching distinction between accepting morality and trying to formulate its principle, and making moralities the subject of descriptive investigation. It is the historian of humanity's manifold cultures and cultural values who speaks:

Hitherto all moralists, with a pedantic and ridiculous seriousness, have wanted to give a "basis" to morality, and each has believed that he has given this "basis" to morality. Morality itself, however, has been regarded as something "given."

That which moralists have called "giving a basis to morality," has proved merely a learned form of good faith in prevailing morality, a new means of expressing prevailing morality, consequently just a phenomenon within one definite morality, a sort of denial that it is lawful for this particular morality to be called in question. In no case has the attempt to "provide a basis for morality" ever involved a testing, analyzing, doubting, and vivisecting of the prevailing moral faith.

The philosophical workers, after the pattern of Kant and Hegel, have to fix and systematize some existing body of valuations, that is to say, creations of value which have become prevalent and are for a time called "the truth." It is for these thinkers to make conspicuous, conceivable, intelligible, manageable what has happened and been esteemed hitherto.

Apart from the value of such assertions as "there is a categorical imperative in us," we can always ask: "What does such an assertion indicate about him who makes it?"

Because moralists have known the moral facts imperfectly, in an arbitrary epitome, perhaps the morality of their environment, their position, their church, their *Zeitgeist*, their climate; because they have been badly instructed with regard to nations, eras, and past ages, and were by no means eager to know about these matters; precisely because of this fact, they did not even come in sight of the real problems of morality, problems which disclose themselves only to a comparison of many kinds of morality.

There are systems of morals which are meant to justify their author in the eyes of other people; systems which are meant to tranquilize him and make him self-satisfied; systems which are meant to enable him to crucify and humble himself. By means of one system of morals, he wishes to take revenge; by means of another, to conceal himself; by means of another, to glorify himself and gain superiority and distinction. In short, systems of morals are only sign languages of the emotions.

What is still necessary is the collection of material, the comprehensive survey and classification of sentiments of worth, distinctions of worth, which live, grow, propagate, and perish; and the attempt, perhaps, to give a clear idea of the recurring and more common forms of these living crystallizations. This is necessary as preparation for a theory of types of morality.

So much as a start. The primary problem is not to formulate the principle of morality, but to recognize the existence and study the natural history of many moralities. An acquaintance with these matters, Nietzsche feels, will reveal the fact that genuine moralities arise from the presence in any group of an aristocratic or ruling-class element. He offers an hypothetical reconstruction of the natural history or genealogy of morals.

Every elevation of the type "man" has hitherto been the work of an aristocratic society, and so it will always be: a society believing in a long gradation of rank and differences of worth among human beings, and requiring slavery in some form or other.

Without the pathos of distance, such as grows out of the difference of classes, out of the constant outlooking and downlooking of the ruling class on subordinates and instruments, out of the constant practice of obeying and commanding, out of the keeping down and keeping at a distance, without these, that other more mysterious pathos could never have arisen: the longing for the continued self-surmounting of man.

To be sure, one must cherish no humanitarian illusions about the origin of aristocratic societies. The truth is hard. Every higher civilization has originated in barbarism. Men, barbarians in every respect, men of prey, still in possession of unbroken strength of will and desire for power, threw themselves upon weaker, more moral, more peaceful races, upon old mellow civilizations in which the final vital force was flickering out in brilliant fireworks of wit and depravity. In the beginnings, the noble caste was always the barbarian caste.

The essential thing in a good and healthy aristocracy is that it should regard itself not as a function of the king or the people but as the significance and highest justification thereof; that it should accept with a clear conscience the sacrifice of a legion of individuals, who, for its sake, must be suppressed and reduced to imperfect men, to slaves and instruments. Its fundamental belief must be that society is not allowed to exist for its own sake, but only as a foundation and scaffolding by which a select class may be able to elevate themselves to their higher duties: like those climbing, sun-seeking plants in Java which encircle a tree till, high above it but supported by it, they can unfold their tops in the open light and exhibit their happiness.

Consider an aristocratic commonwealth, e.g., an ancient Greek city state, as a voluntary or involuntary contrivance for rearing human beings. There men are beside one another, thrown on their own resources, who want to make their species prevail, chiefly because they must prevail or be in danger of extermination. The favor, the abundance, the protection, are lacking under which variations are fostered. The species needs itself as species; as something which by its hardness, its uniformity, its simplicity of structure, can prevail in the struggle against neighbors or rebellious vassals. Experience teaches it what are the qualities to which it owes its continued existence in spite of gods and men. These qualities it calls *virtues*, and these virtues alone it develops to maturity.

These virtues it develops with severity. Every aristocratic morality is intolerant in the education of its youth, in the control of its women, in the customs which control marriage, in the relations between old and young, in the penal laws (which have an eye only for the degenerating). It counts intolerance itself among the virtues.

Thus is established a type, with few but very marked features. The constant struggle with unfavorable conditions is the cause of the type becoming stable and hard.

Finally, however, a happy state of security results, and the enormous tension is relaxed. Perhaps there are no more enemies among neighboring peoples; perhaps the means of life and enjoyment are present in abundance. With one stroke the bond and constraint of the old discipline snaps. It is no longer regarded as a necessary condition of existence and survival. If it would continue, it can do so only as an archaizing "taste." Variations appear suddenly in the greatest exuberance and splendor. The individual dares to be individual and detach himself.

At this turning point of history there manifest themselves a magnificent manifold growth and an extraordinary decay, owing to the savagely opposed and seemingly exploding egoisms which strive for "light and sun" and can no longer assign any limit or restraint to themselves by the hitherto existing morality. It was this morality itself which piled up the enormous strength, which bent the bow in so threatening a manner, but it is now out of date, or getting out of date.

The dangerous and disquieting point has now been reached. The greater, more manifold, more comprehensive life now coming into existence is lived beyond the old morality. The "individual" stands out and is obliged to have recourse to his own law giving, his own arts and artifices for self-preservation, self-elevation, self-deliverance. Nothing but new "whys"; nothing but new "hows." No longer any common formulae; misunderstanding and disregard in league together; decay, deterioration, lofty desire, frightfully entangled; the genius of the race overflowing from all the cornucopias of good and bad; new charms and mysteries peculiar to the still inexhausted, still unwearied, corruption.

Danger, the mother of morality, is present once more. This time the danger point has shifted, into the individual, the neighbor, the friend; into the street, into their own child, into all the most personal and secret recesses of their desires and volitions.

After the fabric of a society seems established and secure against external dangers, it is the fear of our neighbor which creates new perspectives of moral evaluation.

It is by the loftiest and strongest instincts, when they break out and carry the individual above and beyond the average, above and beyond the low level of the herd conscience, that the self-reliance of the community is destroyed. Its belief in itself breaks. Consequently these instincts will be most branded and most defamed.

Strong and dangerous instincts, e.g., the love of enterprise, foolhardiness, revengefulness, astuteness, rapacity, love of power, which, up till then had to be honored and fostered and cultivated because required in the common dangers against common enemies, are now felt to be themselves dangerous, are gradually branded as immoral and given over to calumny. The opposite instincts and inclinations now attain to moral honor. The herd instinct gradually draws its conclusions.

How much danger to the community or its equality is contained in an opinion, a condition, an emotion, a character, a disposition? That is now the moral perspective. Here again fear is the mother of morals.

The lofty, independent spirit, the will to stand alone, are felt to be dangers. Everything that elevates the individual above the herd, and is a source of fear to the neighbor, is henceforth called evil. The tolerant, unassuming, self-adapting, self-equalizing disposition, the middle-of-the road desires, attain to moral distinction and honor.

Under peaceful circumstances there is always less opportunity and less need for training the feelings to severity and rigor. Now every form of severity, even severity in justice, begins to disturb the conscience. A lofty and rigorous nobleness and self-responsibility becomes now almost an offense.

The man of an age of dissolution, of an age which mixes the races with one another; who has the inheritance of a diversified descent in his body, contrary instincts and standards of value which struggle among themselves and are seldom at peace; such a man, of late culture and broken lights, will, as a rule, be a weak man.

His fundamental desire is that the war which is in him should come to an end. Happiness appears to him in the character of a soothing medicine and mode of thought; it is above all things the happiness of repose, of undisturbedness, of repletion, of final unity.

All systems of morals which address themselves to "happiness" are only suggestions for behavior adapted to the degree of danger from themselves in which the individuals live. They are thus recipes for their passions, their good and bad propensities, insofar as the individuals would like to play the master. They are all so many small and great expediences, permeated with the musty odor of old family medicines and old wives' wisdom; all grotesque and absurd because they are generalizations where generalization is not justified.

The rank-and-file man assumes an air of being the only kind of man that is allowable. He glorifies, as the peculiarly human virtues, his qualities, such as public spirit, kindness, deference, industry, temperance, modesty, indulgence, sympathy (by virtue of which he is gentle, endurable, and useful to the herd).

In cases where it is believed that a leader cannot be dispensed with, attempt after attempt is made to replace rulers by summing together clever herd-minded men. All representative constitutions, for example, are of this origin.

There arises what I call the moral hypocrisy of the ruling class. They know no other way to protect themselves from bad conscience than to play the role of executors of older and higher orders. (These "older and higher orders" may be predecessors, the constitution, justice, the law, or God himself.) Or they even justify themselves by maxims drawn from the current opinions of the herd, as, for example, "the first servants of their people," or "instruments of public weal."

The end is quickly approaching; everything decays and produces decay; nothing will endure until the day after tomorrow; nothing, that is, except one species of man, the incurably mediocre. The mediocre alone have a prospect of continuing, of propagating themselves. They will be the men of the future, the sole survivors. "Be like them! Be mediocre!" is now the only morality which has still a significance or obtains a hearing. But it is difficult to preach this morality of mediocrity. It can never avow what it is and what it desires. It has to talk of "moderation," and "dignity," and "duty," and "brotherly love." It will have difficulty in concealing its irony!

But this herding-animal morality is only one kind of morality, beside which, before which, and after which, many other moralities, above all, higher moralities, are or should be possible. Against such a possibility, this herd morality defends itself with all its strength. It says obstinately and inexorably: "I am morality and nothing else is morality."

The first corollary which follows from Nietzsche's conception of the genealogy of morals is what he calls his *immoralism,* or his proposed *transvaluation of values.* Thus:

What will the moralists who appear at this time have to preach? What shall be the message of these sharp on-lookers, these unhurried ones?

What is essential and invaluable in every system of morals, is that it is a long constraint.

A species originates, a type becomes established and strong in the long struggle with essentially unfavorable conditions. On the other hand, species which receive abundant nourishment, a surplus of protection and care, tend to develop variations, become fertile in prodigies and monstrosities.

The essential thing, to repeat, is that there should be a long obedience in the same direction. Thereby results something which makes life worth living; for instance, virtue, art, music, dancing, reason, spirituality; whatever, in short, is transfiguring, refined, or divine.

One may look at every system of morals in this light. It teaches us to hate the lax, the too great freedom. It implants the need for limited horizons, for immediate duties, for narrow perspectives. "Thou must obey some one, and for a long time; otherwise thou wilt come to grief, and lose all respect for thyself."

The tension of soul in misfortune, its shuddering in view of rack and ruin, its inventiveness and heroism in enduring and exploiting misfortune, its depth, mystery, greatness; have these not been bestowed through the discipline of great suffering?

Up to now man has been in the worst hands, has been ruled by the misfits, the physiologically botched, the cunning and revengeful, the so-called *saints*—slanderers of the world, traducers of humanity. The morality of decadence, the will to nothingness, passes as morality *par excellence*. Proof of this: Altruism is considered an absolute value, while egoism meets with hostility everywhere. He who disagrees with me on this point I regard as infected.

For a physiologist, such an opposition of altruism and egoism would leave no room for doubt. If the smallest organ in the body neglects its self-preservation, its recuperative powers, its "egoism," the whole organism will degenerate. The physiologist insists that such decayed parts be cut out. He pities them not at all. But the priest wants precisely the degeneration of mankind; hence he strives to preserve the decayed elements in humanity. This is the price of his rule. This is the "harm that good men do."

When one is no longer serious about self-preservation and the increase of bodily energy, when anemia is made an ideal and contempt of the body is construed as "salvation of the soul," what can all this be, if not a recipe for decadence? Loss of ballast, resistance to natural instincts, "selflessness," these have hitherto been called *morality*.

You want, if possible, to do away with suffering. There is not a more foolish "if possible." We would rather have it increased and made worse. Well-being, as you understand it, is certainly not a goal. The discipline of great suffering is the only discipline that has produced all the elevations of humanity hitherto.

To consider distress as something to be destroyed is sheer idiocy. Generally, it is actually harmful in its consequences, a fatal stupidity, almost as mad as the desire to abolish bad weather out of pity for the poor. In the great economy of the universe the terrors of reality, e.g., the passions, the desires, the will to power, are incalculably more essential than that petty happiness, so-called *goodness.*

It is only among decadents that pity is called a virtue. They are too ready to forget modesty, reverence, and that delicacy of feeling which knows how to keep at a distance. They forget that this sentimental emotion stinks of the mob; that pity is only one step removed from bad manners; that pitying hands may be thrust with destructive results into a great destiny, into a wounded isolation. . . . The overcoming of pity I reckon among the noble virtues.

There is nowadays a sickly irritability and sensitiveness to pain, a repulsive complaining, an effeminizing, which, with the aid of religious and philosophical nonsense, seeks to deck itself out as something superior. There is a regular cult of suffering. The unmanliness of what such groups of visionaries call *sympathy* is, I believe, the first thing that strikes the eye. One must resolutely taboo this latest form of bad taste.

There is a point of diseased mellowness and effeminacy in the history of society, at which society itself takes the part of him who injures it, the part of the criminal. To punish now appears to be somehow "unfair." Is it not sufficient, it is asked, if the criminal be rendered harmless? Why should we still punish? Punishment is barbarous! And so on. With these questions, the herd morality, the morality of fear, draws its ultimate conclusion.

On no point is the ordinary mind of Europe more unwilling to be corrected, than on this matter. People rave nowadays, even under the guise of "science," about coming social conditions in which the "exploiting character" of human relations is to be absent. Particularly is this true of socialistic shallowpates and howling anarchistic dogs. Their words sound to me as if they were promising a mode of life which should refrain from all organic functions. "Exploitation" is not the mark of a depraved or primitive society; it belongs to the nature of the living, as a primary organic function; it is a consequence of the will to power which is precisely the will to life.

You may note that I do not care to see rudeness undervalued. It is by far the most humane form of contradiction, and amid modern effeminacy, it is one of our first virtues.

To be able to be an enemy, to be an enemy, presupposes a strong nature. Strong natures need resistance, accordingly they seek it. The pathos of aggression belongs to strength as much as feelings of revenge and rancor belong to weakness. The strength of the aggressor is determined by the opposition he needs; every increase of strength betrays itself by a search for a more formidable opponent.

To refrain from mutual injury, from violence, from exploitation, to put one's will on a par with others' may result in a kind of good conduct among individuals; but only when the necessary conditions are given, namely, an equality of the individuals in force and worth, and their correlation within one organization.

To take this principle more generally, however, to use it as the fundamental principle of society, would immediately reveal what it actually amounts to, namely, a principle of dissolution and decay. Here one must think profoundly and resist all sentimentality; life itself is essentially appropriation, injury, exploitation, conquest, suppression, severity, obtrusion, incorporation.

Even the organization within which the members treat each other as equal, must, itself, do that toward other organizations which its members refrain from doing to each other; if, that is, it be a living, growing, and not a dying organization. It will endeavor to grow, to gain ground, to attract to itself, to acquire ascendency; not owing to any morality or immorality, but simply because it lives, and because life is precisely will to power.

Fortunately, the world is not built merely on those instincts in which the good-natured herd animal would find his paltry happiness. To demand that everyone become a "good man," a gregarious animal, a blue-eyed benevolent "beautiful soul," or (as Herbert Spencer wished) an altruist, would mean robbing existence of its greatest character, emasculating mankind. And this has been attempted. It is just this that men call *morality*.

The "good" man is the most harmful kind of man. He secures his existence at the cost of truth. He cannot create. He crucifies the man who writeth new values on new tables. He crucifies the whole future of humanity. Whatever harm the slanderers of the world may do, the harm which good men do is the most calamitous of all harm.

Let me say again what I have already said a hundred times. In all our principal moral judgments, that which is sure of itself, that which glorifies itself with praise and blame, that which calls itself good, is the instinct of the herding human animal: the instinct which is coming more and more to the front, coming more and more to dominate other instincts. Morality at present is hearding-animal morality.

All questions of politics, of the social order, of education, have been falsified from top to bottom, because the most harmful men have been taken for great men, and because people were taught to despise the fundamentals of life.

Nietzsche's characteristic doctrines have their basis in these conceptions of the genealogy of morals and the transvaluation of values. His distinction between man and superman, between master morality and slave morality, his reiterated criticisms of the softer, more humanitarian virtues and customs, follow reasonably enough. Perhaps the most famous of all Nietzsche's teachings is in his distinction between master morality and slave morality. Its point is this:

Moral systems must be compelled to bow before the gradations of rank. Their presumption must be driven home, until they thoroughly understand that it is immoral to say that "what is right and proper for one is right and proper for another."

In a tour through the many finer and coarser moralities which have hitherto prevailed, or still prevail, on the earth, I have found certain traits recurring regularly together, until finally two primary types revealed themselves to me: There are master morality and slave morality.

Moral valuations have originated, either in a ruling class pleasantly conscious of being different from the ruled, or in a ruled class, among slaves and dependents of all sorts.

In the master morality, when it is the rulers who determine the notion of "goodness," it is the exalted, proud type of character which is regarded as the distinguishing feature, as that which determines the order of rank. The noble man separates from himself the persons in whom these characteristics are absent; them he despises.

They say: "Thus shall it be." They determine the whither and the why of mankind. They grasp at the future with a creative hand. Whatever is and was becomes for them a means, an instrument, a hammer. Their knowing is creating. Their creating is law-giving. Their will to truth is will to power.

In master morality the antithesis is between "noble" and "despicable." The cowardly, the timid, the no-accounts, the narrowly utilitarian, the distrustful, the self-abasing, the doglike who submit to abuse, the mendicant flatterers, and above all the liars, are despised.

A man who says, "I like that, I take it for my own, I mean to guard it and protect it"; a man who can carry out a resolution, keep hold of a woman, punish and overthrow insolence; a man who has his indignation and his sword; a man whom the weak, the suffering, even the animals, willingly submit to and naturally belong to; such a man is a master by nature.

The noble type of man regards himself as the determiner of values; he does not require to be approved of; he passes the judgment: "What is injurious to me is injurious in itself"; he knows that it is he himself only who confers honor on things; he is a creator of values. He honors whatever he recognizes in himself: such morality is self-glorification. In the foreground there is the feeling of plenitude, of power which seeks to overflow, the consciousness of a wealth which would fain give and bestow.

The noble man honors in himself the powerful one, him who has power over himself, who knows how to speak and how to keep silent, who takes pleasure in subjecting himself to severity and hardness and has reverence for all that is severe and hard. "Wotan placed a hard heart in my breast," says an old Scandinavian saga: it is thus rightly expressed from the soul of a proud Viking.

The noble man is furthest removed from the morality which sees the essence of the moral in sympathy, or in "acting for the good of others." Faith in oneself, pride in oneself, a radical irony and enmity toward "selflessness," belong as definitely to master morality as do scorn and precaution in the presence of sympathy and the "warm heart."

A man of this sort is carved from a single block, which is hard, sweet, fragrant. He enjoys only what is good for him. His desire ceases when the limits of what is good for him are overstepped. . . . Whatever does not kill him makes him stronger. He gathers his material from all he sees, hears, and experiences. He is a selective principle: he rejects much. . . . He reacts slowly to all kinds of stimuli, with that slowness which long caution and pride have bred in him. . . . He is always in his own company, whether mingling with men or books or nature. . . . He honors the thing he chooses.

There is an instinct for rank, which, more than anything else, is the sign of a high rank. The refinement, the goodness, the loftiness of a soul are put to a real test when something of the highest rank passes by but is not yet protected with the awe of authority; something that goes its way like a living touchstone, undistinguished, undiscovered, tentative, perhaps veiled and disguised.

The noble and powerful know how to honor; it is their art, their domain for invention. The profound reverence for age and tradition, the belief and prejudice in favor of ancestors and against newcomers, is typical of master morality. If, contrariwise, men of "modern ideas" believe in "progress" and the "future," and are increasingly lacking in respect for the past, the ignoble origin of these "ideas" is thereby betrayed.

He whose task is to investigate souls will avail himself of many varieties of this very art to determine the ultimate value of a soul, the innate order of rank to which it belongs. He will test it by its instinct for reverence. The vulgarity of many a soul spurts up like dirty water when any holy vessel, any jewel from closed shrines, any book bearing the marks of great destiny, is brought before it. Contrariwise, there is an involuntary silence, a hesitation, a cessation, by which is indicated that a soul feels the nearness of what is worthy of respect.

In the so-called *cultured* classes today, the dealers in "modern ideas," nothing is perhaps so repulsive as their lack of shame, their lack of reverence, the easy insolence of hand and eye with which they touch, finger, and examine everything. It is possible that more tact for reverence exists among the lower classes and peasants than among the newspaper-reading demimonde of "intellect" and "culture."

Much has been achieved when the sentiment of reverence has been finally instilled into the masses, when they realize that they are not allowed to touch everything, that there are some experiences before which they must take off their shoes and restrain their hand.

The master morality is especially foreign and irritating to present-day taste. It is disliked and distrusted for the sternness of its principle that one has duties only to one's equals; that one may act toward persons of a lower rank, toward all that is foreign, just as one pleases; that its values are "beyond good and evil."

It is typical of the master morality to be able and obliged to exercise prolonged gratitude and prolonged revenge, but both only within the circle of one's equals; artfulness in retaliation; a need for enemies as outlets for emotions of envy, quarrelsomeness, arrogance. This, of course, is not "modern morality," and is therefore difficult to realize, to discover.

In contrast to the master morality stands the slave morality:

It is otherwise with the second type of morality; what I have named slave morality. If the abused, the oppressed, the suffering, the unemancipated, the weary, the uncertain-of-themselves, should moralize, what will be the common element in their moral evaluations?

The slave has an unfavorable eye for the virtues of the powerful. He has a skepticism and distrust of everything which they honor. He would fain persuade himself that their happiness is not genuine.

On the other hand, those qualities which serve to alleviate the existence of sufferers are brought into prominence and flooded with light. It is here that sympathy, the kind helping hand, the warm heart, patience, diligence, humility, friendliness, attain to honor. For here these are the most useful equalities, almost the only means of supporting the burden of existence.

Slave morality is essentially the morality of utility. It is oriented around the idea of the "useful." Here is the seat of the origin of the famous antithesis of "good" and "evil," which I have distinguished from the antithesis of "good" and "bad." According to slave morality, the "evil" man rouses fear. According to master morality, the "good" man rouses fear, and seeks to rouse it, while the "bad" man is regarded as the despicable being.

According to slave morality, the good man must be the "safe" man: he must be good-natured, easily hoodwinked, perhaps a little stupid. Wherever slave morality gains the ascendency, language shows a tendency to approximate the significations of the words *good* and *stupid*.

A last fundamental difference: the desire for freedom, the enthusiasm for "liberty" the instinct of being "happy" belong as inherently to slave morality as artifice in reverence and enthusiasm in devotion belong to master morality. Hence, we can understand, love as a passion, romantic love, with its ardors and endurances and binding ties, is a phenomenon of master morality.

Nietzsche never wearied of criticizing those phases of modern morality which smacked of "degeneration" and "slaves." Among the topics singled out for castigation was the nineteenth-century enthusiasm for the emancipation of women. Says Nietzsche:

To be mistaken in the fundamental problem of "man and woman" is the typical sign of a shallow mind. To deny here the profoundest antagonism, the need for hostile tension; to dream here of "equal rights," equal training, equal claims and obligations; to prove oneself shallow at this dangerous spot, may be regarded as suspicious, nay more, as betrayed. Such an one may probably prove "too short" for all the fundamental issues of life, unable to descend into any of the depths.

In no previous age have women been treated with so much respect by men as at present. This belongs to the tendency and fundamental taste of democracy. Is it any wonder that abuse should be made of this respect? Women want more; they learn to make claims; they become rivals for rights. In a word, they lose their modesty. And, let me add, they also lose their taste.

They unlearn their fear of men. But the woman who "unlearns" her fear of men, sacrifices her most womanly instincts. That woman should venture forward when man has ceased to inspire fear, is reasonable enough, and intelligible enough. But what is more difficult to grasp is that precisely thereby woman deteriorates. That is happening these days: let us not deceive ourselves about it.

Wherever the industrial spirit has triumphed over the military and aristocratic spirit, woman strives for the economic and legal independence of a clerk. "Woman as clerk" is inscribed on the portal of that modern society which is in course of formation.

While she thus appropriates new rights, aspires to be master, and inscribes the "progress" of woman on her flags and banners, the very opposite realizes itself with terrible obviousness—woman retrogrades.

There is stupidity in this movement, an almost masculine stupidity, of which a well-bred sensible woman might be heartily ashamed. To lose the ground on which she can most surely achieve victory; to neglect her proper weapons; to let herself go before man where formerly she kept herself in control in artful humility; to neutralize man's faith in a fundamentally different ideal in woman, something eternally feminine; to emphatically and loquaciously dissuade man from the idea that woman must be preserved, protected, and indulged like some delicate, strangely wild, and often pleasant domestic animal; what does all this betoken, if not a disintegration of womanly instincts?

There are, to be sure, enough of idiotic friends and corrupters of woman amongst the learned asses of the male sex, who advise woman to defeminize herself in this manner, and to imitate all the stupidities from which man suffers, who would like to lower woman to "general culture," indeed, even to newspaper reading and meddling with politics.

In their efforts to rise to the ideal woman, to the higher woman, they have really wished to lower the general level of women, and there are no more certain means to this end than university education, trousers, and the rights of voting like cattle. Fundamentally, the "emancipated" and the "emancipators" (for example, that typical old maid, Henrik Ibsen) are anarchists, misbegotten souls whose most deep-rooted instinct is revenge.

Almost everywhere her nerves are being ruined, and she is daily being made more hysterical and more incapable of fulfilling her first and last function, namely, the rearing of robust children. These "friends of woman" wish to "cultivate" her, to make the weaker sex strong by "culture," as if history did not teach that the "cultivating" of mankind and the weakening of mankind have always kept pace with one another.

That which inspires respect in woman, and often also fear, is her real nature, her genuine, carnivora-like cunning and flexibility, her tiger claws beneath the glove, her naïveté in egoism, her untrainableness, her innate wildness, her incomprehensibleness, the extent and deviation of her virtues.

That which, in spite of fear, excites one's sympathy for the dangerous and beautiful in woman, is that she seems more afflicted, more vulnerable, more needful of love and more condemned to disillusion, than any other creature. Fear and sympathy—it is with these feelings that man has hitherto stood in the presence of woman, always with one foot in tragedy which rends while it delights. And all that is now to be at an end? The disenchantment of women is in progress? The tediousness of woman is slowly evolving?

Another object of Nietzsche's criticism was what he describes as "Christian morality." He never tires of railing at it. From among pages and pages, the following citations may be taken as representative:

All the things men have valued heretofore are not even realities. They are mere fantasies; more strictly speaking, they are lies. All the concepts, "God," "soul," "virtue," "sin," "Beyond," "truth," "eternal life," are lies arising from the evil instincts of diseased and harmful natures.

I am the first immoralist. Basically, there are two denials included in this term. First, I deny the type of man who formerly passed as the highest, the "good" man, the "benevolent" man, the "charitable" man. Second, I deny that kind of morality which has become recognized and dominant, namely Christian morality. . . . The second of these denials is the more decisive.

No one before me has felt Christian morality beneath him. To do that one must have height, far vision, depth. Up to now, Christian morality has been the Circe of all thinkers; they stood at her service. What man before me has descended into the caves from which the poisonous fumes of this ideal burst forth? Who before me ever dared to suspect they were caves? What philosopher before me was a real moralist and not a superior swindler, an idealist?

Have you understood me? What defines me is the fact that I unmasked Christian morality. For this reason I needed a word which would contain the idea of a universal challenge: immoralist. Blindness in the face of Christian morality is the essential crime. It is the great uncleanliness.

Christian morality is the most pernicious form of the will to falsehood, the denial of life. It is not error as error which infuriates me here. It is not the age-long lack of "good will," of discipline, of decency, of spiritual courage, which betrays itself in the triumph of Christian morality. It is the ghastly fact that what was unnatural received the highest honors as morality, and remained suspended over man as the law of the categorical imperative. This is the great blundering. To teach contempt of the primal life instincts; to set up a "soul," a spirit, in order to overthrow the body; to teach man to find impurity in sex; to look for the principle of evil in the need for expansion; to see a "higher moral value" in "selflessness," in "objectivity," in "neighbor love"; these things are the will to nothingness, the denial of life, the great nay-saying.

The Jews performed the miracle of the inversion of valuations, by means of which life on earth obtained a new and dangerous charm for a couple of thousand years. Their prophets fused the expressions *rich, godless, wicked, violent, sensual,* into one expression, and for the first time coined the word *world* as a term of reproach. In this inversion of values (which included the use of *poor* as synonymous with *saint* and *friend*) the significance of the Jewish people is to be found. It is with them that slave morality begins.

From the beginning, Christian morality was essentially the surfeit of life which disguised itself under the belief in "another" and "better" life. The hatred of the world, the condemnation of emotion, the fear of beauty, the distrust of sensuality, all these have always appeared to me as the most dangerous forms of the "will to perish," symptoms of the deepest weariness, exhaustion, anemia.

The teachers and preachers and leaders of mankind, including the theologians, have been decadents. Hence their inversion of values into a hostility to life; hence "morality." Here is a definition of *morality:* the idiosyncrasy of decadents actuated by a desire to avenge themselves successfully upon life. I attach great value to this definition.

Have you understood me? The unmasking of Christian morality is a unique event. It breaks the history of mankind in two. Man lives either before or after that. Everything which was until then called the *truth,* is now recognized as the most harmful, spiteful, and concealed falsehood. The sacred pretext, the "improvement of man," is recognized as a ruse to drain life of its blood. This morality is vampirism.

He who unmasks Christian morality unmasks the worthlessness of the values in which men believe. He sees in them only the most fatal kind of abortions; fatal, because they fascinate. The notion of "God" was invented as the counternotion to life. The notion of a "Beyond" was invented to depreciate the only world that exists. The notion of an "immortal soul" was invented to despise the body. The notion of "sin" was invented to mislead our instincts. Finally, the notion of a "good man" has come to mean everything that is weak, ill, misshapen, everything which should be obliterated. The law of selection is thwarted. And all this was believed in as morality! *Ecrasez l'infâme!*

We who hold a different view, we who regard Christian morality and democratic politics to be a degenerating form of organization, where have we to fix our hopes?

In new moralists and a new morality. There is no other alternative. In minds strong enough and original enough to initiate a transvaluation of values, to invert "eternal valuations," lies our only hope. In forerunners, in men of the future, who shall fix the constraints and fasten the knots which will compel millenniums to take new paths; make preparations for vast hazardous enterprises and collective attempts in rearing and educating; put an end to the frightful rule of folly and chance which has hitherto gone by the name of *history;* in such do we fix our hopes.

For these purposes a new type of moralist and ruler will some time be needed, at the very idea of which everything that has existed might look pale and dwarfed. The image of such leaders hovers before our eyes.

But their image fills our hearts with anxiety and gloom. How are they to be born? How are they to be bred? How nurtured to that elevation and power which will feel the present needs as their tasks? Of them is demanded a transvaluation of values. In them is needed a new conscience of steel, a new heart of brass, to bear the weight of such responsibility. There is always the danger that they may be lacking, or miscarry and degenerate. These are our real anxieties and glooms. These are the heavy thoughts and storms which sweep across our skies.

There are few pains so grievous as to have seen an exceptional man miss his way and deteriorate. But he who has the rare eye to see the danger of mankind itself missing its way and deteriorating; he who has recognized the element of wild chance in human affairs; he who has detected the fate that is hidden under the idiotic unwariness and blind confidence of "modern ideas," and still more of Christian morality and democratic politics; suffers from an anguish beyond comparison.

The universal degeneracy of mankind to the level of the ideals of socialistic fools and humanitarian shallowpates, the dwarfing of man to an absolutely gregarious animal, the brutalizing of man into pigmy with equal "rights" and "claims"—this is undoubtedly possible. He who has foreseen this possibility knows another loathing unknown to the rest of mankind.

From these themes, Nietzsche turns to the question of his own significance for the modern mind. Nietzsche on the genealogy of morals is interesting. Nietzsche on the distinction between master morality and slave morality is suggestive. Nietzsche on woman and Christianity is challenging. But Nietzsche on himself is unique:

Idealism is alien to me. Where you see ideal things I see human things, alas all-too-human.

He who would be a creator in good and evil must first be a destroyer, and break values into pieces. I am the most terrible man that has ever existed. But I shall be the most beneficent. I know the joy of annihilation. I am the first immoralist. I am thus the essential destroyer.

I know my destiny. I am not a man. I am a fatality. I am dynamite. Some day my name will be bound up with the recollection of something terrific, a crisis, a profound clash of consciences, a decisive condemnation of all that before me had been believed, required, hallowed.

I am the voice of truth. But my truth is terrible, for hitherto lies have been called truth. "The transvaluation of all values" is my formula for mankind's act of highest self-recognition. I contradict as no one has contradicted before. For when truth engages in a struggle with the falsehoods of ages, we must expect shocks, earthquakes, rearrangements of hills and valleys, such as never yet have been dreamt of. All the mighty forms of the old social structure I blow into space, for they rest on falsehoods. Politics on a grand scale will date from me.

My life task is to prepare humanity for a moment of supreme self-consciousness, a great noontide, a transvaluation of all values, an emancipation from all moral values, a yea-saying, a confidence in all that has formerly been forbidden, despised, and damned; when it will gaze both backwards and forwards, emerge from the tyranny of accident and priesthood, and, for the first time, pose the question of the why and wherefore of humanity as a whole.

But with all this there is nothing in me to suggest the founder of a "religion." Religions are the business of the mob. After coming in contact with a religious man, I have always to wash my hands. I want no "believers." I never address myself to the masses. I do not wish to be a saint: I would rather be a clown. Perhaps I am a clown.

Note on Sources. The Nietzsche materials in this section are quoted, abridged, or paraphrased from many different books, essays, and chapters. The basic "argument" of the section is derived principally from his book, *Beyond Good and Evil*, particularly Chapters 1, 5, and 9; and somewhat also from his book, *The Genealogy of Morals*, particularly essays I and II. The materials taken from those two sources were used to construct the "framework." But a number of passages from his other writings were then fitted into that framework. These passages were taken from his *Zarathustra*, his *Dawn of Day*, his *Joyful Wisdom*, his *Will to Power*, and his *Ecce Homo*.

Reading References. The best thing to do with Nietzsche, having read carefully the selections given here, is to try his *Thus Spake Zarathustra*. This is at first a somewhat difficult book, but it has a strange, exotic charm.

It may be supplemented by chapters from *Beyond Good and Evil* and *The Genealogy of Morals*. Among items that may be consulted with profit, for a beginning, is Will Durant's chapter in his *Story of Philosophy*. A good book on Nietzsche is George A. Morgan's *What Nietzsche Means*. The author of the Philo Vance detective novels was a student of Nietzsche's works. His name was W. H. Wright, and his book *What Nietzsche Taught* is a good introduction. The same goes for H. L. Mencken's *The Philosophy of Friedrich Nietzsche*. Among books of a more academic character may be mentioned W. K. Salter's *Nietzsche the Thinker*.

The following are some books published since 1940:

Bentley, E. R. *A Century of Hero-Worship.*
Bonifazi, C. *Christendom Attacked: A Comparison of Kierkegaard and Nietzsche.*
Borland, H. H. *Nietzsche's Influence on Swedish Literature.*
Brinton, C. *Nietzsche.*
Copleston, F. *Friedrich Nietzsche, Philosopher of Culture.*
Hamblen, E. S. *Friedrich Nietzsche and His New Gospel.*
Heller, E. *The Disinherited Mind.*
Hubben, W. *Four Prophets of Our Destiny.*
Kaufmann, W. A. *Nietzsche: Philosopher, Psychologist, Anti-Christ.*
Knight, G. *Christ and Nietzsche.*
Lavrin, J. *Nietzsche: An Approach.*
Lea, F. F. *The Tragic Philosopher: A Study of Friedrich Nietzsche.*
Mann, T. *Nietzsche's Philosophy in the Light of Contemporary Events.*
Manthey-Zorn, O. *Dionysus: The Tragedy of Nietzsche.*
Morgan, G. A. *What Nietzsche Means.*
Nicholls, R. A. *Nietzsche in the Early Works of Thomas Mann.*
Rayburn, H. A. *Nietzsche: The Story of a Human Philosopher.*
Thompson, R. M. *Nietzsche and Christian Ethics.*
Williams, W. D. *Nietzsche and the French.*

READING QUESTIONS

1. Nietzsche begins by repudiating traditional moral philosophy, as represented e.g., in Paley or Kant or Mill. What such moralists have sought to do. Why Nietzsche will have none of it.
2. A traditional moralist might say that he was trying to formulate a theory of morality. Nietzsche wants a theory of moralities or of types of morality. What is the difference here?
3. If you study a morality with an eye to its genealogy, its natural his-

tory, rather than its defining principle, you will (says Nietzsche) find that it originates during the early aristocratic period of the people whose morality it is. His point here: (a) the pathos of distance, (b) the long constraint, (c) that other more mysterious pathos, (d) the sun-seeking plants in Java, (e) intolerance.

4. Under the protection and control of its early aristocracy a people achieves security. The need for the early morality disappears. A morality emerges expressive of the needs and desires of a more democratic age. His point here: (a) the dangerous and disquieting point, (b) new whys; new hows, (c) fear of the neighbor, i.e., not of an external enemy, (d) the herd instinct, (e) happiness-moralities, (f) the moral hypocrisy of the ruling class, (g) "I am morality and nothing else is morality."

5. Nietzsche believed that, within most of Western civilization, moralities had reached the "democratic," the herding-animal, stage. He took a dim view of such latter-day moralities. His point here: (a) altruism, (b) the discipline of great suffering, (c) pity, (d) sympathy, (e) the criminal, (f) exploitation, (g) rudeness, (h) the "good" man, (i) socialistic shallow-pates and howling anarchistic dogs.

6. When a morality is in its aristocratic phase you have "master-morality." When it is in its democratic, herding-animal phase, you have "slave-morality," i.e., the morality of those who once were slaves. Nietzsche favored the former over the latter. His point here: (a) noble versus despicable, (b) a determiner, a creator of values, (c) an instinct for rank, a sentiment of reverence, (d) "beyond good and evil," (e) "good and bad" versus "good and evil," (f) liberty and happiness, (g) the morality of utility.

7. How wrong-headed is Nietzsche on the subject of women?

8. What is Nietzsche's indictment of Christian morality? If you grant that the indictment ("unmasking") is essentially correct, would you attach as much importance to it as he does?

9. "These are our real anxieties and glooms." Elaborate.

10. Point here: (a) an anguish beyond comparison, (b) loathing unknown to the rest of mankind.

11. Wherein you find Nietzsche (a) most (b) least worth your while. Why?

5. MORALITY GROUNDED IN INTRINSIC GOODNESS —FROM G. E. MOORE

Thus far. Up to this point we have examined claims made by Paley, Kant, Mill, and Nietzsche in reference to the question, What makes an act right? We found in Paley the claim that an act is right if and only if it is according to the will of God; in Kant, that an act is right if the maxim on which it is performed can be consistently universalized; in Mill, that an act is right if it produces more happiness, more pleasure, than any other act possible under the circumstances; and in Nietzsche the claim that such a question is futile and had better be abandoned. Nietzsche would put an end to attempts at formulating an ethical theory. He would replace ethical theory by something different. This distrust of ethical theory has not been without influence.[2] But, if Nietzsche were alive today, the most he would be entitled to say would be, "We've scotched the snake, not killed it." In the present concluding section we are to be concerned with a writer, G. E. Moore, whose book, *Principia Ethica,* has helped greatly to keep alive an interest in ethical theory. The book contains sharp criticism of much traditional ethical theory. If the criticisms are sound, you have to say that much traditional ethical theory has been mistaken and confused, but you do not have to say, as with Nietzsche, that it is "all a mistake," that it would be better to repudiate it than revise it.

Biographical Note. George Edward Moore, was born in 1873 and died in 1958 in his eighty-fifth year. He had become, for some years preceding his death, the best known and most distinguished writer on philosophy in the United Kingdom. He was educated at Dulwich College, and at Trinity College, Cambridge. For six years (1898–1904) he was a Fellow of Trinity College, during which time he published his important book, *Principia Ethica,* 1903. For fourteen years (1911–1925) he was lecturer in moral science in Cambridge University, during which time he published his small book, *Ethics,* 1911. For twenty-six years (1921–1947) he was editor of the imporant English philosophical journal, *Mind.* For fourteen years (1925–1939) he was professor of philosophy in Cambridge University. During the four years 1940–44, he visited the United States and taught at a number of colleges and universities. Those who were fortunate enough to attend any of his courses or seminars remember them as scenes of lively presentation and debate. In 1951 Professor Moore received the Order of Merit, one of his country's most distinguished awards.

Professor Moore published his *Principia Ehica* in 1903, about sixty years ago. No other book has, during those years, exerted as great an influence on the teaching and writing of ethical theory. It has not been necessary to agree with what Professor Moore said. Indeed, many have gone to great lengths to make clear that they do not agree with him. But it has been necessary to take account of his principal contentions. The *Principia*

[2] See Chapter III in Castell, *An Elementary Ethics.*

has not been the sort of book that people can safely ignore. It has, thus, been a challenging book. It may be that more people disagree with the *Principia* than agree with it. It is difficult to be sure. But you can say that, among persons whose professional business it is to have opinions on these matters, more have taken note of what Professor Moore had to say than have ignored him.

Professor Moore's book is not large. It contains only six chapters. The over-all plan is simple. The first chapter contains the fundamental theses. The next three criticize positions which differ in respect to one of these theses. The last two "apply" claims set forth in the first chapter to two important questions.

Let us take a look at the book's first chapter. It has become a famous document, more frequently quoted or quoted from than any other piece of twentieth-century writing in this field. What claims do you find Professor Moore making? They come to something like this:

(1) Ethics investigates the principles and presuppositions which are operative in ethical judgments.

(2) Ethical judgments are of two sorts. Let us call them primary or secondary.

(3) A primary ethical judgment states either that something is intrinsically good, or that it is intrinsically evil.

(4) If something is intrinsically good, then even though it existed alone in the world its existence would be better than its nonexistence.

(5) A secondary or derived ethical judgment states that something is a means to or cause of or condition for something else which is itself intrinsically good.

(6) Intrinsic goodness is a simple, unique, unanalyzable, indefinable quality or property or predicate or object of thought.

(7) The attempt to define it, by reference to any other quality, is the naturalistic fallacy.

(8) Primary ethical judgments are self-evident. If true, they are self-evidently so. Their truth must be directly apprehended or intuited. There is no evidence for them apart from the statement of them.

(9) That restriction (no. 8) does not hold of secondary or derived ethical judgments.

(10) A primary ethical judgment, if true of one instance of a thing, is necessarily true of all instances. It is a universal judgment, not a generalization; a universal truth, not a general truth; true universally, not "true generally" or "generally true."

(11) That claim (no. 10) does not hold of secondary or derived ethical judgments. They are generalizations.

(12) The intrinsic goodness of a complex whole is not necessarily equivalent to the sum of the intrinsic goodnesses of its parts. This is the principle of organic unities.

These have proved to be a lively set of claims. They have given rise to many questions and criticisms. Is it true that all ethical judgments can be shaken down to two fundamental sorts? Is it true that intrinsic goodness is a quality or property of things? Is it, as Professor Moore insists, a non-natural quality? What is a "non-natural" quality? What things are intrinsically good? Is it true that intrinsic goodness is an indefinable notion? Why have so many writers believed that they could define it? Is it true that primary ethical judgments (e.g., "X is intrinsically good") are self-evidently true? That it is a mistake to imagine that reasons or evidence can ever be offered in support of them? True also that they are universal judgments, not generalizations, not hypotheses having increasable and decreasable probability? What "complex wholes" illustrate the principle of organic unities?

Chapters II, III, and IV review and criticize attempts to define goodness in the sense of intrinsic goodness. Each attempt is diagnosed as involving the "naturalistic fallacy," the mistake of imagining that you can, in the last analysis, ever say anything more of intrinsic goodness by way of defining it, than that it is intrinsic goodness; that you can "reduce" it to some quality other than intrinsic goodness; that you can say of all intrinsically good things that they have some quality, other than intrinsic goodness, by virtue of which they are intrinsically good.

Chapter V moves on from goodness to rightness. Here Professor Moore insists that we do clearly have a definable notion; that rightness is to be defined by reference to goodness. Thus, an act is right if and only if it produces more goodness than any other act possible under the circumstances. You can say that. That is what right *means*. But you must not try to push the definition one step further by trying to define goodness. To do so would involve you in the naturalistic fallacy.

Chapter VI returns to the indefinable notion of intrinsic goodness, and asks the fundamental question: What things are intrinsically good? And, among things that are intrinsically good, which are intrinsically the best? It is not easy to be quite sure what Professor Moore says in this interesting and challenging final chapter. He speaks at great length about two matters; namely personal affections and the appreciation of beauty. It is clear that he apprehends these as intrinsically good. It is sometimes not clear whether he apprehends that they are the only things that are intrinsically good; or whether he apprehends that, among all the things which are intrinsically good, these are intrinsically the best.

The following passages are quoted or abridged from Professor Moore's *Principia Ethica*. The book contains a preface and 135 numbered sections. The numbers in parentheses refer you to the sections in the book; the P to the preface; the T.C. to the table of contents.

Let us begin with Professor Moore's distinction between intrinsically good, and, a means to something intrinsically good. Thus one might say that pleasure is intrinsically good, and that money, a means to pleasure, is a means to something intrinsically good.

It is important to distinguish these two judgments. Both may be expressed in the same language. We may say "This is good"; but in the one case good will indicate good as a means: in the other case, good as an end. These are very different assertions to make about a thing. Unless we are clear which we mean, we shall have a poor chance of deciding whether our assertion is true or false. To settle the one is not to settle the other. (17)

This difference is sometimes expressed by the contrast between good in itself and good as a means, intrinsic value and value as a means. (15) . . . To say something is good as a means is to say that its effect is good in itself. (16)

Not necessarily →

Having drawn attention to this distinction between being good and being a means to something good, Professor Moore concentrates on the notion of good:

Everyone understands the question "Is this good?" It is different from the question "Is this pleasant, or desired, or approved?" It has a distinct meaning, even though one may not recognize in what respect it is distinct. When one thinks of intrinsic value, or intrinsic worth, or says that a thing ought to exist, he has before his mind the unique object, the unique property, which I mean by good. Everyone is aware of this notion, although he may not be aware that it is different from other notions of which he is also aware. (13)

We are aware of a certain quality or property which (and not anything else) is what we mainly mean by good. Many different things possess this quality. Things which are good owe their goodness to their common possession of this quality, and not to their common possession of any other quality. (24)

We have then the notion of something being good in the sense of intrinsically good. Professor Moore uses several different phrases to express this notion; for example, intrinsically valuable, intrinsically desirable, ought to exist for its own sake, good in itself, and so on. I propose to use the phrase "intrinsically good." Given the phrase, you may ask what things it applies to, what things are intrinsically good; or you may ask what it means, what it is you say about something when you say that it is intrinsically good. Both questions are fundamentally important. For the time being Professor Moore bears down on the question of meaning:

The question "What is good?" may ask what thing is good or what things are good. But it may have still another meaning, namely how "good" is to be defined. This question, how "good" is to be defined is fundamental in ethics. That which is meant by "good" is, except its converse "bad," the only simple object of thought that is peculiar to ethics. Unless this question (how "good" is to be defined) is understood, and its answer clearly recognized, the rest of ethics is useless as systematic knowledge. (5)

The question how a certain conception, in this case intrinsic goodness, is to be defined, is itself ambiguous. For example there is verbal or nominal definition which aims to tell how people use a certain word; and then there is real or essential definition which aims to set forth the nature or essence of that to which the word refers. Professor Moore wants it clear that he is interested in real or essential, not verbal or nominal.

How is "good" to be defined? It may be thought that this is a verbal question. But this is not the sort of definition I am asking for. Such a definition can never be of ultimate importance except in lexicography. If I wanted that kind of definition I should have to consider how people generally use the word "good"; but my business is not with its customary usage. My business is solely with that object or idea which the word is generally used to stand for. I want to discover the nature of that object or idea. (6)

We have the question clear: What is the real, in contrast to merely verbal, definition of intrinsic goodness? Now for Professor Moore's famous and controversial claim:

If we understand the question in this sense, my answer may seem disappointing. If I am asked "How is good to be defined?" my answer is that it cannot be defined. And that is all I have to say about it. (6)

It may be that that is all he has to say about it. But he is aware that what he has said runs contrary to much traditional ethical theory at this point. Invited into this discussion both Paley and Mill might have said that they could define goodness. Their definitions would not have been the same; but the point is they would have offered definitions. So Professor Moore must expand on his brief but challenging claim:

I do not mean that that which is good (e.g., pleasure, intelligence, etc.) is indefinable. I mean that good itself is indefinable. (9)

To readers who are familiar with philosophic terminology I can express my point by saying that propositions about the good are synthetic, never analytic; and that is no trivial matter. If I am right, then nobody can foist upon us such an axiom as "Pleasure is the only good," or "The good is the desired," on the pretence that this is "the very meaning of the word." (6)

Good, that quality which we assert to belong to a thing when we call it good, is incapable of definition. Good has no definition because it is simple. It is one of those innumerable objects of thought which are indefinable because they are the ultimate terms by reference to which whatever is definable must be defined. (10) They are something which you think of or perceive, and to anyone who cannot think of or perceive them, you can never, by any definition, make their nature known. (7)

Good is a simple notion, just as yellow is a simple notion. You cannot explain to anyone who does not already know it, what yellow is. So, you cannot explain what good is. Yellow and good are simple notions, out of which definitions are composed and with which the power of further defining ceases. (7)

I deny good to be definable. I say that it is not composed of any parts. There is nothing whatsoever which we can substitute for good. That is what I mean when I say that good is indefinable. (8) . . . "Good" has no definition because it is simple and has no parts. (10)

There is no inherent difficulty in the claim that good denotes a simple and indefinable quality. There are many other instances of such qualities. (10)

Consider yellow. We may try to define it by describing its physical equivalent, what kind of light-vibrations must stimulate the normal eye in order that we may see it (yellow). But light-vibrations are not what we mean by yellow. They are not what we perceive. The most we can say is that they correspond to the yellow which we actually perceive. (10)

Consider pleasure. It too is indefinable. It is some one thing, the same in all the degrees and kinds of it that there may be. We may be able to say how it is related to other things: that it is in the mind, that it causes desire, that we are conscious of it, etc. We can describe its relation to other things, but define it we can *not*. (12)

There is, then, a simple, indefinable, unanalysable object of thought. By what name we call this unique object is a matter of indifference, so long as we recognize what it is and that it differs from other objects. The words which are signs of ethical judgments all refer to it; and they are expressions of ethical judgments solely because they do refer to it. (15)

Suppose you were not convinced of Professor Moore's point. So you assemble in your mind all the things you would be willing to say were intrinsically good. Suppose that, in addition to possessing the quality of intrinsic goodness, these things also possessed some other quality, and that their possession of this other quality was, in each case, your reason for calling them intrinsically good. I do not think Professor Moore would deny the possibility of what is here suggested. However, suppose you now proceeded to *define* goodness as *meaning* the possession of this other quality. To possess this other quality, you would say, is what I mean by being intrinsically good. That is how I would define it. Your point would not be that the possession of this other quality is evidence that something is intrinsically good; nor that this other property was a measure or criterion of intrinsic goodness. It would be that "possession of this other quality" is what intrinsic goodness means. You would be trying to deal with a question of meaning, a question in semantics, not a question of evidence or a question in criteriology. If this was your stand, then, I think Professor Moore would accuse you of committing his "naturalistic fallacy." On the title page of his book he quotes from Bishop Butler: "Everything is what it is, and not another thing." His claim that goodness is not definable by reference to anything else, that goodness is goodness and not anything else, is an instance of Butler's general remark. And if you think that goodness is *not* goodness but is something else, you commit the naturalistic fallacy.

It may be that all things which are good are also something else, just as all things which are yellow produce a certain kind of vibration in the light. Ethics aim to discover what *other* properties belong to all things which are good. But when you name those other properties you are not defining good. Those other properties are not the same with goodness. To say that they are is the "naturalistic fallacy." (10)

The naturalistic fallacy consists in identifying the simple notion which we mean by "good" with some other notion. (35)

If a man confuses good, which is not a natural object, with any natural object whatever, then there is a naturalistic fallacy. The reasons why good is not to be considered a natural object may be discussed in another place. But, even if good were a natural object, that would not alter the character of the fallacy; only the name would not be appropriate. I do not care about the name: what I care about is the fallacy. (12)

The naturalistic fallacy has been quite as commonly committed with regard to beauty as with regard to good: its use has introduced as many errors into esthetics as into ethics. (121)

Professor Moore's claim that goodness, in the sense of intrinsic goodness, is an indefinable notion, is not deflationary. To say this about goodness is not to "belittle" it. Thus, it is not to say that goodness is "relative," or obscure, or meaningless, or unknowable; merely that it is indefinable. And if one objects to this, one may well be asked which ethical notion is indefinable; for it would seem that there is going to be one. If you define volume in terms of surface, and surface in terms of plane, and plane in terms of line, and line in terms of point, and point in terms of position, is there any reason to believe that you can continue this regressive analysis indefinitely? If not, you arrive eventually at an indefinable notion. Is there anything paradoxical about the idea that the definable presupposes the indefinable?

Professor Moore's claim that goodness is indefinable is connected with his further claim that judgments in which it is predicated are unprovable. If you say that something is intrinsically good, do not try to define the notion of goodness and do not try to prove the truth of your statement. The provable presupposes the unprovable. It will be remembered that Professor Moore distinguishes between goodness and rightness, and insists that rightness can be defined in terms of goodness—e.g., an act is right if any only if it produces more goodness than any other act possible under the circumstances. Thus you can have two distinct questions: (a) Is X intrinsically good? (b) Is a certain act right? Professor Moore's claim is that you can answer the first question; that your answer is meaningful, and either true or false; that you cannot prove which it is; and that this limitation follows from the nature of proof—as suggested above, the provable presupposes the unprovable. Thus:

For answers to the *first* question ("Is X intrinsically good?") no relevant evidence whatever can be adduced: from no other truth, except themselves alone, can it be inferred that they are either true or false. As for the *second* question ("Is a certain action right?") any answer to it *is* capable of proof or disproof. Indeed, so many considerations are relevant to its truth or falsehood, as to make the attainment of probability very difficult and the attainment of certainty impossible. (P)

If any ethical philosopher offers, for propositions of the first kind ("X is intrinsically good"), any evidence whatever, his reasoning has not the least tendency to establish his conclusions. Not only are his conclusions totally devoid of weight: we have reason to suspect him of confusion; since the offering of irrelevant evidence generally indicates that the philosopher has had before his mind, not the question he professes to answer, but some other entirely different one. (P)

To express the fact that ethical propositions of my *first* class ("X is intrinsically good") are incapable of proof or disproof I have sometimes called them "Intuitions." But I am not an "Intuitionist" in the ordinary sense of the term. The Intuitionist proper maintains that propositions of my *second* class ("A certain action is right or a duty") are incapable of proof or disproof by any inquiry into the results of such actions. I on the contrary maintain that propositions of *this* kind are *not* "Intuitions." (P)

If judgments of intrinsic goodness are true, yet unprovable because they have no evidence beyond themselves, you can say that they are self-evident, meaning that they are their own evidence. Professor Moore warns against imagining that self-evident means "evident to a self."

I am anxious that this should not be misunderstood. The expression "self-evident" means that the proposition is evident or true, by itself alone; that it is not an inference from some other proposition. It does not mean that the proposition is true because it is evident to you or me or all mankind. By saying that a proposition is self-evident we mean that its appearing so to us is not the reason why it is true: for we mean that it has absolutely no reason. (86)

Intrinsic goodness is indefinable. Judgments which predicate intrinsic goodness are unprovable. They are also "universal." This is an additional claim.

One difference between a judgment which asserts that a thing is good in itself, and a judgment that asserts that it is a means to good, consists in the fact that the first, if true of one instance of the thing in question, is necessarily true of all; whereas a thing which has good effects under some circumstances may have bad ones under others. All judgments of intrinsic value are universal in this sense. (18)

Given the concept of intrinsic goodness you can have the question, "What things possess this quality? What things are intrinsically good?" And Professor Moore insists that this is an important and persistent question for ethics. But before raising that question, he extends his account of intrinsic goodness by adding what he calls "the principle of organic unities." This is his thesis about "complex wholes" whose constituent parts are intrinsically good. He says:

There is a vast number of different things, each of which has intrinsic value. There are also many things which are bad, and many that appear to be indifferent. A thing belonging to any of these three classes (good, bad, indifferent) may occur as part of a complex whole which includes other things belonging both to the same class and to the other two classes. (A complex whole may be made up of parts which are themselves good, or bad, or indifferent.) The value of such a complex whole bears no regular proportion to the sum of the values of its parts. (18)

A good thing may exist in such a relation to another good thing that the value of the complex whole thus formed is greater than the sum of the values of the two good things. A complex whole formed of a good thing and an indifferent thing may have greater value than that good thing by itself possesses. The point is that the value of a complex whole must not be assumed to be the same as the sum of the values of its parts. (18)

There are complex wholes whose value is different from the sum of the values of their parts. The relations between such parts and a complex whole which they form, have not hitherto received a separate name. (19) It would be useful that it should have one; and there is a name which might well be appropriated to it. (20) I would propose the name "principle of organic unities." This principle is that the intrinsic value of a whole is neither identical with nor proportional to the sum of the values of its parts. (111)

The title of Chapter I of *Principia Ethica* is "The Subject-matter of Ethics." Since however, the primary subject-matter of ethics is intrinsic goodness, one could think of the chapter as having that title. The book's six chapters would then be strung together as follows: (1) Intrinsic goodness. (2–3–4) Theories which commit the naturalistic fallacy about intrinsic goodness. (5) Relation of intrinsic goodness to rightness. (6) What things are intrinsically good. It is clear from this that the conception introduced in Chapter I, intrinsic goodness, is central to the rest of the book. It is here that the main theses are propounded: There is the notion of intrinsic goodness. It is indefinable. It enters into the definition of every other genuinely ethical notion—e.g., right, duty, virtue, and so on. It is a universal, not a generality. The attempt to define it is the naturalistic fallacy. Judgments which predicate it are unprovable. The principle of organic unities is an important truth about the intrinsic goodness of complex wholes. By applying the "method of isolation," one can arrive at answers to the question "What things are intrinsically good?" The study of ethics must (1) clarify the concept of intrinsic goodness, and (2) enable us to tell what things are intrinsically good.

I propose that we pass over Chapters 2, 3, 4, and 5. They are neither dull nor unimportant, but they are complicated. They contain close analysis and reasoning which do not lend themselves, with justice, to exposition by a few quotations. The following passages from Chapter 6 show Professor Moore addressing himself to the question, "What things are intrinsically good?"

In order to arrive at a correct decision on the question "What things have intrinsic value?" it is necessary to consider what things are such that if they existed by themselves, in absolute isolation, we should yet judge their existence to be good. (112)

In order to obtain a correct answer to the question, "What is good in itself?" we must consider what value things would have if they existed absolutely by themselves. (T.C., 112)

If, now, we use this method of absolute isolation, it appears that the question we have to answer is far less difficult than the controversies of ethics might have led us to expect. Indeed, once the meaning of the question is clearly understood, the answer to it, in its main outlines, appears to be so obvious that it runs the risk of seeming to be a platitude. By far the most valuable things which we can know or can imagine, are certain states of consciousness which may be roughly described as the pleasures of human intercourse and the enjoyment of beautiful objects. No one, probably, who has asked himself the question, has ever doubted that personal affection and the appreciation of what is beautiful in art or nature, are good in themselves; nor, if we consider strictly what things are worth having, purely for their own sakes, does it appear probable that any one will think that anything else has nearly so great a value as the things which are included under those two heads. Personal affections and aesthetic enjoyments include all the greatest, and by far the greatest, goods we can imagine. They are highly complex organic unities, and in discussing the consequences which follow from this fact, and the elements of which they are composed, I hope to confirm and define my position. (113)

All unmixed goods consist in the love of beautiful things or of good persons. (135) . . . I began this survey of great unmixed goods by dividing all the greatest goods we know into the two classes of (a) aesthetic enjoyment and (b) personal affection. (122)

Speaking of things which are intrinsically good, Professor Moore says:

It is only for the sake of these things—in order that as much of them as possible may at some time exist—that anyone can be justified in performing any public or private duty. They are the *raison d'etre* of virtue. They form the rational ultimate end of human action and the sole criterion of social progress. (113)

Note on Sources. The Moore material in this section is quoted or abridged from his book, *Principia Ethica.*

Reading References. As noted, *Principia Ethica*, especially Chapter I. Also a later small volume, *Ethics*, by G. E. Moore. And, over the years, essays on ethical theory now available in his volumes *Philosophical Studies, Some Main Problems of Philosophy*, and *Philosophical Papers*. In the volume, *The Philosophy of G. E. Moore*, edited by Paul Schilpp, there is a charming autobiography by Professor Moore; essays on aspects of his ethical theory by Professors Broad, Edel, Frankena, Garnett, Paton, and Stevenson; and a "Reply to the Critics" by Professor Moore. Professor Frankena's paper, "The Naturalistic Fallacy," published in *Mind* (1939), is highly recommended. Chapter 7 of A. R. White's book, *G. E. Moore: A Critical Approach*, is a usable general account of Professor Moore's ethical theory.

READING QUESTIONS

1. Illustrate Professor Moore's distinction between being intrinsically good and being a means to something intrinsically good.
2. Mention some words or phrases which he uses to express this distinction.
3. Distinguish between a "verbal" and a "real" definition. Which Professor Moore is interested in, so far as concerns the concept of goodness.
4. What is his claim about a real, in contrast to a verbal, definition of goodness?
5. How that (No. 4) claim gives rise to the notion of the naturalistic fallacy.
6. Two things you had better not do, according to Professor Moore, if you say that something (e.g., pleasure) is intrinsically good.
7. Do you see any similarity between Professor Collingwood's notion of absolute presuppositions and Professor Moore's claim about judgments of intrinsic goodness?
8. How Professor Moore would define the concept "right."
9. Wherein, in his definition of right, he both agrees with and differs from the utilitarians.
10. What do you suppose is meant by the distinction between "goodism" and "rightism"?
11. What is Professor Moore's "method of isolation"?
12. In what sense the first and last chapters of his *Principia* form a complementary pair.
13. Having studied this brief account of Professor Moore's book, which part of it would you be most inclined to select for further study? Why.
14. Which of Professor Moore's claims are you (a) most (b) least inclined to accept. Why?
15. Professor Moore's position is sometimes referred to as "Intuitionism." Why?
16. His warning about "intuitionism" and "self-evident."

17. You will hear it said, "Well, there is intuitionism, there is naturalism, and there is emotivism." Elucidate this claim. Would you add, "You pay your money and you take your choice"? Why or why not?

6. EMOTIVISM
—FROM A. J. AYER

From Moore to Ayer. You begin by being able and willing to authorize moral judgments; e.g., stealing is wrong, truth-telling is right, and so on. You then face a question: What fact, common to all your cases of wrong-doing is the reason for calling them cases of wrong-doing? Or, what fact, common to all your cases of right-doing is the reason for calling them cases of right-doing?

Much traditional ethical theory centers in those questions. If you get an answer, you are in a position to say "An act is wrong if and only if. . . ." or "right if and only if. . . ." and supply what is needed to finish the statement. The completed sentence formulates the *principle* which is operative in your moral judgments. Much traditional ethical theory centers in the attempt to formulate the principle of moral judgment.

It will be recalled that Paley, Kant, Mill, and Moore tried each to formulate the principle of morality. Paley did so with reference to the will of God; Mill, with reference to happiness; and Moore with reference to intrinsic goodness. Other end-of-the-rope alternatives would be possible. Let all of them be set down side by side. Then let the question be asked: What *logical* type do these statements belong to? This is Professor Ayer's question. In his hands this question presupposes that there are two possible answers: a statement is either empirical or tautological. He is clear that when you formulate the principle of morality, the resulting proposition is neither empirical nor tautological. His conclusion is that it is not a proposition at all, but a pseudo-proposition; that is to say, it looks like a proposition because it is formulated in words and "reads" like a sentence expressing a proposition, but it is nevertheless not a proposition because to be a proposition it would have to be either empirical or tautological, and it is neither.

If it is not a proposition, then what is it? To say that it is a pseudo-proposition is merely to say that it is not a proposition but looks as though it were. The question remains: what is it? Professor Ayer's point could be expressed by saying that it is a symbol, something used to express what is in the mind; and by distinguishing between two kinds of symbols—cognitive and emotive. A cognitive symbol is one which is used to express what you know or could know; an emotive symbol is one which is used to express what you feel or could feel. His claim would then be that when the principle of morality is expressed in words it is an emotive, not a cognitive symbol. In using it you express what you feel or could feel not what you know or could know. This is the emotive theory about ethical concepts and the judgments in which they occur.

Biographical Note. (see p. 156)

Our business is to give an account of "judgements of value" which is both satisfactory in itself and consistent with our general empiricist principles. We shall set ourselves to show that in so far as statements of value are significant, they are ordinary "scientific" statements; and that in so far as they are not scientific, they are not in the literal sense significant, but are simply expressions of emotion which can be neither true nor false. In maintaining this view, we may confine ourselves for the present to the case of ethical statements. What is said about them will be found to apply, *mutatis mutandis,* to the case of æsthetic statements also.

The ordinary system of ethics, as elaborated in the works of ethical philosophers, contains, first of all, propositions which express definitions of ethical terms, or judgments about the legitimacy or possibility of certain definitions. Secondly, there are propositions describing the phenomena of moral experience, and their causes. Thirdly, there are exhortations to moral virtue. And, lastly, there are actual ethical judgements.

Only the first of our four classes, namely that which comprises the propositions relating to the definitions of ethical terms, can be said to constitute ethical philosophy. The propositions which describe the phenomena of moral experience, and their causes, must be assigned to the science of psychology, or sociology. The exhortations to moral virtue are not propositions at all, but ejaculations or commands which are designed to provoke the reader to action of a certain sort. Accordingly, they do not belong to any branch of philosophy or science. As for ethical judgements, inasmuch as they are neither definitions nor comments upon definitions, nor quotations, we may say that they do not belong to ethical philosophy. A strictly philosophical treatise on ethics should therefore make no ethical pronouncements. But it should, by giving an analysis of ethical terms, show what is the category to which all such pronouncements belong. And this is what we are now about to do.

A question which is often discussed by ethical philosophers is whether it is possible to find definitions which would reduce all ethical terms to one or two fundamental terms. But this question, though it undeniably belongs to ethical philosophy, is not relevant to our present enquiry. We are not now concerned to discover which term, within the sphere of ethical terms, is to be taken as fundamental; whether, for example, "good" can be defined in terms of "right" or "right" in terms of "good," or both in terms of "value." What we are interested in is the possibility of reducing the whole sphere of ethical terms to non-ethical terms. We are enquiring whether statements of ethical value can be translated into statements of empirical fact.

That they can be so translated is the contention of those ethical philosophers who are commonly called subjectivists, and of those who are known as utilitarians. For the utilitarian defines the rightness of actions, and the goodness of ends, in terms of the pleasure, or happiness, or satisfaction, to which they give rise; the subjectivist in terms of the feelings of approval which a certain person, or group of people, has towards them. Each of these types of definition makes moral judgements into a sub-class of psychological or sociological judgements; and for this reason they are very attractive to us. For, if either was correct, it would follow that ethical assertions were not generically different from the factual assertions which are ordinarily contrasted with them.

Nevertheless we shall not adopt either a subjectivist or a utilitarian analysis of ethical terms. We reject the subjectivist view that to call an action right, or a thing good, is to say that it is generally approved of, because it is not self-contradictory to assert that some actions which are generally approved of are not right, or that some things which are generally approved of are not good. And we reject the alternative subjectivist view that a man who asserts that a certain action is right, or that a certain thing is good, is saying that he himself approves of it, on the ground that a man who confessed that he sometimes approved of what was bad or wrong would not be contradicting himself. And a similar argument is fatal to utilitarianism. We cannot agree that to call an action right is to say that of all the actions possible in the circumstances it would cause, or be likely to cause, the greatest happiness, or the greatest balance of pleasure over pain, or the greatest balance of satisfied over unsatisfied desire, because we find that it is not self-contradictory to say that it is sometimes wrong to perform the action which would actually or probably cause the greatest happiness, or the greatest balance of pleasure over pain, or of satisfied over unsatisfied desire. And since it is not self-contradictory to say that some pleasant things are not good, or that some bad things are desired, it cannot be the case that the sentence "x is good" is equivalent to "x is pleasant," or to "x is desired." And to every other variant of utilitarianism with which I am acquainted the same objection can be made. Therefore the validity of ethical judgements is not determined by the felicific tendencies of actions, any more than by the nature of people's feelings; but that it must be regarded as "absolute" or "intrinsic," and not empirically calculable.

We are not denying that it is possible to invent a language in which all ethical symbols are definable in non-ethical terms; what we are denying is that the suggested reduction of ethical to non-ethical statements is consistent with the conventions of our actual language. That is, we reject utilitarianism and subjectivism, not as proposals to replace our existing ethical notions by new ones, but as analyses of our existing ethical notions. Our contention is simply that, in our language, sentences which contain normative ethical symbols are not equivalent to sentences which express psychological propositions, or indeed empirical propositions of any kind.

It is only normative ethical symbols, and not descriptive ethical symbols, that are indefinable in factual terms. There is a danger of confusing these two, because they are commonly constituted by signs of the same sensible form. Thus "x is wrong" may expresses a moral judgement concerning a certain type of conduct, or it may state that a certain type of conduct is repugnant to the moral sense of a particular society. In the latter case, the symbol "wrong" is a descriptive ethical symbol, and the sentence in which it occurs expresses an ordinary sociological proposition; in the former case, the symbol "wrong" is a normative ethical symbol, and the sentence in which it occurs does not, we maintain, express an empirical proposition at all. It is only with normative ethics that we are at present concerned; so that whenever ethical symbols are used in the course of this argument without qualification, they are to be interpreted as symbols of the normative type.

In admitting that normative ethical concepts are not reducible to empirical concepts, we seem to be leaving the way clear for the view that statements of value are not controlled by observation, as ordinary empirical propositions are, but only by a mysterious "intellectual intuition." This would make statements of value unverifiable. For it is notorious that what seems intuitively certain to one person may seem doubtful, or even false, to another. So that unless it is possible to provide some criterion by which one may decide between conflicting intuitions, a mere appeal to intuition is worthless as a test of a proposition's validity. But in the case of moral judgements, no such criterion can be given. Some moralists claim to settle the matter by saying that they "know" that their own moral judgements are correct. But such an assertion is of purely psychological interest, and has not the slightest tendency to prove the validity of any moral judgement. For dissentient moralists may equally well "know" that their ethical views are correct. And, as far as subjective certainty goes, there will be nothing to choose between them. When such differences of opinion arise in connection with an ordinary empirical proposition, one may attempt to resolve them by referring to, or actually carrying out, some relevant empirical test. But with regard to ethical statements, there is, on the "intuitionist" theory, no relevant empirical test. Therefore on this theory ethical statements are held to be unverifiable. They are, of course, also held to be genuine synthetic propositions.

Considering the use which we have made of the principle that a synthetic proposition is significant only if it is empirically verifiable, it is clear that the acceptance of an "absolutist" theory of ethics would undermine the whole of our main argument. And as we have already rejected the "naturalistic" theories which are commonly supposed to provide the only alternative to "absolutism" in ethics, we seem to have reached a difficult position. We shall meet the difficulty by showing that the correct treatment of ethical statements is afforded by a third theory, which is wholly compatible with our radical empiricism.

We begin by admitting that the fundamental ethical concepts are unanalysable, inasmuch as there is no criterion by which one can test the validity of the judgements in which they occur. So far we are in agreement with the absolutists. But, unlike the absolutists, we are able to give an explanation of this fact about ethical concepts. We say that the reason why they are unanalysable is that they are mere pseudo-concepts. The presence of an ethical symbol in a proposition adds nothing to its factual content. Thus if I say to someone, "You acted wrongly in stealing that money," I am not stating anything more than if I had simply said, "You stole that money." In adding that this action is wrong I am not making any further statement about it. I am simply evincing my moral disapproval of it. It is as if I had said, "You stole that money," in a peculiar tone of horror, or written it with the addition of some special exclamation marks. The tone, or the exclamation marks, adds nothing to the literal meaning of the sentence. It merely serves to show that the expression of it is attended by certain feelings in the speaker.

If now I generalise my previous statement and say, "Stealing money is wrong," I produce a sentence which has no factual meaning—that is, expresses no proposition which can be either true or false. It is as if I had written "Stealing money!!"—where the shape and thickness of the exclamation marks show, by a suitable convention, that a special sort of moral disapproval is the feeling which is being expressed. It is clear that there is nothing said here which can be true or false. Another man may disagree with me about the wrongness of stealing, in the sense that he may not have the same feelings about stealing as I have, and he may quarrel with me on account of my moral sentiments. But he cannot, strictly speaking, contradict me. For in saying that a certain type of action is right or wrong, I am not making any factual statement, not even a statement about my own state of mind. I am merely expressing certain moral sentiments. And the man who is ostensibly contradicting me is merely expressing his moral sentiments. So that there is plainly no sense in asking which of us is in the right. For neither of us is asserting a genuine proposition.

What we have just been saying about the symbol "wrong" applies to all normative ethical symbols. Sometimes they occur in sentences which record ordinary empirical facts besides expressing ethical feeling about those facts: sometimes they occur in sentences which simply express ethical feeling about a certain type of action, or situation, without making any statement of fact. But in every case in which one would commonly be said to be making an ethical judgement, the function of the relevant ethical word is purely "emotive."

It is used to express feeling about certain objects, but not to make any assertion about them.

It is worth mentioning that ethical terms do not serve only to express feeling. They are calculated also to arouse feeling, and so to stimulate action. Indeed some of them are used in such a way as to give the sentences in which they occur the effect of commands. Thus the sentence "It is your duty to tell the truth" may be regarded both as the expression of a certain sort of ethical feeling about truthfulness and as the expression of the command "Tell the truth." The sentence "You ought to tell the truth" also involves the command "Tell the truth," but here the tone of the command is less emphatic. In the sentence "It is good to tell the truth" the command has become little more than a suggestion. And thus the "meaning" of the word "good," in its ethical usage, is differentiated from that of the word "duty" or the word "ought." In fact we may define the meaning of the various ethical words in terms both of the different feelings they are ordinarily taken to express, and also the different responses which they are calculated to provoke.

We can now see why it is impossible to find a criterion for determining the validity of ethical judgements. It is not because they have an "absolute" validity which is mysteriously independent of ordinary sense-experience, but because they have no objective validity whatsoever. If a sentence makes no statement at all, there is obviously no sense in asking whether what it says is true or false. And we have seen that sentences which simply express moral judgements do not say anything. They are pure expressions of feeling and as such do not come under the category of truth and falsehood. They are unverifiable for the same reason as a cry of pain or a word of command is unverifiable—because they do not express genuine propositions.

Thus, although our theory of ethics might fairly be said to be radically subjectivist, it differs in a very important respect from the orthodox subjectivist theory. For the orthodox subjectivist does not deny, as we do, that the sentences of a moralizer express genuine propositions. All he denies is that they express propositions of a unique non-empirical character. His own view is that they express propositions about the speaker's feelings. If this were so, ethical judgements clearly would be capable of being true or false. They would be true if the speaker had the relevant feelings, and false if he had not. And this is a matter which is, in principle, empirically verifiable. Furthermore they could be significantly contradicted. For if I say, "Tolerance is a virtue," and someone answers, "You don't approve of it," he would, on the ordinary subjectivist theory, be contradicting me. On our theory, he would not be contradicting me, because, in saying that tolerance was a virtue, I should not be making any statement about my own feelings or about anything else. I should simply be evincing my feelings, which is not at all the same thing as saying that I have them.

The distinction between the expression of feeling and the assertion of feeling is complicated by the fact that the assertion that one has a certain feeling often accompanies the expression of that feeling, and is then, indeed, a factor in the expression of that feeling. Thus I may simultaneously express boredom and say that I am bored, and in that case my utterance of the words, "I am bored," is one of the circumstances which make it true to say that I am express-ing or evincing boredom. But I can express boredom without actually saying that I am bored. I can express it by my tone and gestures, while making a state-ment about something wholly unconnected with it, or by an ejaculation, or without uttering any words at all. So that even if the assertion that one has a certain feeling always involves the expression of that feeling, the expression of a feeling assuredly does not always involve the assertion that one has it. And this is the important point to grasp in considering the distinction between our theory and the ordinary subjectivist theory. For whereas the subjectivist holds that ethical statements actually assert the existence of certain feelings, we hold that ethical statements are expressions and excitants of feeling which do not necessarily involve any assertions.

We have already remarked that the main objection to the ordinary sub-jectivist theory is that the validity of ethical judgements is not determined by the nature of their author's feelings. And this is an objection which our theory escapes. For it does not imply that the existence of any feelings is a necessary and sufficient condition of the validity of an ethical judgement. It implies, on the contrary, that ethical judgements have no validity.

There is, however, a celebrated argument against subjectivist theories which our theory does not escape. It has been pointed out by Moore that if ethical statements were simply statements about the speaker's feelings, it would be impossible to argue about questions of value. To take a typical example: if a man said that thrift was a virtue, and another replied that it was a vice, they would not, on this theory, be disputing with one another. One would be say-ing that he approved of thrift, and the other that *he* didn't; and there is no reason why both these statements should not be true. Now Moore held it to be obvious that we do dispute about questions of value, and accordingly con-cluded that the particular form of subjectivism which he was discussing was false.

It is plain that the conclusion that it is impossible to dispute about ques-tions of value follows from our theory also. For as we hold that such sentences as "Thrift is a virtue" and "Thrift is a vice" do not express propositions at all, we clearly cannot hold that they express incompatible propositions. We must therefore admit that if Moore's argument refutes the ordinary subjectivist theory, it also refutes ours. But, in fact, we deny that it does refute even the ordinary subjectivist theory. For we hold that one really never does dispute about questions of value.

This may seem, at first sight, to be a very paradoxical assertion. For we certainly do engage in disputes which are ordinarily regarded as disputes about questions of value. But, in all such cases, we find, if we consider the matter closely, that the dispute is not really about a question of value, but about a question of fact. When someone disagrees with us about the moral value of a certain action or type of action, we do admittedly resort to argument in order to win him over to our way of thinking. But we do not attempt to show by our arguments that he has the "wrong" ethical feeling towards a situation whose nature he has correctly apprehended. What we attempt to show is that he is mistaken about the facts of the case. We argue that he has misconceived the agent's motive: or that he has misjudged the effects of the action, or its probable effects in view of the agent's knowledge; or that he has failed to take into account the special circumstances in which the agent was placed. Or else we employ more general arguments about the effects which actions of a certain type tend to produce, or the qualities which are usually manifested in their performance. We do this in the hope that we have only to get our opponent to agree with us about the nature of the empirical facts for him to adopt the same moral attitude towards them as we do. And as the people with whom we argue have generally received the same moral education as ourselves, and live in the same social order, our expectation is usually justified. But if our opponent happens to have undergone a different process of moral "conditioning" from ourselves, so that, even when he acknowledges all the facts, he still disagrees with us about the moral value of the actions under discussion, then we abandon the attempt to convince him by argument. We say that it is impossible to argue with him because he has a distorted or undeveloped moral sense; which signifies merely that he employs a different set of values from our own. We feel that our own system of values is superior, and therefore speak in such derogatory terms of his. But we cannot bring forward any arguments to show that our system is superior. For our judgement that it is so is itself a judgment of value, and accordingly outside the scope of argument. It is because argument fails us when we come to deal with pure questions of value, as distinct from questions of fact, that we finally resort to mere abuse.

In short, we find that argument is possible on moral questions only if some system of values is presupposed. If our opponent concurs with us in expressing moral disapproval of all actions of a given type t, then we may get him to condemn a particular action A, by bringing forward arguments to show that A is of type t. For the question whether A does or does not belong to that type is a plain question of fact. Given that a man has certain moral principles, we argue that he must, in order to be consistent, react morally to certain things in a certain way. What we do not and cannot argue about is the validity of these moral principles. We merely praise or condemn them in the light of our own feelings.

If anyone doubts the accuracy of this account of moral disputes, let him try to construct even an imaginary argument on a question of value which does not reduce itself to an argument about a question of logic or about an empirical matter of fact. I am confident that he will not succeed in producing a single example. And if that is the case, he must allow that its involving the impossibility of purely ethical arguments is not, as Moore thought, a ground of objection to our theory, but rather a point in favour of it.

Having upheld our theory against the only criticism which appeared to threaten it, we may now use it to define the nature of all ethical enquiries. We find that ethical philosophy consists simply in saying that ethical concepts are pseudo-concepts and therefore unanalysable. The further task of describing the different feelings that the different ethical terms are used to express, and the different reactions that they customarily provoke, is a task for the psychologist. There cannot be such a thing as ethical science, if by ethical science one means the elaboration of a "true" system of morals. For we have seen that, as ethical judgements are mere expressions of feeling, there can be no way of determining the validity of any ethical system, and, indeed, no sense in asking whether any such system is true. All that one may legitimately enquire in this connection is, What are the moral habits of a given person or group of people, and what causes them to have precisely those habits and feelings? And this enquiry falls wholly within the scope of the existing social sciences.

It appears, then, that ethics, as a branch of knowledge, is nothing more than a department of psychology and sociology. And in case anyone thinks that we are overlooking the existence of casuistry, we may remark that casuistry is not a science, but is a purely analytical investigation of the structure of a given moral system. In other words it is an exercise in formal logic.

When one comes to pursue the psychological enquiries which constitute ethical science, one is immediately enabled to account for the Kantian and hedonistic theories of morals. For one finds that one of the chief causes of moral behaviour is fear, both conscious and unconscious, of a god's displeasure, and fear of the enmity of society. And this, indeed, is the reason why moral precepts present themselves to some people as "categorical" commands. And one finds, also, that the moral code of a society is partly determined by the beliefs of that society concerning the conditions of its own happiness—or, in other words, that a society tends to encourage or discourage a given type of conduct by the use of moral sanctions according as it appears to promote or detract from the contentment of the society as a whole. And this is the reason why altruism is recommended in most moral codes and egotism condemned. It is from the observation of this connection between morality and happiness that hedonistic or eudæmonistic theories of morals ultimately spring, just as the moral theory of Kant is based on the fact, previously explained, that moral precepts have for some people the force of inexorable commands. As each of these theories ignores the fact which lies at the root of the other, both may be criticized as being one-sided; but this is not the main objection to either of them. Their essential defect is that they treat propositions which refer to the causes and attributes of our ethical feelings as if they were definitions of ethical concepts. And thus they fail to recognize that ethical concepts are pseudo-concepts and consequently indefinable.

As we have already said, our conclusions about the nature of ethics apply to æsthetics also. Æsthetic terms are used in exactly the same way as ethical terms. Such æsthetic words as "beautiful" and "hideous" are employed, as ethical words are employed, not to make statements of fact, but simply to express certain feelings and evoke a certain response. It follows, as in ethics, that there is no sense in attributing objective validity to æsthetic judgements, and no possibility of arguing about questions of value in æsthetics, but only about questions of fact. A scientific treatment of æsthetics would show us what in general were the causes of æsthetic feeling, why various societies produced and admired the works of art they did, why taste varies as it does within a given society, and so forth. And these are ordinary psychological or sociological questions. They have, of course, little or nothing to do with æsthetic criticism as we understand it. But that is because the purpose of æsthetic criticism is not so much to give knowledge as to communicate emotion. The critic, by calling attention to certain features of the work under review, and expressing his own feelings about them, endeavours to make us share his attitude towards the work as a whole. The only relevant propositions that he formulates are propositions describing the nature of the work. And these are plain records of fact. We conclude, therefore, that there is nothing in æsthetics, any more than there is in ethics, to justify the view that it embodies a unique type of knowledge.

It should now be clear that the only information which we can legitimately derive from the study of our æsthetic and moral experiences is information about our own mental and physical make-up. We take note of these experiences as providing data for our psychological and sociological generalisations. And this is the only way in which they serve to increase our knowledge. It follows that any attempt to make our use of ethical and æsthetic concepts the basis of a metaphysical theory concerning the existence of a world of values, as distinct from the world of facts, involves a false analysis of these concepts. Our own analysis has shown that the phenomena of moral experience cannot fairly be used to support any rationalist or metaphysical doctrine whatsoever. In particular, they cannot, as Kant hoped, be used to establish the existence of a transcendent god.

This mention of God brings us to the question of the possibility of religious knowledge. We shall see that this possibility has already been ruled out by our treatment of metaphysics. But, as this is a point of considerable interest, we may be permitted to discuss it at some length.

Note on Sources. The passages just quoted are from Chapter 6, "Critique of Ethics and Theology," in the book, *Language, Truth, and Logic.*

Reading References. A second formulation of Emotivism will be found in Professor Charles Stevenson's book, *Ethics and Language.* A good criticism of Emotivism will be found in Professor Brand Blanshard's *Reason and Goodness*, especially Chapter 8. Exposition and criticism of Emotivism will be found in the author's book, *An Elementary Ethics*.

READING QUESTIONS

1. How you would formulate the Emotivist theory.
2. Contrast Emotivism with (a) Utilitarianism (b) Subjectivism.
3. At what point the Emotive theory presupposes the Verifiability theory of meaning.
4. Use the distinction between cognitive and emotive symbols to state the Emotivist position.
5. Contrast Emotivism in ethics with Emotivism in aesthetics.
6. Suggest one criticism of Emotivism in terms of the grounds on which it rests; and one in terms of the consequences which follow from it.
7. Wherein you find Emotivism (a) most (b) least convincing.

A Political Problem

THE PROBLEM STATED

The fact that men have religions, and that most religions include beliefs about God, provided us with the subject matter of our first topic. The fact that men distinguish between appearance and reality, and entertain beliefs about the nature of reality, provided us with the subject matter of our second topic. The fact that men distinguish between knowledge and speculation, and formulate theories to clarify and sharpen this distinction, provided us with the subject matter of our third topic. The fact that men distinguish between right and wrong, and formulate theories to clarify and sharpen this distinction, provided us with the subject matter of our fourth topic. The fact that men live in political organizations, and that political organization involves rights and duties of an imperative nature, provides us with the subject matter of our present topic.

Our subject is the state. Our problem is the justification of its claim to possess sovereign power over the wills of its subjects. Before elaborating upon this problem, we must note three terms, namely, *society*, *state*, and *government*. The term *society* is not easily defined with precision. We could perhaps say, "Any group of people held together by actual or potential common interests." There seems to be intended some such meaning when we say, "Society insists that criminals be punished," or "The interests of society require a certain amount of fair dealing in business." The term *society* should not be confused with the term *state*. By the term *state* is meant a "society organized to make law possible." The state, again, is not the government. Statehood is a kind of organization which a society can exhibit. Government is an organization, within a state, whose function is to make and administer the laws.

344

A government may be elective or hereditary; again, it may be by one man or many men. These distinctions do not apply to the state.

The government of a state differs from the government of a church or university or industrial corporation in the amount of power which it sometimes possesses and always claims over the wills of individuals who compose the state of which it is the government. Thus, the government of a church may claim and sometimes possess the power to stipulate the conditions under which an individual may belong to the church. But it does not usually claim the power to prevent an individual from leaving the church, if he chooses to do so, nor the power to inflict physical punishment upon its members, to dispossess them of their property, to imprison them, to conscript them, or to execute them.

The unique characteristic of the government of a state is that under some circumstances it does claim power to deal in these and other ways with individuals without their consent, even against their wills. This is the claim to possess and exercise sovereignty. There are several interesting things about such a claim. It may be made, but it may be disputed. It may be challenged from within, in which case there is revolt. It may be challenged from without, in which case there is conquest. Or it may be merely evaded, in which case there is crime. The criminal, the invader, the rebel are each differently related to the central claim which defines the government of a state.

We have distinguished between making and making good the claim to possess sovereign power. We need, also, to distinguish between both of these and justifying the claim. It is one thing to make a claim. It is another to enforce it. It is still another to justify it. The problem of the present topic arises out of this distinction between *de facto* and *de jure* claim to possess absolute sovereignty. Upon what is this claim based? If the question of justification be raised, to what shall appeal be made? The authors included in this topic have written with this or a closely related problem in mind. The issue is clearer in some than it is in others, but if, at any time, you have a sense of having lost this point of connection, you can always restate the matter in very simple terms: The government of a state claims absolute sovereignty over its subjects. Upon what grounds can this claim be justified? Then ask yourself what light the author in point is shedding or attempting to shed on this problem.

The first author, James I of Great Britain, sets himself to state "the true grounds of the mutual duty and allegiance betwixt an absolute monarch and his people." This is our question, somewhat differently worded. The second author, Thomas Hobbes, says that he "will consider what are the rights and just power of a sovereign, and what it is that preserveth and dissolveth it." This, too, is our question, somewhat differently worded. The third author, Jean Jacques Rousseau, begins, "Man is born free, and is everywhere in chains. . . . How does this change come about? I do not know. What can make it legitimate? That question I think I can answer." This is again our problem, somewhat differently worded. The fourth author, Edmund Burke, after denying the notion of popular sovereignty, advances the claim that the foundation of the state, meaning its principle of justification, is to be sought among the needs of human nature, and specifically in the need to be coerced and restrained in things that are our duties when we might choose to violate these in the name of supposed rights. This again is our problem. The fifth author, Karl Marx, argues that a state is a society organized to make it possible for one economic class to exploit another economic class; and that government is the agent of the exploiting class. The two economic classes, which he had in mind, he refers to as the "bourgeoisie" and the "proletariat." His small tract, *Manifesto of the Communist Party*, was written to explain to the members of a left-wing group that they should organize and educate the proletariat and help them overthrow the "bourgeois state," and replace it by a "workers' state." The sixth author, Harold Laski, gives a lucid exposition of the basic thesis that a state is a community organized to make government possible, that government exercises a monopoly of coercive violence, and that it does this in enforcing law in the name of the state.

1. THE DIVINE RIGHT OF KINGS —FROM JAMES I

There is little to say by way of introduction to the argument which follows. Many persons have doubtless heard of the doctrine of the divine right of kings; few have had an opportunity to examine a somewhat detailed statement of it. For that reason, it is included here. The author, as will be seen from the biographical note which follows, was king of Scotland at the time this argument was written. Five years later, he became king of Scotland and England, that is, Great Britain. He is aware of the threefold distinction between claiming sovereignty, making good the claim to sovereignty, and justifying the claim to sovereignty. He would justify the claim to sovereignty by an appeal to the will of God, as revealed in the Scriptures and manifested in the order of nature.

Biographical Note. James Stuart, subsequently James VI of Scotland

and James I of Britain, was born in Edinburgh in 1566 and died in England in 1625 at the age of fifty-nine. He was the son of Mary, Queen of Scots. His life may be divided into three periods. (1) Until 1583 he was growing up, getting an education in the classics, the Bible, and Protestant theology, and discovering the vast difference between claiming and exercising supreme power. The question of justifying did not come until later. His mother was forced to abdicate in 1567. Scotland carried on under a regency until 1583, at which time James took matters into his own hands. (2) From 1583 to 1603 his energies were absorbed by a prolonged struggle with the still feudal nobility of Scotland. By the end of twenty years, he had reduced the anarchical baronage of sixteenth-century Scotland to obedience, and had replaced the divided sovereignty which was the essence of feudalism by a strong centralized authority. In fact, he did for Scotland what the Tudors had done for England, what Louis XI had done for France, what Ferdinand and Isabella had done for Spain. During this period, in 1598, he wrote *The True Law of Free Monarchies*, which contains his argument for the divine right of kings. A year later, 1599, he published a treatise, *Demonologie*, denouncing witchcraft and exhorting the civil power to the strongest measures of suppression. (3) In 1603, Queen Elizabeth died closing the Tudor line in England. James VI of Scotland was invited to become James I of Britain, uniting Scotland and England under one throne. His career in England was less successful than it had been in Scotland. By disposition and conviction he was unfitted to succeed to the throne of the Henrys and Elizabeth. The Tudors had been strong monarchs, but they had not written books or made speeches in which they drew on the Bible to justify their absoluteness. They had claimed supremacy and, for the most part, made good their claim; they had not cast about for any subtle or elaborate justification.

The Argument of the Citations. James's argument may be divided into four parts. There is, first, a preamble in which he explains why and how he proposes to expound the doctrine of the divine right of kings. There is, second, a consideration of the duties of a king to his subject. These are explained, and the explanations documented by arguments drawn from the Scriptures and from the order of nature. There is, third, a consideration of the duties of a subject to his king. These are explained, and the explanations documented by arguments drawn from the Scriptures and the order of nature. This third portion of the total argument, "the duty that the lieges owe to their king, and the ground thereof" is the main thing. James's efforts to prove his case reach here a maximum.

The whole doctrine of the divine right of kings is at stake. There is, finally, a consideration of objections to the doctrine. These objections are stated and refuted by arguments drawn from the Scriptures or the order of nature. In disclosing what James considers a relevant objection and a relevant reply, these passages reveal the level at which the entire argument moves. He begins:

My dear countrymen: Accept, I pray you, as thankfully this pamphlet that I offer unto you, as lovingly it is written for your weal. It may be ye miss many things that ye look for in it. But, for excuse thereof, consider rightly that I only lay down herein the true grounds, to teach you the right way, without wasting time upon refuting the adversaries.

My intention is to instruct, not to irritate. The profit I would wish you to make of it, is, to frame all your actions according to these grounds, as may confirm you in the course of honest and obedient subjects to your king in all times coming, as also, when ye shall fall in with any that shall praise or excuse the by-past rebellions that brake forth either in this country, or in any other, ye shall herewith be armed against their siren songs. Whereby ye shall soundly keep the course of righteous judgment, discerning wisely of every action only according to the quality thereof, and not according to your prejudged conceits of the committers. So shall ye, by reaping profit to yourselves, turn my pain into pleasure.

As there is nothing so necessary to be known by the people of any land, next to their knowledge of God, as the right knowledge of their allegiance, according to the form of government established among them, especially in a monarchy, so hath the ignorance and seduced opinion of the multitude (blinded by them who think themselves able to teach and instruct) procured the wreck and overthrow of sundry flourishing commonwealths, and heaped heavy calamities, threatening utter destruction, upon others.

And among others, no commonwealth that ever hath been since the beginning hath had greater need of the true knowledge of this ground, than this our so long disordered and distracted commonwealth. The misknowledge hereof is the only spring from whence hath flowed so many endless calamities, miseries, and confusions; as is better felt by many than the cause thereof well known and deeply considered.

The natural zeal, therefore, that I bear to this my native country, with the great pity I have to see the so-long disturbance thereof, hath compelled me to break silence, to discharge my conscience to you, my dear countrymen, so that, knowing the ground from whence these your many endless troubles have proceeded, ye may, by knowledge and eschewing of the cause, escape and divert the lamentable effects that ever necessarily follow thereupon.

I have chosen, then, only to set down in this short treatise, the true grounds of the mutual duty and allegiance betwixt a free and absolute monarch and his people.

First, I will set down the true grounds, whereupon I am to build, out of the Scriptures, since monarchy is the true pattern of divinity; next, from the law of nature, by divers similitudes drawn out of the same; and will end by answering the most weighty and apparent incommodities that can be objected.

From a statement of his aims and method, he turns to the first part of the argument. What have the Scriptures to say concerning the king's duties to his subjects? He begins:

The king's duty to his subjects is so clearly set down in many places of the Scriptures, and so openly confessed by all good princes, that it needeth not that I be long therein.

Kings are called Gods by the prophetical King David, in the sixth verse of the eighty-second Psalm, because they sit upon God His throne in the earth, and have the count of their administration to give unto Him. Their office is "to minister justice and judgment to the people," as the same David saith; "to advance the good and punish the evil," as he likewise saith; "to establish good laws to his people, and procure obedience to the same," as divers good kings of Judah did; "to procure the peace of the people," as the same David saith; "to decide all controversies that arise among them," as Solomon did; "to be the minister of God for the weal of them that do well, and to take vengeance upon them that do evil," as Saint Paul saith; "to go out and in before his people, as a good pastor," as is said in first Samuel; "that through the prince's prosperity, the people's peace may be procured," as Jeremiah saith.

And therefore, in the coronation of every Christian monarch, they give their oath: first, to maintain the religion presently professed within their country, according to their laws whereby it is established, and to punish all those who should seek to alter or disturb the profession thereof; next, to maintain all the lowable and good laws made by their predecessors, to see them put into execution and the breakers and violators thereof punished according to the tenor of the same; and lastly, to maintain the whole country, and every state therein, in all their ancient privileges and liberties, as well against all foreign enemies as among themselves.

In short, they take each his oath to procure the weal and flourishing of the people, not only by maintaining and executing the old lowable laws of the country, by establishing new laws (as necessity and evil manners will require), but by all other means possible to foresee and prevent all dangers that are likely to fall upon them; and to maintain concord, wealth, and civility among them as a loving father and careful watchman, caring for them more than for himself, knowing himself to be ordained for them, and not they for him, accountable therefore to that great God who placed him as His lieutenant over them, upon the peril of his soul to procure the weal of both souls and bodies as far as in him lieth.

¶ From the Scriptures he turns to the order of nature. What does the order of nature show regarding a king's duties to his subjects? He continues:

By the law of nature the king becomes a natural father to all his lieges. As the father is bound to care for the nourishing, education, and virtuous government of his children, even so is the king bound to care for all his subjects. As all the toil and pain that the father can take for his children will be thought light and well bestowed by him, so the effect thereof redounds to their profit and weal; so ought the king to do toward his people. As the kindly father ought to foresee all the inconveniences and dangers that may arise toward his children, and with the hazard of his own person to press to prevent the same; so ought the king toward his people. As the father's wrath and correction upon any of his children that offendeth ought, by a fatherly chastisement to be seasoned with pity, as long as there is any hope of amendment in them; so ought the king towards any of his lieges that offend in that measure.

In short, as a father's chief joy ought to be in procuring his children's welfare, rejoicing at their weal, sorrowing and pitying at their woe, hazarding for their safety, traveling for their rest, waking for their sleep, thinking (in a word) that his earthly felicity and life standeth and lieth more in them than in himself; so ought a good prince to think of his people.

Having dealt with the question of the king's duties to his subject, he turns to the much more controversial question of the subject's duties to the king. What do the Scriptures say regarding "the other branch of this tie"? He begins:

The other branch of this mutual and reciprocal tie is the duty and allegiance that the lieges owe to their king. The ground hereof I take out of the words of Samuel, dited by God's spirit, when God had commanded him to hear the people's voice in choosing and anointing them a king. Because that place of Scripture is so pertinent for our purpose, I insert herein the very words of the text.

That these words and discourses of Samuel were dited by God's spirit, it needs no further probation than that it is in the Scripture; since the whole Scripture is dited by that inspiration, as Paul saith; which ground no good Christian will or dare deny.

And it came to pass, when Samuel was old, that he made his sons judges over Israel. And his sons walked not in his ways, but turned aside after lucre, and took bribes, and perverted judgment. Then all the elders of Israel gathered themselves together, and came to Samuel unto Ramah, and said unto him: "Behold, thou art old, and thy sons walk not in thy ways: now make us a king to judge us like all the nations." But the thing displeased Samuel, when they said: "Give us a king to judge us." And Samuel prayed unto the Lord. And the Lord said unto Samuel: "Hearken unto the voice of the people in all that they say unto thee: for they have not rejected thee, but they have rejected Me, that I should not reign over them. According to all the works which they have done since the day that I brought them up out of Egypt even unto this day, wherewith they have forsaken Me, and served other gods, so do they also unto thee. Now therefore hearken unto their voice: howbeit yet protest solemnly unto them, and shew them the manner of the king that shall reign over them."

And Samuel told all the words of the Lord unto the people that asked of him a king. And he said: "This will be the manner of the king that shall reign over you: he will take your sons, and appoint them for himself, for his chariots, and to be his horsemen; and some shall run before his chariots. And he will appoint him captains over thousands, and captains over fifties; and will set them to ear his ground, and to reap his harvest, and to make his instruments of war, and instruments of his chariots. And he will take your daughters to be confectionaries, and to be cooks, and to be bakers. And he will take your fields, and your vineyards, and your oliveyards, even the best of them, and give them to his servants. And he will take the tenth of your seed, and of your vineyards, and give to his officers, to his servants. And he will take your menservants, and your maidservants, and your goodliest young men, and your asses, and put them to his work. He will take the tenth of your sheep: and ye shall be his servants. And ye shall cry out in that day because of your king which ye shall have chosen you; and the Lord will not hear you in that day." Nevertheless the people refused to obey the voice of Samuel; and they said: "Nay; but we will have a king over us; that we also may be like all the nations; and that our king may judge us, and go out before us, and fight our battles." And Samuel heard all the words of the people, and he rehearsed them in the ears of the Lord. And the Lord said to Samuel: "Hearken unto their voice, and make them a king."

If ye will consider the very words of the text, as they are set down, it shall plainly declare the obedience that the people owe to their king in all respects.

First, God commanded Samuel to grant the people a king. Then, He commanded Samuel to forewarn them of what some kings will do unto them, that they may not thereafter say, "We would never have had a king of God, had He let us know how we would have been used by him."

Next, Samuel declares unto them what points of justice and equity their king will break in his behavior unto them; and putteth them out of hope that they shall have leave to shake off that yoke which God, through their importunity, hath laid upon them.

Now, the erection of this kingdom and monarchy among the Jews, and the law thereof, may and ought to be a pattern to all Christian and well-founded monarchies, as being founded by God Himself. What liberty, then, can broiling spirits and rebellious minds justly claim against any Christian monarchy? They can claim no greater liberty, on their part, than the people of God might have done. They can point to no greater tyranny than was here forwarned to the people of God; and yet all rebellion was countermanded unto them.

That this proposition, grounded upon the Scripture, may the more clearly appear to be true, we never read that ever the prophets persuaded the people to rebel against the king, howsoever wicked he was.

There never was a more monstrous persecutor and tyrant nor Ahab was. Yet all the rebellion that Elias ever raised against him was to flee to the wilderness, where, for fault of sustentation, he was fed with the corbies.

I think no man will doubt but Samuel, David, Elias, had as great power to persuade the people, had they liked to employ their credit to uproars and rebellions against wicked kings, as had any of our seditious preachers in these days of whatsoever religion, either in this country or in France. (Only love of verity, I protest, has moved me this far to be somewhat satiric.)

I could cite further. Jeremiah threatened the people of God with utter destruction for rebellion against Nebuchadnezzar, the king of Babel, although he was an idolatrous persecutor, a foreign king, a tyrant and usurper of their liberties. Yet, in respect they had once received and acknowledged him for their king, Jeremiah not only commanded them to obey him but even to pray for his prosperity, adjoining the reason to it: because in his prosperity stood their peace.

To end the grounds of my proposition as taken out of the Scripture, let a notable example from the New Testament be considered. That king, whom Paul bids the Romans obey and serve for conscience' sake, was Nero—that bloody tyrant, that infamy to his age, that monster to the world, being also an idolatrous persecutor. If then, idolatry and defection from God, tyranny and the persecution of the Saints, hindered not the spirit of God to command his people under highest pain to give all due and hearty obedience for conscience sake, giving to Caesar what was Caesar's and to God what was God's, what shameless presumption, I say, is it in any Christian people nowadays to claim that unlawful liberty which God refused to his own peculiar and chosen people?

In short, to take up in two or three sentences, grounded upon all these arguments out of the law of God, the duty and allegiance of the people to their lawful king, I say: Their obedience ought to be to him, as to God's lieutenant on earth answerable to God alone, obeying his commands in all things as the commands of God's minister; acknowledging him as a judge set by God over them and having power to judge them; fearing him and loving him; praying for him as their protector, for his continuance if he be good, for his amendment if he be wicked; following his lawful commands and fleeing his fury in his unlawful commands; offering no resistance, but by sobs and tears to God.

Thus the Scriptures. They are clearly on the king's side. What about the order of nature? Does it, too, support the king's claim to absolute sovereignty? He continues:

The agreement of the law of nature with the laws and constitutions of God will by two similitudes easily appear.

The king toward his people is rightly compared (1) to a father of children, and (2) to a head of a body composed of divers members.

As fathers, the good princes and magistrates of the people of God acknowledged themselves to their subjects. And for all other well-ruled commonwealths the style of *pater patriae* was ever used of kings.

Now, for the father's part, consider, I pray you, what duty his children owe to him, and whether, upon any pretext whatsoever, it will not be thought monstrous and unnatural in his sons to rise up against him, to control him, to slay him when they think good, or to cut him off and adopt to themselves any other they please in his room.

Can any pretense of wickedness or rigor on his part be a just excuse for his children to put a hand to him? Even suppose the father hated and wronged the children never so much, will any man, endowed with the least spark of reason, think it lawful for them to meet him with the line? Yea, suppose the father were furiously following his sons with a drawn sword, is it lawful for them to turn and strike back, or to make any resistance but by flight?

I think surely, if there were no more but the example of brute beasts, it may serve well enough to qualify and prove this my argument. For instance, we read often of the pity that storks have to their old and decayed parents. And generally, we know, there are many sorts of beasts and fowls that with violence and many bloody strokes will beat and banish their young ones from them as soon as they perceive them able to fend for themselves; but we never read or hear of any resistance on the part of the young except among the vipers. This proves such persons as unnaturally follow this example to be endowed with a viperous nature.

As for the similitude of the head and the body, the proper office of a king toward his subjects agrees very well with the office of the head toward the body. For, from the head, being the seat of judgment, proceedeth the care and foresight of guiding, and preventing all evil that may come to the body or any part thereof. The head careth for the body; so doeth the king for his people. Discourse and directions flow from the head, execution according thereunto belongs to the rest of the members every one according to his office; so it is bewixt a wise prince and his people. Judgment, coming from the head, may employ the members every one in their own office as long as they are able for it; in case any one of them be affected with any infirmity, it must care and provide for their remedy, so it be curable, and if otherwise, cut them off for fear of infecting the rest. Even so it is betwixt the prince and his people. There is always hope of curing any diseased member by the direction of the head, as long as it is whole; but, by the contrary, if the head be troubled, all the members are partakers of that pain. So it is betwixt the prince and his people.

Now, it may very well fall out that the head will be forced to cut off some rotten members to keep the rest of the body in its integrity: but what state the body can be in, if the head, for any infirmity that can befall it, be cut off, I leave to the reader's judgment.

To conclude these similitudes: If the children may upon any pretext lawfully rise up against their father, cut him off and choose any other they please in his room; if the body may for any infirmity that can be in the head, strike it off—then I cannot deny that the people may rebel, control, displace, or cut off their king.

The case is complete. Both God and nature are on the side of the king who claims absolute sovereignty. "In case any doubts might arise," however, he proposes four possible objections to his argument:

In case any doubts might arise in any part of this treatise, I will conclude with the solution of the principal and most weighty objections.

First, it is cast up by divers who employ their pens upon apologies for rebellions and treasons: every man is born to carry such a natural zeal and duty to his commonwealth that, seeing it so rent and deadly wounded, as whiles it will be by wicked kings, good citizens will be forced, out of said zeal and duty, to put their hand to work for freeing their commonwealth from such a pest.

Whereunto I give two answers: (1) It is a sure axiom in theology that evil should not be done in order that good may come of it. The wickedness, therefore, of the king can never make them that are ordained to be judged by him, to become his judges. If it be not lawful to a private man to revenge his private injury upon a private adversary, how much less is it lawful to the people, or any part of them, to take upon them the use of the sword against the public magistrate?

(2) In place of relieving the commonwealth out of distress, they shall keep double distress and trouble upon it; and so their rebellion shall procure the contrary effects that they pretend for it. For a king cannot be imagined to be so unruly and tyrannous but the commonwealth will be kept in better order by him than it can by his way-taking. For all sudden mutations are perilous in commonwealths, hope being thereby given to all bare men to set

themselves up and fly with other men's feathers, the reins being loosed to all the insolencies that disordered people can commit by hope of impunity because of the looseness of all things.

Second, it is objected: A curse hangeth over the commonwealth where a wicked king reigneth, and, say they, there cannot be a more acceptable deed in the sight of God than to free the country of such a curse.

Whereunto for answer: I grant indeed that a wicked king is sent by God for a curse to his people, and a plague for their sins. But, that it is lawful to them to shake off that curse by their own hand, which God hath laid upon them, that I deny, and may so do justly. Will any deny that the king of Babylon was a curse to the people of God, as was plainly forespoken and threatened unto them in the prophecy of their captivity? What else was Nero to the Christian church in his time? And yet, Jeremiah and Paul commanded the people not only to obey them, but heartily to pray for their welfare. It is certain then, that patience, earnest prayers to God, and amendment of their lives, are the only lawful means to move God to relieve them of that heavy curse.

The third objection: They say that the fortunate success which God hath so often given to enterprises of rebellion proveth plainly that God favored the justness of these quarrels.

To which I answer: It is true indeed that all the success of battles lieth only in God's hands. But, to conclude on that principle that He always gives victory to the just quarrel would prove that the Philistines, and divers other enemies of the people of God, had, in respect to the many victories they obtained over the people of God, justice on their side. It hath been so in many other instances. Therefore, I say, it is oft times a very deceivable argument to judge of the cause by the event.

The last objection is grounded upon the mutual pact and adstipulation betwixt the king and his people at the time of his coronation. For there, they say, was a mutual pact whereupon it followeth that if the contract be broken upon the king's side, the people are no longer bound to keep their part of it, but are thereby freed of their oath.

My answer: I confess that a king at his coronation oath promiseth to discharge honorably and truly the office given him by God over his people. But, presuming that thereafter he breaks his promise unto them never so inexcusably, the question is: Who should be judge? A contract cannot be broken by one party and so free the other party except first a lawful trial and cognition be had by the ordinary judge of the breakers thereof. Otherwise every man may be both party and judge in his own cause: which is absurd once to be thought.

Now (I say) in this contract betwixt the king and his people, God is the only judge, because to Him only the king must make count of his administration. For in His presence, as only judge of oaths, and therefore of coronation oaths, all oaths ought to be made. Since, then, God is the only judge betwixt the two contracting parties, the trial and revenge must only appertain to Him. It follows therefore that God must first give sentence upon the king before the people can think themselves freed of their oath.

The argument stated, the objections met, he concludes:

And as ye see it manifest: the king is overlord of the whole land. . . . In the parliament (which is nothing else but the head court of the king and his vassals) the laws are but craved by his subjects. For, although the king make daily statutes and ordinances, enjoining such pains thereto as he thinks fit, yet it lies in the power of no parliament to make any kind of law or statute without his scepter be to it giving it the force of law. He is master over every person that inhabiteth the land, having power over the life and death of every one of them. For, although a just king will not take the life of any of his subjects without a clear law, yet the laws whereby he taketh them are made by him; so the power flows always from him. . . . Likewise, although a good king will frame his actions to be according to the law, yet he is not bound thereto but of his good will and for good example-giving to his subjects.

Note on Sources. The James I material in this section is quoted, abridged, or paraphrased from his tract, *The True Law of Free Monarchies.* That document will be found in *The Political Works of James I,* edited by C. H. McIlwain.

Reading References. Other items by James I will be found in *The Political Works of James I,* edited by C. H. McIlwain. To this volume Professor McIlwain has contributed a long and enlightening introduction. A history of Great Britain, especially if it included a chapter on the history of Scotland during the period of James VI, would provide good background reading. A book published in recent years is H. G. Stafford's *James VI of Scotland and the Throne of England.*

READING QUESTIONS

1. Why King James proposes to set forth the doctrine of the divine right of kings to govern. Sources from which he proposes to draw his materials.
2. Does he want to justify the claim that governments (a) have a right to a monopoly of legal violence, or (b) should be monarchies? Do these stand or fall together?

3. Why it was good strategy to begin by reviewing a king's duties to his subjects.
4. The story from the Book of Samuel. Does it show that the Lord favored monarchy as a form of government? If not, why does King James cite it?
5. Point of his references to Ahab, Nebuchadnezzar, and Nero. What "men of God" are thereby involved? Cumulative effect in these references.
6. What follows from his "king as father" argument?
7. The moral he draws from storks and vipers.
8. What follows from his "king as head" argument?
9. It is the duty of a good citizen to free the commonwealth from a wicked king. His two rejoinders.
10. A wicked king is a curse to the commonwealth. His rejoinder.
11. The success which God gives to rebellions proves the justness of these quarrels. His rejoinder.
12. If the king breaks his contract with the people, they are no longer bound by it. His rejoinder.
13. Wherein you find King James (a) most (b) least convincing.

2. THE GREAT LEVIATHAN
—FROM THOMAS HOBBES

From James I to Hobbes. King James had published *The True Law of Free Monarchy*, stating the case for the divine right of kings, in 1598. In 1603 he had become king of Great Britain. Throughout his reign, he sought to act upon the assumption that he possessed an absolute sovereignty delegated to him by God. His parliaments resented this notion, but bided their time. In 1625 James I was succeeded by Charles I, who also professed the doctrine of divine rights and tried to live up to it. Indeed, for eleven years, he ruled without parliament. But in 1640, needing extra money to finance some military operations, he convoked his parliament. This parliament continued in session for twenty years. It began by passing the Triennial Act, which required its convocation every three years, and presented, in the Grand Remonstrance, a summary of its objections to Stuart absolutism. In 1642, it conducted a civil war under the leadership of Cromwell. In 1649 it executed Charles I and set up a Commonwealth which lasted eleven years. During the early years of this Commonwealth period, in 1651, Thomas Hobbes published his book, the *Leviathan*.

The *Leviathan* contains a restatement of the case for absolute sovereignty. But this time the argument is not carried out in theological terms. It is not made to rest upon the claim that absolute sovereignty is something delegated to governments by God. It is a statement in naturalistic instead of supernaturalistic terms. It represents, therefore, a step toward the wholly secular statement of the claim that sovereignty is delegated to the government by a people organized as a state.

Biographical Note. In Topic Two, "A Metaphysical Problem," we encountered Hobbes in the role of a propounder of materialism. In the present topic we are to meet him in the role of propounder of what he conceived to be the implications in political theory of his position in metaphysical theory. It will be remembered, from the previous biographical note, that Hobbes was born in 1588 and died in 1679. His political theory acquires considerable persuasiveness when one recalls the tumultuous period during which it was thought out and written down. Hobbes was born ten years before James published the defense of the divine right of kings. He lived to see James I antagonize parliament by those claims, to see Charles I executed by his parliament, to see Cromwell become an absolute dictator under the Commonwealth, to see Charles II (restored to the throne in 1660) gradually alienate his parliament by absolutist claims. When Hobbes died, the reign of Charles II was six years from its close, and the reign of the House of Stuarts was but nine years from its close, for in 1688 the parliament deposed James II, thus putting an end to the Stuart dynasty and the political theory which it had exemplified. All this being so, it would seem that the argument of Hobbes's *Leviathan* reflected two elements in his own experience. He saw that the divine-rights doctrine was a bankrupt troublemaker, but he saw also that some person or persons not only do claim sovereignty, but must needs do so if society is not to disintegrate amid stresses and strains such as had been set up by James I, Charles I, the Civil War, and the Commonwealth, to mention only matters within the society in question.

The Argument of the Citations. There are two thoughts running through Hobbes's argument. Both refer to absolute sovereignty considered as a fact. The first thought is: On what hypothesis can the occurrence of this fact be accounted for? The second thought is: On what principle can this fact be morally justified? Hobbes does not always keep these distinct. He begins with a pretty conceit, in which the body politic is likened to the body physical. From this he passes to an explanation of the formation of states. Out of this he derives a justification of the same. From this he passes to a description of the institution of sovereignty within any state; from this to an inventory of the rights and powers possessed by the person or persons in whom sovereignty is vested; from this to an inventory of the rights and powers reserved by individuals despite the absolute sovereignty supposed to exist in the government. And he ends with the thought that the universities of England would do well to propagate his views. He begins:

Two chief kinds of bodies offer themselves to such as search after their generation and properties: One is called a *natural body;* the other is called a *commonwealth* and is made by the wills and argeement of men.

Nature is imitated by the art of man in many ways; but especially in this, that it can make an artificial animal. For by art is created that great Leviathan called a *commonwealth* or *state*, which is but an artificial man, though of greater stature and strength than the natural man. The sovereignty is an artificial soul, as giving life and motion to the whole body; the magistrates and other officers of judicative and executive are artificial joints; rewards and punishments, by which every joint and member is moved to perform his duty, are the nerves; the wealth and riches of all the particular members are the strength; the people's safety is its business; councilors, by whom all things needful for it to know are suggested unto it, are the memory; equity and laws are its reason and will; concord is its health; sedition is its sickness; and civil war its death.

How and why does it come to pass that men make this "artificial animal" of which Hobbes here speaks? Why do men set up the state, limiting thereby their own liberties by the will of the person or persons in whom an absolute sovereignty is vested? Because of such facts as the following:

Nature hath made men so equal, in the faculties of the body and mind, as though there be found one man sometimes manifestly stronger in body or of quicker mind than another, yet when all is reckoned together, the difference between man and man is not so considerable as that one man can thereupon claim to himself any benefit, to which another may not pretend as well as he. For as to strength of body, the weakest hath strength enough to kill the strongest, either by secret machinations or by confederacy with others that are in the same danger with himself.

From this equality of ability ariseth equality of hope in the attaining of our ends. And therefore, if any two men desire the same thing, which nevertheless they cannot both enjoy, they become enemies; and in the way to their end, which is principally their own conservation and sometimes their own pleasure only, endeavor to destroy or subdue one another.

So that in the first place, I put for a general inclination of all mankind a perpetual and restless desire of power after power that ceaseth only in death. And the cause of this that no man can assure the power and means to live well, which he hath at present, without the acquisition of more.

It may seem strange to some, who have not well weighed these things, that nature should thus dissociate and render men apt to invade and destroy one another. Such persons, not trusting to this inference made from the passions, may therefore desire to have the same confirmed by experience.

Let him therefore consider within himself. When taking a journey, he arms himself. When going to sleep, he locks his doors. Even in his own home, he locks his chests. What opinion has he of his fellow subjects, when he rides armed? Of his fellow citizens, when he locks his doors? Of his children and servants, when he locks his chest? Does he not there as much accuse mankind by his actions, as I do by my words?

Hereby it is manifest, that during the time men live without a common power to keep them all in awe, they are in that condition which is called war; and such a war as is of every man against every man. For war consisteth not in battle only, but in a tract of time wherein the will to contend by battle is sufficiently known.

Whatsoever therefore is consequent to a time of war, where every man is enemy to every man; the same is consequent to the time wherein men live without other security than what their own strength and their own invention shall furnish them withal.

In such condition, there is no place for industry because the fruit thereof is uncertain, and consequently no culture of the earth, no navigation, no use of commodities that may be imported by sea, no commodious buildings, no instruments of moving and removing, no knowledge of the face of the earth, no account of time, no arts, no letters, no society; and, which is worst of all, continual fear of violent death; and the life of man, solitary, poor, nasty, brutish, and short.

To this war of every man against every man this also is consequent, that nothing can be unjust. The notions of right and wrong, justice and injustice have there no place. Where there is no common power, there is no law; where there is no law, there is no injustice. Justice and injustice are faculties of neither the body nor the mind, differing herein from both the senses and the passions. They are qualities that relate to men in society, not in solitude. It is consequent also to the same condition that there be no propriety, no dominion, no mine and thine distinct, but only that to be every man's that he can get, and for so long as he can keep. Thus much for the ill condition which man by mere nature is actually placed in.

It may peradventure be thought that there never was such a time, nor condition of war such as this. And I believe it was never generally so, over all the world. But there are many places where they live so now. However, it may be perceived what manner of life there would be, where there were no common power to fear, by the manner of life that men degenerate into a civil war.

The state, when it comes, is to be a union of wills to the end that law and order may be possible. The intolerable nature of the alternative —"the life of man, solitary, poor, nasty, brutish, and short"—is the justification. The state, man's answer to the threat of chaos, is founded upon a contract. What are the terms of this contract? Who are the parties to this contract? Hobbes continues:

Without the terror of some common power to cause them to be observed, justice, equity, modesty, mercy, doing to others as we would be done to, are contrary to our natural passions that carry us to partiality, pride, revenge, and the like. Covenants without the sword are but words, and of no strength to secure a man at all.

The only way to erect such a common power is for men to confer all their power and strength upon one man or one assembly of men that may reduce their wills unto one will: which is as much as to say, for all to appoint one man or one assembly of men to bear their person, for all to acknowledge themselves to be the authors of whatsoever he shall do or cause to be done, in those things which concern the common peace and safety, for all to submit their wills to his will, and their judgments to his judgment.

This is more than consent or concord. It is a real unity of all in one person or one assembly of persons, made by covenant of every man with every man, as if every man should say to every man, "I give up my right of governing myself to this man or assembly of men on condition that thou give up thy right in like manner." This done, the multitude so united in one person or one assembly of persons is called a *commonwealth*. This is the generation of that great Leviathan, of that mortal god to which we owe (under the immortal God) our peace and defense.

He that carrieth this power is called *sovereign*, and is said to have sovereign power. Everyone besides is said to be his *subject*. In him consisteth the essence of the commonwealth; which, to define it, is "one person of whose acts a great multitude, by mutual covenants one with another, have made themselves everyone the author to the end that he may use the strength and means of all for their peace and defense."

The difference of commonwealth consisteth in the difference of the sovereign. When the representative is one man, then is the commonwealth a monarchy; when an assembly of all, then is the commonwealth a democracy; when an assembly of part only, then is the commonwealth an aristocracy. Other kind of commonwealth there can be none, for either one, or some, or all must have the sovereign power. The difference between these three kinds of commonwealth consisteth not in the difference of power, but in the difference of convenience or aptitude to produce the peace and security of the people; which end they were instituted to. [Hobbes then argues that on six counts of efficiency an absolute monarchy is to be preferred to any other form of sovereignty.]

We have, by now, seen why men set up a state. We have seen the nature of that contract upon which it rests. We have seen the peculiar relation of the sovereign to this contract. He is a beneficiary of it but not a party to it. What follows, if this be so? Hobbes proceeds:

From this institution of a commonwealth are derived all the rights and powers of him or them on whom sovereign power is conferred by the consent of the people.

First, because they covenant, they cannot lawfully make a new covenant among themselves to be obedient to any other, in anything whatsoever, without his permission. They that are subject to a sovereign cannot, without his leave, cast him off and return to the confusion of a disunited multitude, nor transfer to another man or assembly of men; for they are bound every man to every man.

Second, because sovereignty is given by covenant only of one to another and not him to any of them, there can be no breach of covenant on the part of the sovereign. He that is made sovereign maketh no covenant with his subject beforehand. The opinion that any sovereign receiveth his power by covenant, that is on condition, proceedeth from want of understanding this easy truth that covenants, being but words and breath, have no force to oblige any man but what it has from the public sword, that is from the untied hands of that man or assembly of men that hath the sovereignty.

Third, because every subject is by this institution the author of all the actions of the sovereign, it follows that whatsoever the sovereign doth can be no injury to any of his subjects; nor ought he to be accused of injustice by any of them. For he that doth anything by authority of another, doth no injury to him by whose authority he acteth. He that complaineth of injury from his sovereign, complaineth of that whereof he himself is the author, and therefore ought not to accuse any man but himself; nor even himself, since to do injury to oneself is impossible.

Fourth, it follows from what was said last that no sovereign can justly be put to death or otherwise punished in any manner by his subjects. For seeing every subject is the author of the actions of his sovereign, he but punisheth another for the actions committed by himself.

Fifth, it is annexed to sovereignty to be judge of what opinions and doctrines are averse and what are conducive to peace; and, consequently, on what occasions, how far, and what men are to be trusted in speaking to multitudes, and who shall examine the doctrines of all books before they be published. For the actions of men proceed from their opinions; and in the well-governing of opinions consisteth the well-governing of men's actions in order to their peace and concord. And, though in matter of doctrine, nothing ought to be regarded but the truth, yet this is not repugnant to regulating the same by reference to peace. For doctrine repugnant to peace cannot be true. For those men that are so remissly governed that they dare take up arms to defend or introduce an opinion, are still in a state of war. Their condition is not peace, but only a cessation of arms for fear of one another, and they live as it were in the precincts of battle continually. It belongeth therefore to sovereignty to be judge, or to appoint all judges, of opinions and doctrines, as a thing necessary to peace, and to prevent discord and civil war.

Sixth, the whole power of prescribing rules whereby every man may know what goods he may enjoy and what actions he may do without being molested by any of his fellow men, is annexed to sovereignty. For before the constitution of sovereignty, as hath been shown, all men had right to all things, which necessarily causeth war. And therefore, these rules of property and conduct, being necessary to peace and depending on sovereignty, are the act of that power in order to preserve the public peace.

Seventh, the right of hearing and deciding all controversies which may arise concerning law or concerning fact, is annexed to sovereignty. For without such decision of controversies there is no protection of one subject against another, the laws concerning mine and thine are in vain, and to every man remaineth the right to protect himself by his private strength, which is the condition of war and contrary to the end for which commonwealth is instituted.

Eighth, the right of making war and peace, of judging when it is for the public good, of levying money upon the subjects to defray expenses thereof, is annexed to the sovereignty.

Lastly, to sovereignty is committed the power of rewarding every subject with riches or honor or dignity or titles; of punishing every subject by fine, by imprisonment, by corporal punishment, by ignominy, according to the law that sovereignty hath formerly made.

These are the rights which make the essence of sovereignty, and which are the marks whereby one may discern in what man or assembly of men the sovereign power is placed. For these are incommunicable and inseparable. And as the power, so also the honor of the sovereign ought to be greater than that of any or all of the subjects. Though his subjects shine, some more and some less when they are out of his sight, yet in his presence they shine no more than the stars in the presence of the sun.

Such are the rights and powers invested in government by men who form a state. Is this sovereignty absolute? Hobbes is evasive here.

He seems to say, "In a sense, yes"; but, equally clearly, he means also, "In a sense, no." It appears that there are limits which define sovereignty. These take the form of rights reserved by men in case the sovereign should overreach itself. Thus:

As men, for the attaining of peace and conservation of themselves thereby, have made an artificial man which we have called a *commonwealth*, so also have they made artificial chains called *civil laws*, which they themselves by mutual covenants, have fastened at one end to the lips of that man or assembly of men to whom they have given sovereign power, and at the other end to their own ears. These bonds, in their own nature but weak, may nevertheless be made to hold, by the danger though not by the difficulty of breaking them. In relation to these bonds only it is that I am to speak now, of the liberty of subjects. What are the things which, though commanded by the sovereign, the subject may nevertheless justly refuse to do?

If the sovereign (i.e., the government) command a man, though justly condemned, to kill, to wound, or to maim himself; not to resist those that assault him; to refrain from anything without which he cannot live; that man hath the liberty to disobey.

If the sovereign interrogate a man concerning a crime done by himself, he is not bounden, without assurance of pardon, to confess it.

If a man be held in prison, he is not bounded by covenant to subjection. If he can, he may make his escape by any means whatsoever.

If the sovereign command a man to execute any dangerous or dishonorable office, and refusal to obey frustrates the end for which the sovereignty was ordained, there is no liberty to refuse; otherwise there is.

To resist the sword of the commonwealth, in defense of another man, guilty or innocent, no man hath liberty; because such liberty takes away from the sovereign the means of protecting us, and is therefore destructive of the very essence of government. But in case a great many men together have already resisted the sovereign power unjustly, or committed some capital crime, for which every one of them expecteth death, have they not the liberty to join together, and assist and defend one another?

They have, for they but defend their lives, which the guilty as well as the innocent may do. But the offer of pardon taketh from them the plea of self-defense and maketh their perseverance unlawful.

If a subject have a controversy with his sovereign, he hath the same liberty to sue for his rights as if it were against a subject.

If the sovereign, either monarch or assembly, grant any liberty to all or any subject, by virtue whereof he is disabled to provide for their safety, the grant is void.

The obligation of subject to sovereign lasts no longer than the power by which he is able to protect them. For the right men have by nature to protect themselves when none else can protect them, can by no covenant be relinquished.

If a subject be taken prisoner in war, and hath his life and liberty given him on condition he be subject to the victor, he hath liberty to accept the conditions.

If the sovereign shall relinquish the sovereignty without appointing successor, his subjects thereby return to the absolute state of nature.

If the sovereign banish the subject, during banishment he is not subject.

If the sovereign be subdued by war, subjects are delivered from their obligation and become obligated to the victor.

As for other liberties, they depend on the silence of the law. In cases where the sovereign has prescribed no rule, the subject hath the liberty to do or foredo according to his own discretion. And therefore, such liberty is in some places more and in some less, in some times more and in some times less, according as they that have the sovereignty shall think most convenient.

The argument closes with a few observations upon the wisdom of spreading these ideas among the students at the universities, and with the hope that the author may hereafter be left in that peace of mind required for the prosecution of his other studies.

I think what I have writ may be profitably printed, and more profitably taught at the universities, in case they also think so. For, seeing the universities are the fountains of civil and moral doctrine from whence the preachers and gentry, drawing such water as they find, sprinkle the same (both from the pulpit and in their conversation) upon the people, there ought to be great care taken to have it pure, both from the venom of heathen politicians and from the incantations of heathen spirits.

And thus I have brought to an end my discourse on government, occasioned by the disorders of the present time, without partiality, without application, without other design than to set before men's eyes the mutual relation between protection and obedience of which the condition of human nature and the laws both natural and positive, require an inviolable observation.

In the revolution of states there can be no very good constellation for truth of this nature to be born under. Yet I cannot think it will be condemned at this time, either by the public judge of doctrine, or by any that desire the continuance of public peace. And in this hope I return to my uninterrupted speculation of bodies natural, wherein I hope the novelty will as much please as, in the doctrine of this artificial body, it useth to offend.

Note on Sources. The Hobbes material in this section is quoted, abridged, or paraphrased from his *Leviathan.* That volume contains an Introduction, forty-seven chapters, and a Review and Conclusion. The materials in this section are from the Introduction; Chapters 13, 17, 18, 21; and the Review and Conclusion.

Reading References. More by Hobbes is the best commentary on anything by Hobbes. Despite his somewhat archaic English, he is readable and suggestive. There is a refreshing cynicism about him. Further reading in the *Leviathan*, particularly that portion in which Hobbes describes the "kingdom of Darkness," is in order. Sir Leslie Stephen's book, *Hobbes*, in the *English Men of Letters* series, is good. So is Sir G. P. Gooch's book, *Political Thought in England: Bacon to Halifax*, in the *Home University Library* series. An older commentary will be found in the first two chapters of William Graham's *English Political Philosophy: Hobbes to Maine*.

For books published since 1940, see page 119.

READING QUESTIONS

1. It may be, as some have said, that God wills the state; but who, according to Hobbes, makes the state?
2. Why men combine together to make a state.
3. The state is founded upon a contract. The terms of this contract. The parties to this contract. Who is not a party to it?
4. There can be no breach of covenant on the part of the sovereign. Why not? Therefore what?
5. From the way in which a state comes to pass, and sovereignty is instituted, certain consequences follow. Mention any six.
6. According to Hobbes, men authorize government to exercise sovereignty over them; but in doing so they reserve certain rights which they may exercise against the government. Mention any six.
7. Why he recommends the teaching of his doctrines at the universities.
8. Wherein you find Hobbes (a) most (b) least convincing.

3. THE SOCIAL CONTRACT AND THE GENERAL WILL —FROM JEAN JACQUES ROUSSEAU

From Hobbes to Rousseau. Hobbes published his account of the state, in his *Leviathan*, in 1651. It had been written with reference to the Puritan revolution in England in 1649. The intention of the author had been to set forth the principles and presuppositions of that revolution. Between the *Leviathan* in 1651 and Rousseau's *Social Contract* in 1762, there came a second English revolution in 1688. This is referred to, sometimes, as the "bloodless" revolution, because of the fact that James II was deposed, the Stuart line closed, a new monarch invited to come to England from Holland, with little or no actual fighting. This revolution of 1688 was celebrated in the annals of political theory by John Locke in his *Two Treatises of Government.* This book defended the revolution on the ground that government rests upon the consent of the governed, and that what the governed consent to is a satisfactory definition and protection of their natural rights. There is, between sovereign and subject, a contractual relation. If the sovereign violates this contract, revolution is justified. This doctrinal claim that government *is* founded —in contrast to the historical claim that it *was* founded—on a contract was made the central theme of Jean Jacques Rousseau's important and influential little book, *The Social Contract.* Locke and Rousseau together provided the theory upon which the revolutionary movements at the end of the eighteenth century professed to rest. Americans in 1776 and French in 1789 were convinced that their actions were susceptible of justification in terms of the *Two Treatises of Government* and *The Social Contract.* The essence of these books is perhaps expressed in the claims that an ideal government is one which rests upon the consent of the governed; and that community self-government is the imposition by each man on himself of rules and limitations demanded by him of all others.

Biographical Note. Jean Jacques Rousseau was born in Switzerland in 1712, and died in 1778 at the age of sixty-six. His life falls into three periods. (1) During the period from 1712 to 1748 he was acquiring the elements of a formal education and something more than the elements of a worldly education. These matters are set down in his *Confessions.* As might be expected from the haphazard and undisciplined way in which he conducted himself during these years, Rousseau arrived at a state of some maladjustment. The times looked out of joint. The mores looked cramped and artificial. Civilization looked decadent.

(2) During the period from 1749 to 1762 he formulated his criticisms of the then modern world in a series of tracts which have given him his place in the scheme of things. The first of these (1749) was addressed to the question: Have the sciences and arts contributed to purify morals? Rousseau's answer was No. The second (1755), *On the Origin of Inequality Among Men,* argued that the root of inequality is the division of labor within society which permits the strong and wealthy to subject the mass of mankind to toil and poverty. The third (1760), *The New Heloise,* was a protest against the artificialities of marriage and

the family. The fourth (1762), *Émile*, was an indictment of education conceived as discipline and restraint. It stated the case for education, conceived as expression and development. The fifth (1762), *The Social Contract*, was addressed to the problem: Man is born free, and is everywhere in chains. How can this be justified? In these writings, Rousseau touched on important phases of eighteenth-century civilization. His pronouncements were usually in terms of such words as *artificial, unnatural, narrow, selfish, ignoble, crass.* Art, science, society, education, religion, the family, the state—all gave evidence that mankind was paying too great a price for the fruits of "civilized" living.

(3) During the period from 1763 to 1778 he was again a wanderer. The authorities ordered him out of France. He moved to Switzerland. The authorities ordered him out of Switzerland. He moved, at the invitation of David Hume, to England. This proved no better. He returned to France. During the last years of his life his mind became unbalanced. He died suddenly in 1778, two years after the American Revolution had begun and eleven years before the French Revolution began, for both of which in *The Social Contract* he had formulated principles of justification.

The Argument of the Citations. The problem which Rousseau set himself has been stated already. It was this: "Man is born free, and is everywhere in chains. How did this come about? I do not know. What can make it legitimate? That question I think I can answer." It is clear, that Rousseau does not propose to account for the fact that man is everywhere in chains. That is, he is not proposing historical research into origins. Nor is he proposing to remove the chains in question. That is, he is not proposing an argument for anarchism. His question is the more searching one: Granted that men must live in chains (i.e., under laws) what considerations will justify the fact? He begins by rejecting the notion that the right of this condition is to be found in the might that enforces it. Might does not make right. What does, then? His answer is common need, common confrontation with conditions which no individual could handle if left to himself. This idea is contained in the notion of the social contract. The terms of the contract are noted. The attributes of the sovereignty created and sustained by the contract are noted. The role of lawmaker is noted. The nature of law is noted. The separation of powers within government is argued for. The alternative forms of government (monarchy, aristocracy, democracy) are noted, together with their defining virtues and vices. He notes, finally, "the unavoidable and inherent defect which tends ceaselessly to destroy" any

form of political organization in any society. The argument begins as
follows:

Man is born free, and is everywhere in chains. One thinks himself the
master of others, and still remains a greater slave than they. How did this
come about? I do not know. What can make it legitimate? That question I
think I can answer.

The first thing to be clear about is that the restrictions which law
imposes cannot be justified by any appeal to the fact of force which lies
back of them. Might does not make right. Thus:

Suppose that "force" creates "right." The result is a mass of nonsense. For,
if force creates right, then every force that is greater than the first succeeds
to its right. As soon as it were possible to disobey with impunity, disobedience
would become legitimate; and, the strongest being always in the right, the only
thing that would matter (so far as concerns "justification") would be to act
so as to become the strongest.

But what kind of "right" is it that perishes when force fails? If we "must"
obey, there is no question that we "ought" to obey. And, on the principle
that force makes right, if we are not forced to obey, we are under no obligation to do so. A brigand surprises me at the edge of a wood. The pistol he
holds gives him power. Does it also give him right? Even if I could withhold
my purse, am I in conscience bound to give it up? Does his "might" create a
"right"?

Force is a physical power, and I fail to see what moral effect it can have.
To yield to force is an act of necessity, not of will; at most, an act of prudence. In what sense can it be a duty?

"Obey the powers that be." If this means "yield to force," it is a good
precept; but superfluous: I can answer for its never being violated. If it means
"yield, because all power comes from God," the case is no better. All power
comes from God, I admit; but so does sickness. Does that mean that we are
forbidden to call in a doctor?

Let us admit then that force does not create right, and that we are obligated to obey only legitimate powers. In that case my original question recurs:
What is the basis of political obligations?

If might does not make right, if the "chains" are not justified by
the fact that we are forced to wear them, what can we say? Rousseau
shifts from the force which is admittedly necessary to the existence of
law, to the conditions which justify law backed by force. Thus:

Suppose men to have reached the point at which the obstacles in the way of their preservation in the state of nature are greater than the resources at the disposal of each individual. That primitive condition can then subsist no longer, and the human race would perish unless it changed its manner of existence.

The problem is to find a form of association which will protect the person and goods of each individual with the whole common force of all; and in which each, uniting himself with all, may still obey himself alone and remain as free as before. This is the fundamental problem of which the "social compact" provides the solution.

If we disregard what is not of the essence of the social compact we shall find that it reduces itself to the following terms: "Each of us puts his person and his power in common under the supreme direction of the general will; and, in our corporate capacity, we receive each member as a part of the whole."

At one stroke, in place of the individual personality of each contracting party, this act of association creates a collective body, receiving from this act its unity, its common identity, its life, and its will. This public person, so formed by the union of all other persons, takes the name of *body politic*. It is called *state* when passive, *sovereign* when active, and *power* when compared with others like itself. Those who are associated in it take collectively the name of *people*, are severally called *citizens* as sharing in the sovereign power, and *subjects* as being under the laws of the state.

As soon as this multitude is united in one body politic, it becomes impossible to offend against one of the members without attacking the body politic, and still more to offend against the body politic. Duty and interest, therefore, equally obligate the two contracting parties to give each other help.

The social contract creates the state. It thereby creates the "chains" he had referred to. But it does more than that. The chains are seen to be, in principle, self-imposed restrictions; and they bring with them compensating advantages: Thus:

In the social compact there is no real "renunciation" on the part of the individuals. The position in which they find themselves, as a result of the compact, is really preferable to that in which they were before. Instead of a "renunciation," they have made an advantageous exchange; instead of an uncertain and precarious way of living, they have got one that is better and more secure; instead of natural independence, they have got liberty; instead of the power to harm others, they have got security for themselves; instead of their strength, which others might overcome, they have got a right which social union makes invincible.

What a man loses by the social compact is his natural liberty, and an unlimited right to everything he tries to get and succeeds in getting. What he gains is civil liberty and the proprietorship of all he possesses. If we are to avoid mistake in weighing one against the other, we must distinguish natural liberty, bounded only by the strength of the individual, from civil liberty, limited by the general will; and we must distinguish possession, the effect of force, from property, founded only on a positive title.

For such physical inequalities as nature may have set up between men, the social compact substitutes an equality that is moral and legitimate: by it, men who may be unequal in strength or intelligence, become every one equal by convention and legal right.

Under bad governments, this equality is only apparent and illusory: it serves only to keep the pauper in his poverty and the rich man in the position he has usurped. In fact, laws are always of use to those who possess, and harmful to those who have nothing: from which it follows that the social state is advantageous to men only when all have something and none have too much.

The general will alone can direct the state according to the object for which it was instituted, i.e., the common good: for, if the clashing of particular interests made the establishing of societies necessary, the agreement of these interests made it possible. The common element in these different interests is what forms the social tie; and, were there no point of agreement between them all, no society could exist. It is solely on the basis of this common interest that every society should be governed.

There is often a great difference between the "will of all" and the "general will." The latter considers only the common interest; the former takes private interest into account, and is no more than a sum of particular wills. But deduct from the sum of particular wills the plusses and minuses that cancel one another, and the general will remains.

Each individual may have a particular will contrary or dissimilar to the general will which he has as a citizen. His particular interest may speak to him quite different from the common interest; may make him look upon what he owes to the common cause as a gratuitous contribution, the loss of which will do less harm to others than the payment of it is burdensome to himself. He may come to regard the moral person which constitutes the state as a *persona ficta*, because not a man; and, as a result, may wish to enjoy the rights of citizenship without being ready to fulfill the duties of a subject. This, continued, would prove the undoing of the body politic.

The social contract creates sovereignty, i.e., a society organized to define and enforce its laws. The sovereignty inheres in the people. Rousseau proceeds to note several of its defining properties:

In order that the social compact may not be an empty formula, it includes the undertaking, that whoever refuses to obey the general will shall be compelled to do so. In this lies the key to the working of the body politic. This alone legitimizes civil undertakings which, without it, would be absurd, tyrannical and liable to the most frightful abuses. The social compact gives the body politic absolute power over all its members. It is this power, under the direction of the general will, which bears the name of *sovereignty*.

The sovereign, being formed wholly of the individuals who compose it, neither has nor can have any interest contrary to theirs. The sovereign, therefore, need give no guarantee to its subjects. Merely by virtue of what it is, the sovereign is always what it should be.

Sovereignty, being nothing less than the exercise of the general will, is inalienable, and the sovereign, who is no less than a collective being, cannot be represented except by himself. The power may be delegated, but not the general will from which it derives. To be "general," the will need not be unanimous, but every vote must count; any exclusion is a breach of generality. For the same reason that it is inalienable, sovereignty is indivisible.

The social compact sets up among the citizens an equality of such a kind that they all bind themselves to observe the same conditions and should therefore all enjoy the same rights. Thus, from the very nature of the compact, every act of sovereignty binds or favors all the citizens equally; so that the sovereign recognizes only the body of the nation and draws no distinctions between those of whom it is made up.

What, then, is an act of sovereignty? It is not a convention between a superior and an inferior, but a convention between the body politic and each of its members. It is legitimate, because based on the social contract; equitable, because common to all; useful, because it can have no other object than the general good; and stable, because guaranteed by the public force and the supreme power.

The people are sovereign. Granted. But what can they do about it? They can delegate their sovereignty to a legislature and an administration. Of themselves the sovereign people cannot draw up good law nor can they administer it.

But how are the people to "regulate the conditions of society"? By a common agreement? By a sudden inspiration? Has the body politic an organ to declare its will? Who can give it the foresight to formulate and announce its acts in advance? How is it to announce them in the hour of need? How can a blind multitude, who often does not know what is good for it and hence what it wills, carry out for itself so great and difficult an enterprise as a system of legislation?

Of itself, the people always wills the good, but of itself it by no means always sees it. The general will is always in the right, but the judgment which guides it is not always enlightened. It must be got to see things as they are, and, sometimes, as they ought to appear to it. It must be shown the good road it is in search of, secured against the seductive influences of individual wills. It must be taught to see times and places, made to weigh the attractions of present and sensible advantages against the dangers of distant and hidden evils.

All stand equally in need of guidance. Individuals must be compelled to bring their wills into conformity with their reason. The public must be taught to know what is the good which it wills. If that is done, there is a union of understanding and will in the social body. The parts work together, and the whole is raised to its highest power. This makes a legislator necessary.

7. The function of lawmaker needs to be considered. The unique qualifications are noted. The "legislator" is a paradoxical ideal.

To discover the rules of society best suited to nations, a superior intelligence beholding all the passions of men without experiencing any of them, would be needed. This intelligence would have to be wholly unrelated to our nature, while knowing it through and through. Its happiness would have to be independent of our happiness and yet ready to occupy itself with it. It would have to look forward and, working in one century, to be able to enjoy the next. It would take gods to give men laws.

He who dares undertake the making of a people's institutions ought to feel himself capable of changing human nature, of transforming each individual into part of a greater whole, of altering men's constitution for the purpose of strengthening it, of substituting a shared and moral existence for the independent and natural existence which nature has conferred on us all. In a word, he must take away from man his own resources and give him in their stead new ones incapable of being used without the help of other men. The more completely these "natural" resources are annihilated, the greater and more lasting are those which supplant them, and the more stable and perfect are the new institutions.

The office of legislator, which gives form to the state, nowhere enters into its constitution. He who holds command over men (the government), ought not to hold command over the laws. He who holds command over the laws (the legislator) ought not to hold command over men. Else would his laws be the ministers of his passions serving to perpetuate his injustices, and his private aims mar the sanctity of his work.

Thus in the task of legislation we find two things which appear to be incompatible: an enterprise too difficult for human powers, and, for its execution, an authority that is no authority.

The great soul of the legislator is the only miracle that can prove his mission. Any man may engrave on tables, buy an oracle, feign secret connexion with the gods, train a bird to whisper into his ear, or find some other trumpery way to impose on the people. He whose knowledge goes no further may perhaps gather round him a band of fools, but he will never found an empire, and his extravagances will perish with him. Idle tricks form a passing tie; only wisdom can make it lasting.

Provided the miracle of a good law can be performed, what does society have at its disposal? An instrument, essentially, for dealing with general conditions. The particulars must be seen to fall under the law by the wisdom of the executive.

What is a law? When the whole people declares for the whole people, this is what I call a *law*.

The matter about which such decree is made is, like the decreeing will, general. When I say that the matter is "general," I mean that law considers subjects *en masse* and actions in the abstract, never a particular person or action. Thus law may declare that there shall be privileges; but it cannot confer them on any one by name. It may set up classes of citizens. It may specify qualifications for membership of these classes. But, as law, it cannot nominate such and such persons as belonging to these classes. Law may, e.g., establish a monarchical form of government and an hereditary succession. It cannot choose a king or nominate a royal family. In a word, no function which has a particular object in view can be a matter of law.

On this view, we see at once that it can no longer be asked whose business it is to make laws, since they are acts of the general will; nor whether "government is above the law," since governors are part of the state; nor whether laws can be unjust, since no one is unjust to himself; nor how we can be both "free" and at the same time subject to laws, since they are but registers of our wills.

The law unites universality of will with universality of object. What any man commands of his own motion cannot be law. Even what sovereignty commands with regard to some particular matter cannot be law; it is then merely a decree of the government.

Laws are, strictly speaking, the conditions of civil association. The people, being subject to the laws, ought to be their author: the conditions of the society ought to be regulated by those who unite to give it form.

Thus far we have had society, the contract, the sovereign people, the legislator, and laws. We come now to government, what we would call the executive arm of government. It is not to be confused with any of the other terms:

I have argued that the power to make laws belongs to the sovereign people, and can belong to it alone. On the other hand, the power to execute these laws cannot belong to the generality, because such power consists wholly of particular acts which fall outside the competency of lawmaking as such.

The body politic, therefore, needs an agent of its own to bind it together, to set it to work under the direction of the general will, to serve as a means of communication between the (people as) state and the (people as) sovereign. Here we have the basis of government, something which is often confused with the sovereign whose minister it is.

What then is government? It is an intermediate body, set up between the (people as) subjects and the (people as) sovereign, to secure their mutual correspondence, to execute the laws and to maintain liberty. The members of this body are called governors.

Government is hence simply and solely a commission, in which the governors, mere officials of the sovereign people, exercise in their own name the power which is invested in them by the people. This delegated power the sovereign people can limit, modify, or recover at pleasure.

The government gets from the (people as) sovereign the orders which it gives to the (people as) subjects. For the state to be properly balanced there must be an equality between the power of the government and the power of the citizens, for the latter are, on the one hand, sovereign, and, on the other hand, subject.

None of these three terms—*sovereign, subjects, government*—can be altered without the equality being instantly destroyed. If the sovereign tries to govern, if the government tries to give laws, or if the subjects refuse to obey, disorder replaces order, force and will no longer act together, and the state is dissolved into despotism or anarchy.

Government, then, is distinct from society, sovereignty, legislator, law, and so on. Its function is to administer the laws. What form should it have?

There has been at all times much dispute concerning the best form of government. Is it democratic? Aristocratic? Or monarchical? This question, "What, absolutely, is the best form of government?" is unanswerable and indeterminate. The fact is that each is in some cases the best, and in others the worst.

Let us see. Consider first the notion of democracy:

The sovereign people may commit the charge of the government to the whole people or to a majority of the people. The result would be that more citizens would be actual governors than mere private subjects. This form of government is called *democracy*.

If we take the term in the strict sense, there never has been a real democracy, and there never will be. It is unimaginable that the people should remain continually assembled to devote their time to public affairs.

Besides, how many conditions, difficult to unite, would such a form of government presuppose! First, a very small state, where the people can readily be got together and where each citizen can with ease know all the rest. Second, great simplicity of manners, to prevent business from multiplying and raising thorny problems. Third, a large measure of equality in rank and fortune, without which equality of rights and authority cannot long subsist. Fourth, little or no luxury, for luxury either comes of riches or makes them necessary.

Moreover, it is a certainty that promptitude in execution diminishes as more people are put in charge of it. Where prudence is made too much of, not enough is made of fortune; opportunity is let slip, and deliberation results in the loss of its object.

It may be added that no form of government is so subject to civil wars and intestinal agitations as democracy, because there is none which has so strong and persistent a tendency to change to another form, or which demands more vigilance and courage for its maintenance. Were there a people of gods, their government would be democratic. So perfect a government is not for men.

Obviously, pure democracy is unsuited to the needs of the modern state. Another possibility is an elected aristocracy. It holds more promise:

The sovereign people may restrict the government to a small number, so that there are more private citizens than magistrates. This is named *aristocracy*.

There are three sorts of aristocracy: natural, elective, and hereditary. The first is only for simple peoples; the second is the best, and is aristocracy properly so-called; the third is the worst of all governments.

There is much to be said for an elective aristocracy. It has the advantage of keeping clear the distinction between the two powers, sovereignty and government. Besides this, its members are chosen to be governors, not born to this office, as in the case of a pure democracy or an hereditary aristocracy. By this means uprightness, understanding, experience, and all other claims to preeminence become so many guarantees of wise government.

It is more efficient. Assemblies are more easily held; affairs are better discussed and carried out with more order and diligence; the credit of the state is better sustained abroad.

It is more economical. There is no need to multiply instruments, or get twenty thousand men to do what a hundred picked men can do better.

However, if an elective aristocracy does not demand all the virtues needed by popular government, it demands others which are peculiar to itself; for instance, moderation on the side of the rich, and contentment on the side of the poor. If this form of government carries with it a certain inequality of fortune, this is justifiable on the grounds that the administration of public affairs may be entrusted to those who are most able to give them their whole time.

In Rousseau's day the commonest form of government was hereditary monarchy. It has its good points and its bad points. Thus:

The sovereign people may concentrate the whole government in the hands of a single person from whom all others hold their power. This form of government is the most usual, and is called *monarchy*.

No form of government is more vigorous than this. All answer to a single motive power. All the springs of the machine are in the same hands. The whole moves toward the same end. There are no conflicting movements to cancel another. In no constitution does a smaller amount of effort produce a greater amount of action. Archimedes seated quietly on the bank of a river, easily drawing a great floating vessel, stands in my mind for a skillful monarch governing vast estates from his study, moving everything while he seems himself unmoved.

For a monarchical state to have a chance of being well governed, its population and extent must be proportionate to the abilities of its governor. It is easier to conquer than to rule. With a lever long enough, the world could be moved with a single finger; to sustain it requires the shoulders of Hercules.

These are some of the virtues to be expected in monarchy. However, Rousseau goes on to note possible defects:

Everything conspires to take away from a man who is set in authority the sense of justice and reason.

Kings desire to be absolute, and men are always crying out to them from afar that the best means is to get themselves loved by their people. This is all very well, and true enough in some respects. Unfortunately, it will always be derided at court. The power that comes of a people's love is no doubt the greatest; but it is precarious and conditional, and princes will never rest content with it. The best of kings desire to be in a position to be wicked, if they so please, without forfeiting thereby their mastery. Political sermonizers may tell them, to their hearts' content, that the people should be prosperous, numerous, and formidable. Kings know this to be untrue. Their personal interest is that the people should be weak, wretched, and unable to resist them.

There is an essential and inevitable defect which will always rank a monarchy below a republic. It is this. In a republic the people hardly ever raises men who are unenlightened and incapable to the highest positions; whereas, under a monarch, those who rise to power are most often petty blunderers, petty swindlers, petty intriguers, men whose petty talents cause them to get into stations of the greatest eminence at court. The people is far less often mistaken in its choice than the monarch. A man of real worth among the king's ministers is almost as rare as a fool at the head of a republic.

Another disadvantage in monarchical government is the lack of any continuous succession. When one king dies, another is needed. In the case of an elective monarchy, dangerous interregnums occur, and are full of storms; unless, that is, the citizens are upright and disinterested to a degree which seldom goes with this kind of government.

What has been done to prevent these evils? Succession has been made hereditary in certain families. That is to say, men have chosen rather to be ruled by children, monstrosities, or imbeciles than to endure disputes over the choice of good kings. Apparent tranquillity has been preferred to wise administration.

These difficulties have not escaped our political writers. But they are not troubled by them. The remedy, they say, is to obey without a murmur: God sends bad kings in His wrath, and they are to be borne as the scourges of heaven. Such talk is doubtless edifying, but it would be more in place in a pulpit than in a political book. What are we to say of a doctor whose whole art is to exhort the sufferer to patience?

By way of conclusion we may note the fundamental fact from which political instability continually proceeds:

All forms of government contain within them the seeds of destruction and dissolution. As the particular will acts constantly in opposition to the general will, the government continually exerts itself against the sovereign. The greater this exertion becomes, the more the constitution changes. This is the unavoidable and inherent defect which, from the very birth of the body politic, tends ceaselessly to destroy it, as age and death end by destroying the human body.

Such is the natural and inevitable tendency of the best constituted governments. If Sparta and Rome perished, what state can hope to endure for ever? We desire a long-lived form of government? Let us not dream of making it eternal. If we are to succeed, we must not attempt the impossible; nor must we flatter ourselves that we are endowing the work of man with a stability which human conditions do not permit.

The body politic begins to die as soon as it is born, and carries in itself the causes of its own destruction. The state is a work of art, not of nature. It is for men to prolong its life as much as possible, by giving it the best possible constitution. But even the best will have an end.

The life principle of the body politic lies in the sovereign authority. The legislative power is the heart of the state; the executive power is its brain. The brain may become paralyzed, and the body still live. But as soon as the heart ceases to perform its function, the organism is dead. Wherever the laws grow weak as they become old, there is no longer a legislative power, and the state is dead.

Note on Sources. The Rousseau material in this section is quoted, abridged, or paraphrased from his *Social Contract.*

Reading References. The number of books written on Rousseau is large. Each generation has found it necessary to take stock of his ideas. Lord Morley's *Rousseau* is good reading for those who continue to share Lord Morley's typically nineteenth-century rationalism and liberalism. A provocative chapter on *The Social Contract* is to be found in Bernard Bosanquet's *Philosophical Theory of the State.* The author stresses the fact that Rousseau's self-imposed problem was *not* how to justify revolution, but how to justify restraint of the individual by the state. A good biography is to be found in Matthew Josephson's *Jean Jacques Rousseau.* The best comprehensive accounts of Rousseau's ideas are to be found, so far as books written in English are concerned, in C. W. Hendel's two volumes, *Rousseau as Moralist,* and in Matthew Josephson's book.

The following are some books published since 1940:

Cassirer, E. *Rousseau, Kant and Goethe.*
———. *The Question of Jean-Jacques Rousseau.*
Chapman, J. W. *Rousseau: Totalitarian or Liberal.*
Durkheim, E. *Montesquieu and Rousseau: Forerunners of Sociology.*
Feuchtwanger, L. *'Tis Folly To Be Wise* (A novel on Rousseau).
Green, F. C. *Jean Jacques Rousseau: A Critical Study of His Life and Writings.*
Osborn, A. M. *Rousseau and Burke: A Study in the Idea of Liberty in Eighteenth Century Political Thought.*

READING QUESTIONS

1. It is well to distinguish these two matters at the beginning: (a) What it is he does not know. (b) Question he thinks he can answer.
2. Why he turns aside to deal with the "might makes right" doctrine. Any two of his criticisms.
3. Why men exchange the state of nature for a politically organized society.
4. This (No. 3) transition is effected, underwritten, marked, by the "social contract." The terms of this contract. The parties to it.

Does it refer to the setting up of a state or the setting up of a government?

5. Losses and gains to be chalked up to passing from the state of nature to civil society.

6. Those who enter the social contract thereby create a "moral and collective body," a "public person." Is this metaphor?

7. The object of the general will. What, continued, would prove the undoing of the body politic.

8. Whoever refuses to obey the general will shall be compelled to do so. Why this is not tyranny, despotism, arbitrary coercion.

9. Rousseau's answer to the question, "Who are sovereign?" Contrast Rousseau here with James I and Hobbes.

10. Why a people needs a legislator or legislature.

11. Why it would take Gods to give men laws.

12. What a person sets himself to do, who undertakes to give institutions to a people.

13. Why there should be a separation between legislator and (a) the constitution, (b) the executive.

14. So long as laws express the general will, those who obey them obey their own wills. How so (see No. 8).

15. Is a person's relation to the social contract the same as his relation to a law? If not, wherein not?

16. His distinction between state and government. Why this was a revolutionary distinction.

17. The sovereign people may commit the charge of government to the whole people or a majority, to a small number of the people, or to a single person. Rousseau's opinion of each resulting form of government.

18. The unavoidable and inherent defect which tends ceaselessly to destroy the body politic.

19. Why Rousseau would not speak of a democratic or aristocratic or monarchical state. How he would have revised Louis XIV's remark "I am the state."

20. Give a connected account of these notions according to Rousseau: (a) state of nature (b) social contract (c) civil state (d) general will (e) law (f) legislator (g) government (h) dissolution.

21. Wherein you find Rousseau (a) most (b) least convincing.

4. PRINCIPLES OF CONSERVATISM
—FROM EDMUND BURKE

From Rousseau to Burke. Rousseau published *The Social Contract* in 1762. The American Revolution began in 1775. It was scarcely over when the French Revolution began, in 1789. This political restlessness in the colonies and in Europe was accompanied by a sharp demand for parliamentary reform in England. The revolutionary Society for Constitutional Information was organized in 1780. Prime Minister Pitt tried three times, each time in vain, to persuade the House of Commons to consider the case for parliamentary reform. During these years, Tom Paine was gaining his reputation as spokesman for liberal and revolutionary movements in America and Europe. Jeremy Bentham published in 1789 his epoch-making treatise on liberal social reform, *Principles of Morals and Legislation,* in which he argued that customs, laws, institutions, and constitutions should be evaluated in terms of one standard, namely, the greatest happiness of the greatest number.

Such was the climate of opinion in which Edmund Burke wrote his exposition and defense of political conservatism. On all hands he saw, or thought he saw, signs that the old regimes of monarchies and aristocracies were weakening before popular demand for democratic politics. Wherever he looked, he detected "factions now busy amongst us who endeavor to propagate an opinion that the people, in forming their commonwealth, have by no means parted with their power over it." He set himself to stem this tide. He might as well have bade the sun stand still. These democratizing tendencies swept on and left the memory of his plea stranded amid the welter of wars, revolutions, reforms, and changes. If this were all, there would be little need to include Burke among spokesmen of political philosophy. But there is more to Burke than a neglected warning against democratic politics. In his words may be found a careful account of the principles of political conservatism. It is an expression of one of man's perennial needs.

Biographical Note. Edmund Burke was born in Ireland in 1729 and died in England in 1797 at the age of sixty-eight. He received his academic education at Trinity College, Dublin. He spent some time acquiring the rudiments of a legal training in London in the Middle Temple. He entered Parliament in the 1760's and rose there to a position of great prestige. In 1775 he delivered his famous speech, "Conciliation with America." In 1785 he opened his attack on Warren Hastings' India administration with his equally famous speech "The Nabob of Arcot's Debts." In 1790 he published his *Reflections on the French Revolution.* The ideas advanced in this tract were subsequently elaborated in his *Appeal from the New to the Old Whigs,* his *Letter to a Noble Lord* and his *Letter on a Regicide Peace.* The citations in this chapter are, for the most part, from the *Reflections* and the *Appeal* and the *Letters.*

The Argument of the Citations. Burke begins by noting that there are certain "factions now busy amongst us who endeavor to propagate an opinion that 'the people' in forming their commonwealth have by no means parted with their power over it." In other words, the notion of popular sovereignty is being argued for. The substance of such claims is noted. A general criticism is passed upon them. The concept of "the people," upon which the whole argument turns, is then proposed for analysis. What does one mean by *the people?* If by *the people* one means a numerical majority, then certain criticisms may be advanced. At this point the argument is suspended while Burke makes two excursions into recent French history to document his critique of the concept of the people as sovereign. The first aside is addressed to a Frenchman, pointing out the extent to which, in Burke's mind, alternative steps had been possible in France at the time the revolution was launched. Various excesses are noted. "Were all these dreadful things necessary?" he demands. The second aside recounts the fate of the French king and queen and laments the absence of wisdom and decency exhibited by those who put them to death. "Alas, the age of chivalry is gone." From these historical asides, he returns to his criticism of the "barbarous philosophy" which has led to this havoc.

At this point Burke's arguments become positive. He sketches the foundation in which government is laid. From this, there results a more austere conception of the state than is held by those who launch and defend revolution in the name of the "rights of man." Does this commit Burke to a repudiation of the notion of the rights of man? "I am far from denying the real rights of man," he protests. The notion of "real" rights, in contrast to spurious rights, is outlined. This involves a clarification of "real" liberties in contrast to spurious liberties. The "real" rights and liberties, which Burke is prepared to ascribe to "the people" presuppose government by a natural aristocracy. This notion is outlined. It is then contrasted with a sham aristocracy of mere lords and dukes.

The fundamental claim is disclosed at this point: Burke will entertain the notion of rights only in terms of the notion of duties. We have rights because we have duties, and, within limits, we do not choose our duties. They await us in the society into which we are born and in which we grow up. This idea may involve difficult problems and nice distinctions. In all such cases, it is wiser to keep an eye on duties than on rights. The burden of proof rests with those who violate obligations in the name of their rights. This, however, is not to be taken as a categorical denial of all change and reform, merely an insistence that wisdom ordinarily lies

with custom and tradition, and that an individual should address himself
to the problem of extracting the wisdom which these contain. It is folly
to "trade each on his own private stock of reason." This conservative
political philosophy rests upon a recognition of the fact that wise politics
has, in the last analysis, a religious basis. "On religion all our laws and
institutions stand." "The awful author of our being has disposed and
marshalled us by a divine tactic." The argument concludes with several
eloquent paragraphs setting forth the great wisdom which attends the
policy, arising out of these views, of regarding "liberties as an entailed
inheritance" to be held as a sacred trust and passed on intact to one's
posterity.

Opposes

Factions now busy amongst us, in order to divest men of all love for their
country, and remove from their minds all duty with regard to the state, endeavor to propagate an opinion that the "people," in forming their commonwealth, have by no means parted with their power over it. Discuss any of their
schemes, and their answer is, It is the act of the people and that is sufficient.

These theorists hold, that sovereignty, whether exercised by one or many,
did not only originate from the people, but that in the people the same sovereignty constantly and unalienably resides; that the people may lawfully de-
pose kings; not only for misconduct, but without any misconduct at all; that
they may set up any new fashion of government for themselves, or continue
without any government at their pleasure; that the people are essentially their
own rule, and their will the measure of their conduct; that the tenure of rulers
is not a proper subject of contracts, because rulers have duties, but no rights;
and that if a contract *de facto* is made with them in one age, allowing that it
binds at all, it binds only those who are immediately concerned in it, but
does not pass to posterity.

They hold that to a majority of the people belongs the right of altering
the whole frame of their society, if such should be their pleasure. They may
change it, say they, from a monarchy to a republic today and tomorrow
back again from a republic to a monarchy, and so backward and forward as
often as they like. They are masters of the commonwealth, because in substance they are themselves the commonwealth.

The ceremony of cashiering kings, of which these gentlemen talk so
much, can rarely, if ever, be performed without force. It then becomes a case
of war, and not of constitution. Laws are commanded to hold their tongues
amongst arms, and tribunals fall to the ground with the peace they are no
longer able to uphold.

Whilst they are possessed by these notions, it is vain to talk to them of the
practice of their ancestors, the fundamental laws of their country, the fixed
form of a constitution, whose merits are confirmed by the solid test of long

experience, and an increasing public strength and national prosperity. They despise experience as the wisdom of unlettered men, and as for the rest, they have wrought underground a mine that will blow up, at one grand explosion, all examples of antiquity, precedents, charters, and acts of parliament.

Burke now has the political heresy stated. It is the claim that the people are sovereign and need acknowledge no masters save of their own choosing. Those who hold this view are, Burke feels, beyond the reach of argument. Nevertheless, over·against the time when experience shall have disclosed to them the folly of their ways, he proposes to analyze and evaluate their claim:

These doctrines concerning "the people" tend, in my opinion, to the utter subversion, not only of all government, in all modes, but all stable securities to rational freedom, and all the rules and principles of morality itself.

On such principles every individual would have a right to originate what afterwards is to become the act of the majority. Whatever he may lawfully originate, he may lawfully endeavor to accomplish. He has a right therefore to break the ties and engagements which bind him to the country in which he lives, and he has a right to make as many converts to his opinions, and to obtain as many associates in his designs, as he can procure: for how can you know the dispositions of the majority to destroy their government, but by tampering with some part of the body? You must begin by a secret conspiracy, that you may end with a national confederation.

The mere pleasure of the beginning must be the sole guide, since the mere pleasure of others must be the sole ultimate sanction, as well as the sole actuating principle in every part of the progress. Thus, arbitrary will (the last corruption of ruling power) step by step poisons the heart of every citizen. No sense of duty can prevent any man from being a leader or a follower in such enterprises. Nothing restrains the temper; nothing guards the tempted. Nor is the new state, fabricated by such arts, safer than the old. What can prevent the mere will of any person, who hopes to unite the wills of others to his own, from an attempt wholly to overturn it? It wants nothing but a disposition to trouble the established order, to give a title to the enterprise.

By such doctrines, all love to our country, all pious veneration and attachment to its laws and customs, are obliterated from our minds; and nothing can result from this opinion, when grown into a principle, and animated by discontent, ambition, or enthusiasm, but a series of conspiracies and seditions, sometimes ruinous to their authors, always noxious to the state.

There is, it appears, much to be said against this popular doctrine. A few obvious things have already been noted. But nothing fundamental has been offered as yet. Burke moves, accordingly, to the essential point. Everything turns upon the meaning of this phrase, *the people*. So he proceeds:

Believing it a question at least arduous in theory, and in practice very critical, it would become us to ascertain what our incantations are about to call up from darkness and the sleep of ages when the supreme authority of "the people" is in question. Before we attempt to extend or to confine, we ought to fix in our minds, with some degree of distinctness, an idea of what it is we mean, when we say *the people*.

We are so little affected by things which are habitual, that we consider this idea of the decision of a majority as if it were a law of our original nature, but such constructive whole, residing in a part only, is one of the most violent fictions that ever has been or can be made on the principles of artificial incorporation. Out of civil society nature knows nothing of it; nor are men, even when arranged according to civil order, otherwise than by very long training, brought at all to submit to it.

In a state of rude nature there is no such thing as "a people." A number of men in themselves have no collective capacity. The idea of a people is the idea of a corporation. It is wholly artificial, and made like all other legal fictions, by common agreement. What the particular nature of that agreement was, is collected from the form into which the particular society has been cast. Any other is not their covenant.

When men, therefore, break up the agreement which gives its corporate form and capacity to a state, they are no longer a people; they have no longer a corporate existence; they have no longer a legal, coactive force to bind within, nor a claim to be recognized abroad. They are a number of vague, loose individuals and nothing more. With them all is to begin again. Alas! They little know how many a weary step is to be taken before they can form themselves into a mass, which has a true, political personality.

The phrase *the people* cannot be identified with a mere voting majority. Such an idea, namely that a voting majority shall be "the people" is a product of late political experience. Men must have learned much from long trial and error before they can act on that notion. It expresses an agreement or consensus that political experience alone makes possible. If this meaning of the phrase is a product of group experience of state organization, then it cannot be argued to be prior to and more fundamental than state organization. To overlook or to deny this fact is to court much trouble. Thus:

I see as little of policy or utility, as there is of right, in laying down a principle that a majority of men, told by the head are to be considered as "the people," and that as such their will is to be law. What policy can there be in arrangements made in defiance of every political principle? To enable men to act with the weight and character of a people, and to answer the ends for which they are incorporated into that capacity, we must suppose them to be in that state of habitual social discipline, in which the wiser, the more expert, and the more opulent conduct, and by conducting enlighten and protect the weaker, the less knowing, and the less provided with the goods of fortune. When the multitude are not under this discipline, they can scarcely be said to be in civil society.

It is not necessary to teach men to thirst after power. But it is very expedient that by moral instruction, they should be taught, and by their civil constitutions they should be compelled, to put many restrictions upon the immoderate exercise of it, and the inordinate desire for it. The best method of obtaining these great points forms the important, but at the same time the difficult problem to the true statesman. No legislator, at any period of the world, has willingly placed the seat of active power in the hands of the multitude: because there it admits of no control, no regulation, no steady direction whatsoever.

The people are not to be taught to think lightly of their engagements to their governors; else they teach their governors to think lightly of their engagements toward them. In that kind of game in the end the people are sure to be the losers. To flatter them into a contempt of faith, truth, and justice, is to ruin them; for in those virtues consists their whole safety. To flatter any man, or any part of mankind, in any description, by asserting that in engagements he or they are free whilst any other human creature is bound, is ultimately to vest the rule of morality in the pleasure of those who ought to be rigidly submitted to it, to subject the sovereign reason of the world to the caprices of weak and giddy men.

The democratic commonwealth is the foodful nurse of ambition. Under other forms of government it meets with many restraints. Whenever, in states which have a democratic basis, the legislators have endeavored to put restraints upon ambition, their methods were as violent, as in the end they were ineffectual: as violent indeed as any the most jealous despotism could invent. The caution could not very long save the state which it was meant to guard, from the attempts of ambition, one of the natural, inbred, incurable distempers of a powerful democracy.

I am well aware that men love to hear of their power, but have an extreme disrelish to be told of their duty. This is a matter of course; because every duty is a limitation of some power. Indeed arbitrary power is so much to the depraved taste of the vulgar of every description, that almost all dissensions, which lacerate the commonwealth, are not concerning the manner in which it is to be exercised, but concerning the hands in which it is to be placed.

The people are, to a far less extent than are princes and other persons of exalted station, under responsibility to one of the greatest controlling powers on earth, the sense of fame and estimation. The share of infamy that is likely to fall to the lot of each individual in public acts is small indeed; the operation of opinion being in the inverse ratio to the number of those who abuse power. Their own approbation of their own acts has to them the appearance of a public judgment in their favor. A perfect democracy is therefore the most shameless thing in the world. As it is the most shameless, it is also the most fearless.

So far his indictment has been in terms of rather large general issues. He moves to consider more specific outrages, particularly the case of the king and queen. Burke's prose here should be read aloud.

Let those who have the trust of political or of natural authority ever keep watch against the desperate enterprises of innovation; let even their benevolence be fortified and armed. They have before their eyes the example of a monarch, insulted, degraded, confined, deposed; his family dispersed, scattered, imprisoned; his wife insulted to his face like the vilest of the sex, by the vilest of all populace; himself three times dragged by these wretches in an infamous triumph; his children torn from him, in violation of the first right of nature, and given into the tuition of the most desperate and impious of the leaders of desperate and impious clubs; his revenues dilapidated and plundered; his magistrates murdered; his clergy proscribed, persecuted, famished; his nobility degraded in their rank, undone in their fortunes, fugitives in their persons; his armies corrupted and ruined; his whole people impoverished, disunited, dissolved; whilst through the bars of his prison, and amidst the bayonets of his keepers, he hears the tumult of two conflicting factions.

All this accumulation of calamity, the greatest that ever fell upon one man, has fallen upon his head, because he had left his virtues unguarded by caution; because he was not taught that, where power is concerned, he who will confer benefits must take security against ingratitude.

It is now sixteen or seventeen years since I saw the queen of France, then the dauphiness, at Versailles; and surely never lighted on this orb a more delightful vision. I saw her just above the horizon, glittering like the morning star, full of life and splendor and joy. Oh! what a revolution, and what a heart must I have, to contemplate without emotion that elevation and that fall. Little did I dream, when she added titles of veneration to those of enthusiastic, distant, respectful love, that she should ever be obliged to carry the sharp antidote against disgrace concealed in that bosom. Little did I dream that I should have lived to see such disasters fallen upon her in a nation of gallant gentlemen, a nation of men of honor and of cavaliers. I thought ten thousand swords must have leaped from their scabbards to avenge even a look that threatened her with insult!

But alas, the age of chivalry is gone. The age of sophisters, economists, and calculators has succeeded, and the glory of Europe is extinguished for ever. Never, never more shall we behold that generous loyalty to rank and sex, that proud submission, that dignified obedience, that subordination of the heart, which kept alive, even in servitude itself, the spirit of an exalted freedom. The unbought grace of life, the cheap defense of nations, the nurse of manly sentiment and heroic enterprise, is gone. That sensibility of principle, that chastity of honor, which felt a stain like a wound, which inspired courage while it mitigated ferocity, which ennobled whatever it touched, under which vice lost half its evil by losing all its grossness, is gone.

Now all is changed. All the pleasing illusions, which made power gentle and obedience liberal, which harmonized the different shades of life, which by a bland assimilation incorporated into politics the sentiments which beautify and soften private society, are to be dissolved by this new conquering empire of "light and reason." All the decent drapery of life is to be torn off. All the superadded ideas, furnished from the wardrobe of a moral imagination, which the heart owns and the understanding ratifies as necessary to cover the defects of our naked shivering nature and raise it to dignity in our own estimation, are to be exploded as ridiculous, absurd, and antiquated fashion.

Back of all this chaos and cruelty and injustice and folly lies the doctrine of popular sovereignty. That was what Burke set out to criticize. The asides have been intended merely to document his claims:

The pretended "rights of man," which have made this havoc, cannot be the rights of the people. For to be a people, and to have these rights, are things incompatible. The one supposes the presence, the other the absence of a state of civil society. The very foundation of the French commonwealth is false and self-destructive; nor can its principles be adopted in any country, without the certainty of bringing it to the very same condition in which France is found.

On the scheme of this barbarous philosophy, which is the offspring of cold hearts and muddy understandings, which is void of solid wisdom, which is destitute of all taste and elegance, laws are to be supported only by their own terrors and by the concern which each individual may find in them from his own private speculations or can spare to them from his own private interests. In the groves of their academy, at the end of every vista, you see nothing but the gallows.

On the principles of this philosophy institutions can never be embodied in persons. That sort of "reason" which banishes the affections is incapable of filling their place. These public affections, combined with manners, are required, sometimes as supplements, sometimes as correctives, always as aids, to law.

At this point he returns to his original argument. "The people" cannot be the foundation of government, it seems, or he has misread French history of late. What then? If the foundation of coercive government is not to be found in the doctrine of the "rights of man," where then? He settles down to this more positive question:

The dislike I feel to revolutions, the signals for which have so often been given from pulpits; the spirit of change that is gone abroad; the total contempt which prevails of all ancient institutions, when set in opposition to a present sense of convenience, or to the bent of a present inclination—all these considerations make it not unadvisable, in my opinion, to call back our attention to the true principle of laws.

The foundation of government is laid, not in imaginary rights of men, but in political convenience, and in human nature; either as that nature is universal, or as it is modified by local habits and social aptitudes. The foundation of government is laid in a provision for our wants, and in a conformity to our duties; it is to purvey for the one; it is to enforce the other.

Among men's wants is to be reckoned the want of a sufficient restraint upon their passions. Society requires not only that the passions of individuals should be subjected, but that even in the mass and body, as well as in the individuals, the inclinations of men should frequently be thwarted, their will controlled, and their passions brought into subjection. This can only be done by a power out of themselves; not subject to that will and those passions which it is its office to bridle and subdue.

In this sense the restraints on men, as well as their liberties, are to be reckoned among their rights. But as the liberties and the restrictions vary with times and circumstances, and admit of infinite modifications, they cannot be settled upon any abstract rule; and nothing is so foolish as to discuss them upon that principle.

The state ought to be considered as something better than a partnership agreement in a trade of pepper and coffee, calico or tobacco, to be taken up for a little temporary interest, and to be dissolved by the fancy of the parties. It is to be looked on with reverence, because it is not a partnership in things subservient only to the gross animal existence of a temporary and perishable nature.

The state is a partnership in all science, a partnership in all art, a partnership in every virtue and in all perfection. As the ends of such a partnership cannot be attained in many generations, it becomes a partnership not only between those who are living, but between those who are living, those who are dead, and those who are to be born. People will not look forward to posterity who never look backward to their ancestors.

Each contract of each particular state is but a clause in the great primeval

contract of eternal society, linking the lower with the higher natures, connecting the visible and the invisible world according to a fixed compact sanctioned
by the inviolable oath which holds all physical and all moral natures each to
their appointed places.

The "rights of man" are not the foundation of the state. They are
not "prior" to the state. Indeed, they are made possible by the state;
and the foundation of anything is not to be sought in that which the
things in question makes possible. What then does he think about the
"real" rights of men which *proceed* from political organization?

I am far from denying the real rights of men. In denying their false claims
of right, I do not mean to injure those which are real, and are such as their
pretended rights would totally destroy. If civil society be made for the advantage of man, all the advantages for which it is made become his right.

Men have right to the fruits of their industry, and to the means of making
their industry fruitful. They have a right to the acquisitions of their parents;
to the nourishment and improvement of their offspring; to instruction in life,
and to consolation in death. Whatever each man can separately do, without
trespassing upon others, he has a right to do for himself, and he has a right to
a fair portion of all which society, with all its combination of skill and force,
can do in his favor.

In this partnership all men have equal rights, but not to equal things. He
that has but five shilling in the partnership, has as good a right to it as he that
has five hundred pounds has to his larger proportion. But he has not a right
to an equal dividend in the product in the joint stock, and as to the share of
power, authority, and direction which each individual ought to have in the
management of the state, that I must deny to be amongst the direct original
rights of man in civil society; for I have in my contemplation the civil social
man, and no other. It is a thing to be settled by convention.

Circumstances (which with some gentlemen pass for nothing) give in reality to every political principle its distinguishing color and discriminating effect.
The circumstances are what render every civil and political scheme beneficial
or noxious to mankind.

I must be tolerably sure, before I venture publicly to congratulate men
upon a blessing, that they have really received one. Flattery corrupts both the
receiver and the giver, and adulation is not of more service to people than to
kings. I should therefore suspend my congratulations on the acquisition of liberties, until I was informed how it had been combined with government; with
public force; with the discipline and obedience of armies; with the collection
of an effective and well-distributed revenue; with morality and religion; with
solidity and property; with peace and order; with civil and social manners.

All these (in their way) are good things too, and, without them, liberty is not a benefit whilst it lasts, and it is not likely to continue long. The effect of liberty to individuals is that they may do what they please; we ought to see what it will please them to do, before we risk congratulations, which may be soon turned into complaints. Prudence would dictate this in the case of separate, insulated, private men; but liberty, when men act in bodies, is power. Considerate people, before they declare themselves, will observe the use which is made of power, and particularly of so trying a thing as new power in new persons, of whose principles, tempers, and dispositions, they have little or no experience, and in situations where those who appear the most stirring in the scene may possibly not be the real movers.

I flatter myself that I love a manly, moral, regulated liberty as well as any gentleman, be he who he will; and perhaps I have given as good proofs of my attachments to that cause, in the whole course of my public conduct. I think I envy liberty as little as they do, to any other nation. But I cannot stand forward, and give praise or blame to anything which relates to human actions, and human concerns, on a simple view of the object, as it stands stripped of every relation, in all the nakedness and solitude of abstraction.

Is it because liberty in the abstract may be classed amongst the blessings of mankind, that I am seriously to felicitate a madman, who has escaped from the protecting restraint and wholesome darkness of his cell, on his restoration to the enjoyment of life and liberty? Am I to congratulate a highwayman and murderer, who has broke prison, upon the recovery of his natural rights?

If true rights and liberties presuppose government, and therefore, coercion, the question, as in Rousseau, presents itself: What is the best form of government? Again as in Rousseau, the answer is an aristocracy. But where Rousseau had suggested an elective, Burke suggests a natural aristocracy. Thus:

Believe me, those who attempt to level never equalize. In all societies, consisting of various descriptions of citizens, some description must be uppermost. The levelers therefore only change and pervert the natural order of things; they load the edifice of society, by setting up in the air what the solidity of the structure requires to be on the ground. Tailors and carpenters cannot be equal to the situation, into which, by the worst of usurpations, an usurpation on the prerogatives of nature, you attempt to force them.

You will hear it said that all occupations are honorable. If this means only that no honest employment was disgraceful, it does not go beyond the truth. But in asserting that anything is honorable, we imply some distinction in its favor. The occupation of a hairdresser, or of a working tallow chandler, cannot be a matter of honor to any person—to say nothing of a number of other more servile employments. Such men ought not to suffer oppression from the state, but the state suffers oppression, if such as they, either individually or collectively, are permitted to rule. In this you think you are combatting prejudice, but you are at war with nature.

A true natural aristocracy is not a separate interest in the state, or separable from it. It is an essential integrant part of any large body rightly constituted. It is formed out of a class of legitimate presumptions, which, taken as generalities, must be admitted for actual truths. To be bred in a place of estimation; to see nothing low and sordid from one's infancy; to be taught to respect oneself; to be habituated to the censorial inspection of the public eye; to look early to public opinion; to stand upon such elevated ground as to be enabled to take a large view of the widespread and infinitely diversified combinations of men and affairs in a large society; to have leisure to read, to reflect, to converse; to be enabled to draw the court and attention of the wise and learned wherever they are to be found; to be habituated to command and to obey; to be taught to despise danger in the pursuit of honor and duty; to be formed to the greatest degree of vigilance, foresight, and circumspection, in a state of things in which no fault is committed with impunity, and the slightest mistakes draw on the most ruinous consequences; to be led to a guarded and regulated conduct, from a sense that you are considered as an instructor of your fellow citizens in their highest concerns, and that you act as a reconciler between God and man; to be employed as an administrator of law and justice, and to be thereby amongst the first benefactors to mankind; to be a professor of high science, or of liberal and ingenuous art; to be amongst rich traders, who from their success are presumed to have sharp and vigorous understandings, and to possess the virtues of diligence, order, constancy, and regularity, and to have cultivated an habitual regard to commutative justice—these are the circumstances of men that form what I should call a *natural* aristocracy, without which there is no nation.

Men, qualified in the manner I have just described, form in nature, as she operates in the common modification of society, the leading, guiding, and governing part. It is the soul to the body, without which the man does not exist. To give therefore no more importance, in the social order, to such men, than that of so many units, is a horrible usurpation.

When great multitudes act together, under that discipline of nature, I recognize the people. I acknowledge something that perhaps equals, and ought always to guide the sovereignty of convention. In all things the voice of this grand chorus of national harmony ought to have a mighty and decisive influence.

But when you disturb this harmony; when you break up this beautiful order, this array of truth and nature, as well as of habit and prejudice; when you separate the common sort of men from their proper chieftains so as to form them into an adverse army, I no longer know that venerable object called *the people* in such a disbanded race of deserters and vagabonds. For a while they may be terrible indeed, but in such a manner as wild beasts are terrible.

The mind owes to them no sort of submission. They are, as they have been reputed, rebels.

Woe to the country which would madly and impiously reject the service of the talents and virtues, civil, military, or religious, that are given to grace and serve it, and would condemn to obscurity everything formed to diffuse luster and glory around a state. Woe to that country too that, passing into the opposite extreme, considers a low education, a mean contracted view of things, a sordid, mercenary occupation, as a preferable title to command.

He wishes to be clear about one point. His doctrine of a natural aristocracy does not commit him to a theory of government by lords and dukes. Thus:

I am accused of being a man of aristocratic principles. If by *aristocracy* they mean the peers, I have no vulgar admiration, nor any vulgar antipathy, toward them; I hold their order in cold and decent respect. I hold them to be of absolute necessity in the constitution, but I think they are only good when kept within their proper bounds.

I am no friend to aristocracy, in the sense at least in which that word is usually understood. If it were not a bad habit to moot cases on the supposed ruin of the constitution, I should be free to declare that, if it must perish, I would rather by far see it resolved in any other form than lost in that austere and insolent domination.

Do not imagine that I wish to confine power, authority, and distinction to blood and names and titles. There is no qualification for government but virtue and wisdom, actual or presumptive. Wherever they are actually found, they have, in whatever state, condition, profession or trade, the passport of Heaven to human place and honor.

From the notion of a natural aristocracy, Burke returns to his earlier theme that government is justified by reason of the fact that men have duties which they need to have enforced. He desires to point out that "duties" is a basic notion, and that duties are seldom a matter of choice:

Look through the whole of life, and the whole system of duties. Much the strongest moral obligations are such as were never the result of our option.

I cannot too often recommend it to the serious consideration of all men, who think civil society to be within the province of moral jurisdiction, that if we owe to it any duty, it is not subject to our will. Duties are not voluntary. *Duty* and *will* are even contradictory terms.

Men without their choice derive benefits from association; without their choice they are subjected to duties in consequence of these benefits; and without their choice they enter into a virtual obligation as binding as any that is actual. Look through the whole of life and the whole system of duties. Much the strongest moral obligations are such as were never the result of our option.

When we marry, the choice is voluntary, but the duties are not matter of choice. They are dictated by the nature of the situation. Dark and inscrutable are the ways by which we come into the world. The instincts which give rise to this mysterious process of nature are not of our making. But out of physical causes, unknown to us, perhaps unknowable, arise moral duties, which as we are able perfectly to comprehend, we are bound indispensably to perform.

Parents may not be consenting to their moral relation; but consenting or not, they are bound to a long train of burdensome duties toward those with whom they have never made a convention of any sort. Children are not consenting to their relation, but their relation, without their actual consent, binds them to its duties, or rather it implies their consent, because the presumed consent of every rational creature is in unison with the predisposed order of things.

Nor are we left without powerful instincts to make this duty as grateful to us, as it is awful and coercive. Our country is not a thing of mere physical locality. It consists, in a great measure, in the ancient order into which we are born. We may have the same geographical situation, but another country; as we may have the same country, in another soil. The place that determines our duty to our country is a social civil relation.

Obviously, the notion of duties contains problems. There is always the problem of a clash between duties and rights. There is, too, the more difficult problem of a clash between one duty and another, and of deciding when, precisely, one is confronted with a duty. Burke acknowledges all this, but would not emphasize it:

I admit, indeed, that in morals, as in all things else, difficulties will sometimes occur. Duties will sometimes cross one another. Then questions will arise: Which of them is to be placed in subordination? Which of them may be entirely superseded? These doubts give rise to that part of moral science called *casuistry*. It requires a very solid and discriminating judgment, great modesty and caution, and much sobriety of mind in the handling; else there is a danger that it may totally subvert those offices which it is its object only to methodize and reconcile.

Duties, at their extreme bounds, are drawn very fine, so as to become almost evanescent. In that state some shade of doubt will always rest upon these questions, when they are pursued with subtlety. But the very habit of stating these extreme cases is not very laudable or safe, because, in general, it is not right to turn our duties into doubts. They are imposed to govern our conduct, not to exercise our ingenuity; and therefore, our opinions about them ought not to be in a state of fluctuation, but steady, sure, and resolved.

Amongst these nice, and therefore, dangerous points of casuistry, may be reckoned the question so much agitated at the present hour—whether, after the people have discharged themselves of their original power by an habitual delegation, no occasion can possibly occur which may justify the resumption of it. This question, in this latitude, is very hard to affirm or deny, but I am satisfied that no occasion can justify such a resumption, which would not equally authorize a dispensation with any other moral duty, perhaps with all of them together.

However, if, in general, it be not easy to determine concerning the lawfulness of such devious proceedings, which must be ever on the edge of crimes, it is far from difficult to see the perilous consequences of the resuscitation of such a power in the people. The practical consequences of any political tenet go a great way in deciding upon its value. Political problems do not primarily concern truth or falsehood. They relate to good or evil. What in the result is likely to produce evil, is politically false; that which is productive of good politically true.

The natural conservative in him has the floor by now. He cannot abide the thought of all the nice problems in casuistry which he sees rising before him:

I confess, I never liked this continual talk of resistance and revolution, or the practice of making the extreme medicine of the constitution its daily bread. It renders the habit of society dangerously valetudinarian; it is taking periodical doses of mercury sublimate, and swallowing down repeated provocatives of cantharides to our love of liberty.

As it was not made for common abuses, so it is not to be agitated by common minds. The speculative line of demarcation, where obedience ought to end, and resistance must begin, is faint, obscure, and not easily definable. It is not a single act, or a single event, which determines it. Governments must be abused and deranged indeed, before it can be thought of, and the prospect of the future must be as bad as the experience of the past.

The subversion of a government, to deserve any praise, must be considered but as a step preparatory to the formation of something better, either in the scheme of the government itself, or in the persons who administer it, or in both. These events cannot in reason be separated.

This, I think, may be safely affirmed: that a sore and pressing evil is to be removed, and a good, great in its amount and unequivocal in its nature, must be probable almost to certainty, before the inestimable price of our own morals, and the well-being of a number of our fellow citizens, is paid for a revolution. If ever we ought to be economists even to parsimony, it is in the voluntary production of evil. Every revolution contains in it something of evil.

The burden of proof lies heavily on those who tear to pieces the whole frame and contexture of their country, that they could find no other way of settling a government fit to obtain its rational ends, except that which they have pursued by means unfavorable to all the present happiness of millions of people, and to the utter ruin of several hundreds of thousands.

It is not worth our while to discuss, like sophisters, whether, in no case, some evil, for the sake of some benefit, is to be tolerated. Nothing universal can be rationally affirmed on any moral, or any political subject. Pure abstraction does not belong to these matters. The lines of morality are not like ideal lines of mathematics. They are broad and deep as well as long. They admit of exceptions; they demand modifications. These exceptions and modifications are not made by the process of logic, but by the rules of prudence.

This line of argument against emancipation by citing hard cases reaches its high point in the paragraphs which follow:

I would not exclude alteration, but even when I changed, it should be to preserve, not to destroy. I should be led to my remedy by a great grievance. In what I did, I should follow the example of our ancestors. I would make the reparation as nearly as possible in the style of the building. We know that we have made no discoveries, and we think that no discoveries are to be made, in morality; nor many in the great principles of government; nor in the ideas of liberty, which were understood long before we were born, altogether as well as they will be after the grave has heaped its mold upon our presumption, and the silent tomb shall have imposed its law on our pert loquacity.

Prejudice is of ready application in the emergency; it previously engages the mind in a steady course of wisdom and virtue, and does not leave the man hesitating in the moment of decision, sceptical, puzzled, and unresolved. Prejudice renders a man's virtue his habit, and not a series of unconnected acts. Through just prejudice, his duty becomes a part of his nature.

Prescription [i.e., tradition] is the most solid of all titles, not only to property, but, which is to secure that property, to government. All titles terminate in prescription. Nor is prescription of government formed upon blind unmeaning prejudices for man is a most unwise and most wise being. The individual is foolish . . . but the species is wise, and when time is given to it, as a species it almost always acts right.

If you apprehend that on a concession you shall be pushed by metaphysical process to the extreme lines, and argued out of your whole authority, my advice is this: When you have recovered your old, your strong, your tenable position, then face about—stop short—do nothing more—reason not at all—oppose the ancient policy and practice as a rampart against the speculations of innovators on both sides of the question, and you will stand on great, manly, and sure ground.

We are afraid to put men to live and trade each on his own private stock of reason . . . individuals would do better to avail themselves of the general bank and capital of nations and of ages. Thanks to our sullen resistance to innovation, thanks to the cold sluggishness of our national character, we still bear the stamp of our forefathers.

Burke has one last point to make. It is that politics, like morals, is based ultimately on religion. This is the taproot of his conservatism. He begins:

Nothing is more certain than that manners, civilization, and all good things connected with manners and civilization, have, in this European world of ours, depended for ages upon two principles, and were indeed the result of both combined: I mean, the spirit of a gentleman and the spirit of religion.

We know, and what is better, we feel inwardly that religion is the basis of civil society, and the source of all good and all comfort; that on religion, according to our mode, all our laws and institutions stand as upon their base.

The religious sense of mankind, like a wise architect, hath built up the august fabric of states; like a provident proprietor, to preserve the structure from profanation and ruin, as a sacred temple purged from all the impurities of fraud and violence and injustice and tyranny, it hath solemnly and forever consecrated the commonwealth and all that officiate therein.

This consecration is made that all who administer in the government of men should have high and worthy notions of their function and destination; that their hope should be full of immortality; that they should not look to the paltry pelf of the moment, nor to the temporary and transient praise of the vulgar, but to a solid, permanent existence, in the permanent part of their nature, and to a permanent fame and glory, in the example they leave as a rich inheritance to the world.

This principle ought to be impressed, even more strongly, upon the minds of those who compose the collective sovereignty. For the people at large can never become the subject of punishment by any human hand. They ought therefore to be persuaded that they are fully as little entitled and far less qualified, with safety to themselves, to use any arbitrary power whatsoever; that they are not, under a false show of "liberty," tyranically to exact, from those who officiate in the state, an abject submission to their occasional will.

When the people have emptied themselves of all the lust of selfish will, which without religion it is utterly impossible they ever should; when they are conscious that they exercise a power, which to be legitimate must be according to that eternal and immutable law in which will and reason are the same, they will be more capable how they place power in base and incapable hands.

In their nomination to office they will not appoint to the exercise of authority as to a pitiful job, but as to a holy function; not according to their sordid selfish interest, nor to their wanton caprice, nor to their arbitrary will. They will confer that power, which any man may well tremble to give or to receive, on those only in whom they discern a predominant portion of active virtue and wisdom.

Those who form their opinions on such grounds as they ought to form them, conceive that He who gave our nature to be perfected by our virtue willed also the necessary means to its perfection. He willed therefore the state. He willed its connection with the source and original archetype of all perfection.

Those who believe that God willed the state think some part of the wealth of the country is as usefully employed in maintaining a church and a clergy as in fomenting the luxury of individuals. It is the public ornament. It is the public consolation. It nourishes the public hope. The poorest man finds his own importance and dignity in it. It is for the man in humble life—to raise his nature, to put him in mind of a state in which the privileges of opulence will cease, when he will be equal by nature, and may be more than equal by virtue—that his portion of the general wealth of the country is thus employed and sanctified.

The awful author of our being is the author of our place in the order of existence. Having disposed and marshalled us by a divine tactic, not according to our will, but according to His, He has, in and by that disposition, virtually subjected us to act the part which belongs to the place assigned us. We have obligations to mankind at large, which are not in consequence of any special voluntary pact. They arise from the relation of man to man, and the relation of man to God, which relations are not matters of choice.

An "alliance" between church and state in a Christian commonwealth is, in my opinion an idle and a fanciful speculation. An alliance is between two things that are in their nature distinct and independent, such as between two sovereign states. But in a Christian commonwealth, the church and state are one and the same thing, being different integral parts of the same whole.

Religion is so far, in my opinion, from being out of the province or duty of a Christian magistrate that it is, and ought to be, not only his care, but the principal thing in his care; because it is one of the great bonds of human society.

Against infidels [i.e., unbelievers] I would have the laws rise in all their terrors. . . . I would cut up the very root of atheism. The infidels are outlaws of the constitution; not of this country, but of the human race. They are never to be supported, never to be tolerated.

The concluding paragraphs sum up the argument. Rights and liberties are products of the political organization of society. In the political organization of society one is confronted, largely, with matters of tradition—*prescription* is his word—matters of slow growth and gradual change:

> From Magna Charta to the Declaration of Right, it has been the uniform policy of our constitution to claim and assert our liberties as an entailed inheritance from our forefathers and to be transmitted to our posterity; as an estate, specially belonging to the people of this realm without any reference whatever to any other more general or prior right.
>
> By thus regarding our liberties as an entailed inheritance, our constitution preserves a unity in the great multiplicity of its parts. We have an inheritable crown; an inheritable peerage; and a house of commons and a people inheriting privileges, franchises, and liberties, from a long line of ancestors.
>
> This policy appears to me to be the result of profound reflection; or rather, the happy effect of following nature, which is wisdom without reflection, and above it. The idea of inherited liberties, rights, and privileges furnishes a sure principle of conservation and transmission, without at all excluding a principle of improvement. It leaves acquisition free, but it secures what it acquires. Whatever advantages are obtained, are locked fast as in a sort of family settlement, grasped as in a kind of mortmain forever.
>
> We receive, we hold, we transmit our government and our privileges, in the same manner in which we enjoy and transmit our property and our lives. The institutions of policy, the goods of fortune, the gifts of Providence, are handed down to us and from us in the same course and order. Our political system is placed in a just correspondence and symmetry with that mode of existence decreed to a permanent body composed of transitory parts, by the disposition of a stupendous wisdom, molding together the great mysterious incorporation of the human race, the whole at one time, is never old or middle-aged or young, but in a condition of unchangeable constancy moves on through the varied tenor of perpetual decay, fall, renovation, and progression.
>
> By preserving thus the method of nature in the conduct of the state, in what we improve we are never wholly new; in what we retain, we are never wholly obsolete. By adhering in this manner and on those principles to our forefathers, we are guided, not by the superstition of antiquarians but by the spirit of philosophic analogy. In this choice of entailment, inheritance, we have given to our frame of polity the image of a relation in blood; binding up the constitution of our country with our dearest domestic ties; adopting our fundamental laws into the bosom of our family affections; keeping inseparable, and cherishing with the warmth of all their combined and mutually reflected charities, our state, our hearths, our sepulchers, and our altars.
>
> We procure reverence to our civil institutions on the principle upon which nature teaches us to revere individual men, on account of their age, and on account of those from whom they are descended. All your sophisters cannot

produce anything better adapted to preserve a rational and manly liberty than the course we have pursued, who have chosen our nature rather than our speculations, our breasts rather than our inventions, for the great conservatories and magazines of our rights and privileges.

A politic caution, a guarded circumspection, a moral timidity, were among the ruling principles of our forefathers in their most decided conduct. They were not illuminated with that "light of reason," of which the gentlemen of France tell us they have got so abundant a share. They acted under a strong sense of the ignorance and fallibility of mankind. He that made them thus fallible, rewarded them for having in their conduct attended to their nature. Let us imitate their caution, if we wish to deserve their fortune or retain their bequests. Let us add, if we please; but let us preserve what they have left; let us be satisfied to admire, rather than attempt to follow in their desperate flights the aeronauts of France.

Note on Sources. The Burke materials in this section are quoted, abridged, or paraphrased from three sources: his *Reflections on the Revolution in France*, his *Appeal from the New to the Old Whigs*, and his *Letter to a Noble Lord*. The passages from each of these three books do not occur as continuous sequences; that is, you cannot refer any sequence of passages, as a set, to any one of those books. The "themes" were established, and then passages relevant to each "theme" were taken from one or other of the books and strung together.

Reading References. John Maccun has a good book, *The Political Philosophy of Burke*. It is not easy reading. Lord Morley has done the Burke volume in the *English Men of Letters* series. It is easier reading. Chapter 6 in Volume One and Chapter 1 in Volume Two of C. E. Vaughan's *Studies in the History of Political Philosophy* are good. Chapters 8, 10, and 11 in Sir Leslie Stephen's *English Thought in the Eighteenth Century* are also good. An interesting contrast between author and subject will be found in Harold Laski's pages on Burke in *Political Thought in England from Locke to Bentham*. A good recent biography will be found in R. H. Murray's *Edmund Burke*. But better than any of these would be a careful reading of Burke's *Letter to a Noble Lord*, *Appeal from the New to the Old Whigs*, or any hundred pages from his *Reflections*.

The following are some books published since 1940:

Barry, L. *Our Legacy from Burke.*
Canavan, F. P. *The Political Reason of Edmund Burke.*
Cone, C. B. *Burke and the Nature of Politics*, Vol. I.

Copeland, T. W. *Our Eminent Friend Edmund Burke.*
Graubard, S. R. *Burke, Disraeli and Churchill.*
Hoffman, R. J. *Edmund Burke, New York Agent.*
Lucas, F. L. *The Art of Living: Hume, Walpole, Burke, Franklin.*
Mahoney, T. H. D. *Edmund Burke and Ireland.*
Oliver, R. T. *Four Who Spoke Out.*
Osborn, A. M. *Rousseau and Burke: A Study in the Idea of Liberty in Eighteenth Century Political Thought.*
Parkin, C. *The Moral Basis of Burke's Political Thought.*
Reynolds, E. E. *Edmund Burke: Christian Statesman.*
Stanlis, P. J. *Edmund Burke and the Natural Law.*
Utley, T. E. *Edmund Burke.*

READING QUESTIONS

1. Burke says somewhere that God willed (or wills) the state for man so that by the exercise of his virtues he might perfect his nature. Aside from how Burke knew this, what questions would that statement enable you to put to him?
2. He rejects the radical-revolutionary theory of "the people as sovereign." (a) What was that theory? (b) Any three of his reasons for rejecting it.
3. He rejects the radical-revolutionary theory of "the rights of man." (a) What was that theory? (b) Any two of his reasons for rejecting it.
4. Would you say that Burke held the "contract theory" as you find it in either Hobbes or Rousseau?
5. "I am far from denying the real rights of man." His position here. Use what he says about men's right to liberty as an example.
6. His theory of a true natural aristocracy. (a) State it. (b) Does it commit him to dukes and lords? (c) What conception of "the people" it leads him to.
7. Why he would emphasize "the duties of man" rather than "the rights of man."
8. How the notion of duty leads him to the notion of casuistry. Policy he recommends in that connection.
9. Is he categorically opposed to revolution, subversion?
10. Why he defends prejudice and prescription.
11. Why he rejects the notion of an alliance between church and state. What he would do about religious unbelievers.

12. What it means to regard liberties as an "entailed" inheritance. Why he would recommend a people so to regard them. Advantages which we (the English) have derived from so regarding them.

13. Wherein you find Burke (a) most (b) least convincing.

5. PRINCIPLES OF COMMUNISM —FROM KARL MARX

From Burke to Marx. We have been examining important theses about the state propounded by James I, Hobbes, Rousseau, and Burke. James I's thesis was that God gives kings the right to rule over states; and that, in the exercise of this right they are answerable to Him, not to their subjects. This was the doctrine of the divine right of kings. Hobbes' thesis was that states must have governments, and that governments must exercise a monopoly of coercive restraint over their peoples; otherwise there is anarchy or the threat of it, and that is the death of a state. There is not a great difference here between Hobbes and Rousseau. The latter's thesis is that the coercive restraint which a government, acting in the name of the state, exercises over a people, is justified when it is done in the name of the common good. Burke's thesis is that God wills the state, as a mode of living, for men so that by the exercise of their virtues they may perfect their natures. Left to themselves men would not do this. Hence a state needs a government to enforce the exercise of human virtues. A government should consist of a state's natural aristocracy, those who know the good for man and desire that it shall prevail. Each of these writers has more to say than what is here represented by his central thesis.

A lively turn in this protracted argument is introduced by Karl Marx's "economic interpretation" of the life of the state. The thesis is this: a state contains two great economic classes, one of which owns the materials and means of economic production, the other of which works for those who own. Referring to his own period in history, Marx spoke of the bourgeois or capitalist class, and the proletariat or wage-earning class. A society is organized as a state because in that way the bourgeoisie is able to use the government to rule over the proletariat. Between the property-owning class and the wage-earning class there is an irreconcilable antagonism. A government exercises a monopoly of legal violence to further and protect the class interests of the bourgeoisie.

Marx had also an historical thesis about the state. It was to this effect: in earlier times the antagonism had been between the feudal landowning class and the emerging bourgeois capital-owning class. The latter broke the feudal state as a way of achieving their political emancipation. Hence the feudal state was succeeded by the capitalist or bourgeois state. In time, the proletariat will break the bourgeois state as a way of achieving *their* political emancipation. Hence the bourgeois state will be succeeded by the proletariat state. The task of the Communist Party, he says, is to organize the proletariat so that this one-class state may be achieved.

Biographical Note. Marx was born in 1818 and died in 1883 at the age of sixty-five. He was educated in the universities at Bonn and Berlin, beginning with law, but subsequently devoting his entire attention to philosophy. Hegelianism was the fashionable doctrine at the time. It found no favor with young Marx. So, when he graduated and looked about for a job teaching philosophy, he found no openings. For the next few years, amid a life of newspaper work and radical agitation, he devoted his spare time to working out his economic interpretation of history. By 1848 he had joined the Communist League. For it he wrote the celebrated *Manifesto*. Exiled from Germany, from Belgium, from France, he settled in London. From here, in 1864, he organized the First International. In 1867 he published Volume One of *Capital*. The remainder was edited and published by Engels after Marx's death. In life, judged by ordinary standards, he was unhappy, unsuccessful, and largely unknown. In death he has become, like Darwin and Freud and Einstein, one of the makers of the modern mind.

The Argument of the Manifesto. The history of all hitherto existing society is the history of class struggles. In early modern times the bourgeosie triumphed over the feudal masters. They thus became masters of the modern world. An account of their multifarious doings. They have, among other things, brought into being a new class, the proletariat. The class struggle is now between bourgeosie and proletariat. When the latter win out, as they are destined to do, the world will see its first classless society. The bourgeois economy will be replaced by the communist economy. Injustices arising out of the fact that modern society has been, in respect to production and distribution, a capitalist economy, will cease to exist. The text:

A spectre is haunting Europe—the spectre of Communism. All the powers of old Europe have entered into a holy alliance to exorcise this spectre; Pope and Czar, Metternich and Guizot, French Radicals and German police-spies.

Where is the party in opposition that has not been decried as communistic by its opponents in power? Where the Opposition that has not hurled back the branding reproach of Communism, against the more advanced opposition parties, as well as against its reactionary adversaries?

Two things result from this fact.

I. Communism is already acknowledged by all European Powers to be itself a Power.

II. It is high time that Communists should openly, in the face of the whole world, publish their views, their aims, their tendencies, and meet this nursery tale of the Spectre of Communism with a Manifesto of the party itself.

To this end, Communists of various nationalities have assembled in London, and sketched the following manifesto, to be published in the English, French, German, Italian, Flemish and Danish languages.

BOURGEOIS AND PROLETARIANS

The history of all hitherto existing society is the history of class struggles.

Freeman and slave, patrician and plebeian, lord and serf, guild-master and journeyman, in a word, oppressor and oppressed, stood in constant opposition to one another, carried on an uninterrupted, now hidden, now open fight, a fight that each time ended, either in a revolutionary re-constitution of society at large, or in the common ruin of the contending classes.

In the earlier epochs of history, we find almost everywhere a complicated arrangement of society into various orders, a manifold gradation of social rank. In ancient Rome we have patricians, knights, plebeians, slaves; in the middle ages, feudal lords, vassals, guild-masters, journeymen, apprentices, serfs; in almost all of these classes, again, subordinate gradations.

The modern bourgeois society that has sprouted from the ruins of feudal society, has not done away with class antagonisms. It has but established new classes, new conditions of oppression, new forms of struggle in place of the old ones.

Our epoch, the epoch of the bourgeoisie, possesses, however, this distinctive feature; it has simplified the class antagonisms. Society as a whole is more and more splitting up into two great hostile camps, into two great classes directly facing each other: Bourgeoisie and Proletariat.

From the serfs of the middle ages sprang the chartered burghers of the earliest towns. From these burgesses the first elements of the bourgeoisie were developed.

The discovery of America, the rounding of the Cape, opened up fresh ground for the rising bourgeoisie. The East-Indian and Chinese markets, the colonization of America, trade with the colonies, the increase in the means of exchange and in commodities generally, gave to commerce, to navigation, to industry, an impulse never before known, and thereby, to the revolutionary element in the tottering feudal society, a rapid development.

The feudal system of industry, under which industrial production was monopolized by closed guilds, now no longer sufficed for the growing wants of the new markets. The manufacturing system took its place. The guild-masters were pushed on one side by the manufacturing middle-class; division of labor between the different corporate guilds vanished in the face of division of labor in each single workshop.

Meantime the markets kept ever growing, the demand, ever rising. Even manufacture no longer sufficed. Thereupon, steam and machinery revolutionized industrial production. The place of manufacture was taken by the giant, Modern Industry, the place of the industrial middle-class, by industrial millionaires, the leaders of whole industrial armies, the modern bourgeois.

Modern industry has established the world-market, for which the discovery of America paved the way. This market has given an immense development to commerce, to navigation, to communication by land. This development has, in its turn, reacted on the extension of industry; and in proportion as industry, commerce, navigation, railways extended, in the same proportion the bourgeoisie developed, increased its capital, and pushed into the background every class handed down from the Middle Ages.

We see, therefore, how the modern bourgeoisie is itself the product of a long course of development, of a series of revolutions in the modes of production and of exchange.

Each step in the development of the bourgeoisie was accompanied by a corresponding political advance of that class. An oppressed class under the sway of the feudal nobility, an armed and self-governing association in the mediaeval commune, here independent urban republic (as in Italy and Germany), there taxable "third estate" of the monarchy (as in France), afterwards, in the period of manufacture proper, serving either the semifeudal or the absolute monarchy as a counterpoise against the nobility, and, in fact, cornerstone of the great monarchies in general, the bourgeoisie has at last, since the establishment of Modern Industry and of the world-market, conquered for itself, in the modern representative State, exclusive political sway. The executive of the modern State is but a committee for managing the common affairs of the whole bourgeoisie.

The bourgeoisie, historically, has played a most revolutionary part.

The bourgeoisie, wherever it has got the upper hand, has put an end to all feudal, patriarchal, idyllic relations. It has pitilessly torn asunder the motley feudal ties that bound man to his "natural superiors," and has left remaining no other nexus between man and man than naked self-interest, than callous "cash payment." It has drowned the most heavenly ecstasies of religious fervor, of chivalrous enthusiasm, of philistine sentimentalism, in the icy water of egotistical calculation. It has resolved personal worth into exchange value, and in place of the numberless indefeasible chartered freedoms, has set up that single,

unconscionable freedom—Free Trade. In one word, for exploitation, veiled by
religious and political illusions, it has substituted naked, shameless, direct, brutal exploitation.

The bourgeoisie has stripped of its halo every occupation hitherto honored
and looked up to with reverent awe. It has converted the physician, the lawyer,
the priest, the poet, the man of science, into its paid wage-laborers.

The bourgeoisie has torn away from the family its sentimental veil, and
has reduced the family relation to a mere money relation.

The bourgeoisie has disclosed how it came to pass that the brutal display
of vigor in the Middle Ages, which Reactionists so much admire, found its
fitting complement in the most slothful indolence. It has been the first to show
what man's activity can bring about. It has accomplished wonders far surpass-
ing Egyptian pyramids, Roman aqueducts, and Gothic cathedrals; it has conducted expeditions that put in the shade all former Exoduses of nations and
crusades.

The bourgeoisie cannot exist without constantly revolutionizing the instruments of production, and thereby the relations of production, and with
them the whole relations of society. Conservation of the old modes of production in unaltered form, was, on the contrary, the first condition of existence
for all earlier industrial classes. Constant revolutionizing of production, uninterrupted disturbance of all social conditions, everlasting uncertainty and
agitation distinguish the bourgeois epoch from all earlier ones. All fixed, fast-
frozen relations, with their train of ancient and venerable prejudices and opinions, are swept away, all new-formed ones become antiquated before they can
ossify. All that is solid melts into air, all that is holy is profaned, and man is at
last compelled to face, with sober senses, his real conditions of life, and his
relations with his kind.

The need of a constantly expanding market for its products chases the
bourgeoisie over the whole surface of the globe. It must nestle everywhere,
settle everywhere, establish connections everywhere.

The bourgeoisie has through its exploitation of the world-market given a
cosmopolitan character to production and consumption in every country. To
the great chagrin of Reactionists, it has drawn from under the feet of industry
the national ground on which it stood. All old-established national industries
have been destroyed or are daily being destroyed. They are dislodged by new
industries, whose introduction becomes a life and death question for all civilized nations, by industries that no longer work up indigenous raw material,
but raw material drawn from the remotest zones; industries whose products
are consumed, not only at home, but in every quarter of the globe. In place
of the old wants, satisfied by the productions of the country, we find new
wants, requiring for their satisfaction the products of distant lands and climes.
In place of the old local and national seclusion and self-sufficiency, we have
intercourse in every direction, universal inter-dependence of nations. And as

in material, so also in intellectual production. The intellectual creations of individual nations become common property. National one-sidedness and narrow-mindedness become more and more impossible, and from the numerous national and local literatures there arises a world-literature.

The bourgeoisie, by the rapid improvement of all instruments of production, by the immensely facilitated means of communication, draws all, even the most barbarian, nations into civilization. The cheap prices of its commodities are the heavy artillery with which it batters down all Chinese walls, with which it forces the barbarians' intensely obstinate hatred of foreigners to capitulate. It compels all nations, on pain of extinction, to adopt the bourgeois mode of production; it compels them to introduce what it calls civilization into their midst, i.e., to become bourgeois themselves. In a word, it creates a world after its own image.

The bourgeoisie has subjected the country to the rule of the towns. It has created enormous cities, has greatly increased the urban population as compared with the rural, and has thus rescued a considerable part of the population from the idiocy of rural life. Just as it has made the country dependent on the towns, so it has made barbarian and semi-barbarian countries dependent on the civilized ones, nations of peasants on nations of bourgeois, the East on the West.

The bourgeoisie keeps more and more doing away with the scattered state of the population, of the means of production, and of property. It has agglomerated population, centralized means of production, and has concentrated property in a few hands. The necessary consequence of this was political centralization. Independent, or but loosely connected provinces, with separate interests, laws, governments and systems of taxation, became lumped together in one nation, with one government, one code of laws, one national class-interest, one frontier and one customs-tariff.

The bourgeoisie, during its rule of scarce one hundred years, has created more massive and more colossal productive forces than have all preceding generations together. Subjection of Nature's forces to man, machinery, application of chemistry to industry and agriculture, steam-navigation, railways, electric telegraphs, clearing of whole continents for cultivation, canalization of rivers, whole populations conjured out of the ground—what earlier century had even a presentiment that such productive forces slumbered in the lap of social labor?

We see then: the means of production and of exchange on whose foundation the bourgeoisie built itself up, were generated in feudal society. At a certain stage in the development of these means of production and of exchange, the conditions under which feudal society produced and exchanged, the feudal organization of agriculture and manufacturing industry, in one word, the feudal relations of property became no longer compatible with the already developed productive forces; they became so many fetters. They had to burst asunder; they were burst asunder.

Into their places stepped free competition, accompanied by a social and political constitution adapted to it, and by the economical and political sway of the bourgeois class.

A similar movement is going on before our own eyes. Modern bourgeois society with its relations of production, of exchange and of property, a society that has conjured up such gigantic means of production and of exchange, is like the sorcerer, who is no longer able to control the powers of the nether world whom he has called up by his spells. For many a decade past the history of industry and commerce is but the history of the revolt of modern productive forces against modern conditions of production, against the property relations that are the conditions for the existence of the bourgeoisie and of its rule. It is enough to mention the commercial crises that by their periodical return put on its trial, each time more threateningly, the existence of the entire bourgeois society. In these crises a great part not only of the existing products, but also of the previously created productive forces, are periodically destroyed. In these crises there breaks out an epidemic that, in all earlier epochs, would have seemed an absurdity—the epidemic of over-production. Society suddenly finds itself put back into a state of momentary barbarism; it appears as if a famine, a universal war of devastation had cut off the supply of every means of subsistence; industry and commerce seem to be destroyed; and why? Because there is too much civilization, too much means of subsistence, too much industry, too much commerce. The productive forces at the disposal of society no longer tend to further the development of the conditions of bourgeois property; on the contrary, they have become too powerful for these conditions, by which they are fettered, and so soon as they overcome these fetters, they bring disorder into the whole of bourgeois society, endanger the existence of bourgeois property. The conditions of bourgeois society are too narrow to comprise the wealth created by them. And how does the bourgeoisie get over these crises? On the one hand by enforced destruction of a mass of productive forces; on the other, by the conquest of new markets, and by the more thorough exploitation of the old ones. That is to say, by paving the way for more extensive and more destructive crises, and by diminishing the means whereby crises are prevented.

The weapons with which the bourgeoisie felled feudalism to the ground are now turned against the bourgeoisie itself.

But not only has the bourgeoisie forged the weapons that bring death to itself; it has also called into existence the men who are to wield those weapons—the modern working-class—the proletarians.

In proportion as the bourgeoisie, i.e., capital, is developed, in the same proportion is the proletariat, the modern working-class, developed, a class of laborers, who live only so long as they find work, and who find work only so long as their labor increases capital. These laborers, who must sell themselves piecemeal, are a commodity, like every other article of commerce, and are con-

sequently exposed to all the vicissitudes of competition, to all the fluctuations
of the market.

Owing to the extensive use of machinery and to division of labor, the
work of the proletarians has lost all individual character, and, consequently,
all charm for the workman. He becomes an appendage of the machine, and it
is only the most simple, most monotonous, and most easily acquired knack that
is required of him. Hence, the cost of production of a workman is restricted,
almost entirely, to the means of subsistence that he requires for his maintenance, and for the propagation of his race. But the price of a commodity,
and also of labor, is equal to its cost of production. In proportion, therefore,
as the repulsiveness of the work increases, the wage decreases. Nay more, in
proportion as the use of machinery and division of labor increases, in the same
proportion the burden of toil also increases, whether by prolongation of the
working hours, by increase of the work enacted in a given time, or by increased speed of the machinery, etc.

Modern industry has converted the little workshop of the patriarchal
master into the great factory of the industrial capitalist. Masses of laborers,
crowded into the factory, are organized like soldiers. As privates of the industrial army they are placed under the command of a perfect heirarchy of
officers and sergeants. Not only are they the slaves of the bourgeois class, and
of the bourgeois State, they are daily and hourly enslaved by the machine, by
the over-looker, and, above all, by the individual bourgeois manufacturer himself. The more openly this despotism proclaims gain to be its end and aim, the
more petty, the more hateful and the more embittering it is.

The less the skill and exertion or strength implied in manual labor, in
other words, the more modern industry becomes developed, the more is the
labor of men superseded by that of women. Differences of age and sex have
no longer any distinctive social validity for the working class. All are instruments of labor, more or less expensive to use, according to their age and sex.

No sooner is the exploitation of the laborer by the manufacturer, so far
at an end, that he receives his wages in cash, than he is set upon by the other
portions of the bourgeoisie, the landlord, the shopkeeper, the pawnbroker, etc.

The lower strata of the middle class—the small tradespeople, shopkeepers,
and retired tradesmen generally, the handicraftsmen and peasants—all these
sink gradually into the proletariat, partly because their diminutive capital does
not suffice for the scale on which Modern Industry is carried on, and is
swamped in the competition with the large capitalists, partly because their specialized skill is rendered worthless by new methods of production. Thus the
proletariat is recruited from all classes of the population.

The proletariat goes through various stages of development. With its birth
begins its struggle with the bourgeoisie. At first the contest is carried on by
individual laborers, then by the workpeople of a factory, then by the operatives
of one trade, in one locality, against the individual bourgeois who directly ex-

ploits them. They direct their attacks not against the bourgeois conditions of production, but against the instruments of production themselves; they destroy imported wares that compete with their labor, they smash to pieces machinery, they set factories ablaze, they seek to restore by force the vanished status of the workman of the Middle Ages.

At this stage the laborers still form an incoherent mass scattered over the whole country, and broken up by their mutual competition. If anywhere they unite to form more compact bodies, this is not yet the consequence of their own active union, but of the union of the bourgeoisie, which class, in order to attain its own political ends, is compelled to set the whole proletariat in motion, and is moreover yet, for a time, able to do so. At this stage, therefore, the proletarians do not fight their enemies, but the enemies of their enemies, the remnants of absolute monarchy, the landowners, the non-industrial bourgeois, the petty bourgeoisie. Thus the whole historical movement is concentrated in the hands of the bourgeoisie; every victory so obtained is a victory for the bourgeoisie.

But with the development of industry the proletariat not only increases in number, it becomes concentrated in greater masses, its strength grows, and it feels that strength more. The various interests and conditions of life within the ranks of the proletariat are more and more equalized, in proportion as machinery obliterates all distinctions of labor, and nearly everywhere reduces wages to the same low level. The growing competition among the bourgeois, and the resulting commercial crises, make the wages of the workers ever more fluctuating. The unceasing improvement of machinery, ever more rapidly developing, makes their livelihood more and more precarious; the collisions between individual workmen and individual bourgeois take more and more the character of collisions between two classes. Thereupon the workers begin to form combinations (Trades' Unions) against the bourgeois; they club together in order to keep up the rate of wages; they found permanent associations in order to make provision beforehand for these occasional revolts. Here and there the contest breaks out into riots.

Now and then the workers are victorious, but only for a time. The real fruit of their battle lies, not in the immediate result, but in the ever-expanding union of the workers. This union is helped on by the improved means of communication that are created by modern industry, and that place the workers of different localities in contact with one another. It was just this contact that was needed to centralize the numerous local struggles, all of the same character, into one national struggle between classes. But every class struggle is a political struggle. And that union, to attain which the burghers of the Middle Ages, with their miserable highways, required centuries, the modern proletarians, thanks to railways, achieve in a few years.

This organization of the proletarians into a class, and consequently into a political party, is continually being upset again by the competition between the workers themselves. But it ever rises up again, stronger, firmer, mightier. It compels legislative recognition of particular interest of the workers, by taking advantage of the divisions among the bourgeoisie itself. Thus the ten-hour bill in England was carried.

Altogether collisions between the classes of the old society further, in many ways, the course of development of the proletariat. The bourgeoisie finds itself involved in a constant battle. At first with the aristocracy; later on, with those portions of the bourgeoisie itself, whose interests have become antagonistic to the progress of industry; at all times, with the bourgeoisie of foreign countries. In all these battles it sees itself compelled to appeal to the proletariat, to ask for its help, and thus, to drag it into the political arena. The bourgeoisie itself, therefore, supplies the proletariat with its own elements of political and general education, in other words, it furnishes the proletariat with weapons for fighting the bourgeoisie.

Further, as we have already seen, entire sections of the ruling classes are, by the advance of industry, precipitated into the proletariat, or are at least threatened in their conditions of existence. These also supply the proletariat with fresh elements of enlightenment and progress.

Finally, in times when the class-struggle nears the decisive hour, the process of dissolution going on within the ruling class, in fact, within the whole range of old society, assumes such a violent, glaring character, that a small section of the ruling class cuts itself adrift, and joins the revolutionary class, the class that holds the future in its hands. Just as, therefore, at an earlier period, a section of the nobility went over to the bourgeoisie, so now a portion of the bourgeoisie goes over to the proletariat, and in particular, a portion of the bourgeois ideologists, who have raised themselves to the level of comprehending theoretically the historical movements as a whole.

Of all the classes that stand face to face with the bourgeoisie today, the proletariat alone is a really revolutionary class. The other classes decay and finally disappear in the face of modern industry; the proletariat is its special and essential product.

The lower middle-class, the small manufacturer, the shopkeeper, the artisan, the peasant, all these fight against the bourgeoisie, to save from extinction their existence as fractions of the middle class. They are, therefore, not revolutionary, but conservative. Nay more, they are reactionary, for they try to roll back the wheel of history. If by chance they are revolutionary, they are so, only in view of their impending transfer into the proletariat, they thus defend not their present, but their future interests, they desert their own standpoint to place themselves at that of the proletariat.

The "dangerous class," the social scum, that passively rotting mass thrown off by the lowest layers of old society, may, here and there, be swept into the movement by a proletarian revolution; its conditions of life, however, prepare it far more for the part of a bribed tool of reactionary intrigue.

In the conditions of the proletariat, those of old society at large are already virtually swamped. The proletarian is without property; his relation to his wife and children has no longer anything in common with the bourgeois family-relations; modern industrial labor, modern subjection to capital, the same in England as in France, in America as in Germany, has stripped him of every trace of national character. Law, morality, religion, are to him so many bourgeois prejudices, behind which lurk in ambush just as many bourgeois interests.

All the preceding classes that got the upper hand, sought to fortify their already acquired status by subjecting society at large to their conditions of appropriation. The proletarians cannot become masters of the productive forces of society, except by abolishing their own previous mode of appropriation, and thereby also every other previous mode of appropriation. They have nothing of their own to secure and to fortify; their mission is to destroy all previous securities for, and insurances of, individual property.

All previous historical movements were movements of minorities, or in the interest of minorities. The proletarian movement is the self-conscious, independent movement of the immense majority, in the interest of the immense majority. The proletariat, the lowest stratum of our present society, cannot stir, cannot raise itself up, without the whole superincumbent strata of official society being sprung into the air.

Though not in substance, yet in form, the struggle of the proletariat with the bourgeoisie is at first a national struggle. The proletariat of each country must, of course, first of all settle matters with its own bourgeoisie.

In depicting the most general phases of the development of the proletariat, we traced the more or less veiled civil war, raging within existing society, up to the point where that war breaks out into open revolution, and where the violent overthrow of the bourgeoisie lays the foundation for the sway of the proletariat.

Hitherto, every form of society has been based, as we have already seen, on the antagonism of oppressing and oppressed classes. But in order to oppress a class, certain conditions must be assured it under which it can, at least, continue its slavish existence. The serf, in the period of serfdom, raised himself to membership in the commune, just as the petty bourgeois, under the yoke of feudal absolutism, managed to develop into a bourgeois. The modern laborer, on the contrary, instead of rising with the progress of industry, sinks deeper and deeper below the conditions of existence of his own class. He becomes a pauper, and pauperism develops more rapidly than population and wealth. And here it becomes evident, that the bourgeoisie is unfit any longer to be the ruling class in society, and to impose its conditions of existence upon society as an over-riding law. It is unfit to rule, because it is incompetent to assure an existence to its slave within his slavery, because it cannot help letting him sink into such a state that it has to feed him, instead of being fed by him. Society can no longer live under this bourgeoisie, in other words, its existence is no longer compatible with society.

The essential condition for the existence, and for the sway of the bourgeois class, is the formation and augmentation of capital; the condition for capital is wage-labor. Wage labor rests exclusively on competition between the laborers. The advance of industry, whose involuntary promoter is the bourgeoisie, replaces the isolation of the laborers, due to competition, by their revolutionary combination, due to association. The development of Modern Industry, therefore, cuts from under its feet the very foundation on which the bourgeoisie produces and appropriates products. What the bourgeoisie therefore produces, above all, are its own grave-diggers. Its fall and the victory of the proletariat are equally inevitable.

PROLETARIANS AND COMMUNISTS

In what relation do the Communists stand to the proletarians as a whole?

The Communists do not form a separate party opposed to other working-class parties.

They have no interests separate and apart from those of the proletariat as a whole.

They do not set up any sectarian principles of their own, by which to shape and mould the proletarian movement.

The Communists are distinguished from the other working class parties by this only: 1. In the national struggles of the proletarians of the different countries, they point out and bring to the front the common interests of the entire proletariat independently of all nationality. 2. In the various stages of development which the struggle of the working class against the bourgeoisie has to pass through, they always and everywhere represent the interests of the movement as a whole.

The Communists, therefore, are on the one hand, practically, the most advanced and resolute section of the working class parties of every country, that section which pushes forward all others; on the other hand, theoretically, they have over the great mass of the proletariat the advantage of clearly understanding the line of march, the conditions, and the ultimate general results of the proletarian movement.

The immediate aim of the Communists is the same as that of all the other proletarian parties; formation of the proletariat into a class, overthrow of the bourgeois supremacy, conquest of political power by the proletariat.

The theoretical conclusions of the Communists are in no way based on ideas or principles that have been invented, or discovered, by this or that would-be universal reformer.

They merely express, in general terms, actual relations springing from an existing class struggle, from a historical movement going on under our very eyes. The abolition of existing property relations is not at all a distinctive feature of Communism.

All property relations in the past have continually been subject to historical change consequent upon the change in historical conditions.

The French Revolution, for example, abolished feudal property in favor of bourgeois property.

The distinguishing feature of Communism is not the abolition of property generally, but the abolition of bourgeois property. But modern bourgeois private property is the final and most complete expression of the system of producing and appropriating products, that is based on class antagonism, on the exploitation of the many by the few.

 In this sense, the theory of the Communists may be summed up in the single sentence: Abolition of private property.

We Communists have been reproached with the desire of abolishing the right of personally acquiring property as the fruit of a man's own labor, which property is alleged to be the ground work of all personal freedom, activity and independence.

Hard-won, self-acquired, self-earned property! Do you mean the property of the petty artisan and of the small peasant, a form of property that preceded the bourgeois form? There is no need to abolish that; the development of industry has to a great extent already destroyed it, and is still destroying it daily.

Or do you mean modern bourgeois private property?

But does wage-labor create any property for the laborer? Not a bit. It creates capital, i.e., that kind of property which exploits wage-labor, and which cannot increase except upon condition of getting a new supply of wage-labor for fresh exploitation. Property, in its present form, is based on the antagonism of capital and wage-labor. Let us examine both sides of this antagonism.

To be a capitalist, is to have not only a purely personal, but a social status in production. Capital is a collective product, and only by the united action of many members, nay, in the last resort, only by the united action of all members of society, can it be set in motion.

Capital is therefore not a personal, it is a social power.

When, therefore, capital is converted into common property, into the property of all members of society, personal property is not thereby transformed into social property. It is only the social character of the property that is changed. It loses its class-character.

Let us now take wage-labor.

The average price of wage-labor is the minimum wage, i.e., that quantum of the means of subsistence, which is absolutely requisite to keep the laborer in bare existence as a laborer. What, therefore, the wage-laborer appropriates by means of his labor, merely suffices to prolong and reproduce a bare existence. We by no means intend to abolish this personal appropriation of the products of labor, an appropriation that is made for the maintenance and reproduction of human life, and that leaves no surplus wherewith to command the labor of others. All that we want to do away with is the miserable character of this appropriation, under which the laborer lives merely to increase capital, and is allowed to live only in so far as the interest of the ruling class requires it.

In bourgeois society, living labor is but a means to increase accumulated labor. In communist society, accumulated labor is but a means to widen, to enrich, to promote the existence of the laborer.

In bourgeois society, therefore, the past dominates the present; in communist society, the present dominates the past. In bourgeois society capital is independent and has individuality, while the living person is dependent and has no individuality.

And the abolition of this state of things is called by the bourgeois, abolition of individuality and freedom! And rightly so. The abolition of bourgeois individuality, bourgeois independence, and bourgeois freedom is undoubtedly aimed at.

By freedom is meant, under the present bourgeois conditions of production, free trade, free selling and buying.

But if selling and buying disappears, free selling and buying disappears also. This talk about free selling and buying, and all the other "brave words" of our bourgeoisie about freedom in general, have a meaning, if any, only in contrast with restricted selling and buying, with the fettered traders of the Middle Ages, but have no meaning when opposed to the Communistic abolition of buying and selling, of the bourgeois conditions of production, and of the bourgeoisie itself.

You are horrified at our intending to do away with private property. But in your existing society, private property is already done away with for nine-tenths of the population; its existence for the few is solely due to its non-existence in the hands of those nine-tenths. You reproach us, therefore, with intending to do away with a form of property, the necessary condition for whose existence is, the non-existence of any property for the immense majority of society.

In one word, you reproach us with intending to do away with your property. Precisely so; that is just what we intend.

From the moment when labor can no longer be converted into capital, money, or rent, into a social power capable of being monopolized, i.e., from the moment when individual property can no longer be transformed into bourgeois property, into capital, from that moment, you say, individuality vanishes.

You must, therefore, confess that by "individual" you mean no other person than the bourgeois, than the middle-class owner of property. This person must, indeed, be swept out of the way, and made impossible.

Communism deprives no man of the power to appropriate the products of society: all that it does is to deprive him of the power to subjugate the labor of others by means of such appropriation.

It has been objected, that upon the abolition of private property all work will cease, and universal laziness will overtake us.

According to this, bourgeois society ought long ago to have gone to the dogs through sheer idleness; for those of its members who work, acquire nothing, and those who acquire anything, do not work. The whole of this objection is but another expression of the tautology: that there can no longer be any wage-labor when there is no longer any capital.

All objections urged against the Communistic mode of producing and appropriating material products, have, in the same way, been urged against the Communistic modes of producing and appropriating intellectual products. Just as, to the bourgeois, the disappearance of class property is the disappearance of production itself, so the disappearance of class culture is to him identical with the disappearance of all culture.

That culture, the loss of which he laments, is, for the enormous majority, a mere training to act as a machine.

But don't wrangle with us so long as you apply, to our intended abolition of bourgeois property, the standard of your bourgeois notions of freedom, culture, law, etc. Your very ideas are but the outgrowth of the conditions of your bourgeois production and bourgeois property, just as your jurisprudence is but the will of your class made into a law for all, a will, whose essential character and direction are determined by the economic conditions of existence of your class.

The selfish misconception that induces you to transform into eternal laws of nature and of reason, the social forms springing from your present mode of production and form of property—historical relations that rise and disappear in the progress of production—this misconception you share with every ruling class that has preceded you. What you see clearly in the case of ancient property, what you admit in the case of feudal property, you are of course forbidden to admit in the case of your own bourgeois form of property.

Abolition of the family! Even the most radical flare up at this infamous proposal of the Communists.

On what foundation is the present family, the bourgeois family, based? On capital, on private gain. In its completely developed form this family exists only among the bourgeoisie. But this state of things finds its complement in the practical absence of the family among the proletarians, and in public prostitution.

The bourgeois family will vanish as a matter of course when its complement vanishes, and both will vanish with the vanishing of capital.

Do you charge us with wanting to stop the exploitation of children by their parents? To this crime we plead guilty.

But, you will say, we destroy the most hallowed of relations, when we replace home education by social.

And your education! Is not that also social, and determined by the social conditions under which you educate, by the intervention, direct or indirect, of society by means of schools, etc.? The Communists have not invented the intervention of society in education; they do but seek to alter the character of that intervention, and to rescue education from the influence of the ruling class.

The bourgeois clap-trap about the family and education, about the hallowed co-relation of parent and child, becomes all the more disgusting, the more, by the action of Modern Industry, all family ties among the proletarians are torn asunder, and their children transformed into simple articles of commerce and instruments of labor.

But you Communists would introduce community of women, screams the whole bourgeoisie in chorus.

The bourgeois sees in his wife a mere instrument of production. He hears that the instruments of production are to be exploited in common, and, naturally, can come to no other conclusion, than that the lot of being common to all will likewise fall to the women.

He has not even a suspicion that the real point aimed at is to do away with the status of women as mere instruments of production.

For the rest, nothing is more ridiculous than the virtuous indignation of our bourgeois at the community of women which, they pretend, is to be openly and officially established by the Communists. The Communists have no need to introduce community of women; it has existed almost from time immemorial.

Our bourgeois, not content with having the wives and daughters of their proletarians at their disposal, not to speak of common prostitutes, take the greatest pleasure in seducing each other's wives.

Bourgeois marriage is in reality a system of wives in common and thus, at the most, what the Communists might possibly be reproached with, is that they desire to introduce, in substitution for a hypocritically concealed, an openly legalized community of women. For the rest, it is self-evident, that the abolition of the present system of production must bring with it the abolition of the community of women springing from the system, i.e., of prostitution both public and private.

The Communists are further reproached with desiring to abolish countries and nationalities.

The working men have no country. We cannot take from them what they have not got. Since the proletariat must first of all acquire political supremacy, must rise to be the leading class of the nation, must constitute itself the nation, it is, so far, itself national, though not in the bourgeois sense of the word.

National differences, and antagonisms between peoples, are daily more and more vanishing, owing to the development of the bourgeoisie, to freedom of commerce, to the world-market, to uniformity in the mode of production and in the conditions of life corresponding thereto.

The supremacy of the proletariat will cause them to vanish still faster. United action, of the leading civilized countries at least, is one of the first conditions for the emancipation of the proletariat.

In proportion as the exploitation of one individual by another is put an end to, the exploitation of one nation by another will also be put an end to. In proportion as the antagonism between classes within the nation vanishes, the hostility of one nation to another will come to an end.

The charges against Communism made from a religious, a philosophical, and generally, from an ideological standpoint, are not deserving of serious examination.

Does it require deep intuition to comprehend that man's ideas, views, and conceptions, in one word, man's consciousness, changes with every change in the conditions of his material existence, in his social relations and in his social life?

What else does the history of ideas prove, than that intellectual production changes in character in proportion as material production is changed? The ruling ideas of each age have ever been the ideas of its ruling class.

When people speak of ideas that revolutionize society, they do but express the fact, that within the old society, the elements of a new one have been created, and that the dissolution of the old ideas keeps even pace with the dissolution of the old conditions of existence.

When the ancient world was in its last throes, the ancient religions were overcome by Christianity. When Christian ideas succumbed in the 18th century to rationalist ideas, feudal society fought its death-battle with the then revolutionary bourgeoisie. The ideas of religious liberty and freedom of conscience, merely gave expression to the sway of free competition within the domain of knowledge.

"Undoubtedly," it will be said, "religious, moral, philosophical, and juridical ideas have been modified in the course of historical development. But religion, morality, philosophy, political science, and law, constantly survived this change.

"There are, besides, eternal truths, such as Freedom, Justice, etc., that are common to all states of Society. But Communism abolishes eternal truths, it abolishes all religion, and all morality, instead of constituting them on a new basis; it therefore acts in contradiction to all past historical experience."

What does this accusation reduce itself to? The history of all past society has consisted in the development of class antagonisms, antagonisms that assumed different forms at different epochs.

But whatever form they may have taken, one fact is common to all past ages, viz., the exploitation of one part of society by the other. No wonder, then, that the social consciousness of past ages, despite all the multiplicity and variety it displays, moves within certain common forms, or general ideas, which cannot completely vanish except with the total disappearance of class antagonisms.

The Communist revolution is the most radical rupture with traditional property-relations; no wonder that its development involves the most radical rupture with traditional ideas.

But let us have done with the bouregois objections to Communism.

We have seen above that the first step in the revolution by the working class is to raise the proletariat to the position of ruling class, to win the battle of democracy.

The proletariat will use its political supremacy, to wrest, by degrees, all capital from the bourgeoisie, to centralize all instruments of production in the hands of the State, i.e., of the proletariat organized as the ruling class; and to increase the total of productive forces as rapidly as possible.

Of course, in the beginning, this cannot be effected except by means of despotic inroads on the rights of property, and on the conditions of bourgeois production; by means of measures, therefore, which appear economically insufficient and untenable, but which, in the course of the movement, outstrip themselves, necessitate further inroads upon the old social order, and are unavoidable as a means of entirely revolutionizing the mode of production.

These measures will of course be different in different countries.

Nevertheless in the most advanced countries the following will be pretty generally applicable:

1. Abolition of property in land and application of all rents of land to public purposes.

2. A heavy progressive or graduated income tax.

3. Abolition of all right of inheritance.

4. Confiscation of the property of all emigrants and rebels.

5. Centralization of credit in the hands of the State, by means of a national bank with State capital and an exclusive monopoly.

6. Centralization of the means of communication and transport in the hands of the State.

7. Extension of factories and instruments of production owned by the State; the bringing into cultivation of waste lands, and the improvement of the soil generally in accordance with a common plan.

8. Equal liability of all to labor. Establishment of industrial armies, especially for agriculture.

9. Combination of agriculture with manufacturing industries; gradual abolition of the distinction between town and country, by a more equable distribution of population over the country.

10. Free education for all children in public schools. Abolition of children's

factory labor in its present form. Combination of education with industrial production, etc., etc.

When, in the course of development, class distinctions have disappeared, and all production has been concentrated in the hands of a vast association of the whole nation, the public power will lose its political character. Political power, properly so called, is merely the organized power of one class for oppressing another. If the proletariat during its contest with the bourgeoisie is compelled, by the force of circumstances, to organize itself as a class, if, by means of a revolution, it makes itself the ruling class, and, as such, sweeps away by force the old conditions of production, then it will, along with these conditions, have swept away the conditions for the existence of class antagonisms, and of classes generally, and will thereby have abolished its own supremacy as a class.

In place of the old bourgeois society, with its classes and class antagonisms, we shall have an association, in which the free development of each is the condition for the free development of all.

Position of the Communists in Relation to the Various Existing Opposition Parties

Section II [p. 413] has made clear the relations of the Communists to the existing working class parties, such as the Chartists in England and the Agrarian Reformers in America.

The Communists fight for the attainment of the immediate aims, for the enforcement of the momentary interests of the working class; but in the movement of the present, they also represent and take care of the future of that movement. In France the Communists ally themselves with the Social-Democrats, against the conservative and radical bourgeoisie, reserving, however, the right to take up a critical position in regard to phrases and illusions traditionally handed down from the great Revolution.

In Switzerland they support the Radicals, without losing sight of the fact that this party consists of antagonistic elements, partly of Democratic Socialists, in the French sense, partly of radical bourgeois.

In Poland they support the party that insists on an agrarian revolution, as the prime condition of national emancipation, that party which fomented the insurrection of Cracow in 1846.

In Germany they fight with the bourgeoisie whenever it acts in a revolutionary way, against the absolute monarchy, the feudal squirearchy, and the petty bourgeoisie.

But they never cease, for a single instant, to instill into the working class the clearest possible recognition of the hostile antagonism between bourgeoisie and proletariat, in order that the German workers may straightway use, as so many weapons against the bourgeoisie, the social and political conditions that the bourgeoisie must necessarily introduce along with its supremacy, and in order that, after the fall of the reactionary classes in Germany, the fight against the bourgeoisie itself may immediately begin.

The Communists turn their attention chiefly to Germany, because that country is on the eve of a bourgeois revolution, that is bound to be carried out under more advanced conditions of European civilization, and with a more developed proletariat, than that of England was in the seventeenth, and of France in the eighteenth century, and because the bouregois revolution in Germany will be but the prelude to an immediately following proletarian revolution.

In short, the Communists everywhere support every revolutionary movement against the existing social and political order of things.

In all these movements they bring to the front, as the leading question in each, the property question, no matter what its degree of development at the time.

Finally, they labor everywhere for the union and argeement of the democratic parties of all countries.

The Communists disdain to conceal their views and aims. They openly declare that their ends can be attained only by the forcible overthrow of all existing social conditions. Let the ruling classes tremble at a Communistic revolution. The proletarians have nothing to lose but their chains. They have a world to win.

Working men of all countries, unite!

Note on Sources. The above material comprises sections I, II, and IV of Karl Marx and Friedrich Engels, *The Manifesto of the Communist Party.* Section III is omitted.

Reading References. For Marx as philosopher, one can consult Sidney Hook's book, *Toward an Understanding of Karl Marx.* It may be supplemented by the same author's paper on "Marxism" in his volume, *Reason, Social Myth, and Democracy.* Bertrand Russell's *Freedom versus Organization* is also excellent on Marx as theoretical philosopher. A. D. Lindsay's little book, *Karl Marx's Capital* is well worth the effort required to read it.

For Marx as social critic, one can consult Edmund Wilson's book, *To The Finland Station.* This is one of the finest pieces of historical writing so far published upon the revolutionary movement. Less deftly written, but valuable, is Max Nomad's *Apostles of Revolution.*

The standard biography of Marx is by Franz Mehring. Another, not so exhaustive, by Otto Ruhle, is good reading. A short work, *Karl Marx,* by I. Berlin, in the *Home University Library* series, is perhaps the best single item for busy students.

The following are some books published since 1940:

Adams, H. P. *Karl Marx in His Earlier Writing.*

Balz, A. G. A. *The Value Doctrine of Karl Marx.*

Barzun, J. *Darwin, Marx, Wagner.*

Berlin, I. *Karl Marx: His Life and Environment.*

Bernal, J. D. *Marx and Science.*

Bernstein, S. (ed.). *A Centenary of Marxism.*

Bloom, S. F. *The World of Nations.*

Bober, M. M. *Karl Marx's Interpretation of History.* 2nd ed., rev.

Browder, E. R. *Marx and America.*

Cameron, J. M. *Scrutiny of Marxism.*

Cole, G. D. H. *Meaning of Marxism.*

Cornu, A. *Origins of Marxian Thought.*

Dunayevskaya, R. *Marxism and Freedom.*

Eastman, M. *Marxism: Is It a Science?*

Eaton, J. *Marx against Keynes.*

Gesell, S. *Karl Marx in Error.*

Hook, S. (ed.). *Marx and the Marxists.*

Hunt, R. N. C. *Marxism, Past and Present.*

Jackson, J. H. *Marx, Proudhon and European Socialism.*

Kenafick, K. J. *Michael Bakunin and Karl Marx.*

Leontiev, L. A. *Marx's Capital.*

Lindsay, J. *Marxism and Contemporary Science.*

Macek, J. *Essay on the Impact of Marxism.*

Mitrany, D. *Marx against the Peasant.*

Pappenheim, F. *The Alienation of Modern Man.*

Petersen, A. *Karl Marx and Marxian Science.*

Robinson, J. *An Essay on Marxian Economics.*

Schlesinger, R. *Marx: His Time and Ours.*

Schwartzchild, L. *The Red Prussian: The Life and Legend of Karl Marx.*

Sprigge, C. J. S. *Karl Marx.*

Sweezy, P. M. *The Theory of Capitalist Development: Principles of Marxian Political Economy.*

Tsuru, S. *Essays on Marxian Economics.*

Turner, J. K. *Challenge to Karl Marx.*

Wilson, E. *To the Finland Station.*

READING QUESTIONS

1. Marx's footnote definition of (a) bourgeoisie and (b) proletariat.
2. What about the history of all hitherto existing society? Who are the "antagonistic classes" in our epoch?
3. To what medieval economic groups does he trace the bourgeoisie? How did geographical discovery lead to the overthrow of feudalism?
4. Elucidate: "The bourgeoisie is the product of . . . a series of revolutions in the modes of production and exchange."
5. The development of the bourgeoisie as an economic class was accompanied by their political advance. Cite an example.
6. Elucidate: "The executive of the modern state is but a committee for managing the common affairs of the whole bourgeoisie."
7. The bourgeoisie, historically, has played a most revolutionizing part. Mention three examples.
8. They cannot exist without constantly revolutionizing the instruments of production. Why not? (See No. 4 above.)
9. What about the bourgeoisie "during its rule of scarce one hundred years"?
10. Elucidate: "Modern bourgeois society . . . is like the sorcerer. . . ."
11. What "crises" and "epidemics" mark the career of the bourgeois economy? How are they dealt with?
12. What class has the bourgeoisie called into existence? How?
13. The proletariat is recruited from all classes of society. How so?
14. The proletariat goes through various stages of development. Mention two.
15. What "division among the bourgeoisie itself" produced the ten-hour bill in England?
16. The bourgeoisie supplies the proletariat with its own political and general education. Why? With what result?
17. A portion of the bourgeois ideologists goes over to the proletariat. When? Which portion?
18. Why the proletariat is today the only revolutionary class.
19. To the proletariat "law, morality, religion" are so many bourgeois prejudices: Why?
20. "The bourgeoisie is unfit any longer to be the ruling class in society." Why so?
21. Elucidate: "The bourgeoisie produces its own gravediggers."
22. What is the relation of the communist party to the proletarian class?
23. Marx mentions five or six bourgeois objections to communism. Namely. How does he handle any two of these?

24. The 10-point program is suggested as a step toward abolishing what? Show, for any two of these, how they would be that.

25. What is the position of the communists in relation to the various existing opposition parties?

26. This document deals with three groups (bourgeoisie, proletariat, communist). What, briefly, is the relation between bourgeoisie, and proletariat, proletariat and communist, and therefore between bourgeoisie and communist?

6. THE STATE AND SUPREME COERCIVE POWER —FROM H. J. LASKI

From Marx and Engels to Laski. Marx looked upon a society as fundamentally an economy, an economic order, a community of persons organized to make possible production by division of labor and distribution by exchange. If this is the fundamental fact about a society, you have the question: Why, in addition to being an economic order, is a society also, and equally obviously, a political order, a state, a community organized to make law possible? That is to say, if a society is fundamentally a community organized to facilitate production and distribution, economic activities, why is it politically organized at all? Why does an economic order require to be organized as a political order, an order permitting government to use supreme coercive power to enforce laws in the name of the society? Marx, Engels, and the Marxists have their theory about this. It can be seen in Marx' and Engels' *Communist Manifesto,* in Engels' *Socialism: Utopian and Scientific,* and in H. J. Laski's *History of Liberalism.* That theory is advanced to account for what is admitted to be fact, namely that societies *are* political orders—states, communities organized to make law and therefore government possible. This fact, if it is a fact, is itself worth considering, apart from any theory advanced to account for it. Such a consideration is provided in the opening chapter of Professor Laski's book, *The State in Theory and Practice.* His presentation of these matters, apart from the Marxist theory which, in the rest of the book he advances to account for these matters, is a useful concluding summary for this entire chapter. Apart from his Marxism, Professor Laski's statement would read well to Hobbes and Rousseau.

Biographical Note. Harold J. Laski was born in 1893 and died in 1950 at the age of 57. At the time of his death he was the author of more than a score of widely-read books on political questions in the modern world. Among the best-known of these were *The Problem of Sovereignty* (1917), *Authority in the Modern State* (1919), *The Foundations of Sov-*

ereignty (1921), *A Grammar of Politics* (1925) and *The Rise of European Liberalism* (1936). Mr. Laski was educated at Manchester Grammar School and New College, Oxford. During the eleven years 1914–1925, he taught at McGill University, Harvard University, Yale University and Magdalen College, Oxford. In 1926 he became Professor of Political Science in the University of London, retaining that position for many years thereafter. His participation in politics included membership of the Executive Committees of the Fabian Society (1922) and the Labor Party (1936–1949).

Professor Laski begins with a definition of society. On that he will build definitions of state, government, and law.

We have to begin with definitions. We find ourselves living in a society with other men. That society is integrated into a unity we call the state. As a state, its affairs are administered by a body of persons we call the government. What do these terms mean?

A society is a group of human beings living together and working together for the satisfaction of their mutual wants. The basic wants are economic: they must earn their living before they begin to live well. But beyond bare economic needs there is every variety of want—religious, cultural, domestic.

The societies with which we are concerned—such as England, France, Germany, the United States, Russia—are groups of human beings, differentiated from other groups by sharing in certain traditions—political, psychological, linguistic, or whatever they may be—which separate them from the rest of mankind. They are societies which, over a long period of history, have assumed the form of a national state.

At this point we get the definition which is primary in Professor Laski's whole position in his volume, *The State in Theory and Practice*.

A state is a society of this kind which is integrated by possessing a coercive authority legally supreme over any individual or group which is part of the society. A society is a state when the way of life to which both individuals and associations must conform is defined by a coercive authority binding upon them all. The French state, for example, is a territorial society, divided into government and subjects, whether individuals or associations, whose relationships are determined by the exercise of this supreme coercive power.

This supreme coercive power is called sovereignty; and it is by the possession of sovereignty that the state is distinguished from all other forms of human association. A municipality is a territorial society divided into government and subjects; so also may be a trade union or a church. But none of

AN INTRODUCTION TO MODERN PHILOSOPHY

these possesses supreme coercive power. The state gives orders to all and receives orders from none. Its orders are binding upon all who come within its
jurisdiction.

The attribution of sovereignty to the state is description, not valuation.
It says nothing of the wisdom or justice that may or may not be inherent
in the will of the state. It says only that the state is supreme over all other
forms of association because it is formally competent to bind them to obedience
without itself being bound. It may, in fact, be unwise or unjust in what it
commands; but neither unwisdom nor injustice makes any difference to the
formal legal right of the state to exact and enforce obedience to its orders.

The state, then, is a way of organizing the collective life of a given society. Since its coercive power is supreme, there is, in theory, no activity
within its jurisdiction the character of which it may not seek to define.

Anyone who considers the extent of the functions of the modern state
will not be tempted to underestimate the reality of its sovereign power. Defence and police. The control of industry. Social legislation, including functions so far-reaching as education and insurance against sickness and unem-
ployment. The encouragement of scientific research. The operation, with all
its immense consequences, of a system of currency. The power of taxation.
The definition of the terms upon which men may, for their various purposes,
associate together. The maintenance of a system of courts in which its own
legal principles will be given effect no matter what person or persons may be
involved. Merely to take a rapid view of its outstanding functions is to realize the degree to which it pervades and permeates. The modern citizen is
enmeshed at every turn in the network of its operations.

Professor Laski is retracing steps taken by Rousseau in the *Social
Contract:* there is society; some societies are states; a state needs a government. A government, though essential to a state, should not be identified
with a state.

The state needs a body of men to operate, in its name, the supreme coercive authority of which it disposes. This body of men is the government.

The government is the agent of the state. It is not itself the supreme coercive power. It is the mechanism of administration which gives effect to the
purposes of that power. It is not sovereign in the sense in which the state is
sovereign. Its competence is defined by such authority as the state may choose
to confer upon it. If it oversteps that authority it may be called to account.
Even a ruler so powerful as the President of the United States must find authority for the exercise of his will either in the Constitution or in some
power legally granted to him thereunder by Congress. There are even states
which expressly forbid their governments, by Constitutions under which those

governments must act, to take certain types of power or to exercise others in certain ways.

The purpose of distinguishing between state and government is to emphasize the limitation upon the latter so to act that it pay proper regard to the end for which the state exists. That end, however variously defined, is the creation of those conditions under which the members of the state may attain the maximum satisfaction of their desires.

The expedients of limitation—e.g., a written constitution, a bill of rights, the separation of powers, etc.—are all methods which experience has suggested to prevent abuse of the state's sovereign power by the government which acts in its name.

Every government is composed of fallible men. They may deliberately exploit the authority they possess for their own selfish purposes. They may mistake the private interests of a few for the well-being of the whole community. They may be ignorant of the position they confront, or incompetent in handling it. The value of the distinction between state and government is the possibility it offers of creating institutional mechanisms for changing the agents of the state, i.e., the government, when the latter is inadequate to its responsibilities.

Governments exercise, in the name of the state, supreme coercive power, a monopoly of legal violence. For this reason governments need control of armed forces, e.g., police and military.

The state is built upon the ability of its government to operate successfully its supreme coercive power. Its authority depends upon the power to coerce the opponents of the government, to break their wills, to compel them to submit. This emerges as the central fact in the nature of the state.

A state whose purposes are challenged has to respond to the challenge or change its purposes. If it proposes to maintain them, it must do so by force. It must therefore have at its command coercive instruments, separate from the mass of the population, upon whom it can rely to enforce its authority. The basis of sovereignty is the power to use armed forces to compel obedience.

Critical challenge to law involves a threat to order; and every government will use the armed forces to preserve it. Where it cannot use those forces, it must change the law or abdicate. The armed forces are there to protect the sovereignty which the government exercises in the name of the state. Those therefore who control the use of the armed forces are in fact the masters of its sovereignty. From this angle the state may be regarded as a method of organizing the public power of coercion so that the will of the government may prevail.

The legal right to coercion distinguishes the government of a state from the government of all other associations. The authority of a trade union, or a church, over its members, is never a coercive authority. It can only become such when the state decides to support the trade union or the church. The sanction of that support is the knowledge that behind the decision of the state is the coercive power of the armed forces upon whose services its rulers are legally entitled to rely.

My discussion, so far, has not been concerned with the purposes the state announces itself as seeking to fulfil. Whatever its purposes, the state is a powerful organization relying upon its legal title to coerce for the ultimate enforcement of its will. In the last resort, the armed forces are the instrument of this enforcement.

One large and essential task, performed by government acting as agent for state, is the devising, revising, administering, and enforcing of law. A law can be thought of as a command issued by government in the name of state. This defines or describes a law; but it does not enable you to distinguish between a good law and a bad law, does not enable you to criticize a law. Professor Laski moves along from society, state, government, and armed forces to this matter of law; first conceiving of it, as he says, "formally," then as an object of possible criticism.

Once we accept the idea of the state as sovereign, law can be nothing but the will of the state. Granted the nature of sovereignty, law must be that which the state is prepared to enforce. Juristically, the content of the law is a matter of indifference. It may be unwise or mistaken or wrong. The jurist excludes all considerations of what is ethically right or socially expedient. He considers as law only that which emanates from the will of the sovereign. Any other question is meta-jurisprudence, and so outside his province. To translate law into justice takes him from the pure theory of law into political philosophy. He has then to consider questions of value, the answers to which are undiscoverable upon the plane of formal law.

The human mind, it may be said, revolts from a jurisprudence as bare and formal as that. It remembers the long medieval effort to identify law with the will of God. The stoic notion of law as the expression of universal reason. Ulpian's conception of law as the science of distinguishing between right and wrong in human conduct. It rejects the idea of law as simply that behind which there is the sovereign power of the state. It feels that law, to be law, must correspond with something more valid than the will of an authority which grounds its claim to respect upon nothing more than the coercive power at its disposal. As an eminent writer has said, "then one must regard every statute, however absurd, contrary to reason, or despicable, as a true statute, and one is no longer entitled to complain of injustice."

There are two answers. First, any criticism of the pure theory of law is an endeavor to change its postulates because of a dislike of the results to which they formally lead. This is an inadequate methodological procedure. Second, such criticisms are not a theory of what the state actually is. They are a definition of the ends which the state ought to pursue; that is, a criterion by which to judge the practice of states. There is, no doubt, behind them, the whole formidable history of the idea of natural law. They lead from the pure theory of law into political philosophy.

The purposes of a state are always referred, by those who operate its sovereignty, to a criterion of good they are prepared to defend. The defence must be in terms of reason. If it is stated on other grounds, e.g., revelation or force, it has no meaning for those who do not accept the revelation or who deny that force can of itself make a rule of right.

I assume, in this book, that the object of the state must be to fulfil, at the maximum possible, the desires of its citizens.

Thus far: positive law cannot be declared immune to criticism. Positive law therefore presupposes what, in an older language, was called "natural" law; namely, an evaluative principle independent of concrete legislation, with reference to which such legislation can be criticized. Professor Laski has two irons in the fire here. First, he wishes to insist that legislation is not immune to criticism resting upon principles which legislation itself does not supply. The principles upon which you criticize legislation are not themselves the product or outcome of legislation. In the criticism of legislation there are operative principles which are not authorized or certified by legislation. Second, he wishes to indicate what the ultimate principle is, upon which criticism of legislation rests.

If this be true, it follows that the state must aim to satisfy the desires of all its citizens, and to satisfy them in equal measure; unless it can demonstrate, by rational argument, that the good (the desires) of those who are excluded from equal treatment is served by their exclusion. Equality of satisfaction must be the rule. Exceptions can be justified only when it can be rationally shown that the exceptions themselves are a necessary part of the equality aimed at, a logical condition of its fulfilment.

Otherwise the action of the state is biased. Its object is not the maximum possible satisfaction of all citizens but of some only, in whose interest the sovereign power of the state is exerted. Those who exercise the supreme coercive power in the name of the state, must argue that the greater satisfaction secured by the part, results in a greater satisfaction for the rest than could otherwise be secured. When such a case can be made out, differential treatment in the receipt of satisfactions is justified.

When the state maintains such a differentiation it should convince those excluded. Inequalities are not proved to be adequate by securing the assent of those who benefit from them.

Those who make law defend it on the grounds that it is just. They offer arguments to prove that the law which is may be regarded as the law which ought to be. Now, once we admit that there is a law which ought to be, we are admitting the existence of natural law. I take the view that, despite all the difficulties in the way of natural law, the need to postulate it, as an essential part of the philosophy of political obligation, cannot be avoided. None of the arguments by which the critics of natural law have so far sought to destroy it, have been successful. The historical attack on natural law has broken down. The attack of the positivists has broken down. Nor is the relativists attack in any better case. This is not to say that we have an adequate science of natural law. The obstacles in the way are enormous. These obstacles ought to make us humble. But I do not think this humility ought to reconcile us to abandoning the search.

By now Professor Laski has completed his introductory outline. The state is an institution in society which exercises supreme coercive power. The balance of his book is to deal with questions related to the working of this institution in the history of modern nations. Hence the title of the book: *The State in Theory and Practice.* Before moving along from theory to practice, he summarizes his claims as follows:

Let us remind ourselves of the definition with which we started. A state is a society integrated by possessing a coercive authority legally supreme over any individual or group which is part of the society. The state therefore is a special way of exercising power. It is special because it is supreme; and special also because it is coercive. No other authority in society can, save by delegation from the state, dispose of a similar power. Only the state, to put it brutally, has the legal right to kill and imprison its subjects, and to use its armed forces to compel them to accept its decisions.

This state power has to be exercised by men. Those who are entrusted with its exercise constitute the government of the state. Their business is to use the state power for the purposes for which it was instituted. These may be summarized by saying that the end of the state is the satisfaction, at the highest possible level, of its subjects' demands. It follows that the justification of state power, the right to exercise coercive authority, is conditioned by the duty of satisfying demand. The fulfilment of the state purpose can be accomplished only when the incidence of its actions is unbiased. Differential treatment of citizens cannot be justified unless it can be shown that such differentiation secures equally the good of those against whom it works, not less than of those who seem to be benefited by it. These seem to be the assumptions with which we have to start.

Note on Sources. The materials in this section are from Laski's *The State in Theory and Practice*, pp. 8–12, 14–16, 18–23, 78–79, 81–83, 138–139.

Reading References. Further reading should be taken from Professor Laski's *The State in Theory and Practice*, and from other books by him, e.g., *Communism*, *History of Liberalism*, and so forth.

READING QUESTIONS

1. What a state is, according to Professor Laski.
2. How a state gives rise to a government.
3. Why it is well to distinguish between state and government.
4. How the idea of a "state" leads to the idea of "law."
5. How the idea of "law" leads to consideration of questions which "go beyond" law, e.g., into ethics.
6. What is Professor Laski's position in these matters that transcend, go beyond, law?
7. Why his troubled concern over "natural law"?
8. Wherein you find Laski (a) most (b) least convincing.

TOPIC SIX

An Historical Problem

THE PROBLEM STATED

Our first problem arose out of the distinction between nature and God; our second, out of the distinction between appearance and reality; our third, out of the distinction between speculation and knowledge; our fourth, out of the distinction between moral and immoral; our fifth, out of the distinction between society and state. In each case, we have been concerned with the justification for these distinctions, and with the justification for beliefs about the second member of each set. Thus, for example, we distinguish between appearance and reality. With what justification? We proceed to assert beliefs about reality. What beliefs? Upon what grounds can such beliefs be justified?

Our sixth problem arises out of the distinction between event and history. We make this distinction readily enough. We distinguish between the death of Caesar and the history of Rome, between the taking of the Bastille and the history of the French Revolution, between the production of *Hamlet* and the history of Elizabethan drama, between the invention of the steam engine and the history of the Industrial Revolution. We "stumble upon" events in the context of a history. We "understand" events in terms of a history. We "isolate" events within a history. We "abstract" events from a history. We "locate" events by referring them to a history.

What is a *history*? It is not easy to say. We cannot say that a history is "nothing but" the events which "make it up," because an event, in turn, is soon seen to be "nothing but" a moment in its history. These terms are correlative. Each is useless without the other.

If we cannot define *history* in terms of events, except on pain of involving ourselves in a circular definition, can we describe *history* by

432

means of a metaphor? Can we say, that a history is a pattern, a plot, a theme, a motif, a frame, a structure, a plan, a *schema*, an outline? The term *pattern* is perhaps the most neutral of these metaphors. The idea which it is intended to convey is illustrated in the familiar newspaper drawing containing scattered numbers which the reader is invited to connect up by means of lines. The result is a "picture," perhaps of a horse or a man's head. The scattered numbers occur in a pattern. When we first look at them, we do not detect the pattern. Gradually, as we fill in the lines from number to number, we begin to "see" the pattern. It was "there" all the time.

Now, suppose we liken a history to the pattern which is implicit or latent in the scattered numbers in the cartoon. The scattered numbers would be the events. Drawing lines between them would be tracing connections between the events. Seeing the picture which gradually emerges would be grasping the history within which the events occur.

Granted the legitimacy of this pattern metaphor, we can pose the problem of the present topic: What is the pattern which holds the events of history together, which gradually emerges as we fill in the events, which is merely latent in the events considered in their bare particularity? Is there one such pattern which takes in all events? Or many limited patterns? If there are many limited patterns, do they themselves form parts of a more inclusive pattern? If there are many limited patterns, do single events occur in more than one of these? Do they belong equally fundamentally to each of the patterns in which they occur?

We could use this pattern metaphor to avail ourselves of some terminology. The claim that there is "patternedness" we could call historical *rationalism*. The claim that there is one overarching and all-inclusive pattern we could call historical *monism*. The claim that there is more than one pattern, each equally fundamental and irreducible, we could call historical *pluralism*. The claim that there is no pattern, we could call historical *nihilism* or historical *irrationalism*. The claim that we do not know whether there is a pattern we could call historical *skepticism*. The claim that a pattern is something which we arbitrarily impose, one pattern being no more there than any other, we could call historical *subjectivism*.

When we think about events, we use a pattern as an hypothesis. How many facts does it enable us to account for? Does it do this better than any alternative hypothesis? Are there any facts which it ought to account for, but will not? This is not to suggest that historical patterns are merely in our heads. Unless, of course, we would be prepared to admit that the pattern marked out by the planets around the sun, is also merely in our heads; because this pattern we also use as an hypothesis to account for the facts, the observed or recorded positions and changes of the planets.

There are three fundamental types of philosophy of history. The first, historical rationalism, is the claim that there is "patternedness." The second, historical nihilism, is the claim that there is no "patternedness." The third, historical skepticism, is the claim that we do not know whether or not there is "patternedness." What was referred to above as historical subjectivism is a form of historical nihilism. It asserts that the "patternedness" is not there in history, but merely in our heads.

There are accordingly two fundamentally distinct sorts of controversy possible within the field of philosophy of history. (1) The first sort of controversy would be whether historical rationalism, historical nihilism, or historical skepticism can be justified. An extension of this controversy, which would be possible only after historical rationalism had been proved or postulated, would be whether historical monism or historical pluralism has truth on its side. (2) The second sort of controversy, possible only after historical monism or historical pluralism had been proved or postulated, would be over what the pattern is, or what the patterns are, which events hold implicit in their apparent particularity.

The first sort of controversy is not illustrated by any of the authors assembled in this topic. Each of the five is, in his own way, a rationalist. That is, he believes there is a rationale, or pattern, to history. Each differs from the other in respect to what the precise pattern is. Each offers a different interpretation of history. Each reads a different meaning out of the events. The first, reported on by George Santayana, sees in history the realization of God's plan for man's salvation. The second, Kant, sees in history the story of rationality in the social order. The third, Hegel, sees in history the self-realization of the world spirit in the self-realization of individual spirits and nations. The fourth, Engels, sees in history the struggle between economic classes, and the eventual triumph of the proletariat class. The fifth, Spengler, sees in history the recurrence of a cyclical movement which begins in a culture and ends in a civilization.

1. THE BIBLICAL INTERPRETATION OF HISTORY —FROM GEORGE SANTAYANA

Not many persons hold a philosophy of history. The reason may be that they do not know enough history to be able to catch at the notion of a vast pattern detectable amid its manifold particulars. Or it may be that they know too much history, with the result that they are skeptical about any single theme amid so great a welter of particulars. Time was when a majority of persons with any pretensions to historical knowledge would have expressed themselves in no uncertain terms. They would have begun with Creation. They would have continued with the Fall. They would have concluded with the Incarnation, the Crucifixion, the Ascension, the Redemption, the Last Judgment, and the Life to Come. This "golden thread" they would have detected amid the myriad events. This inclusive "meaning" they would have read into or out of the story of the past. In its essentials it has probably been held in the Western world by more people and over a longer period than any other single interpretation of history.

Biographical Note. George Santayana was born in Madrid in 1863 and died in Rome in 1952 at the age of eighty-nine. He lived in the United States from 1872 to 1911 or thereabouts. During that time he obtained his education at Harvard, taught philosophy there for twenty-two years, and taught also for a year (1905–06) at the Sorbonne in Paris. At the time of his death he was the author of a number of widely read books. Among these were the following: *The Sense of Beauty* (1898), *Interpretations of Poetry and Religion* (1900), *The Life of Reason* (1905–06), *Skepticism and Animal Faith* (1923), *The Last Puritan* (1935), and *Persons and Places* (1944).

The Argument of the Citations. The selection which follows is from George Santayana's *Reason in Religion.* It is a report or summary of what might perhaps be called the "biblical" interpretation of history. It should be clear that Santayana does not himself believe this interpretation of history. It requires no comment or summary.

There was in the beginning, so runs the Christian story, a great celestial King, wise and good, surrounded by a court of winged musicians and messengers. He had existed from all eternity, but had always intended, when the right moment should come, to create temporal beings, imperfect copies of himself in various degrees. These, of which man was the chief, began their career in the year 4004 B.C., and they would live on an indefinite time, possibly, that chronological symmetry might not be violated, until A.D. 4004. The opening and close of this drama were marked by two magnificent tableaux.

In the first, in obedience to the word of God, sun, moon, and stars, and earth with all her plants and animals, assumed their appropriate places, and nature sprang into being with all her laws. The first man was made out of clay, by a special act of God, and the first woman was fashioned from one of his ribs, extracted while he lay in a deep sleep. They were placed in an orchard where they often could see God, its owner, walking in the cool of the evening. He suffered them to range at will and eat of all the fruits he had planted save that of one tree only. But they, incited by a devil, transgressed this single prohibition, and were banished from that paradise with a curse upon their head, the man to live by the sweat of his brow and the woman to bear children in labor. These children possessed from the moment of conception the inordinate natures which their parents had acquired. They were born to sin and to find disorder and death everywhere within and without them.

At the same time God, lest the work of his hands should wholly perish, promised to redeem in his good season some of Adam's children and restore them to a natural life. This redemption was to come ultimately through a descendant of Eve, whose foot should bruise the head of the serpent. But it was to be prefigured by many partial and special redemptions. Thus, Noah was to be saved from the deluge, Lot from Sodom, Isaac from the sacrifice, Moses from Egypt, the captive Jews from Babylon, and all faithful souls from heathen forgetfulness and idolatry. For a certain tribe had been set apart from the beginning to keep alive the memory of God's judgments and promises, while the rest of mankind, abandoned to its natural depravity, sank deeper and deeper into crimes and vanities.

The deluge that came to punish these evils did not avail to cure them. "The world was renewed and the earth rose again above the bosom of the waters, but in this renovation there remained eternally some trace of divine vengeance. Until the deluge all nature had been exceedingly hardy and vigorous, but by that vast flood of water which God had spread out over the earth, and by its long abiding there, all saps were diluted; the air, charged with too dense and heavy a moisture, bred ranker principles of corruption. The early constitution of the universe was weakened, and human life, from stretching as it had formerly done to near a thousand years, grew gradually briefer. Herbs and roots lost their primitive potency, and stronger food had to be furnished to man by the flesh of other animals. . . . Death gained upon life, and men felt themselves overtaken by a speedier chastisement. As day by day they sank deeper in their wickedness, it was but right they should daily, as it were, stick faster in their woe. The very change in nourishment made manifest their decline and degradation, since as they became feebler they became also more voracious and bloodthirsty."

Henceforth there were two spirits, two parties, or, as St. Augustine called them, two cities in the world. The City of Satan, whatever its artifices in art, war, or philosophy, was essentially corrupt and impious. Its joy was but a comic mask and its beauty the whitening of a sepulcher. It stood condemned before God and before man's better conscience by its vanity, cruelty, and secret misery, by its ignorance of all that it truly behooved a man to know who was destined to immortality. Lost, as it seemed, within this Babylon, or visible only in its obscure and forgotten purlieus, lived on at the same time the City of God, the society of all the souls predestined to salvation; a city which, however humble and inconspicuous it might seem on earth, counted its myriad transfigured citizens in heaven, and had its destinies, like its foundations, in eternity.

To this City of God belonged, in the first place, the patriarchs and the prophets who, throughout their plaintive and ardent lives, were faithful to what echoes still remained of a primeval revelation, and waited patiently for the greater revelation to come. To the same city belonged the magi who followed a star till it halted over the stable in Bethlehem; Simeon, who divined the present salvation of Israel; John the Baptist, who bore witness to the same and made straight its path; and Peter, to whom not flesh and blood, but the spirit of the Father in Heaven, revealed the Lord's divinity. For salvation had indeed come with the fulness of time, not, as the carnal Jews had imagined it, in the form of an earthly restoration, but through the incarnation of the Son of God in the Virgin Mary, His death upon a cross, His descent into hell, and His resurrection at the third day according to the Scriptures. To the same city belonged finally all those who, believing in the reality and efficacy of Christ's mission, relied on His merits and followed His commandment of unearthly love.

All history was henceforth essentially nothing but the conflict between these two cities: two moralities, one natural, the other supernatural; two philosophies, one rational, the other revealed; two beauties, one corporeal, the other spiritual; two glories, one temporal, the other eternal; two institutions, one the world, the other the church. These, whatever their momentary alliances or compromises, were radically opposed and fundamentally alien to one another. Their conflict was to fill the ages until, when wheat and tares had long flourished together and exhausted between them the earth for whose substance they struggled, the harvest should come; the terrible day of reckoning when those who had believed the things of religion to be imaginary would behold with dismay the Lord visibly coming down through the clouds of heaven, the angels blowing their alarming trumpets, all generations of the dead rising from their graves, and judgment without appeal passed on every man, to the edification of the universal company and his own unspeakable joy or confusion. Whereupon the blessed would enter eternal bliss with God their master and the wicked everlasting torments with the devil whom they served.

The drama of history was thus to close upon a second tableau: long-robed and beatified cohorts passing above, amid various psalmodies, into an infinite luminous space, while below the damned, howling, writhing, and half trans-formed into loathsome beasts, should be engulfed in a fiery furnace. The two cities, always opposite in essence, should thus be finally divided in existence, each bearing its natural fruits and manifesting its true nature.

Let the reader fill out this outline for himself with its thousand details; let him remember the endless mysteries, arguments, martyrdoms, consecrations that carried out the sense and made vital the beauty of the whole. Let him pause before the phenomenon; he can ill afford, if he wishes to understand history or the human mind, to let the apparition float by unchallenged without delivering up its secret. What shall we say of this Christian dream?

Those who are still troubled by the fact that this dream is by many taken for a reality, and who are consequently obliged to defend themselves against it, as against some dangerous error in science or in philosophy, may be allowed to marshal arguments in its disproof. Such, however, is not my intention. Do we marshal arguments against the miraculous birth of Buddha, or the story of Cronos devouring his children? We seek rather to honor the piety and to understand the poetry embodied in those fables. If it be said that those fables are believed by no one, I reply that those fables are or have been believed just as unhesitatingly as the Christian theology, and by men no less reasonable or learned than the unhappy apologists of our own ancestral creeds. Matters of religion should never be matters of controversy. We neither argue with a lover about his taste, nor condemn him, if we are just, for knowing so human a passion. That he harbors it is no indication of a want of sanity on his part in other matters. But while we acquiesce in his experience, and are glad he has it, we need no arguments to dissuade us from sharing it. Each man may have his own loves, but the object in each case is different. And so it is, or should be, in religion. Before the rise of those strange and fraudulent Hebraic pretensions there was no question among men about the national, personal, and poetic character of religious allegiance. It could never have been a duty to adopt a religion not one's own any more than a language, a coinage, or a costume not current in one's own country. The idea that religion contains a literal, not a symbolic, representation of truth and life is simply an impossible idea. Whoever entertains it has not come within the region of profitable philosophizing on that subject. His science is not wide enough to cover all existence. He has not discovered that there can be no moral allegiance except to the ideal. His certitude and his arguments are no more pertinent to the religious question than would be the insults, blows, and murders to which, if he could, he would appeal in the next instance. Philosophy may describe unreason, as it may describe force; it cannot hope to refute them.

The eclectic Christian philosophy thus engendered constitutes one of the most complete, elaborate, and impressive products of the human mind. The ruins of more than one civilization and of more than one philosophy were ransacked to furnish materials for this heavenly Byzantium. It was a myth circumstantial and sober enough in tone to pass for an account of facts, and yet loaded with enough miracle, poetry, and submerged wisdom to take the place of a moral philosophy and present what seemed at the time an adequate ideal to the heart. Many a mortal, in all subsequent ages, perplexed and abandoned in this ungovernable world, has set sail resolutely for that enchanted island and found there a semblance of happiness, its narrow limits give so much room for the soul and its penitential soil breeds so many consolations.

True, the brief time and narrow argument into which Christian imagination squeezes the world must seem to a speculative pantheist childish and poor, involving, as it does, a fatuous perversion of nature and history and a ridiculous emphasis laid on local events and partial interests. Yet just this violent reduction of things to a human stature, this half-innocent, half-arrogant assumption that what is important for a man must control the whole universe, is what made Christian philosophy originally appealing and what still arouses, in certain quarters, enthusiastic belief in its beneficence and finality.

Nor should we wonder at this enduring illusion. Man is still in his childhood; for he cannot respect an ideal which is not imposed on him against his will, nor can he find satisfaction in a good created by his own action. He is afraid of a universe that leaves him alone. Freedom appals him; he can apprehend in it nothing but tedium and desolation, so immature is he and so barren does he think himself to be. He has to imagine what the angels would say, so that his own good impulses (which create those angels) may gain in authority, and none of the dangers that surround his poor life make the least impression upon him until he hears that there are hobgoblins hiding in the wood. His moral life, to take shape at all, must appear to him in fantastic symbols. The history of these symbols is therefore the history of his soul.

Note on Sources. The above passage is quoted from George Santayana's, *Life of Reason*, Volume II: *Reason in Religion*, Chapter 6, "*The Christian Epic.*"

READING QUESTIONS

1. When did men begin their career?
2. Why might their career close in 4004 A.D.?
3. "The opening and close of this drama were marked by two magnificent tableaux." What drama? What tableaux?
4. "They transgressed this single prohibition." Who did? What prohibition? With what result? How is this episode described in theological or biblical language?
5. "It was to be prefigured with many partial and special redemptions." What was? By whom?
6. Why was the deluge sent? What results did it produce?
7. Contrast the City of Satan and the City of God.
8. "Two moralities." Namely?
9. "Two philosophies." Namely?
10. "Two beauties." Namely?
11. "Two glories." Namely?
12. "Two institutions." Namely?

13. Who will behold what with dismay?
14. "Matters of religion should never be matters of controversy." Why?
15. What is the point of Santayana's reference to Buddha and Cronos?
16. "And so it is, or should be, in religion." What is? Agreed?
17. "The idea . . . is an impossible idea." What idea? Why impossible?
18. Who has not come within the region of profitable philosophizing on what subject?
19. What must seem childish and poor to whom?
20. What made the Christian philosophy of history originally appealing?
21. "The history of these symbols is therefore the history of his soul." What symbols? Why "therefore"?

2. HISTORY AS THE EVOLUTION OF A RATIONAL SOCIAL ORDER —FROM IMMANUEL KANT

Kant. The biblical view proposed history as the drama of salvation; man's creation, fall, redemption, and destiny in heaven. This overview died hard; indeed, it may be an exaggeration to say that it is dead yet. But from it to Kant is a shift from an "age of faith" to an "age of reason." Kant wrote toward the end of the eighteenth century, in the period following the rise of modern science, and itself crowded with the American Revolution, the French Revolution, the Encyclopedists, Hume, Voltaire, Condorcet, Rousseau, Tom Paine. These men repudiated what was called the biblical standpoint. What philosophy of history could a man propose that would command their belief? That is the problem which Immanuel Kant tackled in his *Idea of a Universal History*, published in 1784, just three years after his *Critique of Pure Reason*.

Biographical Note. See under "An Epistemological Problem," page 202, and under "An Ethical Problem," page 269.

The Argument of the Citations. Can we find a clue to any plan implicit in human history? Kant replies in the affirmative, and outlines his answer as follows: If creatures are predisposed by nature to develop any latent tendencies, they will do so. Men are predisposed by nature to develop tendencies which will involve the use of their reason. This development will take place in the species as a whole, not in any individual. Nature intends that man should owe to himself alone the development of his rational powers and the sort of happiness that attends their exercise and growth. To this end she has so created man that his distinctively human tendencies can develop only in the antagonism, conflict, give-and-take of life in a society. The highest problem she has set man is, therefore, the formation of a social order in which the fruitfulness of conflict will not be destroyed by conflict. This problem is not only the highest, it is also the hardest and the last. The problem requires for its final solution the formation of a world state. History is the unraveling of nature's plan for establishing this perfect political order.

Whatever difference there may be in our notions of the freedom of the will, it is evident that the manifestations of this will, viz., human actions, are as much under the control of universal laws of nature as any other physical phenomena. It is the province of history to narrate these manifestations; and let their causes be ever so secret, we know that history, simply by taking its station at a distance and contemplating the agency of the human will upon a large scale, aims at unfolding to our view a regular stream of tendency in the great succession of events; so that the very same course of incidents, which taken separately and individually would have seemed incoherent and lawless, yet viewed in their connection never fail to discover a steady and continuous though slow development of certain great predispositions in our nature. Thus for instance deaths, births, and marriages, considering how much they are separately dependent on the freedom of the human will, should seem to be subject to no law according to which any calculation could be made beforehand of their amount; and yet the yearly registers of these events in great countries prove that they go on with as much conformity to the laws of nature as the oscillations of the weather; the latter again are events which in detail are so far irregular that we cannot predict them individually, and yet taken as a whole series we find that they never fail to support the growth of plants, the currents of rivers, and other arrangements of nature in a uniform and uninterrupted course. Individual men, and even nations, are little aware that, while they are severally pursuing their own peculiar and often contradictory purposes, they are unconsciously following the guidance of a natural purpose which is wholly unnoticed by themselves, and are thus promoting and making efforts for a process which, even if they perceived it, they would little regard.

Considering that men, taken collectively as a body, do not proceed like animals under the law of an instinct, nor yet like wholly rational beings under the law of a preconcerted plan, one might imagine that no systematic history of their actions (such, for instance, as the history of bees or beavers) could be possible. At the sight of the actions of man displayed on the great stage of the world, it is impossible to escape a certain degree of disgust; with all the occasional indications of wisdom scattered here and there, we cannot but perceive the whole sum of these actions to be a web of folly, childish vanity, and often even of the idlest wickedness and spirit of destruction. Hence at last one is puzzled to know what judgment to form of our species so conceited of its high advantages. In this perplexity there is no resource for the philos-

opher but this: that, finding it impossible to presume in the human race any
rational purpose of its own, he must endeavor to detect some natural purpose
in such a senseless current of human actions, by means of which a history of
creatures that pursue no plan of their own may yet admit a systematic form
as the history of creatures that are blindly pursuing a plan of nature. Let us
now see whether we can succeed in finding out a clue to such a history, leaving
it to nature to produce a man capable of executing it.

PROPOSITION THE FIRST. All tendencies of any creature to which it is predisposed by nature, are destined in the end to develop themselves perfectly and
agreeably to their final purpose.

External as well as internal (or anatomical) examination confirms this
remark in all animals. An organ which is not to be used, a natural arrangement
that misses its purpose, would be a contradiction in physics. Once departing
from this fundamental proposition, we have a nature no longer tied to laws,
but objectless and working at random; and a cheerless reign of chance steps
into the place of reason.

PROPOSITION THE SECOND. In man, those tendencies which have the use of
his reason for their object are destined to obtain their perfect development
in the species only and not in the individual.

Reason in a creature is a faculty for extending the rules and purposes of
the exercise of all its powers far beyond natural instinct, and it is illimitable
in its plans. It works however not instinctively, but stands in need of trials,
of practice, and of instruction in order to ascend gradually from one degree
of illumination to another. On this account either it would be necessary for
each man to live an inordinate length of time in order to learn how to make
a perfect use of his natural tendencies; or else, supposing the actual case that
nature has limited his term of life, she must then require an incalculable series
of generations (each delivering its quota of knowledge to its immediate successor) in order to ripen the germs which she has laid in our species to that
degree of development which corresponds with her final purpose. Otherwise
man's own natural predispositions must of necessity be regarded as objectless;
and this would at once take away all practical principles, and would expose
nature—the wisdom of whose arrangements must in all other cases be assumed
as a fundamental postulate—to the suspicion of capricious dealing in the case
of man only.

PROPOSITION THE THIRD. It is the will of nature that man should owe
to himself alone everything which transcends the mere mechanical constitution
of his animal existence, and that he should be susceptible of no other happiness or perfection than what he has created for himself, instinct apart, through
his own reason.

Nature does nothing superfluously, and in the use of means to her ends
does not play the prodigal. Having given to man reason, and freedom of the
will grounded upon reason, she had hereby sufficiently made known the pur-

pose which governed her in the choice of the furniture and appointments, intellectual and physical, with which she has accoutered him. Thus provided, he had no need for the guidance of instinct, or for knowledge and forethought created to his hand; for these he was to be indebted to himself. The means of providing for his own shelter from the elements—for his own security, and the whole superstructure of delights which add comfort and embellishment to life—were to be the work of his own hands. So far indeed has she pushed this principle, that she seems to have been frugal even to niggardliness in the dispensation of her animal endowments to man, and to have calculated her allowance to the nicest rigor of the demand in the very earliest stage of existence: as if it had been her intention hereby to proclaim that the highest degree of power—of intellectual perfection—and of happiness to which he should ever toil upwards from a condition utterly savage, must all be wrung and extorted from the difficulties and thwartings of his situation—and the merit therefore be exclusively his own, thus implying that she had at heart his own rational self-estimation rather than his convenience or comfort. She has indeed beset man with difficulties; and in no way could she have so clearly made known that her purpose with man was not that he might live in pleasure; but that by a strenuous wrestling with those difficulties he might make himself worthy of living in pleasure. Undoubtedly it seems surprising on this view of the case that the earlier generations appear to exist only for the sake of the latter—viz., for the sake of forwarding that edifice of man's grandeur in which only the latest generations are to dwell, though all have undesignedly taken part in raising it. Mysterious as this appears, it is however at the same time necessary, if we once assume a race of rational animals, as destined by means of this characteristic reason to a perfect development of their tendencies, and subject to mortality in the individual but immortal in the species.

PROPOSITION THE FOURTH. The means, which nature employs to bring about the development of all the tendencies she has laid in man, is the antagonism of these tendencies in the social state—no farther however than to that point at which this antagonism becomes the cause of social arrangements founded in law.

By antagonism of this kind I mean the unsocial sociality of man; that is, a tendency to enter the social state combined with a perpetual resistance to that tendency which is continually threatening to dissolve it. Man has gregarious inclinations, feeling himself, in the social state, more than man by means of the development thus given to his natural tendencies. But he has also strong antigregarious inclinations prompting him to insulate himself, which arise out of the unsocial desire (existing concurrently with his social propensities) to force all things into compliance with his own humor; a propensity to which he naturally anticipates resistance from his consciousness of a similar spirit of resistance to others existing in himself. Now this resistance it is which awakens all the powers of man. It drives him to master his propensity to indolence, and, in the shape of ambition or avarice, impels him to procure distinction for himself amongst his fellows. In this way arise the first steps from the savage state to the state of culture, which consists peculiarly in the social worth of man: Talents of every kind are now unfolded, taste formed, and by gradual increase of light a preparation is made for such a mode of thinking as is capable of converting the rude natural tendency to moral distinctions into determinate practical principles, and finally of exalting a social concert that had been extorted from the mere necessities of the situation into a moral union founded on reasonable choice. But for these antisocial propensities, so unamiable in themselves, which give birth to that resistance which every man meets with in his own self-interested pretensions, an Arcadian life would arise of perfect harmony and mutual love such as must suffocate and stifle all talents in their very germs. Men, as gentle as the sheep they fed, would communicate to their existence no higher value than belongs to mere animal life, and would leave the vacuum which exists in reference to the final purpose of man's nature, as a rational being, unfilled. Thanks be, therefore, to nature for the enmity, for the jealous spirit of envious competition, for the insatiable thirst after wealth and power! These wanting, all the admirable tendencies in man's nature would remain for ever undeveloped. Man, for his own sake as an individual, wishes for concord; but nature knows better what is good for man as a species, and she ordains discord. He would live in ease and passive content; but nature wills that he shall precipitate himself out of his luxury of indolence into labors and hardships, in order that he may devise remedies against them and thus raise himself above them by an intellectual conquest— not sink below them by an unambitious evasion. The impulses, which she has laid in his moral constitution, the sources of that antisociality and universal antagonism from which so many evils arise, but which again stimulate a fresh reaction of the faculties and by consequence more and more aid the development of the primitive tendencies—all tend to betray the adjusting hand of a wise creator, not that of an evil spirit that has bungled the execution of his own designs, or has malevolently sought to perplex them with evil.

PROPOSITION THE FIFTH. The highest problem for the human species, to the solution of which it is irresistibly urged by natural impulses, is the establishment of a universal civil society founded on political justice.

Since it is only in the social state that the development of all man's tendencies can be accomplished; since such a social state must combine with the utmost possible freedom, and consequent antagonism of its members, the most rigorous determination of the boundaries of this freedom in order that the freedom of such individual may coexist with the freedom of others; and since this as well as all other objects of man's destination should be the work of men's own efforts, on these accounts a society in which freedom under laws is united with the greatest possible degree of irresistible power is the highest problem nature sets for man; because it is only by the solution of this problem that nature can accomplish the rest of her purpose with our species. Into this state of restraint man, who is otherwise so much enamored of lawless freedom, is compelled to enter by necessity, his natural inclinations making it impossible for man to preserve a state of perfect liberty for any length of time in the neighborhood of his fellows. But, under the restraint of a civil community, these very inclinations lead to the best effects—just as trees in a forest, for the very reason that each endeavors to rob the other of air and sun, compel each other to shoot upwards in quest of both; and thus attain a fine erect growth; whereas those which stand aloof from each other under no mutual restraint, and throw out their boughs at pleasure, become crippled and distorted. All the gifts of art and cultivation which adorn the human race —in short, the most beautiful forms of social order—are the fruits of the antisocial principle—which is compelled to discipline itself, and by means won from the very resistance of man's situation in this world to give perfect development to all the germs of nature.

PROPOSITION THE SIXTH. This problem is at the same time the most difficult of all, and the one which is latest solved by man.

The difficulty, which is involved in the bare idea of such a problem, is this: Man is an animal that, so long as he lives amongst others of his species, stands in need of a master. For he inevitably abuses his freedom in regard to his equals; and, although as a reasonable creature he wishes for a law that may set bounds to the liberty of all, yet do his self-interested animal propensities seduce him into making an exception in his own favor whensoever he dares. He requires a master therefore to curb his will, and to compel him into submission to a universal will which may secure the possibility of universal freedom. Now where is he to find this master? Of necessity amongst the human species. But, as a human being, this master will also be an animal that requires a master. Lodged in one or many, it is impossible that the supreme and irresponsible power can be certainly prevented from abusing its authority. Hence it is that this problem is the most difficult of any; nay, its perfect solution is impossible; out of wood so crooked and perverse as that which man is made of, nothing absolutely straight can ever be wrought. An approximation to this idea is therefore all which nature enjoins. That it is also the last of all problems, to which the human species addresses itself, is clear from this—that it presupposes just notions of the nature of a good constitution, great experience, and a will favorably disposed to the adoption of such a constitution; three elements that can hardly, and not until after many fruitless trials, be expected to concur.

PROPOSITION THE SEVENTH. The problem of the establishment of a perfect constitution of society depends upon the problem of a system of international relations adjusted to law; and, apart from this latter problem, cannot be solved.

To what purpose is labor bestowed upon a civil constitution adjusted to law for individual men, i.e., upon the creation of a commonwealth? The same

antisocial impulses, which first drove men to such a creation, is again the cause
—that every commonwealth in its external relations, i.e., as a state in reference
to other states, occupies the same ground of lawless and uncontrolled liberty.
Consequently each must anticipate from the other the same evils which compelled individuals to enter the social state. Nature accordingly avails herself
of the spirit of enmity in man, as existing even in the great national corpora-
tions of that animal, for the purpose of attaining through the inevitable antagonism of this spirit a state of rest and security. That is, by wars, by the
exhaustion of incessant preparations for war, and by pressure of evil consequences which war at last entails even through the midst of peace, she drives
nations to all sorts of experiments and expedients; and finally after devasta-
tions, ruin, and exhaustion of energy, to one which reason should have suggested without the cost of so sad an experience; viz., to quit the condition
of lawless power, and to enter into a federal league of nations, in which even
the weakest member looks for its rights and for protection not to its own
power, or its own adjudication, but to this great confederation, to the united
power, and the adjudication of the collective will. Visionary as this idea may
seem, it is, notwithstanding, the inevitable resource and mode of escape under
that pressure of evil which nations reciprocally inflict; and, hard as it may
be to realize such an idea, states must of necessity be driven at last to the
very same resolution to which the savage man of nature was driven with equal
reluctance—viz., to sacrifice brutal liberty, and to seek peace and security in
a civil constitution founded upon law. All wars therefore are so many tentative essays (not in the intention of man, but in the intention of nature) to bring
about new relations of states, and by revolutions and dismemberments to form
new political bodies. These again, either from internal defects or external
attacks, cannot support themselves, but must undergo similar revolutions, until
at last, partly by the best possible arrangement of civil government within
and partly by common concert and legal compact without, a condition is
attained which, like a well-ordered commonwealth, can maintain itself.

Now, whether (in the first place) it is to be anticipated that states, like
atoms, by accidental shocking together, should go through all sorts of new
combinations to be again dissolved by the fortuitous impulse of fresh shocks,
until at length by pure accident some combination emerges capable of supporting itself; or whether (in the second place) we should assume that nature
is pursuing her course of raising our species gradually from the lower steps
of animal existence to the very highest of a human existence, and that not
by any direct interposition in our favor but through man's own spontaneous
and artificial efforts (spontaneous, but yet extorted from him by his situation),
and in this apparently wild arrangement of things is developing with perfect
regularity the original tendencies she has implanted; or whether (in the third
place) it is more reasonable to believe that out of all this action and reaction
of the human species upon itself nothing in the shape of a wise result will

ever issue, that it will continue to be as it has been, and therefore that it cannot be known before hand but that the discord, which is so natural to our species, will finally prepare for us a hell of evils under the most moral condition of society such as may swallow up this very moral condition itself and all previous advance in culture by a reflex of the original barbaric spirit of desolation; to all this the answer turns upon the following question: Is it reasonable to assume a final purpose in all natural processes and arrangements in the parts, and yet a want of purpose in the whole?

What therefore the condition of savage life effected, viz., checked the development of the natural tendencies in the human species, but then, by the very evils thus caused, drove man into a state where those tendencies could unfold and mature themselves, that same service is performed for states by the barbaric freedom in which they are now existing—viz., by causing the dedication of all national energies and resources to war, it checks the full development of the natural tendencies in its progress; but on the other hand by these very evils and their consequences, it compels our species at last to discover some law of counterbalance to the principle of antagonism between nations, and in order to give effect to this law to introduce a federation of states and consequently an international police corresponding to national internal police.

This federation will itself not be exempt from danger, else the powers of the human race would go to sleep. It will be sufficient that it contain a principle for restoring the equilibrium between its own action and reaction, and thus checking the two functions from destroying each other. Before this last step is taken, human nature—then about half way advanced in its progress —is in the deepest abyss of evils under the deceitful semblance of external prosperity. We are at this time in a high degree of culture as to arts and sciences. We are civilized to superfluity in what regards the graces and decorums of life. But, to entitle us to consider ourselves moralized, much is still wanting. Nothing indeed of a true moral influence can be expected so long as states direct all their energies to idle plans of aggrandizement by force, and thus incessantly check the slow motions by which the intellect of the species is unfolding and forming itself, to say nothing of their shrinking from all positive aid to those motions. But all good, that is not engrafted upon moral good, is mere show and hollow speciousness—the dust and ashes of morality. And in this delusive condition will the human race linger, until it shall have toiled upwards in the way I have mentioned from its present chaotic abyss of political relations.

PROPOSITION THE EIGHTH. The history of the human species as a whole may be regarded as the unraveling of a hidden plan of nature for accomplishing a perfect state of civil constitution for society in its internal relations (and, as the condition of that, in its external relations also) as the sole state of society in which the tendencies of human nature can be all and fully developed.

This proposition is an inference from the preceding. The question arises: Has experience yet observed any traces of such an unraveling in history? I answer: Some little. The entire period of this unraveling is probably too vast to admit of our detecting the relation of the parts to the whole from the small fraction of it which man has yet left behind him.

Meantime our human nature obliges us to take an interest even in the remotest epoch to which our species is destined, provided we can anticipate it with certainty. So much less can we be indifferent to it, inasmuch as it appears within our power by intellectual arrangements to contribute something toward the acceleration of the species in its advance to this great epoch. On this account the faintest traces of any approximation in such a direction becomes of importance to us. At present all states are so artificially interconnected, that no one can possibly become stationary without retrograding with respect to the rest; and thus if not the progress yet the nondeclension of this purpose of nature is sufficiently secured through the ambition of nations. Moreover, civil liberty cannot at this day any longer be arrested in its progress but that all the sources of livelihood, and more immediately trade, must betray a close sympathy with it, and sicken as that sickens; and hence a decay of the state in its external relations. Gradually too this liberty extends itself. If the citizen be hindered from pursuing his interest in any way most agreeable to himself, provided only it can coexist with the liberty of others, in that case the life of general business is palsied, and in connection with that again the powers of the whole. Hence it arises that all personal restriction is more and more withdrawn; religious liberty is established; and thus, with occasional interruptions, arises illumination; a blessing which the human race must win even from the self-interested purposes of its rulers, if they comprehend what is for their own advantage. Now this illumination, and with it a certain degree of cordial interest which the enlightened man cannot forbear taking in all the good which he perfectly comprehends must by degrees mount upwards even to the throne, and exert an influence on the principles of government.

Finally, war itself becomes gradually not only so artificial a process, so uncertain in its issue, but also in the afterpains of inextinguishable national debts so anxious and burthensome; and, at the same time, the influence which any convulsions of one state exert upon every other state is so remarkable in our quarter of the globe—linked as it is in all parts by the systematic intercourse of trade—that at length, those governments, which have no immediate participation in the war, under a sense of their own danger, offer themselves as mediators—though as yet without any authentic sanction of law, and thus prepare all things from afar for the formulation of a great primary state body, such as is wholly unprecedented in all preceding ages. Although this body at present exists only in rude outline, yet already a stirring is beginning to be perceptible in all its limbs—each of which is interested in the maintenance of the whole; even now there is enough to justify a hope that, after many revolutions and remodelings of states, the supreme purpose of nature will be accomplished in the establishment of an international state as the bosom in which all the original tendencies of the human species are to be developed.

PROPOSITION THE NINTH. A philosophical attempt to compose a universal history tending to unfold the purpose of nature in a perfect civil union of the human species is to be regarded as possible, and as capable even of helping forward this very purpose of nature.

At first sight it is apparently an extravagant project—to propose a history of man founded on any idea of the course which human affairs would take if adjusted to certain reasonable ends. On such a plan, it may be thought, nothing better than a romance could result. Yet, if we assume that nature proceeds not without plan even in the motions of human free will, this idea may possibly turn out very useful; and, although we are too shortsighted to look through the secret mechanism of her arrangements, this idea may yet serve as a clue for connecting into something like unity the great abstract of human actions that else seem a chaotic and incoherent aggregate. For, if we take our beginning from Greek history; if we pursue down to our own times its influence upon the formation and malformation of the Roman people as a political body that swallowed up the Greek state, and the influence of Rome upon the barbarians by whom Rome itself was destroyed; and if to all this we add the political history of every other people so far as it has come to our knowledge through the records of the two enlightened nations above mentioned; we shall then discover a regular gradation of improvement in civil polity as it has grown up in our quarter of the globe, which quarter is in all probability destined to give laws to all the rest. If further we direct an exclusive attention to the civil constitution, with its laws, and the external relations of the state, insofar as both, by means of the good which they contained, served for a period to raise and to dignify other nations and with them the arts and sciences, yet again by their defects served also to precipitate them into ruin, but always so that some germ of illumination survived which, being more and more developed by every revolution, prepared continually a still higher step of improvement; in that case, I believe that a clue will be discovered not only for the unraveling of the intricate web of human affairs and for the guidance of future statesmen, but also such a clue as will open a consolatory prospect into futurity, in which at a remote distance we shall discover the human species seated upon an eminence won by infinite toil where all the germs are unfolded which nature has implanted—and its destination upon this earth accomplished. Such a justification of nature, or rather of providence, is no mean motive for choosing this station for the survey of history. For what does it avail to praise and to draw forth to view the magnificence and wisdom of the creation in the irrational kingdom of nature, if that part in the great stage of the supreme wisdom, which contains the object of all this mighty display—viz., the history of the human species— is to remain an eternal objection to it, the bare sight of which obliges us to turn away our eyes with displeasure, and (from the despair which it raises of ever discovering in it a perfect and rational purpose) finally leads us to look for such a purpose only in another world?

My object in this essay would be wholly misinterpreted, if it were supposed that under the idea of a universal history which to a certain degree has its course determined *a priori*, I had any wish to discourage the cultivation of empirical history in the ordinary sense. On the contrary, the philosopher must be well versed in history who could execute the plan I have sketched, which is indeed a most extensive survey of history, only taken from a new station. However, the extreme and, simply considered, praiseworthy circumstantiality, with which the history of every nation is written in our times, must naturally suggest a question of some embarrassment: In what way will our remote posterity be able to cope with the enormous accumulation of historical records which a few centuries will bequeath to them? There is no doubt that they will estimate the historical details of times far removed from their own, the original monuments of which will have long perished, simply by the value of that which will then concern themselves—viz., by the good or evil performed by nations and their governments in a universal view. To direct the eye upon this point as connected with the ambition of rulers and their servants, in order to guide them to the only means of bequeathing an honorable record of themselves to distant ages, may furnish some small motive (over and above the great one of justifying providence) for attempting a philosophic history on the plan I have here explained.

Note on Sources. The above material is quoted from Kant's *Idea of a Universal History*.

Reading References. Kant's *Idea of a Universal History* was published in 1784. It was followed, in 1795 by his essay, *Toward Everlasting Peace*. This latter can be read with profit as an extension of the claims set forth in the former. Among secondary sources, the following are useful: Edward Caird's *Critical Philosophy of Kant*, Volume II, Book II, Chapter 6; and Friedrich Paulsen's *Immanuel Kant*, Part II, Book II, Section II.

READING QUESTIONS

1. What are Kant's views on history and man's free will?
2. Why must the philosopher endeavor to detect some natural purpose in human actions?
3. Be prepared to formulate each numbered proposition (e.g., Proposition the First) as briefly as you can.
4. "This would expose nature, the wisdom of whose arrangements must

in all other cases be assumed, as a fundamental postulate, to the suspicion of capricious dealing with man only."

    (a) What would expose nature thus?

    (b) Why must the wisdom of her arrangements be assumed, in all other cases, as a fundamental postulate?

    (c) What is the wisdom of her arrangements?

    (d) Do you imagine that Kant would criticize the design argument in natural theology?

5. Where, do you suppose, Kant finds out that the arrangement noted in Proposition the Third is the will of nature? What does such an expression mean, if not the will of God? Can nature be said to have a will?

6. What *appears* mysterious, but *is* necessary, if we once assume what?

7. What is the means which nature employs to bring about the development of the tendencies she has laid in man?

8. "No farther, however, than to that point." What point?

9. "Man wishes for concord; but nature knows better, and she ordains discord." Why?

10. What is the highest problem for the human species?

11. "This problem is at the same time the most difficult of all." Elucidate.

12. "This problem depends upon a system of international relations adjusted to law." Elucidate.

13. "The human race will linger in this delusive condition until it shall have toiled upwards in the way I have mentioned." What delusive condition? What way?

14. "The history of the human species may be regarded as the unraveling of a hidden plan of nature." Namely?

15. Of what value is such a history?

16. "I have no wish to discourage, under the idea of a universal history, which is to a certain degree *a priori*, the cultivation of empirical history." Explain.

3. AN IDEALISTIC INTERPRETATION OF HISTORY —FROM G. W. F. HEGEL

From Kant to Hegel. Kant's views on history were published in 1784. They did not command much attention at that time. Hegel's views, however, have been much more widely read and influential. These were set forth in his *Philosophy of History*, delivered as lectures in the University at Berlin for some years prior to his death, and published posthumously in 1837.

Between Kant and Hegel the two great historical events were the

French Revolution and the career of Napoleon. These made a difference, for persons who lived on into the period of reaction under Metternich, in the interpretation of history. The French Revolution, which began as a demand for liberty, seemed to culminate in a demand for licence; and its licence, in turn, seemed to have invoked the heavy-handed regime of Napoleon. The result, in the sphere of practical politics, was a period of illiberalism, of distrust of revolutionary politics, and of fear of the tyranny which they seem to generate. From 1815 to 1830 this distrust was at its height. Hegel's philosophy of history is the attempt to restate the appeal to reason, such as one meets in Kant's pamphlet, by an appeal to reason somewhat disillusioned and chastened by the events which fell between him and Kant. Three things at least Hegel had to do: save the great concept of freedom, by means of the distinction between law and licence; provide recognition of the fact that the argument of history includes a place for the great man, or hero, e.g., Napoleon, whom Hegel referred to as the world-spirit on horseback; and justify the attempt of the reaction to save Europe from licence and tyranny in the name of "rational freedom" or freedom under law.

Biographical Note. Georg Wilhelm Friedrich Hegel was born in 1770 and died in 1831 at the age of sixty-one. He wrote many volumes elucidating the general thesis that reality is spirit manifesting itself in nature, in man, and in their combination which is history. These books are difficult reading, partly because the thought they contain is unfamiliar and elusive, partly because the words they contain are obscure and technical. Early in life, Hegel arrived at the conclusion that the totality of things is an objectification or manifestation of "Geist" or spirit. This Spirit is manifested *as* nature and is present *in* man. With his reasons for this conclusion we are not here concerned. His writings are directed, for the most part, toward elaborating his central thesis, not proving it. In his *Phenomenology of Spirit* he offered an account of nature, of man, of society, of morality, of art, of religion, of philosophy, as so many "fields" in which the nature of "Geist" is disclosed. His *Philosophy of Right* was a treatise on the state and law in which these are analyzed and described to show wherein they disclose the nature of "Geist," spirit. After his death, his disciples published his lectures in a series of volumes, *Philosophy of History, Philosophy of Art, Philosophy of Religion,* in which similarly motivated analyses and descriptions are carried out.

The external facts of Hegel's life are few and unimportant. He was trained for the church. He early became an academic. Outwardly at least, he never ceased to be one. He taught at several universities before he was called to occupy the chair of philosophy in the University at Berlin. He died, at the height of his fame, from an attack of cholera which had broken out in Berlin. His writings provided the great synthesis of European thought between the age of Newton and Kant before him, and Darwin and Marx after him.

The Argument of the Citations. After defending the notion of a philosophy of history against the charge of forcing facts to fit theories, Hegel proposes that history be construed as the realm of mind, in contrast to nature as the realm of matter. In history, mind, or spirit, is engaged in working out the form and substance of freedom. Freedom is the capacity to act. It presupposes rules. Rules which permit the exercise and growth of the capacity to act are rules which define freedom under law, which is true freedom, in contrast to false freedom or licence. The career of spirit has been marked by violence and conflict. This breeds pessimism and cynicism only in little men. Hegel's claim is that they (violence and conflict) are the necessary conditions under which freedom comes into being. The process is blind, in the sense that the successive steps are not marked out in advance. But it is also beneficent in the sense that each step forward, no matter what the cost in individual misery, marks an increase in the conditions which make freedom possible. The pain and sorrow which characterize the history of humanity, the conflicts within states and between states are blind stumblings toward that form of organized living in which spirit will achieve a maximum of realization in the freedom of individuals. This is a kind of long-range optimism; but in the short range it is harsh and blood-thirsty.

The world-spirit makes use of certain individuals to initiate new and difficult turns in the history of civilization. These are the great men, or heroes, of history. They serve a power and an end which transcends them. The goal of history is the evolution of the state, that is, a union of rational wills making possible the continuous exercise and development of freedom. This is the march of God on earth. The state is the organization of the nation. Since there are many nations, war is a necessary ingredient in history. Such conflict purifies and strengthens the national state. There is no judge of the nations, beyond their survival in the strenuous march of God on earth. The world's history is the world's tribunal. Let us make a beginning:

The most general definition that can be given of the philosophical treatment of history is contained in the word *rational*. The *philosophy of history* means the "rationale of history." The only thought which philosophy brings to the contemplation of history is the simple conception of reason; that reason is the sovereign of the world; that the history of the world, therefore, presents us with a "rational" process. This conviction and intuition are an hypothesis in the domain of history as such.

Before elaborating this view of history, Hegel turns to consider a possible objection. May this not lead a man to set up a plan and then force the facts to fit it?

This presupposition that history has an essential and actual goal or end is called an *a priori* view of it. Philosophy is reproached with "*a priori* history-writing." On this point we must go into further detail. This seems to be the legitimate demand that the historian should proceed with impartiality; there should be no prepossession in favor of an idea or opinion, just as a judge should have no special sympathy for one of the contending parties.

Now, in the case of the judge it is admitted that he would administer his office ill and foolishly if he had no interest in justice; indeed, if he did not have an exclusive interest in justice. That is assumed to be his one sole aim. This requirement, which we make of a judge, may be called partiality for justice.

But, in speaking of the impartiality required from an historian, this self-satisfied, insipid, chatter lets the distinction between legitimate, responsible partiality and mere subjective partiality, disappear. It demands that the historian shall bring with him no definite aim, no definite conception by which he may sort out, describe, evaluate events. It demands that he shall narrate them exactly in the casual mode he finds them, in all their incoherent and unintelligent particularity. A history must have an object, e.g., Rome and its fortunes, or the greatness and decline of Rome. This lies at the basis of the events themselves, and therefore at the basis of the critical examination into their comparative importance. A history without some such criticism would be only an imbecile mental digression—not so good as a fairy tale, for even children expect a motif in their stories, at least dimly surmisable, with which events and actions are put in relation.

To presuppose such a theme is blameworthy only when the assumed conception is arbitrarily adopted, and when a determined attempt is made to force events and actions to conform to this conception. For this kind of *a priori* handling of history, however, those are chiefly to blame who profess to be "purely historical," who raise their voice against any attempt to deal philosophically with history. Philosophy is to them a troublesome neighbor; for she is the enemy of all arbitrariness and hasty suggestion.

So much, then, for an objection to his view. He asks of history what a scientist asks of nature, namely, that it be reasonable, that the use of reason on the details of history shall not *ipso facto* mislead a man. This granted, much may be expected. However, this rationality of history is not to be confused with a pious belief in a superintending providence:

The time must come for understanding that rich product of active Reason which world history offers to us. It was for a while the fashion to profess admiration for the wisdom of God as displayed in animals, plants, and isolated occurrences. But, if it be allowed that Providence exhibits itself in such objects and forms of existence, why not also in the world history? Is this too great a matter to be thus regarded? But divine wisdom, that is, reason, is one and the same in the great as well as in the little.

In those to whom such a conception is not familiar, I may at least presume the existence of a belief in reason, a desire, a thirst, for an understanding of it. Indeed, it is the wish for rational insight, not the ambition to amass a mere heap of facts, that should be presupposed in the mind of every learner. If the clear idea of reason, of pervading rationality, is not already in our minds, in beginning the study of history, we should at least have the firm faith that it does exist there, that the scene of intelligence and conscious volition—human history—is not abandoned to chance. . . . To him who looks upon the world rationally, the world in its turn presents a rational aspect. The relation is mutual.

This conviction involves much more than the mere belief in a "superintending Providence." Pious folk are encouraged to see in particular circumstances, something more than mere chance; to acknowledge the "guiding hand" of God when help has unexpectedly come to an individual in great perplexity and need. But these instances of "providential design" are of a limited kind. They concern the accomplishment of nothing more than the desires of the individual in question. But in world history the "individuals" we have to deal with are whole peoples, e.g., the Jews, the Greeks, the Romans. We cannot, therefore, be satisfied with what we may call this "trifling" view of Providence.

But *reason*, whose presence in the world and sovereignty over the world has been maintained, is as vague and indefinite a term as *Providence*. Unless we can characterize it distinctly, unless we can show wherein it consists, we cannot decide whether a thing is rational or irrational. An adequate definition of *reason* is therefore the first desideratum to an inquiry into "reason in history." Without such a definition we can get no further than mere words.

To begin with, it must be observed that world history belongs to the realm of spirit, not to the realm of matter. The term *world*, indeed, includes both physical and psychical. But our concern is not with nature at large. On the stage of world history spirit displays itself in its most concrete reality. The development of spirit is our central theme.

The nature of spirit may be understood by a glance at its direct opposite —matter. As the essence of matter is gravity, so the essence of spirit is freedom. It involves an appreciation of its own nature, a power to know itself as also an energy enabling it to realize itself, to make itself actually that which it is potentially. Accordingly it may be said of world history that it is the exhibition of spirit in the process of working out that which it is potentially.

The spirit which thinks in world history, stripping off the limitations of its several national manifestations and temporal restrictions, lays hold of its actual transcendence and universality, rises to apprehend itself for what it essentially is, while the necessity of nature and the necessity of history but minister to its revelation and are vessels of its honor.

It is the spirit which not merely broods over history as over the waters, but lives in it and is alone its principle of movement. And in the path of that spirit, liberty is the guiding principle and its development the final aim. Such a doctrine—reason in history—will be partly a plausible faith, partly a philosophical insight.

If the essence of spirit is freedom, then the history of the world, if it is the history of spirit, is none other than the progress of the consciousness of freedom.

The [ancient] Orientals had not attained the knowledge that spirit, man as such, is free. And because they did not know this, they lived in bondage. They knew only the freedom of one among the many. That one was therefore only a despot, a tyrant, not a free man. The freedom of that one was only caprice; ferocity, brutal recklessness of passion; or, equally an accident of nature, mildness and tameness of desire.

The consciousness of freedom first arose among the Greeks. And therefore they were free. But they, and the Romans likewise, knew only that some are free, not man as such. They therefore had slaves. Their whole life, and the maintenance of their splendid liberty, was implicated with the institution of slavery. Liberty, among them, was therefore only an accidental, a transient, a limited growth; and this very fact constituted it a rigorous thraldom of our common human nature.

The Germanic peoples, under the influence of Christianity, were the first to realize that man, as man, is free; that it is freedom which constitutes the essence of spirit. To introduce this realization into the various relations of the actual world was a large problem, whose solution required a severe and lengthened process of culture. Slavery did not cease immediately upon the reception of Christianity. Liberty did not all at once predominate in states. Governments and constitutions did not all at once adopt a rational organization, or recognize freedom as their basis. The application of the principle to political relations, the thorough molding and interpenetration of society by it, has been identical with history itself. But the history of the world has been none other than the progress of the consciousness of freedom.

In the process before us, world history, the essential nature of freedom is displayed as coming to a consciousness of itself, as realizing itself. This is the result at which the process of world history has been aiming. To this end have the sacrifices that have ever and anon been laid on the vast altar of the earth, through long lapse of ages, been offered. This is the only aim that sees itself realized and fulfilled; the only pole of repose amid the ceaseless change of events and conditions; the sole efficient principle that pervades the whole. Translating this into the language of religion, we may say that this realization by spirit of the nature and conditions of freedom is God's final aim and purpose with the world.

Freedom, the capacity to act, is the essence of spirit. Spirit is both manifested *as* nature and our bodies, and present *in* us. This "present-in-us" part is latent. We can potentially do many things that we cannot do actually; e.g., "I cannot, actually, play bridge; but, potentially, I can; that is, I can develop that freedom." Now, Hegel asks: By what means does the spirit present *in* humanity develop its freedoms?

If, as we have argued, the history of the world is the history of the further and further realization of freedom, we are moved to pose a question: By what means does freedom develop? By what means is it brought to further and further realization?

A first glance at history convinces us that the actions of men proceed from their needs, their passions, their characters, their abilities. A first glance impresses us, too, with the belief that these needs, passions, private interests, are the sole springs of human action. Here and there may be found, perhaps, some aims of a liberal kind; benevolence, maybe; or noble patriotism. But such aims and virtues are insignificant on the broad canvas of history. They bear only a trifling proportion to the mass of the human race, and their influence is limited accordingly.

Passions, private aims, the satisfaction of selfish desires, are the most effective springs of human action. Let no illusions be cherished on this point. Their power lies in the fact that they respect none of the limitations which justice and morality would impose on them. These natural impulses have a more direct influence over men than the artificial and tedious discipline which tends to order and self-restraint, law and morality.

If I am to exert myself for any object, principle, aim, design, it must in some way or other be mine. In its realization I must find my satisfaction; although the purpose for which I exert myself includes a complication of results, many of which have no interest for me. This is the absolute right of personal existence—to find itself satisfied in its activity and labor. If men are to interest themselves in anything, they must find their individuality gratified by its attainment. Nothing therefore happens, nothing is accomplished, unless individuals seek their own satisfaction in the issue.

We assert, then, that nothing has been accomplished without interest on the part of those who brought it about. If *interest* be called *passion*, where the whole individuality is concentrating all its desires and powers to the neglect or exclusion of all other actual or possible interests or claims, we may affirm without qualification that nothing great has been accomplished in the world without passion.

Two elements, therefore, enter into our investigation: first, the aim, principle, destiny, namely the realization of freedom; second, the complex of human passions. The one the warp, the other the woof, of the vast arras web of world history.

The spirit which is both manifested as and present in humanity must come out, must gain freedom, must achieve the capacity to act. It must learn and master the conditions of its freedom. Now, Hegel has it, the medium in which this spirit works is the totality of blind drives that compose an unenlightened and undisciplined humanity. The spirit must achieve its freedom through and in these drives, or not at all. In themselves these drives are neither good nor bad. They are, it happens, necessary to that freedom which spirit is seeking in the history of humanity.

Passion is by many regarded as a thing of sinister aspect, more or less immoral. Man is required to have no passions. We need only repeat, to silence such pallid moralizing, that nothing great has been accomplished without passion, without the concentration of energy and will upon some private interests —self-seeking, if you will—to the exclusion of all things else.

World history is controlled by a general aim—the realization of the essence of spirit, which is freedom. In the beginning this is only implicit—a profoundly hidden, unconscious instinct. The whole process of history is directed to rendering this unconscious impulse a conscious one. At the very dawn of world history, physical craving, animal instinct, private interest, selfish passion, prejudiced opinion, spontaneously present themselves. This vast congeries of wills, interests, and activities constitute the instruments, the means, the media, of the world spirit for attaining its object.

At this point Hegel introduces a line of thought which is not easy to grasp. But it is central to his philosophy of history. We may approach it by way of what he has already said: The story of humanity is the story of the conquest by the spirit present in humanity of the conditions of its freedom, its power to act. The spirit which is present in man encounters no difficulty in acting, in exerting its will, in the realm of the natural order. And the reason is that "nature" is the realm of law and order. Nature is calculable. She "obeys" rules. When these are known they provide a basis for action. A law in nature is a possible basis for action by men. If there were no law, no order, no pattern, in nature, we could not act. We would be reduced to sheer guesswork; even lower, since if there were no law or order, we could not even guess. When we turn from nature to society, we turn from the realm of law to the realm of freedom. If man is to act in the "medium" of private wills, there must be something corresponding to laws as they are in nature. To this end man needs the state. The *state* may be defined as "society organized to make law possible." Some laws are left without the pressure of the state immediately behind them. Such laws are moral. Law and morality then, between them, are self-imposed limitations for which the justification is that they make it possible to act. They extend the realm of freedom, from the natural into the social order.

The concrete union of the two elements which we find in history—that freedom which is the essence of spirit, and those individual needs and desires which supply the driving power—is liberty under the conditions of law and morality in the state.

A state is well constituted and internally powerful when the private interests of its citizens are one with the common interest of the state, when the one finds its gratification and realization in the other. The epoch during which a state attains this harmonious condition marks the period of its bloom, its vigor, its virtue and prosperity.

I will endeavor to make my point more vivid by means of an example. The building of a house is, on the one hand, a subjective aim and design. On the other hand we have, as means, the several substances required for the undertaking—iron, wood, stone, etc. The elements are used to work up this material—fire to melt the iron, wind to blow the fire, water to drive the wheels to cut the wood, and so on. The result is that the wind which has helped to build the house is shut out by the house. So also are the rains and floods which supplied the water to drive the wheels; and the destructive power of fire, so far as the house is fireproof. The stones and beams obey their law of gravity —press downwards—and so high walls are carried up.

Thus the elements are used according to their natures, and yet cooperate for a product by which their operation is limited. Thus, in the building of a state, where freedom is realized under conditions of law and order, the passions of men are gratified; they develop themselves and their aims in accordance with their natural tendencies, and build up the edifice of human society; thus fortifying a position for law and order against themselves.

Lest anyone should feel that Hegel is growing optimistic, viewing humanity and the state through rosy spectacles, he turns aside to note that the price of freedom is not merely eternal vigilance; it is eternal strife and violence.

When we contemplate this display of passions, and the consequences of their violence, the unreason which is associated with them; when we see the evil, the vice, the ruin that has befallen the most flourishing kingdom which the mind of man ever created, we can scarce avoid being filled with sorrow at this universal taint and corruption. Since, moreover, this perversion and decay are not the work of mere nature, but the work of human will, we are liable to a moral bitterness, a revolt of the good will, as a result of our reflections.

Without rhetorical exaggeration, a simple truthful account of the miseries that have overwhelmed the noblest of nations and the finest exemplars of private virtue, provides a picture of most fearful aspect, excites emotions of the profoundest and most hopeless sadness, counterbalanced by no consolatory results. History appears as the slaughter bench at which the happiness of peoples, the wisdom of states, and the virtue of individuals have been victimized.

In beholding it we endure a mental torture allowing no defense or escape save the consideration that what has happened could not have been otherwise; that it has been a fatality which no intervention could alter. We draw back at last in disgust. We turn from these intolerable sorrows, from these blackened pages of humanity's history, to the more agreeable environment of our own individual life.

The philosophy of history which Hegel has been marking out threatens to end in a kind of pessimism. Spirit is the capacity to act. It is therefore freedom. It is manifested as nature. It is present in humanity. It requires a social order comprising a moral and political order. These orders are the battleground of private passions and private wills controlled by private passions. The spirit must work out its destiny in terms of these factors, or not at all. They are the matter to which it will give the form, the form of freedom. This entails tension and conflict. We turn from it, as from a slaughter bench. But where to? To our own private selves. Only by withdrawing from humanity do we see any prospect of relief from the price which it continuously pays. But we withdraw from the human scene in the name of precisely those human values and ideals which the human scene alone makes possible, and toward which it is the endless struggle. Are we caught here in a vicious circle? The "great man" as hero is Hegel's partial answer. The "great man" is he who "breaks ground" for spirit's further advance.

But whither do we thus retreat? Into the present, formed by our own private aims and interests! In short, we retreat into the selfishness that stands on the quiet shore, enjoying thence in safety the distant spectacle of wreckage and confusion.

To what final aim have these enormous sacrifices been offered? To what paradox, moreover, have we come? We point to the gloomy facts presented by history—but we point to them as the very field which we regard as exhibiting the means for realizing what we have described as the essential destiny, the final aim, of world-history. In what terms can this paradox be resolved? We pick up our analysis again. The steps to which it will lead us will also evolve the conditions required for answering the question suggested by the panorama of sin and suffering that history unfolds.

Those manifestations of vitality on the part of individuals and nations, in which they seek and satisfy their own purposes, are at the same time the means and instruments of a higher and broader purpose of which they know nothing, which they realize unconsciously. This has been questioned, denied, condemned, as mere dreaming and "philosophy." So be it. On this point I announced my view at the very outset: Reason governs the world, and has consequently governed history. All else is subordinate to it, subservient to it, and the means for its development.

In the sphere of world history we see momentous collisions between established, acknowledged duties, laws, rights on the one hand and forces adverse to this fixed system on the other. These forces realize themselves in history. They involve principles different from those on which depend the permanence of a people or a state. They are an essential phase in the creative advance of the world spirit. Great historical men—world figures—are those in whose aims such principles are present.

Caesar belongs to this category. His enemies had the *status quo* and the power conferred by an appearance of justice on their side. Caesar was contending for his own position. But his victory secured for him the conquest of the empire. This realization of his own aim, however, was an independently necessary feature in the history of Rome and of the world. It was not merely his private gain. An unconscious impulse occasioned the accomplishment of that for which the time was ripe.

Such are all great historical men. Their own private aims involve those larger issues which are the will of the world spirit. They derive their purposes from a concealed fount, from that inner spirit still hidden beneath the surface which impinges on the outer world as on a shell and bursts it to pieces; not from the calm, regular course of things sanctioned by the existing order.

Such world figures have no consciousness of the general idea they are unfolding while prosecuting their own private aims. On the contrary, they are practical, political men, but possessed of an insight into the requirements of the time, an understanding of what was ripe for development. It is theirs to realize this nascent principle; the next step forward which their world is to take. It is theirs to make this their aim and spend their energies promoting it. They are the heroes of an epoch; must be recognized as its clear-sighted ones. Their deeds, their words, are the best of their time.

World historical figures form purposes to satisfy themselves, not others. Whatever they might learn from others would limit their role. It is they who best understand. From them others learn; or with them, they acquiesce. For that spirit which, in their persons, takes a fresh step in history is the inmost soul of all individuals; but in them it is in a state of unconsciousness which great men arouse. Their fellows therefore follow them, for they feel the irresistible power of their own indwelling spirit embodied in them.

If we contemplate the fate of the world historical person, whose destiny is to be the agent of the world spirit, we find it to be no happy one. He attains no calm enjoyment. His whole life is labor and trouble, driven by some master passion. And when his object is attained, he falls off like an empty shell from the kernel. He dies early, like Alexander; he is murdered, like Caesar; he is exiled, like Napoleon. This consolation those may draw from history who stand in need of it, vexed at what is great and transcendent, striving to belittle it because it is beyond them.

The special interests of private passion are thus inseparable from the development of general principles. But the principle is not implicated in the opposition and combat through which it comes into being. It remains in the hinterland, untouched. This may be called the cunning of reason; it sets the passions to work for it, while that which develops through the conflict of passions pays the penalty and suffers the loss.

A world historical figure is not so unwise as to permit many wishes to divide his energies. He is devoted to one aim. He frequently overrides great and sacred interests. Such conduct is indeed morally reprehensible, but so mighty a form must trample down many an innocent flower, and crush to pieces many an object in its path.

What pedagogue has not demonstrated of Alexander the Great, or of Julius Caesar, that they were immoral men? Whence the conclusion follows that he—the pedagogue—is a better man than they, because he is not driven by their passion. For proof of this he can point to the fact that he does not conquer Asia, does not vanquish Darius, does not subdue an empire. He enjoys life and lets others enjoy it too.

No man is a hero to his valet. Not because he is no hero, but because his valet is only a valet. World historical figures, waited upon in historical literature by psychological valets, come off poorly. They are brought down to the level—or usually a few degrees below the level—of their biographers, those exquisite discerners of true spirits!

Hegel returns, at this point, to his central thought about the state. It is society organized to make law possible. Under the shadow of political law, we can gradually get moral law. Under the discipline of "legal" law man may rise to "moral" law. Law is the possibility of action. It is therefore the basis of freedom, since freedom is the capacity to act. This Hegelian freedom, with its deification of the state, is sometimes confused with freedom in the sense of "permission" or absence of restraint. He wishes to obviate any such confusion.

In world history, only those people can come under our notice which form a state. For it must be understood that the state is the realization of freedom.

The state exists for its own sake. All the worth which any human being possesses, he possesses only through the state. Thus only is he fully conscious. Thus only is he a partaker of morality—of a just and moral social and political life. The state is the march of God on earth. We have in it the object of history, that in which freedom obtains realization; for only that will which obeys law is free.

In our time various errors are current, respecting the state. We shall mention only one, but one which is the direct contradictory of our principle that the state is the realization of freedom. It is this misconception: that man is free by nature, but that in society, in the state, he must limit this natural freedom. In this sense a "state of nature" is assumed, in which mankind possess their "natural rights," with the unconstrained exercise and enjoyment of their freedom.

This assumption of "natural freedom" and "natural rights" is not, indeed, given the dignity of being an historical fact. It would be difficult to point to any such condition as existing or having existed. Examples of savage social organization can be pointed to; but not in support of this idea, for they are marked by brutal passion and violence, and, however primitive their conditions, they involve social organizations which actually function to restrain freedom.

Freedom does not exist as primitive and natural. On the contrary, freedom must be sought and won, and by an incalculable discipline of intellectual and moral powers. The "state of nature" is a state of injustice and violence, of untamed natural impulse, of inhuman deeds and feelings. Limits are certainly imposed by social organization; but they are limits imposed on emotions and instincts. In more advanced stages, they are limits imposed on self-will, caprice, passion. Limitation of this kind is, in part, the means whereby rational freedom, contrasted with unbridled license, can be obtained.

To the conception of freedom, law and morality are indispensably necessary. They are discovered only by the activity of thought, separating itself from the merely sensuous and developing itself in opposition thereto. They must be introduced and incorporated into the originally desire-controlled will, contrarily to its "natural" inclination. The widespread misapprehension of the true nature of freedom consists in conceiving it to be a constraint imposed upon desire, something pertaining to the individual as such. Thus a limitation of caprice and selfwill is regarded as a limitation of freedom. Instead, we argue, such limitation is the indispensable proviso of freedom. Society and the state, with the law and morality upon which they rest, are the very conditions in which freedom is realized.

The state, its laws and morality, constitute the rights of its members. (Thus wide of the facts is the conception of "natural" rights.) Its natural features, its mountains, its rivers, its forests and fields, are their country, their homeland, their material property. Its history is their history. What their forefathers have produced, belongs to them and lives now in their memory. All is their possession, and they are possessed by it. It constitutes their being. This is the meaning of *patriotism*.

The state, then, is the hero of Hegel's philosophy of history. In it the spirit which is manifested as nature and present in man comes to self-realization. When these unions of wills clash, there is war. This conflict clarifies and strengthens the parties. War, like every other genuine expression of will, has its place in the growth of freedom.

In world history each nation is to be regarded as an individual. For world history is the story of the growth of spirit in its highest forms. The forms which this progress assumes are the characteristic "national spirits" of history; the peculiar tenor of their moral life, their government, their art, religion, science. To realize these successive forms is the boundless impulse of the world spirit, the goal of its irresistible longing. The state is the march of God through the world . . . the world which the spirit has made for itself . . . a great architectonic edifice, a hieroglyph of reason, manifesting itself in reality.

All the worth which any human being possesses, all his "spiritual reality," he possesses only through the state. For his "spiritual reality" consists in this, that his own essential nature—rationality—is objectively present to him. Thus only is he fully conscious. Thus only is he a partaker of morality, of a just and moral social and political life. For truth, in these matters, is the unity of the objective and subjective will; and the objective will is to be found in the state, in its laws and arrangements.

Just as the individual is not a real person unless related to other persons, so the state is not a real state unless it is related to other states.

The relation of one state to another presents, on the largest possible scale, the most shifting play of individual passions, interests, aims, talents, virtues, power, injustice, vice, and mere external chance. It is a play in which even the independence of the state is exposed to accident.

When the wills of the particular state can come to no agreement, the matter can only be settled by war. What shall be recognized as a violation of treaty, of respect, of honor, must remain indefinite since many and various injuries can accrue from the wide range of interests and complex relations among states. A state may identify its majesty and honor with any one of its aspects. And if a state, as a strong individuality, has experienced an unduly protracted internal rest, it will naturally be more inclined to irritability in order to find an occasion for intense activity.

There is an ethical element in war. It must not be regarded as an absolute ill, or as merely an external calamity accidentally based upon the passions of despotic individuals or nations, upon acts of injustice and what ought not to be.

War has the deep meaning that by it the ethical health of nations is preserved and their finite aims uprooted. And as the winds which sweep over the ocean prevent the decay that would result from its perpetual calm, so war protects a people from the corruption which an everlasting peace would bring on it.

In times of peace, civic life becomes more extended, every sphere is hedged in and grows immobile, and at last men stagnate, their particular nature becoming more and more hardened and ossified. Where the organs become still, there is death. Eternal peace is often demanded as an ideal toward which mankind should move. But nations issue forth invigorated from their wars. Nations torn by internal strife win internal peace as the result of war abroad. War indeed causes insecurity of property, but this is a necessary commotion.

From the pulpits one hears much concerning the insecurity, the vanity, the instability of temporal things. Everyone is touched by the words. Yet, let insecurity really come, in the form of Hussars with flashing sabers, and that edification which foresaw all this and acquiesced, now turns upon the enemy with curses. Wars break out whenever necessity demands them; but the seeds spring up anew, and speech is silenced before the grave repetitions of history.

The principles which control the many national spirits are limited. Each nation is guided by its particular principles. No judge exists to adjust differences, save the universal spirit of which these are but moments. Only as a particular individuality can each national spirit win objectivity and self-realization; but states, in their relation one to another, reveal the dialectic, the claims and counterclaims, which arise out of their finitude. Out of this dialectic of history rises the universal spirit, pronouncing its judgment upon the nations of the worlds. For the world's history is the world's tribunal.

Note on Sources. The above material is quoted, abridged, or paraphrased from Hegel's book, *The Philosophy of History*. Except for a few passages, the material comes from his "Introduction" to that book.

Reading References. Hegel has been much written about, but the result is not encouraging. In English, there is a small volume by G. S. Morris, *Hegel's Philosophy of History*. It is more understandable, perhaps, than Hegel's own volumes, *Philosophy of History* and *Philosophy of Right*. The Hegelian conception of the state, and thus the central theme in his philosophy of history, is adopted with modifications by Bernard Bosanquet in his *Philosophical Theory of the State*. A sharply critical and not altogether satisfactory account of the Hegelian notion of the state as the significance of history may be found in L. T. Hobhouse's *The Metaphysical Theory of the State*. It should be offset by a few chapters from M. B. Foster's small volume, *The Political Philosophies of Plato and Hegel*. The fact is that Hegel is difficult to read, and that no expositor has succeeded, as yet, in translating him into the language and idiom of ordinary discourse.

The following are some books published since 1940:

Gray, J. G. *Hegel's Hellenic Ideal.*
Marcuse, H. *Reason and Revolution: Hegel and the Rise of Social Theory.*
Mure, G. R. C. *An Introduction to Hegel.*
————. *A Study of Hegel's Logic.*
Myers, H. *Spinoza-Hegel Paradox.*

READING QUESTIONS

1. What is the *a priori* view of history?
2. On what grounds does Hegel defend himself against any imputation of apriorism?
3. Can you explain his use of the terms *reason, spirit, freedom?*
4. How is he led to introduce questions of private interests and passions?
5. "The one the warp, the other the woof, of the vast arras web of world history." Elucidate.
6. "The concrete union of the two elements is liberty under law and morality." Elucidate.
7. "The state is well constituted and internally powerful when. . . ." Discuss.
8. "I will endeavor to make my point more vivid by means of an example." What is the example?
9. What renders us "liable to a moral bitterness, a revolt of the good will"?
10. What is the role of the great man in history?
11. "No man is a hero to his valet." Why not?

12. "In our time various errors are current respecting the state. We shall mention only one. . . ." Namely?
13. "All the worth which any human being possesses, he possesses only through the state." Elucidate.
14. "There is an ethical element in war." Namely?
15. "The world's history is the world's tribunal." Meaning?

4. AN ECONOMIC INTERPRETATION OF HISTORY —FROM FRIEDRICH ENGELS

From Hegel to Marx and Engels. What came to be called the "idealistic" interpretation of history was the claim that in history, as opposed to in nature, spirit was at work. There is spirit. It manifests itself as matter, the order of nature which the natural sciences study. But it goes beyond that. In addition to being *manifested as* matter, spirit is also *present in* man, the order of human nature, and in all his activities. The German word for "spirit" is "Geist." One therefore spoke of "Geisteswissenschaft," the systematic and orderly study of what spirit does, considered apart from its manifestation as nature. This would give you "history and the social sciences." In all of this, the notion of spirit is ultimate. Given the notion of spirit, you knew how to try to think about "nature," the material order. In this way you arrived at the natural sciences. You knew also how to try to think about man. In this way you arrived at the historical sciences, those inquiries in which spirit set forth the story of its own activities, the activities which it is itself present in.

Now, up to a point, this idealistic interpretation of history satisfied those who wished to extend their thinking beyond history into a philosophy of history. It was an attractive alternative for those who were skeptical of the biblical interpretation of history, but whose skepticism did not lead them to go further and reject also the conception of spirit working in nature and history. If you were able and willing to think of matter, the material order, as somehow produced by or derived from spirit, this speculative idealism held out hopes for you. But the friends of matter have never been willing to do this. They have always insisted that matter is fundamental and primary, and that spirit is produced by, a derivative from, matter. In the beginning was matter in motion. As a result, spirit gets produced. This speculative materialism is felt to underlie the natural sciences, and also the historical and social sciences. This gives you the materialist interpretation of history, the philosophy of history which makes matter primary and history the story of its motions and changes.

Karl Marx and his friend Friedrich Engels set themselves to work out what became a popular and influential version of the materialist interpretation of history. They called it historical materialism, and referred to it as the economic interpretation of history. They offered it as an alternative to all versions of the biblical or theological interpretation of history, and all versions of the Hegelian or idealist interpretation of history. Matter is primary. Man is made of matter. His activities are "material" activities. The most important of his activities are those which he performs upon matter, transforming it into food, clothing, shelter, and other material means to his material existence and well-being. To this end he everywhere finds it necessary to organize into associations and communities whereby his *working* on matter is made more productive of the means of subsistence. The result is an economy, a community of persons organized to make possible production by division of labor and, therefore, distribution by exchange. What men do as members of economies is therefore the fundamental answer to the question, What goes on in history? Hence the phrase economic interpretation of history.

Note on Marx and Engels. These two men worked together at the job of formulating the economic interpretation of history. Engels says that Marx was responsible for the fundamental idea, and for the intellectual drive required to work it out in detail; whereas he himself undertook to set it forth in simple, popular language. If you read their joint tract, *The Communist Manifesto*, published in 1848, you see the Marxist interpretation of history already at work. It tells you what has been happening to man, and what man has been doing about it, throughout human history. Marx himself wrote some historical accounts of events in his own time, basing his narrative on the assumption that his general interpretation of history would be granted; e.g., his *Class Struggles in France*, his *Eighteenth Brumaire of Louis Napoleon*, his *Civil War in France*. Late in the 1870's Engels wrote out a statement of their historical materialism. He later published it in the form of a pamphlet, *Socialism: Utopian and Scientific*. This small document contains the clearest and most straightforward wording of the doctrine, particularly in its third section or chapter. That third section, slightly abridged but not otherwise changed, follows. In it Engels explains how, as members of economies, men have transformed economies from feudal, land-based economies into capitalist or bourgeois economies; and will transform these in turn into proletarian socialist economies. The joint *Manifesto*, and this similar tract by Engels alone, have done more to secure a hearing for the Marxist economic interpretation of history, than any other writings by Marx or Engels or anyone else.

1. The materialist conception of history starts from the proposition that the production of the means to support human life and, next to production, the exchange of things produced, is the basis of all social structure; that the manner in which wealth is distributed and society divided into classes is dependent upon what is produced, how it is produced, and how the products are exchanged. From this point of view the final causes of all social changes and political revolutions are to be sought, not in men's brains, not in man's better insight into eternal truth and justice, but in changes in the modes of production and exchange. They are to be sought, not in the *philosophy*, but in the *economics* of each epoch. The perception that social institutions are unreasonable and unjust, only proves that in the modes of production and exchange changes have silently taken place, with which the social order, adapted to earlier economic conditions, is no longer in keeping. The means of getting rid of the incongruities must be present, in a more or less developed condition, within the changed modes of production themselves. These means are not to be invented by deduction from fundamental principles. They are to be discovered in the facts of the existing system of production.

2. What is, then, the position of modern socialism in this connection?

3. The present structure of society is the creation of the ruling class of today, of the bourgeosie. The mode of production peculiar to the bourgeosie, the capitalist mode, was incompatible with the feudal system. The bourgeoisie broke up the feudal system and built the capitalist order of society, the kingdom of free competition, of personal liberty, of equality before the law of all commodity owners, and all the rest of the capitalist blessings. Thenceforward the capitalist mode of production could develop in freedom. Since steam, machinery, and the making of machines by machinery, transformed the older manufacture into modern industry, the productive forces evolved under the bourgeosie developed with a rapidity and in a degree unheard of before. But just as the older manufacture had come into collision with the feudal system, so now modern industry, comes into collision with the bounds within which the capitalistic mode of production holds it confined. The new productive forces have already outgrown the capitalistic mode of using them. And this conflict between productive forces and modes of production exists independently of the will and actions even of the men that brought it on. Modern socialism is the reflex, in thought, of this conflict in fact.

4. In what does this conflict consist?

5. Before capitalistic production, the system of petty industry obtained generally, based upon the private property of the labourers in their means of production; in the country, the agriculture of the small peasant, freeman or

serf; in the towns, the handicrafts organised in guilds. The instruments of labour were the instruments of single individuals, adapted for the use of one worker, and, therefore, small, dwarfish, circumscribed. They belonged, as a rule, to the producer himself. To concentrate these scattered, limited means of production, to enlarge them, to turn them into the powerful levers of production of the present day, was the rôle of capitalist production and of its upholder, the bourgeosie. Since the fifteenth century this has been worked out through the three phases of simple co-operation, manufacture and modern industry. But the bourgeosie could not transform these puny means of production into mighty productive forces, without transforming them, at the same time, from means of production of the individual into *social* means of production only workable by a collectivity of men. The spinning-wheel, the hand-loom, the blacksmith's hammer were replaced by the spinning machine, the power-loom, the steam-hammer; the individual workshop, by the factory, implying the co-operation of hundreds and thousands of workmen. In like manner, production itself changed from a series of individual into a series of social acts, and the products from individual to social products. The yarn, the cloth, the metal articles that now came out of the factory were the joint product of many workers. No one person could say of them: "I made that; this is *my* product."

6. But where the form of production is that spontaneous division of labour which creeps in gradually and not upon any preconceived plan, there the products take on the form of *commodities*, whose mutual exchange, buying and selling, enable the individual producers to satisfy their wants. And this was the case in the Middle Ages. The peasant, e.g., sold to the artisan agricultural products and bought from him the products of handicraft. Into this society of individual producers, of commodity producers, the new mode of production thrust itself. In the midst of the old division of labour, grown up spontaneously and upon *no definite plan*, arose division of labour upon *a definite plan*, as organised in the factory; side by side with *individual* production appeared *social* production. The products of both were sold in the same market, and, therefore, at prices approximately equal. But organisation upon a definite plan was stronger than spontaneous division of labour. The factories working with the combined social forces of a collectivity of individuals produced their commodities more cheaply than the individual small producers. Individual production succumbed in one department after another. Socialised production revolutionised all the old methods of production. But its revolutionary character was so little recognized that it was introduced as a means of increasing and developing the production of commodities. When it arose, it found ready-made, certain machinery for the production and exchange of commodities; merchants' capital, handicraft, wage labour. Socialised production thus introducing itself as a new form of the production of commodities, the old forms

of appropriation remained in full swing, and were applied to its products as well.

7. In the mediæval stage, the question as to the owner of the product of labour could not arise. The individual producer had, from raw material belonging to himself, and generally his own handiwork, produced it with his own tools, by the labour of his own hands or of his family. There was no need for him to appropriate the new product. It belonged to him, as a matter of course. His property in the product was based *upon his own labour.* Even where external help was used, this was, as a rule, of little importance, and was generally compensated by something other than wages.

8. Then came the concentration of production and producers in large workshops, their transformation into socialised means of production and socialised producers. But the socialised producers and means of production and their products were still treated, after this change, just as they had been before, i.e., as the means of production and the products of individuals. Hitherto, the owner of the instruments of labour had himself appropriated the product, because as a rule it was his own product and the assistance of others was the exception. Now the owner of the instruments of labour appropriated the product, although it was no longer *his* product but the product of the *labour of others.* Thus, the products now produced socially were not appropriated by those who had actually produced the commodities, but by the *capitalists.* The means of production, and production itself, had become in essence socialised. But they were subjected to a form of appropriation which presupposes the private production of individuals, under which every one owns his own product and brings it to market. The mode of production is subjected to this form of appropriation, although it abolishes the conditions upon which the latter rests.

9. This contradiction *contains the germ of the social antagonisms of today.* The greater the mastery obtained by the new mode of production, the more it reduced individual production to an insignificant residuum, *the more clearly was brought out the incompatibility of socialised production with capitalistic appropriation.*

10. The first capitalists found wage labour ready-made for them on the market. But it was exceptional, complementary, necessary, transitory wage labour. The agricultural labourer, though, upon occasion, he hired himself out by the day, had a few acres of his own on which he could live at a pinch. The guilds were so organised that the journeyman of today became the master of tomorrow. But all this changed, as the means of production became socialised and concentrated in the hands of capitalists. The means of production, as well as the product of the individual producer, became more and more worthless; there was nothing left for him but to turn wage worker under the capitalist. Wage labour, formerly the exception, now became the rule of production.

The worker became a wage worker for life. The number of these wage work-ers was further increased by the breaking up of the feudal system, by the dis-banding of the retainers of the feudal lords, the eviction of the peasants from their homesteads, etc. The separation was made complete between the capital-ists possessing the means of production, and the producers, possessing nothing but their labour power. *The contradiction between socialised production and capitalistic appropriation manifested itself as the antagonism of proletariat and bourgeoisie.*

11. The capitalistic mode of production thrust its way into a society of individual producers, whose social bond was the exchange of their products. But in every society based upon the production of commodities, the producers lose control over their social inter-relations. Each man produces for himself and for such exchange as he may require to satisfy his remaining wants. No one knows how much of his particular article is coming on the market, nor how much of it will be wanted. No one knows whether his individual product will meet an actual demand, whether he will be able to make good his cost of pro-duction or even to sell his commodity at all. Anarchy reigns in socialised pro-duction.

12. But the production of commodities has its peculiar laws; and these laws work in and through anarchy. They reveal themselves in exchange, and here they affect the individual producers as laws of competition. They are, at first, unknown and have to be discovered as the result of experience. They work themselves out, therefore, independently of the producers, and in an-tagonism to them, as laws of their particular form of production.

13. In mediæval society, production was directed towards satisfying the wants of the individual. It satisfied the wants of the producer and his family. Where personal dependence existed, it also helped to satisfy the wants of the feudal lord. In all this there was no exchange; the products did not assume the ·character of commodities. The family of the peasant produced what they wanted: clothes and furniture, means of subsistence. Only when it began to produce more than was sufficient to its own wants and the payments in kind to the feudal lord, did it also produce commodities. This surplus became com-modities.

14. The artisans of the towns also supplied the greatest part of their own individual wants. They had gardens and plots of land. They turned their cat-tle out into the communal forest, which, also, yielded them timber and firing. The women spun flax, wool, and so forth. Production for exchange, produc-tion of commodities, was only in its infancy. Hence, exchange was restricted, the market narrow, the methods of production stable.

15. But with the extension of the production of commodities, and espe-cially with the introduction of the capitalist mode of production, the laws of commodity production came into action more openly and with greater force. Old bonds were loosened, old limits broken through, producers more and

more turned into independent, isolated producers of commodities. It became apparent that the production of society at large was marked by absence of plan, by accident, by anarchy; and this anarchy grew greater and greater. But the chief means by which the capitalist mode of production intensified this anarchy of socialised production was the exact opposite of anarchy. It was the increasing organisation of production, upon a social basis, in every individual productive establishment. By this, the old, peaceful, stable condition of things was ended. Wherever this organisation of production was introduced, it brooked no other method of production. The field of labour became a battle ground. The great geographical discoveries, and the colonisation following upon them, multiplied markets and quickened the transformation of handicraft into manufacture. War broke out between the individual producers of particular localities. The local struggles begat in their turn national conflicts, the commercial wars of the seventeenth and eighteenth centuries.

16. Finally, modern industry and the opening of the world market made the struggle universal and gave it an unheard-of virulence. Advantages in conditions of production now decide the existence or non-existence of individual capitalists, as well as of whole industries and countries. He that falls is cast aside. It is the Darwinian struggle of the individual for existence transferred from nature to society. The conditions of existence natural to the animal appear as the final term of human development. The contradiction between socialised production and capitalistic appropriation now presents itself as *an antagonism between the organisation of production in the individual workshop and the anarchy of production in society generally.*

17. The capitalistic mode of production moves in these two forms of antagonism. It is never able to get out of that "vicious circle." This circle is gradually narrowing. The movement becomes more and more a spiral, and must come to an end. It is anarchy in production in society at large that more and more turns the majority of men into proletarians; and it is the proletariat who will finally put an end to anarchy in production. It is the anarchy in social production that turns the perfectibility of machinery into a law by which every individual industrial capitalist must continually perfect his machinery under penalty of ruin.

18. But the perfecting of machinery makes human labour superfluous. The introduction and increase of machinery means the displacement of manual, by a few machine workers. Improvement in machinery means the displacement of the machine workers themselves. It means the production of wage workers in excess of the needs of capital, the formation of an industrial reserve army available when industry is working at high pressure, to be cast out when the crash comes, a constant weight upon the limbs of the working class in its struggle for existence with capital, keeping wages down to the level that suits the interests of capital. Thus machinery becomes the most powerful weapon in the war of capital against the working class; the instruments of labour tear the

means of subsistence out of the hands of the labourer; the product of the worker is turned into an instrument for his subjugation. Thus economising the instrument of labour becomes the waste of labour power, and robbery based upon the normal conditions under which labour functions; machinery, the most powerful instrument for shortening labour time, becomes the means for placing the labourer's time at the disposal of the capitalist. Thus it comes about that overwork of some becomes the condition for the idleness of others, and that modern industry, which hunts after new consumers over the whole world, forces the consumption of the masses at home down to a starvation minimum, and so destroys its own home market. The law that equilibrates the surplus population, the industrial reserve army, to the extent and energy of accumulation, rivets the labourer to capital more firmly than ever. It establishes an accumulation of misery, corresponding with accumulation of capital. Accumulation of wealth at one pole; accumulation of misery, agony of toil, slavery, ignorance, brutality, mental degradation, at the opposite pole.

19. The perfectibility of modern machinery is, by the anarchy of social production, turned into a law that forces the individual industrial capitalist to improve his machinery, to increase its productivity. The possibility of extending production is transformed for him into a compulsory law. The expansive force of modern industry, laughs at all resistance. Such resistance is offered by consumption, by sales, by the markets. The extension of the markets cannot keep pace with the extension of production. The collision becomes inevitable, and as this cannot produce any real solution so long as it does not break the capitalist mode of production, the collisions become periodic. Capitalist production has begotten another "vicious circle."

20. Since 1825, when the first general crisis broke out, the whole industrial and commercial world is thrown out of joint about once every ten years. Commerce is at a standstill, the markets are glutted, products accumulate, hard cash disappears, credit vanishes, factories are closed, workers are in want of the means of subsistence, because they have produced too much of the means of subsistence; bankruptcy follows bankruptcy. The stagnation lasts for years; productive forces and products are wasted and destroyed, until the accumulated commodities finally filter off depreciated in value, until production and exchange gradually begin to move again. Little by little the pace quickens. It becomes a trot. The trot breaks into a canter, the canter grows into the headlong gallop of a steeplechase of industry, commercial credit and speculation, which finally, after breakneck leaps, ends where it began—in the ditch of a crisis. And so over and over again. We have now, since 1825, gone through this five times, and at the present moment (1877) we are going through it for the sixth time.

21. In these crises, the contradiction between socialised production and capitalist appropriation ends in a violent explosion. The circulation of commodities is stopped. Money becomes a hindrance to circulation. The laws of

production and circulation of commodities are turned upside down. The economic collision has reached its apogee. *The mode of production is in rebellion against the mode of exchange.*

22. The socialised organisation of production has become incompatible with the anarchy of production. This is brought home to the capitalists by the concentration of capital that occurs during crises, through the ruin of large and small capitalists. The mechanism of the capitalist mode of production breaks down under the pressure of the productive forces. It is no longer able to turn all this means of production into capital. They lie fallow, and hence the industrial reserve army must also lie fallow. Means of production, means of subsistence, available labourers, all the elements of production and of general wealth, are present in abundance. But abundance becomes the source of distress and want, because it prevents the transformation of the means of production and subsistence into capital. For in capitalistic society the means of production can only function when they have undergone transformation into capital, into the means of exploiting human labour power. The necessity of this transformation into capital of the means of production and subsistence stands like a ghost between these and the workers. It alone prevents the coming together of the material and personal levers of production; it alone forbids the means of production to function, the workers to work and live. The capitalistic mode of production stands convicted of its own incapacity to direct these productive forces. These productive forces press forward to the removal of the existing contradiction, to the *recognition of their character as social productive forces.*

23. This rebellion of the productive forces, this command that their social character shall be recognised, forces the capitalist class to treat them more and more as social productive forces. The period of industrial high pressure, with its inflation of credit, not less than the crash itself, by the collapse of great capitalist establishments, tends to bring about the form of the socialisation of means of production which we meet in joint-stock companies. Many of these means of production and of distribution are, from the outset, so colossal, that, like the railroads, they exclude all other forms of capitalistic exploitation. At a further stage of evolution this form also becomes insufficient. The producers on a large scale in a particular branch of industry in a particular country unite in a "trust," for the purpose of regulating production. They determine the amount to be produced, parcel it out among themselves, and thus enforce the selling price fixed beforehand. But trusts of this kind, as soon as business becomes bad, are generally liable to break up, and, on this account, compel a yet greater concentration of association. The whole of the particular industry is turned into one gigantic joint-stock company; internal competition gives place to the internal monopoly of this one company.

24. In the trusts, competition changes into its opposite—monopoly; and the production without any definite plan of capitalistic society capitulates to the production upon a definite plan of the invading socialistic society. This is

still to the advantage of the capitalists. But in this case the exploitation is so palpable that it must break down. No nation will put up with production conducted by trusts, with so barefaced an exploitation of the community by a small band of dividend mongers.

25. In any case, with trusts or without, the official representative of capitalist society—the state—will ultimately have to undertake the direction of production. This necessity of conversion into state property is felt first in the great institutions for intercourse and communication—the post-office, the telegraphs, the railways.

26. The crises demonstrate the incapacity of the bourgeosie to manage modern productive forces. The transformation of the great establishments for production and distribution into joint-stock companies, trusts and state property, show how unnecessary the bourgeoisie are for that purpose. The social functions of the capitalist are now performed by salaried employees. The capitalist has no further social function than pocketing dividends, tearing off coupons, and gambling on the Stock Exchange, where the different capitalists despoil one another of their capital. At first the capitalistic mode of production forces out the workers. Now it forces out the capitalists, and reduces them, as it reduced the workers, to the ranks of the surplus population, although not immediately into those of the industrial reserve army.

27. But the transformation, into joint-stock companies and trusts, or into state ownership, does not do away with the capitalistic nature of the productive forces. In the joint-stock companies and trusts this is obvious. But the modern state, is only the organisation that bourgeois society takes on to support the conditions of the capitalist mode of production against the encroachments of the workers and of individual capitalists. The modern state is essentially a capitalist machine, the state of the capitalists, the ideal personification of the total national capital. The more it takes over productive forces, the more it becomes the national capitalist, the more citizens it exploits. The workers remain wage workers—proletarians. The capitalist relation is not done away with. It is rather brought to a head. But, brought to a head, it topples over. State ownership of the productive forces is not the solution of the conflict, but concealed within it are the elements of that solution.

28. This solution consists in the recognition of the social nature of the modern forces of production, and therefore in the harmonising of the modes of production, appropriation and exchange with the socialised character of the means of production. And this can only come about by society taking possession of the productive forces which have outgrown all control except that of society as a whole. The social character of the means of production and of the products today reacts against the producers, periodically disrupts production and exchange. But with the taking over by society of the productive forces, the social character of the means of production and of the products will be utilised by the producers with an understanding of its

nature, and instead of being a source of disturbance and periodical collapse, will become the most powerful lever of production itself.

29. Social forces work like natural forces; blindly, forcibly, destructively, so long as we do not understand and reckon with them. But when we understand them, when we grasp their action, their direction, their effects, it depends only upon ourselves to subject them to our own will, and by means of them to reach our own ends. And this holds especially of the mighty productive forces of today. As long as we refuse to understand the nature of these social means of action—and this understanding goes against the grain of the capitalist mode of production and its defenders—so long these forces work in opposition to us, so long they master us.

30. But when their nature is understood, they can, in the hands of the producers working together, be transformed from master demons into willing servants. With this recognition of the real nature of the productive forces of today, the social anarchy of production gives place to a social regulation of production upon a definite plan, according to the needs of the community and of each individual. Then the capitalist mode of appropriation, in which the product enslaves first the producer and then the appropriator, is replaced by the mode of appropriation of the products that is based upon the nature of the modern means of production; upon the one hand, direct social appropriation, as means to the maintenance and extension of production—on the other, direct individual appropriation, as means of subsistence and enjoyment.

31. Whilst the capitalist mode of production transforms the great majority of the population into proletarians, it creates the power which, under penalty of its own destruction, is forced to accomplish this revolution. Whilst it forces on the transformation of the means of production, already socialised, into state property, it shows the way to accomplishing this revolution. *The proletariat seizes political power and turns the means of production into state property.*

32. In doing this, it abolishes itself as proletariat, abolishes class distinctions and antagonisms, abolishes also the state as state. Society thus far, based upon class antagonisms, had need of the state: that is, an organisation of the particular class which was *pro tempore* the exploiting class, an organisation to prevent interference with the existing conditions of production, and therefore, to keep the exploited classes in the condition of oppression corresponding with the given mode of production (slavery, serfdom, wage labour). The state was the official representative of society as a whole. But it was this only in so far as it was the state of that class which represented, for the time being, society as a whole; in ancient times, the state of slave-owning citizens; in the Middle Ages, the feudal lords; in our own time, the bourgeoisie. When it becomes the representative of the whole of society, it renders itself unnecessary. As soon as there is no longer any social class to be held in subjection; as soon as class rule and the individual struggle for existence based

upon our present anarchy in production, with the collisions and excesses arising from these, are removed, nothing remains to be repressed, and a special repressive force, a state, is no longer necessary. The first act by which the state constitutes itself the representative of the whole of society— taking possession of the means of production in the name of society—is its last independent act as a state. State interference in social relations becomes superfluous, and then dies out; the government of persons is replaced by the administration of things, and by the conduct of processes of production. The state is not "abolished." *It dies out.*

33. Since the appearance of the capitalist mode of production, the appropriation by society of the means of production has been dreamed of, by individuals and sects, as the ideal of the future. But it could become possible, could become a historical necessity, only when the actual conditions for its realisation were there. Like every other social advance, it becomes practicable, not by men understanding that the existence of classes is in contradiction to justice, equality, etc., not by the mere willingness to abolish these classes, but by virtue of certain new economic conditions. The separation of society into an exploiting and an exploited class, a ruling and an oppressed class, was the necessary consequence of the deficient and restricted development of production in former times. So long as the total social labour yields a produce which but slightly exceeds that necessary for the existence of all; so long, therefore, as labour engages the great majority of the members of society—so long, of necessity, this society is divided into classes. Side by side with this great majority arises a class freed from directly productive labour, which looks after the general affairs of society, the direction of labour, state business, law, science, art, etc. It is, therefore, the law of division of labour that lies at the basis of the division into classes. But this does not prevent this division into classes from being carried out by violence and robbery, trickery and fraud. It does not prevent the ruling class from consolidating its power at the expense of the working class, turning their social leadership into an exploitation of the masses.

34. But if division into classes has a certain historical justification, it has this only for a given period, under given social conditions. It was based upon the insufficiency of production. It will be swept away by the development of modern productive forces. And the abolition of classes presupposes a degree of historical evolution, at which the existence of any ruling class and, therefore, the existence of class distinction itself has become obsolete. It presupposes, therefore, the development of production to a point where appropriation of the means of production and of the products, of political domination, of the monopoly of culture, and of intellectual leadership by a particular class has become superfluous; economically, politically, intellectually a hindrance to development.

35. This point is now reached. Their political and intellectual bankruptcy

is no longer a secret to the bourgeoisie. Their economic bankruptcy recurs every ten years. In every crisis, society is suffocated beneath its own productive forces and products, which it cannot use, and stands helpless before the absurd contradiction that the producers have nothing to consume, because consumers are wanting. The expansive force of the means of production bursts the bonds that the capitalist mode of production had imposed upon them. Their deliverance from these bonds is the one condition for an unbroken, constantly accelerated development of the productive forces, and therewith for a practically unlimited increase of production. Nor is this all. The socialised appropriation of the means of production does away not only with the artificial restrictions upon production, but also with the waste and devastation of productive forces and products that are at present the concomitants of production, and that reach their height in the crises. Further, it sets free for the community at large a mass of means of production and of products, by doing away with the senseless extravagance of the ruling classes and their political representatives. The possibility of securing for every member of society, by means of socialised production, an existence not only sufficient materially, but guaranteeing to all the free development and exercise of their physical and mental faculties is now for the first time here.

36. With the seizing of the means of production by society, production of commodities is done away with, and, simultaneously, the mastery of the product over the producer. Anarchy in social production is replaced by definite organisation. The struggle for individual existence disappears. Then man is finally marked off from the rest of the animal kingdom, and emerges from mere animal conditions of existence into human ones. The conditions of life which environ man, and which have hitherto ruled man, now come under the control of man, who for the first time becomes the conscious lord of nature, because he has become master of his own social organisation. The laws of his own social action, hitherto standing face to face with man as laws of nature foreign to and dominating him, will then be used with understanding, and so mastered by him. Man's own social organisation, hitherto confronting him as a necessity imposed by nature and history, now becomes the result of his own free action. The forces that have hitherto governed history pass under the control of man himself. Only from that time will man, more and more consciously, make his own history—only from that time will the social causes set in movement by him have, in a constantly growing measure, the results intended by him. It is the ascent of man from the kingdom of necessity to the kingdom of freedom.

37. Let us briefly sum up our sketch of historical evolution.

I. *Mediæval Society*—Individual production on a small scale. Means of production adapted for individual use; hence primitive, ungainly, petty, dwarfed. Production for immediate consumption, either of the producer himself or of his feudal lords. Only where an excess of production over this consumption occurs is such excess offered for sale, enters into exchange. Production of commodities, therefore, is only in its infancy. But already it contains within itself *anarchy in the production of society at large.*

II. *Capitalist Revolution*—Transformation of industry, at first by means of simple co-operation and manufacture. Concentration of the means of production, hitherto scattered, into great workshops. As a consequence, their transformation from individual to social means of production—a transformation which does not, on the whole, affect the form of exchange. The old forms of appropriation remain in force. The capitalist appears. In his capacity as owner of the means of production, he appropriates the products and turns them into commodities. Production has become a *social* act. Exchange and appropriation continue to be *individual* acts, the acts of individuals. *The social product is appropriated by the individual capitalist.* Fundamental contradiction, whence arise all the contradictions in which our present day society moves, and which modern industry brings to light.

A. Severance of the producer from the means of production. Condemnation of the worker to wage labour. *Antagonism between the proletariat and the bourgeoisie.*

B. Growing predominance and increasing effectiveness of the laws governing the production of commodities. Unbridled competition. *Contradiction between socialised organisation in the individual factory and social anarchy in production as a whole.*

C. On the one hand, perfecting of machinery, made by competition compulsory for each individual manufacturer, and complemented by a constantly growing displacement of labourers. *Industrial reserve army.* On the other hand, unlimited extension of production, also compulsory under competition, for every manufacturer. On both sides, unheard of development of productive forces, excess of supply over demand, overproduction, glutting of the markets, crises every ten years, the vicious circle: excess here, of means of production and products—excess there, of labourers, without employment and without means of existence. But these two levers of production and of social well-being are unable to work together because the capitalist form of production prevents the productive forces from working and the products from circulating, unless they are first turned into capital—which their very superabundance prevents. The contradiction has grown into an absurdity. *The mode of production rises in rebellion against the form of exchange.* The bourgeoisie are convicted of incapacity to manage their social productive forces.

D. Partial recognition of the social character of the productive forces forced upon the capitalists themselves. Taking over of the great institutions for production and communication, first by joint-stock companies, later on by trusts, then by the state. The bourgeoisie demonstrated to be a superfluous class. All its social functions performed by salaried employees.

III. *Proletarian Revolution*—Solution of the contradictions. The proletariat seizes the public power, and by means of this transforms the socialised means of production, slipping from the hands of the bourgeoisie, into public property. By this act, the proletariat frees the means of production from the character of capital they have thus far borne, and gives their socialised character freedom to work itself out. Socialised production upon a predetermined plan henceforth possible. The development of production makes the existence of different classes of society thenceforth an anachronism. In proportion as anarchy in social production vanishes, the political authority of the state dies out. Man, at last the master of his own form of social organisation, becomes at the same time the lord over nature, his own master—free.

To accomplish this act of universal emancipation is the historical mission of the modern proletariat. To thoroughly comprehend the historical conditions and thus the nature of this act, to impart to the now oppressed proletarian class a full knowledge of the conditions and of the meaning of the momentous act it is called upon to accomplish, this is the task of the theoretical expression of the proletarian movement, scientific socialism.

Reading References. Professor H. J. Laski's book, *The Rise of European Liberalism,* is a good piece of further reading. It will hand the interested reader on to other books by him and to other books by twentieth-century Marxists. Two alternatives to Marxism as a philosophy of history will be found in Toynbee's *Study of History,* and in R. G. Collingwood's "The Idea of History." The reader who has come this far can find his own way in Toynbee: the terms of the assignment ("a pattern detectable in the details") carries over from our earlier authors. Professor Collingwood, however, proposes a new, or at least different, assignment; namely an exploration and description of the *modes of thinking* which mark the historian's effort to make the past intelligible. When an historian addresses himself to that task, what principles and what presuppositions are operative in his thinking? This is to redefine philosophy's problem in respect to history.

READING QUESTIONS

1. The "materialist" conception of history.
2. Why "economic interpretation of history" or "economic determinism" are usable alternatives to "historical materialism."

3. Use his distinction between "individual" and "social" or "collective" to set forth the transition from a "medieval" economy to a "bourgeois" economy.

4. And his distinction between division of labor upon "no definite plan" vs. "a definite plan."

5. Individual production succumbed to what? Why?

6. In the medieval stage the question of the owner of the product could not arise. (a) Why not? (b) Whereas . . . ?

7. Anarchy reigns in socialized production when the products are *commodities*. (a) What is a commodity? (b) Why the anarchy?

8. What is the Industrial Reserve Army? Where does it come from?

9. "Capitalist production has begotten *another* vicious circle" (a) What was the first one? (b) What is this second one?

10. How the "anarchy" generates trusts, monopolies, state ownership.

11. At first the capitalistic mode of production forces out the workers. Then it forces out the capitalists. How so?

12. Why "state ownership" will not satisfy him.

13. What he wants instead.

14. In doing this, the proletariat abolishes itself as proletariat.

15. The state is not "abolished." It dies out. It withers away.

16. Watch his "Summary" carefully.

5. CULTURES DECLINE INTO CIVILIZATIONS —FROM OSWALD SPENGLER

From Marx and Engels to Spengler. Thus far we have acquainted ourselves with Santayana's description of the popular and wide-spread biblical-Christian conception of human history, with reference to which so much "philosophizing" about history has proceeded. In the beginning God created the world, then created man in the world. Human history is the spread-out story of what has happened to man and what he has done about it. It takes off with the creation and closes with salvation. Our other philosophies of history stand in contrast to that. Kant sees in history the story of nature's efforts, having produced in man an animal capable of living by the use of his rational powers, to force him to develop those powers by posing for him a problem. If he handles the problem it will be because he uses and develops his rational powers. If he does not, those powers may atrophy, but the species will not survive to tell about it. The exercise and development of his rational powers is a mandate of survival from nature to man. Hegel pushes this argument beyond the somewhat "fable" way in which Kant had left it. In Hegel there is no nature having designs on man whereby he will be goaded into developing his rational powers. There is reason in the world. History is the story of how reason develops, and in developing, produces, indeed *is*, the historical world of human beings and human society. The basic thought here is obscure. That spirit manifests itself *as* nature, and is present *in* man and society as developing reason, is not an easily apprehended claim. It may not be a "fable," as Kant's way of conceiving the matter was; but genuinely obscure, in a way that Kant was not. Marx, in setting forth his views on history, took Hegel, not Kant, as his point of departure. This was to accept the more obscure formulation. Marx seems to have clear intentions about this aspect of his relation to Hegel. He says he wanted to turn Hegel right way up; having found him standing on his head, to turn him right way up and stand him on his feet. His materialist conception of history, his historical materialism in contrast to Hegels historical idealism, was the outcome. For reasons which Marx and Engels both make clear, their historical materialism became finally their "economic interpretation of history."

The Communist Manifesto was published by Marx and Engels in 1848. It broached the theory that history discloses a pattern of class struggles moving toward a social revolution which will end the class struggle by ushering in a classless social order based upon a socialist economy. Exactly seventy years later, in 1918, Oswald Spengler published his massive work, *The Decline of the West*. The years between were crowded with events and ideas. These should be recalled to mind in passing from Marx and Engels to Spengler.

1. In the first place, from 1848 to 1918 there was much lively history. Merely the list of wars and revolutions is imposing. In the year 1848 itself, revolutionary uprisings occurred throughout Europe on an unprecedented scale. The Crimean War and the Indian Mutiny came in the 1850's; the American Civil War, in the 1860's; the Franco-Prussian War, the third French revolution, and the rise of the Paris Commune in the 1870's; a number of colonial and "imperialistic" wars, in the 1880's and 1890's, culminating in the Boer War at the opening of the new century; the Russian-Japanese War and the first Russian revolution, in 1904–1905; an intricate tangle of Balkan wars, in the years preceding 1914; the important Chinese revolution, in 1912; the World War, in 1914; the two Russian revolutions under Kerensky and Lenin, in 1917; and the German revolution in 1918. This list is representative, not ex-

haustive. These wars and revolutions formed an accompaniment to enormous population growth, tremendous economic expansion, vast and complex political and social reform movements, the rise of organized labor, the formation of overseas empires by European great powers, and much more besides. Consult the table of contents of any good history of the world since 1848. The cultural history of the period is no less intense. The scientific theories of Darwin, Pavlov, Freud, and Einstein fall between Marx and Spengler. The challenging problem literature of modern England, Russia, France, Germany, and the Scandinavias falls between Marx and Spengler. The heated controversies associated with the names of Colenso, Bradlaugh, Huxley, Pasteur, Dreyfus, Pankhurst, Nietzsche, to name only a few, fall between Marx and Spengler. The movements in the arts associated with such persons as Wagner, William Morris, Rodin, Cézanne, Matisse, and others, fall between Marx and Spengler. The tendencies in modern philosophy covered by such terms as *neo-Hegelianism, neo-positivism, pragmatism, creative evolutionism, instrumentalism, realism, anti-intellectualism,* and so on fall between Marx and Spengler.

2. In the second place, the period from 1848 to 1918 was rich in historical writing. More and, with a few notable exceptions, greater histories were written during these years than during any comparable period in the past. In Germany the latter half of the historical writings of Leopold von Ranke, the historical writings of Theodor Mommsen, of Heinrich von Treitschke, of Eduard Zeller, of Kuno Fischer, of Adolph Harnack, of Theodor Gomperz, to name only a few, fall between Marx and Spengler. So, also, in France, do the historical writings of Jean Victor Duruy, Ernest Renan, Hippolyte Taine, and others. In England the historical writings of Macaulay, Froude, Stubbs, Green, Maine, Gardiner, Lecky, Seeley, Creighton, Acton, Maitland, the Trevelyans, fall within the same period; as, also, in the United States, do the works of John Lothrop Motley, of Francis Parkman, of John Fiske, of James Ford Rhodes, Alfred Mahan, Henry Adams, and others. The point of listing these names is to indicate that a philosophy of history formulated during or at the close of this period had to take account of a vastly increased amount of sheer data. The inviting simplicity presented by the picture of world history between Augustine and Hegel is gone. The man who proposes discourse on these matters now, must be prepared to take account of a greater number and a larger range of facts than confronted his predecessors in other centuries.

3. In the third place, the period from 1848 to 1918 was prolific in

theories or philosophies of history. In England, Carlyle's "great man" theory carried over from a previous generation. It was followed by the hypothesis of geographic determinism and the central role of intellectual progress, in the writings of H. T. Buckle. Buckle was followed by Walter Bagehot, whose *Physics and Politics* proposed an application to human history of categories applied to natural history by Darwin. On the continent philosophies of history were set forth by Hippolyte Taine, by Friedrich Nietzsche, by Anatole France, by Benedetto Croce, by Vilfredo Pareto, and many others. And mention should be made, in the United States, of the interesting and suggestive theory advanced by Henry Adams in his two papers, "The Tendency of History" and "The Rule of Phase Applied to History," and illustrated in his two books, *Mont-Saint-Michel and Chartres* and *The Education of Henry Adams*.

No matter who is read, following Kant, Hegel, Marx and Engels, the history of the world since 1848 would have to be kept in mind. The problem of a philosophy of history remains what it has always been: an hypothesis in the light of which to interpret the events. But, as already noted, the number and range of events known is greater, and the tempo of reflection upon them has been stepped up. In selecting Spengler it is not suggested that valuable alternatives are lacking. Spengler, in our own day, is worth reading, in the wake of Kant and Hegel and Engels. But so, too, are several others, particularly Benedetto Croce, Flinders Petrie, Henry Adams, Vilfredo Pareto, Pitirim Sorokin, Arnold Toynbee, and R. G. Collingwood. If science has been the greatest fertilizer of modern philosophy, history runs it a close second.

Biographical Note. Oswald Spengler was born in Germany in 1880 and died in 1936, at the age of fifty-six. He was educated in the universities at Halle, Munich, and Berlin. He studied mathematics and philosophy particularly, we are told, but, like Francis Bacon, seems to have taken all knowledge for his field. After teaching for seven years in the secondary schools of Germany, he retired to do private tutoring and to write his books. His one great work, *The Decline of the West*, was published, Volume One in 1918 and Volume Two in 1922. Over a hundred thousand copies were sold in Germany in a few years. The *Decline* was followed by two small volumes, *Man and Technics* and *The Hour of Decision*, in which the author formulates a philosophy of life and a call to action, based upon the premise that the argument of the large treatise is substantially correct.

The Argument of the Citations. Spengler begins with the usual questions: "Is there a logic of history? Is there, beyond all the casual and incalculable elements of the separate events, something that we may call a structure of historic humanity? Does world history present certain grand traits?" The first step toward an answer to this question is the critique of what he calls the "ancient-medieval-modern" scheme of history. Reasons for rejecting this "Ptolemaic" view of history. In place of it, the author proposes his "Copernican" view, reminding us of an earlier "Copernican revolution" in philosophy. Granted the Copernican hypothesis in history, he pauses to emphasize the fact that analogy thereby becomes fundamental in historical thinking. The essence of Spengler's Copernican revolution is the distinction between a culture and a civilization, and the claim that history reveals many cultures maturing and declining into civilizations. The culture of the West, declining into the civilization of the West, is a case in point. The book is to tell the story of this decline, once the general theory has been established. One feature of a culture degenerating into a civilization is the emergence of "world cities" and their contributary "provinces." Our own period is then given some attention. Finally, the futility and fate of philosophizing, in our own period, are pointed out.

Is there a logic of history? Is there, beyond all the casual and incalculable elements of the separate events, something that we may call a structure of historic humanity? Does world history present certain grand traits? And if so, what are the limits to which reasoning from such premises may be pushed?

The above quotation shows that Spengler is proposing the same question as Kant, Hegel, Marx, and Engels. Before presenting his own views to the reader, the author pauses to repudiate the usual textbook division of history into ancient, medieval, and modern. He calls this the Ptolemaic view of history, likening it to Ptolemaic astronomy according to which our earth was the center of the universe.

What is world history? An ordered presentation of the past, no doubt. Everyone, if asked, would say that he knew "the form" of history, quite clearly and definitely. He would be under an illusion. The illusion is there because no one has seriously reflected upon the question of the form of world history, still less conceived any doubts as to his knowledge of it. In fact, the common notion of world history is an unproved and subjective affair handed down from generation to generation, and badly in need of a little of that skepticism which, from Galileo onward, has regulated and deepened our ideas of nature.

Thanks to the subdivision of history into "ancient," "medieval," and "modern"—an incredibly jejune and meaningless scheme, which has, however, entirely dominated our historical thinking—we have failed to perceive the true position in the general history of mankind of the little part world that has developed in Western Europe from the time of the Roman Empire, to judge of its relative importance, and to estimate its direction.

The ages that are to come will find it difficult to believe that such a scheme, with its simple rectilinear progression and its meaningless proportions, becoming more preposterous with each century, incapable of bringing into itself the new fields of history as they come into the light of our knowledge, was never wholeheartedly attacked.

The criticisms that it has long been the fashion for historical students to level at this scheme mean nothing. They have only obliterated the scheme without substituting any other for it. To toy with such phrases as "the Greek middle ages" or "Germanic antiquity" does not help us to form a clear picture in which China and Mexico, the empire of Axum and that of the Sassanids have their proper places. And the expedient of shifting the initial point of "modern history" from the Crusades to the Renaissance, or from the Renaissance to the French Revolution, only goes to show that the scheme is still regarded as unshakably sound.

It is not only that the ancient-medieval-modern scheme circumscribes the area of history. What is worse, it rigs the stage. Western Europe is treated as a steady pole, and great histories of millenial duration and mighty far-away cultures are made to revolve around this pole in all modesty. We select a single patch of ground, for no better reason, it seems, than because we live on it, and make it the center of the historical system. From it all the events of history receive their light; from it their importance is judged. But this phantom "world history," which a breath of skepticism would dissipate, is acted out only in our own West European conceit.

We have to thank this conceit of ours for the immense optical illusion whereby distant histories, such as those of China and Egypt, are made to shrink to mere episodes while in the neighborhoods of our own position the decades since Luther or Napoleon loom large as Brocken specters.

For the cultures of the West, it is evident that Athens, Florence, or Paris, is more important than Lo-Yang or Pataliputra. But is it permissible to found a scheme of world history on such estimates? The Chinese historian is equally entitled to frame a world history in which Caesar, the Crusades, the Renaissance, Frederick the Great are passed over in silence as insignificant. From the morphological point of view, why should our eighteenth century be more important than any of the sixty centuries that preceded it? Is it not ridiculous to oppose a "modern" history of a few centuries to an "ancient" history which covers as many millennia? This is no exaggeration. Do we not, for the sake of keeping the hoary scheme of ancient-medieval-modern, dispose of Egypt and Babylon as a prelude to classical history? Do we not relegate the vast cultures of India and China to footnotes? Do we not entirely ignore the great American cultures?

As mentioned above, this ancient-medieval-modern scheme is to be repudiated as Ptolemaic and replaced by a Copernican view of history.

The most appropriate designation for this ancient-medieval-modern scheme of history, in which great cultures are made to follow orbits around us, is the Ptolemaic system of history. The system that is put forward in this book, in place of it, I regard as the Copernican system in the historical sphere. It admits no privileged position to the classical culture, or the Western culture, as against the cultures of India, Babylon, China, Egypt, the Arabs, Mexico. Each of these non-Western cultures, being separate worlds, count, in point of mass for just as much in the general picture of history as the classical culture, while they frequently surpass it in point of spiritual greatness and soaring power.

I see, in place of that empty figment of ancient-medieval-modern, the drama of a number of mighty cultures, each springing from the soil of a mother region; each stamping its material in its own image; each having its own idea, its own passions, its own life, its own will and feeling, its own death. Here indeed are colors, lights, movements, that no eye has yet discovered.

Here cultures, peoples, languages, truths, gods, bloom and age as the oaks and the stone pines. Each culture has its own new possibilities of self-expression, which arise, ripen, decay, and never return. There is not just one sculpture, one painting, one mathematics, one physics, one religion, one morality, one philosophy, but many, each different from the others, each limited in duration, each having its special type of growth and decline. Each grows with the same superb aimlessness as the flowers of the field. I see world history as a picture of endless formations and transformations. The professional historian sees it as a sort of tapeworm industriously adding onto itself one epoch after another.

The substitution of the Copernican for the Ptolemaic view of history effects an unmeasurable widening of horizon. This idea once attained, the rest is easy. To this single idea one can refer all those separate problems of religion, art, philosophy, morals, politics, economics with which the modern mind has busied itself so passionately and so vainly. This idea is one of those truths that have only to be expressed with clarity to become indisputable. It is capable of transforming the world outlook of one who fully understands it. It immensely deepens the world historical picture. By its aid we are enabled to follow the broad lines into the future, a privilege till now permitted only to the physicist.

The Copernican view, then, resolves history into a number of different epochs. Each epoch, it is to be argued, begins as a "culture" and ends as a "civilization." The first step will be to clarify these terms *culture* and *civilization*. Do the epochs have any common characteristics? Does each have a "life" of its own?

Is it possible to find in life a series of stages which must be traversed? For everything organic, the notions of birth, youth, age, lifetime, death, are fundamentals. May not these notions possess, in the realm of history, a meaning which no one has yet extracted? In short, is all history founded upon general biographic archetypes?

At this point Spengler develops the thought that a history of many different epochs will develop analogies between one epoch and another. Something in one epoch will be "analogous" to something in another epoch. How reliable is the analogy?

The means whereby to identify dead forms is mathematical law. The means whereby to understand living forms is analogy.

From any technique of analogies we are far distant. It is neither a principle nor a sense of historic necessity, but simple inclination, that governs the choice of the analogies we draw. They throng up without scheme or unities. If they do hit upon something that is apt, it is thanks to luck, more rarely to instinct, never to a principle. No one has hitherto set himself to work out a technique or method for striking upon apt and revealing analogies in the region of world history. Nor has anyone had the slightest inkling that there is here a root, in fact the only root, from which can come a broad solution of the problems of history.

Insofar as they lay bare the structure of history, analogies might be a blessing to historical thought. Their technique, developing under the influence of a comprehensive idea, might eventuate in inevitable conclusions and logical mastery. But, as hitherto understood and practiced, they have been a curse, for they have enabled historians to follow their own tastes, instead of realizing that their first task was the symbolism of history and its analogies. Superficial in many cases, these analogies are worse than superficial in others, while occasionally they are bizarre to the point of perversity.

Napoleon has hardly ever been discussed without a side glance at Caesar and Alexander. Napoleon himself conceived of his situation as akin to Charlemagne's. The French Revolutionary Convention spoke of Carthage when it meant England, and the Jacobins styled themselves Romans. Cecil Rhodes, the organizer of British South Africa, felt himself akin to the Emperor Hadrian. And so on, through an indefinitely long list.

I have not hitherto found anyone who has carefully considered the morphological relationship that binds together the expression forms of all branches of a single culture; who has, e.g., gone beyond politics to grasp the ultimate and fundamental ideas in mathematics, ornamentation, architecture, philosophy, literature, craftsmanship, etc., within a single culture.

Who among historians realizes that there are deep uniformities between the differential calculus and the dynastic principle of politics in the age of Louis XIV; between the classical city state and Euclidean geometry; between the space perspective of Western oil painting and the conquest of space by railroad; between telephone and long-range weapon; between contrapuntal music and credit economics? Yet, viewed from this morphological standpoint, such things as the Egyptian administrative system, the classical coinage, analytical geometry, the cheque, the Suez Canal, the book printing of the Chinese, the Prussian army, the Roman road engineering, can be made uniformly understandable as symbols.

The historian, then, despite risks, must be prepared to make large use of analogies. He will be interested in noting what things in epoch A are "contemporary" with things in epoch B. The word *contemporary* in Spengler's use means happening in one epoch at relatively the same point as in another epoch. Two events can be contemporary, in this sense, even if the epochs in question are several centuries apart. However, the whole point of working up these analogies is to throw light on the common characteristics of an epoch. Now, an epoch, it was said, begins as a culture and ends as a civilization. Accordingly, we turn to these two key terms.

If we are to discover the form in which the destiny of Western culture will be accomplished, we must first be clear as to what a culture is. What are its relations to visible history? How far may we point to peoples, tongues and epochs, battles and ideas, states and goods, arts and crafts, sciences, laws, economic types, great men, great events, world ideas, as symbols of a culture?

Every culture has its own civilization. In this book, these two words are used in a periodic sense, to express an organic succession. The civilization is the destiny of the culture. In this principle we obtain the viewpoint from which the problems of historical morphology become capable of solution. Civilizations are the most external and artificial states of which a species of developed humanity is capable. Civilizations are a conclusion, death following upon life, rigidity following expansion. They are an end, irrevocable, yet, by an inward necessity reached again and again. They consist in a progressive taking-down of forms that have become dead.

To the culture belongs gymnastics, the joust, the tournament. To the civilization belongs sport. Art itself becomes a sport, to be played before a highly intelligent audience of connoisseurs or buyers; and this, whether the feat consist in mastering absurd instrumental tone masses and taking harmonic fences, or in some *tour de force* of coloring. Then a new fact philosophy appears, which can spare only a smile for metaphysical speculations; and a new literature that is a necessity for the megalopolitan palate and nerves but is both unintelligible and ugly to the provincial.

What is the hallmark of a politic of civilization, in contrast to a politic of culture? It is, for the classical and the West European, money. The money spirit penetrates the historical forms of the people's existence. Though the forms persist, the great political parties cease to be more than reputed centers of decision. The decisions in fact lie elsewhere. A small number of superior heads, whose names are often little known, settle everything, while below them are the great mass of second-rate politicians selected through a franchise to keep alive the illusion of popular self-determination.

Imperialism is to be taken as the typical symbol of passing away. Imperialism is civilization unadulterated. The energy of culture-man is directed inwards; of civilization-man, outwards. In this form the destiny of the West is now set. Thus I see in Cecil Rhodes a man of the age. He stands for the political style of a far-ranging future. His phrase "expansion is everything" is the Napoleonic reassertion of the tendency of every civilization that has fully ripened. It is not a matter of choice. The expansive tendency is a doom which grips man of the world-city stage.

Rhodes is to be regarded as the precursor of a Western type of Caesar whose day is to come, though yet distant. He stands midway between Napoleon and the force-men of the next centuries. It was only before his maps that he could fall into a sort of poetic trance, this son of a parson who, sent out to South Africa without means, made a gigantic fortune and employed it as the engine of political aims.

His idea of a trans-African railway from Cape to Cairo, his project of a South African empire, his hold on the hard metal souls of the mining magnates, his capital planned as the future residence of an all-powerful statesman who yet stood in no definite relation to the state, his wars, his diplomatic deals, his road systems, his syndicates, his armies, all this is the prelude of a future which is still in store for us and with which the history of Western man will be definitely closed.

The civilization of an epoch crystallizes always into the "world city" and the "province": megalopolis and its surrounding territory. What about these two units of social organization?

World city and province, the two basic ideas of every civilization, bring up a wholly new form-problem of history, the very problem that we are living through today with hardly any notion of its immensity. In place of a people true to a type, born of the soil and grown on the soil, there is a new sort of nomad, cohering unstably in fluid masses, the parasitical city dweller, traditionless, utterly matter-of-fact, without religion, clever, unfruitful, contemptuous of the countryman. This is a great stride toward the end. What does it signify? France and England have already taken the step. Germany is beginning to do so. After Syracuse, Athens, Alexandria, comes Rome. After Madrid, Paris, London, come Berlin and New York. It is the destiny of whole regions that lie outside the circle of one of these great cities to become "provinces."

The world city means cosmopolitanism in place of home, matter-of-fact coldness in place of reverence for tradition, scientific irreligion in place of the older religion of the heart, society in place of the state, "natural" in place of hard-earned rights. It was in the conception of money, entirely disconnected from the notion of the fruitful earth, that the Romans had the advantage over the Greeks. Thereafter any high ideal of life becomes largely a question of money. Unlike the Greek stoicism, Roman stoicism presupposes a private income. Unlike the social and moral ideals of the eighteenth century, the ideals of the twentieth century are matters for millionaires. To the world city belongs not a folk, but a mass.

The uncomprehending hostility of the mass of the world city to all the traditions of the culture—nobility, church, privilege, dynasties, conventions in art, limits of knowledge—the keen and cold intelligence that confounds the wisdom of the peasant, the new-fashioned naturalism in sex and society, the reappearance of *panem et circenses* in the form of wage disputes and large-scale organized spectator sports, all these things betoken the definite closing down of the culture and the setting in of the civilization, antiprovincial, late, futureless, but inevitable.

At this level civilizations enter upon a stage of depopulation. The whole pyramid of culture vanishes. It crumbles from the summit, first the world cities, then the provinces, and finally the land itself whose best blood has incontinently poured into the towns. At last only the primitive blood remains alive, but robbed of its strongest and most promising elements. The residue is the Fellah type.

Thus far: Has history a logic? Repudiation of the Ptolemaic theory of history. Proposal of the Copernican theory. History deals with great epochs. Hence analogy as the historical method. Epochs begin as cultures and end as civilizations. The world city and its province characterize the end of an epoch. With these general ideas in mind Spengler turns to the particular subject of his book: the history of our own times or, as he calls it, *The Decline of the West*. We live at the end of an epoch. We live in a civilization, not in a culture. And his massive book is an inductive survey of the evidence for this claim. He says:

Our narrow task, then, is to determine, from such a survey of world history, the state of Western Europe and America for the epoch, 1800-2000; to establish the chronological position of this period in the cultural history of the West; to indicate its significance as a chapter that it found in the story of every culture; and to make clear the meaning of its political, artistic, intellectual, and social expression forms.

Every culture is a four-act drama with an ascending movement of religion, aristocracy, and art, and a descending movement of irreligion, democracy, socialism, and the great city. The culture of the West, whose "decline" is referred to in the title of this book, originated in that feudal system of lord and serf which Roman conquest left like a network over Europe. Its basis is a stolid peasantry, bearing on its back the economic life of the world.

Considered in the spirit of analogy the period appears as chronologically parallel to the epoch we call *Hellenism;* and its present culmination, marked by the World War, corresponds to the transition from the Hellenistic to the Roman age. Rome, with its rigorous realism, uninspired, barbaric, disciplined, practical, will always give us, working as we must by analogies, the key to our own future.

Long ago we should have seen in the classical culture a development which is the counterpart of our own, differing indeed in surface detail, but similar as regards the power driving the great organism toward its end. We might have established the correspondence, item by item, from the Trojan War and the Crusades, Homer and the *Nibelungenlied,* through Doric and Gothic, Dionysian and Renaissance, Polycletus and Bach, Athens and Paris, Aristotle and Kant, Alexander and Napoleon, to the world city and imperialism.

The transition from culture to civilization was accomplished for the classical world in the fourth century A.D.; for the Western world in the nineteenth century. From these periods onwards, the great decisions take place. And they take place in three or four world cities that have absorbed into themselves the whole content of history.

Let it be realized, then, that the nineteenth and twentieth centuries, hitherto looked upon as an ascending straight line of world history, are in reality a stage of life which may be observed in every culture that has ripened to its limit. Let it be realized, then, that the future of the West is not a limitless tending upwards and onwards toward our present ideals, but a single phenomenon of history, strictly limited and defined as to form and duration, covering a few centuries and, in essentials, calculated from available precedents.

He who does not understand that this outcome is obligatory, that our choice is between willing this and willing nothing, between cleaving to this destiny or despairing of the future; he who cannot feel that there is grandeur in the achievements of powerful intelligence, in the energy and discipline of metal-hard natures, in battles fought with the coldest and abstractest means; he who is obsessed with the ideals of past ages, must forego all desire to comprehend history, to live through history, or to make history.

So much, then, for a few of the analogies by means of which Spengler locates the West and the period of its decline. He turns to some of the characteristic phenomena of the period. Here we can only quote a few scattered items from an enormous mass comprising two stout volumes. For example, the press:

A more appalling caricature of freedom cannot be imagined. There is today no need to impose military service on people. Whip their souls with articles, telegrams, pictures, till they clamor for weapons and force their leaders into a conflict. In preparation for the World War the press of whole countries was brought financially under the control of a few world cities, and the peoples belonging to them reduced to an unqualified intellectual slavery.

As for the modern press, the sentimentalist may beam with contentment when it is constitutionally "free." But the realist merely asks at whose disposal it is. For the multitude, that is true which it continually reads and hears. Its "truth" is a product of the press. What the press wills is true. Three weeks of press work, and the truth is acknowledged by everybody. The press and the news service keep whole peoples and continents under a deafening drumfire of theses, catchwords, standpoints, scenes, feelings.

Or the modern omnipresent machine:

These machines become less and less human; more ascetic, mystic, esoteric. They weave over the earth an infinite web of subtle forces, currents, tensions. Their bodies become ever more immaterial, ever less noisy. The wheels, rollers, levers, are vocal no more. All that matters draws itself into the interior. The center of this artificial and complicated realm is the engineer, the priest of the machine.

Or the modern masses:

. . . the fluid megalopolitan populace; the newspaper readers of our time; the "educated" who makes a cult of intellectual mediocrity and a church of advertisement; the man of the theaters and places of amusement, of sport and "best sellers," of expressionism, the movies, theosophy, dances, poker, and racing. The Roman *panem et circenses* we have in our wage disputes and football games.

Such "men" constitute the "masses." The masses reject the matured culture of our epoch. The mass is formless. It persecutes with hatred all distinctions of rank, the orderliness of tradition, of property, of knowledge. They are the new nomads of cosmopolis. They recognize no past and possess no future. They are the end.

Or modern art:

It is all irretrievably over with the arts of the West. What is practiced as art today is impotence and falsehood: a faked music, filled with artificial noisiness of massed instruments; a faked painting, full of idiotic, exotic, and show-card effects; a lying plastic that steals from Assyria, Egypt, Mexico, indifferently. For Western people there can no longer be any question of great painting or great music. We are today playing out a tedious game with dead forms to keep up the illusion of a living art.

Coming, at last, to philosophy, the story makes unpalatable reading. To begin with, Herr Spengler dislikes and distrusts the "thinker" type:

There are born destiny men and causality men. A whole world separates the man born to prosper, to rule, to fight, to dare, to organize, from the man who is destined by the power of his mind or the defect of his blood to be an intellectual—the saint, the priest, the scholar, the idealist. The eye for men and situations, the belief in his star, things which every born man of action possesses, are something wholly different from the belief in the "correctness of a standpoint," and are denied to the critical, meditative man. Even the footfall of the fact man sounds different from that of the thinker.

With that as a beginning, one can expect what follows: Modern philosophers are nobodies and busybodies:

It still remains to consider the relation of a morphology of world history to philosophy. For me the test to be applied to a thinker is his eye for the great facts of his own time. Only this can settle whether he is merely a clever architect of systems and principles, versed in definitions and analyses, or one in whom the soul of his time speaks in his works and intuitions.

A philosopher who cannot grasp and command actuality will never be of the first rank. The early Greek philosophers were merchants and politicians *en grande*. The desire to put his political ideas into practice nearly cost Plato his life. Confucius was several times a minister of state. Pythagoras organized an important political movement. Goethe, besides being an executive minister, was interested in the Suez and Panama Canals and their effects upon the economy of the world. Hobbes was one of the originators of a plan for winning South America for England. Leibnitz, without doubt the greatest intellect in Western philosophy, founder of the differential calculus and the analysis situs, conceived or cooperated in a number of major political schemes.

Turning from men of this world to the "philosophers" of today, one is dismayed and ashamed. What they do not possess is real standing in actual life. Their personalities are poor. Their political and practical outlook is commonplace. Not one of them has intervened effectively in politics, in the development of modern techniques, in matters of communication, in economics, or in any other big actuality, with a single act or a single compelling idea. Not one of them counts in mathematics, in physics, in politics. Why is it that the mere idea of calling upon one of them to prove his intellectual eminence in government, diplomacy, large-scale organization, the direction of any big colonial or commercial or transport concern, is enough to evoke our pity? This insufficiency indicates, not that they possess profundity but that they lack weight. I look around in vain for an instance in which a modern "philosopher" has made a name by even one deep or far-seeing pronouncement on an important question of the day. I see nothing but provincial opinions of the same kind as any one else's. Whenever I take up a work by a modern philosopher I find myself asking: Has he any idea of the actualities of world politics, world-city problems, capitalism, the future of the state, the relation of techniques to the course of civilization, Russia, science? Goethe would have understood all this and reveled in it. There is not one living philosopher capable of taking it in. This sense for actualities is, of course, not the same thing as the content of a philosophy; but, I repeat, it is an infallible symptom of its necessity, fruitfulness and importance.

We must allow ourselves no illusions as to the gravity of this negative result. We have lost sight of the final significance of effective philosophizing. We have descended from the perspective of the bird to that of the frog. We confuse philosophy with preaching, with agitation, with novel-writing, with lecture-room jargon. It were better to become a colonist or an engineer, to do something that is real and true, than to chew over once more the old dried-up themes under cover of some "new wave of philosophic thought"; better to construct an aero-engine than a new theory of apperception that is not wanted. It is indeed a poor life's work to restate once more the views of a hundred predecessors on the will or on psychophysical parallelism. This may be a profession. It is emphatically not a philosophy. A doctrine that does not attack and affect the life of one's period is no doctrine, and had better not be taught.

To me, the depths and refinement of mathematical and physical theories are a joy. By comparison, the aesthete and the physiologist are fumblers. I would sooner have the fine mind-begotten forms of a fast steamer, a steel structure, a precision lathe, the subtlety and elegance of many chemical and optical processes, than all the pickings and stealings of present-day "arts and crafts."

This is a situation that regularly repeats itself at a certain historical level. I maintain that today many an inventor, many a diplomat, many a financier, is a sounder philosopher than all those who practice the dull craft of experimental psychology. It would have been absurd in a Roman of intellectual eminence, who might, as consul or praetor, have led armies, organized provinces, built cities and roads, to want to hatch out some new variant of post-Platonic philosophy at Athens. Consequently no one did so. It was not in harmony with the tendency of the age. Therefore it attracted only third-class men of the kind that always advances as far as the Zeitgeist of the day before yesterday.

I prefer one Roman aqueduct to all the Roman temples and statues. I love the Colosseum and the giant vault of the Palatine, for they display the real Rome and the grand practical sense of her engineers. It was not for nothing, that the genuine Roman despised the "artist" and the "philosopher." The time for art and philosophy had passed; they were exhausted, used up, superfluous, and his instinct for the realities of life told him so. One Roman law weighed more than all the lyrics and school metaphysics of the time put together.

Modern philosophy, like modern art, is played out. With Kant and Schopenhauer, the curtain went down for the last time. What remains is merely the possibility of becoming competent and understanding historians of philosophy.

Systematic philosophy closed with the end of the eighteenth century. Kant put its utmost possibilities in forms that are grand and, for the Western soul, final. He is followed, as Plato and Aristotle were followed, by a specifically megalopolitan philosophy that is not speculative, but practical, irreligious, social-moral. This philosophy begins in the West with Schopenhauer. He was the first to make the will-to-live a central thought. It is the same will-to-live that was Schopenhauer-wise denied in *Tristan* and Darwin-wise asserted in *Siegfried;* that led Marx to an economic and Darwin to a biological hypothesis which have together subtly transformed the world-outlook of the Western megalopolis; and that produced a series of tragedies from Hebbel to Ibsen and Hardy. It has embraced, therefore, all the possibilities of a philosophy, and has exhausted them.

We have not chosen our time. We cannot help it if we are born in the early winter of a civilization, instead of in the golden summer of a culture. Everything depends upon seeing our own position clearly; on realizing that we may lie to ourselves about it but cannot evade it. He who does not acknowledge this ceases to be counted among the men of his generation.

One must begin, therefore, by asking what today is possible and what is not. In the case of a genuine adept this question is answered in advance by a kind of instinct.

Systematic philosophy, then, lies far behind us, and ethical philosophy has been wound up. But a third possibility, corresponding to the classical skepticism, still remains. And it can be brought to light by the hitherto unknown methods of historical morphology. Classical skepticism was ahistoric. Our skepticism, a symbol of the autumn of spirituality, is historical. Its solutions are got by treating everything as relative, as historical. Classical skepticism is the negation of philosophy, declaring it to be useless. Our skepticism, on the contrary, regards the history of philosophy as, in the last resort, philosophy's gravest theme. This is *skepsis* in the true sense; for, where classical skepticism is led to renounce absolute standpoints by contempt for the past, we are led to do so by comprehension of the past.

It is our task to sketch out this unphilosophical philosophy—the last that the West will know. Skepticism is the expression of a pure civilization, and it dissipates the world picture of the culture that has gone before. For us, its success will lie in resolving all the older problems into one, the historical. With that, the claim of higher thought to possess general and eternal truths falls to the ground. Truths are truths only in relation to a particular mankind. Thus, my own philosophy is able to express and reflect only the Western mind, and that mind only in its present civilized phase by which its conception of the world, its practical range, and its sphere of effect, are specified.

Note on Sources. The above material is quoted, abridged, or paraphrased from Spengler's *The Decline of the West;* for the most part, from his "Introduction" to that book.

Reading References. An introductory account of Spengler and his *Decline* is to be found in Will Durant's book *Adventures in Genius.* This book was reissued under the title *Great Men of Literature.* A book on Spengler's interpretation of history, *Civilization or Civilizations*, has been written by E. H. Goddard and P. A. Gibbons. A volume of selections from the *Decline*, with introduction and notes by Edwin F. Dakin, has been published under the title *Today and Destiny.* The *Decline* itself is not easy reading. The author's style and his esoteric references slow things up. The two short books, *Man and Technics* and *The Hour of Decision* are much less encumbered.

READING QUESTIONS

1. What is the Ptolemaic view of history?
2. Why is it so named?

3. Give three of Spengler's criticisms of this view.
4. What is the Copernican view of history?
5. Why is it so named?
6. Why is Spengler led to a consideration of analogy in history?
7. Name one or two he suggests.
8. In what sense does he propose to use the word *contemporary?*
9. What distinguishes a culture from its civilization?
10. What is a world city?
11. Name two or three from history.
12. How does Spengler characterize world cities?
13. What, roughly, is the period of the decline in our case?
14. What about the press in our day?
15. Or the machine?
16. Or the masses?
17. Or the fine arts?
18. What is a causality man?
19. Some items in Spengler's appraisal of modern philosophers.
20. "A third possibility . . . still remains." Namely?

An Aesthetic Problem

THE PROBLEM STATED

We sometimes refer to poems, pictures, musical compositions and statues as works of art; and the activity which produces them as art. Is it possible to define these terms, *art* and *work of art?* What fact about any activity would be our reason for calling it art? What fact about any object would be our reason for calling it a work of art? There would seem to be *some* reason. On some occasions we withhold these terms; on others, we are in doubt. Such behavior on our part would suggest that we at least "know what we are talking about" when we use, or refuse, or are in doubt about using, the terms *art* and *work of art*. If there is *no* detectable reason for using these terms, why do we do so? Why do we refuse to do so? Why do we hesitate to do so?

In an inquiry of this kind, we might begin with judgments which we would be able and willing to authorize. Take for example Matthew Arnold's poem, "Dover Beach." Is it a work of art? If so, why? If not, why not? Let the reader settle these questions for himself. Let him mention a dozen items, *any* dozen—poems, pictures, musical compositions, statues—about which he would be prepared to say "These are works of art. Whatever else they are, they are works of art. Whatever other items are works of art, at least *these* are. Whatever other items are *not* works of art, at least these *are*. And the activity which produced them is art." If the reader cannot or will not authorize *any* such judgments, then for him the problem dealt with in this Topic does not arise. But there is no *prima facie* reason to believe that the reader is thus either unable or unwilling. Why should he be?

Suppose, then, that these aesthetic judgments are forthcoming. "This and this and this are works of art; and the activity which produced them is art." Such judgments are data. Given them, the question arises: What fact, common and peculiar to these and similar objects, is the reason for calling them works of art? And the activities, art? An answer to this question would define, set limits to, the class "work of art" and "art." Whatever satisfied the definition would fall inside these classes; whatever did not, would fall outside these classes. As these definitions took shape, they would suggest further questions; and as these questions were answered, the answers could be added on to the original definitions. The outcome would constitute a theory of art. The English word *theory* is said to be derived from the Greek word *theoria,* meaning a looking at, a viewing, a beholding. A theory of art is a looking at the particulars which together make up "the world of art."

In the authors brought together in this Topic you have persons attempting to think about aesthetic judgments, definitions, and theories. They are endeavoring to define and theorize about art; or to theorize about the attempt to define and theorize about art. The first author, Eugene Véron, proposes the hypothesis that art is an activity in which the agent expresses his feelings or emotions, and does this subject to the limitations imposed by some medium, e.g., words, sounds, lines, colors, or stone. This theory of art as expression stands in contrast to an older theory of art as imitation. The second author, Leo Tolstoy, would include communication as well as expression. There must be communication as well as expression, if the activity is to be art, and the outcome a work of art. The third, R. G. Collingwood, reverts to the first position, art as expression of emotion, and offers a more intimate and detailed account of the character of this activity. Criticism sets in with the fourth author, Professor John Hospers. Professor Hospers gives reasons for doubting that "expression of emotion" will enable one to formulate a definition of art or work of art. The fifth author, Professor Morris Weitz, rejects the entire enterprise of defining the terms *art* or *work of art;* he claims that these terms are essentially and in principle impossible to define. His point, to speak in metaphor, is that these terms are "alive" and "growing"; and that therefore *any* attempt to "contain" them by a definition or a theory is bound to be unsatisfactory.

1. ART AS EXPRESSION OF EMOTION
—FROM EUGENE VÉRON

A good beginning can be made with Eugene Véron (1825–1889). His book, *Aesthetics,* was published in 1878. It was translated into

English a year later, but is now out of print and difficult to come by. This is regrettable because it has the virtues of simplicity and clarity. Whether you agree with Véron or not, at least you know where he stands. If you agree, he leaves you free to develop beyond him if you see the necessity for doing so. If you disagree, he leaves you "in the clear" with respect to what it is you disagree with. These are helps, when one is making a beginning.

His proposal is that a work of art is an emotive symbol, something whereby the artist expresses his emotions, his feelings. An emotive symbol can be contrasted with a cognitive symbol, something whereby one expresses what one knows or believes, in contrast to what one feels. It is one thing to have emotions and to express them: this calls for an emotive symbol. It is another to have knowledge or belief, and to express them: this calls for a cognitive symbol. If emotions are to be expressed, a symbol or vehicle must be created enabling them to be expressed. Art is the activity of creating these emotionally expressive symbols. The symbol is the work of art.

Véron distinguishes sharply between this way of conceiving art and the older way which thought of art as the activity of producing a copy or imitation of some original. According to this Imitation Theory an artist looks at a man or a mountain and paints "what he sees." The result would be an imitation or copy or "picture" of some "original." On this way of thinking, the work of art would be something of a cognitive symbol. It would tell you what you would know if you knew the original. You could gauge its excellence by comparing it with the original. On this way of thinking a good camera might produce a better work of art than any painter could do. Compared to an original, a photograph can be more accurate than a painting. Even greater accuracy could be obtained by holding a mirror up to an original. Véron's essential claim would rule out mirror-images, photographs, contrived echoes, tape-recordings, and so on as not works of art, and the activity of producing them as not art. The artist must have a certain feeling or emotion. The work of art must express that feeling or emotion.

This primary claim enables Véron to distinguish between decorative and expressive art. The latter is art proper. It is not to be judged by its power to please, but by its power to express. The claim—art as creation of emotive symbol—enables him also to develop the notions of artistic integrity and artistic style. Integrity demands that one express the emotions one has; not, e.g., the feelings one "ought to" have, or would like to have. Style is the way in which the person one basically is, determines the way in which one gives expression to the emotions one has. These are a few of the good things to be had from a reading of Véron's statement of the Emotive Theory of Art. No matter what awkward questions that theory may give rise to, there is no dismissing it out of hand on the grounds that it does not lead one to think at all fruitfully about art.

Art, far from being the blossom and fruit of civilization, is rather its germ. It began to give evidence of its existence so soon as man became self-conscious, and is to be found clearly defined in his very earliest works.

By its psychological origin it is bound up with the constituent principles of humanity. The salient and essential characteristic of man is his incessant cerebral activity, which is propagated and developed by countless acts and works of varied kind. The aim and rule of this activity is the search after *the best;* that is to say, the more and more complete satisfaction of physical and moral wants. This instinct, common to all animals, is seconded in man by an exceptionally well-developed faculty to adapt the means to the end.

The effort to satisfy physical wants has given birth to all the industries that defend, preserve, and smooth the path of life; the effort to satisfy the moral wants—of which one of the most important is the gratification of our cerebral activity itself—has created the arts, long before it could give them power sufficient for the conscious elaboration of ideas. The life of sentiment preceded the manifestations of intellectual life by many centuries.

The gratification, *in esse* or *in posse,* of either real or imaginary wants, is the cause of happiness, joy, pleasure, and of all the feelings connected with them; the contrary is marked by grief, sadness, fear, etc.: but in both cases there is emotion to give more or less lively evidence by means of exterior signs. When expressed by gesture and rhythmic movement, such emotion produces the dance; when by rhythmic notes, music; when by rhythmic words, poetry.

As man is essentially sympathetic and his joy or pain is often caused as much by the good or evil fortunes of others as by his own; as, besides, he possesses in a very high degree the faculty of combining series of fictitious facts, and of representing them in colors even more lively than those of reality: it results that the domain of art is of infinite extent for him. For the causes of emotion are multiplied for every man—not only by the number of similar beings who live around him and are attached to him by the more or less closely knit bonds of affection, alliance, similitude of situation or community of ideas and interests; but also, by the never-ending multitude of beings and events that are able to originate or direct the imaginings of poets.

To these elements of emotion and moral enjoyment must be added the combinations of lines, of forms and of colors, the dispositions and opposition of light and shade, etc. The instinctive search after this kind of emotion or pleasure, the special organ of which is the eye, has given birth to what are called the arts of design—sculpture, painting and architecture.

We may say then, by way of general definition, that art is the manifestation of emotion, obtaining external interpretation, now by expressive arrangements of line, form or color, now by a series of gestures, sounds, or words governed by particular rhythmical cadence.

We must conclude, from our definition, that the merit of a work of art can be measured by the power with which it manifests or interprets the emotion that was its determining cause, and that, for a like reason, must constitute its innermost and supreme unity.

Imitation is not the aim of art. The poet arranging his verses, the musician composing his airs and harmonies, are well aware that their real object is not imitation. This distinction is perhaps less clear in matters of painting and sculpture. Some artists, and these not the least capable, are convinced that when they have a model before them, their one duty is to imitate it, copy it. And indeed they do nothing else; and, by virtue of such imitation, they succeed in producing works of incontestable artistic value.

Here we have simply a misunderstanding. If an artist were really able to reduce himself to the condition of a copying machine; if he could so far efface and suppress himself as to confine his work to the servile reproduction of all the details of an object or event, the only value his work would possess would be that of a more or less exact *procès verbal*, and it would perforce remain inferior to reality. Where is the artist who would attempt to depict sunlight without taking refuge in some legerdemain, calling to his aid devices which the true sun would despise? But enough of this. Just because he is endowed with sensibility and imaginative power, the artist, in presence of the facts of nature or the events of history, finds himself, whether he will or not, in a peculiar situation. However thorough a realist he may think himself, he does not leave himself to chance. Now, choice of subject alone is enough to prove that some preference has existed, the result of a more or less predeterminate impression, and of a more or less unconscious agreement between the character of the object and that of the artist. This impression and agreement he sets to work to embody in outward form; it is the real aim of his work, and its possession gives him his claim to the name of artist. Without wishing or even knowing it, he molds the features of nature to his dominant impression and to the idea that caused him to take pencil in hand. His work has an accidental stamp, in addition to that of the permanent genius which constitutes his individuality. Poet, musician, sculptor and architect, all pay more or less strict obedience to the same law. To it, point all those rules of artistic composition which pedantic academicism has subtly multiplied until they contradict each other.

The more of this personal character that a work possesses; the more harmonious its details and their combined expression; the more clearly each part communicates the impression of the artist, whether of grandeur, of melancholy or of joy; in fine, the more that expression of human sensation and will predominates over mere imitation, the better will be its chance of obtaining sooner or later the admiration of the world—always supposing that the sentiment expressed be a generous one, and that the execution be not of such a kind as to repel or baffle connoisseurs. It is not of course impossible that an artist endowed with an ill-regulated or morbid imagination may place himself outside all normal conditions and condemn himself to the eternal misapprehension of the public. Impressions that are too particular, eccentric feelings, fantastic execution or processes, which do nothing to raise the intrinsic value or power of inspiration of a work, may give it so strange and ultra-individual a character that it may become impossible for us to arrive at its real merit. The best qualities, when exaggerated, become faults; and that very personality or individuality which, when added to imitative power, results in a work of art, produces when pushed to extravagance nothing but an enigma.

We see, then, that the beautiful in art springs mainly from the intervention of the genius of man when excited by special emotion.

A work is beautiful when it bears strong marks of the individuality of its author, of the permanent personality of the artist, and of the more or less accidental impression produced upon him by the sight of the object or event rendered.

In a word, it is from the worth of the artist that that of his work is derived. It is the manifestation of the faculties and qualities he possesses which attracts and fascinates us. The more sympathetic power and individuality that these faculties and qualities display, the easier is it for them to obtain our love and admiration. On the other hand, we, for a similar reason, reject and contemn bold and vulgar works that by their shortcomings demonstrate the moral and intellectual mediocrity of their authors, and prove the latter to have mistaken their vocation.

Consequently, then, beauty in art is a purely human creation. Imitation may be its means, as in sculpture and painting; or, on the other hand, it may have nothing to do with it, as in poetry and music. This beauty is of so peculiar a nature that it may exist even in ugliness itself; inasmuch as the reproduction of an ugly model may be a beautiful work of art, by the ensemble of qualities which the composition of it may prove are possessed by its author.

The theory of imitation is but the incomplete and superficial statement of the ideas which we are here advocating. What is it that we admire in imitation? The resemblance? We have that much better in the object itself. But how is it that the similitude of an ugly object can be beautiful? It is obvious that between the object and its counterfeit some new element intervenes. This element is the personality, or, at least, the skill of the artist. This latter, indeed, is what they admire who will have it that beauty consists in imitation. What these applaud, in fact, is the talent of the artist. If we look below the surface and analyze their admiration we shall find that it is so; whether they mean it or not, what they praise in a work is the worker.

This was the opinion of Bürger, who says: "In works which interest us the authors in a way substitute themselves for nature. However common or vulgar the latter may be, they have some rare and peculiar way of looking at it. It is Chardin himself whom we admire in his representation of a glass of water. We admire the genius of Rembrandt in the profound and individual character which he imparted to every head that posed before him. Thus did they seem to him, and this explains everything simple or fantastic in his expression and execution."

After all this, we need not stop to refute the theory which would found artistic beauty upon the imitation of "beautiful nature."

The only beauty in a work of art is that placed there by the artist. It is both the result of his efforts and the foundation of his success. As often as he is struck by any vivid impression—whether moral, intellectual, or physical—and expresses that impression by some outward activity by poetry, music, sculpture, painting or architecture—in such a way as to cause its communication with the soul of spectator or auditor; so often does he produce a work of art the beauty of which will be in exact proportion to the intelligence and depth of the sentiment displayed, and the power shown in giving it outward form.

The union of all these conditions constitutes artistic beauty in its most complete expression. We may define aesthetics as the science of beauty in art. It is the science whose object is the study and elucidation of the manifestations of artistic genius.

There are two distinct kinds of art: decorative and expressive. The main object of decorative art is the gratification of the eye and ear. Its chief means to perfection of form are harmony and grace of contour, diction or sound. Such art rests upon the desire for beauty, and has nothing in view beyond the peculiar delight caused by the sight of beautiful objects. It has produced admirable works in the past, and may produce them again on condition that its inspiration be sought in actual and existing life, and not in the imitation of works sanctified by time.

Modern art has no tendency in this latter decorative direction. Decorative beauty no longer suffices for us in art. Something more has been required. The chief characteristic of modern art is power of expression. Through form this, the second kind of art, traces the moral life, and endeavors to occupy man, body and soul, but with no thought of sacrificing the one to the other.

The moral life is but the general result of the conditions of the physical. The one is bound to the other by necessary connections which cannot be broken without destroying both. The first care of the artist should be to seek out and grasp the methods of manifestation so as to comprehend and master their unity.

Art, thus understood, demands intellectual faculties higher and more robust than if founded solely upon an ideal of beauty. Art founded upon the latter notion would be sufficiently served by one possessing an acute sense of the beautiful—the degree of his sensibility being indicated by the plastic perfection of his work. But expressive art demands a capability of being moved by many sentiments, demands the power to penetrate beneath outward appearances and to seize a hidden thought, the power to grasp either the permanent characteristic or the particular and momentary emotion; in a word, it demands that complete eloquence of representation which art might have dispensed with while it confined itself to the investigation or delineation of a single expression, but which became indispensable the moment the interpretation of the entire man became its object.

We may say, too, that modern art is doubly expressive; because, while the artist is indicating by form and sound the sentiments and ideas of the personages whom he introduces, he is also by the power and manner of such manifestation giving an unerring measure of his own sensibility, imagination, and intelligence.

Expressive art is in no way hostile to beauty; it makes use of it as one element in the subjects which require it, but its domain is not enclosed within the bounds of such a conception. It is not indifferent to the pleasures of sight and hearing, but it sees something beyond them. Its worth must not be measured only by perfection of form, but also and chiefly, by the double power of expression which we have pointed out, and, we must add, by the value of the sentiments and ideas expressed. This latter point is too often and wrongly ignored by artists.

Between two works which give evidence of equal facility to grasp the accents and characteristics of nature, and equal power to bring out both the inner meaning of things and the personality of the artist—we, for our part, would prefer that one of which the *Conception* showed the more vigorous intelligence and elevated feeling. The art critics seem to have made it one of their principles to take no account of choice of subject, but only to look at the technical result. Such a principle is plausible rather than true. The individuality of the author can never be excluded from a work, and choice of subject is frequently one of the points by which this individuality is most clearly indicated.

It is true, of course, that elevation of sentiment can never take the place of art talent. On this point we cannot too strongly condemn the practice of academic juries who, on the one hand, reward mere mechanical labor simply because it has been exercised upon what are called classic subjects; and, on the other, persecute more independent artists to punish their obstinacy in deserting the beaten track. Nothing, then, can be further from our thoughts than to require critics to substitute, in every case, consideration of the subject for that of the work itself; or to condemn *a priori* all artists who remain faithful to the traditions, ideas, and sentiments of the past. In these, indeed, some find their only inspiration. We only wish to affirm our conviction that choice of subject is not so indifferent a matter as some say it is, and that it must be taken into account as of considerable weight in determining an opinion of a work of art.

This is one consequence of the distinction between decorative and expressive art. The former, solely devoted to the gratification of eye and ear, affords no measure of its success beyond the pleasure which it gives. The latter, whose chief object is to express the feelings and ideas, and, through them, to manifest the power of conception and expansion possessed by the artist, must obviously be estimated, partly at least, by the moral or other value of the ideas and sentiments in question. And, as the value of a work depends directly upon the capability of its author, and as many artists have been about equal in their technical ability, we must be ready to acknowledge that moral and intellectual superiority is a real superiority, and is naturally marked by the possession of an instinctive and spontaneous power of sympathy.

Style is the man. Get some one who *can* read, to read a page of Demosthenes *and* of Cicero, of Bossuet and of Massillon, of Corneille and of Racine, of Lamartine and of Victor Hugo. You will notice that no two of them sound the same. Apart from the subjects or ideas, which may be identical, each one has an air, an accent, which can never be confounded or replaced. In some of them we find elegance, finesse, grace, the most seductive and soothing harmony; in others, a force and *élan* like the sound of a trumpet.

Style only exists by virtue of *the law of separation.* "A being only exists in consequence of his separation from other beings. . . . This law of successive detachment—which alone renders progress possible—may be proved to influence the course of religion, of politics, of literature and of art." It is by style, by the manner of comprehension, of feeling and interpretation, that epochs, races, schools and individuals are separated and distinguished one from the other. In all the arts, analogous differences are to be found; plainly marked, in proportion as a more or less extensive field is offered for the development of artistic personality. Michelangelo and Raphael, Leonardo and Veronese, Titian and Correggio, Rubens and Rembrandt, resembled each other no more and no less than Beethoven resembled Rossini; Weber, Mozart; or Wagner resembles Verdi. Each has his own style, his peculiar mode of thinking and feeling, and of expressing those feelings and thoughts.

Why have mediocre artists no style? For the same reasons that they are mediocrities. The particular characteristic of mediocrity is commonness or vulgarity of thought and feeling. At each moment in the evolution of a social system, there is a general level which marks, for that moment, the average value of the human psyche and intellect. Such works as rise above this general level imply an amount of talent or genius in proportion to the amount of superior elevation and spontaneity which they display. Mediocrity comes up to the general level, but does not pass it; thus the mediocre artist thinks and feels like the ordinary run of mankind, and has nothing to "separate" him from the crowd. He may have a manner, an ensemble of habits of working, peculiar to himself; but he can have no style in the accurate sense of the word. Facilities not style; for the latter is a product, a reverberation from the soul itself, and can no more be artificially acquired than can the sonorousness of bronze or silver be acquired by lead. . . .

Style, which is a simple reflection of the artist's personality, is naturally found in the work of every artist who possesses any personality. The indescribable quality, the *je ne sais quoi*, is precisely the assemblage of qualities, the condition of being and temperament which caused Rubens to see things differently from Rembrandt. The two extracted, from one and the same object or subject, emotions widely different though congenial to their respective natures; just as a tightened string in a concert room will vibrate in response to the note which it would itself produce if struck. The one thing needful is the power to vibrate, which is too often wanting.

The question of style is important. We might even say that it includes the whole of esthetics, which is in fact the question of personality in art. . . .

Truth and *personality:* these are the alpha and omega of art formulas; *truth* as to facts, and the *personality* of the artist. But, if we look more closely, we shall see that these two terms are in reality but one. Truth as to fact, so far as art is concerned, is above all the truth of our own sensations, of our own sentiments. It is truth as we see it, as it appears modified by our own temperaments, preferences, and physical organs. It is, in fact, our personality itself. Reality, as given by the photographer, reality taken from a point of view without connection with us or our impressions, is the negation of art. When this kind of truth predominates in a work of art, we cry, "There is realism for you!" Now, realism partakes of the nature of art, only because the most downright of realists must, whether he will or not, put something of his own individuality into his work. When, on the other hand, the dominant quality is what we call human or personal truth, then we at once exclaim, "Here is an artist!"

And the latter is the right meaning of the word. Art consists essentially in the predominance of subjectivity over objectivity; it is the chief distinction between it and science. The man intended for science is one whose imagination has no modifying influence over the results of his direct observation. The artist, on the other hand, is one whose imagination, impressionability—in a word, personality—is so lively and excitable that it spontaneously transforms everything, dyeing them in its own colors, and unconsciously exaggerating them in accordance with its own preferences.

We think ourselves justified, then, in calling art the direct and spontaneous manifestation of human personality. But we must not omit also the fact that personality—individual and particular as it is from some points of view—is nevertheless exposed to many successive and temporary modifications caused by the various kinds of civilization through which it has had to pass.

Note on Sources. The above material is from Véron's book, *Aesthetics*, published in 1878, and translated in 1879. A few brief passages have been deleted.

READING QUESTIONS

1. Bear the following in mind: "We may say then, by way of general definition, that art is the manifestation of emotion, obtaining external interpretation, now by expressive arrangements of line, form or color, now by a series of gestures, sounds, or words. . . . If our definition is exact, we must conclude from it that the merit of a work of art can be finally measured by the power with which it manifests or interprets the emotion which was its determining cause. . . ." Use any particular work of art to illustrate Véron's two claims.
2. Use the Emotive Theory to distinguish between art and a work of art.
3. Why, if you hold the Emotive Theory, you would be constrained to criticize the Imitation Theory.
4. Any two criticisms, your own or Véron's, of the Imitation Theory of art.
5. He says that the Imitation Theory is only an incomplete and superficial statement of the Emotive or Expression Theory. How so?
6. Véron's distinction between decorative and expressive art.
7. Véron: "We may say that modern art is doubly expressive." How so?
8. Why the Emotive Theory is much concerned with style and personality.
9. Distinguish between an emotive symbol and a cognitive symbol. Which is this: $2 + 2 = 4$. Why?
10. If you were in doubt whether a given symbol were emotive or cognitive, how would you settle the matter?
11. Distinguish between the Emotive Theory in aesthetics and in ethics. Is it a sounder theory in aesthetics than in ethics? Why, or why not.
12. Wherein you find the Emotive Theory of Art (a) most (b) least, convincing.

2. ART AS COMMUNICATION OF EMOTION —FROM LEO TOLSTOY

From Véron to Tolstoy. Véron published his reflections on art and works of art in 1878. The book was read, almost at once, by the Russian novelist Leo Tolstoy. By 1878 Tolstoy was himself a well-known European novelist, the author of *War and Peace* and *Anna Karenina*. There was no question but that these were works of art and their author an artist. It is not irrelevant therefore that Véron's thesis made a considerable impression upon Tolstoy. That a man is an artist does not *guarantee* his answer to the question "What is art?" But it at least makes it difficult to say that, in addressing himself to this question, he "does not know what he is talking about." Tolstoy read and thought about this question: What, as artist, was he seeking to do when he produces his great novels? In 1896 he published his conclusions in the small but important book, *What Is Art?*

Biographical Note. Leo Tolstoy was born in 1828 and died in 1910, aged eighty-two. He was born into one of the great families of the Russian aristocracy. His three books, *Childhood, Boyhood,* and *Youth,* give a vivid account of the life of a privileged young aristocrat. After completing his university education, he spent time in military service, following it with a period of European travel. He was married in 1863, and for fifteen years led a happy, successful, productive life, earning wealth and world-wide fame as a novelist. To this period belong his *War and Peace* and his *Anna Karenina*. Beginning in 1878, and lasting until his death in 1910, he became increasingly alienated from modern civilization in most of its "important" phases. Stages in this rejection of modern civilization are set forth in a series of small books which combine vivid autobiography with social and cultural criticism—e.g., *My Confession, What I Believe, What Then Shall We Do? The Kingdom of God Is Within You,* and *What Is Art?* These essays in criticism and repudiation contain one of the most impressive attempts by any modern writer to formulate a "philosophy of life."

The Argument. In this book Tolstoy admits that Véron's Emotive Theory of Art is correct as far as it goes; but he insists that it does not go far enough. What it says is necessary but not sufficient. If you stop short with Véron's claim that art is the expression of emotion, you have told only half the story. You must go on and add that it is the *communication* of emotion; the intentional successful communication to reader or listener or spectator of emotion felt by the artist. He has some refinements on this, but communication of emotion is the essential point. Tolstoy, like Véron, defends this thesis against the older idea of art as imitation. He also defends it, at great length, against the older thesis that art is the creating of beauty. Indeed the book gives the impression that Tolstoy's principle *bête noir* is the notion that there is any necessary connection between art and beauty.

The claim that art is the communication of emotion enables Tolstoy to distinguish between art and non-art; e.g., between a picture of a sunset and a sunset. A picture of a sunset, provided it communicates the emotion which the artist felt about the sunset, is a work of art. But the sunset itself, unless we think of it as the work of a Divine Artist, is not and cannot be a work of art. Once we have a principle that enables us to distinguish between art and non-art, we can raise the further question of the distinction, within art, between good art and bad art. This question Tolstoy handles by referring to the quality, the character, the nature, of the emotion communicated. If it is one kind of emotion, you have good art; if another kind, bad art. Friends of the Emotive Theory of Art have taken less kindly to Tolstoy's way of distinguishing, within art, between good and bad. Indeed, they have been amused or scandalized by the conclusions which he arrived at when he applied this secondary principle to specific works of art; e.g., when he found that his own great novels were art but perhaps neither good nor great.

In order to define art correctly it is necessary first of all to cease to consider it as a means to pleasure, and to consider it as one of the conditions of human life. Viewing it in this way we see that art is a means of intercourse between man and man.

Every work of art causes the receiver to enter into a certain kind of relationship both with him who produced or is producing the art, and with all those who receive the same artistic impression.

Speech transmitting the thoughts and experiences of men serves as a means of union among them. Art serves a similar purpose. The peculiarity of the latter consists in this, that whereas by words a man transmits his thoughts by art he transmits his feelings.

The activity of art is based on the fact that a man receiving through his sense of hearing or sight another man's expression of feeling, is capable of experiencing the emotion which moved the man who expressed it. To take the simplest example: one man laughs, and another who hears becomes merry, or a man weeps, and another who hears feels sorrow. A man is excited or irritated, and another man seeing him is brought to a similar state of mind. By his movements or by the sounds of his voice a man expresses courage and determination or sadness and calmness, and this state of mind passes on to others. A man suffers, manifesting his sufferings by groans and spasms, and this suffering transmits itself to other people; a man expresses his feelings of admiration, devotion, fear, respect, or love, to certain objects, persons, or phenomena, and others are infected by the same feelings of admiration, devotion, fear, respect, or love, to the same objects, persons, or phenomena.

It is on this capacity of man to receive another man's expression of feeling and to experience those feelings himself, that the activity of art is based.

If a man infects another directly, immediately, by his appearance or by the sounds he gives vent to at the time he experiences the feeling; if he causes another man to yawn when he himself cannot help yawning, or to laugh or cry when he himself is obliged to laugh or cry, or to suffer when he himself is suffering—that does not amount to art.

Art begins when one person with the object of joining another or others to himself in one and the same feeling, expresses that feeling by certain external indications. To take an example: a boy, having experienced fear on encountering a wolf, relates that encounter, and in order to evoke in others the feeling he has experienced, describes himself, his condition before the encounter, the surroundings, the wood, his own lightheartedness, and then the wolf's appearance, its movements, the distance between himself and the wolf, and so forth. All this, if only the boy when telling the story again experiences the feelings he had lived through, and infects the hearers and compels them to feel what he had experienced—is art. Even if the boy had not seen a wolf but had frequently been afraid of one, and if wishing to evoke in others the fear he had felt, he invented an encounter with a wolf and recounted it so as to make his hearers share the feelings he experienced when he feared the wolf, that also would be art. And in the same way it is art if a man, having experienced either the fear of suffering or the attraction of enjoyment (whether in reality or in imagination), expresses these feelings on canvas or in marble so that others are infected by them. And it is also art if a man feels, or imagines to himself, feelings of delight, gladness, sorrow, despair, courage, or despondency, and the transition from one to another of these feelings, and expresses them by sounds so that the hearers are infected by them and experience them as they were experienced by him.

The feelings with which the artist infects others may be very strong or very weak, very important or very insignificant, very bad or very good: feelings of love of one's country, self-devotion and submission to fate or to God expressed in a drama, raptures of lovers described in a novel, feelings of voluptuousness expressed in a picture, courage expressed in a triumphal march, merriment evoked by a dance, humor evoked by a funny story, the feeling of quietness transmitted by an evening landscape or by a lullaby, or the feeling of admiration evoked by a beautiful arabesque—it is all art.

If only the spectators or auditors are infected by the feelings which the author has felt, it is art.

To evoke in oneself a feeling one has once experienced and having evoked it in oneself then by means of movements, lines, colors, sounds, or forms expressed in words, so to transmit that feeling that others experience the same feeling—this is the activity of art.

Art is a human activity consisting in this, that one man consciously by means of certain external signs, hands on to others feelings he has lived through, and that others are infected by these feelings and also experience them.

Art is not the manifestation of some mysterious Idea of beauty or God; it is not a game in which man lets off his excess of stored-up energy; it is not the expression of man's emotions by external signs; it is not the production of pleasing objects; and, above all, it is not pleasure; but it is a means of union among men joining them together in the same feelings, and indispensable for the life and progress towards well-being of individuals and of humanity.

As every man, thanks to man's capacity to express thoughts by words, may know all that has been done for him in the realms of thought by all humanity before his day, and can in the present, thanks to this capacity to understand the thoughts of others, become a sharer in their activity and also himself hand on to his contemporaries and descendants the thoughts he has assimilated from others as well as those that have arisen in himself; so, thanks to man's capacity to be infected with the feelings of others by means of art, all that is being lived through by his contemporaries is accessible to him, as well as the feelings experienced by men thousands of years ago, and he has also the possibility of transmitting his own feelings to others.

If people lacked the capacity to receive the thoughts conceived by men who preceded them and to pass on to others their own thoughts, men would be like wild beasts or like Kasper Hauser.[1]

And if men lacked this other capacity to be infected by art, people might be almost more savage still, and above all more separated from, and more hostile to, one another.

And therefore the activity of art is most important, as important as the activity of speech itself and as generally diffused.

As speech does not act on us only in sermons, orations, or books, but in all those remarks by which we interchange thoughts and experiences with one another, so also art in the wide sense of the word permeates our whole life, but it is only to some of its manifestations that we apply the term in the limited sense of the word.

We are accustomed to understand art to be only what we hear and see in theaters, concerts, and exhibitions; together with buildings, statues, poems, and novels. But all this is only the smallest part of the art by which we communicate with one another in life. All human life is filled with works of art of every kind—from cradle-song, jest, mimicry, the ornamentation of houses, dress, and utensils, to church services, buildings, monuments, and triumphal

---

[1] "The foundling of Nuremberg," found in the marketplace of that town on 23rd May 1828, apparently some sixteen years old. He spoke little and was almost totally ignorant even of common objects. He subsequently explained that he had been brought up in confinement underground and visited by only one man, whom he saw but seldom.

processions. It is all artistic activity. So that by art, in the limited sense of the word, we do not mean all human activity transmitting feelings but only that part we for some reason select from it and to which we attach special importance.

This special importance has always been given by men to that part of this activity which transmits feelings flowing from their religious perception, and this small part they have specifically called art, attaching to it the full meaning of the word.

That was how men of old—Socrates, Plato, and Aristotle—looked on art. Thus did the Hebrew prophets and the ancient Christians regard art. Thus it was, and still is, understood by the Mohammedans, and thus it still is understood by religious folk among our own peasantry.

Some teachers of mankind—e.g., Plato in his *Republic*, the primitive Christians, the strict Momammedans, and the Buddhists—have gone so far as to repudiate all art.

People viewing art in this way (in contradiction to the prevalent view of to-day which regards any art as good if only it affords pleasure) held and hold that art (as contrasted with speech, which need not be listened to) is so highly dangerous in its power to infect people against their wills, that mankind will lose far less by banishing all art than by tolerating each and every art.

Evidently such people were wrong in repudiating all art, for they denied what cannot be denied—one of the indispensable means of communication without which mankind could not exist. But not less wrong are the people of civilized European society of our class and day in favoring any art if it but gives people pleasure.

Formerly people feared lest among works of art there might chance to be some causing corruption, and they prohibited art altogether. Now they only fear lest they should be deprived of any enjoyment art can afford, and they patronize any art. And I think the last error is much grosser than the first and its consequences far more harmful.

. . .

Art in our society has become so perverted that not only has bad art come to be considered good, but even the very perception of what art really is has been lost. In order to be able to speak about the art of our society it is, therefore, first of all necessary to distinguish art from counterfeit art.

There is one indubitable sign distinguishing real art from its counterfeit—namely, the infectiousness of art. If a man without exercising effort and without altering his standpoint, on reading, hearing, or seeing another man's work experiences a mental condition which unites him with that man and with others who are also affected by that work, then the object evoking that condition is a work of art. And however poetic, realistic, striking, or interesting, a work may be, it is not a work of art if it does not evoke that feeling (quite distinct from all other feelings) of joy and of spiritual union with another (the author) and with others (those who are also infected by it).

It is true that this indication is an *internal* one and that there are people who, having forgotten what the action of real art is, expect something else from art (in our society the great majority are in this state), and that therefore such people may mistake for this aesthetic feeling the feeling of diversion and a certain excitement which they receive from counterfeits of art. But though it is impossible to undeceive these people, just as it may be impossible to convince a man suffering from colour-blindness that green is not red, yet for all that, this indication remains perfectly definite to those whose feeling for art is neither perverted nor atrophied, and it clearly distinguishes the feeling produced by art from all other feelings.

The chief peculiarity of this feeling is that the recipient of a truly artistic impression is so united to the artist that he feels as if the work were his own and not some one else's—as if what it expresses were just what he had long been wishing to express. A real work of art destroys in the consciousness of the recipient the separation between himself and the artist, and not that alone, but also between himself and all whose minds receive this work of art. In this freeing of our personality from its separation and isolation, in this uniting of it with others, lies the chief characteristic and the great attractive force of art.

If a man is infected by the author's condition of psyche, if he feels this emotion and this union with others, then the object which has effected this is art; but if there be no such infection, if there be not this union with the author and with others who are moved by the same work—then it is not art. And not only is infection a sure sign of art, but the degree of infectiousness is also the sole measure of excellence in art.

The stronger the infection the better is the art, as art, speaking of it now apart from its subject-matter—that is, not considering the value of the feelings it transmits.

And the degree of the infectiousness of art depends on three conditions: (1) On the degree of individuality of the feeling transmitted; (2) on the degree of clearness with which the feeling is transmitted; (3) on the sincerity of the artist, that is, on the degree of force with which the artist himself feels the emotion he transmits.

The more individual the feeling transmitted the more strongly does it act on the recipient; the more individual the state of psyche into which he is transferred the more pleasure does the recipient obtain and therefore the more readily and strongly does he join in it.

Clearness of expression assists infection because the recipient who mingles in consciousness with the author is the better satisfied the more clearly that feeling is transmitted which, as it seems to him, he has long known and felt and for which he has only now found expression.

But most of all is the degree of infectiousness of art increased by the degree of sincerity in the artist. As soon as the spectator, hearer, or reader, feels that the artist is infected by his own production and writes, sings, or plays, for himself, and not merely to act on others, this mental condition of the artist infects the recipient; and, on the contrary, as soon as the spectator, reader, or hearer, feels that the author is not writing, singing, or playing, for his own satisfaction—does not himself feel what he wishes to express, but is doing it for him, the recipient—resistance immediately springs up, and the most individual and the newest feelings and the cleverest technique not only fail to produce any infection but actually repel.

I have mentioned three conditions of contagion in art, but they may all be summed up into one, the last, sincerity; that is, that the artist should be impelled by an inner need to express his feeling. That condition includes the first; for if the artist is sincere he will express the feeling as he experienced it. And as each man is different, his feeling will be individual; and the more individual it is—the more the artist has drawn it from the depths of his nature— the more sympathetic and sincere will it be. And this same sincerity will impel the artist to find clear expression for the feeling which he wishes to transmit.

Therefore this third condition—sincerity—is the most important of the three. It is always complied with in peasant art, and this explains why such art always acts so powerfully; but it is a condition almost entirely absent from our upper-class art, which is produced by artists actuated by personal aims of covetousness or vanity.

Such are the three conditions which divide art from its counterfeits, and which also decide the quality of every work of art considered apart from its subject-matter.

The absence of any one of these conditions excludes a work from the category of art and relegates it to that of art's counterfeits. If the work does not transmit the artist's peculiarity of feeling and is therefore not individual, if it is unintelligibly expressed, or if it has not proceeded from the author's inner need for expression—it is not a work of art. If all these conditions are present even in the smallest degree, then the work even if a weak one is yet a work of art.

The presence in various degrees of these three conditions: individuality, clearness, and sincerity, decides the merit of a work of art as art, apart from subject-matter. All works of art take order of merit according to the degree in which they fulfil the first, the second, and the third, of these conditions. In one the individuality of the feeling transmitted may predominate; in another, clearness of expression; in a third, sincerity; while a fourth may have sincerity and individuality but be deficient in clearness; a fifth, individuality and clearness, but less sincerity; and so forth, in all possible degrees and combinations.

Thus is art divided from what is not art, and thus is the quality of art, as art, decided, independently of its subject-matter, that is to say, apart from whether the feelings it transmits are good or bad.

But how are we to define good and bad art with reference to its content or subject-matter?

.   .   .

A few days ago I was returning home from a walk feeling depressed. On nearing the house I heard the loud singing of a large choir of peasant women. They were welcoming my daughter, celebrating her return home after her marriage. In this singing, with its cries and clanging of scythes, such a definite feeling of joy, cheerfulness, and energy, was expressed, that without noticing how it infected me I continued my way towards the house in a better mood and reached home smiling and in good spirits. That same evening a visitor, an admirable musician, famed for his execution of classical music and particularly of Beethoven, played us Beethoven's sonata, Opus 101. For the benefit of those who might attribute my judgment of that sonata of Beethoven to non-comprehension of it, I should mention that for a long time I used to attune myself to delight in those shapeless improvizations which form the subject-matter of the works of Beethoven's later period. But I had only to consider the question of art seriously, and to compare the impression I received from Beethoven's later works, with those pleasant, clear, and strong, musical impressions which are transmitted, for instance, by the melodies of Bach (his arias), Haydn, Mozart, Chopin (when his melodies are not overloaded with complications and ornamentation), of Beethoven himself in his earlier period, and above all, with the impressions produced by folk-songs,—Italian, Norwegian, or Russian,—by the Hungarian *csárdás*, and other such simple, clear, and powerful music, for the obscure, almost unhealthy, excitement from Beethoven's later pieces, which I had artificially evoked in myself, to be immediately destroyed.

On the completion of the performance (though it was noticeable that every one had become dull) those present warmly praised Beethoven's profound production in the accepted manner, and did not forget to add that formerly they had not been able to understand that last period of his, but that they now saw he was really then at his very best. And when I ventured to compare the impression made on me by the singing of the peasant women—an impression which had been shared by all who heard it—with the effect of this sonata, the admirers of Beethoven only smiled contemptuously, not considering it necessary to reply to such strange remarks.

But for all that, the song of the peasant women was real art transmitting a definite and strong feeling, while the 101st sonata of Beethoven was only an unsuccessful attempt of art containing no definite feeling and therefore not infectious.

For my work on art I have this winter read diligently, though with great effort, the celebrated novels and stories praised by all Europe, written by Zolá,

Bourget, Huysmans, and Kipling. At the same time I chanced on a story in a child's magazine, by a quite unknown writer, which told of the Easter preparations in a poor widow's family. The story tells how the mother managed with difficulty to obtain some wheat-flour, which she poured on the table ready to knead. She then went out to procure some yeast, telling the children not to leave the hut and to take care of the flour. When the mother had gone, some other children ran shouting near the window calling those in the hut to come to play. The children forgot their mother's warning, ran into the street, and were soon engrossed in the game. The mother on her return with the yeast finds a hen on the table throwing the last of the flour to her chickens, who were busily picking it out of the dust of the earthen floor. The mother, in despair, scolds the children, who cry bitterly. And the mother begins to feel pity for them—but the white flour has all gone. So to mend matters she decides to make the Easter cake with sifted rye-flour, brushing it over with white of egg and surrounding it with eggs. "Rye-bread we bake is as good as a cake," says the mother, using a rhyming proverb to console the children for not having an Easter cake of white flour, and the children, quickly passing from despair to rapture, repeat the proverb and await the Easter cake more merrily even than before.

Well! the reading of the novels and stories by Zolá, Bourget, Huysmans, Kipling, and others, handling the most harrowing subjects, did not touch me for one moment, and I was provoked with the authors all the while as one is provoked with a man who considers you so naïve that he does not even conceal the trick by which he intends to take you in. From the first lines one sees the intention with which the book is written, the details all become superfluous, and one feels dull. Above all, one knows that the author had no other feeling all the time than a desire to write a story or a novel, and so one receives no artistic impression. On the other hand I could not tear myself away from the unknown author's tale of the children and the chickens, because I was at once infected by the feeling the author had evidently experienced, re-evoked in himself, and transmitted.

.   .   .

Beethoven's *Ninth Symphony* is considered a great work of art. To verify its claim to be such I must first ask myself whether this work transmits the highest religious feeling. I reply in the negative, since music in itself cannot transmit those feelings; and therefore I ask myself next: Since this work does not belong to the highest kind of religious art, has it the other characteristic of the good art of our time—the quality of uniting all men in one common feeling—does it rank as Christian universal art? And again I have no option but to reply in the negative; for not only do I not see how the feelings transmitted by this work could unite people not specially trained to submit themselves to its complex hypnotism, but I am unable to imagine to myself a crowd of normal people who could understand anything of this long, confused, and artificial production, except short snatches which are lost in a sea of what is incomprehensible. And therefore, whether I like it or not, I am compelled to conclude that this work belongs to the rank of bad art. It is curious to note in this connection, that attached to the end of this very symphony is a poem of Schiller's which (though somewhat obscurely) expresses this very thought, namely, that feeling (Schiller speaks only of the feeling of gladness) unites people and evokes love in them. But though this poem is sung at the end of the symphony, the music does not accord with the thought expressed in the verses; for the music is exclusive and does not unite all men, but unites only a few, dividing them off from the rest of mankind.

Note on Sources. The above material is quoted, with a few minor deletions, from Chapters 5 and 15 and 16 of Aylmer Maude's translation (1898) of Tolstoy's *What Is Art?*

Reading References. Tolstoy's book is short enough and challenging enough to be read through. Discussions will be found in most manuals on Aesthetics. H. W. Garrod's book *Tolstoï's Theory of Art* is a standard work. Israel Knox's paper "Tolstoï's Esthetic Definition of Art," in the *Journal of Philosophy*, Volume 27 (1930) is worthwhile.

READING QUESTIONS

1. The use which Tolstoy makes of the distinction between transmitting thoughts and transmitting feelings.
2. It is on *this* capacity . . . that the activity of art is based. Namely.
3. How he distinguishes real art from counterfeit art.
4. "The degree of infectiousness of art depends on three conditions." Namely.
5. Why the third condition is the most important of the three.
6. Apart from reference to what he calls "the subject-matter," how would he distinguish between good art and poor art?
7. What he means by subject-matter. How he would use subject-matter to distinguish between good art and bad art.
8. Tolstoy's addition to Véron's position. Does this addition represent a step forward or backward?
9. Why Tolstoy would be constrained to deal polemically with the notion that art is imitation, and the notion that art is creation of beauty.
10. Wherein you find Tolstoy's position (a) most (b) least satisfactory.

3. ART AS EXPRESSION OF EMOTION
—FROM R. G. COLLINGWOOD

From Véron and Tolstoy to Collingwood. We began our examination
of Emotivism with a statement by Eugene Véron: art is the expression of
emotion. Tolstoy revised Véron's position slightly by insisting that expression, while necessary, is not sufficient: there must be communication
of emotion; the expression must be infectious; and the more infectious,
the more art. With Professor Collingwood, the reader is invited to return
to Véron, and pick up again the aesthetic principle that art is an activity
in which an agent expresses, or works at expressing, the emotional charge
which marked his experience. This re-take of the original formulation
was worked out in Professor Collingwood's interesting and important
book, *The Principles of Art*, published in 1937. This book contains one
of the twentieth century's most astute and persuasive statements of the
Emotive Theory in Aesthetics.

Biographical Note. (See page 248).

The Argument of the Citations. Much of our experience, perhaps
all of it, is marked by a certain "feeling tone," what Professor Collingwood calls its "emotional charge." For example, one lives through a
love affair, or an earthquake or a military battle. One is thereby open
to the question, "How does it *feel* to be in love, to encounter an earthquake, to engage an enemy in battle? What emotional charge marked
the experience?" One may try to answer this question by *describing*
the feelings. That would not be art. But one might compose a poem,
or a piece of music, or paint a picture, in which one endeavored not to
describe the feelings but to express them. That would be tackling the
problem by producing or trying to produce a work of art. The author's
emphasis here is on *expressing;* an activity which he does not want
confused with describing or communicating, or arousing, or betraying,
the emotion. These other activities might occur, but their occurrence
would not be necessary to making the expressing-activity to be art. It
is basic and essential. It is the art-activity. Its product or creation is the
art-object, or work of art.

Our first question is this. Since the artist proper has something to do with
emotion, and what he does with it is not to arouse it, what is it that he does?
It will be remembered that the kind of answer we expect to this question is an

answer derived from what we all know and all habitually say; nothing original or recondite, but something entirely commonplace.

Nothing could be more entirely commonplace than to say he expresses them. The idea is familiar to every artist, and to every one else who has any acquaintance with the arts. To state it is not to state a philosophical theory or definition of art; it is to state a fact or supposed fact about which, when we have sufficiently identified it, we shall have later to theorize philosophically. For the present it does not matter whether the fact that is alleged, when it is said that the artist expresses emotion, is really a fact or only supposed to be one. Whichever it is, we have to identify it, that is, to decide what it is that people are saying when they use the phrase. Later on, we shall have to see whether it will fit into a coherent theory.

They are referring to a situation, real or supposed, of a definite kind. When a man is said to express emotion, what is being said about him comes to this. At first, he is conscious of having an emotion, but not conscious of what this emotion is. All he is conscious of is a perturbation or excitement, which he feels going on within him, but of whose nature he is ignorant. While in this state, all he can say about his emotion is: "I feel. . . . I don't know what I feel." From this helpless and oppressed condition he extricates himself by doing something which we call expressing himself. This is an activity which has something to do with the thing we call language: he expresses himself by speaking. It has also something to do with consciousness: the emotion expressed is an emotion of whose nature the person who feels it is no longer unconscious. It has also something to do with the way in which he feels the emotion. As un-expressed, he feels it in what we have called a helpless and oppressed way; as expressed, he feels it in a way from which this sense of oppression has vanished. His mind is somehow lightened and eased.

This lightening of emotions which is somehow connected with the ex-pression of them has a certain resemblance to the "catharsis" by which emotions are earthed through being discharged into a make-believe situation; but the two things are not the same. Suppose the emotion is one of anger. If it is effectively earthed, for example by fancying oneself kicking some one down stairs, it is thereafter no longer present in the mind as anger at all: we have worked it off and are rid of it. If it is expressed, for example by putting it into hot and bitter words, it does not disappear from the mind; we remain angry; but instead of the sense of oppression which accompanies an emotion of anger not yet recognized as such, we have that sense of alleviation which comes when we are conscious of our own emotion as anger, instead of being conscious of it only as an unidentified perturbation. This is what we refer to when we say that it "does us good" to express our emotions.

The expression of an emotion by speech may be addressed to some one; but if so it is not done with the intention of arousing a like emotion in him. If there is any effect which we wish to produce in the hearer, it is only the effect which we call making him understand how we feel. But, as we have already seen, this is just the effect which expressing our emotions has on ourselves. It makes us, as well as the people to whom we talk, understand how we feel. A person *arousing* emotion sets out to affect his audience in a way in which he himself is not necessarily affected. He and his audience stand in quite different relations to the act, very much as physician and patient stand in quite different relations towards a drug administered by the one and taken by the other. A person expressing emotion, on the contrary, is treating himself and his audience in the same kind of way: he is making his emotions clear to his audience, and that is what he is doing to himself.

It follows from this that the expression of emotion, simply as expression, is not addressed to any particular audience. It is addressed primarily to the speaker himself, and secondarily to any one who can understand. Here again, the speaker's attitude towards his audience is quite unlike that of a person desiring to arouse in his audience a certain emotion. If that is what he wishes to do, he must know the audience he is addressing. He must know what type of stimulus will produce the desired kind of reaction in people of that particular sort; and he must adapt his language to his audience in the sense of making sure that it contains stimuli appropriate to their peculiarities. If what he wishes to do is to express his emotions intelligibly, he has to express them in such a way as to be intelligible to himself; his audience is then in the position of persons who overhear him doing this. Thus the stimulus-and-reaction terminology has no applicability to the situation.

The means-and-end, or technique, terminology too is inapplicable. Until a man has expressed his emotion, he does not yet know what emotion it is. The act of expressing it is therefore an exploration of his own emotions. He is trying to find out what these emotions are. There is certainly here a directed process: an effort, that is, directed upon a certain end; but the end is not something foreseen and preconceived, to which appropriate means can be thought out in the light of our knowledge of its special character. Expression is an activity of which there can be no technique.

Expressing an emotion is not the same thing as describing it. To say "I am angry" is to describe one's emotion, not to express it. The words in which it is expressed need not contain any reference to anger as such at all. Indeed, so far as they simply and solely express it, they cannot contain any such reference. The curse of Ernulphus, as invoked by Dr. Slop on the unknown person who tied certain knots, is a classical and supreme expression of anger; but it does not contain a single word descriptive of the emotion it expresses.

This is why, as literary critics well know, the use of epithets in poetry, or even in prose where expressiveness is aimed at, is a danger. If you want to express the terror which something causes, you must not give it an epithet like "dreadful." For that describes the emotion instead of expressing it, and your language becomes frigid, that is inexpressive, at once. A genuine poet, in his moments of genuine poetry, never mentions by name the emotions he is expressing.

Some people have thought that a poet who wishes to express a great variety of subtly differentiated emotions might be hampered by the lack of a vocabulary rich in words referring to the distinctions between them; and that psychology, by working out such a vocabulary, might render a valuable service to poetry. This is the opposite of the truth. The poet needs no such words at all; the existence or nonexistence of a scientific terminology describing the emotions he wishes to express is to him a matter of perfect indifference. If such a terminology, where it exists, is allowed to affect his own use of language, it effects it for the worse.

The reason why description, so far from helping expression, actually damages it, is that description generalizes. To describe a thing is to call it a thing of such and such a kind: to bring it under a conception, to classify it. Expression, on the contrary, individualizes. The anger which I feel here and now, with a certain person, for a certain cause, is no doubt an instance of anger, and in describing it as anger one is telling truth about it; but it is much more than mere anger: it is a peculiar anger, not quite like any anger that I ever felt before, and probably not quite like any anger I shall ever feel again. To become fully conscious of it means becoming conscious of it not merely as an instance of anger, but as this quite peculiar anger. Expressing it, we saw, has something to do with becoming conscious of it; therefore, if being fully conscious of it means being conscious of all its peculiarities, fully expressing it means expressing all its peculiarities. The poet, therefore, in proportion as he understands his business, gets as far away as possible from merely labelling his emotions as instances of this or that general kind, and takes enormous pains to individualize them by expressing them in terms which reveal their difference from any other emotion of the same sort.

This is a point in which art proper, as the expression of emotion, differs sharply and obviously from any craft whose aim it is to arouse emotion. The end which a craft sets out to realize is always conceived in general terms, never individualized. However accurately defined it may be, it is always defined as the production of a thing having characteristics that could be shared by other things. A joiner, making a table out of these pieces of wood and no others, makes it to measurements and specifications which, even if actually shared by no other table, might in principle be shared by other tables. A physician treating a patient for a certain complaint is trying to produce in him a condition which might be, and probably has been, often produced in others, namely, the condition of recovering from that complaint. So an "artist" setting out to produce a certain emotion in his audience is setting out to produce not an individual emotion, but an emotion of a certain kind. It follows that the means appropriate to its production will be not individual means but means of a certain kind: that is to say, means which are always in principle replaceable by other similar means. As every good craftsman insists, there is always a "right way" of performing any operation. A "way" of acting is a general pattern to which various individual actions may conform. In order that the "work of art" should produce its intended psychological effect, therefore, whether this effect be magical or merely amusing, what is necessary is that it should satisfy certain conditions, possess certain characteristics: in other words be, not this work and no other, but a work of this kind and of no other.

This explains the meaning of the generalization which Aristotle and others have ascribed to art. We have already seen that Aristotle's *Poetics* is concerned not with art proper but with representative art, and representative art of one definite kind. He is not analyzing the religious drama of a hundred years before, he is analyzing the amusement literature of the fourth century, and giving rules for its composition. The end being not individual but general (the production of an emotion of a certain kind) the means too are general (the portrayal, not of this individual act, but of an act of this sort; not, as he himself puts it, what Alcibiades did, but what anybody of a certain kind would do). Sir Joshua Reynolds' idea of generalization is in principle the same; he expounds it in connexion with what he calls "the grand style," which means a style intended to produce emotions of a certain type. He is quite right; if you want to produce a typical case of a certain emotion, the way to do it is to put before your audience a representation of the typical features belonging to the kind of thing that produces it: make your kings very royal, your soldiers very soldierly, your women very feminine, your cottages very cottagesque, your oak-trees very oakish, and so on.

Art proper, as expression of emotion, has nothing to do with all this. The artist proper is a person who, grappling with the problem of expressing a certain emotion, says, "I want to get this clear." It is no use to him to get something else clear, however like it this other thing may be. Nothing will serve as a substitute. He does not want a thing of a certain kind, he wants a certain thing. This is why the kind of person who takes his literature as psychology, saying "How admirably this writer depicts the feelings of women, or bus-drivers, or homosexuals . . . ," necessarily misunderstands every real work of art with which he comes into contact, and takes for good art, with infallible precision, what is not art at all.

Finally, the expression of emotion must not be confused with what may be called the betraying of it, that is, exhibiting symptoms of it. When it is said that the artist in the proper sense of that word is a person who expresses his emotions, this does not mean that if he is afraid he turns pale and stammers; if he is angry he turns red and bellows; and so forth. These things are no doubt called expressions; but just as we distinguish proper and improper senses of the word "art," so we must distinguish proper and improper senses of the word "expression," and in the context of a discussion about art this sense of expression is an improper sense. The characteristic mark of expression proper is lucidity or intelligibility; a person who expresses something thereby becomes conscious of what it is that he is expressing, and enables others to become conscious of it in himself and in them. Turning pale and stammering is a natural accompaniment of fear, but a person who in addition to being afraid also turns pale and stammers does not thereby become conscious of the precise quality of his emotion. About that he is as much in the dark as he would be if (were that possible) he could feel fear without also exhibiting these symptoms of it.

Confusion between these two senses of the word "expression" may easily lead to false critical estimates, and so to false aesthetic theory. It is sometimes thought a merit in an actress that when she is acting a pathetic scene she can work herself up to such an extent as to weep real tears. There may be some ground for that opinion if acting is not an art but a craft, and if the actress's object in that scene is to produce grief in her audience; and even then the conclusion would follow only if it were true that grief cannot be produced in the audience unless symptoms of grief are exhibited by the performer. And no doubt this is how most people think of the actor's work. But if his business is not amusement but art, the object at which he is aiming is not to produce a preconceived emotional effect on his audience but by means of a system of expressions, or language, composed partly of gesture, to explore his own emotions: to discover emotions in himself of which he was unaware, and, by permitting the audience to witness the discovery, enable them to make a similar discovery about themselves. In that case it is not her ability to weep real tears that would mark her out a good actress; it is her ability to make it clear to herself and her audience what the tears are about.

This applies to every kind of art. The artist never rants. A person who writes or paints or the like in order to blow off steam, using the traditional materials of art as means for exhibiting the symptoms of emotion, may deserve praise as an exhibitionist, but loses for the moment all claim to the title of artist. Exhibitionists have their uses; they may serve as an amusement, or they may be doing magic. The second category will contain, for example, those young men who, learning in the torment of their own bodies and minds what war is like, have stammered their indignation in verses, and published them in the hope of infecting others and causing them to abolish it. But these verses have nothing to do with poetry.

Thomas Hardy, at the end of a fine and tragic novel in which he has magnificently expressed his sorrow and indignation for the suffering inflicted by callous sentimentalism on trusting innocence, spoils everything by a last paragraph fastening his accusation upon "the president of the immortals." The note rings false, not because it is blasphemous (it offends against no piety worthy of the name) but because it is rant. The case against God, so far as it exists, is complete already. The concluding paragraph adds nothing to it. All it does is to spoil the effect of the indictment by betraying a symptom of the emotion which the whole book has already expressed; as if a prosecuting counsel, at the end of his speech, spat in the prisoner's face.

The same fault is especially common in Beethoven. He was confirmed in it, no doubt, by his deafness; but the cause of it was not his deafness but a temperamental inclination to rant. It shows itself in the way his music screams and mutters instead of speaking, as in the soprano part of the Mass in D, on the layout of the opening pages of the *Hammerklavier* Sonata. He must have known his failing and tried to overcome it, or he would never have spent so many of his ripest years among string quartets, where screaming and muttering are almost, one might say, physically impossible. Yet even there, the old Adam struts out in certain passages of the *Grosse Fuge*.

It does not, of course, follow that a dramatic writer may not rant in character. The tremendous rant at the end of *The Ascent of F6*, like the Shakesperian [1] ranting on which it is modelled, is done with tongue in cheek. It is not the author who is ranting, but the unbalanced character he depicts; the emotion the author is expressing is the emotion with which he contemplates that character; or rather, the emotion he has towards that secret and disowned part of himself for which the character stands.

Note on Sources. The materials used in this section are quoted from R. G. Collingwood's book, *The Principles of Art,* Book I, Chapter VI, "Art as Expression."

Reading References. By all means, extend your acquaintance with Collingwood's own statement in *The Principles of Art* by reading the whole of Book I, "Art and Not-Art." Books II and III are equally valuable, but more difficult to follow. Collingwood's *Principles* can be supplemented by relevant chapters in Professor C. J. Ducasse's *The Philosophy of Art* and Professor E. F. Carritt's *The Theory of Beauty.*

READING QUESTIONS

1. Contrast Tolstoy and Collingwood on the question, "What is art?"
2. Collingwood's distinction between *expressing* and *arousing.* Which is a craft?
3. Between *expressing* and *betraying.*
4. Between *expressing* and *describing.*
5. Indicate some of the advantages which attend the study of the Emotive Theory of Art.

[1] Shakespeare's characters rant (1) when they are characters in which he takes no interest at all, but which he simply uses as pegs on which to hang what the public wants, like Henry V; (2) when they are meant to be despicable, like Pistol; or (3) when they have lost their heads, like Hamlet in the graveyard.

6. Indicate the sense in which Emotivism in Aesthetics may be compared *and* contrasted with Empiricism or Utilitarianism, in their respective philosophical disciplines.

7. Some persons object to the notion that a work of art is an emotive symbol, created to express emotion. Unless you *were* the artist, or yourself knew him rather well, how could you know (a) that he was expressing emotion, or (b) what emotion he was expressing? Would the same objection hold for a cognitive symbol, e.g., $2 + 2 = 4$, or "The earth is spherical?"

8. Having read Véron and Tolstoy and Collingwood: (a) What is your principal reservation with reference to the Emotive Theory in Aesthetics? (b) If you reject it, do you have an alternative which you would propose in its place?

9. Wherein you find Collingwood (a) most (b) least convincing.

4. CRITIQUE OF EXPRESSIONISM —FROM JOHN HOSPERS

From Collingwood to Hospers. Any friend of Emotivism in Aesthetics will find a paper, presented by Professor John Hospers to the Aristotelian Society in 1954, both challenging and valuable. The title of Professor Hospers' paper was "The Concept of Artistic Expression." His purpose was to show that the use of "expression" in the statement of the Emotive Theory, gives rise to difficult questions. This was to be expected. The key notions in any fundamental philosophical theory may be relied on to give trouble. They turn out to be vague, obscure, ambiguous, and metaphorical. What made Professor Hospers' paper something of a "hatchet-job" was his patience in tracking down bothersome questions which the notion of *expression* gives rise to.

To see how this comes about, let us retrace our steps to the point where we began, namely by identifying certain activities as art, and the embodiments of these activities as works of art. These identifications are primary data. As initially arrived at, they are pre-analytical. Once obtained, they may be subjected to conceptual analysis with a view to detecting what they have in common. Professor Hospers emphasizes this point when he says, e.g., "It is, I think, more certain that these men (Bach, Shakespeare, Cezanne, Poe, Eliot, etc.) were artists than that any single theory of art, such as the expression theory, is true"; and again: "If we accept as being artists those men who have created unquestionably great works of art . . ." The point is worth emphasizing: if you cannot tell chalk from cheese there is no future in asking what marks them as essentially different. If you cannot tell art from non-art, or good art from bad art, you have no *data* about which to ask philosophical questions or propose philosophical theses. This was Hegel's point in speaking of philosophy as a "night owl" which takes flight *after* the heat and battle of the day is over, i.e., after the pre-analytical data have been assembled. To put the matter simply: if you don't know *what* you are talking about (e.g., artist, art, work of art) don't propound theories about it.

But suppose you *can* identify examples of artist, art, work of art. Proponents of Emotivism, e.g., Véron, Tolstoy, Collingwood, were willing to assume this initial responsibility. Having done so, they then proposed the Emotive Theory about these examples. An artist is one who expresses his emotions in the creation of a poem, a picture, a statue, a musical composition, etc. Art is the activity of doing this. What is thereby created is a work of art. It is clear that the concepts of *express, expressing, expression*, are here essential vehicles. Let me suggest an analogy. Suppose you identify certain actions as "moral" and propose the theory that an action is moral if and only if it is done because believed to be right; or, going a step further, that an act is right if and only if it produces more pleasure than pain. There are essential vehicles here; e.g., "done because believed," or "right," or "produces more pleasure than." If you raise difficult questions about these essential vehicles you will embarrass these theories. That is Professor Hospers' strategy. He pitches on the concept of *expression* and proceeds to raise "hard questions" about it. And there is no denying that some, perhaps all, of his questions *are* hard to deal with if you subscribe to Emotivism as a theory about artists, art, and works of art. It should be clear that in this strategy Professor Hospers is raising what might be called "second-order" questions; that is, questions about the theory, not about pre-analytical data which the theory purports to deal with; and that the questions bear down on the concept of *expression*.

Biographical Note. Professor John Hospers is a member of the department of philosophy in Brooklyn College. His writings include: *Meaning and Truth in the Arts* (1946), *An Introduction to Philosophical Analysis* (1953), and *Human Conduct: an introduction to the problems of ethics* (1961). He has taught at the University of Minnesota, the University of California (Los Angeles) and elsewhere.

The Argument of the Citations. The paper, as reprinted, contained four sections. Sections I and III are given below. In Section I Professor Hospers concentrates on *express* as the name for the activity which the artist performs. In Section II, he concentrates on *express* as the name for what the work of art does, and particularly on the notion that its power to evoke something in us is a criterion of expressiveness in it. In section III he returns to the activity of the artist and concentrates on *express* as meaning *communicate;* e.g., to express a feeling is to communicate it. In Section IV he returns to the work of art, and concentrates on *express* as the name for what it does, regardless of its relation to the artist or to the beholder. At the end of this final section, after pummelling the concept of expression till one wonders how the poor word will ever get back on its feet, Professor Hospers remarks: ". . . in the field of aesthetics, where there are probably more promises and fewer fulfillments than anywhere else in philosophy, I am impelled to be suspicious of the promissory note, especially when the date due is repeatedly postponed, and to be content only with the cold hard cash of fulfillment." One does not begrudge Professor Hospers the right to his flourish; but flourish it is, because "second order" questions, or "third order" questions, can be used to raise just as much hob in ethics or logic or metaphysics or any other field of philosophy; and because, if you want "cold hard cash" in *any* of these fields, when second-order pressure or third-order pressure is being applied, you are going to be disappointed. When that hour strikes, aesthetics is no more a Cinderella than her sister-disciplines.

The expression theory of art, in one form or another, has dominated the esthetic scene for the past two centuries as much, perhaps, as the imitation theory had done previously. It is often assumed without question that the distinctive function of the artist is to express emotions; that if the artist does not express in his work, what he does is to that extent less entitled to be called art; and that all art must be expressive of something or other, so much so that a non-expressive work of art is a contradiction in terms. Nor has the predominance of expression been limited to art; it has been extended to all objects of beauty. It is said that all truly beautiful objects are expressive, and some have even asserted their identity: beauty *is* expression.

In all this the terms "express," "expressive," and "expression" are, of course, all-important. It is of the utmost consequence, then, that we know what these terms are being used to mean. What is artistic expression? What does an artist do when he expresses? What is it for a work of art to be expressive? In this paper I shall try to do no more than give a brief critical examination of the principal senses which can be given to the notion of expression as it occurs in the literature of esthetics.

What, then, is expression? One answer seems obvious, though we shall see that it is not the only possible one: expression is an activity of the artist in the process of artistic creation; expressing is something that the artist *does.*

What precisely is it that the artist does when he expresses? On this point accounts differ from one another considerably, and I can do no more than mention a few main points to indicate briefly the area in which esthetic philosophers are working when they discuss expression.

Most accounts of the expressive process emphasize the confusion and chaos with which the process begins in the artist's mind; gradually replaced by clarity and order as it approaches completion. Collingwood [in *The Principles of Art*], for example, says:

> When a man is said to express emotion, what is being said about him comes to this. At first, he is conscious of having an emotion, but not conscious of what that emotion is. All he is conscious of is a perturbation or excitement, which he feels going on within him, but of whose nature he is ignorant. While in this state, all he can say about his emotion is: "I feel . . . I don't know what I feel." From this helpless and oppressed condition he extricates himself by doing something which we call expressing himself.

At this point, he writes, he paints, or he carves in stone, and from doing this his emotions become channeled in the exercise of a medium, and his oppressed state is relieved; his inner turbulence ceases, and what was inchoate becomes clear and articulate.

Although Collingwood does not make clear what sense of the phrase "what it is" he is employing when he says that the artist does not know what his emotion is, let us assume that the process he is describing is in general clear enough and turn to another aspect of the expressive process which is usually included, namely, its springs in the artist's unconscious life. William James says:

> A man's conscious wit and will are aiming at something only dimly and inaccurately imagined. Yet all the while the forces of organic ripening within him are going on to their own prefigured result, and his conscious strainings are letting loose subconscious allies behind the scenes which in their way work toward rearrangement, and the rearrangement toward which all these deeper forces tend is pretty surely definite, and definitely different from what he consciously conceives and determines. It may consequently be actually interfered with (jammed as it were) by his voluntary efforts slanting toward the true direction. When the new center of energy has been subconsciously incubated so long as to be just ready to burst into flower, "hands off" is the only word for us; it must burst forth unaided.

In all this, the expression of feeling or emotion is to be distinguished sharply from the deliberate *arousing* of it; accounts are fairly unanimous on this point. A writer of fiction, for example, may deliberately attempt to arouse feelings in his readers, which he does not experience himself. In this case he is expressing nothing, but cold-bloodedly adopting what devices he can to arouse feelings in others, remaining himself unmoved. Because the artist, while expressing his feeling, is clarifying it to himself, he cannot before expressing it know or state what he is going to express; therefore he cannot *calculate* in advance what effects he wants to produce and then proceed to produce them. If he could, he would have no need to express, since the emotion would already be clear to him. "Until a man has expressed his emotion," says Collingwood, "he does not yet know what emotion it is. The act of expressing it is therefore an exploration of his own emotions. He is trying to find out what these emotions are." The novelist who tries deliberately and consciously to arouse a certain emotion in his audience cannot, on the expression theory, be an artist; expression is the activity of an artist, while arousal is the activity of a clever craftsman or a trained technician.

In the foregoing characterization of the expressive process, attention has been given primarily to what is going on in the artist; and this, indeed, is the center of emphasis in the Croce-Collingwood school of aesthetics. Though they do talk about the artistic medium, and insist that what the artist expresses must be conceived in the medium the artist is going to use—be it words or paints or musical tones—they tend to view the artist's actual manipulation of a physical medium outside himself as an accident or an afterthought. That such a bias, though perhaps affecting most accounts of expression, is no essential part of the expression theory is brought out most clearly by John Dewey in his account of expression in *Art as Experience*. Dewey conceives expression, as (one is tempted to add) he conceives of everything else, as an interaction between the organism and its environment: more specifically, in the case of art, as the recalcitrance of the medium and the artist's attempt to bend the medium to his will. To talk about expression in terms of the artist alone is to omit half the story; no amount of talk about the artist's inner experiences is enough.

> There is no expression without excitement, without turmoil. Yet an inner agitation that is discharged at once in a laugh or a cry, passes away with its utterance. To discharge is to get rid of, to dismiss; to express is to stay by, to carry forward in development, to work out to completion. A gush of tears may bring relief, a spasm of destruction may give outlet to inward rage. But where there is no administration of objective conditions, no shaping of materials in the interest of embodying the excitement, there is no expression. What is sometimes called an act of self-expression might better be termed one of self-exposure; it discloses character—or lack of character —to others. In itself, it is only a spewing forth.

We have already distinguished expressing from arousing; Dewey asks us now to make another distinction, from the opposite direction, between expressing and discharging, getting rid of, or as Dewey puts it, "spewing forth." Esthetic theory, says Dewey, has made the mistake of supposing that the mere giving way to an impulsion, native or habitual, constitutes expression. Such an act is expressive not in itself but only in reflective interpretation on the part of some observer—as the nurse may interpret a sneeze as the sign of an impending cold. As far as the act itself is concerned, it is, if purely impulsive, just a boiling over. While there is no expression, unless there is urge from within outwards, the welling up must be clarified and ordered by taking into itself the values of prior experiences before it can be an act of expression. And these values are not called into play save through objects of the environment that offer resistance to the direct discharge of emotion and impulse. Emotional discharge is a necessary but not a sufficient condition of expression.

There are many questions which one might ask of the above accounts as descriptions of what goes on when artists create. But as a psychological account I shall leave it largely unquestioned. It becomes of interest for the philosopher when it is presented, as it often is, as a theory of art. And as such there are a few questions which should be put to it:

1. Expression theories usually speak of *emotions* as what is being expressed, although sometimes the phrase "expression of *feelings*" is used; but the meaning of these two terms, and their relation to one another, is not usually made clear. But let that pass: cannot other things be expressed as well, such as ideas? One wants to know more about *what* it is that the artist *qua* artist is expressing, and, if some things are appropriate for artistic expression and not others, why.

2. But no matter what the artist is said to be expressing, why should one assume that the artist in his distinctively artistic activity is always expressing? Why not say that he is sometimes representing, for example, or just playing around with tones or colors? Many composers do not begin with emotions or feelings at all, but with fragments of melody which they then develop. For them feelings do not particularly enter the picture at all, except possibly feelings of frustration at delays and jubilation at having finished the job. Artists have been creating great works of art for many centuries, yet only in the last two centuries or less would it have been customary, or even seemed natural, to say that *the* distinctive activity of the artist was that of expression.

Indeed, if we accept as being artists those men who have created unquestionably great works of art—Bach, Shakespeare, Cézanne, and so on—it is by no means clear that the creative processes through which they passed can be adequately labeled under the heading of "expression." In the first place, in the case of most artists we have very little idea of what their creative processes were like, since we have no record of them. And in the second place, even when we have such records, whether by the artist himself or his biographers, they do not always point to the kind of thing set forth by the expression theory. For example, what was Shakespeare doing—was he, necessarily and always, expressing? There are doubtless creative experiences in the life of every artist which could be described by talking about an inner turbulence gradually becoming clarified and ordered, and emotions being released through the manipulation of an artistic medium; but I suspect that, as a general description of artistic activity, this is far too narrow, and is a bit too reminiscent of the mystical concept of genius fostered by the Romantic era. I doubt whether Shakespeare was always expressing feelings; sometimes he probably wrote, although he did not feel like it, to meet a deadline, or to have money coming in for the next month, or because the plot he had borrowed from somewhere else intrigued him and he wondered how he could incorporate it into a five-act drama. The motivation, the ends and aims, as well as the inner springs of artistic activity are, I am sure, a very mixed lot; and to assume that the artist *qua* artist is always expressing seems just as one-sided as the earlier assumption that he is always imitating nature or human action.

The written records left by artists, when we have them, sometimes seem flatly to contradict the expression theory—even though artists as a whole probably tend to glamorize themselves and like to leave the impression that they are solitary geniuses engaged in mysterious acts of self-expression. Thus, Poe gives us an account of cold-blooded calculation in the composition of his poem "The Raven," which is such a far cry from the description of the artistic process given us by the expression theory that it would be difficult to make it fit in at any point. And T. S. Eliot said in *The Sacred Wood* that "poetry is not a turning loose of emotion but an escape from emotion." One may, of course, say that if these men did not go through the process described by the theory, they were therefore not true artists; but this is surely to allow an *a priori* dogma to take precedence over cold facts. It is, I think, more certain that these men were artists than that any single theory of art, such as the expression theory, is true. And if the theory is presented, not as an *a priori* pronouncement but as an actual account of the creative process in artists, it will have to stand the empirical test, namely: in all cases of admitted works of art, was the process of its creation such as the expression theory describes? And I do not see any evidence that it holds true in all cases.

3. If it is true that not all great art was created in the way the theory describes, it is, I think, even more plainly true that not everything created in the way the theory describes is great art. Let us assume that Shakespeare, Virgil, Mozart, Rembrandt, and Hokusai all went through the throes of creation as described by the expression theory; the same can be said of any number of would-be poets, painters, and composers whom one has never heard of for the very good reason that they have never produced anything worth looking at twice. I do not mean, now, the deliberate hacks and quacks, the detective-story writers who spin out half a dozen books a year with an eye on next season's market—these could be accused of trying to arouse emotions in others instead of expressing emotions of their own; I mean the host of deeply earnest would-be artists with delusions of grandeur, so dedicated to Art that they would starve if need be to give proper expression to their genius—but who have neither genius nor, sometimes, even talent. The same turmoil and excitement, the same unpredictability of outcome, the feelings of compulsion and dedication, the surcease from emotion from working in a medium, are experienced not alone by the great creators of art but by their hosts of adoring imitators and camp-followers as well as the supreme individualists who sigh and die alone, ignored and unrecognized but devoted

still. This is indeed the most disconcerting fact about the expression theory as a criterion of art: that [according to Harold Osborne in *Aesthetics and Criticism*]

> . . . all the characteristic phenomena of inspiration are described in undistinguishable terms by good and bad artists alike. Nor has the most penetrating psychological investigation succeeded in detecting any general differences between the mental processes which accompany the creation of a masterpiece and the inspirations of a third-rate botcher.

4. In any case, can anything at all relating to the artistic process be validly used as a criterion for evaluating the artistic product? Even if all artists did in fact go through the process described by the expression theory, and even if nobody but artists did this, would it be true to say that the work of art was a good one *because* the artist, in creating it, went through this or that series of experiences in plying his medium? Once the issue is put thus baldly, I cannot believe that anyone could easily reply in the affirmative; it seems much too plain that the merits of a work of art must be judged by what we can find in the work of art, quite regardless of the conditions under which the work of art came into being. Its genesis is strictly irrelevant; what we must judge is the work before us, not the process of the artist who created it. And yet much critical writing seems to be beset by the delusion that the artist's creative processes are relevant to judging his product—that a bad work is excused or a great work enhanced by considerations of how hard he tried or whether the conditions of work were unfavorable or whether he was inspired or in a mystical trance, and so on. And, perhaps, such considerations do excuse the *artist*, but they do not change the value of the work of art. It is a moral condemnation of Fitzgerald that he was lazy and indolent, and could have composed many poems like the *Rubaiyat* but failed to do so; but this is no criticism of the *Rubaiyat* itself; and it may be praise of Mozart's genius that every note in a concerto of his popped into his head in one afternoon, but not praise of his work—the concerto would be just as great if it had taken him ten years to complete. Even Collingwood, when he is distinguishing false art from art proper, does so on the basis of the artistic process: the artist is one who, during creation, expresses emotions formerly unclear to himself, while the false artist is the one who tries to evoke in others emotions which he does not feel. And I cannot emphasize too strongly that, however much this may be a criterion for judging the artist as a man (and I am not saying that it is a good one), it is not a criterion for judging his work. To fudge the distinction between these two is to fall victim to the process-product ambiguity with a vengeance: the word "art" is normally used to name both a process and the product of that process, and because of this fact formulas like "art is expression" can be made to sound true and reasonable; the misfortune here is that this ambiguity, so obvious once it is pointed out,

may help to make people think that any considerations about the artistic process can be relevant to judging the merits of the artistic product.

Our conclusion is, then, that when we make a judgment of esthetic value upon a work of art, we are in no way judging the process, including any expressive process, which led to its completion, and therefore the act of expression does not enter into a critical judgment. If we do not know what the process was like, we need not on that account hold our judgment of the work in abeyance; and if we do happen to know what it was like, we should not let this sway our judgment of the work of art. But there *are* times when we *seem* to invoke the process as a criterion of judgment, and these we should now briefly examine. Here is an example from Dewey [in *Art as Experience*]:

> If one examines into the reason why certain works of art offend us, one is likely to find that the cause is that there is no personally felt emotion guiding the selecting and assembling of the materials presented. We derive the impression that the artist . . . is trying to regulate by conscious intent the nature of the emotion aroused.

One example of this occurs, I suppose, when we feel that a novel is "plot-ridden"—for example, that the novelist has forced his characters into conformity with the demands of a plot which he had outlined in full before giving much thought to his characters. This feeling, I take it, is familiar enough. But is our criticism here really of the author's creative processes? Are we blaming the novel because he outlined the plot first and then manufactured the characters to fit the plot? I do not think so: we criticize the work because the actions that these characters are made to perform are not such as characters of this kind would do; in other words, they oversimplify and falsify human nature, and it is because of this that we are offended. If the characters strike us as real human beings, we do not care what process the artist went through in creating them: whether he thought of the plot first and the characters afterward, or whatever it may have been.

The same considerations apply in other cases where we seem to make use of the process in criticizing the product. For example, we say, "One must feel that the work of art came out of the artist's own experience, that he himself lived through the things he was describing," or we say, "I don't like this work because I don't feel that the artist was being *sincere* when he wrote it." Now, living through something and being sincere about something are things we say about people; are we not therefore using the process in evaluating the product? Again, I think not. Perhaps we do require that the characters in the drama behave as if the dramatist had personally experienced all their emotions and shared all their fates; but as long as we feel this, must we reverse our judgment if we should subsequently discover that the dramatist had felt none of these things at all, or only a small part of them? Shakespeare could hardly have gone through the experiences of Hamlet, Macbeth, Iago, Cleopatra, Lear, Goneril, Prospero and Coriolanus in one lifetime, but what difference does this make as long as he could present us with a series of vivid, powerful, convincing characterizations? Or suppose we praise a work, say *Uncle Tom's Cabin*, for its sincerity. Does it really change our critical judgment when we know that Mrs. Stowe was weeping tears during many of the hours in which she wrote it, and if we should discover that it was written by a wealthy Southern slaveowner on a wager to prove how well he could present the feelings of "the other side," would it alter our critical judgment of his work? It would alter our judgment about the author, surely; it would change our judgment about the author's sincerity, and it would probably make us attribute to the author much more ingenuity than we now attribute to Mrs. Stowe. But our judgment of the work would not be changed; or, at any rate, I submit, it *should* not—for the novel, after we have made this discovery, would be just the same as before; not a jot or a tittle of it would be changed by our discovery. And as long as it is the *work* which we are judging, surely our judgment should remain unchanged as long as the work is unchanged.

What difference does it make *what* emotions the artist felt, so long as the work of art is a good one? If the artist was clever enough to compose a work of art without expressing emotion in anything like the manner described by the expression theory, or even if he felt nothing at all, this is of no importance so long as we find the work an enduring source of esthetic satisfaction. It may be true as an empirical fact about artists, that *unless* they really feel something, unless they are or have been on fire with emotion, or unless they have deep perturbations which demand resolution, they are not able to create great works of art. This may sometimes be true, though I doubt whether it is true in all cases. But even if it were true in all cases, we need still have no interest in the artist's creative processes as such; knowing facts about the artist's processes would at best be a good indicator of his having created great works of art, which we might then go on to examine, and test the correlation between process and product. To know (supposing it to be true) that a work of art could be produced only when the artist went through this or that kind of creative process would be to know an interesting correlation, but it would not be a means of judging the work of art itself. Even if Bach's Preludes and Fugues had been produced by machinery, would they not be as great as before?—and this in spite of the fact that there were no artist's emotions to be expressed because there was no artist. For appreciating the work of art, the artist's biography is not essential: "by their works shall ye know them."

But we may long since have become impatient with the line of reasoning just pursued. What we have been talking about all through it (it will be said) is evocation—trying to analyze expression in terms of certain effects, of whatever kind, evoked in the listener or reader or observer. And whatever expression is, it is not evocation; no theory of expression is merely a theory about evocation. So we shall have to look elsewhere if we want a sensible meaning for the term "expression," when used to characterize not artistic processes but works of art.

Why is this evocation-talk inadequate, one might ask, to deal with expression? One could imagine the following reply: To say that a work of art expresses something is not to say that the artist underwent certain creative processes, nor to say that the listener had certain experiences. Rather, it is to say that the artist had communicated something *to* the listener by means of his work. Expression is not just something evoked in us, it is something which the artist *did* which he then *communicated* to us. Thus far we have dealt with the two aspects—artist and audience—in isolation from each other; but we should have considered them both together; this has been our error. Let us pursue this line of thought a little.

The typical kind of view here is one hallowed by tradition; we might describe it roughly as follows: The artist feels a powerful emotion which he expresses by creating a work of art, in such a way that we, the audience, on reading or seeing or hearing the work of art, feel the same emotion ourselves. Whether the artist did this by intent—i.e., whether in creating he wanted us to feel this emotion, which is what Collingwood denies that a true artist will do—or whether he was working something out within himself without thinking of an audience, does not matter at this point; the important thing is that, whether by intent or not, whether he created with an audience in mind or only to express what he felt, the artist put something into his work which we, the audience, can get out of it; and what we get out is the same thing that he put in. In this way whatever it is that he put in is communicated to us who get it out. Expression is thus a "two-way deal" involving both the artist and his audience.

The language used just now in characterizing the view is deliberately crude, for I do not know how else to describe it with any accuracy. Indeed, this is the very feature of it which makes it, on reflection, extremely difficult to defend. Nor is it easy to remedy it by employing a more sophisticated language in formulating it, for the sophisticated terms usually turn out to be metaphorical. Yet these metaphors seem to be basic to the theory.

For example, it is said that the artist, by means of his work, *transmits* his emotion to us. But what is meant by "transmit" here? When water is transmitted through a pipe, the same water that comes into the pipe at one end comes out at the other; this is perhaps a paradigm case of transmission. When we speak of electricity as being transmitted through a wire, there is not in the same sense something that comes in at one end and out at the other, but at any rate there is a continuous flow of electricity; or if the word "flow" is itself metaphorical, it is perhaps enough to remark that at any point between its two ends the wire will affect instruments and produce shocks. When we transfer this talk about transmission from these contexts to works of art, we may tend to imagine a kind of wire connecting the work of art with the artist at one end and with the audience at the other; or, if we do not actually have such an image, at any rate the term "transmit" takes its meaning from situations such as we have just described; and the question arises, what does it mean in the very different context of art? If it is not like these orthodox cases of transmission, what makes it transmission? What is one committing himself to when he says that in art emotion is transmitted?

A metaphor that may seem to do better justice to the theory is that of deposition. The artist has, as it were, *deposited* his emotion in the work of art, where we can withdraw it at any time we choose. It is somewhat like the dog burying a bone, which another dog may dig up at his own pleasure. But of course, the artist has not literally buried or deposited emotion in his work; he has, rather, with or without the divine agonies of inspiration, painted in oils or written a complicated set of notes on paper. It is true that on seeing the one or hearing the other performed we may have certain feelings; but in no literal sense has the artist *put* them there in the way that we put money into the bank to withdraw at a later time. Moreover, the bone that is dug up is one and the same bone that was previously buried; whereas the emotion which we feel (I shall not say "extract") when we hear or see the work of art cannot be one and the same numerical emotion as the one which the artist felt (I shall not say "put in").

Let us then substitute the metaphor of *conveying*. Whatever it is that the artist is said to be conveying to his audience, of what does such conveyance consist? One person conveys the ball to another by throwing it; the postman conveys letters from the postoffice to one's door. Is a material continuum necessary for conveyance—the postman between the postoffice and the house, the moving conveyor-belt for trays and machinery? If something mysteriously disappeared at one place and reappeared at another, would it be said to be conveyed? If the emotion ceases in the artist and turns up in the audience when they examine his work, has the artist's emotion been conveyed? Again it is not clear exactly what is involved in the talk about conveying. And even if the emotion ceased in the artist and thereupon occurred in the audience, would it be the same emotion that occurred in the two? In all the cases of conveyance—the ball, the letter, the water through the pipe —it is one and the same thing that is conveyed from the one person or place to the other. This condition is not fulfilled in the case of emotion. One and the same emotion could no more occur in both artist and observer than the same pain can be passed along from one person to another by each person in a row successively pricking his finger with the same pin.

Though the language of the expression theory leaves the impression that it is one and the same emotion which occurs in both artist and observer, on the analogy with the other examples, this is surely not essential to the theory; perhaps it is enough that they be two emotions of the same kind or class.

It may be enough that the artist in composing may feel an emotion of kind X, and the observer on seeing it may feel another emotion of kind X. This probably occurs often enough. But suppose it does; is *this* sufficient for saying that X is conveyed from the one to the other? Is this watered-down formulation really what the theory means when it says that art expresses emotion?

Let us, then, speak simply of "communication." The word "communicate" is somewhat more elastic than the previous ones—people can communicate in person, by wireless, even telepathically—but it is also more vague and difficult to pin down. We could spend many hours discussing criteria for communication. Since we cannot do this here, let us take an example in which we would probably agree that communication had occurred. A student summarizes the contents of a difficult essay, and the author looks at the summary and says, "That's it exactly!" Similarly, one might say that an emotion had been communicated if the listener to a symphony described a movement as "haunting, tinged with gentle melancholy, becoming by degrees hopeful, ending on a note of triumph" and the composer said, "Exactly so! that's just what I meant to communicate."

I have some doubts about whether even this last example would satisfy us as being a "communication of emotion." At any rate, what the listener did here was intellectual, not emotional—he *recognized* the emotions rather than experiencing them himself; and perhaps this suffices for communication, but it is worth pointing out that in the traditional expression theory the listener does not merely recognize the feeling, he himself *has* the feeling. But, so as not to spend more time tinkering with the highly vulnerable terminology of the expression theory (in the form we are considering in this section), let me state some objections that could be raised to any formulation of it known to me.

1. There are many experiences which the artist undergoes in the process of creation—the divine agonies of inception, the slow working through of ideas to fruition, and the technical details of execution—which the audience need not and probably should not share. This part of the artist's creative activity need in no sense be communicated. For example, much of the creative process may be agonizing or even boring, but the audience on viewing or hearing the work of art should not feel either agonized or bored. At most, then, it is only a selection of the artist's experiences in creation that should be communicated. One should not speak as if somehow the artist's whole experience in creation were somehow transferred bodily to the observer or listener.

2. Even for the part that the artist wants to communicate to his audience, it is not necessary that he be feeling this at the time of creation, as the theory so often seems to imply. When the artist is under the sway or spell of an emotion, he is all too inclined to be victim and not master of it, and therefore

not to be in a good position to create a work of art, which demands a certain detachment and distance as well as considerable lucidity and studied self-discipline. Wordsworth himself said that the emotion should be recollected in tranquillity; and others, such as Eliot, have gone further and expunged emotion from the account altogether. Perhaps, then, it might be held essential only that the artist *have had* the emotion at some time or other. But if all that is required is that the artist have some emotion or other of type X, then, since most people of any sensitivity have experienced a considerable part of the gamut of human emotions, including some from type X or any other one chooses to mention, this feature in no way distinguishes the artist from other people, and the theory loses all its punch; it becomes innocuous and, like all highly diluted solutions, uninteresting and undistinctive.

3. To say that the audience should feel the same kind of emotion as the artist seems often to be simply not true. Perhaps, in lyric poems and some works of music, the listener may feel an emotion of the same kind as the artist once felt; but in many cases this is not so at all. Even when we do feel emotions in response to works of art (and most of the time what we experience should not, I think, be called "emotions" at all, at least if our attitude is esthetic), they are often of a quite different sort: if the author has expressed anger, we feel not anger but (perhaps) horror or repulsion; if he has expressed anguish, we may feel not anguish but pity.

Often it seems quite clear that the audience emotion should be quite different from anything that was or sometimes even could have been in the mind of the artist. We may experience fascination, horror, or sympathy when seeing *Hamlet* because of what we feel is the oedipal conflict unconsciously motivating his inaction; but this response, a result of Freudian psychology, could hardly have been in the mind of Shakespeare. And why indeed should it have been? It is enough that his drama can be consistently interpreted in this way, perhaps even giving it an added coherence; it is enough that he wrote a drama capable of arousing such feelings; it is not necessary that he have experienced them himself.

4. Epistemologically the most ticklish point for the expression theory is simply this: how can we ever know for sure that the feeling in the mind of the artist was anything like the feeling aroused in a listener or observer? Our judgments on this point, in cases where we do have evidence, have notoriously often been mistaken. We might feel absolutely certain that Mozart felt joy when he composed the Haffner Symphony, and be amazed to discover that during this whole period of his life he was quite miserable, full of domestic dissension, poverty, and disease. A happy composition does not imply a happy composer. Strictly speaking the only way we can know how a composer felt is to ask him, and then only if he is not lying. If he is dead, we have to consult his autobiography, if any, or other written records, if any, and hope that they do not misrepresent the facts and that they do not

tell us what the composer or biographer wanted us to think rather than what really was the case. And of course [as Harold Osborne said in *Aesthetics and Criticism*] they often do this: "Artists who are dead have rarely left satisfactory psychological records, and the difficulties of appealing to living artists, whose motives and intentions are often mixed and their powers of introspective analysis small, are overwhelming."

This consequence is fatal if the expression theory is made a criterion of good art. For it would follow that if we do not know whether the emotion experienced by a listener is of the same kind as that experienced by the artist, we do not know whether or not this is a good work of art. Therefore in those cases where we have no records or they are of dubious value, we must hold our judgment of the work of art in abeyance. And such a consequence, it would seem, makes the theory in this form pass the bounds of the ridiculous.

"But," it may be said, "we don't have to find out from the artist himself or from written records what emotion the artist felt—we can tell this from seeing or hearing the work of art." But this is precisely what we cannot do. Though in this area conviction is strong and subjective feelings of certainty run high, our inferences from works of art to artists are as likely as not to be mistaken. We cannot tell from just listening to the symphony how Mozart felt; the work simply provides no safe clue to this. The best we can do is guess, after hearing the composition, what he was feeling; and then, if the available evidence should point to the conclusion that he actually was feeling so at the time, our inference would have been correct for at least this instance. But once we do this, we are already checking our inference (made from hearing the work) against the empirical evidence, and it is the evidence that is decisive.

We might, in the light of these objections, wish to revise the theory so as not to require that the audience should feel what the artist felt, but only what the artist wanted or *intended* the audience to feel. But when this is done, difficulties again confront us: (1) The same difficulties that attend our knowing how the artist felt are also present, though sometimes in lesser degree, in knowing what he intended. (2) The artist's whole intention may have misfired; he may have intended us to feel one thing, but if even the most careful and sensitive listeners for generations fail to feel anything like this when they hear his composition, shall we still say that we should feel what the artist intended us to feel? (3) The moment we abandon the stipulation that the audience should feel, not as the artist felt but as the artist intended the audience to feel, we seem to abandon anything that could be called the expression theory. For it is characteristic of the expression theory that the artist must have felt something which he "conveys" through his work and which we on observing the work also feel; if he did not feel it, but only tried to make us feel it or intended us to feel it, this is no longer an expression of feeling on his part but a deliberate attempt to evoke it in others—in other words, not expressing but arousing.

It may seem that in the last few pages we have been flogging a dead horse; yet if one examines much critical writing he must be aware how far from dead this horse is. Critics and laymen alike are dominated, quite unconsciously, by the metaphors of transmission, conveyance, and the like, the emotion in the analogy being usually a kind of liquid that is transmitted bodily from artist to audience. Although when made explicit this kind of formulation would doubtless be rejected, it is precisely these metaphors which are at the very roots (to use another metaphor) of the expression theory in the form we have been considering in this section. And the very strong objections to the theory seem seldom to be realized.

But then, one might say, why should the expression theory be held in any such form as this? What we have been discussing in this section concerns communication between artist and audience; and a theory of communication, one might say, is no more a theory of expression than a theory of evocation is. For an artist to *express* something, however irrelevant this may be to a judgment of its value, is one thing; for him to *communicate* it to an audience is another. For a work to be expressive is one thing; for an audience to feel so-and-so is another. If this is so—if reference to an audience has no place in a theory of expression—it immediately rules out both the evocation forms of the theory which we discussed, and the communication forms which we have been discussing.

Note on Source. The material in the above section is quoted from Sections I and III of John Hospers' paper, "The Concept of Artistic Expression," *Proceedings of the Aristotelian Society 1954–55.*

Reading References. The student would do well to browse in one or more of the following collections of readings in aesthetics: E. F. Carritt, *Philosophies of Beauty from Socrates to Robert Bridges,* 1931. S. K. Langer, *Reflections on Art,* 1958. M. Rader, *A Modern Book of Aesthetics,* 3rd edition, 1960. E. Vivas and M. Krieger, *The Problems of Aesthetics,* 1953. M. Weitz, *Problems in Aesthetics,* 1959.

READING QUESTIONS

1. What it means to say that *expression* is an "essential vehicle" in the statement of the Emotive Theory of Art.
2. Elucidate: "These identifications are primary data . . . pre-analytical."
3. Hegel's point in comparing philosophy to a night owl.
4. What it means to say that Professor Hospers raises "second-order"

questions. What would be an example of a first-order question? A third-order question?

5. Any two difficulties which Professor Hospers raises for *express* when that word refers to the activity which the artist performs.

6. Any two difficulties which he raises for *express* when that word is used to mean communicate.

7. Professor Hospers raises second-order questions about Emotivism in Aesthetics. Suggest, by analogy, how you might employ the same strategy against, say, Utilitarianism in ethics, or Empiricism in Theory of Knowledge.

5. REPUDIATION OF TRADITIONAL AESTHETIC THEORY —FROM MORRIS WEITZ

From Hospers to Weitz. Our first three authors—Véron, Tolstoy, Collingwood—propounded the Emotive Theory about the arts and works of art. Our fourth author, Professor Hospers, selected one of the essential vehicles of that theory—the concept of expression—and subjected it to considerable criticism. Our fifth author, Professor Weitz, is more drastic in his treatment of the question to which the other four addressed themselves. If he is correct, they are in a worse state of confusion than they would seem to be aware of. Three of them are stating a theory and the fourth is criticizing it. Three of them are addressing themselves to a common question— "What is art?"—to use the title of Tolstoy's book, and proposing an answer. The fourth is criticizing their answer; even, if you will, rejecting their answer. But to criticize or reject an answer is to leave open the possibility that the question makes sense, that it is susceptible of being answered. Professor Weitz proposes a clean sweep. He is convinced that the question itself is wrong-headed, and should not be asked. If this is so, then *no* answer will satisfy. If you are asking the wrong question, or an essentially pointless or meaningless or "impossible" question, then your trouble is more deep-rooted. There is no use in seeking *any* answer; what you must do is abandon the question. Professor Weitz is of the opinion that the question rests on a false or at least indefensible presupposition. If a person asks whether you have stopped beating your wife, you may reject the question on the grounds that it presupposes that you had been doing so, whereas you hadn't; or that you have a wife, whereas you haven't. You would say "That question does not, because it cannot, arise." Professor Hospers had not proposed any such drastic criticism of the Emotive Theory. He seemed to allow the question, but disallow the answer. He bore down on one particular answer to the question "What is art?" Professor Weitz would rule out *all* answers to that question because he would rule out the question. As a Spanish proverb has it, these are major words.

Biographical Note. Morris Weitz was born in 1916. He is at present (1963) a professor of philosophy in Ohio State University. He is the author of *Philosophy of the Arts* (1950) and the editor of an anthology of readings in Aesthetics, *Problems in Aesthetics* (1959). The article repudiating traditional aesthetic theory, "The Role of Theory in Esthetics," was published in *The Journal of Aesthetics and Art Criticism* (1956).

The Argument of the Citations. The traditional question— What is art?—presupposes that works of art have some property or set of properties in common by virtue of which they are works of art. This Professor Weitz denies; works of art do not have *any* such common property or set of properties by virtue of which they are works of art. They are simply works of art, and that is the end of the matter. If you presuppose that there are *any* conditions which are necessary and sufficient to being a work of art—other than *being* a work of art—you are mistaken. As long as you entertain this false presupposition you will continue to be misled into posing the question "What makes a work of art to be a work of art?" and, in consequence, misled into proposing answers to your question. If you are convinced by Professor Weitz here, and abandon the presupposition, your question will die on the vine.

Then what will you do? Professor Weitz would have you begin all over again with a radically different question. Don't ask "What is art?", instead ask "What kind of concept is your concept of art? How do you conceive of your concept of art?" Two alternatives confront you here: a concept can be either "closed" or "open." A concept, of art or anything else, is closed when you do not entertain the possibility of amending it, extending it, revising it. It is fixed. You "stipulate" that it is not to be altered in any way for any reason. If cases occur which seem as though they ought to be included but don't exactly fit, you close them out. If cases occur which seem as though they ought not to be included yet they do exactly fit, you rule them in. In proceeding thus you are, or may be, deliberately arbitrary, not to say "high-handed." You operate on the Humpty-Dumpty principle: "*I* stipulate the concept: let the cases fall where they may." Suppose you are a teacher and you stipulate that an *A* student shall be one who has a photographic memory, writes legibly, and never fails to show appreciation of your lectures; and you *hold* to this concept. You keep it closed. Professor Weitz would have you ask whether *this* is the way you conceive of your concept of art. As you conceive of your concept of art, would you say that you hold it thus "closed?" If you do, he would, I think, ask you *why* you do; and warn you against the dangers of having a "closed" mind on the question.

In contrast, a concept may be "open." You put it together as you go along. It is "open" to revision, amendment, extension. You "stipulate" nothing in advance. Instead, you "study the field," modifying your concept where you have to, retaining it where you can. Here you don't "stipulate" the concept; you form it and reform it. On these terms you may have no criterion or set of criteria of what constitutes an *A* student held in defiance of what your experience may bring forth. This does not mean that any and every student is an *A*. It means that your concept of an *A* student is not deliberately and unalterably fixed: you are "open" to what the field may produce. Professor Weitz would have you ask whether *this* is the way you conceive of your concept of art. Would you say that you hold it thus "open?" If you do, he would, I think, commend you for having an "open" (*not* a "vacant") mind on the question.

If your concept is "open," and you define it, you will treat your definition as, say, a scientist or a detective treats an hypothesis. If, however, it is "closed," and you define it, you will treat your definition more in the way a geometer treats a concept in geometry.

This is tempting business. The notion of definitions as hypotheses has great charm. On reading Professor Weitz's paper, one might feel a reservation in reference to his sweeping condemnation of his predecessors. It is not clear that they conceived of their conceptions of art as "closed." That is not the conception one has of one's conception of them. When great writers with an interest in philosophy turn their minds to questions connected with art, their thought is often characterized by considerable passion; there is such a thing as intellectual passion. And it may be that their manner of expressing themselves expresses both intellect and passion. Where this is so, one does well in reading them to proceed not only cautiously but *con amore*, with a mind held open by a combination of affection and respect.

Theory has been central in aesthetics and is still the preoccupation of the philosophy of art. Its main concern remains the determination of the nature of art which can be formulated into a definition of it. It construes definition as the statement of the necessary and sufficient properties of what is being defined, where the statement purports to be a true or false claim about the essence of art, what characterizes and distinguishes it from everything else. Each of the great theories of art converges on the attempt to state the defining properties of art. Each claims that it is the true theory because it has formulated correctly into a real definition the nature of art; and that the others are false because they have left out some necessary or sufficient property. Many theorists contend that their enterprise is no mere intellectual exercise but a necessity for any understanding of art and our proper evaluation of it. Unless we know what art is, they say, what are its necessary and sufficient properties, we cannot begin to respond to it adequately or to say why one work is good or better than another. Aesthetic theory, thus, is important not only in itself but for the foundations of both appreciation and criticism. Philosophers, critics, and even artists who have written on art, agree that what is primary in aesthetics is a theory about the nature of art.

Is aesthetic theory, in the sense of a true definition or set of necessary and sufficient properties of art, possible? If nothing else does, the history of aesthetics itself should give one enormous pause here. For, in spite of the many theories, we seem no nearer our goal today than we were in Plato's time. Each age, each art-movement, each philosophy of art, tries over and over again to establish the stated ideal only to be succeeded by a new or revised theory, rooted, at least in part, in the repudiation of preceding ones. Even today, almost everyone interested in aesthetic matters is still deeply wedded to the hope that the correct theory of art is forthcoming. We need only examine the numerous new books on art in which new definitions are proffered; or, in our own country especially, the basic textbooks and anthologies to recognize how strong the priority of a theory of art is.

I want to plead for the rejection of this problem. I want to show that theory—in the requisite classical sense—is *never* forthcoming in aesthetics, and that we would do much better as philosophers to supplant the question, "What is the nature of art?," by other questions, the answers to which will provide us with all the understanding of the arts there can be. I want to show that the inadequacies of the theories are not primarily occasioned by any legitimate difficulty such e.g., as the vast complexity of art, which might be corrected by further probing and research. Their basic inadequacies reside instead in a fundamental misconception of art. Aesthetic theory—all of it— is wrong in principle in thinking that a correct theory is possible because it radically misconstrues the logic of the concept of art. Its main contention— that "art" is amenable to real or any kind of true definition—is false. Its attempt to discover the necessary and sufficient properties of art is logically misbegotten for the simple reason that such a set and, consequently, such a formula about it, is never forthcoming. Art, as the logic of the concept shows, has no set of necessary and sufficient properties, hence a theory of it is logically impossible and not merely factually difficult. Aesthetic theory tries to define what cannot be defined in its requisite sense. But in recommending the repudiation of aesthetic theory I shall not argue from this, as too many others have done, that its logical confusions render it meaningless or worthless. On the contrary, I wish to reassess its role and its contribution primarily in order to show that it is of the greatest importance to our understanding of the arts.

Let us now survey briefly some of the more famous extant aesthetic theories in order to see if they do incorporate correct and adequate statements about the nature of art. In each of these there is the assumption that it is the true enumeration of the defining properties of art, with the implication that previous theories have stressed wrong definitions. Thus, to begin with, consider a famous version of Formalist theory, that propounded by Bell and Fry. It is true that they speak mostly of painting in their writings but both assert that what they find in that art can be generalized for what is "art" in the others as well. The essence of painting, they maintain, is the plastic elements in relation. Its defining property is significant form, i.e., certain combinations of lines, colors, shapes, volumes—everything on the canvas except the representational elements—which evoke a unique response to such combinations. Painting is definable as plastic organization. The nature of art, what it *really* is, so their theory goes, is a unique combination of certain elements (the specifiable plastic ones) in their relations. Anything which is art is an instance of significant form; and anything which is not art has no such form.

To this the Emotionalist replies that the truly essential property of art has been left out. Tolstoy, Ducasse, or any of the advocates of this theory, find that the requisite defining property is not significant form but rather the expression of emotion in some sensuous public medium. Without projection of emotion into some piece of stone or words or sounds, etc., there can be no art. Art is really such embodiment. It is this that uniquely characterizes art, and any true, real definition of it, contained in some adequate theory of art, must so state it.

The Intuitionist disclaims both emotion and form as defining properties. In Croce's version, for example, art is identified not with some physical, public object but with a specific creative, cognitive and spiritual act. Art is really a first stage of knowledge in which certain human beings (artists) bring their images and intuitions into lyrical clarification or expression. As such, it is an awareness, non-conceptual in character, of the unique individuality of things; and since it exists below the level of conceptualization or action, it is without scientific or moral content. Croce singles out as the defining essence of art this first stage of spiritual life and advances its identification with art as a philosophically true theory or definition.

The Organicist says to all of this that art is really a class of organic wholes consisting of distinguishable, albeit inseparable, elements in their causally efficacious relations which are presented in some sensuous medium.

What is claimed is that anything which is a work of art is in its nature a unique complex of interrelated parts—in painting, for example, lines, colors, volumes, subjects, etc., all interacting upon one another on a paint surface of some sort. At one time it seemed to me that this organic theory constituted the one true and real definition of art.

My final example is the most interesting of all. This is the theory of Parker. In his writings on art, Parker persistently calls into question the traditional simple-minded definitions of aesthetics. "The assumption underlying every philosophy of art is the existence of some common nature present in all the arts." "All the so popular brief definitions of art—'significant form,' 'expression,' 'intuition,' 'objectified pleasure'—are fallacious, either because, while true of art, they are also true of much that is not art, and hence fail to differentiate art from other things; or else because they neglect some essential aspect of art." But instead of inveighing against the attempt at definition of art itself, Parker insists that what is needed is a complex definition rather than a simple one. "The definition of art must therefore be in terms of a complex of characteristics. Failure to recognize this has been the fault of all the well-known definitions." His own version is the theory that art is essentially three things: embodiment of wishes and desires imaginatively satisfied, language, which characterizes the public medium of art, and harmony, which unifies the language with the layers of imaginative projections. Thus, for Parker, it is a true definition to say of art that it is ". . . the provision of satisfaction through the imagination, social significance, and harmony. I am claiming that nothing except works of art possesses all three of these marks."

Now, all of these sample theories are inadequate in many different ways. Each purports to be a complete statement about the defining features of all works of art and yet each of them leaves out something which the others take to be central. Some are circular, e.g., the Bell-Fry theory of art as significant form which is defined in part in terms of our response to significant form. Some of them, in their search for necessary and sufficient properties, emphasize too few properties, like (again) the Bell-Fry definition which leaves out subject-representation in painting, or the Croce theory which omits inclusion of the very important feature of the public, physical character, say, of architecture. Others are too general and cover objects that are not art as well as works of art. Organicism is surely such a view since it can be applied to *any* causal unity in the natural world as well as to art. Still others rest on dubious principles, e.g., Parker's claim that art embodies imaginative satisfactions, rather than real ones; or Croce's assertion that there is nonconceptual knowledge. Consequently, even if art has one set of necessary and sufficient properties, none of the theories we have noted or, for that matter, no aesthetic theory yet proposed, has enumerated that set to the satisfaction of all concerned.

Then there is a different sort of difficulty. As real definitions, these theories are supposed to be factual reports on art. If they are, may we not ask, Are they empirical and open to verification or falsification? For example, what would confirm or disconfirm the theory that art is significant form or embodiment of emotion or creative synthesis of images? There does not even seem to be a hint of the kind of evidence which might be forthcoming to test these theories; and indeed one wonders if they are perhaps honorific definitions of "art," that is, proposed redefinitions in terms of some *chosen* conditions for applying the concept of art, and not true or false reports on the essential properties of art at all.

But all these criticisms of traditional aesthetic theories—that they are circular, incomplete, untestable, pseudo-factual, disguised proposals to change the meaning of concepts—have been made before. My intention is to go beyond these to make a much more fundamental criticism, namely, that aesthetic theory is a logically vain attempt to define what cannot be defined, to state the necessary and sufficient properties of that which has no necessary and sufficient properties, to conceive the concept of art as closed when its very use reveals and demands its openness.

The problem with which we must begin is not "What is art?," but "What sort of concept is 'art'?" Indeed, the root problem of philosophy itself is to explain the relation between the employment of certain kinds of concepts and the conditions under which they can be correctly applied. If I may paraphrase Wittgenstein, we must not ask, What is the nature of any philosophical "X"?, or even, according to the semanticist, What does "X" mean?, a transformation that leads to the disastrous interpretation of "art" as a name for some specifiable class of objects; but rather, What is the use or employment of "X"? What does "X" do in the language? This, I take it, is the initial question, the begin-all if not the end-all of any philosophical problem and solution. Thus, in aesthetics, our first problem is the elucidation of the actual employment of the concept of art, to give a logical description of the actual functioning of the concept, including a description of the conditions under which we correctly use it or its correlates.

My model in this type of logical description or philosophy derives from Wittgenstein. It is also he who, in his refutation of philosophical theorizing in the sense of constructing definitions of philosophical entities, has furnished contemporary aesthetics with a starting point for any future progress. In his new work, *Philosophical Investigations*, Wittgenstein raises as an illustrative question, What is a game? The traditional philosophical, theoretical answer would be in terms of some exhaustive set of properties common to all games. To this Wittgenstein says, let us consider what we call "games": "I mean board-games, card-games, ball-games, Olympic games, and so on. What is common to them all?—Don't say: 'there *must* be something common, or they would not be called "games"' but *look and see* whether there is anything common to all.—For if you look at them you will not see something that is common to *all*, but similarities, relationships, and a whole series of them at that . . ."

Card games are like board games in some respects but not in others. Not all games are amusing, nor is there always winning or losing or competition. Some games resemble others in some respects—that is all. What we find are no necessary and sufficient properties, only "a complicated network of similarities overlapping and crisscrossing," such that we can say of games that they form a family with family resemblances and no common trait. If one asks what a game is, we pick out sample games, describe these, and add, "This and *similar things* are called 'games.' " This is all we need to say and indeed all any of us knows about games. Knowing what a game is is not knowing some real definition or theory but being able to recognize and explain games and to decide which among imaginary and new examples would or would not be called "games."

The problem of the nature of art is like that of the nature of games, at least in these respects: If we actually look and see what it is that we call "art," we will also find no common properties—only strands of similarities. Knowing what art is is not apprehending some manifest or latent essence but being able to recognize, describe, and explain those things we call "art" in virtue of these similarities.

But the basic resemblance between these concepts is their open texture. In elucidating them, certain (paradigm) cases can be given, about which there can be no question as to their being correctly described as "art" or "game," but no exhaustive set of cases can be given. I can list some cases and some conditions under which I can apply correctly the concept of art but I cannot list all of them, for the all-important reason that unforeseeable or novel conditions are always forthcoming or envisageable.

A concept is open if its conditions of application are emendable and corrigible; i.e., if a situation or case can be imagined or secured which would call for some sort of *decision* on our part to extend the use of the concept to cover this, or to close the concept and invent a new one to deal with the new case and its new property. If necessary and sufficient conditions for the application of a concept can be stated, the concept is a closed one. But this can happen only in logic or mathematics where concepts are constructed and completely defined. It cannot occur with empirically-descriptive and normative concepts unless we arbitrarily close them by stipulating the ranges of their uses.

I can illustrate this open character of "art" best by examples drawn from its sub-concepts. Consider questions like "Is Dos Passos' *U. S. A.* a novel?," "Is V. Woolf's *To the Lighthouse* a novel?," "Is Joyce's *Finnegan's Wake* a novel?" On the traditional view, these are construed as factual problems to be answered yes or no in accordance with the presence or absence of defining properties. But certainly this is not how any of these questions is answered. Once it arises, as it has many times in the development of the novel from Richardson to Joyce (e.g., "Is Gide's *The School for Wives* a novel or a diary?"), what is at stake is no factual analysis concerning necessary and sufficient properties but a decision as to whether the work under examination is similar in certain respects to other works, already called "novels," and consequently warrants the extension of the concept to cover the new case. The new work is narrative, fictional, contains character delineation and dialogue but (say) it has no regular time-sequence in the plot or is interspersed with actual newspaper reports. It is like recognized novels, A, B, C . . . , in some respects but not like them in others. But then neither were B and C like A in some respects when it was decided to extend the concept applied to A to B and C. Because work N + 1 (the brand new work) is like A, B, C . . . N in certain respects—has strands of similarity to them—the concept is extended and a new phase of the novel engenderd. "Is N + 1 a novel?," then, is no factual, but rather a decision problem, where the verdict turns on whether or not we enlarge our set of conditions for applying the concept.

What is true of the novel is, I think, true of every sub-concept of art: "tragedy," "comedy," "painting," "opera," etc., of "art" itself. No "Is X a novel, painting, opera, work of art, etc.?" question allows of a definitive answer in the sense of a factual yes or no report. "Is this *collage* a painting or not?" does not rest on any set of necessary and sufficient properties of painting but on whether we decide—as we did!—to extend "painting" to cover this case.

"Art," itself, is an open concept. New conditions (cases) have constantly arisen and will undoubtedly constantly arise; new art forms, new movements will emerge, which will demand decisions on the part of those interested, usually professional critics, as to whether the concept should be extended or not. Aestheticians may lay down similarity conditions but never necessary and sufficient ones for the correct application of the concept. With "art" its conditions of application can never be exhaustively enumerated since new cases can always be envisaged or created by artists, or even nature, which would call for a decision on someone's part to extend or to close the old or to invent a new concept. (E.g., "It's not a sculpture, it's a mobile.")

What I am arguing, then, is that the very expansive, adventurous character of art, its ever-present changes and novel creations, makes it logically impossible to ensure any set of defining properties. We can, of course, choose to close the concept. But to do this with "art" or "tragedy" or "portraiture," etc., is ludicrous since it forecloses on the very conditions of creativity in the arts.

Of course there are legitimate and serviceable closed concepts in art. But these are always those whose boundaries of conditions have been drawn for a *special* purpose. Consider the difference, for example, between "tragedy" and "(extant) Greek tragedy." The first is open and must remain so to allow for the possibility of new conditions, e.g., a play in which the hero is not noble or fallen or in which there is no hero but other elements that are like those of plays we already call "tragedy." The second is closed. The plays it can be applied to, the conditions under which it can be correctly used are all in, once the boundary, "Greek," is drawn. Here the critic can work out a theory or real definition in which he lists the common properties at least of the extant Greek tragedies. Aristotle's definition, false as it is as a theory of all the plays of Aeschylus, Sophocles, and Euripides, since it does not cover some of them, properly called "tragedies," can be interpreted as a real (albeit incorrect) definition of this closed concept; although it can also be, as it unfortunately has been, conceived as a purported real definition of "tragedy," in which case it suffers from the logical mistake of trying to define what cannot be defined—of trying to squeeze what is an open concept into an honorific formula for a closed concept.

What is supremely important, if the critic is not to become muddled, is to get clear about the way in which he conceives his concepts; otherwise he goes from the problem of trying to define "tragedy," etc., to an arbitrary closing of the concept in terms of certain preferred conditions or characteristics which he sums up in some linguistic recommendation that he mistakenly thinks is a real definition of the open concept. Thus, many critics and aestheticians ask, "What is tragedy?," choose a class of samples for which they may give a true account of its common properties, and then go on to construe this account of the chosen closed class as a true definition or theory of the whole open class of tragedy. This, I think, is the logical mechanism of most of the so-called theories of the subconcepts of art: "tragedy," "comedy," "novel," etc. In effect, this whole procedure, subtly deceptive as it is, amounts to a transformation of correct criteria for *recognizing* members of certain legitimately closed classes, of works of art into recommended criteria for *evaluating* any putative member of the class.

The primary task of aesthetics is not to seek a theory but to elucidate the concept of art. Specifically, it is to describe the conditions under which we employ the concept correctly. Definition, reconstruction, patterns of analysis are out of place here since they distort and add nothing to our understanding of art. What, then, is the logic of "X is a work of art"?

As we actually use the concept, "Art" is both descriptive (like "chair") and evaluative (like "good"); i.e., we sometimes say, "This is a work of art," to describe something and we sometimes say it to evaluate something. Neither use surprises anyone.

What, first, is the logic of "X is a work of art," when it is a descriptive utterance? What are the conditions under which we would be making such an utterance correctly? There are no necessary and sufficient conditions but there are the strands of similarity conditions, i.e., bundles of properties, none of which need be present but most of which are, when we describe things as works of art. I shall call these the "criteria of recognition" of works of art. All of these have served as the defining criteria of the individual traditional theories of art; so we are already familiar with them. Thus, mostly, when we describe something as a work of art, we do so under the conditions of there being present some sort of artifact, made by human skill, ingenuity, and imagination, which embodies in its sensuous, public medium—stone, wood, sounds, words, etc.—certain distinguishable elements and relations. Special theorists would add conditions like satisfaction of wishes, objectification or expression of emotion, some act of empathy, and so on; but these latter conditions seem to be quite adventitious, present to some but not to other spectators when things are described as works of art. "X is a work of art and contains *no* emotion, expression, act of empathy, satisfaction, etc.," is perfectly good sense and may frequently be true. "X is a work of art and . . . was made by no one," or . . . "exists only in the mind and not in any publicly observable thing," or . . . "was made by accident when he spilled the paint on the canvas," in each case of which a normal condition is denied, are also sensible and capable of being true in certain circumstances. None of the criteria of recognition is a defining one, either necessary or sufficient, because we can sometimes assert of something that it is a work of art and go on to deny any one of these conditions, even the one which has traditionally been taken to be the basic, namely, that of being an artifact: Consider, "This piece of driftwood is a lovely piece of sculpture." Thus, to say of anything that it is a work of art is to commit oneself to the presence of *some* of these conditions. One would scarcely describe X as a work of art if X were not an artifact, or a collection of elements sensuously presented in a medium, or a product of human skill, and so on. If none of the conditions were present, if there were no criteria present for recognizing something as a work of art, we would not describe it as one. But, even so, no one of these or any collection of them is either necessary or sufficient.

The elucidation of the descriptive use of "Art" creates little difficulty. But the elucidation of the evaluative use does. For many, especially theorists, "This is a work of art" does more than describe; it also praises. Its conditions of utterance, therefore, include certain preferred properties or characteristics of art. I shall call these "criteria of evaluation." Consider a typical example of this evaluative use, the view according to which to say of something that it is a work of art is to imply that it is a *successful* harmonization of elements. Many of the honorific definitions of art and its sub-concepts are of this form. What is at stake here is that "Art" is construed as an evaluative term which is either identified with its criterion or justified in terms of it. "Art" is defined in terms of its evaluative property, e.g., successful harmonization. On such a view, to say "X is a work of art" is (1) to say something which is taken *to mean* "X is a succesful harmonization" (e.g., "Art *is* significant form") or (2) to say something praiseworthy *on the basis* of its successful harmonization. Theorists are never clear whether it is (1) or (2) which is being put forward. Most of them, concerned as they are with this evaluative use, formulate (2), i.e., that feature of art that *makes* it art in the praise-sense, and then go on to state (1), i.e., the definition of "Art" in terms of its art-making feature. And this is clearly to confuse the conditions under which we say something evaluatively with the meaning of what we say. "This is a work of art," said evaluatively, cannot mean "This is a successful harmonization of elements"—except by stipulation—but at most is said in virtue of the art-making property, which is taken as a (the) criterion of "Art," when "Art" is employed to assess. "This is a work of art," used evaluatively, serves to praise and not to affirm the reason why it is said.

The evaluative use of "Art," although distinct from the conditions of its use, relates in a very intimate way to these conditions. For, in every instance of "This is a work of art" (used to praise), what happens is that the criterion of evaluation (e.g., successful harmonization) for the employment of the concept of art is converted into a criterion of recognition. This is why, on its evaluative use, "This is a work of art" implies "This has P," where "P" is some chosen art-making property. Thus, if one chooses to employ "Art" evaluatively, as many do, so that "This is a work of art and not (aesthetically) good" makes no sense, he uses "Art" in such a way that he refuses to *call* anything a work of art unless it embodies his criterion of excellence.

There is nothing wrong with the evaluative use; in fact, there is good reason for using "Art" to praise. But what cannot be maintained is that theories of the evaluative use of "Art" are true and real definitions of the necessary and sufficient properties of art. Instead they are honorific definitions, pure and simple, in which "Art" has been redefined in terms of chosen criteria.

But what makes them—these honorific definitions—so supremely valuable is not their disguised linguistic recommendations; rather it is the *debates* over the reasons for changing the criteria of the concept of art which are built into the definitions. In each of the great theories of art, whether correctly understood as honorific definitions or incorrectly accepted as real definitions, what is of the utmost importance are the reasons proffered in the argument for the respective theory, that is, the reasons given for the chosen or preferred criterion of excellence and evaluation. It is this perennial debate over these criteria of evaluation which makes the history of aesthetic theory the important study it is. The value of each of the theories resides in its attempt to state and to justify certain criteria which are either neglected or distorted by previous theories. Look at the Bell-Fry theory again. Of course, "Art is significant form" cannot be accepted as a true, real definition of art; and most certainly it actually functions in their aesthetics as a redefinition of art in terms of the chosen condition of significant form. But what gives it its aesthetic importance is what lies behind the formula: In an age in which literary and representational elements have become paramount in painting, *return* to the plastic ones since these are indigenous to painting. Thus, the role of the theory is not to define anything but to use the definitional form, almost epigrammatically, to pin-point a crucial recommendation to turn our attention once again to the plastic elements in painting.

Once we, as philosophers, understand this distinction between the formula and what lies behind it, it behooves us to deal generously with the traditional theories of art; because incorporated in every one of them is a debate over and argument for emphasizing or centering upon some particular feature of art which has been neglected or perverted. If we take the aesthetic theories literally, as we have seen, they all fail; but if we reconstrue them, in terms of their function and point, as serious and argued-for recommendations to concentrate on certain criteria of excellence in art, we shall see that aesthetic theory is far from worthless. Indeed, it becomes as central as anything in aesthetics, in our understanding of art, for it teaches us what to look for and how to look at it in art. What is central and must be articulated in all the theories are their debates over the reasons for excellence in art—debates over emotional depth, profound truths, natural beauty, exactitude, freshness of treatment, and so on, as criteria of evaluation—the whole of which converges on the perennial problem of what makes a work of art good. To understand the role of aesthetic theory is not to conceive it as definition, logically doomed to failure, but to read it as summaries of seriously made recommendations to attend in certain ways to certain features of art.

Note on Source. The material quoted in this section is from Morris Weitz's article, "The Role of Theory in Esthetics," published in *The Journal of Aesthetics and Art Criticism*, volume XV, 1956.

Reading References. See under Hospers, p. 543.

READING QUESTIONS

1. What is Professor Weitz's purpose in reviewing six "great theories of art"? Name them. Which had he held at one time?
2. "I plead for the rejection of *this* problem." Namely? Why?
3. Use he makes of Wittgenstein's point about games.
4. "A concept is open if its conditions of application are emendable and corrigible." (a) Illustrate his point here; (b) Is this concept of "open" itself open or closed?
5. Why he thinks that the concept of art is an open concept.
6. His point in the contrast between tragedy and extant Greek tragedy.

7. What does he means by "honorific" definitions of art? What makes them "so supremely valuable"?

8. Why, and under what condition, we should deal generously with traditional theories of art.

9. The title of Professor Weitz's paper is "The Role of Theory in Esthetics." Suggest what might go into a paper on "The Role of Theory in Ethics" and "The Role of Theory in Epistemology."

10. Wherein you find Professor Weitz (a) most (b) least convincing.

INDEX